Typefaces for Books

James Sutton & Alan Bartram

Typefaces for Books

The British Library . London 1990

© 1990 James Sutton & Alan Bartram
First published 1990 by
The British Library
Great Russell Street
London WC1B 3DG

British Library Cataloguing in Publication Data

Sutton, James

Typefaces for books.
1.Typefaces
I. Title   II. Bartram, Alan *1932–*   III. British Library
686.224

ISBN 0 7123 0190 9
ISBN 0 7123 0201 8 pbk

Set in Lasercomp Ellington light, with bold
(main text 10 on 13½ pt, captions 9 on 12 pt and 8 on 10½ pt)

Main headings set in 16 pt Linotron 202 Stempel Schadow bold
and 28 pt Shelley Allegro Script (condensed 15%)

Monotype Lasercomp setting by
August Filmsetting, Haydock, St Helens

Linotype Linotron 202 setting by
Nene Phototypesetters, Northampton

Designed by Alan Bartram
Made and printed in Great Britain by
BAS Printers Limited, Over Wallop, Stockbridge, Hampshire
Printed on Diane smooth coated cartridge 135 gm²

Contents

Acknowledgements 6
Introduction 7
1 The Technical Background 8
2 The Historical Background 10
3 The Type Families 16
4 Book Making 18
5 **Specimen Settings** 73
6 Points of Style 282
7 Copyfitting 284
8 Rules, Signs and Symbols 286
Bibliography 287
Index 288

Where the specimens
will also serve for
the alternative system,
this is indicated
in italic

Monotype

Albertina 76
Apollo 80
Baskerville *(and Linotype Baskerville No 2)* 84
Bell 88
Bembo 90
Berkeley Old Style *(and Linotype version)* 94
Bodoni *(and Linotype version)* 98
Bodoni Book *(and Linotype version)* 100
Calisto 108
Calvert 110
Century Schoolbook 118
Clarion 122
Ehrhardt 128
Ellington 132
Fournier 134
Franklin Gothic *(and Linotype version)* 138
Futura 140
Galliard 144
Garamond 148
Garamond (Simoncini) *(and Linotype version)* 150
Gill Sans *(and Linotype version)* 154
Goudy Old Style *(and Linotype version)* 158
Grotesque 215 *(and Linotype version)* 162
Helvetica 166
Horley Old Style 170
Imprint 172
Ionic 176
Italian Old Style 180
Janson 182
Joanna 188
Melior 196
Meridien *(and Linotype version)* 200
Modern Extended 202
Modern Wide 204
Octavian 206
Old Style 208
Optima *(and Linotype version)* 212
Palatino 216
Perpetua *(and Linotype version)* 222
Photina 224
Plantin 228
Plantin Light 230
Poliphilus 236
Rockwell *(and Linotype version)* 238
Sabon 242
Scotch Roman 246
Spectrum 252
Times 256
Trump Medieval 260
Univers 264
Van Dijck 268
Walbaum 274
Zapf International *(and Linotype version)* 280

Linotype

Akzidenz-Grotesk 74
Aldus 78
Basilia Haas 82
Baskerville 86
Bembo 92
Berling 96
Bauer Bodoni 102
Breughel 104
Caledonia *(and Monotype version)* 106
Cartier 112
Caslon 540 114
Century Expanded 116
New Century Schoolbook 120
Concorde 124
Egyptian 505 126
Ehrhardt 130
Fournier 136
Futura 142
Galliard 146
Garamond (Stempel) *(and Monotype version)* 152
Glypha 156
Granjon 160
Guardi 164
Neue Helvetica 168
Imprint 174
Iridium 178
Janson 184
Janson Text 186
Joanna 190
Kennerley 192
Lectura 194
Melior 198
Old Style S 210
Orion 214
Palatino 218
Pegasus 220
Pilgrim 226
Plantin 232
Plantin Light 234
Rotation 240
Sabon 244
Scotch 2 248
Serifa *(and Monotype version)* 250
Stempel Schadow 254
Times 258
Trump Medieval 262
Univers 266
Versailles 270
Video 272
Walbaum 276
Linotype Walbaum 278

Acknowledgements

We are particularly grateful to The Monotype Corporation and to Linotype Ltd for supplying fonts. René Kerfante and Robin Nicholas of Monotype, and Alan Shelley of Linotype, have been especially helpful.

We must also acknowledge the contribution of our typesetters, David Lockett and Tony Fairhurst of August Filmsetting, and Norman Tilley of Nene Phototypesetters. Their understanding of our aims has been essential, and their dedication to the project well beyond the call of duty.

Numerous others have provided help in many ways, including Nicolas Barker, Ron Costley, Elizabeth Hunter (British Library Photographic Section), Robin Kinross, Christopher Legota, John Lewis, George Mackie, Ruari McLean, John Mitchell, David Paisey, John Taylor, Judy Taylor, John Trevitt.

Our publishers Jane Carr, Anne Young, and particularly our editor David Way, must be commended for their patience and help in what, unsurprisingly, proved at moments to be a somewhat fraught project.

The copy fitting tables on pages 284-6 are reproduced by kind permission of Linotype Ltd.

The text used for the specimen settings is taken from *Clea*, the fourth volume of the Alexandria Quartet, by Lawrence Durrell (Faber & Faber 1960), and is reproduced by permission.

Finally, we acknowledge our debt to Jan Tschichold, whose title page for *Typographische Gestaltung* was the model for ours.

Introduction

So with a great musician ... one is no longer aware that the performer is a pianist at all because ... his playing has become so transparent ... that one no longer sees the performer himself – he is simply a window opening upon a great work of art.

MARCEL PROUST *The Guermantes Way*

A window was Proust's image for the great interpretive artist and gives a clue to the qualities we look for in book typography. While display faces can be extrovert, colourful and rich in character, book faces must be transparent, allowing the reader to hear the author's voice without distortion or interference.

It is in answering this little question of the author's voice that the book typographer's task lies. He must invent an accent, a tone, and decide on the volume: should he whisper or shout or sing? Whatever he decides he must keep in mind that he is making a window through which the reader can see the view as clearly as possible and be quite unconscious of the proportions of the glazing bars.

However, one cannot quite avoid the subconscious effect of those glazing bars and the view looks rather different when seen through sans serif plate glass, a white sash window of Baskerville or the leaded casements of William Morris.

In between these extremes there are hundreds of typefaces with far less obvious differences, but these differences are serious enough to require a bulky book to examine even the most important of them.

Why are these minute variations important? Again the clearest analogy is with the tone of the voice. How different the same words sound when spoken by a shepherd or a stockbroker, an archbishop or a schoolboy. But can we locate and identify these nuances in book faces?

This book tries to help by providing over one hundred types in a variety of settings so that realistic visual comparisons can be made.

We also show examples of book faces in use, drawn from a very wide range of sources and over a long period. Although these are largely from the age of metal, many typefaces in use today are based, some very closely, on old designs, and to understand a typeface thoroughly it is essential to make the aquaintance of its ancestors. And *our* ancestors, the type-cutters and book designers of the past, tackled most of the tasks we face and show us their more or less happy solutions for our instruction and delight. This is the way traditions are handed down and typography is a tradition craft which has accepted change slowly.

Such changes are largely the result of the taste of the time interacting with technical advances in paper, ink, presses or type manufacture. The recent developments of filmsetting and offset printing have created opportunities to extend the range of faces. The changes are so dramatic that the highly-respected type designer Hermann Zapf argues – with considerable logic – that historical revivals and types designed for metal are unsuitable models for types printed by today's techniques. Our view is more relaxed. If the type succeeds in being readable and attractive, its origins (or lack of them) are of no consequence. Equally, there is no intrinsic reason why filmsetting types derived from hot-metal designs, while necessarily *different* from their models, need necessarily be *worse*. Many who lament design changes made to classics such as Bembo, Ehrhardt or Baskerville in their adaptation to digital forms overlook the fact that the original hot-metal versions were merely based on the types created by (or for) those illustrious names, and were in no real sense copies of the original. That they were so successful indicates that, first and foremost, they were well-tailored to the machine-setting systems; just as, today, our types are being tailored to the requirements of the astounding advances in current technology.

This is a book for typographic designers and those professionally interested in type design rather than for the general reader. We hope it will be a useful tool to make choice easier and more discriminating, and even that it might result in books which *are* for the general reader being more attractive and more readable. So many titles are published each year that critics (and others) have said there are too many. But no one has complained that books are too carefully designed.

Until the twentieth century the latest design was generally the only text type in use. Our century's chattering repertoire is unprecedented. This babel has been created mainly for commercial reasons, in the hope that the new and distinctive voices are beguiling enough to sell the typesetting systems that produce them. Many speak in the foreign languages of display types, but, even among the book types, not all the voices speak in desirable or attractive accents. Our selection ultimately can only be a personal one. We have further limited our specimens to those available on the Monotype Lasercomp and Linotron/Linotronic systems because these are perhaps the systems most generally used for serious book-work. Many of the fifty or so other systems on the market produce typefaces of excellent quality; but our book would be an unsafe and possibly disastrous guide to use for them.

There are four basic categories of film typesetters.

1. Photo/Optic

Font is kept on film. Characters are projected optically for exposure on film or paper. The entire character is exposed as a unit. Characters are enlarged, reduced, exposed and positioned on film or paper. Some machines offer a large number of sizes from one master image; others reproduce only a few sizes, or even one size, from the master. Photo/Optic systems give high quality resolution at lower speeds than other categories, but are now largely obsolete.

2. Photo/Scan

As with Photo/Optic systems, storage is photographic, but characters are scanned and generated piecemeal. The completed character is built up from dots or lines, exposed by a digitized light source onto a cathode ray tube, where they are lined up and exposed onto the film, paper, or printing plate.

It is much faster than Photo/Optic. Characters can be modified (condensed, slanted, emboldened etc).

3. Digital/CRT/Scan

Master characters are stored digitally (that is, each character is a specific combination of on-and-off electrical digits, which are arranged in grid form). These digitized masters are achieved by scanning photographic masters – but the machine itself holds no photographic images. The digitized characters are generated onto film or paper via a cathode ray tube (CRT), in much the same way as in Photo/Scan devices. The system is capable of extremely high speeds. Fewer moving parts result in greater reliability. It can accommodate large fonts (allowing small caps, non-lining figures, alternative, swash and more pi characters). It can modify type (condense, slant, make bolder etc). Characters can be

positioned above or below a base line (and sized to become superior or inferior, although such figures are too light). It requires a minimum of operator attention. However, originating digitized fonts is costly.

The Linotron 202, used for the Linotype settings in this book, is a Digital/CRT/Scan system.

4. Laser/Scan

Fonts are stored digitally and projected by a laser directly onto the output film or paper, without any intermediate cathode ray tube. Hyphenation and justification information, and other composition programmes, are also stored digitally.

It can operate at extremely high speeds. Few moving parts ensure good reliability. It can accommodate large fonts, and characters can be positioned above or below a base line. It achieves good quality up to very large sizes, and requires a minimum of operator attention. The original manufacture of digitized fonts is costly.

The Lasercomp, used for the Monotype settings in this book, is a Laser/Scan system. The earlier Lasercomp models stored a separate font for each size of each typeface, but later models can produce sizes 5-96 pt from a single master. The Linotronic 300, also a Laser/Scan system, produces sizes up to 186 pt.

The new technology and type design

Most typesetting machines today have fonts stored as a grid in digital form, either on magnetic tape or floppy disks. This has important implications in the design and appearance of the typefaces. Inherently, characters produced from digital fonts reflect the pattern of the grid from which the designs are built up, and have a saw-tooth or stepped appearance to the profile of curved or angled characters. The generation of characters via a CRT softens the edges a little, making the effect less apparent; but direct laser projection produces a sharper image which reveals these imperfections. Vector fonts were developed to minimise the problem. The profile of a character is produced from specific recorded points on the character outline; these points are examined as a group by the typesetting system, and the shape averaged out. This method considerably reduces the amount of digital data required for each font, and enables only one font to be used for all sizes.

Although the character image is improved, the specific recorded points are joined by straight lines, resulting in a facetted profile. For display sizes, therefore, the number of recorded points is doubled, the number of facets thereby increased, and the curve profiles considerably improved.

A further improvement has been achieved by recording the specific points around the perimeter as before, but joining the points by fitting together 'fluid' segments. The formation is achieved by complex algorithms, and produces the exact shape of the original character drawing. This improvement becomes particularly noticeable above 12 pt sizes.

Despite such refinements, the use of one master font for all sizes has major drawbacks. It dictates a compromise design. If the type has been designed for filmsetting and/or digitising, this factor will be a major consideration right from the initial conception, and the problem will be less apparent. But for types derived from hot-metal designs, small sizes will usually be too light, and large display sizes rather coarse. For this reason, some type styles have fonts which are designed for limited ranges of sizes; but few firms would buy two or three fonts if they can get away with one. It is a shortcoming which more advanced technology may eventually solve.

Current systems allow flexibility of letterspacing. This can be ill-used, and result in ugly and illegible spacing which is too tight, or too loose, and which defeats the careful considerations of the type designer, but the facility is of great benefit in display sizes above about 18 pt, where some tightening of the letterspacing is usually an advantage, especially in italic.

Some of the effects made possible by this new technology are undesirable. Instead of buying in a font of small caps (if these are available), some firms economise by reducing full-sized capitals. Our examples show how these electronically-generated substitutes are too light in relation to the caps and lower case. Slanted roman is similarly produced, to save buying true italic. Fractions are sometimes cobbled up by reducing full-sized figures; like similarly-produced superior figures, they are too light.

On the other hand, slanted small caps, slanted non-lining figures and slanted bold can be produced (at any angle in one degree increments from 1 to 45 degrees on the Linotronic 300 and later models of the Lasercomp; at only $14\frac{1}{2}$ degrees on early Lasercomps and 12 degrees on the Linotron 202). These, although sometimes awkward-looking, can be useful if the type family does not include the genuine article.

Any electronic condensing or expanding of types should be done with caution.

Desktop publishing (DTP)

At the moment, DTP covers a number of processes which are used mostly in the production of reports, catalogues and brochures rather than books. However, it is a rapidly developing area and before long there could be significant applications in the field of bookwork proper.

Because developments are so rapid, any attempt at covering DTP typefaces in a book of this nature runs the serious risk of being almost immediately misleading or out of date. But some points can be made.

Where the author merely creates on his word-processor the floppy disk which is used to drive a conventional typesetter, the types shown in this book – assuming the author's processor produces work compatible with his typesetter's Linotron or Lasercomp – are exactly what he will get. However, if the author uses a more sophisticated system – even the comparatively high-quality PostScript – which produces final camera-ready copy by means of a laser printer, then our samples will be misleading, due to the lower degree of resolution of current DTP setting systems. Most of today's typesetting machines or image setters produce type in digital form. (Image setters are also capable of handling graphic images using the same laser technology.) Each character is made up of very fine dots or 'pixels' which are stored in the computer memory. Conventional typesetting machines may have a resolution of between 1000 and 2400 lines to the inch (high resolution). Most laser printers which produce the output from desktop publishing systems work on a much lower resolution of 200, 300 or 600 lines to the inch. This lower resolution results in a coarser image, which may be perfectly satisfactory for many purposes but which may have the effect of distorting the shapes of the letter forms in subtle ways. The development of higher resolution systems is being intensively researched.

Most typefaces offered for DTP are currently derived from designs already developed for high resolution systems, and virtually all the types shown in this book are available in PostScript form. The production of entirely new designs in a lengthy process. Such adaptation of existing forms to new techniques has been a feature throughout the history of printing: Gutenberg followed the black letter manuscript forms, the early printers in Italy adapted the Carolingian hand, the early filmsetting systems used designs adapted from hot-metal types. In the same way, desktop publishing systems are drawing on designs from conventional typesetting systems; but typefaces specially devised for PostScript and other computer systems are already making their appearance.

1440, Mainz. The invention of printing

The series of technical inventions and developments traditionally accredited to Gutenberg at Mainz around 1440 were of colossal importance in shaping the modern world. Prints had been taken from woodblocks many years earlier, but printing by movable, interchangeable, re-usable type was the foundation of the modern printing industry, and Gutenberg's methods were only superseded in the early nineteenth century. By training possibly a goldsmith, his work was of the highest technical standard and his ingenuity made his printed books the equal of the manuscripts they rivalled.

His type forms scarcely reflect the importance of his innovative techniques, for they differed little from those used in the manuscripts his inventions were eventually almost entirely to supersede. The script he took as his model for the 42-line Bible of 1455 was Textura, the most sombre and majestic script then current in northern Europe (fig. 1). It gives the page a noble authority, but its close-packed, heavy, vertical strokes and easily confused letterforms make words static and rigid and therefore hard to read. Five years later, for the

1. **Textura.** From a French manuscript of 1365
2. **Renaissance script.** From a Florentine manuscript of 1455

Catholicon, he used a far less impressive type with weak characterless letterforms, but it was small like a modern book and the shapes of the letters were round, open and legible.

Textura was one of the last monuments of the Middle Ages. In Italy the Renaissance awakened a new demand for the writings of classical authors. Before the invention of printing these had been transcribed from manuscripts of the twelfth century and earlier, written in late Carolingian minuscule. The fifteenth-century scribes mistook this for the bookhand of Rome and enthusiastically modelled their own script upon Carolingian. In their writing we at once recognize the model on which the first roman types were based. The letters are round, open, clear, sane and secular, and are known as Humanistic Book Script (fig. 2). In contrast to the awesome blackness of Textura, with its close-packed vertical strokes of similar shape, the Italian manuscript books are light and graceful, with plenty of white space between the words and lines. Even more important, the letters themselves are perfectly distinct shapes, well formed and regular, with the minuscule serifs carefully shaped to correspond with those of the capital letters. These serifs are not easily made by the pen, and owe their shape to the imitation of serifs on carved roman capitals.

1460, Subiaco and Rome

Printing was brought to Italy, the artistic and commercial centre of the Renaissance, by Germans, and Gutenberg's typography is reflected in the early Roman types of the 1460s. By 1465, Sweynheym and Pannartz at Subiaco were using Roman shapes expressed in gothic terms, with pen-made forms dominating strokes and serifs of capitals and lower case. The letters are rather condensed in shape and set close, giving the page a dark appearance.

On moving to Rome in 1467 the German printers cut a new type which had no gothic characteristics. It became known soon afterwards simply as roman type and was thus differentiated from gothic. It was imitated elsewhere in Italy and abroad. Though imperfect in design and roughly made it was recognized as a type of the new age.

1470, Venice and Nicholas Jenson (fig. 3)

Among the Venetian printers, however, the great merits of the new letter were not at once victorious: although roman was thought appropriate for classical texts, gothic was used for liturgical, legal and vernacular works. The finest early Venetian version of the roman letter was cut by the Frenchman Nicholas Jenson. Even Jenson returned to gothic typography, though the two styles seem to us totally different in appearance and association: one, the dark, constricted, highly formalized expression of the Middle Ages: the other, an open, freely-drawn product of the Renaissance.

3. **Venetian.** Cicero *Epistolae*. da Spira, Venice 1469

4. **Italian Old Face.** Francesco Colonna *Hypnerotomachia Poliphili.* Aldus Manutius, Venice 1499

5. **French Old Face.** Francesco Colonna *Hypnerotomachia Poliphili.* Jacques Kerver, Paris 1546

6. **Dutch Old Face.** Salmasius *Pliny.* Utrecht 1689

3 dictuɤ.Prędimus eum non modo non fecit:fed cum
et poffet rem impedire:fi ut numeraret̃ poftularet tac
affenfus eft qui & locutus honorifice nõ decreuerat fu
ad bos Fauonius acceffit. Quare pro cuiufǫ natura &
agendę:bis ǫ tantū uolūtatē oftēderunt pro fententia
nõ pugnarūt.Curioni uero ǫ de fuaɤ actionū curfu
Furuius & Lentulus ut debuerūt quafi coɤ res eff& :ı
et laborarūt.Balbi quoǫ Cornelii operam & fedulitat
cum Curione uehementer locutus eft:& eum fi aliter

4 parato di ornamenti,& di pompe,& fumptuofi ueftimē
& culto,piu che regio,cum exquifitiffimo exornato p̃-
néte uenerante,di tenera,& florentiffima ætatula q̃ iu-
che, cum uirginei allectabuli,& cœlefti ,& illuftri afpe-
ɤcum decentiffimo famulitio obfequiofe tute fe dapati
nte tute le thereutice paftophore,pyrgophore,& le anti
deuano ,cum trophæi di militare decoramenti in hafta
pofiti,cum la thoraca dil furiale Pyroente,cum laltre-

5 pefle mefle en troupe, ainfi que chacun fe trouuoit.
des perfonnages,& le fon des inftrumens,haultzbois,
& chalemies,eftoient fi grans, qu'il fembloit que l'air
de felicité viuoient les bienheureux en tout foulas & p
& fuyuant les triumphes, parmy les beaux champs
fleurs de toutes les coleurs, odeurs, & faueurs qu'il|el
aromatifantes que toutes les fortes d'efpices que natuı
(certes)plus belles que nulle peincture:& fans iamais e

6 cipere poffent , provincia abieris. Nihil itac
aut antiquius effe duximus *vir Nobiliffime &̃*
fime, quam fedulo curare, ut tamen opus
communibus typis noftris defcriptum , & fe
nomine , materiæque gravitate Te dignum i
fronte Tuum referret nomen. Hoc vero, c
bi fiftimus , effe quis negabit ? Tibi ftrenuioı
fii laudes explicare fi aggrederemur , de no

1495, Venice. The classic typeface takes shape (fig. 4)

Fourteen years after Jenson's death a new roman appeared, also in Venice, which attracted little notice after the sixteenth century until quite recently, in the 1920s, when Stanley Morison supervised the revival and recutting of historic types at the Monotype Corporation. In 1495 the great Renaissance publisher Aldus Manutius brought out a book with a new design of capitals. Though roughly cut, they blended a good deal better with the lower case than the obtrusive capitals of Jenson's roman. Later the same year Aldus published Bembo's *De Aetna*, using the same capitals but with a new lower case cut by his great punch-cutter Francesco Griffo of Bologna.

The Aldine roman is the archetype of the forms which during the sixteenth century established their ascendancy over gothic throughout Europe. The quality of Aldine roman was due to the imagination and judgement of Francesco Griffo; and Aldus as an accurate scholar and highly successful publisher became valued and imitated internationally. It was this success which made his stylistic innovations so influential.

N *ulla mora, ad nutus diuæ tremefactus Apollo*
C *onſtitit, atque oculis late agmina circunspexit,*
E *t ſubito inſidias ſenſit, peditemque retraxit,*
Q *uem contra impulerat dextra impiger. atque periclo*
R *eginam eripuit. tum Maia Atlantide cretus*
L *ittoreum caueæ conſeſſum uocibus implet,*
R *eginam captam ingeminans. fremit undique turba*

7. **Italic.** *Vida de Arte Poetica*. Arrighi, Rome 1527

A further achievement of Aldus was the invention of italic, derived from the cursive script developed during the fifteenth century in Florence and in the Papal Chancery at Rome. Pocket classics with their whole text printed in compressed, sloping lower case and upright capitals appeared soon after 1500. They were an immediate success, chiefly because of their scholarly accuracy, and their low cost; the latter was partly due to economies in paper which the new type form made possible. But the Aldine italic (several versions of which were cut by Francesco Griffo) for all its technical mastery has not been followed by later designers. It is rather cramped, and a whole book in it must have been almost painful to read. Few books were printed with italic texts after 1550.

Modern italics are carefully designed for use as an auxiliary alphabet, closely associated with their romans. They are mainly based on type derived from scribes such as Arrighi (himself also a type designer: see fig. 7) and Tagliente, or upon the italics cut by Robert Granjon in the late sixteenth century.

1540, France (fig. 5)

During the second quarter of the sixteenth century the leadership in typographic design moved to France. Books produced by the Estiennes, Geoffrey Tory, Simon de Colines, Jean de Tournes and Jacques Kerver were of such magnificence and distinction that their epoch became known as the Golden Age of French typography. The page became lighter and more brilliant and the illustrations and borders of printer's flowers had a new delicacy and sophistication.

The new roman type established during these years was primarily the work of the great type-cutter and founder Claude Garamond. In his early years he based his designs on Griffo's roman and Arrighi's italic. About 1530 he set up as an independent type founder and during the 1540s cut several roman fonts of type which set a style for European printers for a century. The letter was still Aldine but with a new grace and civilized assurance.

1680, The Netherlands and England (fig. 6)

The success of Garamond's types in his own day (and now) can be attributed to their technical excellence, as much as to their noble design. They were used throughout Europe, as Garamond and his follower Granjon were pioneer exporters of punches and matrices to printers who could not afford to employ their own type-cutters. The great seventeeth-century publishers of the Netherlands used French types before they developed their own robust workaday versions. Christopher van Dijck and Bartholomaeus and Dirk Voskens, working as freelance punch-cutters during the middle of the seventeenth century, cut some of the finest types of this kind. By the end of the century, the Dutch style was universally accepted.

William Caslon, the first British type-founder to satisfy the growing demand from British printers, followed the Dutch model in his splendid roman started in 1725. This type met with immediate and enduring success not only because of its inherent merits, but because it supplied British printers with type where formerly they had to import it. Caslon met their needs so satisfactorily for most of the eighteenth century that changes in style were slow to make any impact. In spite of the typographical innovations of Baskerville and F A Didot, Caslon remained 'the' roman for most British printers until well into the nineteenth century.

Caslon marks the end of the first stage of type development, during which the roman alphabet of caps, lower case and italic gradually established itself as the standard means of expression for the printed word in Europe. The changes of form in these letters show how designers for more than two hundred years and in different countries made the alphabet respond to their wishes, and the needs of their times.

Insofar as it throws light on a changing world, one might suggest that Aldus supplied Renaissance intellectuals, Garamond, French noblemen, and the Dutch printers, the rising mercantile classes. But the variations are changes in emphasis only, and the line of development from Griffo to Caslon is unbroken.

1700, France. A new approach to old forms (fig. 8)

A radical change in emphasis was made in France at the end of the seventeenth century. An exclusive Royal roman was cut by Philippe Grandjean for Louis XIV. It was based on the Academy's model roman, a cold mathematically-drawn alphabet. The result on the printed page was a haughty brilliance appropriate to its purpose.

1750, England (fig. 9)

Although intended to be exclusive to the Imprimerie Royale, the new roman was copied, and its character influenced designers of the eighteenth century, including the first original contributor to type design in England, John Baskerville. He had little commercial success in his lifetime though versions of his types are among the most popular book faces today. He was a Birmingham japanner, a letter-cutter and a writing master, and in his roman of 1754 these disciplines were reflected in magnificently controlled, generously proportioned letterforms. It is an original design of great distinction, which echoes the architecture of the Augustan Age in its serenity and masculinity.

Baskerville made a number of important innovations in ink and papermaking and printing. Passing wove paper through hot copper cylinders produced a smooth white surface that showed off the black type magnificently. He also developed a new open typographic style with wide margins and leading between lines. This gave the page an austere brilliance. Instead of illustration, the letters decorate the pages.

1790, Britain (fig. 10)

The trends in letter design developed by Baskerville were taken a stage further by William Martin and Richard Austin at the end of the century. Fry's Baskerville, Bell and Scotch Roman are designs which accentuate the sharpness of Baskerville's roman. Whereas Baskerville's type shows his background as a writing master and letter-cutter, his followers' work is very much the product of the engraving tool and matches the woodcuts and copper plates of the illustrators of the time.

8. **Early Transitional**. Académie des inscriptions et belles lettres *Les Médailles des principaux événements du règne de Louis XIV*. Imprimerie Royale, Paris 1702

9. **Transitional.** John Baskerville *Preface to Milton*. Birmingham 1758

10. **Late Transitional.** Goldsmith *Poems*. William Bulmer, London 1795

11. **Modern.** Horace *Works*. G Bodoni, Parma 1791

8 année, eſtant reparti de Breſt mieux accompa
de l'Isle de Tabago, au commencement de D
s'approcha de la Place, & la fit attaquer. Il y
conſidérable, & on ne doutoit point que le Sié
ſement le ſecond jour du ſiége, la troiſiéme b
ba ſur le magaſin à poudres, y mit le feu, & fit
Vice-Amiral Hollandois, quinze Officiers, &

9 *man* and *Italic* are all I have hitherto
ed; if in theſe he has left room for i
ment, it is probably more owing to tha
which divided his attention, than to a
cauſe. I honor his merit, and only
derive ſome ſmall ſhare of Reputatio

10 Or onward, where the rude Carinthian boor
Against the houseless stranger shuts the doc
Or where Campania's plain forsaken lies,
A weary waste, expanding to the skies;
Where-e'er I roam, whatever realms to see,

11 Tentaris numeros. Vt melius, quidquid erit, pat
Seu plures hiemes, seu tribuit Iuppiter ultimam
Quae nunc oppositis debilitat pumicibus mare
Tyrrhenum; sapias, vina liques, et spatio brevi
Spem longam reseces. Dum loquimur, fugerit in
Aetas: carpe diem, quam minimum credula post

1800. France, Italy, Germany (fig. 11)

European admiration for Baskerville's typography resulted in a design at the turn of the century which heralded a new age. The types of Didot, Bodoni and, later, Walbaum concentrated on brilliant contrast and striking effect. They were types designed to impress the eye. The fine hairlines and the abrupt and exaggerated changes from thick to thin demanded careful handling, a sophisticated printing technique and smoother paper of the highest quality; given these the new style was certainly astonishing.

The letters themselves are beautifully designed shapes drawn with sophisticated and rather aristocratic taste. They were, however, the expression of the French revolution as much as of fine neo-classical printing and the Napoleonic empire. But letters which have no reference to written forms tend to lack the subtle rhythms of a good text face. The brilliance and novelty of the new design led to its wide use for general printing throughout the nineteenth century, but its inherent weaknesses and the declining standards of the printing industry resulted eventually in a miserable grey mediocrity.

1820, Britain and the Industrial Revolution

The first truly original design of advertising type appeared in 1817 when Vincent Figgins brought out a form with slab serifs and sledgehammer even weight. It has been described as a typical expression of an age which saw *The Times* being produced on a steam press (in 1814). Letters were no longer mere symbols for sounds but abstract shapes of compelling power which could not be ignored. This new typography, which relied on a single word to get the attention of the passer-by, demanded impact rather than legibility from the typeface.

Clearly, such forceful, even brutal, shapes have little to do with bookwork, certainly not as text types (though they have their uses for chapter headings or title pages). But from 1930 onwards, lighter versions of these slab-seriffed forms have been developed which are sympathetic for books on certain subjects, such as architecture. The trend in the design of these text weights has been from the almost pure geometry of Rockwell, to more subtle shapes which hold together better in lines of text. Usually, several weights of bold are also provided, sometimes also condensed versions.

1840, Britain

In the 1840s the harshness of the slab-seriffed forms was softened. Capitals and lower case were better proportioned, the serifs bracketed and the exaggeration toned down. These types, known as clarendons or ionics, had a very great success and still have, but their greatest importance today lies in the use they are put to in their smaller sizes. Their 'normal' looking yet solid and open shapes make them excellent for rough printing on poor quality paper, and most faces

12 & 13. Two advertisements from the Museum of English Rural Life, University of Reading, show the kind of work for which the new display types were designed. Here, egyptians and fat faces (grossly emboldened moderns) rule supreme. Both 1826.

14. Playbill of c.1880. Some of the vigour has given way to fussy and inventive decoration, but clarendons, egyptians and grotesques still command attention, in usage far removed from bookwork.

for printing the text of newspapers (as well as faces for 'old generation' typewriters) are of this form. Their original usage included punchy display work, but they were also employed for an entirely new concept: the bold text type. Providing more emphasis than italic, this was used to pick out important words and phrases within text, as well as for subheadings.

Except as headings, the bolder clarendons have little place in bookwork today, and are unlikely to be used where great refinement or elegance is required. But the lighter forms, being clearly and strongly drawn, are popular for children's books.

1820 onwards. Britain, Germany, USA

By far the most significant of these nineteenth-century types made a modest first appearance in 1816 when the first sans-serif specimen was put out by the Caslon foundry. The new design looks timid and rather ungainly and was probably intended for sub-headings and short lines of text under the shadow of punchier types. For some time it was used in this way and was available in caps only. By the 1830s lower case forms were in use in Germany, and soon afterwards in the USA, but not widely in Britain until the 1870s. By the end of the century every founder had a full range of grotesques (as sans-serif type had come to be known) ranging from light to ultra bold, condensed to expanded. This weight range was the greatest strength of the design.

Grotesques were devised for display and jobbing work. The idea of using them in bookwork would have appalled publishers and readers. It sometimes still does. But, unlike romans, grotesques could be designed in every imaginable way, capable of use in the most varied circumstances. The brash and bullying letterforms have now been tamed, particularly during the second half of the twentieth century, and many eminently readable and subtle designs have been introduced. Particular care has been taken to create letterforms which hold together well as text.

Mild inconsistencies between letters of the same alphabet frequently gave the Victorian forms a characteristic vigour. There was no desire for the methodical and rational approaches so prevalent in the twentieth century. Today's designers strain to create ever greater regularity and conformity between the letters of any one alphabet, and also to achieve greater family likeness between the different weights of a type style. Even Helvetica, widely considered the ultimate classic grotesque when introduced in 1951, has undergone refinement.

1916, England. 1927, Germany. A return to fundamentals

In their quest for the rainbow gold of ultimate perfection, twentieth century designers tried new approaches to serif-less letters. One, characteristically German, relied on geometry. Another, characterisitically English, relied on tradition. In both cases, letterforms were pared down to their basic skeleton: a 'return to fundamentals' characteristic of the period.

These new versions were designed to avoid the exuberance of nineteenth-century forms, but none made very satisfactory text types. Of the German geometric school, Paul Renner's Futura of 1927 was one of the first, and the best. Its strict geometry and intellectual basis, while avoiding Victorian waywardness, was subtly modified by sensitivity and feeling.

Of the English humanistic sans, Johnston's Railway Type of 1916, designed for London Underground, was the first. Important but somewhat clumsy, it was never intended for text setting. Its originality lies in its proportions, which were based on classical letterforms, not Victorian grotesques. Gill's sans-serif of 1928 was a far subtler and more refined development. Both designs were basically seriffed letters, stripped of their serifs, and made more or less monoline.

Both Futura and Gill Sans were very successful, eventually fathering enormous families of weights and variations. Futura (but not Gill Sans) was widely travestied by inferior and insensitive adaptations.

1890 onwards. England and the private presses

The deterioration of bookwork in the nineteenth century provoked William Morris to found the Kelmscott Press in 1891. Dedicated to reviving the highest standards of printing, it led Morris to experiment with paper, ink and binding as well as commissioning illustrations from Burne-Jones and engraving rich borders. Morris also drew two original typefaces: Golden, inspired by Jenson's roman, and Chaucer (also named Troy in a larger size), based on fourteenth-century German manuscript forms. Neither type nor typography bears much relationship to modern practice, but Morris's achievements earned him devoted disciples whose own private press work at length forced the printing trade to improve standards.

These private presses also commissioned new type designs. Some of the best were later acquired by Monotype or Linotype, and developed for machine setting. The quality of these text types influenced entirely new designs commissioned by the two firms themselves, introduced in parallel with the re-worked classic faces produced by Monotype under Stanley Morison. Unlike those revivals, the new designs show no direct influence of any particular historical example. This less 'revivalist' approach has been even more prevalent since the advent of filmsetting. However, national characteristics – for instance, the living calligraphic tradition in Germany – are sometimes evident in the designs.

The abundance of systems devised to force type styles into meaningful groups indicates that none is totally satisfactory. We have chosen the traditional historical approach as being more useful to designers attempting to match typeface to period or atmosphere.

Type names without brackets indicate modern designs directly reflecting historical forms.

Type names within brackets indicate those partially influenced by historical forms.

1470 **Venetian**

Gradual change from thick to thin strokes; oblique stress; serifs strong and steeply sloped (those on caps having almost no brackets, those on lower case almost only brackets). M has serifs on the inside, e has small eye with oblique bar.

Italian Old Style   (Guardi)
Kennerley

1495 **Italian Old Face**

Calligraphic stress; thicks and the triangular bracketted serifs at an oblique angle. Letter width narrower than Venetian, with round forms generally oval. Close fitting. Open counters, fairly long ascenders and descenders. Cap height slightly less than ascenders. Crossbar of e high and horizontal.

Bembo	(Albertina)	(Palatino)
Poliphilus	(Aldus)	(Spectrum)
	(Berling)	
	(Goudy Old Style)	

1540 **French Old Face**

Based on the Italian types. Balance of capitals, lower case and italic more fully harmonised. Gradual smooth transition from stem to serif. More rounded triangular serifs.

Garamond   (Galliard)   (Sabon)
Granjon

1680 **Dutch Old Face**

Somewhat weightier than French old face, with bigger body to lower case letters. Stress and serifs basically as previous old faces. Sprightly and sometimes irregular italic.

Ehrhardt	Plantin	(Imprint)
Janson	Van Dijck	(Times)
Janson Text	(Caslon 540)	

1700 **Early Transitional**

Strong vertical emphasis, fairly abrupt change from thick to thin. Flat unbracketted serifs. Caps and ascenders of equal height.

Fournier

1750 **Transitional**

Generously proportioned. Round letters approaching circular. Softer forms than early transitional, but more contrast between thicks and thins than in old face designs. Generally vertical stress. Rounded serifs slightly angled, slightly bracketted.

Baskerville

1790 **Late Transitional**

Sharper, more contrasting forms than classic transitional. Vertical stress, giving letters generally a condensed appearance. Horizontal bracketted serifs, tapered and pointed.

Bell   Modern Wide   Scotch Roman
Caledonia   Scotch 2
Modern Extended

1800	**Modern**			
	Strong contrast between thicks and hairline thins, giving extreme vertical stress. Horizontal unbracketted serifs. Caps same height as ascenders. Round letters circular in their outer shapes.	Bodoni	Walbaum	(Basilia Haas)

1820	**Egyptian**			
	Often little or no weight difference between strokes normally thick or thin, although bolder weights force greater variations. Slab, rectangular serifs, no bracketting. Letter widths more regular than in classic text types. Weight ranges from ultra bold to thin.	Calvert Egyptian 505	Glypha Rockwell	Serifa

1820	**Grotesque**			
	An egyptian without serifs. Letter widths more regular than in classic text types. Originally monoline in construction, but extreme weights force more contrast. Often rich somewhat irregular forms. Weight ranges from ultra bold to thin.	Akzidenz-Grotesk Franklin Gothic Grotesque 215 Helvetica		Univers Video

1840	**Clarendon**			
	Originally bold in weight. Strong bracketted serifs with rounded or square-cut tips. Often very rich forms in their bolder versions, with distinct contrast between thicks and thins, though can be almost monoline.	Century Expanded Century Schoolbook		Clarion Ionic

1916	**Sans Serif**			
	Serif-less letter of classical proportions. Often geometric or semi-geometric in construction, and virtually monoline.	Futura	Gill Sans	Optima

Twentieth-century romans
not conforming to any particular grouping

1925	Horley Old Style	1952	Melior	1969	Concorde	1981	Berkeley Old Style
				1969	Lectura	1981	Breughel
1929	Perpetua	1956	Trump Medieval				
				1971	Photina	1982	Old Style S
1930/58	Joanna	1957	Meridien	1971	Rotation		
						1984	Versailles
1934/53	Pilgrim	1963/75	Octavian	1972	Iridium		
						1988	Calisto
1937	Pegasus	1964	Apollo	1974	Orion		
1937	Stempel Schadow					1990	Ellington
		1967	Cartier	1977	Zapf International		

RIGHT
The Holy Bible
Cambridge 1763
printed by John Baskerville
(title page)
reduced from approx 500 mm deep

OPPOSITE
Benjamin Kennedy
Public School Latin Grammar
London 1900
actual size

Baskerville's title page is so grand and commanding that criticism of any kind seems impertinent. However, appearance has ridden roughshod over utility in that the design hardly reflects the sense of the words. Do we need twelve punctuation marks? The only necessary one is in MAJESTY's. We certainly do not need so many sizes of roman, and the use of caps, small caps and italic is somewhat willful. But what splendour!

Kennedy's Latin Grammar is shown not just to contrast the ugly with the beautiful but to introduce the subject of the following pages. Here can be seen a host of typographic problems unsuccessfully tackled. The result is clumsy and repellent with mean line spacing and type size, bad word spacing, and letter spacing used in an unhappy attempt at emphasis. But the problem was daunting and the quantity of information packed in is horribly impressive.

THE

CONTAINING THE

OLD TESTAMENT

AND

THE NEW:

Tranflated out of the

AND

With the former TRANSLATIONS

Diligently Compared and Revifed,

By His MAJESTY's Special Command.

APPOINTED TO BE READ IN CHURCHES.

CAMBRIDGE,

Printed by *JOHN BASKERVILLE*, Printer to the UNIVERSITY.

M DCC LXIII.

CUM PRIVILEGIO.

'The history of printing', said Stanley Morison 'is in large measure the history of the title page'. The title page is generally regarded as *the* major challenge, where book designers display their higher skills. Accordingly, accounts of book design invariably focus on them and other decorative material such as jackets, bindings and illustrations, while the far more important and demanding problems of textual presentation so woefully mismanaged in the Latin grammar shown here are largely or entirely ignored. The following pages are a brief attempt at addressing this subject.

This is not a treatise on book design and certainly not a history. We deal here only with a few basic principles of textual articulation. By illustrating some successful (and a few unsuccessful) solutions, we hope the reader will wish to extrapolate the results as guidance in solving *his* or her problems.

The pages chosen (which incidentally show a large range of types in use) are from a wide variety of books covering over five hundred years of printing; from private presses or limited editions to 'trade' books and paperbacks. Some of the solutions, created within a scheme of things no longer entirely valid, may be of little direct help, but outmoded styles and conventions can sometimes clarify our own viewpoint.

Until the mid-nineteenth century, book printers had little choice in the type they used – although much could be achieved with ingenuity, as Baskerville's title page shows. Today, overwhelmed by choice, we can play all kinds of tunes with our types, sing in innumerable voices. Modern equipment also allows us to mix (economically) styles and sizes in text setting as never before. The books we illustrate on the following pages play many tunes, in many voices, and will, we hope, suggest ways of exploiting the unprecedented riches of filmsetting; although our choice is largely governed by a belief that good book design, acting as a conduit between author and reader, should exhibit an engineering-style elegance, with neat, clean and economical solutions to problems, and elimination of unnecessary fuss.

We begin with the handling of straightforward text, and various special editorial requirements. The particular problems of poetry and plays are examined, then information typography, including the use of symbols. Following this we look at type in relation to illustrations and diagrams. Finally we show developments in this century: the Bauhaus (and other) rethinking, and progress towards the integrated spread.

Today, many people are involved in the creation of a successful book. Author, publisher, publisher's editor, typesetter, originator and printer, possibly an illustrator or photographer or picture researcher, possibly a cartographer: all must play their part. It is often left to the designer, however, to provide what John Lewis has called 'a guiding intelligence'. And without this, no book can be respected as a piece of book making.

238   *Latin Wordlore.*   § 59.

A.   α) ŏ   β) ĭ   γ) ĕŏ   δ) ĭŏ   ε) ŭŏ, vŏ, īvŏ, tīvŏ, vĭ.

II. **c.**

c is a stable suffix, denoting Individuality in Substantives: Permanent Condition or Relation in Adjectives. Often, however, the individuality or condition denoted is of a disparaging kind: as in senex, senec-io, cimex, culex, pulex; caecus, flaccus, luscus, mancus, truncus, &c. So in **c-ulo c** is deminutive, but in **c-undo** it denotes permanent activity.

S.   α) cĭ ĭc   β) cŏ cĭŏ ĭcŏ tĭcŏ   γ) āc ōc   δ) īc īcŏ
         ε) ūcŏ.

A.   α) cŏ ĭcŏ tĭcŏ lĭcŏ   β) ācĭ ōcĭ   γ) ācŏ ācĕŏ

Adjectives:

α) ŏ: *V.* fid-us, *faithful*; viv-us, *alive* . . . with Cpp. naufrăg-us, *shipwrecked*; profug-us, *fugitive* . . . *D.* re-us, *accused*; nov-us, *new*; me-us, tu-us, su-us . . .

β) ĭ: ī-s; quī-s; qui; iug-is . . . Cpp. bimar-is . . .

γ) ĕŏ: *D.* implying '*Formed of:*' aur-eus, *golden*; argent-eus, *of silver*; '*Exhibiting:*' lūt-eus, *muddy*; lūt-eus, *of deep yellow*; '*Belonging to:*' virgin-eus, *maiden, maidenlike*, &c.
     Note.—ēŏ represents Gr. ειος, Pythagor-ēus, El-ēus, *of Elis*.

δ) ĭŏ: *D.* imply generally '*Having the quality*' of, or '*Belonging to:*' mart-ius, patr-ius, reg-ius, pluv-ius, &c. &c.; some Cpp. egreg-ius, exim-ius. Aer-ius, aether-ius are Greek, having the sense of L. ēŭs. Alius, Gr. ἄλλος=al-yus; medius, Gr. μέσσος=med-yus; **i** being **i**-consonans. Add plebe-ius=plebe-yus.

ε) ŭŏ: *V.* with some in **vŏ, īvŏ**, chiefly *V.*, may imply '*Active quality:*' contig-uus, *adjoining*; contin-uus, &c.; gna-vus, *knowing*; proter-vus, *frolicsome*; sae-vus, *raging*, &c.; noc-uus or noc-ivus, *hurtful*, &c.: or may have Passive use: divid-uus, *parted*; ingen-uus, *freeborn*; mut-uus, *exchanged* (between two persons or parties), *mutual*; relic-uus, *left*; rig-uus, irrig-uus, *watered*; vid-uus, *widowed*; ca-vus, *hollow*; sal-vus *safe*; adopt-ivus, *chosen, adoptive*; especially those in **t-īvŏ**, having the Supine or participial suffix **t**: captivus, *captured*; fes-tivus, *festive*; fugi-tivus, na-tivus, praeroga-tivus, vo-tivus, &c. &c. Aes-tivus, *of summer*, supposes a verb aedĕre (Gr. αἰθ-), *to heat*; tempes-tivus, *seasonable*, is abnormal; mor-tuus (=mor-tivus), *dead*; ann-uus is a rare Denom.; mens-tr-uus seems to be for mens-trius from mensis, *month*. **vĭ**: brevis, Gr. βραχύς; gravis, Sk. *gurus*, Gr. βαρύς; lĕ-vis, Sk. *laghus*, Gr. ἐλαχύς, *light*; lē-vis, Gr. λειƒός, *smooth*; sua-vis, Sk. *svâdus*, Gr. ἡδύς.

II. **c.**

Substantives.

α) cĭ: lanx, merx (faeci- fauci- . . .): ĭc (ix) *V.* appendix: ĭc (ex), *V.* vert-ex, vort-ex, *D.* ram-ex. See pp. 95–6 (most unc.).

β) cŏ: *V.* fŏ-cus, *hearth*; fū-cus, *drone*; es-ca, *food*, *D.* iuven-cus -ca; cĭŏ-, *V.* sola-cium; *D.* un-cia (from unus); ĭcŏ: *D.* vil-īcus, *steward*; vil-ica, *steward's wife*; man-īca, *handcuff*; ped-īca, *fetter, springe*, &c.; tĭcŏ, *V.* can-tĭcum: *D.* viaticum, *provision for journey*.

γ) *D.* forn-ax, *furnace*; lim-ax, *snail*; cel-ox, *yacht*.

δ) īc, p. 96 (most unc. rad-ix, &c.): but *V.* in **trīc- trix**, Fem. as mere-trix, vic-trix, &c. (see **R**); īcŏ: *V. D.* mend-īcus, -īcă, *beggar*; lect-īca, *litter*, and others.

ε) lact-ūca, *lettuce* (some unc.).

Adjectives.

α) cŏ: *V. D.* par-cus, pau-cus, pris-cus, rau-cus, sic-cus, &c. (some unc.): ĭcŏ: most *D.* imply '*Pertaining to:*' bell-īcus, publ-īcus, &c.; some *V.* med-īcus, *of healing* (as Subst. *physician*). Many Gentilia; Scythīcus, &c. tĭco: *D.* rus-tĭcus, aqua-tĭcus, &c. *V.* vena-tĭcus; lico: *D.* fame-lĭcus.

β) ācĭ: *V.* imply '*Inclined to*,' '*Capable of:*' aud-ax, *daring*; ĕd-ax, *devouring*; fĕr-ax, *fruitful*, &c. &c.: ōcĭ: *V.* '*Inclined to:*' fĕr-ox, *haughty*; vēl-ox, *swift*.

γ) ācŏ: mer-ācus, *pure* (op-ācus, *shady*, unc.); Subst. clo-āca, *sewer* (clu=lu). ācĕŏ: *D.* '*Consisting of:*' farr-aceus, *of flour*, and some others.

RIGHT
The Holy Bible
Cambridge 1763
printed by John Baskerville
(title page shown on page 18)
reduced from approx 500 mm deep

OPPOSITE
Herodotus
Nonesuch Press
London 1935
printed by Cambridge University Press
reduced from approx 300 mm deep

Baskerville's opening page of Genesis shows careful relationships between the summary (in italic), the main text, and the footnotes, with keys to references, verse numbers and sub-paragraphs discreetly but clearly signalled. Symbols, not numbers, are used to flag the footnotes because these contain so many figures already. But the heading, loose and clumsily-arranged, is further weakened by distracting side notes, including Archbishop Ussher's chronology from the Creation repeated three times. Even taking into account the stylistic conventions of the day, the whole heading area is really rather a mess.

The Nonesuch *Herodotus* consists of main text and a large number of notes and commentary arranged to be read in parallel with it. A double spread displays the main narrative framed on three sides by the notes that decorate the page as well as serving their function. The use of italic for the notes not only creates a different 'colour' but also – because of its condensation – allows an acceptable number of characters within the somewhat narrow columns.

The types Francis Meynell chose were Plantin Light (with specially-cut long ascenders) for the text, and, surprisingly, Perpetua with Felicity italic for the notes.

THE FIRST

BOOK OF *MOSES,*

CALLED

GENESIS.

Year before the } 4004
common Year } of CHRIST }
Julian Period - - 710
Cycle of the Sun 10

Cycle of the Moon - 7
Indiction - - - - 5
Creat. from Tifri - 1
Dominical Letter - B

Before CHRIST 4004.

CHAP. I.

1 *The creation of heaven and earth, 3 of the light, 6 of the firmament, 9 of the earth separated from the waters, 11 and made fruitful, 14 of the sun, moon, and stars, 20 of fish and fowl, 24 of beasts and cattle, 26 of man in the image of God. 29 Also the appointment of food.*

IN the [a] beginning [b] God created the heaven and the earth.

2 And the earth was without form, and void; and darkness *was* upon the face of the deep: [c] and the Spirit of God moved upon the face of the waters.

3 ¶ And God said, [d] Let there be light: and there was light.

4 And God saw the light, that it *was* good: and God divided * the light from the darkness.

5 And God called the light Day, and the darkness he called Night: † and the evening and the morning were the first day.

6 ¶ And God said, [e] Let there be a ‡ firmament in the midst of the waters; and let it divide the waters from the waters.

7 And God made the firmament; and divided the waters which *were* under the firmament, from the waters which *were* [f] above the firmament: and it was so.

8 And God called the firmament Heaven: and the evening and the morning were the second day.

9 ¶ And God said, [g] Let the waters under the heaven be gathered together unto one place, and let the dry-*land* appear: and it was so.

10 And God called the dry-*land* Earth; and the gathering together of the waters called he Seas: and God saw that it *was* good.

11 ¶ And God said, Let the earth bring forth ‖ grass, the herb yielding seed, *and* the fruit-tree yielding fruit after his kind, whose seed *is* in it *self,* upon the earth: and it was so.

12 And the earth brought forth grass, *and* herb yielding seed after his kind, and the tree yielding fruit, whose seed *was* in it *self,* after his kind: and God saw that it *was* good.

13 And the evening and the morning were the third day.

14 ¶ And God said, Let there be [h] lights in the firmament of the heaven, to divide § the day from the night: and let them be for signs, and for seasons, and for days, and for years.

15 And let them be for lights in the firmament of the heaven, to give light upon the earth: and it was so.

16 And God made two great lights; the greater light * to rule the day, and the lesser light to rule the night: *he made* [i] the stars also.

17 And God set them in the firmament of the heaven, to give light upon the earth;

18 And to [k] rule over the day, and over the night, and to divide the light from the darkness: and God saw that it *was* good.

19 And the evening and the morning were the fourth day.

20 ¶ And God said, [l] Let the waters bring forth abundantly the † moving creature that hath ‡ life, and ‖ fowl *that* may fly above the earth in the § open firmament of heaven.

21 And [m] God created great whales, and every living creature that moveth, which the waters brought forth abundantly after their kind, and every winged fowl after his kind: and God saw that it *was* good.

22 And God blessed them, saying, [n] Be fruitful, and multiply, and fill the waters in the seas, and let fowl multiply in the earth.

23 And the evening and·the morning were the fifth day.

24 ¶ And God said, Let the earth bring forth the living creature after his kind, cattle, and creeping thing, and beast of the earth after his kind: and it was so.

25 And God made the beast of the earth after his kind, and cattle after their kind, and every thing that creepeth upon the earth after his kind: and God saw that it *was* good.

26 ¶ And God said, [o] Let us make man in our image, after our likeness: and [p] let them have dominion over the fish of the sea, and over the fowl of the air, and over the cattle, and over all the earth, and over every creeping thing that creepeth upon the earth.

27 So God created man in his *own* image, [q] in the image of God created he him: [r] male and female created he them.

28 And God blessed them, and God said unto them, [s] Be fruitful, and multiply, and replenish the earth, and subdue it: and have dominion over the fish of the sea, and over the fowl of the air, and over every living thing that * moveth upon the earth.

29 ¶ And God said, Behold, I have given you every herb † bearing seed, which *is* upon the face of all the earth, and every tree, in the which *is* the fruit of a tree yielding seed: [t] to you it shall be for meat.

Before CHRIST 4004.

[a] John 1. 1. [b] Psal. 33. 6. & 89. 11, 12. & 102. 25. & 136. 5. & 146. 6. Isa. 44. 24. Jer. 10. 12. & 51. 15. Zech. 12. 1. Acts 14. 15. & 17. 24. Heb. 11. 3. [c] Psal. 33. 6. Isa. 40. 13, 14. [d] 2 Cor. 4. 6. * Heb. *between the light and between the darkness.* † Heb. *and the evening was, and the morning was,* &c. [e] Psal. 136. 5. Jer. 10. 12. & 51. 15. ‡ Heb. *expansion.* [f] Psal. 148. 4. [g] Job 26. 10. & 38. 8. Psal. 33. 7. & 104. 9. & 136. 6. Prov. 8. 29. Jer. 5. 22. ‖ Heb. *tender grass.* [h] Deut. 4. 19. Psal. 136. 7. § Heb. *between the day and between the night.* * Heb. *for the rule of the day,* &c. [i] Job 38. 7. [k] Jer. 31. 35. [l] 2 Esdr. 6. 47. † Or, *creeping.* ‡ Heb. *soul.* ‖ Heb. *let fowl fly.* § Heb. *face of the firmament of heaven.* [m] Psal. 104. 26. [n] ch. 8. 17. & 9. 1. [o] ch. 5. 1. & 9. 6. Wisd. 2. 23. 1 Cor. 11. 7. Ephes. 4. 24. Col. 3. 10. [p] Psal. 8. 6. [q] 1 Cor. 11. 7. [r] ch. 5. 2. Mal. 2. 15. Matth. 19. 4. Mark 10. 6. [s] ch. 9. 1. * Heb. *creepeth.* † Heb. *seeding seed.* [t] ch. 9. 3. Psal. 104. 14, 15.

B

*2 * 1 ANTIQUITY OF EGYPT*

The priority of Egypt is accepted by Aristotle and Diodorus and most other Greeks, although some upheld the claims of the Ethiopians, the Scythians or the Chaldæans. Modern scholarship has usually supported Egypt or Sumer (which corresponds to the Greek Chaldæa), but Elam and the Indus valley are other possible sites for the first civilisation, and the few prehistoric remains of Chinese culture indicate a relationship to the Indian.

*2 * 2 BECOS*

The Phrygians spoke an Indo-European language. The word becos, which is authenticated from other Greek sources, should therefore come from the same root as the English «bake». It first appears in Greek in a fragment of Hipponax, who alludes to eating «the becos of the Cypriotes and the pyron of the Amathusians», as though becos were a Cypriote word; but he may be using it as Greek slang, if indeed the text is not corrupt (Strabo, viii. 340; ed. Knox, fr. 81, p. 57 in Edmonds' Loeb edn. of Theophrastus' Characters).

*2 * 3 Hephæstus represents the god whom the Egyptians called Ptah; he was the patron of craftsmen, especially of masons and smiths, because of his creative activities, and thus could be associated with the divine artisan of the Greeks.*

*3 * 1 LEARNING OF HELIOPOLIS*

Heliopolis, «City of the Sun», was the Greek name for the city called On or Onu in Egyptian (it is written Ywnw, but the pronunciation is known from transliterations into cuneiform, Hebrew and Greek). It had no importance except as a religious centre, the focus of the principal sun-cult of this period. A hall attached to the temple served as a theological university, somewhat like the mosque of El Azhar at Cairo, and from here came, it was said, the teachers of Pythagoras, Solon, Plato and Eudoxus (Strabo, xvii. 806). The resurrection of ancient religious ideas shows that the priests of the Saite period conducted a certain amount of historical research, but in an uncritical spirit, to judge by confusions and contradictions in their religious texts; their knowledge of the early dynastic religion of Egypt was vague and uncertain. The tone of Egyptian religion had changed; the cult of Isis and Osiris was now supreme and was rapidly absorbing all others, mythology was interpreted symbolically by the philosophic, while the populace relied for salvation upon spells, incantations, magical figures and amulets. The decay of mystical religion was balanced in the usual way by a rise of ethical thought; «wisdom literature» developed the moral ideas of the nation to a height previously unparalleled (Peet, Comparative Study of the Literature of Egypt, Palestine and Mesopotamia, p. 99).

*3 * 2 GODS UNKNOWABLE*

Literally translated, the sentence runs: «all men know equally about these». It has been argued that Herodotus means that they all have the same beliefs, but if so his construction is very slipshod and his book contains many passages which prove he did not think so. Xenophanes had already expressed the opinion: «Nor is there anyone who knows about the gods». To the Greeks, who had no revealed religion, certainty was both unattainable and unimportant on such matters; the way to please the gods, said the oracle of Delphi, was to follow «the custom of the state».

*4 * 1 CALENDAR*

The Greek calendar was based on lunar months, alternately of twenty-

---

of discovery: he took two children of the common sort, and gave them over to a herdsman to bring up at his folds, strictly charging him to let no one utter a word in their presence, but to keep them in a sequestered hut, and from time to time introduce goats to their apartment, see that they got their fill of milk, and in all other respects look after them. His object herein was to know, after the indistinct babblings of infancy were over, what word they would first articulate. It happened as he had anticipated. The herdsman obeyed his orders for two years, and at the end of that time, on his one day opening the door of their room and going in, the children both ran up to him with outstretched arms, and distinctly said "Becos". When this first happened the herdsman took no notice; but afterwards when he observed, on coming often to see after them, that the word was constantly in their mouths, he informed his lord, and by his command brought the children into his presence. Psammetichus then himself heard them say the word, upon which he proceeded to make inquiry what people there was who called anything "becos", and hereupon he learnt that "becos" was the Phrygian name for bread.[2] In consideration of this circumstance the Egyptians yielded their claims, and admitted the greater antiquity of the Phrygians.

That these were the real facts I learnt from the priests of Hephæstus[3] at Memphis. The Greeks, among other foolish tales, relate that Psammetichus had the children brought up by women whose tongues he had previously cut out; but the priests said their bringing up was such as I have stated above.

3. I got much other information also from conversation with these priests while I was at Memphis, and I even went to Heliopolis and to Thebes, expressly to try whether the priests of those places would agree in their accounts with the priests at Memphis. The Heliopolitans have the reputation of being the most learned of all the Egyptians.[1] What they told me concerning their religion it is not my intention to repeat, except the names of their deities, for I believe all men know as little about the gods.[2] If I relate anything else concerning them, it will only be when compelled to do so by the course of my narrative.

4. Now with regard to mere human matters, the accounts which they gave, and in which all agreed, were the following. The Egyptians, they said, were the first to discover the solar year, and to portion out its course into twelve parts. They obtained this knowledge from the stars. (To my mind they contrive their year much more cleverly than the Greeks, for these last every other year intercalate a whole month, to preserve the seasons, but the Egyptians, dividing the year into twelve months of thirty days each, add every year a space of five days besides, whereby the circuit of the seasons is made to return with uniformity.)[1] The Egyptians, they went on to affirm, first brought into use the names of the twelve gods,[2] which the Greeks adopted from them; and first erected altars, images, and temples to the gods; and also first engraved upon stone the figures of living creatures.[3] In most of these cases they proved to me that what they said was true. And they told me that the first man who ruled over Egypt was Min,[4] and that in his

---

Middle Kingdom, were ordered on a lunar basis, and the state religious festivals continued so. The people therefore used them as the basis of a second calendar, to get the seasons correct (L. Borchardt, Altägypt. Zeitmessung, 1920; Scharff, Grundzüge der äg. Vorgeschichte, 1927, p. 55, in Morgenland, 12).

*4 * 2 Each religious centre in Egypt had its own theology but they agreed in grouping gods in nines on the basis of the trinity comprised by mother, father and son. Perhaps Herodotus added a fourth trinity to complete his total of twelve, but the gods he enumerates do not fit into any Egyptian grouping.*

*4 * 3 PRIORITY OF EGYPTIAN ART*

Some close connection must have existed between the Sumerian part of Mesopotamia and Egypt, from shortly before the unification of the kingdom to the Third Dynasty, to judge by the similarities of their art. Perhaps development proceeded equally in the two countries, under mutual influence, for neither appears plainly as the originator; their early chronology cannot yet be correlated without a possible error of several centuries, but it seems likely that the Third Dynasty may have coincided with the «Royal Tombs» at Ur at approximately 2700, while the earliest Sumerian works of art may date shortly before 3000. Nor has Sumerian art been traced to its primitive essays with the same wealth of examples as remains from predynastic Egypt (Scharff, Grundzüge der äg. Vorgeschichte, 1927; Childe, New Light on the Most Ancient East, 1934; Ill. London News, May 19 and June 9, 1934, pp. 761, 776, 910, 919).

*4 * 4 MIN*

Mena, the Menes of most Greek authors, is usually taken for a legendary figure compounded of two or three different kings, founders of the first dynasty of united Egypt. The name perhaps occurs on a tablet from Naqada (Newberry, in Brunton, Great Ones of Anc. Egypt, 1929, p. 47); it might mean «Firm», and so may have been used by one or more of them as a subsidiary title (for their tombs see Borchardt, Ä.Z. 36, 1898, p. 87; R.L.V. iv, 2, p. 463, pl. 218). The late Egyptian tradition is preserved by Manetho: «The First Dynasty, after the dead demigods, consisted of eight kings, of whom the first was Menes the Thinite; he reigned 62 years and died from a wound received from a hippopotamus».

nine and of thirty days, but as the true length of a lunar month amounts to forty-four minutes and three seconds in excess of twenty-nine and a half days, they were obliged to add an intercalary month at intervals of eight years or so to bring their year into closer conformity with the solar seasons. The Egyptians took a solar calendar which had twelve months of thirty days each, with five extra days, which were added very early in the dynastic period. They thus approximated so closely to the true calendar as to have two complete extra years in every 1459; they never considered any nearer approximation, even when Ptolemy Euergetes pressed them to accept a system of 365¼ days.

The Egyptian year began (in theory always, in practice only at these intervals of 1460 years), when Sirius rose immediately before sunrise on the Egyptian horizon (n. on 142). This solar calendar probably came into use in the year 2781 or 2776, at the beginning of a cycle in the Old Kingdom, but the Egyptian temple services, even under the

Polyglot Bible
Antwerp 1572
printed by Christopher Plantin
reduced from approx 400 mm deep

Plantin's *Polyglot Bible* shows four
related texts and two subsidiary texts
clearly and with grave elegance. The
woodcut initials decorate the page which
is otherwise fairly austere, although the
different 'colours' of the text types result
in an unusual richness. Verses are flagged
within the texts by a pleasantly decorative little device. The column widths are
varied in order to accommodate differing
lengths of text in the same depth. The
vertical rules are designed to marshal the
reference numbers and are also reminiscent of the ruled lines in a medieval
manuscript bible. The initial capital in
the lower text appears high, and there are
strange gaps in the Hebrew main text,
where verses are indicated, as if to make
up the measure. The spaces in the lower
texts, however, allow one to find each
item easily.

It is interesting to compare this spread
with the preceding example – Meynell's
Herodotus. Both are virtuoso examples of
copyfitting and typesetting of parallel
texts; the Polyglot Bible has the additional problem of different languages –
and their varied lengths.

CAPVT PRIMVM.

1 IN principio creauit Deus cælum & terrá. * Terra autem
erat inanis & vacua : & tenebræ erant super faciē abyssi:
& spiritus Dei ferebatur su-
per aquas. * Dixitq́, Deus, Fiat lux. Et facta est
4 lux. * Et vidit Deus lucem quòd esset bona:&
5 diuisit lucem à tenebris. * Appellauitq́, lucem
diem;& tenebras nocte. Factumq́; est vespere
6 & mane dies vnus. * Dixit quoque Deus, Fiat
firmamentū in medio aquarum ; & diuidat a-
7 quas ab aquis. * Et fecit Deus firmamentū,
diuisitq́; aquas quæ erant sub firmamento, ab
his quæ erant super firmamentū. Et factum est
8 ita. * Vocauitq́; Deus firmamentū,cælum: &
factum est vespere, & mane dies secundus.
9 * Dixit verò Deus , Congregentur aquæ quæ
sub cęlo sunt, in locum vnum:& appareat ari-
10 da. Et factum est ita. * Et vocauit Deus arida,
terram: congregationesq́; aquarum appellauit
11 maria. Et vidit Deus quòd esset bonum. *
ait, Germinet terra herbā virentem & facientem semen; & lignum pomiferū faciens fructū
iuxta genus suum, cuius semen in semetipso sit
12 super terram. Et factū est ita. *Et protulit terra
herbam virenté, & faciente semen iuxta genus
suū;lignumq́; faciens fructū; & habens vnum-
quodq́; sementem secundū speciem suam .
13 vidit Deus quòd esset bonum. * Et factum est
14 vespere & mane dies tertius. *Dixit aute Deus,
Fiant luminaria in firmamento cæli ; & diuidant diem ac nocte ; & sint in signa & tépora
15 & dies & annos: *Vt luceát in firmaméto cæli,
16 & illuminent terrá.Et factum est ita. * Fecitq́,
Deus duo luminaria magna: luminare maius,
vt præesset diei: & luminare minus,vt præesset
17 nocti: & stellas. * Et posuit eas Deus in firmaméto cæli,vt lucerét super terrá: *Et præessent
18 diei ac nocti;& diuiderent lucem ac tenebras.
19 * Et vidit Deus quòd esset bonū. * Et factum est
20 vespere, & mane dies quartus. * Dixit etiam
Deus,Producant aquæ reptile animæ viuentis,
& volatile super terram sub firmamento cæli.

תרגום אונקלוס

בקדמין

CAPVT PRIMVM.

IN principio fecit Deus cælum & terræ. * At terra erat inuisibilis et incōposita, et tenebræ super abyssum: & spiritus Dei ferebatur super aquam. * Et dixit Deus, Fiat lux, & facta est lux. * Et vidit Deus lucē, quòd bona: & diuisit Deus inter lucem, & inter tenebras. * Et vocauit Deus lucē diē: & tenebras vocauit noctē: & factū est vespere; & factū est mane, dies vnus. * Et dixit Deus, Fiat firmamentū in medio aquæ: & sit diuidēs inter aquā, & aquā. * Et fecit Deus firmamentū, & diuisit Deus inter aquā; quæ erat sub firmamēto: & inter aquā; quæ super firmamentū. * Et vocauit Deus firmamentū cælū: & vidit Deus, quòd bonū. Et factū est vespere, & factū est mane, dies secūdus. * Et dixit Deus, Cōgregetur aqua quæ sub cælo, in cōgregationē vnā; & appareat arida. Et factū est ita, et cōgregata est aqua quæ sub cælo, in cōgregationes suas: et apparuit arida. * Et vocauit Deus aridā, terrā: et cōgregationes aquarū, vocauit maria. Et vidit Deus quòd bonū. * Et dixit Deus, Germinet terra herbā fæni seminātē semē secundū genus et secundū similitudinē: & lignū pomiferū faciens fructū, cuius semen ipsius in ipso secundū genus super terrā. Et factum est ita. * Et protulit terra herbā fæni seminātē semen secundū genus & secundū similitudinē: & lignū pomiferū faciens fructū, cuius semē eius in ipso, secundum genus super terrā. Et vidit Deus quòd bonū. * Et factū est vespere, & factū est mane, dies tertius. * Et dixit Deus: Fiant luminaria in firmamento cæli, vt luceant super terrā, ad diuidendum inter diē, & inter noctē; & sint in signa, & in tēpora, & in dies, & in annos. * Et sint in illuminatione in firmamento cæli, vt luceant super terram. Et factū est ita. * Et fecit Deus duo luminaria magna: luminare magnū in principatus diei: & luminare minus in principatus noctis: et stellas. * Et posuit eas Deus in firmamēto cæli: vt lucerēt super terrā, * Et præessent diei, & nocti, & diuiderēt inter lucē et inter tenebras: et vidit Deus quòd bonū. * Et factū est vespere, & factū est mane, dies quartus. * Et dixit Deus, Producant aquæ reptila animarū viuentiū, & volatilia volātia super terrā; secundū firmamentū cæli: & factū est ita.

Ἐν ἀρχῇ ἐποίησεν ὁ θεὸς τὸν οὐρανὸν καὶ τὴν γῆν. ἡ δὲ γῆ ἦν ἀόρατος καὶ ἀκατασκεύαστος, καὶ σκότος ἐπάνω τῆς ἀβύσσου. καὶ πνεῦμα θεοῦ ἐπεφέρετο ἐπάνω τοῦ ὕδατος. * καὶ εἶπεν ὁ θεός, γενηθήτω φῶς· καὶ ἐγένετο φῶς. * καὶ εἶδεν ὁ θεὸς τὸ φῶς, ὅτι καλόν· καὶ διεχώρισεν ὁ θεὸς ἀνὰ μέσον τοῦ φωτὸς, καὶ ἀνὰ μέσον τοῦ σκότους. * καὶ ἐκάλεσεν ὁ θεὸς τὸ φῶς ἡμέραν, καὶ τὸ σκότος ἐκάλεσε νύκτα. καὶ ἐγένετο ἑσπέρα, καὶ ἐγένετο πρωί, ἡμέρα μία. * καὶ εἶπεν ὁ θεός, γενηθήτω στερέωμα ἐν μέσῳ τοῦ ὕδατος, καὶ ἔστω διαχωρίζον ἀνὰ μέσον ὕδατος καὶ ὕδατος. * καὶ ἐποίησεν ὁ θεὸς τὸ στερέωμα, καὶ διεχώρισεν ὁ θεὸς ἀνὰ μέσον τοῦ ὕδατος, ὃ ἦν ὑποκάτω τοῦ στερεώματος, καὶ ἀνὰ μέσον τοῦ ὕδατος τοῦ ἐπάνω τοῦ στερεώματος. * καὶ ἐκάλεσεν ὁ θεὸς τὸ στερέωμα οὐρανόν. καὶ εἶδεν ὁ θεός, ὅτι καλόν. καὶ ἐγένετο ἑσπέρα, καὶ ἐγένετο πρωί, ἡμέρα δευτέρα. * καὶ εἶπεν ὁ θεός, συναχθήτω τὸ ὕδωρ τὸ ὑποκάτω τοῦ οὐρανοῦ εἰς συναγωγὴν μίαν, καὶ ὀφθήτω ἡ ξηρά. καὶ ἐγένετο οὕτως. καὶ συνήχθη τὸ ὕδωρ τὸ ὑποκάτω τοῦ οὐρανοῦ εἰς τὰς συναγωγὰς αὐτῶν, καὶ ὤφθη ἡ ξηρά. * καὶ ἐκάλεσεν ὁ θεὸς τὴν ξηράν, γῆν· καὶ τὰ συστήματα τῶν ὑδάτων ἐκάλεσε θαλάσσας. καὶ εἶδεν ὁ θεός, ὅτι καλόν. * καὶ εἶπεν ὁ θεός, βλαστησάτω ἡ γῆ βοτάνην χόρτου σπεῖρον σπέρμα κατὰ γένος καὶ καθ᾽ ὁμοιότητα, καὶ ξύλον κάρπιμον ποιοῦν καρπόν, οὗ τὸ σπέρμα αὐτοῦ ἐν αὐτῷ κατὰ γένος ἐπὶ τῆς γῆς. καὶ ἐγένετο οὕτως. καὶ ἐξήνεγκεν ἡ γῆ βοτάνην χόρτου σπεῖρον σπέρμα κατὰ γένος καὶ καθ᾽ ὁμοιότητα, καὶ ξύλον κάρπιμον ποιοῦν καρπόν, οὗ τὸ σπέρμα αὐτοῦ ἐν αὐτῷ κατὰ γένος ἐπὶ τῆς γῆς. καὶ εἶδεν ὁ θεὸς ὅτι καλόν. * καὶ ἐγένετο ἑσπέρα καὶ ἐγένετο πρωί, ἡμέρα τρίτη. * καὶ εἶπεν ὁ θεός, γενηθήτωσαν φωστῆρες ἐν τῷ στερεώματι τοῦ οὐρανοῦ εἰς φαῦσιν ἐπὶ τῆς γῆς, τοῦ διαχωρίζειν ἀνὰ μέσον τῆς ἡμέρας καὶ ἀνὰ μέσον τῆς νυκτός· καὶ ἔστωσαν εἰς σημεῖα, καὶ εἰς καιροὺς, καὶ εἰς ἡμέρας, καὶ εἰς ἐνιαυτούς· * καὶ ἔστωσαν εἰς φαῦσιν ἐν τῷ στερεώματι τοῦ οὐρανοῦ, ὥστε φαίνειν ἐπὶ τῆς γῆς. καὶ ἐγένετο οὕτως. * καὶ ἐποίησεν ὁ θεὸς τοὺς δύο φωστῆρας τοὺς μεγάλους, τὸν φωστῆρα τὸν μέγαν εἰς ἀρχὰς τῆς ἡμέρας, καὶ τὸν φωστῆρα τὸν ἐλάσσω εἰς ἀρχὰς τῆς νυκτός, καὶ τοὺς ἀστέρας. * καὶ ἔθετο αὐτοὺς ὁ θεὸς ἐν τῷ στερεώματι τοῦ οὐρανοῦ, ὥστε φαίνειν ἐπὶ τῆς γῆς, καὶ ἄρχειν τῆς ἡμέρας καὶ τῆς νυκτός, καὶ διαχωρίζειν ἀνὰ μέσον τοῦ φωτὸς καὶ ἀνὰ μέσον τοῦ σκότους. καὶ εἶδεν ὁ θεὸς ὅτι καλόν. * καὶ ἐγένετο ἑσπέρα καὶ ἐγένετο πρωί, ἡμέρα τετάρτη. * καὶ εἶπεν ὁ θεός, ἐξαγαγέτω τὰ ὕδατα ἑρπετὰ ψυχῶν ζωσῶν, καὶ πετεινὰ πετόμενα ἐπὶ τῆς γῆς, κατὰ τὸ στερέωμα τοῦ οὐρανοῦ. καὶ ἐγένετο οὕτως.

CHALDAICAE PARAPHRASIS TRANSLATIO.
CAPVT PRIMVM.

IN principio creauit Deus cælum & terram. ' Terra autem erat deserta & vacua: & tenebræ super faciem abyssi: & spiritus Dei insufflabat super faciem aquarum. ' Et dixit Deus, Sit lux: & fuit lux. ' Et vidit Deus lucem quòd esset bona. Et diuisit Deus inter lucem & inter tenebras. ' Appellauitque Deus lucem diem, & tenebras vocauit noctem. Et fuit vespere & fuit mane dies vnus. ' Et dixit Deus, Sit firmamentum in medio aquarum: & diuidat inter aquas & aquas. ' Et fecit Deus firmamentum: & diuisit inter aquas quæ erant subter firmamentum: & inter aquas quæ erant super firmamentum: & fuit ita. ' Et vocauit Deus firmamentum cælum. Et fuit vespere & fuit mane, dies secundus. ' Et dixit Deus, Congregentur aquæ quæ sub cælo sunt, in locum vnum: & appareat arida. Et fuit ita. '' Et vocauit Deus aridam terram: & locum congregationis aquarum appellauit maria. Et vidit Deus quòd esset bonum. '' Et dixit Deus, Germinet terra germinationem herbæ, cuius filius sementis seminatur: arboremque fructiferam facientem fructum secundum genus suum; cuius filius sementis in ipso sit super terram. Et fuit ita. '' Et produxit terra germen herbæ, cuius filius sementis seminatur secundum genus suum; & arborem facientem fructum, cuius filius sementis in ipso secundum genus suum. Et vidit Deus quòd esset bonum. '' Et fuit vespere & fuit mane, dies tertius. '' Et dixit Deus, Sint luminaria in firmamento cæli, vt diuidant inter diem & noctem: & sint in signa & in tempora: & vt numerentur per ea dies & anni. '' Et sint in luminaria in firmamento cæli ad illuminandum super terram: & fuit ita. '' Et fecit Deus duo luminaria magna: luminare maius, vt dominaretur in die: & luminare minus, vt dominetur in nocte: & stellas. '' Et posuit eas Deus in firmamento cæli ad illuminandum super terram: '' Et vt dominarentur in die & in nocte: & vt diuiderent inter lucē & tenebras: & vidit Deus quòd esset bonū. '' Et fuit vespere & fuit mane, dies quartus. '' Et dixit Deus, Serpant aquæ reptile animæ viuētis: & auem quæ volat super terrā super faciē aëris firmamenti cælorum.

RIGHT
Polyglot Bible
Antwerp 1572
printed by Christopher Plantin
(dedication)
reduced from approx 400 mm deep

OPPOSITE
Lord Clarendon
History of the Great Rebellion
Oxford University Press
1702-4
reduced from approx 420 mm deep

Plantin's dedication is an early example of Roman inscriptional typography but with two upper and lower case paragraphs introduced: one in semi-bold and both justified. The two styles sit oddly together on the page but there is no lack of confidence and dignity.

Monumental too is Lord Clarendon's great history of Cromwell's rebellion. The text types were cut by the Dutchman Peter Walpergen, at Oxford, for the University Press, and though many of the characters are odd and irregular the whole page suggests an authority entirely suited to the author's words.

While Plantin achieves a variation of 'colour' on the page by different weights and sizes of roman, and lines of caps, variation is here achieved not only by the engravings, but also by the italic – whose lighter texture forms a bridge between the delicacy of the engraving and the weightier roman text.

SERENISS. PRINCIPI

D. MATTHIAE

ARCHIDVCI AVSTRIÆ,

DVCI BVRGVNDIAE, &c.

IMPERATOR. F. FR.Q.

BELGICÆ PROREGI.

Hoc ſacrum quinquelingue Bibliorũ opus, quod ad ſtabiliendum Eccleſię ſtatum, controuerſias in religione tollendas , Rex Catholicus pietati ſuę teſtandę diuulgari iuſsit, iuuítque;

Quódque Dei in primis, & clariſſ. Theologorum ope, immenſo ſumptu & labore ſuo, Chriſtophorus Plantinus feliciter typis ſuis vulgauit, ita vt Sanctiſſ. D. N. Pontificis, Regum , Principúmque , & penè vniuerſi orbis iudicio , tanti operis comprobata dignitas ſit:

IDEM CHRISTOPH. PLANTINVS

ARCHITYPOGRAPHVS REGIVS

Celſit. ſuæ perpetuus cliens

D. D.

THE

Hiſtory of the Rebellion, &c.

BOOK I.

Deut. iv. 7, 8, 9.

For what Nation is there ſo great, who hath God ſo nigh unto them, as the Lord our God is in all things that we call upon him for?

And what Nation is there ſo great that hath Statutes, and Judgments ſo righteous as all this Law, which I ſet before you this day?

Only take heed to thy ſelf, and keep thy ſoul diligently, leaſt thou forget the things which thine eyes have ſeen.

THAT Poſterity may not be Deceived by the proſperous Wickedneſs of thoſe times of which I write, into an Opinion, that nothing leſs than a general Combination, and univerſal Apoſtacy in the whole Nation from their Religion, and Allegiance, could, in ſo ſhort a time, have produced ſuch a total and prodigious Alteration, and Confuſion over the whole Kingdom; And that the Memory of thoſe, who, out of Duty and Conſcience, have oppoſed that Torrent, which did overwhelm them, may not looſe the recompence due to their Virtue, but having undergone the injuries and reproaches of this, may find a vindication in a better age: It will not be unuſeful for the information of the Judgement and Conſcience of men, to preſent to the world a full and clear Narration of the Grounds, Circumſtances, and Artifices of this Rebellion; not only from the time ſince the flame hath been viſible in a Civil war, but, looking farther back, from thoſe former paſſages and accidents, by which the Seed-plots were made and framed, from whence thoſe miſcheifs have ſucceſſively grown to the height, they have ſince arrived at.

The Preface of the Author.

AND in this enſuing Hiſtory, though the hand and judgement of God will be very viſible, in infatuating a People (as ripe and prepared for Deſtruction) into all the perverſe actions of Folly and Madneſs, making

A 2

the

Address from the Papal Legate
Leonello Chieregato
to King Henry VII
Rome 1490
printed by Eucharius Silber
actual size

Eric Gill
An Essay on Typography
London 1931, re-set 1954
actual size

Special problems apart, the basic task of
the book typographer is to present a text
in its clearest and most appropriate form.
This 1490 page uses a rich dark type in
justified lines with little leading and no
indication of paragraphs.

   Eric Gill's essay is well leaded and
evenly word-spaced (allowed by ranging
left), with paragraphs and sub-paragraphs
clearly marked. The small number of
words in a line make easy reading.

   Because the running heads are in
Joanna's remarkably narrow italic, they
are visually considerably less emphatic
than the same-sized roman of the text;
but the folios are rather too noticeable
and would perhaps be better placed at
the foot of the page.

   Although the two examples are so
different in appearance (and characteristic of their times), both follow ancient
practices in using frequent word breaks,
contractions and ampersands to avoid
undue variation in word spacing or line
length.

instructifqʒ claſſibus Gallico Tyrenoqʒ pelagò
Meſſanam ſimul delati:uariaqʒ deinde fortuna
uſi:licet diuerſo tpe: Ptolæmaidem puenientes
chriſtianoꝜ illã obſidentiũ exercitũ:& aĩcs au-
xerũt:atqʒ urbi capiundæ maximo adiumento
fuere.Cóuenit Hedoardus quoqʒ Henrici Re-
gis Angliæ filius cũ Ludouico FrancoꝜ Rege:
& uno eodéqʒ tpe ille ex Maſſilienſi portu í afri-
cã.hic ex Anglia í Aſiã maximis paratiſſimiſqʒ
claſſibus nauigart cóiuncturi ſe una Ptolæmai-
de ſicut condixerãt. Exemplo quidé ſunt explo
ratiſſimo hæ duæ regales domus ueſtræ:q̃tum
chriſtianoꝜ principũ concordia res chriſtiana
floruerit:q̃tumue diſcordia fuerit afflicta.Con-
cordibus náqʒ Anglis & Frãcis recepta eſt Pto-
læmais . Victus maximo prælio ſtrenuiſſimus
ille Saladinus SarracenoꝜ tyrannus:Aſcaló:&
Gaza urbes inſignes a Saladino deletæ inſtau-
ratæ ſũt:pluraqʒ alia ꝓſpere geſta. Ex eoꝜ uero
diſcordia interrupta eſt Hieroſolymæ obſidio:
receſſũ ex Aſia:ita labefactata Reſp.ut nõ ſine
lachrymis aſſerere auſim iteſtía FrãcoꝜ Anglo
rũqʒ bella totã Aſiã de manibus nr̃is eripuiſſe:
In Europãqʒ ímaniſſimis chriſti hoſtibus trãſi-
tũ:ſecundoſqʒ ſucceſſus præbuiſſe. Nec poſthac
uel torpentibus uel diſſidentibus inuicem reli
quis etiã chriſtianis principibus de repellendo

spite of our preoccupation with merely physical convenience, we have inherited an alphabet of such pre-eminent rationality and dignity as the Roman. A good example is the inscription on Trajan's Column at Rome, of which a plaster cast is in the Victoria & Albert Museum, London. ¶ Lettering is for us the Roman alphabet and the Roman alphabet is lettering. Whatever the Greeks or the Germans or the Russians or the Czecho-slovaks or other people may do, the English language is done in Roman letters, and these letters may be said to have reached a permanent type about the first century A.D. ¶ Though in the course of the centuries innumerable variations in detail have been made, Roman letters have not changed essentially. Fourteen hundred years after the cutting of the Trajan inscription the tablet in Henry VII's chapel was inscribed, and no Roman would have found any difficulty in reading the letters. Eighteen hundred years after the time of Trajan & four hundred years after Henry VII, Roman letters are still made, and in almost the same way (e.g. the Artillery Monument, Hyde Park Corner).

¶ But, although the Roman alphabet has remained essentially unchanged through the centuries, customs & habits of work have changed a great deal. In the time of the Romans, say A.D. 100, when a man said the word 'letters' it is probable that he

immediately thought of the kind of letters he was accustomed to seeing on public inscriptions. Altho' all sorts of other kinds of lettering existed (on wax tablets, on papyrus, &c.) the most common kind of formal lettering was the inscription on stone. The consequence was that when he made letters 'as well as he could' it was the stone inscription letter that he took as his model. He did not say: Such & such a tool or material naturally makes or lends itself to the making of such and such forms. On the contrary, he said: Letters *are* such and such forms; therefore, whatever tools & materials we have to use, we must make these forms as well as the tools and material will allow. This order of procedure has always been the one followed. The mind is the arbiter in letter forms, not the tool or the material. This is not to deny that tools and materials have had a very great influence on letter forms. But that influence has been secondary, and for the most part it has been exerted without the craftsman's conscious intention.

¶ If we admit, as it seems we must admit, that in Roman times the public inscription in stone was the chief model for all forms of letters, we shall expect to find that when they began to make lettering with a pen, on paper or on skin, the forms of letters would be imitations of inscription forms: and this is precisely what we do find. A good

Lewis Carroll
Alice's Adventures in Wonderland
London 1867
reduced from approx 185 mm deep

Gill's typography was the rational craftsman's reaction to industrially-produced work of mid and late Victorian England. This spread from *Alice in Wonderland*, famous for the playful 'mouse's tale', shows most of the faults which Gill and, of course, Morris before him, found so unbearable. The splendid modern roman of Bodoni has here degenerated into a weak and character-less derivation. The justified lines result in very open word spacing and the lines are over-leaded. The skill and care shown in the typographic interpretation of Carroll's original manuscript 'tail' is in remarkable contrast to this joyless

Alice thought the whole thing very absurd, but they all looked so grave that she did not dare to laugh ; and as she could not think of anything to say, she simply bowed, and took the thimble, looking as solemn as she could.

The next thing was to eat the comfits : this caused some noise and confusion, as the large birds complained that they could not taste theirs, and the small ones choked and had to be patted on the back. However, it was over at last, and they sat down again in a ring, and begged the Mouse to tell them something more.

" You promised to tell me your history, you know," said Alice, " and why it is you hate—C and D," she added in a whisper, half afraid that it would be offended again.

" Mine is a long and a sad tale !" said the Mouse, turning to Alice, and sighing.

" It *is* a long tail, certainly," said Alice, looking down with wonder at the Mouse's tail ; " But why do you call it sad ?" And she kept on puzzling about it while the Mouse was speaking,

so that her idea of the tale was something like this :——" Fury said to

        a mouse, That
            he met
              in the
                house,
            ' Let us
            both go
            to law :
        I will
      prosecute
    you.—
        Come, I'll
          take no
            denial ;
          We must
              have a
                trial :
                  For
                really
                this
                morning
                    I've
                  nothing
                  to do.'
              Said the
            mouse to
            the cur,
              ' Such a
                trial,
              dear sir,
            With no
          jury or
        judge,
        would be
          wasting
          our breath.'
            ' I'll be
            judge,
          I'll be
        jury,'
        Said
          cunning
        old Fury ;
          ' I'll try
          the whole
            cause,
              and
            condemn
            you
          to
            death."

uninviting page, which is so absurdly inappropriate for the subject that it is almost as if it were deliberate.

Whistler's elegant arrangement shows a painter raising book typography to the rather precious heights of aestheticism, even when using everyday and unre-markable type and paper. What made Whistler's page distinctive and influential was its simplicity, the careful arrangement of text on the page and the huge margins. The quirky and often pro-vocatively-placed margin notes in minute type are demonstrations of Whistler's ego rather than of his concern for the reader; they also demonstrate some of the same skills in typesetting seen in Carroll's 'tail'.

The Civil Tribunal of the Seine condemned Mr. Whistler to pay 1000 francs damages with interest. You will form your own conclusions, gentlemen; but I am of opinion that the Court had some difficulty in justifying this award. Our opponent pleaded the trouble Lady Eden had been put to, the fatigue and inconvenience involved in sitting to an artist so fastidious, careful, and exacting as Mr. Whistler. The Court, however, disregarded this plea, and justified its award by saying, " Mr. Whistler failed to supply what he agreed to supply; Sir William Eden has a right to damages since he is not to have Lady Eden's portrait."

He is not to have it, I am quite sure; but he has compensation—he has the money he ventured for the portrait. And before assessing damages, the Court must remember the respective proceedings of patron and client in this matter.

I need not go into the details which Mr. Whistler has several times given you of the relations between himself and his client. But here again the Court might be influenced by certain scruples. Here, they might say, was the father of a family who wished to bequeath to his children a portrait of their mother, desiring it to be preserved as an heirloom. Would this be true in the case of Sir William Eden? I regret to have to say no. You know, gentlemen,

" Je ne veux pas revenir sur le récit qui a été fait plusieurs fois par M. Whistler lui-même des rapports qui ont eu lieu entre l'artiste et l'amateur. Ici encore, il y a un scruple que pourrait avoir la Cour. Elle pourrait se dire : Voilà un père de famille qui voulait léguer à ses enfants le portrait de leur mère, qui voulait que ce fût conservé comme un héritage de famille et que ce soit un dépôt sacré se transmettant de génération en génération. Il y a là une satisfaction morale qui peut dans une certaine mesure se traduire par des dommages et intérêts. Mais est-ce le cas de Sir William Eden? J'ai le regret d'être obligé de répondre : Non. Vous savez, Messieurs, que je n'aime pas à mettre en cause directement la personne des adver-saires, je trouve que souvent cela est inutile, que c'est parfois dangereux,

38

mais là je suis dans la nécessité de vous dire ce qu est Sir William dans le rapport que cela a avec la question que vous avez à résoudre, c'est à dire la question des dommages et intérêts. Sir William Eden qui se donne comme un amateur est en réalité un amateur spéculateur de tableaux. Vous allez voir

that, as a rule, I avoid personalities in dealing with my adversaries. They are often irrelevant, and sometimes dangerous. But it is my duty to tell you what Sir William is, as this has a direct bearing on the question of damages you will have to decide. Sir William Eden, who poses as a patron of art, is, in fact, an amateur picture dealer. I shall show you that he does not have his wife's portrait painted for his family, or with any idea of handing it down to his children. His commissions are speculations. He offers the portraits of his wife and children for sale and makes a profit on them. I have communicated certain documents to my adversary which, from a moral point of view, are overwhelming in this connec-tion. The first of these is a letter from Messrs Boussod Valadon. It is written from the London house of the firm to Mr. Webb, Mr. Whistler's solicitor, and is as follows :

que ce n'est pas du tout pour sa famille qu'il fait faire le portrait de sa femme pour le transmettre à ses enfants, et cela pour une raison bien simple c'est que le portrait de sa femme et même le portrait de ses enfants, il les met en vente, il en tire argent, il en fait des spéculations ! J'ai communiqué à cet égard à mon adver-saire des pièces qui sont accablantes au point de vue moral."

October 8, 1897.

DEAR SIR—In reply to your letter I beg to state that shortly after the lawsuit in Paris, Sir William Eden, who has been in the habit of paying us occasional visits for some years past, came into our gallery to see some pictures we were exhibiting. He spoke of the lawsuit, and I mentioned that I had seen Lady Eden's portrait at the Salon. From what I had heard, I knew that Sir William did not care for the picture, but, knowing its commercial value, I told him I was ready to make him an offer of £200 for it on behalf of my firm. He declined it, on the grounds that the picture was worth a great deal more. I then said : Well, we will give you £250. He replied that

39

James McNeill Whistler
The Baronet and the Butterfly
New York 1899
reduced from approx 200 mm deep

The Diary of Virginia Woolf
Vol V 1936-1941
ed Anne Olivier Bell
Hogarth Press
London 1984
reduced from approx 235 mm deep

Letters and diaries give designers the same problems as setting straight narrative, but with various additional complications such as editors' (and sometimes authors') footnotes, subject and running heads, dates, places and folios. There is also the overriding need to make readable and orderly a mass of chaotic material not usually intended by the author for publication.

In this example the various elements are elegantly orchestrated, from the running heads to the neat footnotes; later marginal notes of the author are inset into the text. Editorial explanations are in square brackets and linkages in italics. The styling throughout the book reflects the writer's helter-skelter prose.

Unobtrusive editing and sensitive design are equally responsible for this admirable achievement.

---

repeat the fact that my head is a tight wound ball of string. To unwind it, I lie on my Heal chair bed & doze of an evening. But the noise worries me. The 2 houses next door are down; we are shored up. There are patches of wall paper where there used to be hotel bedrooms. Thus the Southampton Row traffic gets at me; & I long for 37 Mecklenburgh Sq: but doubt if we shall get it. Pritchard is negotiating with the Bedfords.[1] A talk about the future with John. He is harassed by the lean year. Cant live in London on £500 minus his mothers interest &c. 37 is a large seeming & oh so quiet house, where I could sleep anywhere. But it dont do to dwell on it. & there would be the horror of the move in August.

Day Lewis came one day; thrust in on the wake of Elizabeth. A stocky sturdy man. truculent. a little like Muggins 40 yrs ago, as I think George called Malcolm Macnaghten. "Priestley lolling on the beach" was discussed.[2] I made him laugh by repeating that word. I wish I could repeat more words. Boswell did it. Could I turn B. at my age? "I'm doing films for the gas people . . . I live a purely country life. A rather too arty home. Devonshire." I infer some rupture with the Bugger Boys.

should it be lōl ling or lolling?

Boswell at Sissinghurst. Gwen walking through the Bluebell woods, speaking of her youth—a little to justify herself. Had been advertiser to a scent shop. had done welfare work. Her daughter Jiccy meets a prostitute outside the Berkeley whom she has deliv[er]ed. "Must just speak to Bessy" she says to the youth who's treating her—"Its her beat." G. a little shocked.[3] And I liked the soft cream & yellow flowers on the sunny grass & the bend stooping like a picture. And the thread of bright blue bells: & Vita in her breeches.

We are going to Brittany by the way after Whitsun. A whole 2 weeks rambling. Now that'll fill my dry cistern of a head. But this is nothing

1. Although the Woolfs' lease of 52 Tavistock Square ran until 1941, the din and disturbance caused by the adjacent demolitions compelled them to move. On 9 May they saw over and resolved upon 37 Mecklenburgh Square, and their solicitor-tenant Mr Pritchard—who agreed to move with them—attempted (unsuccessfully in the event) to persuade their landlords, the Duke of Bedford Estates, to accept the early surrender of their current lease.
2. Elizabeth Bowen came to tea with VW on 3 May; they were joined by the poet Cecil Day Lewis (1904-72), who was currently writing the script for a projected documentary film on colliers for the British Commercial Gas Association. The High Court judge Sir Malcolm MacNaghten (1869-1955) had been at Eton and Cambridge with George Duckworth. The Woolfs saw J. B. Priestley's play *Johnson Over Jordan* at the Saville Theatre on 4 May.
3. The Woolfs had gone to Sissinghurst on 8 May *en route* from Rodmell to London. Gwen St Aubyn's daughter Jessica (b. 1918) is (1983) mystified by this story.

like so bad as The Years. A nun writes to invite me to stage a meeting of Outsiders in Hyde Park. I stop to answer her. Gertler tonight.[4]

Thursday 25 May

A queer little note to run off in a hurry: L. is bargaining for 37 M. Sq upstairs: I'm packing. We're off: & very likely I shant write much more in this now so tidy studio. Tidied for Ben to work in. I must pack upstairs. Brittany & Rodmell for 3 weeks.

Party last night. G. Keyneses: Eth Wn & her underworld friend. Ben Nicolson.[5]

Interrupted by parties come to see the house. The first day its in the agents hands. Shall we end our lives looking in that great peaceful garden; in the sun? I hope so.

On the afternoon of 25 May the Woolfs drove to Rodmell for Whitsuntide, and on 5 June crossed the Channel to Dieppe for a motor tour of Normandy and Brittany. They visited Les Rochers, Mme de Sévigné's château near Vitré, and continued to Vannes and round the Brittany peninsula to Dinan and Bayeux. (Their itinerary is briefly recorded by LW (Diary, LWP, Sussex); the notebook to which VW refers does not survive). They returned to Monks House on 19 June and to Tavistock Square on Thursday 22 June.

Friday 23 June

Back to London again after 4 weeks. Two spent driving about Brittany. I kept notes in a little square ruled pocketbook in my bag; a good method perhaps, if carried out in London; but I doubt if its worth sticking them here. Perhaps a few, for like pressed leaves they somehow bring back the whole forgotten hedge. So soon forgotten in bulk. The London uproar at once rushes in. Okampo today; John; then I must go to Penman. We have 37 M[ecklenburgh] S[quare]: & this is still unlet.[6]

4. For the nun's letter, see MHP, Sussex, LVP (Books). VW had asked Gertler to dine as she 'was anxious to get your account of the way [Roger Fry] struck younger painters.' (*VI VW Letters*, no. 3501.) See also *Moments of Being*, p. 85: 'May 15th 1939. . . . Last night Mark Gertler dined here and denounced the vulgarity, the inferiority of what he called "literature"; compared with the integrity of painting.'
5. The Woolfs' dinner guests were Maynard Keynes's younger brother the surgeon and bibliophile Geoffrey Langdon Keynes (1887-1982) and his wife Margaret, *née* Darwin. Elizabeth Williamson, her friend Leonie Leontineff (?), and Benedict Nicolson—to whom VW was to lend her 'studio' while she was away—came in afterwards.
6. Victoria Ocampo (1880-1979), the wealthy Argentine founder and publisher of the literary review *Sur*, was an extravagant admirer of VW, whom she met in 1934 (see

Kenneth Clark
Ruskin Today
Penguin 1982 (Peregrine Books 1967)
actual size

The Ruskin anthology seems a simpler problem. That it appears so is largely a measure of the skilled and restrained design. Hans Schmoller's well-judged sensitive tyography, to be seen in hundreds of Penguins in the 1960s and 1970s, is demonstrated here, with Bembo used in a pleasant and readable line. The paragraph marks, numerals and section titles discreetly link and at the same time separate the extracts, while the source note is a model of reticence. Editorial requirements which could have created visual problems have, by subtle design, been made correctly subservient to the main text.

---

tempered evidently, hating humbug of all sorts, shrewd, perhaps a little selfish, highly intellectual, the powers of the mind not brought out with any delight in their manifestation, or intention of display, but flashing out occasionally in a word or a look.'[1]

From *Praeterita*, II, § 66

¶ 13
FIRST LOVE

The entirely inscrutable thing to me, looking back on myself, is my total want of all reason, will, or design in the business: I had neither the resolution to win Adèle,[2] the courage to do without her, the sense to consider what was at last to come of it all, or the grace to think how disagreeable I was making myself at the time to everybody about me. There was really no more capacity nor intelligence in me than in a just fledged owlet, or just open-eyed puppy, disconsolate at the existence of the moon.

From *Praeterita*, I, § 210

¶ 14
TRAVEL BY COACH

The poor modern slaves and simpletons who let themselves be dragged like cattle, or felled timber, through the countries they imagine themselves visiting, can have no conception whatever of the complex joys, and ingenious hopes, connected with the choice and arrangement of the travelling carriage in old times. The mechanical questions first, of strength – easy rolling – steady and safe poise of persons and luggage; the general stateliness of effect to be obtained for the abashing of plebeian beholders; the cunning

1. The actual words of Ruskin's Journal written on 22 June 1840.
2. Adèle was the eldest of the four daughters of Mr Domecq, old Mr Ruskin's partner, who came to stay at Herne Hill, and as Ruskin said 'reduced me to a mere heap of white ashes in four days'. Ruskin fell passionately in love with her, but could not propose to her, partly from timidity, partly because she was a Catholic. His passion brought on a mild attack of tuberculosis, on account of which he was removed from Oxford and taken on the journey to Italy mentioned in the next seven extracts. His poem entitled 'To Adèle' was published in *Friendship's Offering* for 1840.

design and distribution of store-cellars under the seats, secret drawers under front windows, invisible pockets under padded lining, safe from dust, and accessible only by insidious slits, or necromantic valves like Aladdin's trapdoor; the fitting of cushions where they would not slip, the rounding of corners for more delicate repose; the prudent attachments and springs of blinds; the perfect fitting of windows, on which one-half the comfort of a travelling carriage really depends; and the adaptation of all these concentrated luxuries to the probabilities of who would sit where, in the little apartment which was to be virtually one's home for five or six months; – all this was an imaginary journey in itself, with every pleasure, and none of the discomfort, of practical travelling. . . .

For a family carriage of this solid construction, with its luggage, and load of six or more persons, four horses were of course necessary to get any sufficient way on it; and half-a-dozen such teams were kept at every post-house. . . .

The French horses, and more or less those on all the great lines of European travelling, were properly stout trotting cart-horses, well up to their work and over it; untrimmed, long-tailed, good-humouredly licentious, whinneying and frolicking with each other when they had a chance; sagaciously steady to their work; obedient to the voice mostly, to the rein only for more explicitness; never touched by the whip, which was used merely to express the driver's exultation in himself and them, – signal obstructive vehicles in front out of the way, and advise all the inhabitants of the villages and towns traversed on the day's journey, that persons of distinction were honouring them by their transitory presence.

From *Praeterita*, I, §§ 123 and 125

¶ 15
SCHAFFHAUSEN

And then, with Salvador was held council in the inn-parlour of Strasburg, whether – it was then the Friday afternoon – we should push on to-morrow for our Sunday's rest to Basle, or to Schaffhausen.

Two examples show unusual solutions to the articulation of text. Richard Hollis uses overlapping columns in this conversation, set in egyptian and grotesque to suggest different voices. The design mirrors the informality and simplicity of the text, and even suggests the physical presence of two people seated opposite each other.

David Hockney: an interview

Questions put by Mark Glazebrook

M.G.   At art schools in the early sixties I seem to remember that the word literary was a sort of dirty word. Despite the connections between surrealism and abstract expressionism, literary painting was a heresy, in the temple of orthodox modern art. Did you feel any qualms about your blatantly literary sources . . . Blake, Whitman, Cavafy, the Brothers Grimm, and your early tendency to do narrative painting ?

D.H.   Well not really, I mean I didn't worry about it then. I never ever worried about it in my etchings, simply because in my etchings I use line and I think a line can somehow tell a story. So the etchings are still literary in that they actually tell stories, whereas the paintings stopped being literary about when I went to California in 1964. From then on I don't think I painted from literary sources, whereas before then I'd painted a number of pictures from poems, Whitman, Auden, Blake . . . Cavafy.

What chiefly attracted you about Cavafy's poems ? Was it their references to art ; or their candidness about love or sensuality, or . . .

Well, I'll tell you who introduced the poems to me—there's one of them in the back of a Lawrence Durrell novel Justine, I think it's called 'The City'. The person who told me about them and read them to me was Adrian Berg. He found some in a magazine, and read them to me one night years ago and I thought they were terrific, absolutely terrific. One of the poems he read was called 'Waiting for the Barbarians', which is marvellous, absolutely marvellous, and made me want to read some more. Then I went to Bradford on a holiday from the Royal College – I found in the library there a complete volume of his poems, translated by John Mavrogordato, and I read it from cover to cover. Later on when illustrating the poems I finally chose only the ones about love, whereas I had intended to do 'Waiting for the Barbarians' really. One day I will. He wrote poems about the politics of the Ptolemys in ancient Alexandria and they're rather interesting.

Of course they do refer to art a good deal – the art of poetry and visual art.

Yes. The last line of the last poem in the book is about a man who looks at a picture of a beautiful youth. The writer, remember, is tired of writing and he cannot concentrate, so he breaks off and looks at the picture. The line is 'From Art's toil we rest again in art' and I felt that that was a fantastic line to end the book on. Stephen Spender as a matter of fact thought the poem was a little naughty. But I liked it and I wanted to put it in.

The style of the poems is very distinctive . . .

What strikes you straight away is they're so clear and precise and that's what I liked about Whitman in a sense. I thought they were rather similar. They seemed to me very clear and I liked that clarity.

Could we come back to the question of how your recent paintings became more visual – how the change came about ? At a sort of intermediary point they were very much related to stylistic devices. Then they became more purely visual as though you were reacting more to naturalistic beauty in landscape or still life.

They became more and more visual. I'll tell you what happened. In 1965 or 1966 in California I began to paint California as it really appeared to me. In 1965 for instance, I had been in Colorado when I did that picture of the Rocky Mountains. But I invented it. It wasn't how they appeared. It was how I thought they might appear, in a geography book or something. The ideas were really still artistic in that way and I think I just felt at times they should become more . . . instead of being inward I just wanted them to come outward a bit, and become more about life as it was. That's when I started doing the portraits and the paintings began to get more realistic, I began to be interested in light and things like that. Since then in many ways they have got more ordinary, I mean more conventional. As a matter of fact, ironically, I was thinking, when I've finished the pictures I'm working on now, of doing one or two of what I call my technical pictures.

I was just wondering about that, about how much this purely visual thing was the shape of things to come, and of course the painting you're working on now with two figures seated in a chair looking at a landscape as though it was a cinema is almost a return to the idea of the painting within a painting.

Yes it is. And certainly that was the starting-off point. It was me being amused by this constructed landscape and people looking at it. But then on the other hand it's rather a straightforward picture of Vichy, the town and people sat in it. But it's more of a technical picture than the portraits, like the portrait of Henry Geldzahler or the Isherwood portrait.

Could we now move to the question of inspiration from other artists of the past or present ? You seem to me to have had from very early on a strong capacity to digest a number of influences and make your own thing out of them. I mean in the early sixties you absorbed something from abstract expressionism, Dubuffet and Francis Bacon as well as from anonymous graffiti. Is there any one artist who has influenced you more strongly than any other ?

The artist who influenced me most strongly I think not just as an artist but as a person, is Ron Kitaj. It's partly because I've always admired his art enormously; I think he's one of the great artists; and also because he opened my eyes a great deal and I always think of things beginning from particular moments when I discussed things with him. I think of my painting beginning properly then. So that in that sense the influence was big and very important. Stylistically of course his influence has

8

9

Stefan Themerson
Kurt Schwitters on a time chart
Typographica 16
Lund Humphries
London 1967
reduced from approx 420 mm deep

Stefan Themerson's page is a great deal more ambitious, and takes the articulation of text to its limits. However, he uses only one type style, in two weights. The time sequence, meaning, and jerky exclamatory style are all given visible expression. Such complex articulation would rarely be possible in normal bookwork – but it is a useful reminder that text consists of meaningful phrases, whose arbitrary splitting is unhelpful: a point to be borne in mind when handling, for instance, long chapter titles. This example may be bizarre, but it is not arbitrary.

But... revenons à nos moutons!

1910   1920

SARAJEVO | THE FIRST WORLD WAR

Five years before Sarajevo (Mussolini was then only 26), a bio-seismograph called MARINETTI felt the vibration going on in the walls of the simmering kettle, and burst out with his Angry-Young-Man's FUTURIST MANIFESTO:

We are out to glorify war:

the only health-giver of the world!

Militarism! Patriotism!

The Destructive Arm of the Anarchist!

Ideas that kill!

Contempt for women!

('Figaro', Paris, 1909)

Seven years later, in 1916, the same sensitivity of some other artists' nervous systems made them move in the opposite direction.

Their art too ——— **had to be young**

it had to be new,

it had to integrate all the experimental

tendencies of the Futurists and Cubists.

Above everything, however, their art had to be international.
For they believed in **an International of the Spirit**

and not in different national concepts.

No Italian Pride for them!

They **hated the senseless, systematic massacre of**

modern warfare.

The bankruptcy of ideas having destroyed the

concept of Humanity to its very innermost depth,

the instincts and hereditary backgrounds

are now emerging pathologically.

(Richard Huelsenbeck, 'Dada Lives', Transition 25)

(I am quoting from Transition)

(I am quoting from Hugo Ball: Dada Diary, 12 June 1916)

Since no art, politics, or religious faith, seems adequate to dam this torrent,

there remains only the blague & the bleeding pose!

What we are celebrating is at once

a buffoonery

& a Requiem Mass.

(idem: 3 March 1916)

Kurt Schwitters' sympathies were with them, not with Marinetti. At least not with Marinetti's conclusions. As to Marinetti's premises, emotional and theoretical, it would be unwise to dismiss them off-handedly. He inspired the editor of a socialist daily *Avanti* and the author of a flamboyant novel *Claudia Particella* (English title: *Cardinal's Mistress*) – Benito Mussolini, (**It is Marinetti who instilled in me the feeling of the ocean and the power of the machine'**) and he equally inspired a number of poets (Mayakovsky in Russia; T. Peiper, B. Jasieński, A. Wat, A. Stern, in Poland) none of whom was 'fascist'. Some of those who knew him say that Marinetti was a jolly good fellow and the fact that he was admired by Il Duce, who was admired by Ezra Pound, should not be taken too seriously. Well . . . I don't know. Anyway some of his theorizing seem to be right up to date, something pretty near the province of what is today called 'linguistic philosophy': it is all about the functioning of words, about handling grammar, syntax and style.

(a number of inches to the left of this time-chart) It is rather amusing that what Milton wrote about RHYME – – Marinetti, 250 years later, and in a not less boisterous mood, wrote about ADJECTIVES,

and all forms of the verb OTHER THAN THE INFINITIVE:

Rhyme being no necessary adjunct   by **stripping it of all adjectives**

or true ornament   & by **isolating it,**

of poem   the **noun,**

or good verse,   **worn out by the multiple contrasts**

but the invention of a barbarous age,   **& by the weight of classical**

to set off wretched matter   **& decadent adjectives,**

& lame metre.   **can be brought back to its absolute values.**

Adjectives (isolated) in brackets will give the atmosphere of the story.

The different forms of the verb should be eliminated.

The infinitive is the very movement of the new lyricism.

Synoptic tables of lyrical values will permit us to follow simultaneously several currents.

'The Verse' Preface to 'Paradise Lost'

The Holy Bible
The Doves Press
London 1903-5
reduced from approx 330 mm deep

The Doves Bible spread shows the Magnificat and the Benedictus displayed within the text and set one phrase per line. The paragraph marks so dear to the private presses are emphatic and decorative, but do not unduly interrupt the flow of the narrative. There are no verse numbers, but book and chapter are indicated in the margins.

There is pattern-making going on here, but not solely for its own sake, and the spread is very carefully considered.

Luke 1 as soon as the voice of thy salutation sounded in mine ears, the babe leaped in my womb for joy. And blessed is she that believed: for there shall be a performance of those things which were told her from the Lord. ⟨ And Mary said,

My soul doth magnify the Lord,
And my spirit hath rejoiced in God my Saviour.
For he hath regarded the low estate of his handmaiden:
For behold, from henceforth all generations shall call me blessed.
For he that is mighty hath done to me great things;
And holy is his name.
And his mercy is on them that fear him
From generation to generation.
He hath shewed strength with his arm;
He hath scattered the proud in the imagination of their hearts.
He hath put down the mighty from their seats,
And exalted them of low degree.
He hath filled the hungry with good things;
And the rich he hath sent empty away.
He hath holpen his servant Israel,
In remembrance of his mercy,
(As he spake to our fathers),
To Abraham, and to his seed for ever.

And Mary abode with her about three months, & returned to her own house. ⟨ Now Elisabeth's full time came that she should be delivered; & she brought forth a son. And her neighbours and her cousins heard how the Lord had shewed great mercy upon her; & they rejoiced with her. And it came to pass, that on the eighth day they came to circumcise the child; and they called him Zacharias, after the name of his father. And his mother answered and said, Not so; but he shall be called John. And they said unto her, There is none of thy kindred that is called by this name. And they made signs to his father, how he would have him called. And he asked for a writing table, and wrote, saying, His name is John. And they marvelled all. And his mouth was opened immediately, & his tongue loosed, and he spake, and praised God. And fear came on all that dwelt round about them: and all these sayings were noised abroad throughout all the hill country of Judea. And all they that heard them laid them up in their hearts, saying, What manner of child shall this be! And the hand of the Lord was with him. And his father Zacharias was filled with the Holy Ghost, and prophesied, saying,

Blessed be the Lord God of Israel;
For he hath visited and redeemed his people,
And hath raised up a horn of salvation for us

In the house of his servant David;   Luke 1
(As he spake by the mouth of his holy prophets,
Which have been since the world began:)
That we should be saved from our enemies,
And from the hand of all that hate us;
To perform the mercy promised to our fathers,
And to remember his holy covenant;
The oath which he sware to our father Abraham,
That he would grant unto us, that we being delivered out of the hand of our enemies,
Might serve him without fear,
In holiness and righteousness before him,
All the days of our life.
And thou, child, shalt be called the prophet of the Highest:
For thou shalt go before the face of the Lord
To prepare his ways;
To give knowledge of salvation unto his people
By the remission of their sins,
Through the tender mercy of our God;
Whereby the dayspring from on high hath visited us,
To give light to them that sit in darkness and in the shadow of death,
To guide our feet into the way of peace.

And the child grew, and waxed strong in spirit, & was in the deserts till the day of his shewing unto Israel. ⟨ And it came to pass in those days, that there 2 went out a decree from Cesar Augustus, that all the world should be taxed. (And this taxing was first made when Cyrenius was governor of Syria.) And all went to be taxed, every one into his own city. And Joseph also went up from Galilee, out of the city of Nazareth, into Judea, unto the city of David, which is called Bethlehem; (because he was of the house & lineage of David:) to be taxed with Mary his espoused wife, being great with child. And so it was that, while they were there, the days were accomplished that she should be delivered. And she brought forth her firstborn son, and wrapped him in swaddling clothes, and laid him in a manger; because there was no room for them in the inn. And there were in the same country shepherds abiding in the field, keeping watch over their flock by night. And lo, the angel of the Lord came upon them, and the glory of the Lord shone round about them: & they were sore afraid. And the angel said unto them, Fear not: for behold, I bring you good tidings of great joy, which shall be to all people. For unto you is born this day in the city of David a Saviour, which is Christ the Lord. And this shall be a sign unto you; Ye shall find the babe wrapped in swaddling clothes, lying in a manger. And suddenly there was with the angel a multitude of the heavenly host praising God, and saying,

A Ferrier
Epitaphs
'Le Tombeau de Marguerite'
by Ronsard
Paris 1559
actual size

Poetry in this sixteenth-century book has been set in italic, perhaps consciously following Aldus's example (compare it with the illustration on page 36); but the decoration at the head and the ornate initial give the page richness, and the lines of prose in a grave roman increase the almost flowery effect of the italic. The 'reverse indenting' of the new sentence in the poem is odd, and looks like a clumsy afterthought involving a second pass through the press. But the whole design is grand and intimate at the same time.

Both these books have generous margins, creating a feeling of opulence. The French example exploits its right-hand margin to incorporate a potentially awkward, but here well-handled, side note.

3

LE TOMBEAV DE MARGVERI-
TE DE FRANCE, DVCHESSE
DE SAVOYE.

Enſemble celuy de treſauguſte & treſſaincte
memoire, FRANÇOIS premier de ce nom,
& de Meſſieurs ſes enfans.

H! que ie ſuis marry que la Muſe
  Françoiſe
Ne peult dire ces mots comme faiĉt la
  Gregeoiſe,
* *Ocymore, dyſpotme, oligochronien:*
Certes ie les dirois du ſang Valeſien,
Qui de beauté de grace & de luſtre reſemble
Au liz qui naiſt fleuriſt & ſe meurt tout enſemble.
Ce Monarche François, François premier du nom,
Nourriſſon de Phœbus, des Muſes le mignon,
Qui deſſous ſa royale & auguſte figure
Cachoit auec Pithon les Graces & Mercure,
Qui ſçauoit les ſecrets de la terre & des cieux,
Veit, ainſi que Priam, deuant ſes propres yeux
(Hé qui pourroit du ciel corrompre l'influance!)
Enterrer ſes enfans en leur premiere enfance.

                                A ÿ

***Ces motz Grecs** ſeront trouuez fort nouueaux: mais d'autāt que noſtre lāgage ne pouuoit exprimer ma conception, i'ay eſté forcé d'en vſer, qui ſignifiét vne vie de petite duree. Filoſofie & Mathematique ont eſte auſſi eſtranges au commencemēt: mais l'vſage les a par traiĉt de temps adoulcis, & rendus noſtres.

The opening page of Virgil's *Georgics* in this edition of Aldus shows the first great publisher's solution to the problem of setting a classic text in a convenient economical pocket-sized format. He uses a beautiful springy italic, based on Renaissance script, partly no doubt to save space. Italic caps had not yet been deemed necessary, and the fit of the roman caps is loose, although a feature is made of this at the beginning of every line. The initial and the letter-spaced caps are carry-overs from manuscript books.

Baskerville's *Virgil* is a de luxe edition and demonstrates the sober prosperity of the mid-eighteenth century. Splendid press work, fine smooth paper and a classic type make the page memorable, and the expansive margins herald a new era in presentation of text which is actually enhanced by the absence of decorations or illustration. The dropped initial is an even more vestigial reminder of manuscript books than the example opposite. How much more satisfactory is the opening here, compared with the same printer's bible on page 18. By any standards, this is a fine piece of design.

17

OVIDII NASONIS
PERIOCHA·

Quid faciat lætas segetes, quæ sydera seruet
Agricola, ut facilem terram proscindat aratris,
Semina quo iacienda modo, cultus'q; locorum
Edocuit messes magno olim fœnore reddi·

P·V·M·GEORGICON LIBER PRI-
MVS AD MOECENATEM·

Vid faciat lætas segetes, quo syde
re terram
Vertere Mœcenas, ulmis'q; ad=
iungere uites.
Conueniat, quæ cura boum
quis cultus habendo

Sit pecori, at'q; apibus quanta experientia parcis,
Hinc canere incipiam. Vos o clarissima mundi
Lumina, labentem cœlo quæ ducitis annum,
Liber, et alma Ceres, uestro si munere tellus
Chaoniam pingui glandem mutauit arista,
Pocula'q; inuentis Acheloia miscuit uuis,
Et uos agrestum præsentia numina Fauni,
Ferte simul, Fauni'q; pedem, Dryades'q; puellæ,
Munera uestra cano· tu'q; o cui prima frementem
Fudit equum magno tellus percussa tridenti
Neptune, & cultor nemorum, cui pinguia Cææ
Tercentum niuei tondent dumeta iuuenci,
Ipse nemus linquens patrium, saltus'q; Lycæi

c

P. VIRGILII MARONIS

AENEIDOS

LIBER PRIMUS.

I L L E ego, qui quondam gracili modulatus avena
Carmen ; et egreſſus ſilvis, vicina coegi
Ut quamvis avido parerent arva colono :
Gratum opus agricolis : at nunc horrentia Martis

5 ARMA, virumque cano, Trojæ qui primus ab oris
Italiam, fato profugus, Lavinaque venit
Litora : multum ille et terris jactatus et alto,
Vi ſuperum, ſævæ memorem Junonis ob iram :
Multa quoque et bello paſſus, dum conderet urbem,
10 Inferretque Deos Latio : genus unde Latinum,
Albanique patres, atque altæ mœnia Romæ.
   Muſa, mihi cauſas memora, quo numine læſo,
Quidve dolens Regina Deum, tot volvere caſus
Inſignem pietate virum, tot adire labores
15 Impulerit. tantæne animis cœleſtibus iræ?
   Urbs antiqua fuit, Tyrii tenuere coloni,
Carthago, Italiam contra, Tiberinaque longe
Oſtia, dives opum, ſtudiiſque aſperrima belli :
Quam Juno fertur terris magis omnibus unam
20 Poſthabita coluiſſe Samo. hic illius arma,
Hic currus fuit : hoc regnum Dea gentibus eſſe,

O

Si

Molière
Le Cocu Imaginaire
with engravings by Oppenor,
Boucher and Blondel
Paris 1784
reduced from approx 280 mm deep

Molière's verse, the lines shared among the characters in the play, forces an openness on the typography, an openness augmented by the short scenes. The strong caps and rules, and the italic stage directions, further disguise the static quality of formal iambic hexameters, and the page reflects the light bounce of the dialogue.

SCENE II.

CELIE, LA SUIVANTE *de Célie.*

LA SUIVANTE.

CE changement m'étonne.

CELIE.

Et lorfque tu fçauras
Par quel motif j'agis, tu m'en eftimeras.

LA SUIVANTE.

Cela pourroit bien être.

CELIE.

Apprend donc que Lélie
A pû bleffer mon cœur par une perfidie,
Qu'il étoit en ces lieux fans . . . .

LA SUIVANTE.

Mais il vient à nous.

SCENE III.

LELIE, CELIE, LA SUIVANTE *de Célie.*

LELIE.

AVant que pour jamais je m'éloigne de vous,
Je veux vous reprocher au moins en cette place . . . . .

CELIE.

Quoi! me parler encore ? avez-vous cette audace ?

LELIE.

Il eft vray qu'elle eft grande, & votre choix eft tel,
Qu'à vous rien reprocher je ferois criminel.

Vivez, vivez contente, & bravez ma memoire
Avec le digne époux qui vous comble de gloire.

CELIE.

Oui, traître, j'y veux vivre; & mon plus grand défir,
Ce feroit que ton cœur en eût du déplaifir.

LELIE.

Qui rend donc contre moi ce courroux légitime ?

CELIE.

Quoi tu fais le furpris & demandes ton crime ?

SCENE IV.

CELIE, LELIE, SGANARELLE *armé de pied en cap,* LA SUIVANTE *de Célie.*

SGANARELLE.

GUerre, guerre mortelle à ce larron d'honneur
Qui fans miféricorde a fouillé notre honneur.

CELIE *à Lélie, lui montrant Sganarelle.*

Tourne, tourne les yeux, fans me faire répondre.

LELIE.

Ah! je vois . . . .

CELIE.

Cet objet fuffit pour te confondre.

LELIE.

Mais pour vous obliger bien plûtôt à rougir.

SGANARELLE *à part.*

Ma colére à préfent eft en état d'agir,
Deffus fes grands chevaux eft monté mon courage;
Et, fi je le rencontre, on verra du carnage.

Jan Tschichold's design for a projected German edition of *Romeo and Juliet* achieves maximum effect with apparently little effort. Less is more. The result is a quiet mastery which is never dull.

These two designs make an interesting comparison. Both use initial caps, which sit awkwardly in the Molière, whereas they enrich Tschichold's design. Both set the characters' names in caps, although those in the Molière are too large. (Tschichold's text has erratic capitalisation, following neither normal German usage nor the First Folio of 1623.) Long s's are used in both; they were current in 1784, in 1964 deliberately archaic. Stage directions are in italic in both; but in Tschichold's design the placing and size of the act and scene numbers is typically elegant and economical.

II.1

Ein offener platz, der an Capulets garten ſtößt.
Romeo tritt auf.

ROMEO.

Kann ich von hinnen, da mein herz hier bleibt?
Geh, froſtge erde, ſuche deine ſonne!
Er erſteigt die mauer und ſpringt hinunter.
Benvolio und Mercutio treten auf.
BENVOLIO. He, Romeo! he, vetter!
MERCUTIO. Er iſt klug
Und hat, mein ſeel, ſich heim ins bett geſtohlen.
BENVOLIO. Er lief hieher und ſprang die gartenmauer
Hinüber. Ruf ihn, freund Mercutio.
MERCUTIO. Ja, auch beſchwören will ich. Romeo!
Was? Grillen! Toller! Leidenſchaft! Verliebter!
Erſcheine du, geſtaltet wie ein ſeufzer;
Sprich nur ein reimchen, ſo genügt mirs ſchon;
Ein ach nur jammre, paare lieb und triebe;
Gib der gevattrin Venus Ein gut wort,
Schimpf eins auf ihren blinden ſohn und erben,
Held Amor, der ſo flink gezielt, als könig
Kophetua das bettlermädchen liebte.
Er höret nicht, er regt ſich nicht, er rührt ſich nicht.
Der aff iſt tot; ich muß ihn wohl beſchwören.
Nun wohl: Bei Roſalindens hellem auge,
Bei ihrer purpurlipp und hohen ſtirn,
Bei ihrem zarten fuß, dem ſchlanken bein,
Den üppgen hüften und der region,
Die ihnen nahe liegt, beſchwör ich dich,
Daß du in eigner bildung uns erſcheineſt.
BENVOLIO. Wenn er dich hört, ſo wird er zornig werden.

28

MERCUTIO. Hierüber kann ers nicht; er hätte grund,
Bannt ich hinauf in ſeiner dame kreis
Ihm einen geiſt von ſeltſam eigner art
Und ließe den da ſtehn, bis ſie den trotz
Gezähmt und nieder ihn beſchworen hätte.
Das wär beſchimpfung! Meine anrufung
Iſt gut und ehrlich; mit der liebſten namen
Beſchwör ich ihn, bloß um ihn herzubannen.
BENVOLIO. Komm! Er verbarg ſich unter jenen bäumen
Und pflegt' des umgangs mit der feuchten nacht.
Die lieb iſt blind, das dunkel iſt ihr recht.
MERCUTIO. Iſt liebe blind, ſo zielt ſie freilich ſchlecht.
Nun ſitzt er wohl an einen baum gelehnt
Und wünſcht, ſein liebchen wär die reife frucht
Und fiel ihm in den ſchoß. Doch, gute nacht,
Freund Romeo! Ich will ins federbett;
Das feldbett iſt zum ſchlafen mir zu kalt.
Kommt, gehn wir!
BENVOLIO. Ja, es iſt vergeblich, ihn
Zu ſuchen, der nicht will gefunden ſein. *Ab.*

II.2

Capulets garten.
Romeo kommt.

ROMEO.

Der narben lacht, wer wunden nie gefühlt.
Julia erſcheint oben an einem fenſter.
Doch ſtill, was ſchimmert durch das fenſter dort?
Es iſt der oſt, und Julia die ſonne! —
Geh auf, du holde ſonn! ertöte Lunen,

29

Shakespeare
Romeo und Julia
1964
reduced from approx 215 mm deep

Shakespeare
Nonesuch Press
London 1953
actual size

Francis Meynell's *Othello* for the Nonesuch Press required margin notes to indicate variants in the four quarto and first folio texts, as well as references to additional notes on the text (grouped at the end of the play) signalled by asterisks. Stage directions are shown in italic, so are, irritatingly, characters' names within speeches. Square brackets indicate omission of words and modern readings are in italic.

All this is well-surbordinated to the main text; only the mannered paragraph markings before each speaker's name really distract, although their (inconsistent) abbreviation is eccentric in a de luxe edition.

To win the Moore againe.
For 'tis most easie

The inclining Th'inclyning *Desdemona* to subdue
In any honest Suite. She's fram'd as fruitefull
As the free Elements. And then for her

wer't to To win the Moore, were to renownce his Baptisme,
All Seales, and Simbols of redeemed sin:
His Soule is so enfetter'd to her Love,
That she may make, unmake, do what she list,
Even as her Appetite shall play the God,
With his weake Function. How am I then a Villaine,
To Counsell *Cassio* to this paralell course,

hell! Directly to his good? Divinitie of hell,

will their blackest When divels will the blackest sinnes put on,
They do suggest at first with heavenly shewes,

while As I do now. For whiles this honest Foole

fortunes, Plies *Desdemona*, to repaire his Fortune,
And she for him, pleades strongly to the Moore,
Ile powre this pestilence into his eare:

lust; That she repeales him, for her bodies Lust'
And by how much she strives to do him good,
She shall undo her Credite with the Moore.
So will I turne her vertue into pitch,
And out of her owne goodnesse make the Net,

enmesh em all: That shall en-mash them all.
How now *Rodorigo*?

Enter Rodorigo.

¶RODORIGO. I do follow heere in the Chace, not like
a Hound that hunts, but one that filles up the Crie.

I ha bin My Money is almost spent; I have bin to night exceed-

[And] ingly well Cudgell'd: And I thinke the issue will bee,

paines, as that comes to, and no money at all, and with that wit returne to Venice. I shall have so much experience for my paines; And so, with no money at all, and a little more Wit, re-turne againe to Venice.

that ha not ¶IAGO. How poore are they that have not Patience?
What wound did ever heale but by degrees?

knowest Thou know'st we worke by Wit, and not by Witch-craft
And Wit depends on dilatory time:

Dos't not go well? *Cassio* hath beaten thee, *has beaten*
And thou by that small hurt hath casheer'd *Cassio*: *hast casheird*
Though other things grow faire against the Sun,
Yet Fruites that blossome first, will first be ripe: *But fruites*
Content thy selfe, a-while. Introth 'tis Morning; *awhile; bi'the masse tis morning;*
Pleasure, and Action, make the houres seeme short.
Retire thee, go where thou art Billited:
Away, I say, thou shalt know more heereafter:
Nay get thee gone. *Exit Rodorigo.* *[Exit Rodorigo.]*
Two things are to be done: *Some things*
My Wife must move for *Cassio* to her Mistris:
Ile set her on my selfe, a while, to draw the Moor *on. My selfe awhile,*
 apart, *the while*
And bring him jumpe, when he may *Cassio* finde
Soliciting his wife: I, that's the way:
Dull not Device, by coldnesse, and delay. *Exit.* *(Exeunt.)*

ACTUS TERTIUS. SCENA PRIMA.

Enter Cassio, Musitians, and Clowne. *(Before the castle.)*

¶CASSIO. Masters, play heere, I wil content your
 paines,
Something that's briefe: and bid, goodmorrow
 General.

¶CLO. Why Masters, have your Instruments bin in *ha your..bin at*
Naples, that they speake i'th'Nose thus?

¶MUS. How Sir? how? *★(Boy.) How*

¶CLO. Are these I pray you, winde Instruments? *pray, cald wind*

¶MUS. I marry are they sir.

¶CLO. Oh, thereby hangs a tale.

¶MUS. Whereby hangs a tale, sir?

¶CLOW. Marry sir, by many a winde Instrument that
I know. But Masters, heere's money for you: and
the Generall so likes your Musick, that he desires you *you of all loves, to make*
for loves sake to make no more noise with it.

¶MUS. Well Sir, we will not.

¶CLO. If you have any Musicke that may not be
heard, too't againe. But (as they say) to heare Musicke,
the Generall do's not greatly care.

¶MUS. We have none such, sir. *ha none*

Shakespeare
Everyman Library
London 1906 (1966 reprint)
actual size

The Nonesuch is an edition for scholars and bibliophiles. The Everyman Library Shakespeare is for – Everyman. Apparently typographically undistinguished, it is in fact a very easy read – far easier than the Nonesuch. Running heads giving acts and scenes are more easily picked out. Characters' names and stage directions are clear, easily noted and undistracting. Space-saving measures – this is an economically-produced edition for the mass market – are easily accepted. Here, a set of standards had to be devised which worked throughout, with little scope for fine-tuning. And they work very well: tidily, clearly and legibly, though a little tight for the prose speeches. Neither so elegant nor so space-consuming as Tschichold's solution (see page 39), it yet demonstrates again that *less* is lucid; *more* can be counter-productive.

doth not the appetite alter? a man loves the meat in his youth that he cannot endure in his age. Shall quips and sentences and these paper bullets of the brain awe a man from the career of his humour? No, the world must be peopled. When I said I would die a bachelor, I did not think I should live till I were married. Here comes Beatrice. By this day! she's a fair lady: I do spy some marks of love in her.

Enter Beatrice.

Beat. Against my will I am sent to bid you come in to dinner.

Bene. Fair Beatrice, I thank you for your pains.

Beat. I took no more pains for those thanks than you take pains to thank me: if it had been painful, I would not have

Bene. You take pleasure, then, in the message?   [come.

Beat. Yea, just so much as you may take upon a knife's point, and choke a daw withal. You have no stomach, signior: fare you well.   [*Exit.*

Bene. Ha! 'Against my will I am sent to bid you come in to dinner;' there's a double meaning in that. 'I took no more pains for those thanks than you took pains to thank me;' that's as much as to say, Any pains that I take for you is as easy as thanks. If I do not take pity of her, I am a villain; if I do not love her, I am a Jew. I will go get her picture.   [*Exit.*

ACT III—SCENE I

Leonato's orchard.

Enter Hero, Margaret, and Ursula.

Hero. Good Margaret, run thee to the parlour;
There shalt thou find my cousin Beatrice
Proposing with the prince and Claudio:
Whisper her ear, and tell her, I and Ursula
Walk in the orchard, and our whole discourse
Is all of her; say that thou overheard'st us;
And bid her steal into the pleached bower,
Where honeysuckles, ripen'd by the sun,
Forbid the sun to enter; like favourites,
Made proud by princes, that advance their pride
Against that power that bred it: there will she hide her,
To listen our propose. This is thy office;
Bear thee well in it, and leave us alone.

Marg. I'll make her come, I warrant, you, presently.   [*Exit.*

Hero. Now, Ursula, when Beatrice doth come,
As we do trace this alley up and down,
Our talk must only be of Benedick.

300

When I do name him, let it be thy part
To praise him more than ever man did merit:
My talk to thee must be, how Benedick
Is sick in love with Beatrice. Of this matter
Is little Cupid's crafty arrow made,
That only wounds by hearsay.

Enter Beatrice, behind.
                        Now begin;
For look where Beatrice, like a lapwing, runs
Close by the ground, to hear our conference.

Urs. The pleasant'st angling is to see the fish
Cut with her golden oars the silver stream,
And greedily devour the treacherous bait:
So angle we for Beatrice; who even now
Is couched in the woodbine coverture.
Fear you not my part of the dialogue.

Hero. Then go we near her, that her ear lose nothing
Of the false sweet bait that we lay for it.

[*Approaching the bower.*
No, truly, Ursula, she is too disdainful;
I know her spirits are as coy and wild
As haggerds of the rock.

Urs.   But are you sure
That Benedick loves Beatrice so entirely?

Hero. So says the prince and my new-trothed lord.

Urs. And did they bid you tell her of it, madam?

Hero. They did entreat me to acquaint her of it;
But I persuaded them, if they loved Benedick,
To wish him wrestle with affection,
And never to let Beatrice know of it.

Urs. Why did you so? Doth not the gentleman
Deserve as full as fortunate a bed
As ever Beatrice shall couch upon?

Hero. O god of love! I know he doth deserve
As much as may be yielded to a man:
But Nature never framed a woman's heart
Of prouder stuff than that of Beatrice;
Disdain and scorn ride sparkling in her eyes,
Misprising what they look on; and her wit
Values itself so highly, that to her
All matter else seems weak: she cannot love,
Nor take no shape nor project of affection,
She is so self-endeared.

Urs.   Sure, I think so;
And therefore certainly it were not good

301

41

Ronda & Granada. *Route* 103.—*Jaen—Granada.* 363

in the Plaza del Mercado; a clean and comfortable inn. Pop. 22,000. Jaen (*Jayyàn*) was à little independent kingdom under the Moors, consisting of 268 square leagues. *Gien*, in Arabic, is said to signify fertility. Its position is most picturesque; the castle standing like a sentinel commands the gorge of the mountain approach from Granada. The surrounding jumble of mountains is called *del Viento, La Pandera*, and *Jabalcuz*. The two latter are the local barometers. Thus says the proverb—

Cuando Jabalcuz tiene capuz
Y La Pandera montera,
Llovera aunque Dios no quiera.

Jaen is a bishopric conjointly with Baeza. The cathedral is built after the style of its metropolitan at Granada and Malaga. It was originally a mosque, which was pulled down in 1492, the present edifice having been commenced in 1532 by Pedro de Valdelvira. The plan (in the Græco-Roman style) is noble and regular, the W. façade standing between two fine towers. The sacristy and *Sagrario* are elegant. Notice the silver custodia by Juan Ruiz, and the statue of San Eufrasio. The grand relic of Jaen is *El Santo Rostro*, or the Santa Faz, a Holy Face of our Saviour, impressed on the handkerchief of *la Veronica*, which is said to have been lent to the suffering Saviour on the road to Calvary. It was borne by St. Ferdinand at the head of his army. It is shown to the public on Good Friday, and on the day of the Ascension of the Virgin: to great personages it is privately shown on other occasions.

Visit the old Gothic *Church of San Julian*, also the *Church of San Miguel*, where obs. the fine portal by Valdelvira.

The charming Alameda commands splendid views over the surrounding Alps. The *Fuente de la Magdalena* can also be visited; it bursts from the rock as if struck by the wand of Moses. The walk to the mineral springs near the *Jabalcuz* ($1\frac{1}{4}$ m.) is delightful. Jaen surrendered itself to St. Ferdinand in 1246. Here it was that Ferdinand IV. suddenly died (aged 25), on the 7th Sept., 1312, having been summoned to appear before the judgment-seat of God upon that day, by two brothers, Juan and Pedro Carvajal, who were executed *thirty* days before by order of the King, without sufficient evidence of guilt having been brought home to them. Ferdinand having thus died as predicted, is called *El Emplazado*, "the cited one."

The road to Granada was opened in 1828. The first portion runs through a well-watered valley full of figs, pomegranates, apricot-trees, and vineyards. The gorge then becomes wilder and narrower, and is carried through the *Puerta de Arenas*, the sandy gate of Granada, by a tunnel 35 yards long.

$22\frac{1}{4}$ m. *Campillo de Arenas*. Pop. 1200.

The road continues through wild mountain scenery, with here and there a farm-house surrounded by its luxuriant *huerta*, to beautiful Granada, which it enters by the Plaza del Triunfo.

GRANADA.

INDEX.

		Page
§ 1.	Hotels, Cafés, Casinos, Consuls, Theatres, Post and Telegraph, Baths, Carriages, Guides, Shops .	363
§ 2.	Sight-seeing, Historical Notice. .	365
§ 3.	The Alhambra, Generalife, House of Madame Calderon	366
§ 4.	Museo, Cuarto Real, Public Walks, Markets. Archbishop's Palace .	378
§ 5.	Cathedral	380
§ 6.	Zacatin, Fuente de los Avellanos, Albaicin, Gates, Cartuja Convent, Hospitals	383
§ 7.	San Geronimo, Old Houses and Churches	385
§ 8.	Excursions	386

§ 1. HOTELS, CAFÉS, CASINO, CONSULS, THEATRES, POST AND TELEGRAPH, BATHS, CARRIAGES, GUIDES, SHOPS.

31 m. GRANADA. The station is half-an-hour's drive to the Alhambra. *Hotels:* Fonda de los Siete Suelos; beautifully situated upon the Alhambra Hill. Fonda de Washington Irving, on the Alhambra Hill, immediately facing the Siete Suelos Hotel; charges at both these hotels, 40 reals per day. Engage rooms beforehand at the hotels on the hill. Fonda de la Victoria, on the Puerta Real, in the centre of the

LAGO D'ISEO. *39. Route.* 225

though not completed until the 17th century. — A little to the N. is San Francesco (Pl. B, 3; adm. 10-4 by the side-entrance to the left of the choir), with Gothic façade; 3rd chapel on the right, *Moretto*, *SS. Margaret, Francis, and Jerome (signed 1530); over the high-altar, *Romanino*, **Madonna and saints, a masterpiece of brilliant colouring (about 1511; in an older frame, 1502).

The *Casa Fortunato*, an elegant little palazzo in the Venetian high-Renaissance style (16th cent.), should be noticed in the Via Dolzani (Pl. B, 3; No. 3, on the right). — Not far off, 38 Via del Palazzo Vecchio, is the *Palazzo Fanti* (now *Ragnoli*), with a fine Renaissance portal.

Beside the Porta Milano (Pl. A, 2) is a bronze equestrian statue of *Garibaldi*. About 1/2 M. beyond the gate lies the pretty *Campo Santo*, to which an avenue of cypresses leads from the highroad. Monument to the patriots of 1849. Fine view from the tower.

A picturesque walk may be taken in the gardens beneath the **Castello** (Pl. C, D, 2). The view (best towards evening) extends in clear weather to Monte Rosa on the W. The ascent to the castle begins at the Piazza Tito Speri (p. 221).

STEAM TRAMWAYS run from Brescia viâ *Lograto* to (20 1/2 M.) *Soncino* (p. 217); viâ (21 1/2 M.; 2 hrs.) *Medole*, in the church of which is a fine late work by Titian (Christ appearing to the Virgin), and (25 1/2 M.) *Guidizzolo*, on the battlefield of Solferino (p. 218; 2 1/4 hrs.), to (43 1/2 M.) *Mantua* (p. 257; 4 hrs.); to the *Alpine Valleys* described in the next route; and to *Toscolano* on the Lago di Garda (comp. p. 234).

39. The Brescian Alps.

1. Lago d'Iseo and Val Camonica.

RAILWAYS from Brescia. 1. To *Iseo*, 15 M., in 1 hr. (fares 1st cl. 1 fr., 3rd cl. 60 c.; continuation to *Edolo* under construction). 2. To *Paratico* on the Lago d'Iseo, 23 1/2 M., in 1 3/4-2 hrs. (fares 4 fr. 45, 3 fr. 10 c., 2 fr.; carriages changed at Palazzolo). — STEAM TRAMWAYS. 1. From *Chiari* and *Rovato* (p. 218) to *Iseo*, 12 M., in 1 1/4-1 1/2 hr. (the shortest route from Milan; fares 1 fr. 40, 95 c.). 2. From *Bergamo* to *Sarnico* (comp. p. 216). 3. From *Lovere* to *Cividate*, 13 1/2 M., in 1 3/4-2 hrs. (fares 1 fr. 35, 90 c.). — STEAMER on Lago d'Iseo between *Sarnico* and *Lovere* thrice daily in 2 3/4-3 hrs. and between *Iseo* and *Lovere* 4 times in 1 3/4-2 hrs.; Sunday tickets (p. xvii) are issued between April and Nov. and cheap return tickets on market days (Tues., Frid., Sat.). *Marone* is the only intermediate station touched at by all the boats. — POST OMNIBUS from *Pisogne* to *Edolo*, 34 M., daily in 7 hrs. and from *Cividate-Camuno* to *Edolo*, 21 1/2 M., twice daily in 4 1/4-4 1/2 hrs.

FROM BRESCIA TO ISEO. — *Brescia*, see p. 219. 7 1/2 M. *Paderno Franciacorta*; 12 1/2 M. *Provaglio d'Iseo*; 15 M. *Iseo* (p. 226).

FROM BRESCIA TO PARATICO. — From Brescia to (18 M.) *Palazzolo*, see p. 217. Our line here diverges to the N.E. 24 M. *Paratico*, with the ruined *Castello dei Lantieri*, lies on the left bank of the *Oglio*, which here issues from Lago d'Iseo. Immediately opposite lies **Sarnico** (*Cappello*, plain but good), a prettily situated place, connected with Paratico by a bridge.

The ***Lago d'Isēo** (*Lacus Sebinus*; 610 ft. above the sea; 15 1/2 M. long, 1 1/4-3 M. broad, and about 820 ft. deep in the centre) has an area of 24 square miles. Its banks are green with luxuriant

BAEDEKER. Italy I. 13th Edit. 15

ABOVE
Richard Ford
A Handbook for Travellers in Spain
John Murray
London 1878
actual size

ABOVE RIGHT
Karl Baedeker
Northern Italy, Handbook for Travellers
Leipzig 1906
actual size

OPPOSITE
Italy
Michelin Green Guide
Left: 1959; right: 1983
actual size

These four examples show how information typography has developed over the last hundred years. Murray in two columns set solid is adjective-rich but mean on space and margins. A grey page, but the labour of extracting information from it is as much the fault of the author as of the designer.

Baedeker is more succinct. The minimum of description and the maximum of facts are carefully and clearly organised, using a medley of simple typographic devices.

Both Murray and Baedeker were for the leisured traveller with ample time to stroll through their calm pages. Michelin is for the car-bound tourist in a hurry, reading on the move. Emphasis is on sightseeing rather than transport. Simple typographic devices again make for clarity and rapid use. But the effect of the unleaded text in the earlier edition is a little heavy. The later version has been lightened visually (and often Americanised editorially), and reads more easily though the type size is no bigger. Here, the related variants of one typeface, Univers, have been exploited but, strangely, the town heading is messier and takes up two lines rather than one, with an unnecessary rule.

The distinctive Michelin format (about the same as a folded Michelin map) is well-thought out, both for its single-column setting and for ease of handling.

*AREZZO (concluded)

CHIEF THINGS TO SEE (tour: 2 hours)

Church of S. Francesco (St. Francis).—This church is large, being designed for preaching; it was built for the Franciscans in the 14th century, in the Gothic style. These monks, as guardians of the Holy Places, particularly venerated the Holy Cross. They asked Piero della Francesca to decorate the chancel of their church.

Frescoes of Piero della Francesca*.—These frescoes of the Legend of the Holy Cross, executed from 1452 to 1466, form an admirable whole. It is a noble and powerful masterpiece of well-balanced composition, with soft tones (pale greys and blues and reddish-browns) and gentle lights.

South Wall: on the tympanum, the death and burial of Adam; his son Seth plants a branch of the Tree of Paradise on his grave. The Queen of Sheba prostrates herself before a beam of the bridge made from this tree; she has a vision of Christ crucified on this wood; she explains her vision to Solomon, who has the beam buried. Below, the victory of Constantine over Maxentius under the sign of the Cross (A.D. 312).

Central Wall: the Jews make the Cross with wood from the beam which they have unearthed. Below, the dream of Constantine: "By this sign you shall be victorious."

North Wall: The Empress Helen finds the three crosses of Calvary; that of Christ is identified by the resurrection of a dead man. Below, the victorious Heraclius kills Chosroes, who had stolen the Cross.

On leaving the church you will notice inside the façade an oculus fitted with a splendid stained-glass window bearing the arms of Berry with *fleurs-de-lys*; Guillaume de Marcillat, a native of the Berry, has depicted St. Francis offering roses to the Pope in mid-January.

Piazza Grande*.—This is surrounded by mediaeval houses with battlemented towers, the galleried Romanesque apse of S. Maria della Pieve, the court house (end of 18th century), the palace of the Lay Brotherhood, half-Gothic and half-Renaissance, and the 16th century galleries, which used to be closed to the common people.

The "Saracen's Tournament" takes place in this square on the first Sundays in June and September. The best horsemen of Arezzo attack a dummy figure with lances before a great crowd of "extras" in 14th century costumes.

Church of S. Maria della Pieve*.—A tall campanile, known as that "of the hundred holes" because of its many windows, stands over this fine Romanesque church. The **façade***, inspired by the Pisan Romanesque style (*p. 28*), is highly decorative with its three tiers of small columns, adorned with various patterns and standing more closely together as the height increases; there is a small statue-column in the centre of the uppermost tier. The Virgin, flanked by two angels, appears in the tympanum of the central doorway. Symbols of the twelve months of the year, treated in a lively style, adorn the upper arch.

On the high altar is a remarkable 14th century polyptych by the Sienese Pietro Lorenzetti.

The **Via dei Pileati**, with its palaces, Gothic towers and old houses, is curious. At the corner of a cross street the Palazzo Pretorio (14th–15th century) is adorned with the coats of arms of Podestàs or Florentine Governors.

OTHER THINGS TO SEE

Archaeological Museum* (M).—Open to visitors from 9 a.m. to 5 p.m. Its collection of Aretian vases made in the Roman period is remarkable. It also contains coins and an exceptional collection of Etruscan bronze statuettes (6th–5th century B.C.). Alongside the museum are the remains of the Roman amphitheatre.

Duomo (Cathedral) (D).—This large building has a pretty Renaissance doorway in its south front. Inside are some fine **works of art***: stained-glass windows by Marcillat and the "arch" (or tomb) of St-Donat (14th century) at the high altar.

Church of S. Domenico (St. Dominic) (B).—This 13th century Gothic church has an asymmetrical façade. On it you will notice frescoes by Spinello Aretino and, at the high altar, an admirable **Crucifix*** by Cimabue.

Casa del Vasari (Vasari Mansion) (A). *Apply to the porter.* The house was gorgeously decorated in 1540 by Vasari, a painter, sculptor, architect and writer and a symbol of the Renaissance with his versatile talent. He was the author of *Lives of the Most Excellent Painters, Sculptors and Writers*, a basic work on the history of Italian Primitive art and of the Renaissance.

Church of S. Maria delle Grazie (St. Mary of the Graces).—1¼ miles by car southwards along the Via Mecenate. In front of the church is a light, graceful **portico*** by the Florentine Benedetto di Maiano (15th century). Inside the church a retable by Andrea della Robbia frames a picture by Spinello Aretino, "St. Mary of the Graces".

ASCOLI PICENO ** Marches—Michelin map no. 988 16.

Ascoli, an austere but picturesque town, lies in a narrow valley at the confluence of the Castellano and the Tronto, which themselves flow in deep valleys. It is rich in Romanesque and mediaeval buildings. A great part of it is still enclosed in finely proportioned ramparts.

Ascoli has two specialities: paper-making and the preparation of stuffed olives.

CHIEF THINGS TO SEE (tour: 1 hour)

Piazza del Popolo.**—The "Square of the People", elongated and well-proportioned and paved with large flagstones, is surrounded by Gothic buildings and Renaissance arcades. It is usually quiet but becomes lively on market days. On summer evenings the square is filled with strollers enjoying the cool air or sitting on the café terraces and looking at the illuminated façades.

Palazzo del Popolo* (People's Palace).—The People's Palace is an austere 13th century building dominated by a tower. The façade was modified at the Renaissance by the addition, by Cola dell' Amatrice, of an imposing doorway (1548) surmounted by a statue of Pope Paul III. The palace, which has a Renaissance inner courtyard, contains a museum.

Church of S. Francesco* (St. Francis).—This interesting church was begun in 1263 and consecrated in 1371. The apse is particularly curious with its seven Lombard apsidials, two hexagonal towers and a dome over the transept crossing. A Gothic doorway on one side, though it has a semicircular arch, is completed by a Renaissance niche holding the statue of Pope Julius II.

Loggia dei Mercanti* (Loggia of the Merchants).—The Loggia of the Merchants abuts on the south front of the church of St. Francis. It is light and graceful and was built at the beginning of the 16th century under Tuscan influence, revealed by the shape of the capitals.

Quartiere Vecchio* (Old Quarter).—This lies between the Corso Mazzini and the Tronto river. The main street is the Via delle Torri, prolonged by the Via Solesta; these two streets are lined with old houses and shops. At the entrance to the Via delle Torri is the Renaissance façade of **S. Agostino (B)**, a church which contains a Christ bearing the Cross in a moving fresco by Cola dell' Amatrice (beyond the second altar on the left). Two proud towers stand opposite the church. The Via delle Torri ends at the church of S. Pietro Martiri (14th century).

AREZZO

Cavour (Vial) .... BY
Grande (Piazza) .... BY
Italia (Corso) .... ABYZ

Madonna del Prato (V.) .... AZ 3
Mecenate (Viale) .... AZ 4
Niccolò Aretino (Via) ..... AZ 5
Pellicceria (Via) .... BY 6
Pescioni (Via) .... BZ 7
S. Clemente (Via) .... AY 12
Sasso Verde (Via) .... BY 13

---------- S. FRANCESCO
---------- PIAZZA GRANDE *
---------- STA MARIA DELLA PIEVE *

■ ADDITIONAL SIGHTS

Archaeological Museum* (Museo Archeologico) (AZ M¹). — Open 9 am to 2 pm (1 pm Sundays and holidays); closed Mondays. The collections of Aretian vases made in the Roman period and of Etruscan bronze statuettes, dating from the 6-5C BC, are outstanding.

Cathedral (Duomo) (BY D). — This cathedral was built between 1286 and 1510 but has a modern façade. There is a Romanesque-Gothic doorway (1319-1337) in its south front.

Inside are fine **works of art***: stained glass windows by Marcillat (Expulsion of the Money-Changers from the Temple), a fresco by Piero della Francesca of Mary Magdalen in the north aisle, the 14C tomb *(arca)* of St. Donatus at the high altar and 16C marble pulpits.

St. Dominic's Church (San Domenico) (BY B). — This 13C Gothic church has an asymmetrical façade. Inside, you will notice frescoes by the Duccio school and by Spinello Aretino and his followers and, at the high altar, an admirable **Crucifix***, an early work (1260-65) by Cimabue.

Vasari's Mansion (Casa del Vasari) (AY A). — Open 8 am to 2 pm weekdays; 9 am to 1 pm Sundays and holidays; closed Mondays. The house was gorgeously decorated in 1540 by Vasari, a painter, sculptor, architect and writer and a symbol of the Renaissance with his versatile talent. Also exhibited are works by Tuscan mannerists.

Church of St. Mary of Grace (Santa Maria delle Grazie). — 1 km - 3/4 mile — southwards along the Viale Mecenate (AZ). In front of the church is a light, graceful **portico*** by the Florentine, Benedetto da Maiano (15C). Inside the church a marble altarpiece by Andrea della Robbia frames a picture by Parri di Spinello, St. Mary of Grace.

Museum of Mediaeval and Modern Art (AY M²). — Open 9 am to 2 pm (1 pm Sundays and holidays); closed Mondays. The gallery and the museum are both in the 15C Bruni Palace. Works by Margarito d'Arezzo, Guido da Siena, Parri di Spinello, Bartolomeo della Gatta, Luca Signorelli, Cigoli, Vasari, Salvator Rosa and Gaspard Dughet may be seen. The 19C is represented by some of the most famous painters of the Macchiaioli school: Fattori, Signorini... There are also coins, bronzes, glass, arms and ceramics (remarkable collection of the Renaissance period and of the 17 and 18C).

ASCOLI PICENO ** Marches

Michelin map 988 16 — Pop 56 200

Ascoli, an austere but picturesque town lies in a narrow valley at the confluence of the Castellano and the Tronto. The town is rich in Roman and mediaeval buildings.

■ MAIN SIGHTS *time: 1 hour*

Piazza del Popolo.** — The People's Square, elongated and well proportioned and paved with large flagstones, is surrounded by Gothic buildings and Renaissance arcades. The square is the favourite meeting-place of the people and it provides the scene for the Carnival and the parade leading up to the Quintana festival on the first Sunday in August.

People's Palace* (Palazzo del Popolo). — The People's Palace is an austere 13C building dominated by a tower. An imposing doorway (1549) surmounted by a statue of Pope Paul III was added by Cola dell' Amatrice at the Renaissance. The palace has a Renaissance inner court.

St. Francis' Church* (San Francesco). — This interesting church was begun in 1262 and consecrated in 1371. The apse is particularly curious with its seven Lombard apsidioles, two hexagonal towers and a dome over the transept crossing. A statue of Pope Julius II surmounts a Romanesque doorway on the right. The cloisters are on the north side of the church.

BELOW
John Bourke
*The Baroque Churches of Central
Europe*
Faber and Faber
2nd edition, London 1962
actual size

OPPOSITE
Nikolaus Pevsner
*The Buildings of England:
Cumberland and Westmorland*
Penguin Books
Harmondsworth 1967 reprinted 1973
actual size

Narrative guides should read comfortably as continuous text but at the same time contain a good deal of information, which must be lightly signalled without interrupting the flow. Both these examples succeed. Bourke's page is airy and graceful with an entirely appropriate use of Walbaum. In extended descriptions, noteworthy features are numbered (within the paragraph), facilitating on-the-spot use. In the text size and weight, but within brackets, these numbers are surprisingly easy to pick out, but they do not disrupt the page.

THE CHURCHES

the result that the dome is felt as slightly oppressive and some of the other parts (e.g. the diagonal corner chapels) as somewhat dwarfed.

Altomünster, 1763–6 (15 m. E. of Augsburg, 12 m. N.W. of Dachau; from both, as also from Munich, rail and bus connections). Abbey church (Benedictine foundation eighth century for monks and nuns: since 1485 Brigittine). The last of Fischer's churches, he died before its completion. A type of wall-pillar church of complicated design; to a large octagonal nave are added three eastward sections—a 2-storey section quadrilateral on plan, an apsidal choir and (above and behind) a second choir. The Brigittines being a double Order of monks and nuns, the problem was to construct a church in which three groups (monks, nuns, and lay brothers) could take part in the services unseen, and so undisturbed, by one another; to which had to be added and accommodated the lay folk. Fischer's solution produced, not an oddity as might be thought, but an interior which combines certain well-known features of his churches with other surprising and beautiful vistas.

Noteworthy features. Exterior: The tower and its helm are very shapely. The greatly extended E. limb should be noted. *Interior:* (1) The arrangement to meet the accommodation needs can be clearly made out. We enter the main octagon (with two tiers of galleries), immediately E. of which is the 2-storey section with lay-brothers' choir below and nuns' choir above, then the apsidal sanctuary, then (above and behind the high altar, now used as the parish altar) the monks' choir with stalls and altar. The whole lay-out of the greatest interest as an attempt to meet unusual monastic requirements in a way satisfactory both practically and aesthetically. (2) The decoration is of varying quality. The delicate and restrained stucco work by *Jakob Rauch* (1773), the frescoes by *Josef Mages* (1768), especially fine in the drawing and colouring, that in the nave saucer dome depicting scenes, actual and legendary, from the history of the Order; the two chief altars by *J. B. Straub*, late and fanciful but good.

84

SOUTHERN GERMANY

Other churches of J. M. Fischer

Altomünster was Fischer's last great work; he died, as we have seen, while it was being completed. Of his other, lesser but always interesting and beautiful churches, attention is directed to the following. The first four all show variations of the central octagon theme of which we have spoken and which found its perfect expression at *Rott-am-Inn*.

Rinchnach, 1727–9 (12 m. N.E. Deggendorf, on the Regen-Passau road). The nave is a new construction; choir and tower were taken over from the fifteenth-century church and baroquized. Fine stucco work (artist unknown) and frescoes by *Andreas Heindl*.

Unering, 1751 (4 m. N.W. Starnberg on isolated hill) with interior of great charm; good harmonious contemporary furnishings and nave fresco.

Aufhausen, 1736–51 (12 m. S.E. Regensburg, 16 m. S.W. Straubing). One of Fischer's strongest interiors, its appeal predominantly architectural. Here (as at the contemporary *Ingolstadt Franziskanerkirche* before its total destruction by bombs) the narrow sides of the octagon are pierced by arches at ground and at gallery level so that the diagonal axes thrust through to the outer walls, as later at *Rott*.

Bichl, 1751–3 (just N. *Benediktbeuern*) with frescoes by *J. J. Zeiller*, and high altar with a notable group of St George and the Dragon by *J. B. Straub*. Side altars 1709. No stucco.

Dominikus Zimmermann

In *Dominikus Zimmermann* we have a figure who differs in certain important ways from *J. M. Fischer*. Fischer was an architect pure and simple and his churches were decorated by a variety of artists. Zimmermann, having been trained and achieved distinction as stucco artist and designer of altars as well as architect, united in his own person the practice of several arts. Again, he worked in frequent co-operation with his brother, the painter *Johann Baptist Zimmermann*, who contributed the frescoes to all

85

Such well thought-out writing (or editing) is an essential ingredient of good textual presentation.

Pevsner's enthusiastic prose, chock-a-block with information, is economically presented by Schmoller in practical Plantin. Very handsome, with meticulous detailing, the design breathes new life into a classical approach. It relies heavily on caps and small caps, as against the widespread use of italic in *Baroque Churches.*

The problem of a potentially-awkward footnote here seems to disappear. In the margin, roman figures indicate illustrations, italic figures are map references.

Italy
Michelin Red Guide
Clermont-Ferrand 1986
actual size

The Michelin Red Guide uses almost as many symbols as words to convey a mass of information which in narrative would have occupied many pages. It is nontheless very pleasant to use because the complicated typography is well-controlled and the symbols are clear.

---

cusped Y-type. W wall with three stepped lancets, W doorway with naturalistic leaf capitals. In the S porch also one stiff-leaf capital. In the chancel S wall SEDILIA and PISCINA as they ought to be (and who would occupy the three seats at Warwick Bridge ?), in the N wall Easter-Sepulchre-like recess with the founder's tomb. Henry Howard (of Corby Castle) died in 1842. – STAINED GLASS. The side windows clearly by *Hardman*, who mostly worked to Pugin's designs, though these windows were done after Pugin's death (dates commemorated 1860, 1865, 1867).

Former METHODIST CHURCH, Warwick, on the way to St Leonard. A fine pedimented front with just a simple door surround and no front windows. The date 1847 is surprisingly late for so Georgian a design.

WARWICK HALL. Of *c.*1930, by *Guy Elwes*, neo-Georgian. The stables are real Georgian. The house preceding the present one was built in 1828.

HOLME EDEN HALL. *Dobson* in 1837 built this sumptuous Early Tudor mansion for Peter Dixon, one of the founders of the great cotton mills at Carlisle.* It bristles with ornamental chimneys, and has a porch-tower, bays, and mullioned windows. The skyline seen from a distance is superb.

WHOOF HOUSE, 1¾ m. W, on the A-road. In the garden stands the splendid six-light C17 Gothic-Revival E window of *43* Arthuret church. The composition is three plus three lights, each with a segmental arch and above intersecting tracery, and in the mid-spandrel an oval. Arthuret (*see* p. 61) was rebuilt from 1609 onwards. But such an oval looks 1650–75 rather than 1610.

WASDALE HALL *see* STRANDS

WASDALE HEAD *1000*

CHURCH. Very small, of nave and chancel in one, with a bell-cote. Plain mullioned windows. – Victorian IRON BRACKETS for oil lamps. – PLATE. Cup of 1565.

WASTWATER *see* WASDALE HEAD

WATENDLATH *see* GRANGE

WATERFOOT *see* POOLEY BRIDGE (W), p. 284

* But Manner and Whellan say 1833 by *James Stewart* of Carlisle.

ARDORE MARINA 89037 Reggio di Calabria – ✪ 0964.
Roma 711 – Catanzaro 107 – ◆Reggio di Calabria 89.
Euro Hotel, S : 1 km ✆ 61025, ≤, ᵭ₆, ℀ – ⵚ☰⛱wc ⋔wc ☎ ⓟ – ⛩ ⴹ ℀
Pas carta 19/27000 – ☵ 4500 – **56 cam** 60000 – P 44/64000.

AREMOGNA L'Aquila – Vedere Roccaraso.

ARENZANO 16011 Genova ⑨⑧⑧ ③ – 11 257 ab. – Stazione balneare, a.s. Pasqua, giugno-settembre e Natale – ✪ 010.
ᵣ₉ Della Pineta (chiuso martedi ed ottobre) a Punta San Martino ✆ 9127296, O : 1 km.
⊞ via Cambiaso 1 ✆ 9127581
Roma 527 – Alessandria 77 – ◆Genova 28 – ◆Milano 151 – Savona 23.
Gd H. Arenzano, ✆ 9126351, ≤, « Giardino con ⤵ » – ⵚ ⓟ – ⛩
60 cam.
Ena, ✆ 9127379, ≤, ⚓ – ⵚ ⋔wc ☎ ⴹ ℀ rist
Pas (chiuso da ottobre ad aprile) 22/30000 – ☵ 6000 – 25 cam 31/47000 – P 52/55000.
Miramare, ✆ 9127325, ≤ – ⵚ ⛱wc ⋔wc ☎ ⟺ ⴹ ⓞ VISA ℀ rist
chiuso da dicembre al 9 gennaio – Pas 20000 – ☵ 5000 – **45 cam** 30/45000 – P 58000, b.s. 48000.
Lazzaro e Gabriella, ✆ 9124259, Coperti limitati; prenotare – ☰ ⴹ ⓞ VISA
chiuso lunedi e dal 15 dicembre al 15 gennaio – Pas carta 30/53000.
Otello, ✆ 9127026.
Parodi, ✆ 9126637 – ☰
chiuso martedi e dal 15 al 30 ottobre – Pas carta 17/26000.

ARESE 20020 Milano ②①⑨ ⑧ – 15 790 ab. alt. 160 – ✪ 02.
Roma 593 – Como 36 – ◆Milano 16 – Varese 50.
Castanei, viale Alfa Romeo NO : 1,5 km ✆ 9380053 – ⓟ VISA ℀
chiuso domenica – Pas carta 17/30000.
ALFA-ROMEO (Sede) via Alfa Romeo ✆ 93391

AREZZO 52100 P ⑨⑧⑧ ⑮ – 91 691 ab. alt. 296 – ✪ 0575.
Vedere : Chiesa di San Francesco (affreschi di Piero della Francesca★★★) – Chiesa di Santa Maria della Pieve★ (facciata★★) – Piazza Grande★ – Museo Archeologico★ AZ M1 – Duomo (opere d'arte★) BY D – Chiesa di San Domenico (crocifisso★★) BY B – Chiesa di Santa Maria delle Grazie (portico★) AZ.
⊞ piazza Risorgimento 116 ✆ 20839.
A.C.I. viale Luca Signorelli 24/a ✆ 23253.
Roma 218 ④ – ◆Ancona 211 ② – ◆Firenze 81 ④ – Forli 136 ① – ◆Milano 376 ④ – ◆Perugia 74 ③ – Rimini 153 ①.

Pianta pagina a lato

Minerva, via Fiorentina 6 ✆ 27891, Telex 573535 – ⵚ ☰ ⓞ ☎ ⟺ ⓟ – ⛩ ⴹ ⓞ VISA ℀
Pas (chiuso dal 1° al 18 agosto) carta 22/31000 (15%) – ☵ 7500 – **100 cam** 47/75000 – P 70/75000. AY n
Etrusco, via Fleming 39 ✆ 381483 – ⵚ ☰ ⓣⓥ ☎ ⟺ ⓟ – ⛩ ⴹ ⓞ VISA ℀ rist
Pas 18000 – ☵ 4500 – **80 cam** 43/65000. 1 km per ④
Continentale, piazza Guido Monaco 7 ✆ 20251 – ⵚ ☰ rist ⛱wc ⋔wc ☎ ᵭ – ⛩ ⴹ ⓞ E VISA ℀ rist
Pas (chiuso domenica sera e dal 10 al 25 luglio) carta 18/27000 – ☵ 6000 – **78 cam** 38/61000 – P 70/75000. AZ r
Europa senza rist, via Spinello 43 ✆ 357701 – ⵚ ☰ ⛱wc ⋔wc ☎ ℀
☵ 7500 – **45 cam** 46/75000. AZ u
Da Cecco, corso Italia 215 ✆ 20986 – ⵚ ⋔wc ᵭ ⴹ ⓞ E VISA
Pas (chiuso lunedi e dal 1° al 23 agosto) carta 18/24000 – ☵ 4000 – **42 cam** 30/48000 – P 48000. AZ e
Buca di San Francesco, piazza San Francesco 1 ✆ 23271, « Ambiente d'intonazione trecentesca » – ⴹ ⓞ BY c
chiuso lunedi sera, martedi e luglio – Pas carta 23/33000 (15%).
Le Tastevin, via de' Cenci 9 ✆ 28304 – ☰ ⴹ ⓞ E VISA ℀ AZ x
chiuso lunedi e dal 5 al 27 agosto – Pas carta 20/30000.
Spiedo d'Oro, via Crispi 12 ✆ 22873 – ☰ ℀ AZ a
chiuso giovedi e dal 1° al 15 luglio – Pas carta 14/21000 (12%).

sulla superstrada dei 2 Mari SE : 8 km per ② :
Il Torrino, ⊠ 52100 ✆ 360264, ⚓ – ⓟ ⴹ ⓞ E VISA ℀
chiuso lunedi – **Pas** carta 18/30000.

Vedere anche : *Giovi* per ① : 8 km.
Chiassa Superiore per ① : 9 km.

84

Tycho Brahe
De Mundi Aetherei recentoribus
phaenominis
Uraniburg 1577
reduced from approx 240 mm deep

Technical books have a long history and were particularly in demand during the Renaissance. This astronomical treatise uses a simple diagram keyed to the long footnote in italics, while the main text is set in a handsome roman. The arabesque initial gives the page grace, as well as marking a new chapter, and the style is perfectly appropriate for a science book for connoisseurs.

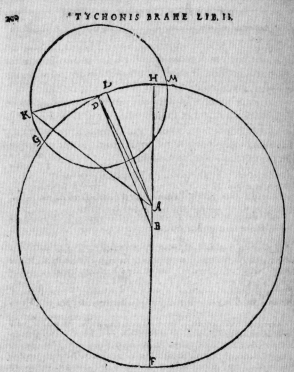

The Shell Encyclopedia of Sailing
ed Michael W Richey
Stanford Maritime
(produced by Rainbird Publishing)
London 1980
reduced from approx 280 mm deep

In contrast to the decoratively elegant book on mathematics for a leisured gentleman of cultivated tastes, this spread from *The Shell Encyclopedia of Sailing* presents serious instruction for the reading sailor. The tools by which this is achieved include clear diagrams set against disciplined typography, grids, alignments across the page, and minimum 'business' in the treatment of type. This is book engineering. Any elegance is incidental, and of the engineering mode: neat, economical of means, functional.

Performance and yacht design

means of compass and protractor; or mathematically, with the help of a hand-held calculator, solving the three following, relatively simple, equations:

1. $V_T = \sqrt{(V_A^2 + V_S^2 - 2V_A V_S \cos\beta)}$

2. $\sin\gamma = \dfrac{\sin\beta}{V_T} V_A$

and lastly the already known equation:

3. $V_{mg} = V_S \cos\gamma$

The result of the calculation can be plotted in terms of V_{mg} versus V_T. The large number of circular dots in fig. 15 illustrate such results obtained in close-hauled conditions, while sailing a full-scale 5.5-Metre boat. The measurements were taken in a variety of wind and sea conditions, on two different waters, as indicated.

The object of these particular full-scale trials was to establish the degree of correlation between the theoretically derived performance curve (the thick continuous line) based on model tests, and the performance actually achieved by helmsmen attempting to reach the best performance in given conditions.

It is evident from the scattered points of performance measurements that a yacht can rarely be sailed at optimum except momentarily and by chance. In fact on a few occasions only the actually measured performance figures coincide with the theoretical curve; which, it should not be forgotten, applies to smooth-water conditions. This thick continuous line curve, enveloping the measured points that lie within or to the left of the curve, can be regarded as an ultimate yardstick – very difficult to match in practice.

In fact, it is not easy to establish the optimum performance curve from full-scale trials. It takes a long time, and a large number of test runs must be recorded, to gather enough data to plot such a curve with a reasonable degree of accuracy. The whole idea of full-scale measurements which appears to be simple in principle, is difficult in realization. It requires a great deal of skill, on the part of experimenters, to execute the tests and interpret the results correctly. There are many reasons for the difficulties usually encountered, which are clearly reflected in the scattered test data of 5.5-Metre boats in fig. 15. Continual variations of wind and water flow greatly affect the air and water sensors and this in turn complicates the measurements (*see* photograph). Because of these changes in apparent wind speed V_A and its direction, the helmsman is not able to distinguish immediately and exactly enough what changes have occurred in the true wind. Recorded variations of wind speed V_T alone, in the order of 10 ft/sec – 50% of the mean speed of about 20 ft/sec – are fairly common

172

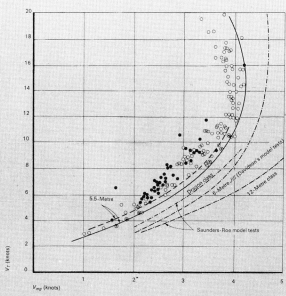

Fig. 15 Close-hauled results for some racing keelboats. (The open circles and the solid curve are the results of full-scale trials in Southampton Water; the solid circles and dashed curve are the results of full-scale trials in the King George VI Reservoir; the crosses are results based on model tests in the National Physical Laboratory, Teddington, Middlesex)

Because sails develop lift, the airflow in their proximity is distorted and thus to avoid unreliable readings, wind sensors must be positioned with some care. To reduce the effect of the distorted airflow the sensors are placed at a distance from the sails, although some desirable positions are precluded because of their interference with boat handling (as in the photograph (below), where a Dragon is being tested by Southampton University). Similar problems arise when testing the hull with water-speed sensors that are operating close to it or its appendages

Performance and yacht design

over intervals of 2 minutes. This being so, the sail forces must also be subject to large fluctuations, and sheeting angles may not be matched correctly to the best performance requirements. The hull speed responds more or less slowly to these varying wind forces transmitted through the rig, depending on the weight (mass) of the hull. The time response of the measuring instruments, together with the helmsman's response to their pointers or merit indicators, is also an important factor. It is therefore highly unlikely that a yacht can be kept moving consistently well, 'on target', in such a variable environment. Some degree of departure from the optimum is inevitable.

– ways of presenting boat performance
The question of the sensitivity of performance to departures from, say, optimum sheeting angle δ, defined in fig. 16, now becomes relevant. To show its significance, the simple example of the Finn-type dinghy, driven by a single sail, has been chosen. (Obviously, the more sails there are to be considered, the more difficult the tuning problem becomes.)

Fig. 16 shows that over the lower windspeed range, up to 2–3 on the Beaufort scale, the optimum sheeting angle δ remains fairly constant and at a relatively low value; but as the wind speed V_T increases so does the sheeting angle, quite sharply. The two thin, broken-line curves in fig. 14 may help to answer another practical question: how much boat performance deteriorates when the helmsman does not pay enough attention to the variation in wind strength and maintains the sheeting angle constant, regardless. These two curves, which just touch the optimum

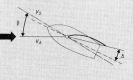

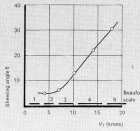

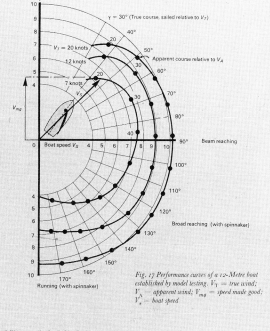

Fig. 17 Performance curves of a 12-Metre boat established by model testing. V_T = true wind; V_A = apparent wind; V_{mg} = speed made good; V_s = boat speed

Fig. 16 Finn-type dinghy (left). Optimum course sailed β and optimum sheeting angle δ for one particular kicking strap (boom vang) tension (Marchaj, Aerohydrodynamics of Sailing). Note: the sheeting angle δ is measured between the boom and the centreline of the hull.

V_{mg} (thick continuous-line) curve twice along its length, give the attainable V_{mg}, assuming in one case the sheeting angle $\delta = 10°$ constant, and in the other $\delta = 18°$ constant. It can now be appreciated that in both cases the potential sail efficiency is fully exploited in only a small range of wind speed V_T. Below and above that particular wind strength, at which the thin curves coincide with the optimum curve, the V_{mg} speed increasingly deteriorates. Correct sail adjustment to suit the variety of wind conditions appears, therefore, to offer a dramatic degree of performance improvement.

Performance calculations, whether the data originates from model tests or full-scale trials, can be presented in a variety of ways, depending on their intended use – by the yacht designer, racing crew, or a yacht-research establishment. Fig. 17, for instance, gives an overall picture of the performance of a ballasted racing yacht of 12-Metre class, sailing in calm water on courses ranging from close-hauled to running, and in true wind speeds $V_T = 7$, 12, and 20 knots. The three performance curves plotted were built up by drawing the boat speed vectors V_S from the origin 0, at each relevant γ angle and wind speed V_T for which the calculations were made. As an example, only one such V_S vector is shown in fig. 17. It indicates that, at wind velocity V_T = 7 knots, the optimum boat speed V_S is 6.5

173

Pristella   Characidae
– *riddlei*   PRISTELLA, X-RAY FISH, WATER GOLDFINCH
4cm. (1½in.)
This fish comes from the north east of South America. Not
the most colourful of fishes, undoubtedly its attraction lies
in the shape, posture and contrasting black and white
markings of its dorsal and anal fins. The fins are large and
held well from the body which is darkish green above and,
in the latter half of the body, with a light, almost
transparent belly. There is a dark line running horizontally
which is picked out above in the posterior half of the body
by a parallel yellow line. The tail fin is a delicate reddish
pink. It is a good member of the community tank where it
helps to accentuate the colours of brighter fish. It requires a
high proportion of live food in its diet and temperatures
between 24–26 C. Sexing is relatively simple. Viewed
against a bright light, the body cavity can be seen within the
living body and is pointed in males, more rounded in
females. Matched pairs breed but only with difficulty.
Plenty of weed with not too deep water, about 10–15cm.,
and a high temperature of 26 C. Parents tend to eat young
so must be removed. **134**

Prochilodus   Curimatidae   ⊕
– *insignis*   SERGEANT CHARACIN, FLAG-TAILED
PROCHILODUS   15cm. (6in.)
A native of the Amazon, this fish reaches some 15cm. in
captivity. The body is a silver grey. It is noticeable because
of its striped tail and anal fins. The dark horizontal stripes
in the tail are separated by white, the base colour.
   It has a sucking mouth similar in appearance to that of
the Kissing Gourami, *Helostoma temminckii,* with which it
feeds in the mud of the river bottom. It consumes algae and,
in captivity, boiled spinach. Not aggressive but jumps high,
so keep the tank covered.
– *taeniurus*   SILVER PROCHILODUS   15cm. (6in.)
This native Amazonian has a dark green body shading to a
yellow undercarriage. The posterior half of the fish is
divided by a horizontal line which commences below the
dorsal fin and extends as far as the tail. The dorsal fin has a
large dark spot. The tail fin has horizontal bands of black
with dark tips to the lobes and the pelvic fins are blood red.

Promicrops   Serranidae   Ψ
– *lanceolatus*   TIGER or QUEENSLAND GROUPER
3m. (9ft 10in.)   ✂
Although it grows very large indeed, young ones can be
kept in captivity in normal-sized tanks, but outgrow them
quickly. The black body is decorated with yellow patches in
the juveniles. Comes from the Indo-Pacific region. At full
size, they are the terror of divers, so beware. Requires live
food. This fish does not breed in captivity.

Protein Skimmers or **Protein Foam Removers**
Basically these work by frothing the water with a stream of
fine bubbles. The dissolved impurities, resulting from
protein breakdown of waste products, respond by making a
stable foam which rises to the surface from where it can be
periodically removed. Rarely necessary except in very large
aquaria. Water changes are simpler, easier to manage, and
far less expensive. See *Management of the Marine
Aquarium.*

Protopteridae   AFRICAN LUNGFISH
This family, together with Ceratodontidae and
Lepidosirenidae, makes up the lungfishes. They have a pair
of lungs lying below but communicating with the
oesophagus. Like other lungfish they bury themselves in
burrows in the mud during the dry season. The male guards
the eggs which are laid in burrows. The young have external
gills which later disappear. See *Protopterus.*

Protopterus   Protopteridae   ⊕
– *annectens*   AFRICAN LUNGFISH   91cm. (3ft)
Rarely kept by aquarists because of its size, it is
nevertheless an interesting fish with an elongated brown
body and an almost white belly, peppered with dark dots.
The pectoral and pelvic fins have been modified to form thin
worm-like extensions which are moved in a circular motion.
Not only can it survive dry conditions by using air, but it
must get air even when in water and will drown if not able to
surface.
   A hardy aquarium inmate, providing it is kept in clean
water anywhere between 20–31 C. It is carnivorous,
normally eating small fish but will take raw meat in
captivity.

PSETTUS DIAMONDFISH see *Monodactylus argenteus*

Pseudobalistes   Balistidae   Ψ
– *fuscus*   JIGSAW or BLUE-LINED TRIGGERFISH
50cm. (20in.)
This fish from the Pacific Ocean grows to 50cm. in length.
Its orange body is patterned with blue lines. A dark patch
separates the eyes, marks the base of the dorsal fin and the
tail. It can vary this colour, actually becoming black with
anger. It naturally feeds on crustacea and shelled echino-
derms, and likes temperatures around 24°C.

Pseudochromidae   DWARF GROUPERS, DOTTYBACKS
A small family of marine fish closely related to *Serranidae.*
They are active little fish with small anal and dorsal fins
each with only three spines. They, like Serranidae, tend to
lie in wait for their prey, hiding in small holes in rocks or
coral. See *Pseudochromis.*

LEFT
David J Coffey
The Encyclopedia of Aquarium Fish
Pelham Books
(produced by Rainbird Publishing)
London 1977
reduced from 240 mm deep

This specialist encyclopedia for the
popular market uses only one text type,
in roman, italic, bold, bold italic and
small caps; but with a disciplined use of
space, the signalling of different kinds of
information (scientific names, generic
names, English names, English words,
families and cross-references) is entirely
adequate for the purpose. Symbols
indicate characteristics such as fresh-
water, marine, aggressive and so on.

OPPOSITE
Christopher Wright
Dutch Painting in the Seventeenth Century
Lund Humphries
London 1989
reduced from 265 mm deep

The scholar's catalogue of Dutch painters
is a massive reference list presented as
succinctly as possible. The three most
important grades of information (artist,
location, title) are differentiated. Preceding each title is a bullet which signals
both it and its group of information.
Small triangles indicate further references in other literature.
   The presentation of such information
requires close co-operation between
author, editor and designer (and a
sympathetic typesetter). As with the
encyclopedia, using the full range of
fonts (and, additionally here, changing
the type size for the main headings)
would have been a costly operation
without the facilities of current filmsetting machines. Changes of type family
could equally easily have been achieved,
had this been thought desirable. The
increased capacity and flexibility of
filmsetting offer temptation to indulge in
the wildest excesses; but restraint is
usually more effective.

Manchester CITY ART GALLERY
● *A party of falconers outside the gates of a castle*
Signed: J Lingelbach
Assheton Bennett Cat.1965 no.33; Concise Cat.1980 no.1979.471, ill.
>Burger-Wegener no.169

Nottingham CASTLE MUSEUM
● *Village festival with peasants merry making*
Signed: L Lingelbach
Inv.no.04-92
Cat.1904 no.27
>Burger-Wegener no.113
Exh. Hull 1961 no.64; London, RA 1962 no.116; Newcastle 1983 no.64, ill.; Philadelphia/Berlin/London, RA 1984 no.63 pl.45

Royal Collection
● *A mountebank and other figures before a locande and a Capriccio view of the Piazza del Popolo, Rome*
False monogram: KDJ
Cat.1982 no.97 pl.86
>Burger-Wegener no.12
● *Embarkation of Charles II at Scheveningen, 1660*
Cat.1982 no.98 pl.87
>Burger-Wegener no.208

National Trust
—AUDLEY END
● *Street scene*
Cat.1973, Great Drawing Room no.10, as attributed
—WADDESDON MANOR
● *Riding scene*
Signed: J Lingelbach
Cat.1967 no.63, ill.
> Burger-Wegener no.192

Linsen, Jan (Hermafrodito)

*b.*Hoorn 1602/3; *w.*Rome 1624; *d.*at sea ?1635

Lisse, Dirck van der

b.?Breda; *w.*The Hague from 1639; *d.*The Hague 1669

Cambridge FITZWILLIAM MUSEUM
● *Landscape with Diana and Actaeon*
Monogram: DVL
Cat.1960 no.407 pl.35

Glasgow ART GALLERY
● *Landscape with Mercury, Argus and Io*
Cat.1961 no.595; Plates 1961 p.60

Leeds TEMPLE NEWSAM HOUSE
● *Diana and Callisto*
Concise Cat.1976 no.7/36

London VICTORIA AND ALBERT MUSEUM
● *Landscape with a rustic bridge and cattle*
Monogram: DVL
Cat.1973 no.212; pl.p.172

Royal Collection
● *A woman*
Monogram: DVL
Cat.1982 no.99 pl.84

Loef, Jacob Gerritsz. van

*b.*Enkhuizen ? *c.*1607; *d.*Enkhuizen ? after 1648

London GREENWICH
● *De Witte in action against Dunkerkers off the coast of Nieuwport in 1641*
Inv.no.1962-69
Cat.1988 no.BHC0271, ill.
Preston 1974 p.25
● *De Witte in action against Dunkerkers off the coast of Nieuwport in 1641*
Signed and dated 1643
Inv.no.1962-70
Cat.1988 no.BHC0272, ill.
Preston 1974 p.25 pl.38

Loeninga, Allaert van

*w.*Middelburg ?1639; *d.*?1649/50

Lois, Jacob

*b.*Rotterdam *c.*1620; *d.*Rotterdam 1676

Loncke, Jacob Lambrechts

*b.*Zierikzee *c.*1580; *d.*?after 1646

Loo, Jacob van

*b.*Sluis 1614; *d.*Paris 1670

Glasgow ART GALLERY
● *Susanna and the Elders*
Signed: J van Loo fecit
Cat.1962 no.623; Plates 1961 p.60

Loo, Lambert Joukes van

*w.*Friesland *c.*1660

Looten, Jan

*b.*Amsterdam 1618; *d.*London or York *c.*1680

Cheltenham ART GALLERY
● *Wooded landscape with a bridge*
Falsely signed and dated: Hobbema pinx 1686
Cat.1988 no.1943.28, ill.

Leeds TEMPLE NEWSAM HOUSE
● *Wooded landscape*
Concise Cat.1976 no.22.76/48

London NATIONAL GALLERY
● *River landscape*
Cat.1960 no.901; Plates 1958 p.184; Illustrated Cat.1986 p.329

Royal Collection
● *Landscape with a bridge*
Cat.1963 no.413 pl.62, as attributed
● *Landscape with figures by a bridge*
Cat.1963 no.414
● *Landscape with an estuary*
Cat.1963 no.415
● *Wooded landscape*
Cat.1963 no.416

Lorme, Anthonie de

*b.*Tournai *c.*1610; *d.*Rotterdam 1673

Dublin NATIONAL GALLERY
● *Church interior*
Signed and dated: A de Lorme 1650
Cat.1986 no.516 pl.99
● *Interior of St Laurenskerk, Rotterdam*
Cat.1986 no.558 pl.98

National Trust
—BRODIE CASTLE
● *Church interior*
Signed and dated 1654
Guide 1986 p.22

Ludeking, David

*w.*Amsterdam 1650s

Ludick, Lodewijk van

*b.*Amsterdam 1629; *d.*Amsterdam before 1697

Luessinck, Johan

*b.*Zutphen 1644; *d.c.*1711

Lundens, Gerrit

*b.*Amsterdam 1622; *d.*Amsterdam 1683

London NATIONAL GALLERY
● *The militia company of Captain Banning Cocq*
(reduced copy of Rembrandt's *Night Watch*)
Cat.1960 Inv.no.289, as after Rembrandt; Plates 1958 p.281; Illustrated Cat.1986 p.339
On long-term loan to Amsterdam, Rijksmuseum

Lust, A. de

*w.*17th century

Cambridge FITZWILLIAM MUSEUM
● *Flower piece*
False signature: J de Heem
Cat.1960 no.313, as attributed
—(BROUGHTON COLLECTION)
● *Glass vase of flowers*
Inv.no.PD.35-1966

Oxford ASHMOLEAN MUSEUM
● *A vase of flowers*
Falsely signed: R Ruysch 166..
Ward Cat.1950 no.50 pl.p.115; Cat.1961 no.W50; Cat.1980 no.A574
Exh. London, RA 1952/3 no.557
● *Still-life with peaches and grapes*
Signed: a d lust
Ward Cat.1950 no.51, pl.p.116; Cat.1961 no.W51; Cat.1980 no.A575

William Turner
A New Herbal
1551
reduced from approx 280 mm deep

Both these examples show illustration used for descriptive as well as decorative purposes. In William Turner's herbal the typography and particularly the woodcut initials are so dark and sumptuous that the pictures of plants seem pale ghosts. In fact, those hopelessly overwrought

The vertues of the reede.

He roote of the common hedge rede, called in latin Canna: by it selfe, oz layde to wyth hys knoppes: dzaweth out shyueres, and pzyckes. Yt also swageth the payne of the ioyntes, and membzes owte of ioynte, layde to wyth vynegre. The greene leues bz oosed, and layd to, heleth cholerycke inflammacyones, and other inflammaciones also. The asshes of the barke layd to wyth vynegre, heleth the fallynge of the heyze. the downe, that is in the toppe ot the reede like floures: yf it come into a mannes eare, maketh hym defe.

Of Follfoote/ oz Asarabacca.

Sarum is called in greke, asaron: in english folfote (because it hath a roũd leafe, lyke a folis fote) and asarabacca in duche, hasell wurt: because it groweth abowte hasell tree rootes: in frenche, cabaret. Folfoote groweth only in gardynes in Englande: but it groweth wylde in certayne places of Germanye. Folesoote is a well sauoringe herbe, and vsed to be put in garlandes. It hath leues lyke vnto yuy, but lesse, and rounder by a great dele: with purple floures, lyke ÿ floures of henbane: and they growe but a lytle from the root, ꝛ haue a good sauour, out of the which cõmeth sede, like gzapes. It hath many rootes ful of knottes, smal, one lieng ouer an other, not vnlike vnto grasse rootes, but much smaler, well sauozinge, hote, and bytyng vehemently the tonge.

Asara Bacca.

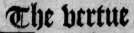

The vertue
of Folfoot.

He nature of this herbe is hote, and it prouoketh water: it heleth ÿ dzopsy, and the olde sciatica. the rootes pzonoke downe a womans sikenes, takẽ in the quantyte of bi. dzammes with mede: and they purge, as nesing pouder called whyte Helleboz doth. Galene sayth: that folefoote is lyke vnto Acozus in strenght: but that thys is moze stronge, and vehement.

Galene

Of great saint Johnes wurte.

Ascyron.

Alene, and Paule conteyne ascyzon vnder andzosemo: but dioscozides descrybeth thes herbes seuerally, ꝛ so maketh them sondzy herbes. Ascyzon called also ascaroides is a kynde of hyperici, called in englishe saint Johns grasse, oz saynt Johns wur t: But it differrith in greatnes. foz it hath greater leues, stalkes, and mo bzaunches, then saynt Johns grasse hathe. I haue marked also thys difference: that ascyzon hathe a four squared stalke, and leues wyth very fewe holes in them: whiche I haue not sene in Hyperico. the herbe may be called in englyshe great saynt Johns grasse. I haue sene it dyuerse tymes in syon parke.

The vertues.

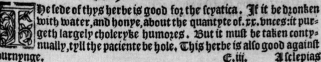

He sede of thys herbe is good foz the scyatica. If it be dzonken with water, and honye, about the quantyte of. xx. vnces: it purgeth largely cholerycke humozes. But it must be taken contynually, tyll the paciente be hole. This herbe is also good against burnynge.

E.iij. Asclepias

initials – themselves like exotic plant forms – appear to serve no useful purpose at all.

The illustrations in *The Englishman's Flora* have been gathered from about the same period, but their size and relationship to the light, self-effacing page strike a proper balance. This calm and satisfying appearance conceals a great deal of careful detail, and much information of different kinds is arranged and visually ordered by the subtle changes of type size, select punctuation, use of small caps and italics, and spacing.

If ever you have to cut a Lime – not for logs, since Lime wood smells rather unpleasant in the fire – it ought to be worth experimenting with the fibre of the inner bark, which is 'white, moyst, and tough, serving very well for ropes, trases, and halters' (Gerard). Ropes of lime bark used to be woven in Devon and Cornwall and in Lincolnshire (125).

A small plant may have a hundred local names. Since trees give timber, and timber is sold and is an essential of life, the names of one species do not vary a great deal. Turner, in the second part of his *Herbal* (1562), wrote of the 'Lind tre'. Lyte called it Linden or Linden tree. 'Line' was common in the sixteenth century. 'Lin' survived in Yorkshire, 'Line' in Lincolnshire, 'Lind' in Scotland. 'Whitewood' has been recorded in Worcestershire and 'Pry' was an old Essex name. Linnaeus – Carl Linné – owed his family name, very aptly for a botanist, to the tall Lime, or Linden, which guarded the family home.

XXII. Malvaceae

1. Musk Mallow. *Malva moschata* L.   92, H 34

Thrusting its pink flowers (sometimes they are white) and its delicately cut leaves out of the grass along a road, the Musk Mallow is among the prettiest of all English plants – pretty as *Sidalcea* – and it does well, and looks well, in gardens. Musky it is. You do not notice the smell out of doors, but take the flowers into a warm room, and the musk soon becomes obvious.

2. Common Mallow. *Malva sylvestris* L.   102, H 40 3. Dwarf Mallow. *Malva neglecta* Waler.   90, H 25

Local names. BILLY BUTTONS, Som; BREAD AND CHEESE, Dor, Som; BREAD AND CHEESE AND CIDER, Som; BUTTER AND CHEESE, Dev, Som; CHEESE-CAKE FLOWERS, Yks; CHEESE FLOWER, Som, Wilts, Suss; CHUCKY CHEESE, Som; CUSTARD CHEESES, Lincs; FAIRY CHEESES, Som, Yks; FLIBBERTY GIBBET, Som; FRENCH MALLOW, Corn; GOOD NIGHT AT NOON, Som; HORSE BUTTON, Donegal; LADY'S CHEESE, Dor; LOAVES OF BREAD, Dor, Som.

MALLACE, Dev, Som, Hants, I o W, Bucks; MALLOW-HOCK, Som; MARSH-MALLICE (by confusion with the name of *Althaea officinalis*), Dev, Som, Shrop, Lakes, N'thum; MAWS, Notts, N'thum, Scot; OLD MAN'S BREAD AND CHEESE, Som; PANCAKE PLANT, Som, Lincs; RAGS AND TATTERS, Dor, Som; ROUND DOCK, Som; TRUCKLES OF CHEESE, Som.

108

These two Mallows are very much a species of waste and wayside; but rather than the gay flowers, it was the disk of nutlets which caught the fancy, the 'knap or round button, like unto a flat cake' (Gerard), and like a cheese. Children still eat these disks or 'cheeses', as they are known from Cornwall to the Border (cf. the name *fromages* in France). Crisp and slimy, they taste not unlike monkey-nuts.

Like the Marsh Mallow and the Tree Mallow, the Common Mallow is

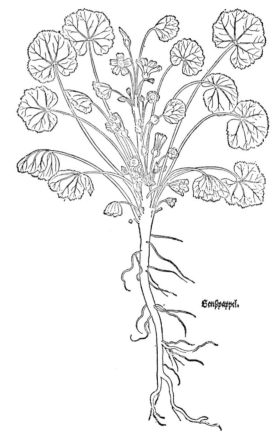

Senßpappel.

15 Dwarf Mallow   *Malva sylvestris*

109

Geoffrey Grigson
An Englishman's Flora
Paladin
St Albans 1975
reduced from approx 200 mm deep

Since the days of manuscript books, words and pictures have been happily combined, but to succeed fully the type needs to be very carefully related to the character of the illustration, whether it be woodcut, fine engraving, line drawing or photograph. These three examples show woodcuts ranging from fairly coarse to delicately detailed; but whether robust children's book or fine edition of *The Chase*, with Bewick's masterly engravings, the accompanying type has been well chosen in relation to the text and the pictures.

XIV.

Sit oneri, erit uſui.

ALs een Schip in de Zee gaet, ſoo ſet men het Boot in het groote Schip, het welck aldaer een groote ruymte neemt, ende de Bootgeſellen ſeer in de wech is; dan moet nochtans mee varen, niet tegenſtaende alle ongerijf ende ongemack datmer af lijdt, om dat men daer mede noodigh moet aen het landt gaen, als men in de Haven komt: daerom dat men met reden zeydt:

Die wat ſpaert / die wat heeft.

van de Sinne-poppen.   14

Sit oneri, erit uſui.

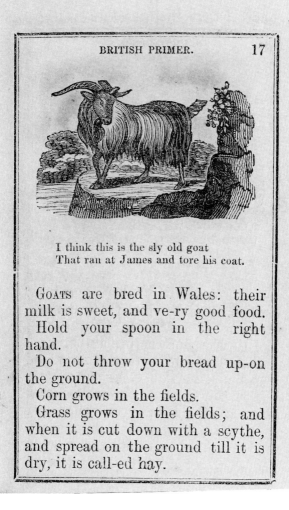

Verdraeght geduldelijck, wat laſt en ongerief,
Van dat u in de noodt, kan dienſtigh zijn en lief.

XV. *Reve*

BRITISH PRIMER.   17

I think this is the sly old goat
That ran at James and tore his coat.

GOATS are bred in Wales: their milk is sweet, and ve-ry good food.
Hold your spoon in the right hand.
Do not throw your bread up-on the ground.
Corn grows in the fields.
Grass grows in the fields; and when it is cut down with a scythe, and spread on the ground till it is dry, it is call-ed hay.

Roemer Visscher
Sinne-poppen
Amsterdam 1614
woodcuts by Claes Visscher
actual size

Richardson's British Primer; or,
the Young Child's First Book
Derby 1846
reduced from approx 140 mm deep

OPPOSITE
William Somerville
The Chase
William Bulmer
London 1796
wood engravings by Thomas Bewick
reduced from approx 290 mm deep

Nor will it less delight the attentive sage,

To observe that instinct, which, unerring, guides

The brutal race, which mimicks reason's lore,

And oft transcends. Heaven-taught, the roebuck swift

Loiters, at ease, before the driving pack,

And mocks their vain pursuit; nor far he flies,

But checks his ardour, till the steaming scent,

That freshens on the blade, provokes their rage.

Urged to their speed, his weak deluded foes

Soon flag fatigued; strain'd to excess each nerve,

Each slacken'd sinew fails; they pant, they foam:

Then o'er the lawn he bounds, o'er the high hills

Plantin's design for Geffrey Whitney's *Book of Emblems* combines the various elements into an agreeable harmonious page. The woodcuts are grandly framed with printer's flowers. The main text, quotations and references are set in a fine roman and related italic, and placing, indentation and line spacing are models of professionalism; although today's tastes might prefer a happier relationship across the spread.

There is an odd inconsistency in setting names sometimes in spaced caps and sometimes in upper and lower case.

42   *Venter, pluma, Venus, laudem fugiunt.*

WHY flieſt thow hence? and turn'ſte awaie thie face?
  Thow glorie brighte, that men with fame doeſt crowne:
GLO. Bycauſe, I haue noe likinge of that place,
Where ſlothfull men, doe ſleepe in beddes of downe:
  And fleſhlie luſte, doth dwell with fowle exceſſe,
  This is no howſe, for glorie to poſſeſſe.

But, if thow wilte my preſence neuer lacke,
SARDANAPAL, and all his pleaſures hate,
Driue VENVS hence, let BACCHVS further packe,
If not, behowlde I flie out of thie gate:
  Yet, if from theiſe, thow turne thie face awaie,
  I will returne, and dwell with thee for aie.

Propert. 4. 11.   *Magnum iter aſcendo, ſed dat mihi gloria vires:*
              Non iuuat ex facili lecta corona iugo.

Ouid. 1. Pont. 6   *Cernis vt ignauum corrumpant otia corpus?*
              Vt capiant vitium, ni moueantur aquæ?

Mens

Mens immota manet.   43

To Sir ROBERT IERMYN *Knight.*

Pſalm. 41.
Quemadmodum
deſiderat Ceruus
ad fontes aquarũ
Ita deſiderat ani-
ma mea ad te
Deus, &c.

BY vertue hidde, beholde, the Iron harde,
  The loadeſtone drawes, to poynte vnto the ſtarre:
Whereby, wee knowe the Seaman keepes his carde,
And rightlie ſhapes, his courſe to countries farre:
  And on the pole, dothe euer keepe his eie,
  And withe the ſame, his compaſſe makes agree.

Which ſhewes to vs, our inward vertues ſhoulde,
Still drawe our hartes, althoughe the iron weare:
The hauenlie ſtarre, at all times to beholde,
To ſhape our courſe, ſo right while wee bee heare:
  That Scylla, and Charybdis, wee maie miſſe,
  And winne at lengthe, the porte of endleſſe bliſſe.

Virg. in Ætna.
*Eſt merito pietas ho-
mini tutiſſima virtus.*

     Conſcia mens recti famæ mendacia ridet.

     Sufficit & longum probitas perdurat in æuum,
       Perq; ſuos annos hinc bene pendet amor.

Ouid. 4. Faſt.

Ouid. de medic.
faciei.

F 2   *Deſide-*

Jean Second
Les Baisers
The Hague 1770
engravings by Charles Eisen
reduced from approx 220 mm deep

Les Baisers shows a simpler task executed with great assurance and refinement. The delicate copper engravings are well-matched by both heading and text type. The line spacing and the placing on the page, with generous margins, are all speaking with the same voice: and here the spread *is* co-ordinated. As so often, one wonders at the intrusive full points in the headings.

Ch. Eisen inv. delin.   1770.   C. Baquoy Sculp.

XX. BAISER.

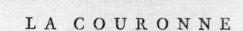

LA COURONNE
DE FLEURS.

Renversé doucement dans les bras de Thaïs,
Le front ceint d'un léger nuage,
Je lui disois : lorsque tu me souris,
Peut-être sur ma tête il s'élève un orage.
Que pense-t-on de mes écrits?
Je dois aimer mès vers, puisqu'ils sont ton ouvrage.
Occuperai-je les cent voix
De la vagabonde Déesse?

LES BAISERS. 119

A ses faveurs pour obtenir des droits,
Suffit-il, ô Thaïs, de sentir la tendresse?
Thaïs alors sur de récens gazons
Cueille des fleurs, en tresse une couronne.
Tiens, c'est ainsi que je répons;
Voilà le prix de tes chansons,
Et c'est ma main qui te le donne :
Renonce, me dit-elle, à l'orgueil des lauriers;
Laisse ces froids honneurs qu'ici tu te proposes;
Il faut des couronnes de roses
A qui peignit l'Amour et chanta les baisers.

William Morris
News from Nowhere
Kelmscott Press
London 1892
reduced from approx 200 mm deep

'Well, I lay it down that a book quite unornamented can look actually and positively beautiful, if it be so to say, architecturally good.' Morris may not have had these pages in mind when he made that pronouncement, but their richness and vigour, and his enthusiasm for the medieval dream, are infectious. The woodcut borders, initials and illustration are well matched by the heavy Venetian type, and the design is executed with such conviction that Morris's unbelievable world is almost credible.

Beatrix Potter
The Story of Miss Moppet
Frederick Warne
London 1916
actual size

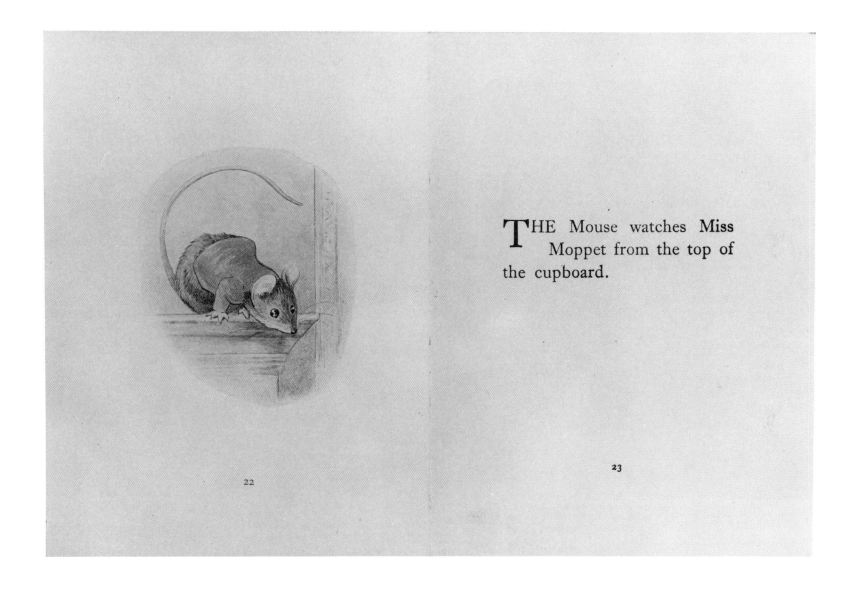

THE Mouse watches **Miss** Moppet from the top of the cupboard.

22

23

The apparent simplicity of Beatrix Potter's books conceals perfect judgement, and is all the more impressive for its minimal design. Any imperfection would jar; but the straightforward, ordinary, matter-of-fact text, and the jewel-like pictures, all placed dead-pan in (almost) the centre of the page, are totally convincing. In that 'almost' lies the secret.

William Morris is famous as an artist-craftsman involved in every aspect of book production. Beatrix Potter wrote and illustrated and was deeply involved with the design of hers, being extremely particular about the balance of picture, text and space. The dropped initial, which seems to link picture and text, besides making each spread a separate 'incident' as in a slide show, was her idea. The style was established in the privately-printed edition of her first book, *Peter Rabbit*, in 1901.

RIGHT
G Heym
Umbra Vitae
Leipzig 1924
woodcuts by Ludwig Kirchner
actual size

OPPOSITE
J Bobrowski
Mäusefest
Raamin Press
Hamburg 1974
illustrations by Roswitha Quadflieg
reduced from approx 285 mm deep

A close relationship between woodcut and typeface produces a powerful effect in the first example. Nothing would better suit these dark, expressive and almost archaic woodcuts than the heavy grotesque, forming strong, free blocks of type. The vertical stress of this condensed form echoes the format of the page.

By contrast, the fine textures of the neatly-framed *Mäusefest* engravings are unified with a closely-related justified block of light grotesque, all placed within generous margins.

Although these two examples are from limited edition 'art' books, their lessons for us, working at a humbler level, could not be clearer.

MIT DEN FAHRENDEN SCHIFFEN

Mit den fahrenden Schiffen
Sind wir vorübergeschweift,
Die wir ewig herunter
Durch glänzende Winter gestreift.
Ferner kamen wir immer
Und tanzten im insligen Meer,
Weit ging die Flut uns vorbei,
Und Himmel war schallend und leer.

Sage die Stadt,
Wo ich nicht saß im Tor,
Ging dein Fuß da hindurch,
Der die Locke ich schor?
Unter dem sterbenden Abend
Das suchende Licht
Hielt ich, wer kam da hinab,
Ach, ewig in fremdes Gesicht.

dasselbe, und das, denk ich, ist gerade so sehr
verwunderlich. Es wird schon eher so sein, daß
du jeden Tag anders bist, obwohl du doch immer
durch die gleiche Tür kommst und es immer dunkel ist, bevor du hier Platz genommen hast. Aber
nun sei mal still und paß gut auf. Siehst du, es ist
immer dasselbe.

Moise hat eine Brotrinde vor seine Füße fallen
lassen, da huschen die Mäuschen näher, ein Streck-
chen um das andere, einige richten sich sogar auf
und schnuppern ein bischen in die Luft. Siehst
du, so ist es. Immer dasselbe.

Walter de la Mare
Love
Faber and Faber
London 1943
reduced from approx 220 mm deep

Trade books cannot afford the luxury of few words on a page, but these two examples show that high standards can be achieved even within the constraints of normal publishing. Barnett Freedman's lithograph sits very well against the page of Perpetua, which is a little small for continuous reading but acceptable in an anthology; while the nicely-placed rubbing, powerful though it is, does not overwhelm the strong setting in Plantin. In the anthology, square brackets neatly differentiate the folios from the (slightly larger) section numbers.

Both these excellent examples are typical of the best productions of this period in British book making.

203

Thus the heavens and the earth were finished, and all the host of them. . . . And the Lord God formed man of the dust of the ground, and breathed into his nostrils the breath of life; and man became a living soul.

And the Lord God planted a garden eastward in Eden; and there he put the man whom he had formed. And out of the ground made the Lord God to grow every tree that is pleasant to the sight, and good for food; the tree of life also in the midst of the garden, and the tree of knowledge of good and evil. And a river went out of Eden to water the garden; and from thence it was parted, and came into four heads. . . .

And the Lord God took the man, and put him into the garden of Eden to dress it and to keep it. And the Lord God commanded the man, saying, Of every tree of the garden thou mayest freely eat: But of the tree of the knowledge of good and evil, thou shalt not eat of it; for in the day that thou eatest thereof thou shalt surely die. . . .

And the Lord God caused a deep sleep to fall upon Adam, and he slept: and he took one of his ribs, and closed up the flesh instead thereof; and the rib, which the Lord God had taken from man, made he a woman, and brought her unto the man. And Adam said, This is now bone of my bones, and flesh of my flesh: she shall be called Woman, because she was taken out of Man. Therefore shall a man leave his father and mother, and shall cleave unto his wife: and they shall be one flesh. And they were both naked, the man and his wife, and were not ashamed. . . .

Now the serpent was more subtil than any beast of the field which the Lord God had made. And he said unto the woman, Yea, hath God said, Ye shall not eat of every tree of the garden? And the woman said unto the serpent, We may eat of the fruit of the trees of the garden: but of the fruit of the tree which is in the midst of the garden, God hath said, Ye shall not eat of it, neither shall ye touch it, lest ye die. And the serpent saith unto the woman, Ye shall not surely die: For God doth know that in the day ye eat thereof, then your eyes shall be opened, and ye shall be as gods, knowing good and evil.

And when the woman saw that the tree was good for food, and that it was pleasant to the eyes, and a tree to be desired to make one wise, she took of the fruit thereof, and did eat, and gave also unto her husband with her; and he did eat. And the eyes of them both were opened,

[173]

Kenneth Lindley
Of Graves and Epitaphs
Hutchinson
London 1965
reduced from approx 240 mm deep

The hand, and less frequently eye, of God appear on numerous tombstones, the hand usually reaching out of the clouds to receive a soul into the upper regions. At Llanddewy, Monmouthshire, a realistic hand, complete with sleeve in the tradition of the typographic 'fist', points a finger out of a painted cloud which bears a distinct resemblance to an anatomical model of the human brain. Unfortunately the rest of the composition has flaked off, but the gothic motifs which surround the panel are typical of the date, 1846. An original version of the hand of God appears on a headstone of 1852 at Twyning, Gloucestershire. This is designed and cut with a fine sense of style, and a simplicity which is more reminiscent of the best work of the present century than the then prevailing fashion for elaboration. The clouds are shown as a collection of spirals, like the volutes on an Ionic capital, and flat strips are cut at slightly varying angles to represent rays of light. The beautifully cut, but broken, hand points to a scroll bearing the words 'The trumpet shall sound and the dead shall be raised'. The eye of God appears as the central feature on a headstone set against the boundary wall at Bury St Edmunds. The cloud in which it appears is upheld on either side, and below it as well as down each side of the stone are realistic floral garlands.

Another 'eye of God' worth mentioning is at Withington, Gloucestershire. In this instance the eye appears on a band of light emerging from clouds which are drawn up like a curtain. A cherub is sliding down the beams towards a band of floral decoration. This symbol continues in use until at least the middle of the nineteenth century. An example dated 1837 can be seen at St Mark's, Swindon, where it accompanies a bow, quiver and oak branch on a well-preserved stone. The pronouncements upon the subject of religious images by Victorian clergymen led to the increasing use of symbols of grief and affection many of which are familiar through their continued use. Weeping willows (whole or in twig form) have had a long run of popularity but, numerically, clasped hands have priority. The slightly ludicrous appearance of a welcoming handshake into Heaven does not seem to have worried anyone, and there are plenty of examples to be seen in municipal cemeteries as well as churchyards. Although they are by no means peculiar to tombstones, birds and more especially plants have been used for so long and in such profusion for the decoration of monuments that they must be given special mention in this context. As has already been noted the bird,

symbolising the Holy Spirit, occurs on many stones and it is frequently given such a naturalistic rendering as to take its place without any incongruity among the common plants with which it is surrounded. In late Victorian times pairs of birds, with or without nests, were used as emblems of affection, the symbolism being taken still further on occasion to include entwined beaks. As with many other motifs, birds occasionally occur on a number of stones in one locality where they were the work of a particular mason. One such group exists in a part of Berkshire, with a good specimen at Buckland, near Faringdon.

Woodgate Baptist, Loughborough, Leicestershire, 1818

The growth of stone flowers has been so rampant for several centuries as to defy classification. Plants were things which the village mason understood. Many eighteenth-century examples are cut with an astonishing realism which has much in common with such medieval masterpieces as the Southwell Chapter House capitals, and yet they are passed unnoticed in hundreds of village churchyards. The Cotswolds

Elizabeth David
A Book of Mediterranean Food
Penguin Books
Harmondsworth 1955
actual size

This Penguin paperback was also designed and illustrated to the highest standards. John Minton's evocative line drawing is the perfect complement to Schmoller's carefully-considered typography. The confidence of a master is shown in the quite justified toleration of what, in lesser hands, would be the awkward two lines (one of them a heading) at the bottom of the left-hand page. Throughout the book, full-page Minton drawings create section dividers.

Lamb and Mutton

* * * * * * * * * * * * * * * * * * *

The Ideal Cuisine

' "You are quite right," the Count was saying to Mr Heard. "The ideal cuisine should display an individual character; it should offer a menu judiciously chosen from the kitchen-workshops of the most diverse lands and peoples – a menu reflecting the master's alert and fastidious taste. Is there anything better, for instance, than a genuine Turkish pilaff? The Poles and Spaniards, too, have some notable culinary creations. And if I were able to carry out my ideas on this point I would certainly add to my list a few of those strange Oriental confections which Mr Keith has successfully taught his Italian chef. There is suggestion about them; they conjure up visions of that rich and glowing East which I would give many years of my remaining life to see." '

South Wind
by Norman Douglas

GIGOT À LA PROVENÇALE

A recipe from an old French cookery book which I have left

78

MEAT

in its original French; as the author rather severely remarks, this dish is supportable only to those who are accustomed to the cooking of the *Midi*.

'On insère symétriquement dans la partie charnue d'un gigot de moyenne grosseur douze gousses d'aïl, et deux fois autant de filets d'anchois bien lavés et employés en guise de lardons. Le gigot ainsi préparé est graissé d'huile et cuit à la broche. Tandis que le gigot est à la broche on épluche d'autre part plein un litre de gousses d'aïl qu'on fait blanchir dans l'eau bouillante.

'Elles doivent y être plongées à trois reprises différentes, en changeant l'eau à chaque fois, après quoi, on les laisse refroidir dans l'eau froide, et l'on achève leur cuisson dans une tasse de bouillon. Le gigot étant rôti à point, on dégraisse avec soin le jus qu'il a rendu, on en assaisonne les gousses d'aïl, et l'on sert le gigot sur cette garniture.

'Ce mets n'est supportable que pour ceux qui sont habitués à la cuisine du Midi, dans laquelle l'aïl fait partie obligée de presque tous les mets. '

ARNÍ SOUVLÁKIA (lamb on skewers)

Cut a piece of lamb from the leg into inch cubes. Season with salt, pepper, lemon juice, and marjoram.* Thread the meat on to skewers and grill them. Serve them on a thick bed of parsley, on the skewers, with quarters of lemon.

Eaten on the terrace of a primitive Cretan taverna, flavoured with wood smoke and the mountain herbs, accompanied by the strong red wine of Crete, these kebabs can be the most poetic of foods. Exquisitely simple, they are in fact of Turkish origin, like many Greek dishes, although the Greeks do not always care to admit it.

* In Greece wild marjoram is used; it is called *rígani* and has a much stronger perfume than our marjoram. *Origanum* means in Greek 'the joy of the mountains'.

79

Dessau
Brochure for
the Dessau Travel Bureau
designed by Joost Schmidt
1931
reduced from
approx 230 mm deep

Photographs set different problems. In this layout by Joost Schmidt, the photograph divides the page horizontally, creating two areas for type. The Baroque script is interrupted by a bold modern which echoes the verticals of the arcade, and which is centred on the x-height of the script rather than sitting on the base line. A grotesque (badly-set with disturbingly wide word spacing) is used in the area below the photograph, headed by the picture caption in a smaller size. The folio matches this text type, and the black circle with numeral reversed out takes its weight from the heavy shadow on the left of the illustration.

The mixture of freedom, the daring combination of unexpected types, the tensions between margins and type, and (above all) the powerful use of space, all announce a radical departure in book design.

die alte Residenzstadt der Herzöge von Anhalt besitzt zahlreiche **Bau- und Kunstwerke** vergangener Epochen, die schöne und eigentümliche Stadtbilder schaffen.'

Großer Markt
Seit der Gründung Dessaus am Ende des XII. Jahrhunderts bildet der Große Markt den Kern der Stadt. An den Langseiten stehen im Norden die „Buden", im Süden die Hofkammer — um 1700 von holländischen Baumeistern errichtet in den Formen des Barockklassizismus. Rechts ragt der Turm und das Dach der Schloß- und Marienkirche herüber. Rückwärts schließen die Bürgerhäuser der Zerbster Straße mit Renaissancegiebeln den Markt ab. Das Bronzedenkmal des „Alten Dessauers" ist eine Wiederholung des Schadowschen Originals in Berlin.

1

Jahrbuch des Deutschen Metallarbeiters
Verlag der Deutschen Arbeitsfront
Berlin 1942
actual size

This Second World War handbook demonstrates that Tschichold and the Bauhaus designers before him had only partial success in their efforts to bring a rational and orderly approach to book design. Grey unleaded text, cramped and awkwardly-placed illustrations, poor quality photographs and mediocre press work result in a muddled and incoherent book, which seems to have happened rather than been designed, and could have appeared in the 1880s. For a technical handbook, this approach seems particularly lamentable.

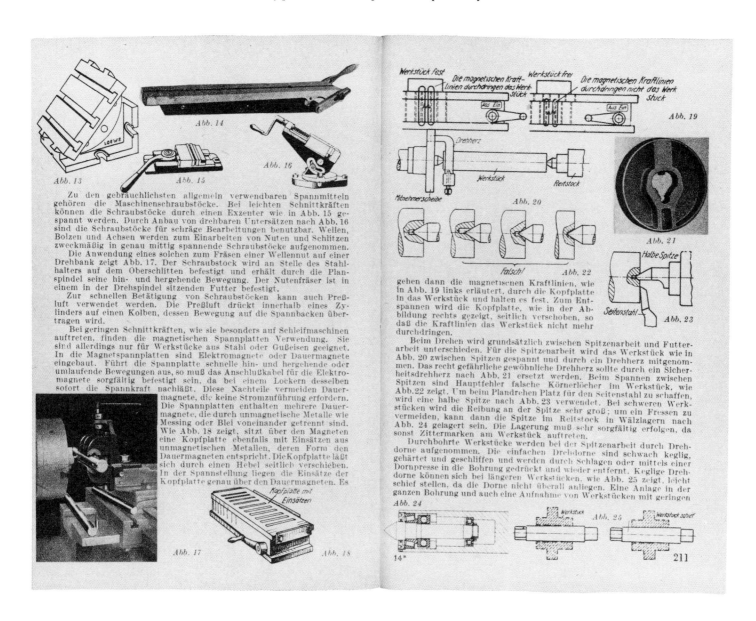

OPPOSITE

Bauhaus Books No 1
1926
reduced from approx 415 mm deep

The sort of solution the Bauhaus had offered can be seen here. Text and photographs are clearly organised in a dynamic and painterly design. However, doctrine forbade capital letters, and clarity and readability were thus sacrificed. The overweight unleaded text is even less legible than in the handbook.

taube mit fotoapparat (1908) foto und klischee: dr. neubronner

taubenaufnahmen 1908 fotos und klischees: dr. neubronner

moholy-nagy:
geradlinigkeit des geistes - umwege der technik

absehbare und unergründliche beziehungen entstehen gleicherweise unter kosmischer determination. die chemisch-fysisch-transzendenten einflüsse der wechselwirkenden beziehungen verdichten sich verschieden, je nach gesetzlichem ablauf. einmal zur blauen farbe, ein anderesmal zu einem aggregatzustand und ein drittes mal zur sublimation des geistes. das denken - als funktionelles ergebnis von körper uud weltallbeziehungen - ist in seinen erscheinungen ein stetiges, ein immer von neuem entstehendes fänomen. geist ist immanente emanation menschlichen daseins.

unter dieser determination der kosmisch entstehenden beziehungen darf es nicht verwirrend scheinen, über eine identität menschlichen denkens aller zeiten zu reden. selbst die formalen variationen des denkens, die sogenannte „geistige haltung", sind in verschiedenen epochen zwangsläufig wiederkehrend. innerhalb dieser zwangsläufigkeit ist jede leistungsreihe von der zeitbedingten umwegigkeit technischer eroberungen abhängig, d. h. das gehirn arbeitet rascher als die ausführende hand. man kann diesen zustand schlagwortartig fassen: geradlinigkeit des geistes - umwege der technik. die „geradlinigkeit" ist nicht ein eindimensionales gerichtetsein auf das spannungsvolle, ökonomische, sublimierte allein, sondern vielmehr eine kosmische expansion, die nach jedem punkt hin den kürzesten weg nimmt.

„umwege der technik" bedeutet, daß praktisch alle wege, die man zur erreichung eines zieles einschlägt, länger und komplizierter sind, als sie - vom geiste aus gesehen - sein müßten, d. h. alles könnte besser als bisher gemacht werden, denn: die inspiration am anfang jeder tat - die geniale eingebung als zentrumbildende expansion - ist nur von zeit und umständen (auch technik) bedingte form des urgedankens.

ein beispiel: man wünscht immer mehr zu sehen als die augen fassen können. das fernrohr reicht bis zum nächsten dorf; das mikroskop in die spalten der zelle; der fernseher bis zum kap der guten hoffnung; die nächste station wird der mond sein. umwegigkeit der technik hier (heute erkennbar): das problem des fernsehens nach anderen planeten mit linsensystemen schaffen zu wollen, statt es z. b. durch elektrisch-magnetisch-fotografische reagenzen zu lösen. die konsequenz: alle kommenden observatorien werden unzulänglich sein, wenn sie auf traditionelle weise ausgerüstet werden.

●

um solche umwegigkeit auf ein minimum zu reduzieren, versucht man die eigene arbeit vom urgedanken her zu kontrollieren.

so kommt es, daß man manchmal einer these besessen ist. sie gibt anlaß zur arbeit, mit ihr begründet man weitläufige konstellationen bis zu einer die ganze arbeit beherrschenden fixen idee.

man kann gegen diese herrschaft der idee gar nicht opponieren. denn: möge die basis noch so „launenhaft" scheinen, alles ist schließlich zur erhöhung der aktivität

da. ein arbeitsichernder wahn, der mit logisch-kausalen konsequenzen operiert.

das ist oft die genesis einer fruchtbringenden theorie. sie ist anregung und gleichzeitig kontrolle.

●

ich war einige jahre von der wichtigkeit der „produktion-reproduktion"-these erfüllt. ich habe fast das ganze leben damit zu meistern gesucht. sie führte mich im einzelnen zu der analyse der reproduzierenden „instrumente", zu verständnis und vorschlägen mechanischer musik; andererseits brachte sie mir grundlegende erkenntnisse auf fotografischem gebiet.

eine ergänzungsidee (vielleicht mehr als das, weil weniger mechanistisch, weil breit auslegbar) führt mich wieder zu optischen dingen: geradlinigkeit des geistes - umwege der technik.

seitdem für mich das problem: malerei - foto - film in die fase des optisch gesetzmäßigen trat, erhellen sich mir die umwegigkeitsformen des uralten wunsches: farbige gestaltung als bannen von licht. der immanente geist sucht: licht, licht! der umweg der technik findet: pigment. (ein zwischenstadium, das erst durch das licht leben gewinnt.) es ist ein verhängnis der menschheitsgeschichte, daß die geistigen emanationen zu falscher auswirkung verleitet werden. nämlich entgegen individueller elastizität und immer vorwärtsschreitender neigung des einzelnen richtet sich die menschliche gemeinschaft - als summe von individuen - nach der überlieferung angeblich unfehlbarer erfahrungen. angebliche unfehlbarkeiten verdichten sich zu fester existenz und die geheiligte existenz treibt zur eigenen rechtfertigung. das ist traditionsgebundenheit, geistige massenlähmung, zeitbedingte umwegigkeit. das war auch das schicksal der pigmententdeckung. die erste verwendung heiligte den zufall, der im pigment eine art lichtlagerungsstätte, wenn auch in grobmateriell abtastbaren komplexen, gefunden hat. alle lichtgestaltung umwegt bis heute auf diesen spuren abendländischer malerei, obwohl seit der ersten laterna magica, seit der ersten camera obscura sich direkte wege des lichtbannens ergaben: projektorisch-reflektorische spiele mit farbig flutendem licht, flüssiges, immaterielles schweben, durchsichtiger farbenfall von leuchtenden garben, vibrieren des raumes mit schillernder lichtemulsion. umwege der technik: von der manuellen darstellung zum grafischen stehbild. vom stehbild zur kinematografie. vom flächigen zum plastischen. vom stummen zum sprechenden. vom undurchdringlichen zum durchscheinenden. vom kontinuierlichen zum simultanen. vom pigment zum licht.

●

mit fieber erarbeiten geist und auge die neuen dimensionen des sehens, die heute schon foto und film, plan und wirklichkeit bieten. die details für morgen. heute die übung des sehens.

geradlinigkeit des geistes - umwege der technik: auf der fotografischen ausstellung in frankfurt a. m. 1926 waren fotografien zu sehen, die durch brieftauben ausgeführt worden sind. für diesen zweck wurden um 1907 herum kleine fotografische apparate mit automatischer auslösung konstruiert, und das über hundert jahre nach montgolfiers erfindung! nach den versuchen mit lenkbaren ballons, nach den versuchen lilienthals und der brüder wright. die kleinen wunderbaren fotografien: stadtaufnahmen, stark divergierende häuser, schienenstränge, plätze mit winzigen menschenfigürchen, eisbahn mit wimmelnden eisläufern, machen - als vorahnung wichtiger verwendungsmöglichkeiten dieser art sichten - dem erfinder dr. neubronner (cronberg im taunus) ehre. und doch: was ist der liliputapparat und sein automatischer auslöser mit seiner zufallssicherheit gegenüber den apparaten, die - in den boden eines flugzeugs eingebaut - sicherheit selbst für kartografische institute bieten.

2 junkers-luftbilder
(das untere ist aus vielen einzelfotos zusammengestellt)

georg muche:
bildende kunst und industrieform

die enge verbindung moderner bildender kunst - insbesondere der malerei - mit der technischen entwicklung im 20.jahrhundert scheint nach einer außerordentlich bedeutungsvollen zeit schöpferischen austauschs auf geistig durchaus polar gelagerten gebieten mit überraschender konsequenz zur gegenseitigen abstoßung führen zu müssen. die illusion, daß die bildende kunst in der schöpferischen art technischer formgestaltung aufzugehen hätte, zerschellt in dem augenblick, in dem sie die grenze der konkreten wirklichkeit erreicht. die mit imposant eindeutiger geste aus der künstlerischen utopie in das verheißene gebiet der technischen gestaltung herausgeführte abstrakte malerei scheint ganz plötzlich ihre vorausgesagte bedeutung als formbestimmendes element zu verlieren, weil die formgestaltung des mit technischen mitteln erzeugten industrieproduktes sich nach einer gesetzmäßigkeit vollzieht, die nicht von den bildenden künsten abgeleitet werden kann. es zeigt sich, daß die technisch-industrielle entwicklungsfolge auch in bezug auf die formgestaltung absolut eigenartig ist. der versuch, die technische produktion mit den bildnerischen gesetzen im sinne der abstrakten gestaltung zu durchdringen, hat zu einem neuen stil geführt, in dem das ornament als unzeitgemäße ausdrucksform vergangener handwerkskulturen keine anwendung findet, der aber trotzdem dekorativ bleibt. einen nur dekorativen stil glaubte man aber gerade vermeiden zu können, weil die besondere art der schöpferischen erforschung elementarer formgesetze durch die ab-

Laszlo Moholy-Nagy
Vision in Motion
Paul Theobald
Chicago 1947, 2nd edition 1961
reduced from approx 280 mm deep

Early Bauhaus doctrine distorted some good ideas. This came to be recognised, and the theories were laced with some more pragmatic solutions, particularly in the treatment of text.

Moholy-Nagy, one-time Bauhaus teacher, was fully aware of the problems of book typography, and in particular the need to develop a modern integrated page using the freedom won by the early Bauhaus experiments. In the Foreword to *Vision in Motion*, he commented: 'Through the publisher's generosity, I was able to make some progress toward a new book form on which I have been experimenting for twenty-five years. I have always held that – for a better visual communication – text and illustration should be welded together. Illustrations should *accompany* the copy and not be searched for. In this book I use a layout which seems better adapted to the present printing technique of machine typesetting and letterpress than the conventional book form of previous periods. Here, all the illustrations are placed where mentioned in the text, either small-sized on the large margin, or larger-sized within the main text or on the opposite page. The result is (at least this was intended) a functional fluidity and greater legibility, that is, a better communication. In the first chapter, where no pictures have been used, the illustrations become verbal, in the form of quotations or remarks. These are set in italics in order to separate them from the captions and text.

'This book is integrated in its text and illustrations, but it also considers the impatient reader, who, at first unwilling to plow through the written arguments, may enjoy the pictorial material. Stirred by this, he may then proceed to read brief captions, glossaries, and footnotes until his appetite is whetted to explore the main text.'

The recognition of these problems is still difficult for very few have as yet the proper attitude for it. But because the idea of vision in motion and the subconscious relationships have far-reaching implications, every creative worker in his field willy-nilly tries to find the means for their exposition.

cubism

Cubism, without being entirely conscious of its role, became a potent instrument in this process of indoctrination. Like Einstein in physics, Freud in psychoanalysis, the cubist painters had a tremendous impact. Their work introduced a whole new outlook.

Cubism is "vision in motion," a new essay at two-dimensional rendering of rotated objects.

An analysis of cubism can best start with the paintings of Cézanne. By leaving out of his pictures the nonessentials, a device which characterizes his aquarelles and especially his so-called "unfinished" canvases, he demonstrated a kind of scientific inquiry into painting—the precise observation of visual elements like "isolated cultures" in a biological test tube. Cézanne tried to say with less more than his predecessors had said previously with much.

The effort to show only the essentials was carried further by the early cubists in stereometrizing of the objects. (Yet Cézanne had prepared even for this development by stating that the painter who can paint a sphere, cylinder and cone, can paint everything.) The bizarre name "cubism" originated with some Braque and Picasso landscapes which did not show too much deviation from nature, except that windows and doors were left out of buildings. The resulting shapes were rather cube-like, hence the name. The attitude in these landscapes toward light was more remarkable than the prismatic simplification of the shapes. Contrary to what had been done in the past, these pictures did not follow the natural conditions of lighting but deliberately used light and shadow effects, a kind of shading, in order to define the objects in a geometric clarity. The "cubist" painter was more interested in rendering the objects in the most economical way than in the light and shadow relationships as determined by the casual position of the sun. With that he became independent of the servile type of observation to which, for example, the documentary photographer was subordinated. Photographic emulsion rendered shadow and light exactly at the spots where they appeared at the time of the exposure, but the cubist carried through the task of rendering without any consideration of such accidental circumstances. He rendered the object in its *true* nature, in its totality. With this, he unbound himself from the dictates of naturalistic renderings; from the pressure of conventional, repetitive, and imitative demands to a growing consciousness of the autonomous interpreting power of the artist.●

● *As a young boy Alexander Kostellow, a Persian artist, now Professor at Pratt Institute, went to Paris in order to learn to draw and paint. When he returned to Persia his teacher there asked him to draw a bird. He did it as he had learned in Europe. The teacher reprimanded him: "Do you know that, to draw something as it is, is very vulgar?"*

Fig. 145. Pablo Picasso, 1943
Still life
Though a late work of Picasso, it demonstrates clearly the pre-cubist principle of "distortion", signifying a composite view of the objects

From Giotto to Cézanne every painter has assured the spectator that his rendering of nature is without "distortion". But this was only a pious wish since a draftsman always has to simplify his subject when he translates it into linear form. And the painter has to interpret the objects in colors; has to leave out details; has to set a dark object into a light surrounding and a light object into a dark one if he wishes to emphasize them. By these subtle manipulations the painter "distorts".

If the painter feels that in a still life a changed relationship of objects would improve his composition, he—of course —changes the position of those objects and no one would complain. But the common belief is that such a rearrangement should not be allowed in the case of that sacrosanct—the human body. But after all, face lifting and beauty surgery are commonly practiced today and one should not wonder that the painter may desire—for a more expressive purpose—those privileges of the surgeon. There is only a shade of difference between "distortion" of a color scheme and of actual parts of the human face, or other such "immutables".

116

Fig. 146. A. E. Brinkman, 1930
The south cross nave of the monastery church in Ottobeuren
This is a composite view produced by assembled perspectives in depth and height. The photograph re-creates the movement of the eyes as they wander from the benches upward to the ceiling

Fig. 147. Paul Cézanne, 1903
Still life
Observe the peculiar distortion of the jug, which bulges more on the right side than on the left. The same is true of the bottle

The next step in the development of cubism was the bird's-eye view, giving a more inclusive vista. To see an object frontally means to see it in elevation. From above not only the elevation can be seen, but also the plan and some of the sides. Also from above, the original shapes are seen with greater clarity than in the central-perspective-vistas and vanishing point renderings which distort the real proportions. One sees "truer". Instead of an egg shape one sees the undistorted sphere; instead of an oval, the circle.•

This attempt at better and more perfect rendering was only a preliminary step. Suddenly, the view from above changed into a view from everywhere.

The classical rendering on the static plane, on the painted surface, showed only one aspect, one view. But in reality objects can be seen from the front, profile, three-quarter profile, and from the back. A person is really defined in his three-dimensionality when he is seen from every angle. This definition can be accomplished either by turning the person or moving around him. Cézanne already indicated this problem. He painted objects in the very same painting from different viewpoints: the one from above, the other frontally, the third from the side. He painted also a bottle, for example, in a peculiar distortion which can be explained as a composite view, that is, seen simultaneously from the front and side.••

• *Photography, which had indirectly given impetus to early cubism, later learned from it. In the twenties it started to favor bird's, frog's, and fish's-eye views. It even tried to give up the traditional horizon line because it cut the object in undesirable ways. Casual horizon lines caused confusion. They rarely contribute to a better explanation of the object. Today, photographs often are taken from above on an inclined surface or against a curved background, eliminating the horizon line. This allows a concentration on the object itself which no longer is cut haphazardly. Also, the contemporary photographer uses any number of light sources at various angles if they help him define his object better. Interesting enough the old-timers—"the sun-worshipers"—violently oppose such a step.*

•• *For a long time this treatment was only interpreted as a kind of expressionistic distortion. At the writing of "the new vision" (1925-1928) I was not yet able to comment on this aspect of "distortion."*

Fig. 148. In front of the Depot, St. Anton, 1935
This picture (a fish-eye view) was taken with a Robin Hill camera, which has a wide angle lens of 180 degrees
In the second World War, the fish-eye view became especially important in the cartography of large territories

Fig. 149. O Milton Halbe, 1942
Head, multiviewed

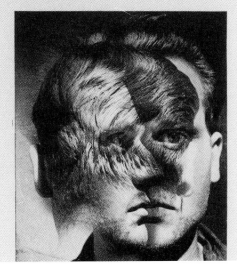

117

To achieve his aims, Moholy-Nagy found it necessary to use three distinct typefaces: Bodoni Book and italic for the text (sub-headings in Bodoni bold), an egyptian (Memphis) for captions, and Century italic for footnotes. The result is an interesting example of intellectual 'systems design' rather than visually-balanced pages.

Vergnügungspavillon

Schweizerische Landesausstellung, Zürich, 1939

Architekt   Hans Fischli
Zürich

1 Theater / Théâtre / Theatre
2 Spielsaal / Salle de jeux / Casino
3 Bureau / Office
4 Galerie / Galerie / Gallery
5 Direktion / Direction / Management
6 Lager / Dépôt / Stores
7 Kanzlei / Chancellerie / Secretary
8 Garderobe / Vestiaire / Cloakroom
9 Eingang / Entrée / Entrance
10 Kasse / Caisse / Ticket Office
11 Festwiese / Champ de fêtes / Green
12 Buden / Baraques foraines / Shooting galleries
13 Bar
14 Tanzpodium / Podium réservé à la dance / Dance floor

15 Buffet / Counter
16 Küche / Cuisine / Kitchen
17 Bühneneingang / Entrée en scène / Stage door
18 Schiebedach / Toit coulissant / Sliding roof

Rechts / A droite / Right:

Die Dachöffnung bot vielfältige Attraktionsmöglichkeiten
L'ouverture du toit offrait de multiples possibilités d'attraction
The opening in the roof offered a wealth of possibilities for attractions

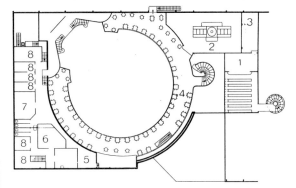

Grundriß 1. Stock / Plan du 1er étage / First-floor plan 1:550

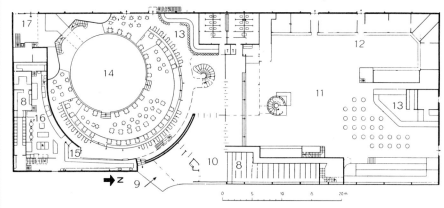

Grundriß Erdgeschoß / Plan du rez-de-chaussée / Ground-floor plan 1:550

Schnitt / Coupe / Section 1:550

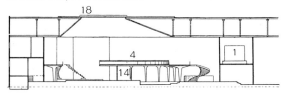

Vergnügungspavillon

Thema

Die Aufgabe bestand in der Schaffung eines Vergnügungszentrums, in welchem der Gesellschaftstanz, Variété und andere Attraktionen zur Darbietung kommen konnten. Der Pavillon wurde von der Ausstellungsleitung so situiert, daß er als Baukörper mit anderen Bauten in Verbindung gebracht wurde und dadurch nicht dominierte.

Form

Den als eigentliches Dancing eingerichteten zentralen Teil des Pavillons bildete die im südlichen Flügel angelegte große Tanzfläche für Gesellschaftstanz, Variété und tänzerische Attraktionen. Um die Tanzfläche in Kreisringen angeordnete Sitzplätze, die von Ring zu Ring treppenartig anstiegen, boten dem Besucher volle Sicht auf die Attraktionen. Die über den Sitzplätzen ebenfalls kreisförmig angelegte Galerie erreichte man vom Parterre aus über eine Wendeltreppe. Auf der Galerie lagen die Büroräume, Garderobe sowie der Spielsaal und ein Kleintheater. Tanzfläche und Sitzplätze im Parterre waren durch halbkreisförmige, halbhohe Wände von den Wirtschaftsräumen abgeschirmt. Im Rücken des westlichen Teils der Zuschauerringe befand sich mit Sicht auf die Tanzfläche die Weinbar. Durch eine Glaswand vom Dancing getrennt, jedoch durch einen direkten Zugang mit diesem in Verbindung stehend, war der für populäre Attraktionen bestimmte Teil des Pavillons mit Festwiese, Budenstadt und Bierbar. Architektonisch wurde der Gegensatz der beiden Vergnügungteile durch verschiedene Raumhöhen ausgedrückt. Ein wesentliches attraktives Moment bildete im Dancing-Teil die große, trichterförmige Öffnung in der Decke, welche mit der Kreisbewegung der Sitzplatzanordnung, der Tanzfläche und der Galerie ein architektonisches Zusammenspiel ergab. Die Öffnung konnte bei ungünstigem Wetter durch ein Schiebedach geschlossen werden.
Die Eingangspartie wurde betont und sichtbar gemacht durch einen markanten Einschnitt, der die Idee der Kreisform nach außen trug. Im Raum dieses kubischen Einschnittes trug eine vertikale Rohrkonstruktion dekorative Ausstellungselemente sowie die Leuchtschrift.

Die äußere Form des Pavillons, der gleichzeitig einer der größten Holzbauten der Ausstellung war, bildete einen auf dem Rechteck aufgebauten Kubus, der – gegen außen völlig abgeschlossen – eine künstliche Belichtung im Innern notwendig machte. Da die benachbarten Anbauten keine selbständige architektonische Form des Pavillons zuließen, mußte der Eingangsseite besondere gestalterische Aufmerksamkeit gegeben werden. Die Fassade des Tanzteils, die durch verschieden farbige, schräg geschnittene Blechzylinder und große, exzentrische, flächige Kreisformen ein attraktives Element bildete, stellte als Gestaltung ein künstlerisch bemerkenswertes Beispiel dar. Tages- und künstliche Belichtung ergaben durch wechselnde Schattenformen phantastische optische Veränderungen der plastischen Trichter. Durch die konsequente Anwendung der Kreisform verbanden sich Innen- und Außenraum zu einer architektonischen Einheit.
Ebenso bemerkenswert war die Durchgestaltung der Fassade des Teils für populäre Attraktionen. Eine hoch liegende durchgehende Verglasung gab eine straffe Führung und bildete zusammen mit den darunter liegenden Kipptoren, die, völlig geöffnet, Einblick in die Halle boten, das Schaufenster dieses Pavillonteils.

Konstruktion

Verschraubte Fassadenstützen in Holz auf Pfahlfundation. Außen vertikale Holzschalung. 3 m hohe Holzfachwerkbinder mit einer Spannweite von 28 m bildeten die Dachträger des 72 m langen Pavillons. Durchmesser der trichterförmigen Deckenöffnung unten 18,60 m, oben 7 m. Perronstützen aus verleimten Brettern als Galerieträger. Decke und Wände Stoffbespannung.

46

Richard P Lhose
Neue Ausstellungsgestaltung
Verlag für Architektur
Erlenbach-Zürich 1953
reduced from approx 230 mm deep

Gesamtansicht der Fassade des Tanzteils. Wand weiß, Trichter weiß, gelb, dunkelblau, Kanten der Trichter weiß, rot, dunkelblau, gelb. Flächenformen sepiabraun.

Vue générale de la façade du dancing. Paroi blanche, entonnoirs blancs, jaunes et bleu fonce, bords des entonnoirs blancs, rouges, bleu foncé et jaunes. Formes circulaires brun sépia.

View of dance hall façade. Wall white, funnels white, yellow, dark blue, edges of funnels white, red, dark blue, yellow. Flat surfaces sepia.

Thème

L'architecte était chargé de la création d'un centre d'amusement, comprenant des locaux de danse, de présentation de variétés et autres attractions. Le pavillon fut situé de manière à faire corps avec d'autres bâtiments de l'exposition.

Présentation

Le dancing même constituait la partie prédominante du pavillon. Installé dans l'aide sud de ce dernier, il se composait de pistes pour danse, variétés et attractions. Des rangées de sièges les encerclaient et formaient une série de cercles concentriques progressivement surélevés. Un escalier en colimaçon menait à la galerie, également circulaire, qui dominait les sièges. On y trouvait les bureaux, des garderobes, une salle de jeux et un petit théâtre. Au rez-de-chaussée, des parois semi-circulaires n'allant que jusqu'à mi-hauteur du local, séparaient la piste de danse et les sièges des locaux réservés à la restauration. Un bar, avec vue sur la piste de danse, se trouvait dans le fond de la partie occidentale. Une paroi vitrée avec portes mettait le dancing en communication directe avec la partie du pavillon réservée aux attractions populaires. Celle-ci comprenait une pelouse de fêtes, des stands forains, une brasserie. La différence de hauteur des plafonds des deux parties du bâtiment soulignait la diversité de caractère de ces dernières. Une ouverture en entonnoir avait été faite dans le plafond du dancing; placée dans l'axe de la piste de danse, des cercles de sièges et de la galerie, elle faisait partie du mouvement architectural de l'ensemble et donnait à celui-ci une note attrayante. Par mauvais temps, un toit coulissant fermait cette ouverture.

L'entrée était soulignée par une embrasure bien marquée; cette dernière prolongeait au dehors l'idée du cercle, laquelle avait servi de base à la division et à l'aménagement intérieurs. Dans cette embrasure se trouvait une construction tubulaire porteuse d'éléments décoratifs et d'enseignes lumineuses.

Le pavillon, l'un des plus grands bâtiments en bois de l'exposition, avait la forme d'un parallélépipède rectangle; ses parois pleines impli-

Vergnügungspavillon

Following the revolutionary experiments of the 1920s and 1930s, when so many of the traditions of book design were challenged and the problems re-defined, a new set of standards emerged, commonly known as Swiss Typography. Similar ideas were developed in design schools at Ulm, Chicago and elsewhere. The style consists of careful analysis of the text, rigorous discipline in arranging the material to a grid, and extreme simplicity of typographic means. Great reliance is placed on the printer, not least in demanding hyper-accurate guillotining.

Characteristically, only one type, often in only one size, is used, with its related bold. In this example, even the three languages are undifferentiated except by position and order, and here, perhaps, less *is* less.

However, the spread demonstrates very clearly the powerful logic and high professionalism of the Swiss style at its best. In its cool way, it is subtle and sensitive. Would that more books today exhibit some of the intellectual rigour deployed here.

100 Years of Russian Art
1889-1989
ed David Elliott
and Valery Dudakov
Lund Humphries
London 1989
reduced from 265 mm deep

SEREBRIAKOVA, Zinaida Yevgenyevna / 1884–1967
Painter and graphic artist. Studied at studio of Tenisheva, St Petersburg (1901) under Repin and workshop of Braz (1903–5). From 1910 participated in exhibitions including World of Art. Member of World of Art. Visited Italy (1902–3), Paris (1905), Switzerland (1914) and Morocco (1928, 1932). Lived in St Petersburg, and in Kharkov (1981–20). In 1924 moved to Paris. Exhibited abroad.

184   Sleeping Peasant Woman 1917, *Ill. in col. p.125*
Oil on canvas, 77.5×138cm
Collection O.I.Rybakova

185   Self Portrait with Children 1917–18
Watercolour on board, 57×47cm
Collection Ye.B. and A.F.Chudnovsky

186   Portrait of Sergei Ernst 1922, *Ill. below*
Tempera on paper, 55×44cm
Collection I.A. and Ya.A.Rzhevsky

Zinaida Serebriakova: **Portrait of Sergei Ernst** 1922
Cat.186

SEROV, Valentin Aleksandrovich / 1865—1911
Painter, graphic artist, sculptor and theatre designer. Studied in Paris (1873–4, 1878–80) under Repin, at Academy of Arts, St Petersburg (1880–5) under Chistyakov, and in Munich and Paris (until 1875). From 1890 participated in exhibitions including TPKhv, MTKh, World of Art, SRKh. Visited The Netherlands, Belgium, Germany, Italy, France, Greece and Spain. Member of TPKhv (1894–9) and World of Art (from 1899). Designed sets for Mamontov's opera company, and worked for Marinsky Theatre (1908) and Diaghilev. Taught at MUZhVZ (1897–1909). One-man show in 1914.

187   The Rape of Europa 1910, *Ill. below*
Ceramic, white, cast 1915, 24×29×22cm
Collection V.A. Dudakov and M.K.Kashuro

Valentin Serov: **The Rape of Europa** 1910
Cat.187

188   Diana and Actaeon, sketch for a wall painting in the house of V.V.Nosov in Moscow 1911, *Ill. p.26*
Watercolour, pencil and charcoal on paper mounted on board, 62×49cm
Collection A.V.Smolyannikov

SHCHEKOTIKHINA-POTOTSKAYA
Aleksandra Vasilyevna / 1892–1967
Theatre designer, ceramics painter and sculptor. Studied at Drawing School of OPKh (1908–15), St Petersburg under Roerich, Bilibin, whom she married, Tsionglinsky and Shchuko. Visited Greece, Italy and France (1913). In Paris worked at studios of Denis, Vallotton and Sérusier (1913). Designed sets and costumes for theatre (1912–20) including costumes for Diaghilev's production of Stravinsky's *Rite of Spring* (1913). From 1913 participated in exhibitions including World of Art, Community of Artists, House of Arts, State Ceramics Factory. Worked at State Ceramics Factory as painter and produced agitational ceramics (1918–23). Lived in Paris (1925–36). Worked at Leningrad Ceramics Factory (1936–53). Was one of the most outstanding ceramic artists in USSR. Produced several models for sculptures including *Snow Maiden*. One-woman shows in Paris (1926) and Leningrad (1955).

189   Plate 'The Pupil' 1923
'GFZ 1923'. On base inscription 'To a design by Shchekotikhina' and signature of factory artist N.Sverchkov. Painted over glaze. Diameter 22cm
Collection T.Rubinshteyn

Ingrid Brandt, geb. 1959, studiert seit 1979 europäische und ostasiatische Kunstgeschichte sowie mittlere und neuere Geschichte. 1982 absolvierte sie ein Praktikum in der Abteilung Asiatische Kunst des Rijksmuseums Amsterdam. Im folgenden Beitrag erläutert sie die Bedeutung des Baumes in den Mythen Chinas und Indiens. Neben der Beseelung des Baumes spielt dort vor allem das Motiv des kosmischen Weltenbaumes eine Rolle, in der hinduistischen Vorstellung auch als „umgekehrter Baum", dessen Wurzeln im Himmel verankert sind. Im Buddhismus bekommt der schon früher als Fruchtbarkeits-Symbol verehrte Baum eine besondere Bedeutung durch das Ereignis der Erleuchtung, das sich unter ihm vollzog. Die Autorin fügt einen Ausblick·auf die Kultur Japans an und schließt mit Überlegungen zum Wandel allgemeinverbindlicher mythologischer Vorstellungen zu subjektiven, lyrisch-expressiven Gestaltungsweisen, einer häufig anzutreffenden Entwicklung, wie sie sich in der chinesischen Kunst am Beispiel des Baum-Motivs besonders gut verdeutlichen läßt.

Bild des Kosmos und des Menschen

er Baum
Kultur und Mythos Chinas
nd Indiens

In *China* wurde 1978 mit einem der größten Aufforstungsprojekte der Welt begonnen: ein „Schutzwaldgürtel", für den 1983 auf einer Fläche von mehr als einer Million Hektar Bäume angepflanzt wurden, soll sich vom Nordosten des Landes über eine Länge von 7 000 Kilometern bis nach Nordwestchina erstrecken, um die gefürchteten Stürme aus Sibirien und der Gobi-Wuste abzumildern. Eine weitere Maßnahme zur Aufforstung wurde im Dezember 1982 vom Nationalen Chinesischen Volkskongress erlassen: Jeder arbeitsfähige Chinese wurde verpflichtet, pro Jahr mindestens drei Bäume zu pflanzen. Diese staatlichen Anordnungen sollen wiedergutmachen, was durch den jahrhundertelangen Raubbau an Bäumen und Wäldern Chinas angerichtet wurde.

Doch trotz dieses Raubbaus und der damit verursachten fast völligen Wald- und Baumlosigkeit des Landes, vor allem auch derjenigen Provinzen, die als Zentren der chinesischen Kultur bezeichnet werden (Süd-Shansi, Honan, Hopei und Shantung), hat der Baum in der Geistesgeschichte des chinesischen Volkes eine bedeutende Rolle gespielt.

Baummythen im alten China

Die Mythen des alten China, in deren Mittelpunkt der Baum steht, gründen auf der Überzeugung, daß Pflanzen, die leben, wachsen und sterben wie der Mensch, ebenso beseelt sind wie dieser, daß ihre Seele aus der einen universalen Seele entspringt, die den ganzen Kosmos durchdringt, und zu ihr wieder zurückkehrt.

Die Mehrzahl der Baumlegenden berichten von Geistern, die in den Bäumen wohnen. Diese *Baumgeister* nehmen nie die Gestalt des Baumes selbst an, sondern sind entweder anthropomorph oder zoomorph, treten also als Mensch oder Tier in Erscheinung, oder aber sie sind amorph, d. h. gestaltlos. In diese beiden Gruppen lassen sich die Pflanzenlegenden, im besonderen die Baumlegenden, einteilen.

Eine Vielzahl der Legenden schreibt den Bäumen *menschliche* Eigenschaften zu. So wird von blutenden Bäumen berichtet, die, über tausend Jahre alt, bei dem Versuch, sie zu fällen oder niederzubrennen, Angst- und Schmerzensschreie ausstießen. Neben diesen finden sich

Abb. 1
Dachziegel mit Maulbeerbaum
Han-Dynastie
Nelson Gallery, Kansas
(Aus: Sullivan, Abb. 146)

Hans Gercke
Der Baum in Mythologie
Kunstgeschichte und
Gegenwartskunst
Braus
Heidelberg 1985
reduced from approx 300 mm deep

Both these examples react against the extreme purity of the 'Swiss' method, aiming for a less austere and more varied appearance. The grid is still employed, but modified by the use of indents; typographic discipline is maintained but there is now a mix of serifed and grotesque types, and rules are used for,

effectively, decorative reasons. The Russian Art catalogue marries slightly letterspaced Headline Bold caps with Ehrhardt – not an obvious combination but unexpectedly successful here. The German book summons back Bauhaus-weight rules, but uses them in a most disciplined way. It is printed on recycled

paper of indifferent quality. Accepting this, its strong design and the choice of Times for text have been well judged.

In both examples, the lessons of the typographic 'revolution' have not at all been forgotten, nor has the extreme purity of the Swiss school; the lessons have been digested, developed, built on.

5 | Specimen Settings

Notes

1 The different treatment of the series numbers reflects the greater importance Monotype put on them. Our descriptions follow the manufacturers'; typesetters frequently use different terms, for example 'roman' may become 'regular', and the range of bold weights can be most confusing. Series numbers clarify requirements.

2 Original designers (in brackets) and dates are given, the dates being for the 'basic core' weights; extreme weights and variations are often added over a period of years or decades. Even a single weight can take years to develop; hence our dates may differ slightly from those elsewhere. Our Linotype dates come from Linotype sources; Monotype from various sources.

3 Copyfitting codes and factors are for normal (manufacturer's recommended) letterspacing. If spacing is tightened or opened out, copyfitting will be affected accordingly.
Copyfitting systems and tables are on pages 284-285.

4 The range shown under any type style is complete at the time of writing, but new weights and variations are being continually introduced.

5 Some typefaces include characters for children learning to read (agyIl149). These are variously known as open, educational or infant characters. We indicate where these are available.

6 Unless otherwise stated, all setting uses manufacturer's recommended spacing.

7 Pica point sizes are used.

8 Captions are in 7pt of the type illustrated.

9 Letterspacing of Monotype specimens is expressed in Monotype's 96 units to the em.
Letterspacing of Linotype specimens is expressed in Linotype's 54 units to the em. NOTE: for *word* spacing, Linotype use an 18 unit per em system.

10 Where the first line of the text setting is in small caps, these are letterspaced 3 units Mono, 1 unit Lino.

11 For unjustified setting, word spacing is 24 units Mono and 4 units Lino. This is the spacing most typesetting firms work to for unjustified setting, but the optimum Mono spacing is 21 units.

12 We have not attempted to show kerning – the overlapping of awkward pairs of characters such as To, Ty, Ya (To, Ty, Ya). Some typesetting firms have a very sophisticated kerning programme, others are able to create a limited programme for specific purposes. This facility is particularly useful in large or display sizes.

13 The Monotype setting has been done on a Lasercomp (digital storage, laser scan).
The Linotype setting has been done on a Linotron 202 (digital storage, electronic CRT scan). The more recent Linotronic 300 has laser scan, but typeface designs, sizes and fit are effectively the same.

14 Apparently similar designs from other manufacturers may differ significantly in design detail, or size. Our examples are not, therefore, to be taken as a guide for type set by any system other than Lasercomp or Linotron/Linotronic.

15 We show the output one may expect from good quality typesetting firms, without introducing exceptional micro adjustments. While small programmes can be created to correct recurring spacing problems, to achieve optically perfect spacing of caps or small caps, for example, would require individual attention to every instance.

16 It should be noted that typesetting firms will sometimes adjust the fit of numerals or punctuation to suit their own preferences. In our settings, for instance, the Monotype question and exclamation marks, and some punctuation, are tighter to their preceding letter than some setters prefer.

17 Our examples of sloped roman are achieved with normal width letters, but their appearance can often be improved by simultaneously condensing the forms. Moreover, if the equipment is able to vary the angle of slope, this, too, could be beneficially exploited.

18 The colour or apparent darkness of text on the printed page varies according to the paper chosen. This book is printed on a smooth coated cartridge. A gloss coated stock or a soft cartridge would have given different results.

Linotype **Akzidenz-Grotesk**

roman (05003), **italic** (13003)
black (09003)
Berthold: roman 1898, italic 1967, black 1909
Copyfitting code 121/117/142

Range also includes light, bold, condensed,
bold condensed, black condensed

ABCDEFGHIJKLMNOP
QRSTUVWXYZ abcdefg
hijklmnopqrstuvwxyz
1234567890
fifl ()[]&£$.,;:-!?''

ABCDEFGHIJKLMNOP
QRSTUVWXYZ abcdefg
hijklmnopqrstuvwxyz
1234567890
fifl ()[]&£$.,;:-!?''

ABCDEFGHIJKLMNOP
QRSTUVWXYZ abcdefg
hijklmnopqrstuvwxyz
1234567890
fifl ()[]&£$.,;:-!?''

24 on 27pt

74

These examples show *normal* letterspacing and the effect of *reduced* letterspacing on roman setting *as well as on words in italic*: they also show the appearance of figures, for example 28 May 1964, within text. These & the ampersand are not included in the setting opposite.
Normal letterspacing

These examples show *normal* letterspacing and the effect of *reduced* letterspacing on roman setting *as well as on words in italic*: they also show the appearance of figures, for example 28 May 1964, within text. These & the ampersand are not included in the setting opposite.
Minus one unit spacing

These examples show *normal* letterspacing and the effect of *reduced* letterspacing on roman setting *as well as on words in italic*: they also show the appearance of figures, for example 28 May 1964, within text. These & the ampersand are not included in the setting opposite.
Minus two units spacing

WALKING ALONG THE MALL WE WONDERED WHO ALL THOSE
WALKING ALONG THE MALL WE WONDERED WHO ALL
WALKING ALONG THE MALL WE WONDERED WHO
Capitals: normal letterspacing/plus 4 units/plus 9 units

Walking along the Mall we wondered who all those men were – tall hawk-featured men perched on balconies and high places, scanning the city with heavy binoculars. WHAT WERE THEY SEEKING SO EARNESTLY? Who were they – so composed and steely-eyed? Timidly we stopped a POLICEMAN TO ASK HIM. 'They are publishers' he said mildly. Publishers! Our hearts stopped beating. 'They are on the look out for new talent.' Great God! It was for *us* they were waiting and watching!
Text with reduced caps normal letterspacing/plus 3 units

WALKING ALONG THE MALL we wondered who all those men were
WALKING ALONG THE MALL we wondered who all those men were
True italic/sloped roman

Walking along the Mall we wondered who all those men were – tall hawk-featured men perched on balconies and high places, scanning the city with heavy binoculars. What were they seeking so earnestly? Who were they – so composed and steely-eyed? Timidly we stopped a policeman to ask him. 'They are publishers' he said mildly. Publishers! Our hearts stopped beating. 'They are on the look out for new talent.' Great God! It was for *us* they were waiting and watching! Then the kindly policeman lowered his voice confidentially and said in hollow and reverent tones: *'They are waiting for the new Trollope to be born!'* Do you remember, at these words, how heavy our suitcases suddenly felt? How our blood slowed, our footsteps lagged? Brother Ass, we had been bashfully thinking of a kind of illumination such as Rimbaud dreamed of – a nagging poem
8 on 9pt

Walking along the Mall we wondered who all those men were – tall hawk-featured men perched on balconies and high places, scanning the city with heavy binoculars. What were they seeking so earnestly? Who were they – so composed and steely-eyed? Timidly we stopped a policeman to ask him. 'They are publishers' he said mildly. Publishers! Our hearts stopped beating. 'They are on the look out for new talent.' Great God! It was for *us* they were waiting and watching! Then the kindly policeman lowered his voice confidentially and said in hollow and reverent tones: *'They are waiting for the new Trollope to be born!'* Do you remember, at these words, how heavy our suitcases suddenly felt? How our blood slowed, our footsteps lagged? Brother Ass, we had been bashfully
8 on 10.5pt

Walking along the Mall we wondered who all those men were – tall hawk-featured men perched on balconies and high places, scanning the city with heavy binoculars. What were they seeking so earnestly? Who were they – so composed and steely-eyed? Timidly we stopped a policeman to ask him. 'They are publishers' he said mildly. Publishers! Our hearts stopped beating. 'They are on the look out for new talent.' Great God! It was for *us* they were waiting and watching! Then the kindly policeman lowered his voice confidentially and said in hollow and reverent tones: *'They are waiting for the new Trollope to be born!'* Do you remember, at these words, how heavy our suitcases suddenly felt? How our blood slowed, our footsteps lagged? Brother Ass, we had been bashfully thinking of a kind of illumination such as Rimbaud dreamed of – a nagging poem which was not didactic or expository but which *infected* – was not simply a rationalised intuition, I mean, clothed in isinglass! We had come to the wrong shop, with the wrong change! A chill struck us as we saw the mist falling in Trafalgar Square, coiling round us its tendrils of ectoplasm! A million muffin-eating moralists were waiting, not for us, Brother Ass, but for the plucky and tedious Trollope! (If you are dissatisfied with your form, reach for the *curette*.) Now do you wonder if I laugh a little off-key? Do you ask yourself what

9 on 11pt

Walking along the Mall we wondered who all those men were – tall hawk-featured men perched on balconies and high places, scanning the city with heavy binoculars. What were they seeking so earnestly? Who were they – so composed and steely-eyed? Timidly we stopped a policeman to ask him. 'They are publishers' he said mildly. Publishers! Our hearts stopped beating. 'They are on the look out for new talent.' Great God! It was for *us* they were waiting and watching! Then the kindly policeman lowered his voice confidentially and said in hollow and reverent tones: *'They are waiting for the new Trollope to be born!'* Do you remember, at these words, how heavy our suitcases suddenly felt? How our blood slowed, our footsteps lagged? Brother Ass, we had been bashfully thinking of a kind of illumination such as Rimbaud dreamed of – a nagging poem which was not didactic or expository but which *infected* – was not simply a rationalised intuition, I mean, clothed in isinglass! We had come to the wrong shop, with the wrong change! A chill struck us as we saw the mist falling in Trafalgar

10 on 12pt

Walking along the Mall we wondered who all those men were – tall hawk-featured men perched on balconies and high places, scanning the city with heavy binoculars. What were they seeking so earnestly? Who were they – so composed and steely-eyed? Timidly we stopped a policeman to ask him. 'They are publishers' he said mildly. Publishers! Our hearts stopped beating. 'They are on the look out for new talent.' Great God! It was for *us* they were waiting and watching! Then the kindly policeman lowered his voice confidentially and said in hollow and reverent tones: *'They are waiting for the new Trollope to be born!'* Do you remember, at these words, how heavy our suitcases suddenly felt? How our blood slowed, our footsteps lagged? Brother Ass, we had been bashfully thinking of a kind of illumination such as Rimbaud dreamed of – a nagging poem which was not didactic or expository but which *infected* – was not simply a rationalised

11 on 13pt

Walking along the Mall we wondered who all those men were – tall hawk-featured men perched on balconies and high places, scanning the city with heavy binoculars. What were they seeking so earnestly? Who were they – so composed and steely-eyed? Timidly we stopped a policeman to ask him. 'They are publishers' he said mildly. Publishers! Our hearts stopped beating. 'They are on the look out for new talent.' Great God! It was for *us* they were waiting and watching! Then the kindly policeman lowered his voice confidentially and said in hollow and reverent tones: *'They are waiting for the new Trollope to be born!'* Do you remember, at these words, how heavy our suitcases suddenly felt? How our blood slowed, our footsteps lagged? Brother Ass, we had been bashfully thinking of a kind of illumination such as Rimbaud dreamed of – a nagging poem which was not didactic or expository but which *infected* – was not simply a rationalised intuition, I mean, clothed in isinglass! We had come to the wrong shop, with the wrong change!

9 on 12pt

Walking along the Mall we wondered who all those men were – tall hawk-featured men perched on balconies and high places, scanning the city with heavy binoculars. What were they seeking so earnestly? Who were they – so composed and steely-eyed? Timidly we stopped a policeman to ask him. 'They are publishers' he said mildly. Publishers! Our hearts stopped beating. 'They are on the look out for new talent.' Great God! It was for *us* they were waiting and watching! Then the kindly policeman lowered his voice confidentially and said in hollow and reverent tones: *'They are waiting for the new Trollope to be born!'* Do you remember, at these words, how heavy our suitcases suddenly felt? How our blood slowed, our footsteps lagged? Brother Ass, we had been bashfully thinking of a kind of illumination such as Rimbaud dreamed of – a nagging poem which was not didactic or expository but which *infected* – was not simply a rationalised intuition, I mean, clothed in isinglass! We had come to the wrong shop, with the wrong change!

10 on 13.5pt

Walking along the Mall we wondered who all those men were – tall hawk-featured men perched on balconies and high places, scanning the city with heavy binoculars. What were they seeking so earnestly? Who were they – so composed and steely-eyed? Timidly we stopped a policeman to ask him. 'They are publishers' he said mildly. Publishers! Our hearts stopped beating. 'They are on the look out for new talent.' Great God! It was for *us* they were waiting and watching! Then the kindly policeman lowered his voice confidentially and said in hollow and reverent tones: *'They are waiting for the new Trollope to be born!'* Do you remember, at these words, how heavy our suitcases suddenly felt? How our blood slowed, our footsteps lagged? Brother Ass, we had been bashfully thinking of a kind of illumination such as Rimbaud dreamed of – a nagging poem which was not didactic or exposi-

11 on 14.5pt

Monotype ALBERTINA

664 roman and italic
Monotype 1966 (Chris Brand)
Copyfitting factor 39.0/35.8

The second Monotype face designed for
phototypesetting

ABCDEFGHIJKLMNOP
QRSTUVWXYZ abcdefg
hijklmnopqrstuvwxyz
1234567890
ff fi fl ffi ffl ()[]&£$.,;:-!?''

ABCDEFGHIJKLMNOP
QRSTUVWXYZ abcdefg
hijklmnopqrstuvwxyz
1234567890
ff fi fl ffi ffl ()[]&£$.,;:-!?''

24 on 27pt

These examples show *normal* letterspacing and the effect of *reduced*
letterspacing on roman setting *as well as on words in italic*: they also
show the appearance of figures, for example 28 May 1964, within text.
These & the ampersand are not included in the setting opposite.
Normal letterspacing

These examples show *normal* letterspacing and the effect of *reduced*
letterspacing on roman setting *as well as on words in italic*: they also
show the appearance of figures, for example 28 May 1964, within text.
These & the ampersand are not included in the setting opposite.
Minus one unit spacing

These examples show *normal* letterspacing and the effect of *reduced*
letterspacing on roman setting *as well as on words in italic*: they also
show the appearance of figures, for example 28 May 1964, within text.
These & the ampersand are not included in the setting opposite.
Minus two units spacing

WALKING ALONG THE MALL WE WONDERED WHO ALL THOSE MEN
WALKING ALONG THE MALL WE WONDERED WHO ALL THOSE
WALKING ALONG THE MALL WE WONDERED WHO ALL
Capitals: normal letterspacing/plus 9 units/plus 18 units

WALKING ALONG THE MALL WE WONDERED WHO ALL THOSE MEN WERE
WALKING ALONG THE MALL WE WONDERED WHO ALL THOSE MEN WERE
WALKING ALONG THE MALL WE WONDERED WHO ALL THOSE MEN
Small caps: normal letterspacing/plus 6 units/plus 12 units

WALKING ALONG THE MALL WE WONDERED WHO ALL THOSE MEN WERE
WALKING ALONG THE MALL WE WONDERED WHO ALL THOSE MEN WERE
True small caps/reduced capitals

WALKING ALONG THE MALL we wondered who all those men were
WALKING ALONG THE MALL we wondered who all those men were
True italic/sloped roman

Walking along the Mall we wondered who all those men were – tall hawk-featured
men perched on balconies and high places, scanning the city with heavy binoculars. What were
they seeking so earnestly? Who were they – so composed and steely-eyed? Timidly we stopped
a policeman to ask him. 'They are publishers' he said mildly. Publishers! Our hearts stopped
beating. 'They are on the look out for new talent.' Great God! It was for *us* they were waiting and
watching! Then the kindly policeman lowered his voice confidentially and said in hollow and
reverent tones: *'They are waiting for the new Trollope to be born!'* Do you remember, at these words,
how heavy our suitcases suddenly felt? How our blood slowed, our footsteps lagged? Brother Ass,
we had been bashfully thinking of a kind of illumination such as Rimbaud dreamed of – a
nagging poem which was not didactic or expository but which *infected* – was not simply a

8 on 9pt

WALKING ALONG THE MALL WE WONDERED WHO ALL THOSE MEN WERE – TALL HAWK-FEATURED
men perched on balconies and high places, scanning the city with heavy binoculars. What were
they seeking so earnestly? Who were they – so composed and steely-eyed? Timidly we stopped
a policeman to ask him. 'They are publishers' he said mildly. Publishers! Our hearts stopped
beating. 'They are on the look out for new talent.' Great God! It was for *us* they were waiting and
watching! Then the kindly policeman lowered his voice confidentially and said in hollow and
reverent tones: *'They are waiting for the new Trollope to be born!'* Do you remember, at these words,
how heavy our suitcases suddenly felt? How our blood slowed, our footsteps lagged? Brother Ass,
we had been bashfully thinking of a kind of illumination such as Rimbaud dreamed of – a

8 on 10.5pt

Walking along the Mall we wondered who all those men were – tall hawk-featured men perched on balconies and high places, scanning the city with heavy binoculars. What were they seeking so earnestly? Who were they – so composed and steely-eyed? Timidly we stopped a policeman to ask him. 'They are publishers' he said mildly. Publishers! Our hearts stopped beating. 'They are on the look out for new talent.' Great God! It was for *us* they were waiting and watching! Then the kindly policeman lowered his voice confidentially and said in hollow and reverent tones: *'They are waiting for the new Trollope to be born!'* Do you remember, at these words, how heavy our suitcases suddenly felt? How our blood slowed, our footsteps lagged? Brother Ass, we had been bashfully thinking of a kind of illumination such as Rimbaud dreamed of – a nagging poem which was not didactic or expository but which *infected* – was not simply a rationalised intuition, I mean, clothed in isinglass! We had come to the wrong shop, with the wrong change! A chill struck us as we saw the mist falling in Trafalgar Square, coiling around us its tendrils of ectoplasm! A million muffin-eating moralists were waiting, not for us, Brother Ass, but for the plucky and tedious Trollope! (If you are dissatisfied with your form, reach for the *curette*.) Now do you wonder if I laugh a little off-key? Do you ask yourself what has turned me into nature's bashful little aphorist? We who are, after all, simply poor co-workers in the psyche of our nation, what can we expect but the natural automatic

9 on 11pt

Walking along the Mall we wondered who all those men were – tall hawk-featured men perched on balconies and high places, scanning the city with heavy binoculars. What were they seeking so earnestly? Who were they – so composed and steely-eyed? Timidly we stopped a policeman to ask him. 'They are publishers' he said mildly. Publishers! Our hearts stopped beating. 'They are on the look out for new talent.' Great God! It was for *us* they were waiting and watching! Then the kindly policeman lowered his voice confidentially and said in hollow and reverent tones: *'They are waiting for the new Trollope to be born!'* Do you remember, at these words, how heavy our suitcases suddenly felt? How our blood slowed, our footsteps lagged? Brother Ass, we had been bashfully thinking of a kind of illumination such as Rimbaud dreamed of – a nagging poem which was not didactic or expository but which *infected* – was not simply a rationalised intuition, I mean, clothed in isinglass! We had come to the wrong shop, with the wrong change! A chill struck us as we saw the mist falling in Trafalgar Square, coiling around us its tendrils of ectoplasm! A million muffin-eating moralists were waiting, not for us, Brother Ass, but for the plucky and tedious Trollope! (If

10 on 12pt

Walking along the Mall we wondered who all those men were – tall hawk-featured men perched on balconies and high places, scanning the city with heavy binoculars. What were they seeking so earnestly? Who were they – so composed and steely-eyed? Timidly we stopped a policeman to ask him. 'They are publishers' he said mildly. Publishers! Our hearts stopped beating. 'They are on the look out for new talent.' Great God! It was for *us* they were waiting and watching! Then the kindly policeman lowered his voice confidentially and said in hollow and reverent tones: *'They are waiting for the new Trollope to be born!'* Do you remember, at these words, how heavy our suitcases suddenly felt? How our blood slowed, our footsteps lagged? Brother Ass, we had been bashfully thinking of a kind of illumination such as Rimbaud dreamed of – a nagging poem which was not didactic or expository but which *infected* – was not simply a rationalised intuition, I mean, clothed in isinglass! We had come to the wrong shop, with the wrong change! A chill struck us as

11 on 13pt

WALKING ALONG THE MALL WE WONDERED WHO ALL THOSE MEN WERE – TALL HAWK-featured men perched on balconies and high places, scanning the city with heavy binoculars. What were they seeking so earnestly? Who were they – so composed and steely-eyed? Timidly we stopped a policeman to ask him. 'They are publishers' he said mildly. Publishers! Our hearts stopped beating. 'They are on the look out for new talent.' Great God! It was for *us* they were waiting and watching! Then the kindly policeman lowered his voice confidentially and said in hollow and reverent tones: *'They are waiting for the new Trollope to be born!'* Do you remember, at these words, how heavy our suitcases suddenly felt? How our blood slowed, our footsteps lagged? Brother Ass, we had been bashfully thinking of a kind of illumination such as Rimbaud dreamed of – a nagging poem which was not didactic or expository but which *infected* – was not simply a rationalised intuition, I mean, clothed in isinglass! We had come to the wrong shop, with the wrong change! A chill struck us as we saw the mist falling in Trafalgar Square, coiling around us its tendrils of ectoplasm! A million muffin-eating moralists were waiting, not for us, Brother Ass, but for the plucky and tedious Trollope! (If you are dissatisfied with your form, reach for the *curette*.) Now do you wonder if I laugh a little off-key? Do you ask yourself what has turned me into nature's bashful little aphorist? We who are, after all,

9 on 12pt

WALKING ALONG THE MALL WE WONDERED WHO ALL THOSE MEN WERE – tall hawk-featured men perched on balconies and high places, scanning the city with heavy binoculars. What were they seeking so earnestly? Who were they – so composed and steely-eyed? Timidly we stopped a policeman to ask him. 'They are publishers' he said mildly. Publishers! Our hearts stopped beating. 'They are on the look out for new talent.' Great God! It was for *us* they were waiting and watching! Then the kindly policeman lowered his voice confidentially and said in hollow and reverent tones: *'They are waiting for the new Trollope to be born!'* Do you remember, at these words, how heavy our suitcases suddenly felt? How our blood slowed, our footsteps lagged? Brother Ass, we had been bashfully thinking of a kind of illumination such as Rimbaud dreamed of – a nagging poem which was not didactic or expository but which *infected* – was not simply a rationalised intuition, I mean, clothed in isinglass! We had come to the wrong shop, with the wrong change! A chill struck us as we saw the mist falling in Trafalgar Square, coiling around us its tendrils of ectoplasm! A million

10 on 13.5pt

WALKING ALONG THE MALL WE WONDERED WHO ALL THOSE MEN WERE – tall hawk-featured men perched on balconies and high places, scanning the city with heavy binoculars. What were they seeking so earnestly? Who were they – so composed and steely-eyed? Timidly we stopped a policeman to ask him. 'They are publishers' he said mildly. Publishers! Our hearts stopped beating. 'They are on the look out for new talent.' Great God! It was for *us* they were waiting and watching! Then the kindly policeman lowered his voice confidentially and said in hollow and reverent tones: *'They are waiting for the new Trollope to be born!'* Do you remember, at these words, how heavy our suitcases suddenly felt? How our blood slowed, our footsteps lagged? Brother Ass, we had been bashfully thinking of a kind of illumination such as Rimbaud dreamed of – a nagging poem which was not didactic or expository but which *infected* – was not simply a rationalised intuition, I mean, clothed in isinglass! We

11 on 14.5pt

Linotype ALDUS

roman (05004), **italic** (13004)
Stempel 1954 (Hermann Zapf)
Copyfitting code 122/123

A lighter version of Palatino, with additional
modifications. (There is also now a light
variant of Palatino itself, designed by Zapf in
1985)

ABCDEFGHIJKLMNOP
QRSTUVWXYZ abcdefg
hijklmnopqrstuvwxyz
1234567890 1234567890
fifl ()[]&£$.,;:-!?''

*ABCDEFGHIJKLMNOP
QRSTUVWXYZ abcdefg
hijklmnopqrstuvwxyz
1234567890 1234567890
fifl ()[]&£$.,;:-!?''*

24 on 27pt

These examples show *normal* letterspacing and the effect of *reduced*
letterspacing on roman setting *as well as on words in italic*: they also
show the appearance of figures, for example 28 May 1964, within text.
These & the ampersand are not included in the setting opposite.
Normal letterspacing

These examples show *normal* letterspacing and the effect of *reduced*
letterspacing on roman setting *as well as on words in italic*: they also
show the appearance of figures, for example 28 May 1964, within text.
These & the ampersand are not included in the setting opposite.
Minus one unit spacing

These examples show *normal* letterspacing and the effect of *reduced*
letterspacing on roman setting *as well as on words in italic*: they also
show the appearance of figures, for example 28 May 1964, within text.
These & the ampersand are not included in the setting opposite.
Minus two units spacing

WALKING ALONG THE MALL WE WONDERED WHO ALL
WALKING ALONG THE MALL WE WONDERED WHO ALL
WALKING ALONG THE MALL WE WONDERED WHO
Capitals: normal letterspacing/plus 4 units/plus 9 units

WALKING ALONG THE MALL WE WONDERED WHO ALL THOSE MEN WERE
WALKING ALONG THE MALL WE WONDERED WHO ALL THOSE MEN
WALKING ALONG THE MALL WE WONDERED WHO ALL THOSE
Small caps: normal letterspacing/plus 3 units/plus 6 units

WALKING ALONG THE MALL WE WONDERED WHO ALL THOSE MEN WERE
WALKING ALONG THE MALL WE WONDERED WHO ALL THOSE MEN WERE
True small caps/reduced capitals

*WALKING ALONG THE MALL we wondered who all those men were
WALKING ALONG THE MALL we wondered who all those men were*
True italic/sloped roman

Walking along the Mall we wondered who all those men were – tall hawk-featured men
perched on balconies and high places, scanning the city with heavy binoculars. What were
they seeking so earnestly? Who were they – so composed and steely-eyed? Timidly we
stopped a policeman to ask him. 'They are publishers' he said mildly. Publishers! Our
hearts stopped beating. 'They are on the look out for new talent.' Great God! It was
for *us* they were waiting and watching! Then the kindly policeman lowered his voice
confidentially and said in hollow and reverent tones: *'They are waiting for the new
Trollope to be born!'* Do you remember, at these words, how heavy our suitcases suddenly
felt? How our blood slowed, our footsteps lagged? Brother Ass, we had been bashfully
thinking of a kind of illumination such as Rimbaud dreamed of – a nagging poem which
8 on 9pt

WALKING ALONG THE MALL WE WONDERED WHO A THOSE MEN WERE – TALL HAWK-
featured men perched on balconies and high places, scanning the city with heavy
binoculars. What were they seeking so earnestly? Who were they – so composed and
steely-eyed? Timidly we stopped a policeman to ask him. 'They are publishers' he said
mildly. Publishers! Our hearts stopped beating. 'They are on the look out for new talent.'
Great God! It was for *us* they were waiting and watching! Then the kindly policeman
lowered his voice confidentially and said in hollow and reverent tones: *'They are waiting
for the new Trollope to be born!'* Do you remember, at these words, how heavy our
suitcases suddenly felt? How our blood slowed, our footsteps lagged? Brother Ass,
8 on 10.5pt

Walking along the Mall we wondered who all those men were – tall hawk-featured men perched on balconies and high places, scanning the city with heavy binoculars. What were they seeking so earnestly? Who were they – so composed and steely-eyed? Timidly we stopped a policeman to ask him. 'They are publishers' he said mildly. Publishers! Our hearts stopped beating. 'They are on the look out for new talent.' Great God! It was for *us* they were waiting and watching! Then the kindly policeman lowered his voice confidentially and said in hollow and reverent tones: *'They are waiting for the new Trollope to be born!'* Do you remember, at these words, how heavy our suitcases suddenly felt? How our blood slowed, our footsteps lagged? Brother Ass, we had been bashfully thinking of a kind of illumination such as Rimbaud dreamed of – a nagging poem which was not didactic or expository but which *infected* – was not simply a rationalised intuition, I mean, clothed in isinglass! We had come to the wrong shop, with the wrong change! A chill struck us as we saw the mist falling in Trafalgar Square, coiling round us its tendrils of ectoplasm! A million muffin-eating moralists were waiting, not for us, Brother Ass, but for the plucky and tedious Trollope! (If you are dissatisfied with your form, reach for the *curette*.) Now do you wonder if I laugh a little off-key? Do you ask yourself what has

9 on 11pt

WALKING ALONG THE MALL WE WONDERED WHO ALL THOSE MEN WERE – TALL hawk-featured men perched on balconies and high places, scanning the city with heavy binoculars. What were they seeking so earnestly? Who were they – so composed and steely-eyed? Timidly we stopped a policeman to ask him. 'They are publishers' he said mildly. Publishers! Our hearts stopped beating. 'They are on the look out for new talent.' Great God! It was for *us* they were waiting and watching! Then the kindly policeman lowered his voice confidentially and said in hollow and reverent tones: *'They are waiting for the new Trollope to be born!'* Do you remember, at these words, how heavy our suitcases suddenly felt? How our blood slowed, our footsteps lagged? Brother Ass, we had been bashfully thinking of a kind of illumination such as Rimbaud dreamed of – a nagging poem which was not didactic or expository but which *infected* – was not simply a rationalised intuition, I mean, clothed in isinglass! We had come to the wrong shop, with the wrong change! A chill struck us as we saw the mist falling in Trafalgar Square, coiling round us its tendrils of ectoplasm! A million muffin-eating moralists were waiting, not for us, Brother Ass, but for the plucky and tedious Trollope! (If you are dissatisfied with your form, reach for the *curette*.)

9 on 12pt

Walking along the Mall we wondered who all those men were – tall hawk-featured men perched on balconies and high places, scanning the city with heavy binoculars. What were they seeking so earnestly? Who were they – so composed and steely-eyed? Timidly we stopped a policeman to ask him. 'They are publishers' he said mildly. Publishers! Our hearts stopped beating. 'They are on the look out for new talent.' Great God! It was for *us* they were waiting and watching! Then the kindly policeman lowered his voice confidentially and said in hollow and reverent tones: *'They are waiting for the new Trollope to be born!'* Do you remember, at these words, how heavy our suitcases suddenly felt? How our blood slowed, our footsteps lagged? Brother Ass, we had been bashfully thinking of a kind of illumination such as Rimbaud dreamed of – a nagging poem which was not didactic or expository but which *infected* – was not simply a rationalised intuition. I mean, clothed in isinglass! We had come to the wrong shop, with the wrong change! A chill struck us as we saw the mist falling in Trafalgar

10 on 12pt

WALKING ALONG THE MALL WE WONDERED WHO ALL THOSE MEN WERE – tall hawk-featured men perched on balconies and high places, scanning the city with heavy binoculars. What were they seeking so earnestly? Who were they – so composed and steely-eyed? Timidly we stopped a policeman to ask him. 'They are publishers' he said mildly. Publishers! Our hearts stopped beating. 'They are on the look out for new talent.' Great God! It was for *us* they were waiting and watching! Then the kindly policeman lowered his voice confidentially and said in hollow and reverent tones: *'They are waiting for the new Trollope to be born!'* Do you remember, at these words, how heavy our suitcases suddenly felt? How our blood slowed, our footsteps lagged? Brother Ass, we had been bashfully thinking of a kind of illumination such as Rimbaud dreamed of – a nagging poem which was not didactic or expository but which *infected* – was not simply a rationalised intuition, I mean, clothed in isinglass! We had come to the wrong shop, with the wrong change! A

10 on 13.5pt

Walking along the Mall we wondered who all those men were – tall hawk-featured men perched on balconies and high places, scanning the city with heavy binoculars. What were they seeking so earnestly? Who were they – so composed and steely-eyed? Timidly we stopped a policeman to ask him. 'They are publishers' he said mildly. Publishers! Our hearts stopped beating. 'They are on the look out for new talent.' Great God! It was for *us* they were waiting and watching! Then the kindly policeman lowered his voice confidentially and said in hollow and reverent tones: *'They are waiting for the new Trollope to be born!'* Do you remember, at these words, how heavy our suitcases suddenly felt? How our blood slowed, our footsteps lagged? Brother Ass, we had been bashfully thinking of a kind of illumination such as Rimbaud dreamed of – a nagging poem which was not didactic or expository but which *infected* – was not simply a rationalised intuition, I

11 on 13pt

WALKING ALONG THE MALL WE WONDERED WHO ALL THOSE MEN were – tall hawk-featured men perched on balconies and high places, scanning the city with heavy binoculars. What were they seeking so earnestly? Who were they – so composed and steely-eyed? Timidly we stopped a policeman to ask him. 'They are publishers' he said mildly. Publishers! Our hearts stopped beating. 'They are on the look out for new talent.' Great God! It was for *us* they were waiting and watching! Then the kindly policeman lowered his voice confidentially and said in hollow and reverent tones: *'They are waiting for the new Trollope to be born!'* Do you remember, at these words, how heavy our suitcases suddenly felt? How our blood slowed, our footsteps lagged? Brother Ass, we had been bashfully thinking of a kind of illumination such as Rimbaud dreamed of – a nagging poem which was not didactic or expository

11 on 14.5pt

Monotype Apollo

645 roman and italic
665 semi-bold
Monotype 1964 (Adrian Frutiger)
Copyfitting factor 41.4/39.2/44.6

The first Monotype type designed for
phototypesetting

Educational characters available

ABCDEFGHIJKLMNOP
QRSTUVWXYZ abcdefg
hijklmnopqrstuvwxyz
1234567890
()[]&£$.,;:-!?''

ABCDEFGHIJKLMNOP
QRSTUVWXYZ abcdefg
hijklmnopqrstuvwxyz
1234567890
()[]&£$.,;:-!?''

ABCDEFGHIJKLMNOP
QRSTUVWXYZ abcdefg
hijklmnopqrstuvwxyz
1234567890
()[]&£$.,;:-!?''

24 on 27pt

These examples show *normal* letterspacing and the effect of *reduced*
letterspacing on roman setting *as well as on words in italic*: they also
show the appearance of figures, for example 28 May 1964, within text.
These & the ampersand are not included in the setting opposite.

Normal letterspacing

These examples show *normal* letterspacing and the effect of *reduced*
letterspacing on roman setting *as well as on words in italic*: they also
show the appearance of figures, for example 28 May 1964, within text.
These & the ampersand are not included in the setting opposite.

Minus one unit spacing

These examples show *normal* letterspacing and the effect of *reduced*
letterspacing on roman setting *as well as on words in italic*: they also
show the appearance of figures, for example 28 May 1964, within text.
These & the ampersand are not included in the setting opposite.

Minus two units spacing

WALKING ALONG THE MALL WE WONDERED WHO ALL THOSE MEN
WALKING ALONG THE MALL WE WONDERED WHO ALL
WALKING ALONG THE MALL WE WONDERED WHO

Capitals: normal letterspacing/plus 9 units/plus 18 units

WALKING ALONG THE MALL WE WONDERED WHO ALL THOSE MEN WERE
WALKING ALONG THE MALL WE WONDERED WHO ALL THOSE MEN WERE
WALKING ALONG THE MALL WE WONDERED WHO ALL THOSE MEN

Small caps: normal letterspacing/plus 6 units/plus 12 units

WALKING ALONG THE MALL we wondered who all those men were
WALKING ALONG THE MALL we wondered who all those men were

True italic/sloped roman

WALKING ALONG THE MALL WE WONDERED WHO ALL THOSE MEN WERE
WALKING ALONG THE MALL WE WONDERED WHO ALL THOSE MEN WERE

True small caps/reduced capitals

Walking along the Mall we wondered who all those men were – tall hawk-featured
men perched on balconies and high places, scanning the city with heavy binoculars. What
were they seeking so earnestly? Who were they – so composed and steely-eyed? Timidly
we stopped a policeman to ask him. 'They are publishers' he said mildly. Publishers!
Our hearts stopped beating. 'They are on the look out for new talent.' Great God! It was
for *us* they were waiting and watching! Then the kindly policeman lowered his voice
confidentially and said in hollow and reverent tones: *'They are waiting for the new Trollope
to be born!'* Do you remember, at these words, how heavy our suitcases suddenly felt? How
our blood slowed, our footsteps lagged? Brother Ass, we had been bashfully thinking of a
kind of illumination such as Rimbaud dreamed of – a nagging poem which was not didactic

8 on 9pt

WALKING ALONG THE MALL WE WONDERED WHO ALL THOSE MEN WERE – TALL
hawk-featured men perched on balconies and high places, scanning the city with heavy
binoculars. What were they seeking so earnestly? Who were they – so composed and
steely-eyed? Timidly we stopped a policeman to ask him. 'They are publishers' he said
mildly. Publishers! Our hearts stopped beating. 'They are on the look out for new talent.'
Great God! It was for *us* they were waiting and watching! Then the kindly policeman
lowered his voice confidentially and said in hollow and reverent tones: *'They are waiting for
the new Trollope to be born!'* Do you remember, at these words, how heavy our suitcases
suddenly felt? How our blood slowed, our footsteps lagged? Brother Ass, we had been

8 on 10.5pt

Walking along the Mall we wondered who all those men were – tall hawk-featured men perched on balconies and high places, scanning the city with heavy binoculars. What were they seeking so earnestly? Who were they – so composed and steely-eyed? Timidly we stopped a policeman to ask him. 'They are publishers' he said mildly. Publishers! Our hearts stopped beating. 'They are on the look out for new talent.' Great God! It was for *us* they were waiting and watching! Then the kindly policeman lowered his voice confidentially and said in hollow and reverent tones: *'They are waiting for the new Trollope to be born!'* Do you remember, at these words, how heavy our suitcases suddenly felt? How our blood slowed, our footsteps lagged? Brother Ass, we had been bashfully thinking of a kind of illumination such as Rimbaud dreamed of – a nagging poem which was not didactic or expository but which *infected* – was not simply a rationalised intuition, I mean, clothed in isinglass! We had come to the wrong shop, with the wrong change! A chill struck us as we saw the mist falling in Trafalgar Square, coiling around us its tendrils of ectoplasm! A million muffin-eating moralists were waiting, not for us, Brother Ass, but for the plucky and tedious Trollope! (If you are dissatisfied with your form, reach for the *curette*.) Now do you wonder if I laugh a little off-key? Do you ask yourself what has turned me into nature's bashful little aphorist? We who are, after all, simply poor

9 on 11pt

Walking along the Mall we wondered who all those men were – tall hawk-featured men perched on balconies and high places, scanning the city with heavy binoculars. What were they seeking so earnestly? Who were they – so composed and steely-eyed? Timidly we stopped a policeman to ask him. 'They are publishers' he said mildly. Publishers! Our hearts stopped beating. 'They are on the look out for new talent.' Great God! It was for *us* they were waiting and watching! Then the kindly policeman lowered his voice confidentially and said in hollow and reverent tones: *'They are waiting for the new Trollope to be born!'* Do you remember, at these words, how heavy our suitcases suddenly felt? How our blood slowed, our footsteps lagged? Brother Ass, we had been bashfully thinking of a kind of illumination such as Rimbaud dreamed of – a nagging poem which was not didactic or expository but which *infected* – was not simply a rationalised intuition, I mean, clothed in isinglass! We had come to the wrong shop, with the wrong change! A chill struck us as we saw the mist falling in Trafalgar Square, coiling around us its tendrils of ectoplasm! A million muffin-eating mor-

10 on 12pt

Walking along the Mall we wondered who all those men were – tall hawk-featured men perched on balconies and high places, scanning the city with heavy binoculars. What were they seeking so earnestly? Who were they – so composed and steely-eyed? Timidly we stopped a policeman to ask him. 'They are publishers' he said mildly. Publishers! Our hearts stopped beating. 'They are on the look out for new talent.' Great God! It was for *us* they were waiting and watching! Then the kindly policeman lowered his voice confidentially and said in hollow and reverent tones: *'They are waiting for the new Trollope to be born!'* Do you remember, at these words, how heavy our suitcases suddenly felt? How our blood slowed, our footsteps lagged? Brother Ass, we had been bashfully thinking of a kind of illumination such as Rimbaud dreamed of – a nagging poem which was not didactic or expository but which *infected* – was not simply a rationalised intuition, I mean, clothed in isinglass! We had come to

11 on 13pt

WALKING ALONG THE MALL WE WONDERED WHO ALL THOSE MEN WERE – TALL hawk-featured men perched on balconies and high places, scanning the city with heavy binoculars. What were they seeking so earnestly? Who were they – so composed and steely-eyed? Timidly we stopped a policeman to ask him. 'They are publishers' he said mildly. Publishers! Our hearts stopped beating. 'They are on the look out for new talent.' Great God! It was for *us* they were waiting and watching! Then the kindly policeman lowered his voice confidentially and said in hollow and reverent tones: *'They are waiting for the new Trollope to be born!'* Do you remember, at these words, how heavy our suitcases suddenly felt? How our blood slowed, our footsteps lagged? Brother Ass, we had been bashfully thinking of a kind of illumination such as Rimbaud dreamed of – a nagging poem which was not didactic or expository but which *infected* – was not simply a rationalised intuition, I mean, clothed in isinglass! We had come to the wrong shop, with the wrong change! A chill struck us as we saw the mist falling in Trafalgar Square, coiling around us its tendrils of ectoplasm! A million muffin-eating moralists were waiting, not for us, Brother Ass, but for the plucky and tedious Trollope! (If you are dissatisfied with your form, reach for the *curette*.) Now do you wonder if I laugh a little off-key? Do

9 on 12pt

WALKING ALONG THE MALL WE WONDERED WHO ALL THOSE MEN WERE – tall hawk-featured men perched on balconies and high places, scanning the city with heavy binoculars. What were they seeking so earnestly? Who were they – so composed and steely-eyed? Timidly we stopped a policeman to ask him. 'They are publishers' he said mildly. Publishers! Our hearts stopped beating. 'They are on the look out for new talent.' Great God! It was for *us* they were waiting and watching! Then the kindly policeman lowered his voice confidentially and said in hollow and reverent tones: *'They are waiting for the new Trollope to be born!'* Do you remember, at these words, how heavy our suitcases suddenly felt? How our blood slowed, our footsteps lagged? Brother Ass, we had been bashfully thinking of a kind of illumination such as Rimbaud dreamed of – a nagging poem which was not didactic or expository but which *infected* – was not simply a rationalised intuition, I mean, clothed in isinglass! We had come to the wrong shop, with the wrong change! A chill struck us as we saw the mist falling in

10 on 13.5pt

WALKING ALONG THE MALL WE WONDERED WHO ALL THOSE MEN were – tall hawk-featured men perched on balconies and high places, scanning the city with heavy binoculars. What were they seeking so earnestly? Who were they – so composed and steely-eyed? Timidly we stopped a policeman to ask him. 'They are publishers' he said mildly. Publishers! Our hearts stopped beating. 'They are on the look out for new talent.' Great God! It was for *us* they were waiting and watching! Then the kindly policeman lowered his voice confidentially and said in hollow and reverent tones: *'They are waiting for the new Trollope to be born!'* Do you remember, at these words, how heavy our suitcases suddenly felt? How our blood slowed, our footsteps lagged? Brother Ass, we had been bashfully thinking of a kind of illumination such as Rimbaud dreamed of – a nagging poem which was not didactic or expository but which *infected* – was not

11 on 14.5pt

MONOTYPE APOLLO

Linotype **Basilia Haas**

roman (05446), **italic** (13446)
bold (07446)
Haas 1978 (André Gürtler)
Copyfitting code 134/134/138

Range also includes medium, medium italic,
bold italic, black, black italic

ABCDEFGHIJKLMNOP
QRSTUVWXYZ abcdefg
hijklmnopqrstuvwxyz
1234567890
fifl () [] &£$.,;:-!?''

ABCDEFGHIJKLMNOP
QRSTUVWXYZ abcdefg
hijklmnopqrstuvwxyz
1234567890
fifl () [] &£$.,;:-!?''

ABCDEFGHIJKLMNOP
QRSTUVWXYZ abcdefg
hijklmnopqrstuvwxyz
1234567890
fifl () [] &£$.,;:-!?''

24 on 27pt

These examples show *normal* letterspacing and the effect of *reduced*
letterspacing on roman setting *as well as on words in italic*: they also
show the appearance of figures, for example 28 May 1964, within text.
These & the ampersand are not included in the setting opposite.
Normal letterspacing

These examples show *normal* letterspacing and the effect of *reduced*
letterspacing on roman setting *as well as on words in italic*: they also
show the appearance of figures, for example 28 May 1964, within text.
These & the ampersand are not included in the setting opposite.
Minus one unit spacing

These examples show *normal* letterspacing and the effect of *reduced*
letterspacing on roman setting *as well as on words in italic*: they also
show the appearance of figures, for example 28 May 1964, within text.
These & the ampersand are not included in the setting opposite.
Minus two units spacing

WALKING ALONG THE MALL WE WONDERED WHO ALL THOSE
WALKING ALONG THE MALL WE WONDERED WHO ALL
WALKING ALONG THE MALL WE WONDERED WHO
Capitals: normal letterspacing/plus 4 units/plus 9 units

Walking along the Mall we wondered who all those men were – tall
hawk-featured men perched on balconies and high places, scanning the
city with heavy binoculars. WHAT WERE THEY SEEKING SO EARNESTLY?
Who were they – so composed and steely-eyed? Timidly we stopped a
POLICEMAN TO ASK HIM. 'They are publishers' he said mildly. Publishers!
Our hearts stopped beating. 'They are on the look out for new talent.'
Great God! It was for *us* they were waiting and watching! Then the
Text with reduced caps normal letterspacing/plus 3 units

WALKING ALONG THE MALL we wondered who all those men were
WALKING ALONG THE MALL we wondered who all those men were
True italic/sloped roman

Walking along the Mall we wondered who all those men were – tall hawk-
featured men perched on balconies and high places, scanning the city with heavy
binoculars. What were they seeking so earnestly? Who were they – so composed
and steely-eyed? Timidly we stopped a policeman to ask him. 'They are
publishers' he said mildly. Publishers! Our hearts stopped beating. 'They are
on the look out for new talent.' Great God! It was for *us* they were waiting and
watching! Then the kindly policeman lowered his voice confidentially and said in
hollow and reverent tones: *'They are waiting for the new Trollope to be born!'* Do
you remember, at these words, how heavy our suitcases suddenly felt? How our
blood slowed, our footsteps lagged? Brother Ass, we had been bashfully thinking
8 on 9pt

Walking along the Mall we wondered who all those men were – tall hawk-
featured men perched on balconies and high places, scanning the city with heavy
binoculars. What were they seeking so earnestly? Who were they – so composed
and steely-eyed? Timidly we stopped a policeman to ask him. 'They are
publishers' he said mildly. Publishers! Our hearts stopped beating. 'They are
on the look out for new talent.' Great God! It was for *us* they were waiting and
watching! Then the kindly policeman lowered his voice confidentially and said in
hollow and reverent tones: *'They are waiting for the new Trollope to be born!'* Do
you remember, at these words, how heavy our suitcases suddenly felt? How our
8 on 10.5pt

Walking along the Mall we wondered who all those men were — tall hawk-featured men perched on balconies and high places, scanning the city with heavy binoculars. What were they seeking so earnestly? Who were they — so composed and steely-eyed? Timidly we stopped a policeman to ask him. 'They are publishers' he said mildly. Publishers! Our hearts stopped beating. 'They are on the look out for new talent.' Great God! It was for *us* they were waiting and watching! Then the kindly policeman lowered his voice confidentially and said in hollow and reverent tones: *'They are waiting for the new Trollope to be born!'* Do you remember, at these words, how heavy our suitcases suddenly felt? How our blood slowed, our footsteps lagged? Brother Ass, we had been bashfully thinking of a kind of illumination such as Rimbaud dreamed of — a nagging poem which was not didactic or expository but which *infected* — was not simply a rationalised intuition, I mean, clothed in isinglass! We had come to the wrong shop, with the wrong change! A chill struck us as we saw the mist falling in Trafalgar Square, coiling round us its tendrils of ectoplasm! A million muffin-eating moralists were waiting, not for us, Brother Ass, but for the plucky and tedious Trollope! (If you are dis-

9 on 11pt

Walking along the Mall we wondered who all those men were — tall hawk-featured men perched on balconies and high places, scanning the city with heavy binoculars. What were they seeking so earnestly? Who were they — so composed and steely-eyed? Timidly we stopped a policeman to ask him. 'They are publishers' he said mildly. Publishers! Our hearts stopped beating. 'They are on the look out for new talent.' Great God! It was for *us* they were waiting and watching! Then the kindly policeman lowered his voice confidentially and said in hollow and reverent tones: *'They are waiting for the new Trollope to be born!'* Do you remember, at these words, how heavy our suitcases suddenly felt? How our blood slowed, our footsteps lagged? Brother Ass, we had been bashfully thinking of a kind of illumination such as Rimbaud dreamed of — a nagging poem which was not didactic or expository but which *infected* — was not simply a rationalised intuition, I mean, clothed in isinglass! We had come to the wrong shop, with

10 on 12pt

Walking along the Mall we wondered who all those men were — tall hawk-featured men perched on balconies and high places, scanning the city with heavy binoculars. What were they seeking so earnestly? Who were they — so composed and steely-eyed? Timidly we stopped a policeman to ask him. 'They are publishers' he said mildly. Publishers! Our hearts stopped beating. 'They are on the look out for new talent.' Great God! It was for *us* they were waiting and watching! Then the kindly policeman lowered his voice confidentially and said in hollow and reverent tones: *'They are waiting for the new Trollope to be born!'* Do you remember, at these words, how heavy our suitcases suddenly felt? How our blood slowed, our footsteps lagged? Brother Ass, we had been bashfully thinking of a kind of illumination such as Rimbaud dreamed of — a nagging poem

11 on 13pt

Walking along the Mall we wondered who all those men were — tall hawk-featured men perched on balconies and high places, scanning the city with heavy binoculars. What were they seeking so earnestly? Who were they — so composed and steely-eyed? Timidly we stopped a policeman to ask him. 'They are publishers' he said mildly. Publishers! Our hearts stopped beating. 'They are on the look out for new talent.' Great God! It was for *us* they were waiting and watching! Then the kindly policeman lowered his voice confidentially and said in hollow and reverent tones: *'They are waiting for the new Trollope to be born!'* Do you remember, at these words, how heavy our suitcases suddenly felt? How our blood slowed, our footsteps lagged? Brother Ass, we had been bashfully thinking of a kind of illumination such as Rimbaud dreamed of — a nagging poem which was not didactic or expository but which *infected* — was not simply a rationalised intuition,

9 on 12pt

Walking along the Mall we wondered who all those men were — tall hawk-featured men perched on balconies and high places, scanning the city with heavy binoculars. What were they seeking so earnestly? Who were they — so composed and steely-eyed? Timidly we stopped a policeman to ask him. 'They are publishers' he said mildly. Publishers! Our hearts stopped beating. 'They are on the look out for new talent.' Great God! It was for *us* they were waiting and watching! Then the kindly policeman lowered his voice confidentially and said in hollow and reverent tones: *'They are waiting for the new Trollope to be born!'* Do you remember, at these words, how heavy our suitcases suddenly felt? How our blood slowed, our footsteps lagged? Brother Ass, we had been bashfully thinking of a kind of illumination such as Rimbaud dreamed of — a nagging poem which was not didactic or expository but which *infected* — was not simply a rationalised intuition,

10 on 13.5pt

Walking along the Mall we wondered who all those men were — tall hawk-featured men perched on balconies and high places, scanning the city with heavy binoculars. What were they seeking so earnestly? Who were they — so composed and steely-eyed? Timidly we stopped a policeman to ask him. 'They are publishers' he said mildly. Publishers! Our hearts stopped beating. 'They are on the look out for new talent.' Great God! It was for *us* they were waiting and watching! Then the kindly policeman lowered his voice confidentially and said in hollow and reverent tones: *'They are waiting for the new Trollope to be born!'* Do you remember, at these words, how heavy our suitcases suddenly felt? How our blood slowed, our footsteps lagged? Brother Ass, we had been bashfully thinking of a kind of illumi-

11 on 14.5pt

Monotype **Baskerville**

169 roman and italic
312 bold
Monotype 1923
Copyfitting factor 41.6/36.2/46.8

Range also includes semi-bold, semi-bold italic, bold italic

Linotype Baskerville No.2 is similar, but uses the slightly lighter and narrower bold of Linotype Baskerville. Copyfitting code 125/106/137. Range also includes medium, medium italic, bold italic, black, black italic

A regularised version of John Baskerville's 1757 Virgil Great Primer fount. It is difficult to realise today that Baskerville's types were never generally popular until Monotype's 1923 cutting

ABCDEFGHIJKLMNOP
QRSTUVWXYZ abcdefg
hijklmnopqrstuvwxyz
1234567890 1234567890
ff fi fl ffi ffl ( )[] & £ $.,;:-!?''

ABCDEFGHIJKLMNOP
QRSTUVWXYZ abcdefg
hijklmnopqrstuvwxyz
1234567890 1234567890
ff fi fl ffi ffl ( ) [ ] & £ $.,;:-!?''

ABCDEFGHIJKLMNOP
QRSTUVWXYZ abcdefg
hijklmnopqrstuvwxyz
1234567890 1234567890
ff fi fl ffi ffl ()[] & £ $.,;:-!?''

24 on 27pt

These examples show *normal* letterspacing and the effect of *reduced* letterspacing on roman setting *as well as on words in italic*: they also show the appearance of figures, for example 28 May 1964, within text. These & the ampersand are not included in the setting opposite.

Normal letterspacing

These examples show *normal* letterspacing and the effect of *reduced* letterspacing on roman setting *as well as on words in italic*: they also show the appearance of figures, for example 28 May 1964, within text. These & the ampersand are not included in the setting opposite.

Minus one unit spacing

These examples show *normal* letterspacing and the effect of *reduced* letterspacing on roman setting *as well as on words in italic*: they also show the appearance of figures, for example 28 May 1964, within text. These & the ampersand are not included in the setting opposite.

Minus two units spacing

WALKING ALONG THE MALL WE WONDERED WHO ALL
WALKING ALONG THE MALL WE WONDERED WHO
WALKING ALONG THE MALL WE WONDERED

Capitals: normal letterspacing/plus 9 units/plus 18 units

WALKING ALONG THE MALL WE WONDERED WHO ALL THOSE MEN WERE
WALKING ALONG THE MALL WE WONDERED WHO ALL THOSE MEN
WALKING ALONG THE MALL WE WONDERED WHO ALL THOSE

Small caps: normal letterspacing/plus 6 units/plus 12 units

WALKING ALONG THE MALL WE WONDERED WHO ALL THOSE MEN WERE
WALKING ALONG THE MALL WE WONDERED WHO ALL THOSE MEN WERE

True small caps/reduced capitals

WALKING ALONG THE MALL we wondered who all those men were
WALKING ALONG THE MALL we wondered who all those men were

True italic/sloped roman

Walking along the Mall we wondered who all those men were – tall hawk-featured men perched on balconies and high places, scanning the city with heavy binoculars. What were they seeking so earnestly? Who were they – so composed and steely-eyed? Timidly we stopped a policeman to ask him. 'They are publishers' he said mildly. Publishers! Our hearts stopped beating. 'They are on the look out for new talent.' Great God! It was for *us* they were waiting and watching! Then the kindly policeman lowered his voice confidentially and said in hollow and reverent tones: '*They are waiting for the new Trollope to be born!*' Do you remember, at these words, how heavy our suitcases suddenly felt? How our blood slowed, our footsteps lagged? Brother Ass, we had been bashfully thinking of a kind of illumination such as Rimbaud dreamed of – a nagging

8 on 9pt

WALKING ALONG THE MALL WE WONDERED WHO ALL THOSE MEN WERE – TALL HAWK-featured men perched on balconies and high places, scanning the city with heavy binoculars. What were they seeking so earnestly? Who were they – so composed and steely-eyed? Timidly we stopped a policeman to ask him. 'They are publishers' he said mildly. Publishers! Our hearts stopped beating. 'They are on the look out for new talent.' Great God! It was for *us* they were waiting and watching! Then the kindly policeman lowered his voice confidentially and said in hollow and reverent tones: '*They are waiting for the new Trollope to be born!*' Do you remember, at these words, how heavy our suitcases suddenly felt? How our blood slowed, our footsteps lagged? Brother Ass, we had been

8 on 10.5pt

Walking along the Mall we wondered who all those men were – tall
hawk-featured men perched on balconies and high places, scanning the city with
heavy binoculars. What were they seeking so earnestly? Who were they – so
composed and steely-eyed? Timidly we stopped a policeman to ask him. 'They are
publishers' he said mildly. Publishers! Our hearts stopped beating. 'They are on
the look out for new talent.' Great God! It was for *us* they were waiting and
watching! Then the kindly policeman lowered his voice confidentially and said in
hollow and reverent tones: '*They are waiting for the new Trollope to be born!*' Do you
remember, at these words, how heavy our suitcases suddenly felt? How our blood
slowed, our footsteps lagged? Brother Ass, we had been bashfully thinking of a
kind of illumination such as Rimbaud dreamed of – a nagging poem which was
not didactic or expository but which *infected* – was not simply a rationalised intuition, I mean, clothed in isinglass! We had come to the wrong shop, with the wrong
change! A chill struck us as we saw the mist falling in Trafalgar Square, coiling
around us its tendrils of ectoplasm! A million muffin-eating moralists were waiting, not for us, Brother Ass, but for the plucky and tedious Trollope! (If you are
dissatisfied with your form, reach for the *curette*.) Now do you wonder if I laugh a
little off-key? Do you ask yourself what has turned me into nature's bashful little

9 on 11pt

Walking along the Mall we wondered who all those men were –
tall hawk-featured men perched on balconies and high places, scanning
the city with heavy binoculars. What were they seeking so earnestly? Who
were they – so composed and steely-eyed? Timidly we stopped a policeman to ask him. 'They are publishers' he said mildly. Publishers! Our
hearts stopped beating. 'They are on the look out for new talent.' Great
God! It was for *us* they were waiting and watching! Then the kindly
policeman lowered his voice confidentially and said in hollow and reverent tones: '*They are waiting for the new Trollope to be born!*' Do you remember,
at these words, how heavy our suitcases suddenly felt? How our blood
slowed, our footsteps lagged? Brother Ass, we had been bashfully thinking
of a kind of illumination such as Rimbaud dreamed of – a nagging poem
which was not didactic or expository but which *infected* – was not simply a
rationalised intuition, I mean, clothed in isinglass! We had come to the
wrong shop, with the wrong change! A chill struck us as we saw the mist
falling in Trafalgar Square, coiling around us its tendrils of ectoplasm! A

10 on 12pt

Walking along the Mall we wondered who all those men
were – tall hawk-featured men perched on balconies and high
places, scanning the city with heavy binoculars. What were they
seeking so earnestly? Who were they – so composed and steely-
eyed? Timidly we stopped a policeman to ask him. 'They are publishers' he said mildly. Publishers! Our hearts stopped beating.
'They are on the look out for new talent.' Great God! It was for *us*
they were waiting and watching! Then the kindly policeman lowered his voice confidentially and said in hollow and reverent tones:
'*They are waiting for the new Trollope to be born!*' Do you remember, at
these words, how heavy our suitcases suddenly felt? How our blood
slowed, our footsteps lagged? Brother Ass, we had been bashfully
thinking of a kind of illumination such as Rimbaud dreamed of – a
nagging poem which was not didactic or expository but which
infected – was not simply a rationalised intuition, I mean, clothed in

11 on 13pt

WALKING ALONG THE MALL WE WONDERED WHO ALL THOSE MEN WERE – TALL
hawk-featured men perched on balconies and high places, scanning the city with
heavy binoculars. What were they seeking so earnestly? Who were they – so
composed and steely-eyed? Timidly we stopped a policeman to ask him. 'They are
publishers' he said mildly. Publishers! Our hearts stopped beating. 'They are on
the look out for new talent.' Great God! It was for *us* they were waiting and
watching! Then the kindly policeman lowered his voice confidentially and said in
hollow and reverent tones: '*They are waiting for the new Trollope to be born!*' Do you
remember, at these words, how heavy our suitcases suddenly felt? How our blood
slowed, our footsteps lagged? Brother Ass, we had been bashfully thinking of a
kind of illumination such as Rimbaud dreamed of – a nagging poem which was
not didactic or expository but which *infected* – was not simply a rationalised intuition, I mean, clothed in isinglass! We had come to the wrong shop, with the wrong
change! A chill struck us as we saw the mist falling in Trafalgar Square, coiling
around us its tendrils of ectoplasm! A million muffin-eating moralists were waiting, not for us, Brother Ass, but for the plucky and tedious Trollope! (If you are
dissatisfied with your form, reach for the *curette*.) Now do you wonder if I laugh a

9 on 12pt

WALKING ALONG THE MALL WE WONDERED WHO ALL THOSE MEN WERE –
tall hawk-featured men perched on balconies and high places, scanning
the city with heavy binoculars. What were they seeking so earnestly? Who
were they – so composed and steely-eyed? Timidly we stopped a policeman to ask him. 'They are publishers' he said mildly. Publishers! Our
hearts stopped beating. 'They are on the look out for new talent.' Great
God! It was for *us* they were waiting and watching! Then the kindly
policeman lowered his voice confidentially and said in hollow and reverent tones: '*They are waiting for the new Trollope to be born!*' Do you remember,
at these words, how heavy our suitcases suddenly felt? How our blood
slowed, our footsteps lagged? Brother Ass, we had been bashfully thinking
of a kind of illumination such as Rimbaud dreamed of – a nagging poem
which was not didactic or expository but which *infected* – was not simply a
rationalised intuition, I mean, clothed in isinglass! We had come to the
wrong shop, with the wrong change! A chill struck us as we saw the mist

10 on 13.5pt

WALKING ALONG THE MALL WE WONDERED WHO ALL THOSE MEN
were – tall hawk-featured men perched on balconies and high
places, scanning the city with heavy binoculars. What were they
seeking so earnestly? Who were they – so composed and steely-
eyed? Timidly we stopped a policeman to ask him. 'They are publishers' he said mildly. Publishers! Our hearts stopped beating.
'They are on the look out for new talent.' Great God! It was for *us*
they were waiting and watching! Then the kindly policeman lowered his voice confidentially and said in hollow and reverent tones:
'*They are waiting for the new Trollope to be born!*' Do you remember, at
these words, how heavy our suitcases suddenly felt? How our blood
slowed, our footsteps lagged? Brother Ass, we had been bashfully
thinking of a kind of illumination such as Rimbaud dreamed of – a
nagging poem which was not didactic or expository but which

11 on 14.5pt

Linotype **Baskerville**

roman (05456), **italic** (13456)
bold (07456)
Linotype 1930 (G W Jones)
(bold: 1939, C H Griffith)
Copyfitting code 132/114/137

Range also includes bold italic

The original hot metal design was a fairly true recutting of the Deberney & Peignot version cast from matrices made from Baskerville's punches

ABCDEFGHIJKLMNOP
QRSTUVWXYZ abcdefg
hijklmnopqrstuvwxyz
1234567890 1234567890
fifl ()[]&£$.,;:-!?"

ABCDEFGHIJKLMNOP
QRSTUVWXYZ abcdefg
hijklmnopqrstuvwxyz
1234567890 1234567890
fifl ()[]&£$.,;:-!?"

ABCDEFGHIJKLMNOP
QRSTUVWXYZ abcdefg
hijklmnopqrstuvwxyz
1234567890 1234567890
fifl ()[]&£$.,;:-!?"

24 on 27pt

These examples show *normal* letterspacing and the effect of *reduced* letterspacing on roman setting *as well as on words in italic*: they also show the appearance of figures, for example 28 May 1964, within text. These & the ampersand are not included in the setting opposite.
Normal letterspacing

These examples show *normal* letterspacing and the effect of *reduced* letterspacing on roman setting *as well as on words in italic*: they also show the appearance of figures, for example 28 May 1964, within text. These & the ampersand are not included in the setting opposite.
Minus one unit spacing

These examples show *normal* letterspacing and the effect of *reduced* letterspacing on roman setting *as well as on words in italic*: they also show the appearance of figures, for example 28 May 1964, within text. These & the ampersand are not included in the setting opposite.
Minus two units spacing

WALKING ALONG THE MALL WE WONDERED WHO ALL
WALKING ALONG THE MALL WE WONDERED WHO
WALKING ALONG THE MALL WE WONDERED
Capitals: normal letterspacing/plus 4 units/plus 9 units

WALKING ALONG THE MALL WE WONDERED WHO ALL THOSE MEN
WALKING ALONG THE MALL WE WONDERED WHO ALL THOSE MEN
WALKING ALONG THE MALL WE WONDERED WHO ALL THOSE
Small caps: normal letterspacing/plus 3 units/plus 6 units

WALKING ALONG THE MALL WE WONDERED WHO ALL THOSE MEN
WALKING ALONG THE MALL WE WONDERED WHO ALL THOSE MEN WERE
True small caps/reduced capitals

WALKING ALONG THE MALL we wondered who all those men were
WALKING ALONG THE MALL we wondered who all those men
True italic/sloped roman

Walking along the Mall we wondered who all those men were – tall hawk-featured men perched on balconies and high places, scanning the city with heavy binoculars. What were they seeking so earnestly? Who were they – so composed and steely-eyed? Timidly we stopped a policeman to ask him. 'They are publishers' he said mildly. Publishers! Our hearts stopped beating. 'They are on the look out for new talent.' Great God! It was for *us* they were waiting and watching! Then the kindly policeman lowered his voice confidentially and said in hollow and reverent tones: *'They are waiting for the new Trollope to be born!'* Do you remember, at these words, how heavy our suitcases suddenly felt? How our blood slowed, our footsteps lagged? Brother Ass, we had been bashfully thinking of a kind of illumination such as
8 on 9pt

WALKING ALONG THE MALL WE WONDERED WHO ALL THOSE MEN WERE – TALL HAWK-featured men perched on balconies and high places, scanning the city with heavy binoculars. What were they seeking so earnestly? Who were they – so composed and steely-eyed? Timidly we stopped a policeman to ask him. 'They are publishers' he said mildly. Publishers! Our hearts stopped beating. 'They are on the look out for new talent.' Great God! It was for *us* they were waiting and watching! Then the kindly policeman lowered his voice confidentially and said in hollow and reverent tones: *'They are waiting for the new Trollope to be born!'* Do you remember, at these words, how heavy our suitcases suddenly felt? How our blood slowed, our footsteps
8 on 10.5pt

Walking along the Mall we wondered who all those men were – tall hawk-featured men perched on balconies and high places, scanning the city with heavy binoculars. What were they seeking so earnestly? Who were they – so composed and steely-eyed? Timidly we stopped a policeman to ask him. 'They are publishers' he said mildly. Publishers! Our hearts stopped beating. 'They are on the look out for new talent.' Great God! It was for *us* they were waiting and watching! Then the kindly policeman lowered his voice confidentially and said in hollow and reverent tones: *'They are waiting for the new Trollope to be born!'* Do you remember, at these words, how heavy our suitcases suddenly felt? How our blood slowed, our footsteps lagged? Brother Ass, we had been bashfully thinking of a kind of illumination such as Rimbaud dreamed of – a nagging poem which was not didactic or expository but which *infected* – was not simply a rationalised intuition, I mean, clothed in isinglass! We had come to the wrong shop, with the wrong change! A chill struck us as we saw the mist falling in Trafalgar Square, coiling round us its tendrils of ectoplasm! A million muffin-eating moralists were waiting, not for us, Brother Ass, but for the plucky and tedious Trollope! (If you are dissatisfied with your form, reach

9 on 11pt

Walking along the Mall we wondered who all those men were – tall hawk-featured men perched on balconies and high places, scanning the city with heavy binoculars. What were they seeking so earnestly? Who were they – so composed and steely-eyed? Timidly we stopped a policeman to ask him. 'They are publishers' he said mildly. Publishers! Our hearts stopped beating. 'They are on the look out for new talent.' Great God! It was for *us* they were waiting and watching! Then the kindly policeman lowered his voice confidentially and said in hollow and reverent tones: *'They are waiting for the new Trollope to be born!'* Do you remember, at these words, how heavy our suitcases suddenly felt? How our blood slowed, our footsteps lagged? Brother Ass, we had been bashfully thinking of a kind of illumination such as Rimbaud dreamed of – a nagging poem which was not didactic or expository but which *infected* – was not simply a rationalised intuition, I mean, clothed in isinglass! We had come to the wrong shop, with the wrong change! A chill struck

10 on 12pt

Walking along the Mall we wondered who all those men were – tall hawk-featured men perched on balconies and high places, scanning the city with heavy binoculars. What were they seeking so earnestly? Who were they – so composed and steely-eyed? Timidly we stopped a policeman to ask him. 'They are publishers' he said mildly. Publishers! Our hearts stopped beating. 'They are on the look out for new talent.' Great God! It was for *us* they were waiting and watching! Then the kindly policeman lowered his voice confidentially and said in hollow and reverent tones: *'They are waiting for the new Trollope to be born!'* Do you remember, at these words, how heavy our suitcases suddenly felt? How our blood slowed, our footsteps lagged? Brother Ass, we had been bashfully thinking of a kind of illumination such as Rimbaud dreamed of – a nagging poem which was not didac-

11 on 13pt

WALKING ALONG THE MALL WE WONDERED WHO ALL THOSE MEN WERE – tall hawk-featured men perched on balconies and high places, scanning the city with heavy binoculars. What were they seeking so earnestly? Who were they – so composed and steely-eyed? Timidly we stopped a policeman to ask him. 'They are publishers' he said mildly. Publishers! Our hearts stopped beating. 'They are on the look out for new talent.' Great God! It was for *us* they were waiting and watching! Then the kindly policeman lowered his voice confidentially and said in hollow and reverent tones: *'They are waiting for the new Trollope to be born!'* Do you remember, at these words, how heavy our suitcases suddenly felt? How our blood slowed, our footsteps lagged? Brother Ass, we had been bashfully thinking of a kind of illumination such as Rimbaud dreamed of – a nagging poem which was not didactic or expository but which *infected* – was not simply a rationalised intuition, I mean, clothed in isinglass! We had come to the wrong shop, with the wrong change! A chill struck us as we saw the mist falling in Trafalgar Square, coiling round us its tendrils of ectoplasm! A million muffin-eating moralists were waiting, not for us, Brother Ass, but for the

9 on 12pt

WALKING ALONG THE MALL WE WONDERED WHO ALL THOSE MEN were – tall hawk-featured men perched on balconies and high places, scanning the city with heavy binoculars. What were they seeking so earnestly? Who were they – so composed and steely-eyed? Timidly we stopped a policeman to ask him. 'They are publishers' he said mildly. Publishers! Our hearts stopped beating. 'They are on the look out for new talent.' Great God! It was for *us* they were waiting and watching! Then the kindly policeman lowered his voice confidentially and said in hollow and reverent tones: *'They are waiting for the new Trollope to be born!'* Do you remember, at these words, how heavy our suitcases suddenly felt? How our blood slowed, our footsteps lagged? Brother Ass, we had been bashfully thinking of a kind of illumination such as Rimbaud dreamed of – a nagging poem which was not didactic or expository but which *infected* – was not simply a rationalised intuition, I mean,

10 on 13.5pt

WALKING ALONG THE MALL WE WONDERED WHO ALL THOSE men were – tall hawk-featured men perched on balconies and high places, scanning the city with heavy binoculars. What were they seeking so earnestly? Who were they – so composed and steely-eyed? Timidly we stopped a policeman to ask him. 'They are publishers' he said mildly. Publishers! Our hearts stopped beating. 'They are on the look out for new talent.' Great God! It was for *us* they were waiting and watching! Then the kindly policeman lowered his voice confidentially and said in hollow and reverent tones: *'They are waiting for the new Trollope to be born!'* Do you remember, at these words, how heavy our suitcases suddenly felt? How our blood slowed, our footsteps lagged? Brother Ass, we had been bashfully thinking of a kind of illumination such as

11 on 14.5pt

LINOTYPE BASKERVILLE

Monotype **Bell**

341 roman and italic
1235 bold
Monotype 1931 (bold: 1988)
Copyfitting factor 41.0/38.0/43.9

Range also includes semi-bold

The hot metal design was a facsimile from
punches cut in 1788 by Richard Austin for
John Bell

Alternative characters:

JkKQR
AÆhJKN
QRTV

ABCDEFGHIJKLMNOP
QRSTUVWXYZ abcdefg
hijklmnopqrstuvwxyz
1234567890
ff fi fl ffi ffl () [] & £ $. , ; : - ! ? " "

ABCDEFGHIJKLMNOP
QRSTUVWXYZ abcdefg
hijklmnopqrstuvwxyz
1234567890
ff fi fl ffi ffl () [] & £ $. , ; : - ! ? " "

ABCDEFGHIJKLMNOP
QRSTUVWXYZ abcdefg
hijklmnopqrstuvwxyz
1234567890
ff fi fl ffi ffl () [] & £ $. , ; : - ! ? " "

24 on 27pt

These examples show *normal* letterspacing and the effect of *reduced*
letterspacing on roman setting *as well as on words in italic:* they also
show the appearance of figures, for example 28 May 1964, within text.
These & the ampersand are not included in the setting opposite.
Normal letterspacing

These examples show *normal* letterspacing and the effect of *reduced*
letterspacing on roman setting *as well as on words in italic:* they also
show the appearance of figures, for example 28 May 1964, within text.
These & the ampersand are not included in the setting opposite.
Minus one unit spacing

These examples show *normal* letterspacing and the effect of *reduced*
letterspacing on roman setting *as well as on words in italic:* they also
show the appearance of figures, for example 28 May 1964, within text.
These & the ampersand are not included in the setting opposite.
Minus two units spacing

WALKING ALONG THE MALL WE WONDERED WHO ALL
WALKING ALONG THE MALL WE WONDERED WHO
WALKING ALONG THE MALL WE WONDERED
Capitals: normal letterspacing/plus 9 units/plus 18 units

WALKING ALONG THE MALL WE WONDERED WHO ALL THOSE MEN WERE
WALKING ALONG THE MALL WE WONDERED WHO ALL THOSE MEN WERE
WALKING ALONG THE MALL WE WONDERED WHO ALL THOSE MEN
Small caps: normal letterspacing/plus 6 units/plus 12 units

WALKING ALONG THE MALL WE WONDERED WHO ALL THOSE MEN WERE
WALKING ALONG THE MALL WE WONDERED WHO ALL THOSE MEN WERE
True small caps/reduced capitals

WALKING ALONG THE MALL we wondered who all those men were
WALKING ALONG THE MALL we wondered who all those men were
True italic/sloped roman

Walking along the Mall we wondered who all those men were – tall hawk-featured
men perched on balconies and high places, scanning the city with heavy binoculars. What
were they seeking so earnestly? Who were they – so composed and steely-eyed? Timidly
we stopped a policeman to ask him. 'They are publishers' he said mildly. Publishers!
Our hearts stopped beating. 'They are on the look out for new talent.' Great God! It was
for *us* they were waiting and watching! Then the kindly policeman lowered his voice
confidentially and said in hollow and reverent tones: *'They are waiting for the new Trollope to
be born!'* Do you remember, at these words, how heavy our suitcases suddenly felt? How our
blood slowed, our footsteps lagged? Brother Ass, we had been bashfully thinking of a kind
of illumination such as Rimbaud dreamed of – a nagging poem which was not didactic or

8 on 9pt

WALKING ALONG THE MALL WE WONDERED WHO ALL THOSE MEN WERE – TALL HAWK-
featured men perched on balconies and high places, scanning the city with heavy binoculars.
What were they seeking so earnestly? Who were they – so composed and steely-eyed?
Timidly we stopped a policeman to ask him. 'They are publishers' he said mildly.
Publishers! Our hearts stopped beating. 'They are on the look out for new talent.' Great
God! It was for *us* they were waiting and watching! Then the kindly policeman lowered his
voice confidentially and said in hollow and reverent tones: *'They are waiting for the new
Trollope to be born!'* Do you remember, at these words, how heavy our suitcases suddenly
felt? How our blood slowed, our footsteps lagged? Brother Ass, we had been bashfully

8 on 10.5pt

Walking along the Mall we wondered who all those men were – tall hawk- featured men perched on balconies and high places, scanning the city with heavy binoculars. What were they seeking so earnestly? Who were they – so composed and steely-eyed? Timidly we stopped a policeman to ask him. 'They are publishers' he said mildly. Publishers! Our hearts stopped beating. 'They are on the look out for new talent.' Great God! It was for *us* they were waiting and watching! Then the kindly policeman lowered his voice confidentially and said in hollow and reverent tones: *'They are waiting for the new Trollope to be born!'* Do you remember, at these words, how heavy our suitcases suddenly felt? How our blood slowed, our footsteps lagged? Brother Ass, we had been bashfully thinking of a kind of illumination such as Rimbaud dreamed of – a nagging poem which was not didactic or expository but which *infected* – was not simply a rationalised intuition, I mean, clothed in isinglass! We had come to the wrong shop, with the wrong change! A chill struck us as we saw the mist falling in Trafalgar Square, coiling around us its tendrils of ectoplasm! A million muffin-eating moralists were waiting, not for us, Brother Ass, but for the plucky and tedious Trollope! (If you are dissatisfied with your form, reach for the *curette*.) Now do you wonder if I laugh a little off-key? Do you ask yourself what has turned me into nature's bashful little aphorist? We who are, after all, simply poor

9 on 11pt

Walking along the Mall we wondered who all those men were – tall hawk-featured men perched on balconies and high places, scanning the city with heavy binoculars. What were they seeking so earnestly? Who were they – so composed and steely-eyed? Timidly we stopped a policeman to ask him. 'They are publishers' he said mildly. Publishers! Our hearts stopped beating. 'They are on the look out for new talent.' Great God! It was for *us* they were waiting and watching! Then the kindly policeman lowered his voice confidentially and said in hollow and reverent tones: *'They are waiting for the new Trollope to be born!'* Do you remember, at these words, how heavy our suitcases suddenly felt? How our blood slowed, our footsteps lagged? Brother Ass, we had been bashfully thinking of a kind of illumination such as Rimbaud dreamed of – a nagging poem which was not didactic or expository but which *infected* – was not simply a rationalised intuition, I mean, clothed in isinglass! We had come to the wrong shop, with the wrong change! A chill struck us as we saw the mist falling in Trafalgar Square, coiling around us its tendrils of ectoplasm! A million muffin-eating mor-

10 on 12pt

Walking along the Mall we wondered who all those men were – tall hawk-featured men perched on balconies and high places, scanning the city with heavy binoculars. What were they seeking so earnestly? Who were they – so composed and steely-eyed? Timidly we stopped a policeman to ask him. 'They are publishers' he said mildly. Publishers! Our hearts stopped beating. 'They are on the look out for new talent.' Great God! It was for *us* they were waiting and watching! Then the kindly policeman lowered his voice confidentially and said in hollow and reverent tones: *'They are waiting for the new Trollope to be born!'* Do you remember, at these words, how heavy our suitcases suddenly felt? How our blood slowed, our footsteps lagged? Brother Ass, we had been bashfully thinking of a kind of illumination such as Rimbaud dreamed of – a nagging poem which was not didactic or expository but which *infected* – was not simply a rationalised intuition, I mean, clothed in isinglass! We had come to

11 on 13pt

WALKING ALONG THE MALL WE WONDERED WHO ALL THOSE MEN WERE – TALL hawk-featured men perched on balconies and high places, scanning the city with heavy binoculars. What were they seeking so earnestly? Who were they – so composed and steely-eyed? Timidly we stopped a policeman to ask him. 'They are publishers' he said mildly. Publishers! Our hearts stopped beating. 'They are on the look out for new talent.' Great God! It was for *us* they were waiting and watching! Then the kindly policeman lowered his voice confidentially and said in hollow and reverent tones: *'They are waiting for the new Trollope to be born!'* Do you remember, at these words, how heavy our suitcases suddenly felt? How our blood slowed, our footsteps lagged? Brother Ass, we had been bashfully thinking of a kind of illumination such as Rimbaud dreamed of – a nagging poem which was not didactic or expository but which *infected* – was not simply a rationalised intuition, I mean, clothed in isinglass! We had come to the wrong shop, with the wrong change! A chill struck us as we saw the mist falling in Trafalgar Square, coiling around us its tendrils of ectoplasm! A million muffin-eating moralists were waiting, not for us, Brother Ass, but for the plucky and tedious Trollope! (If you are dissatisfied with your form, reach for the *curette*.) Now do you wonder if I laugh a little off-key? Do

9 on 12pt

WALKING ALONG THE MALL WE WONDERED WHO ALL THOSE MEN WERE – tall hawk-featured men perched on balconies and high places, scanning the city with heavy binoculars. What were they seeking so earnestly? Who were they – so composed and steely-eyed? Timidly we stopped a policeman to ask him. 'They are publishers' he said mildly. Publishers! Our hearts stopped beating. 'They are on the look out for new talent.' Great God! It was for *us* they were waiting and watching! Then the kindly policeman lowered his voice confidentially and said in hollow and reverent tones: *'They are waiting for the new Trollope to be born!'* Do you remember, at these words, how heavy our suitcases suddenly felt? How our blood slowed, our footsteps lagged? Brother Ass, we had been bashfully thinking of a kind of illumination such as Rimbaud dreamed of – a nagging poem which was not didactic or expository but which *infected* – was not simply a rationalised intuition, I mean, clothed in isinglass! We had come to the wrong shop, with the wrong change! A chill struck us as we saw the mist falling in Trafalgar

10 on 13.5pt

WALKING ALONG THE MALL WE WONDERED WHO ALL THOSE MEN were – tall hawk-featured men perched on balconies and high places, scanning the city with heavy binoculars. What were they seeking so earnestly? Who were they – so composed and steely-eyed? Timidly we stopped a policeman to ask him. 'They are publishers' he said mildly. Publishers! Our hearts stopped beating. 'They are on the look out for new talent.' Great God! It was for *us* they were waiting and watching! Then the kindly policeman lowered his voice confidentially and said in hollow and reverent tones: *'They are waiting for the new Trollope to be born!'* Do you remember, at these words, how heavy our suitcases suddenly felt? How our blood slowed, our footsteps lagged? Brother Ass, we had been bashfully thinking of a kind of illumination such as Rimbaud dreamed of – a nagging poem which was not didactic or expository but which *infected* – was not

11 on 14.5pt

Monotype **Bembo**

270 roman and italic
428 bold
Monotype 1929 (bold: 1932)
Copyfitting factor 40.9/37.0/45.0

Range also includes semi-bold, semi-bold italic, bold italic, extra bold, extra bold italic

Derived from Aldus Manutius's *De Aetna* roman of 1495, with capitals lightened and regularised. The italic is from revised chancery types used and probably designed by Giovantonio Tagliente

Educational characters available

Also shown here is the long-tailed R. This is actually the standard form; the alternative short-tailed R is shown in the alphabet

R *R* **R**

ABCDEFGHIJKLMNOP
QRSTUVWXYZ abcdefg
hijklmnopqrstuvwxyz
1234567890 1234567890
fffiflffiffl ()[]&£$.,;:-!?''

ABCDEFGHIJKLMNOP
QRSTUVWXYZ abcdefg
hijklmnopqrstuvwxyz
1234567890 1234567890
fffiflffiffl ()[]&£$.,;:-!?''

ABCDEFGHIJKLMNOP
QRSTUVWXYZ abcdefg
hijklmnopqrstuvwxyz
1234567890 1234567890
ff fi fl ffi ffl ()[]&£$.,;:-!?''

24 on 27pt

These examples show *normal* letterspacing and the effect of *reduced* letterspacing on roman setting *as well as on words in italic*: they also show the appearance of figures, for example 28 May 1964, within text. These & the ampersand are not included in the setting opposite.

Normal letterspacing

These examples show *normal* letterspacing and the effect of *reduced* letterspacing on roman setting *as well as on words in italic*: they also show the appearance of figures, for example 28 May 1964, within text. These & the ampersand are not included in the setting opposite.

Minus one unit spacing

These examples show *normal* letterspacing and the effect of *reduced* letterspacing on roman setting *as well as on words in italic*: they also show the appearance of figures, for example 28 May 1964, within text. These & the ampersand are not included in the setting opposite.

Minus two units spacing

WALKING ALONG THE MALL WE WONDERED WHO ALL
WALKING ALONG THE MALL WE WONDERED WHO
WALKING ALONG THE MALL WE WONDERED

Capitals: normal letterspacing/plus 9 units/plus 18 units

WALKING ALONG THE MALL WE WONDERED WHO ALL THOSE MEN WERE
WALKING ALONG THE MALL WE WONDERED WHO ALL THOSE MEN WERE
WALKING ALONG THE MALL WE WONDERED WHO ALL THOSE MEN

Small caps: normal letterspacing/plus 6 units/plus 12 units

WALKING ALONG THE MALL WE WONDERED WHO ALL THOSE MEN WERE
WALKING ALONG THE MALL WE WONDERED WHO ALL THOSE MEN WERE

True small caps/reduced capitals

WALKING ALONG THE MALL we wondered who all those men were
WALKING ALONG THE MALL we wondered who all those men were

True italic/sloped roman

Walking along the Mall we wondered who all those men were – tall hawk-featured men perched on balconies and high places, scanning the city with heavy binoculars. What were they seeking so earnestly? Who were they – so composed and steely-eyed? Timidly we stopped a policeman to ask him. 'They are publishers' he said mildly. Publishers! Our hearts stopped beating. 'They are on the look out for new talent.' Great God! It was for *us* they were waiting and watching! Then the kindly policeman lowered his voice confidentially and said in hollow and reverent tones: '*They are waiting for the new Trollope to be born!*' Do you remember, at these words, how heavy our suitcases suddenly felt? How our blood slowed, our footsteps lagged? Brother Ass, we had been bashfully thinking of a kind of illumination such as Rimbaud dreamed of – a nagging poem which was not didactic or expository but

8 on 9pt

WALKING ALONG THE MALL WE WONDERED WHO ALL THOSE MEN WERE – TALL HAWK-featured men perched on balconies and high places, scanning the city with heavy binoculars. What were they seeking so earnestly? Who were they – so composed and steely-eyed? Timidly we stopped a policeman to ask him. 'They are publishers' he said mildly. Publishers! Our hearts stopped beating. 'They are on the look out for new talent.' Great God! It was for *us* they were waiting and watching! Then the kindly policeman lowered his voice confidentially and said in hollow and reverent tones: '*They are waiting for the new Trollope to be born!*' Do you remember, at these words, how heavy our suitcases suddenly felt? How our blood slowed, our footsteps lagged? Brother Ass, we had been bashfully thinking of a kind of

8 on 10.5pt

Walking along the Mall we wondered who all those men were – tall hawk-featured men perched on balconies and high places, scanning the city with heavy binoculars. What were they seeking so earnestly? Who were they – so composed and steely-eyed? Timidly we stopped a policeman to ask him. 'They are publishers' he said mildly. Publishers! Our hearts stopped beating. 'They are on the look out for new talent.' Great God! It was for *us* they were waiting and watching! Then the kindly policeman lowered his voice confidentially and said in hollow and reverent tones: '*They are waiting for the new Trollope to be born!*' Do you remember, at these words, how heavy our suitcases suddenly felt? How our blood slowed, our footsteps lagged? Brother Ass, we had been bashfully thinking of a kind of illumination such as Rimbaud dreamed of – a nagging poem which was not didactic or expository but which *infected* – was not simply a rationalised intuition, I mean, clothed in isinglass! We had come to the wrong shop, with the wrong change! A chill struck us as we saw the mist falling in Trafalgar Square, coiling around us its tendrils of ectoplasm! A million muffin-eating moralists were waiting, not for us, Brother Ass, but for the plucky and tedious Trollope! (If you are dissatisfied with your form, reach for the *curette*.) Now do you wonder if I laugh a little off-key? Do you ask yourself what has turned me into nature's bashful little aphorist? We who are, after all, simply poor

9 on 11pt

Walking along the Mall we wondered who all those men were – tall hawk-featured men perched on balconies and high places, scanning the city with heavy binoculars. What were they seeking so earnestly? Who were they – so composed and steely-eyed? Timidly we stopped a policeman to ask him. 'They are publishers' he said mildly. Publishers! Our hearts stopped beating. 'They are on the look out for new talent.' Great God! It was for *us* they were waiting and watching! Then the kindly policeman lowered his voice confidentially and said in hollow and reverent tones: '*They are waiting for the new Trollope to be born!*' Do you remember, at these words, how heavy our suitcases suddenly felt? How our blood slowed, our footsteps lagged? Brother Ass, we had been bashfully thinking of a kind of illumination such as Rimbaud dreamed of – a nagging poem which was not didactic or expository but which *infected* – was not simply a rationalised intuition, I mean, clothed in isinglass! We had come to the wrong shop, with the wrong change! A chill struck us as we saw the mist falling in Trafalgar Square, coiling around us its tendrils of ectoplasm! A million muffin-eating moralists

10 on 12pt

Walking along the Mall we wondered who all those men were – tall hawk-featured men perched on balconies and high places, scanning the city with heavy binoculars. What were they seeking so earnestly? Who were they – so composed and steely-eyed? Timidly we stopped a policeman to ask him. 'They are publishers' he said mildly. Publishers! Our hearts stopped beating. 'They are on the look out for new talent.' Great God! It was for *us* they were waiting and watching! Then the kindly policeman lowered his voice confidentially and said in hollow and reverent tones: '*They are waiting for the new Trollope to be born!*' Do you remember, at these words, how heavy our suitcases suddenly felt? How our blood slowed, our footsteps lagged? Brother Ass, we had been bashfully thinking of a kind of illumination such as Rimbaud dreamed of – a nagging poem which was not didactic or expository but which *infected* – was not simply a rationalised intuition, I mean, clothed in isinglass! We had come to the wrong shop,

11 on 13pt

WALKING ALONG THE MALL WE WONDERED WHO ALL THOSE MEN WERE – TALL hawk-featured men perched on balconies and high places, scanning the city with heavy binoculars. What were they seeking so earnestly? Who were they – so composed and steely-eyed? Timidly we stopped a policeman to ask him. 'They are publishers' he said mildly. Publishers! Our hearts stopped beating. 'They are on the look out for new talent.' Great God! It was for *us* they were waiting and watching! Then the kindly policeman lowered his voice confidentially and said in hollow and reverent tones: '*They are waiting for the new Trollope to be born!*' Do you remember, at these words, how heavy our suitcases suddenly felt? How our blood slowed, our footsteps lagged? Brother Ass, we had been bashfully thinking of a kind of illumination such as Rimbaud dreamed of – a nagging poem which was not didactic or expository but which *infected* – was not simply a rationalised intuition, I mean, clothed in isinglass! We had come to the wrong shop, with the wrong change! A chill struck us as we saw the mist falling in Trafalgar Square, coiling around us its tendrils of ectoplasm! A million muffin-eating moralists were waiting, not for us, Brother Ass, but for the plucky and tedious Trollope! (If you are dissatisfied with your form, reach for the *curette*.) Now do you wonder if I laugh a little off-key? Do you ask

9 on 12pt

WALKING ALONG THE MALL WE WONDERED WHO ALL THOSE MEN WERE – tall hawk-featured men perched on balconies and high places, scanning the city with heavy binoculars. What were they seeking so earnestly? Who were they – so composed and steely-eyed? Timidly we stopped a policeman to ask him. 'They are publishers' he said mildly. Publishers! Our hearts stopped beating. 'They are on the look out for new talent.' Great God! It was for *us* they were waiting and watching! Then the kindly policeman lowered his voice confidentially and said in hollow and reverent tones: '*They are waiting for the new Trollope to be born!*' Do you remember, at these words, how heavy our suitcases suddenly felt? How our blood slowed, our footsteps lagged? Brother Ass, we had been bashfully thinking of a kind of illumination such as Rimbaud dreamed of – a nagging poem which was not didactic or expository but which *infected* – was not simply a rationalised intuition, I mean, clothed in isinglass! We had come to the wrong shop, with the wrong change! A chill struck us as we saw the mist falling in Trafalgar Square,

10 on 13.5pt

WALKING ALONG THE MALL WE WONDERED WHO ALL THOSE MEN were – tall hawk-featured men perched on balconies and high places, scanning the city with heavy binoculars. What were they seeking so earnestly? Who were they – so composed and steely-eyed? Timidly we stopped a policeman to ask him. 'They are publishers' he said mildly. Publishers! Our hearts stopped beating. 'They are on the look out for new talent.' Great God! It was for *us* they were waiting and watching! Then the kindly policeman lowered his voice confidentially and said in hollow and reverent tones: '*They are waiting for the new Trollope to be born!*' Do you remember, at these words, how heavy our suitcases suddenly felt? How our blood slowed, our footsteps lagged? Brother Ass, we had been bashfully thinking of a kind of illumination such as Rimbaud dreamed of – a nagging poem which was not didactic or expository but which *infected* – was not simply a

11 on 14.5pt

MONOTYPE BEMBO

Linotype **Bembo**

roman (05023), **italic** (13023)
bold (07023)
Monotype 1929 (bold: 1932)
Copyfitting code 130/115/145

Range also includes medium, medium italic,
bold italic, black, black italic

Educational characters available

See Monotype Bembo

ABCDEFGHIJKLMNOP
QRSTUVWXYZ abcdefg
hijklmnopqrstuvwxyz
1234567890 1234567890
fifl ()[]&£$.,;:-!?''

ABCDEFGHIJKLMNOP
QRSTUVWXYZ abcdefg
hijklmnopqrstuvwxyz
1234567890 1234567890
fifl ()[]&£$.,;:-!?''

ABCDEFGHIJKLMNOP
QRSTUVWXYZ abcdefg
hijklmnopqrstuvwxyz
1234567890 1234567890
fifl ()[]&£$.,;:-!?''

24 on 27pt

These examples show *normal* letterspacing and the effect of *reduced*
letterspacing on roman setting *as well as on words in italic*: they also
show the appearance of figures, for example 28 May 1964, within text.
These & the ampersand are not included in the setting opposite.
Normal letterspacing

These examples show *normal* letterspacing and the effect of *reduced*
letterspacing on roman setting *as well as on words in italic*: they also
show the appearance of figures, for example 28 May 1964, within text.
These & the ampersand are not included in the setting opposite.
Minus one unit spacing

These examples show *normal* letterspacing and the effect of *reduced*
letterspacing on roman setting *as well as on words in italic*: they also
show the appearance of figures, for example 28 May 1964, within text.
These & the ampersand are not included in the setting opposite.
Minus two units spacing

WALKING ALONG THE MALL WE WONDERED WHO ALL
WALKING ALONG THE MALL WE WONDERED WHO
WALKING ALONG THE MALL WE WONDERED
Capitals: normal letterspacing/plus 4 units/plus 9 units

WALKING ALONG THE MALL WE WONDERED WHO ALL THOSE MEN WERE
WALKING ALONG THE MALL WE WONDERED WHO ALL THOSE MEN
WALKING ALONG THE MALL WE WONDERED WHO ALL THOSE
Small caps: normal letterspacing/plus 3 units/plus 6 units

WALKING ALONG THE MALL WE WONDERED WHO ALL THOSE MEN WERE
WALKING ALONG THE MALL WE WONDERED WHO ALL THOSE MEN WERE
True small caps/reduced capitals

WALKING ALONG THE MALL we wondered who all those men were
WALKING ALONG THE MALL we wondered who all those men
True italic/sloped roman

Walking along the Mall we wondered who all those men were – tall hawk-
featured men perched on balconies and high places, scanning the city with heavy
binoculars. What were they seeking so earnestly? Who were they – so composed and
steely-eyed? Timidly we stopped a policeman to ask him. 'They are publishers' he said
mildly. Publishers! Our hearts stopped beating. 'They are on the look out for new
talent.' Great God! It was for *us* they were waiting and watching! Then the kindly
policeman lowered his voice confidentially and said in hollow and reverent tones: *'They
are waiting for the new Trollope to be born!'* Do you remember, at these words, how heavy
our suitcases suddenly felt? How our blood slowed, our footsteps lagged? Brother Ass,
we had been bashfully thinking of a kind of illumination such as Rimbaud dreamed of
8 on 9pt

WALKING ALONG THE MALL WE WONDERED WHO ALL THOSE MEN WERE – TALL HAWK-
featured men perched on balconies and high places, scanning the city with heavy
binoculars. What were they seeking so earnestly? Who were they – so composed and
steely-eyed? Timidly we stopped a policeman to ask him. 'They are publishers' he said
mildly. Publishers! Our hearts stopped beating. 'They are on the look out for new
talent.' Great God! It was for *us* they were waiting and watching! Then the kindly
policeman lowered his voice confidentially and said in hollow and reverent tones: *'They
are waiting for the new Trollope to be born!'* Do you remember, at these words, how heavy
our suitcases suddenly felt? How our blood slowed, our footsteps lagged? Brother Ass,
8 on 10.5pt

Walking along the Mall we wondered who all those men were – tall hawk-featured men perched on balconies and high places, scanning the city with heavy binoculars. What were they seeking so earnestly? Who were they – so composed and steely-eyed? Timidly we stopped a policeman to ask him. 'They are publishers' he said mildly. Publishers! Our hearts stopped beating. 'They are on the look out for new talent.' Great God! It was for *us* they were waiting and watching! Then the kindly policeman lowered his voice confidentially and said in hollow and reverent tones: *'They are waiting for the new Trollope to be born!'* Do you remember, at these words, how heavy our suitcases suddenly felt? How our blood slowed, our footsteps lagged? Brother Ass, we had been bashfully thinking of a kind of illumination such as Rimbaud dreamed of – a nagging poem which was not didactic or expository but which *infected* – was not simply a rationalised intuition, I mean, clothed in isinglass! We had come to the wrong shop, with the wrong change! A chill struck us as we saw the mist falling in Trafalgar Square, coiling round us its tendrils of ectoplasm! A million muffin-eating moralists were waiting, not for us, Brother Ass, but for the plucky and tedious Trollope! (If you are dissatisfied with your form, reach for the *curette*.) Now do you wonder if I laugh

9 on 11pt

Walking along the Mall we wondered who all those men were – tall hawk-featured men perched on balconies and high places, scanning the city with heavy binoculars. What were they seeking so earnestly? Who were they – so composed and steely-eyed? Timidly we stopped a policeman to ask him. 'They are publishers' he said mildly. Publishers! Our hearts stopped beating. 'They are on the look out for new talent.' Great God! It was for *us* they were waiting and watching! Then the kindly policeman lowered his voice confidentially and said in hollow and reverent tones: *'They are waiting for the new Trollope to be born!'* Do you remember, at these words, how heavy our suitcases suddenly felt? How our blood slowed, our footsteps lagged? Brother Ass, we had been bashfully thinking of a kind of illumination such as Rimbaud dreamed of – a nagging poem which was not didactic or expository but which *infected* – was not simply a rationalised intuition. I mean, clothed in isinglass! We had come to the wrong shop, with the wrong change! A chill struck us as we saw the mist falling in Trafalgar

10 on 12pt

Walking along the Mall we wondered who all those men were – tall hawk-featured men perched on balconies and high places, scanning the city with heavy binoculars. What were they seeking so earnestly? Who were they – so composed and steely-eyed? Timidly we stopped a policeman to ask him. 'They are publishers' he said mildly. Publishers! Our hearts stopped beating. 'They are on the look out for new talent.' Great God! It was for *us* they were waiting and watching! Then the kindly policeman lowered his voice confidentially and said in hollow and reverent tones: *'They are waiting for the new Trollope to be born!'* Do you remember, at these words, how heavy our suitcases suddenly felt? How our blood slowed, our footsteps lagged? Brother Ass, we had been bashfully thinking of a kind of illumination such as Rimbaud dreamed of – a nagging poem which was not didactic or expository but which *infected* – was

11 on 13pt

WALKING ALONG THE MALL WE WONDERED WHO ALL THOSE MEN WERE – TALL hawk-featured men perched on balconies and high places, scanning the city with heavy binoculars. What were they seeking so earnestly? Who were they – so composed and steely-eyed? Timidly we stopped a policeman to ask him. 'They are publishers' he said mildly. Publishers! Our hearts stopped beating. 'They are on the look out for new talent.' Great God! It was for *us* they were waiting and watching! Then the kindly policeman lowered his voice confidentially and said in hollow and reverent tones: *'They are waiting for the new Trollope to be born!'* Do you remember, at these words, how heavy our suitcases suddenly felt? How our blood slowed, our footsteps lagged? Brother Ass, we had been bashfully thinking of a kind of illumination such as Rimbaud dreamed of – a nagging poem which was not didactic or expository but which *infected* – was not simply a rationalised intuition, I mean, clothed in isinglass! We had come to the wrong shop, with the wrong change! A chill struck us as we saw the mist falling in Trafalgar Square, coiling round us its tendrils of ectoplasm! A million muffin-eating moralists were waiting, not for us, Brother Ass, but for the plucky and tedious Trollope! (If you are dis-

9 on 12pt

WALKING ALONG THE MALL WE WONDERED WHO ALL THOSE MEN WERE – tall hawk-featured men perched on balconies and high places, scanning the city with heavy binoculars. What were they seeking so earnestly? Who were they – so composed and steely-eyed? Timidly we stopped a policeman to ask him. 'They are publishers' he said mildly. Publishers! Our hearts stopped beating. 'They are on the look out for new talent.' Great God! It was for *us* they were waiting and watching! Then the kindly policeman lowered his voice confidentially and said in hollow and reverent tones: *'They are waiting for the new Trollope to be born!'* Do you remember, at these words, how heavy our suitcases suddenly felt? How our blood slowed, our footsteps lagged? Brother Ass, we had been bashfully thinking of a kind of illumination such as Rimbaud dreamed of – a nagging poem which was not didactic or expository but which *infected* – was not simply a rationalised intuition. I mean, clothed in isinglass! We had come to the wrong shop, with the

10 on 13.5pt

WALKING ALONG THE MALL WE WONDERED WHO ALL THOSE MEN were – tall hawk-featured men perched on balconies and high places, scanning the city with heavy binoculars. What were they seeking so earnestly? Who were they – so composed and steely-eyed? Timidly we stopped a policeman to ask him. 'They are publishers' he said mildly. Publishers! Our hearts stopped beating. 'They are on the look out for new talent.' Great God! It was for *us* they were waiting and watching! Then the kindly policeman lowered his voice confidentially and said in hollow and reverent tones: *'They are waiting for the new Trollope to be born!'* Do you remember, at these words, how heavy our suitcases suddenly felt? How our blood slowed, our footsteps lagged? Brother Ass, we had been bashfully thinking of a kind of illumination such as Rimbaud dreamed of – a nagging poem

11 on 14.5pt

Monotype **Berkeley Old Style**

1114 medium and medium italic
1115 bold
ITC 1981 (Tony Stan)
Copyfitting factor 41.0/38.7/41.3

Range also includes book, book italic, bold
italic, black, black italic

The Linotype version is similar (copyfitting
code 123/115/126)

Based upon Goudy's Californian, designed for
The University of California in 1939

ABCDEFGHIJKLMNOP
QRSTUVWXYZ abcdefg
hijklmnopqrstuvwxyz
1234567890
ff fi fl ffi ffl () []&£$.,;:-!?''

ABCDEFGHIJKLMNOP
QRSTUVWXYZ abcdefg
hijklmnopqrstuvwxyz
1234567890
ff fi fl ffi ffl () []&£$.,;:-!?''

ABCDEFGHIJKLMNOP
QRSTUVWXYZ abcdefg
hijklmnopqrstuvwxyz
1234567890
ff fi fl ffi ffl () [] &£$.,;:-!?''

24 on 27pt

These examples show *normal* letterspacing and the effect of *reduced*
letterspacing on roman setting *as well as on words in italic*: they also
show the appearance of figures, for example 28 May 1964, within text.
These & the ampersand are not included in the setting opposite.

Normal letterspacing

These examples show *normal* letterspacing and the effect of *reduced*
letterspacing on roman setting *as well as on words in italic*: they also
show the appearance of figures, for example 28 May 1964, within text.
These & the ampersand are not included in the setting opposite.

Minus one unit spacing

These examples show *normal* letterspacing and the effect of *reduced*
letterspacing on roman setting *as well as on words in italic*: they also
show the appearance of figures, for example 28 May 1964, within text.
These & the ampersand are not included in the setting opposite.

Minus two units spacing

WALKING ALONG THE MALL WE WONDERED WHO ALL THOSE MEN
WALKING ALONG THE MALL WE WONDERED WHO ALL
WALKING ALONG THE MALL WE WONDERED WHO

Capitals: normal letterspacing/plus 9 units/plus 18 units

Walking along the Mall we wondered who all those men were – tall hawk-
featured men perched on balconies and high places, scanning the city
with heavy binoculars. WHAT WERE THEY SEEKING SO EARNESTLY? Who were
they – so composed and steely-eyed? Timidly we stopped a policeman to
ask him. 'THEY ARE PUBLISHERS' he said mildly. Publishers! Our hearts
stopped beating. 'They are on the look out for new talent.' Great God! It
was for *us* they were waiting and watching! Then the kindly policeman

Text with reduced capitals normal letterspacing/plus 6 units

WALKING ALONG THE MALL we wondered who all those men were
WALKING ALONG THE MALL we wondered who all those men were

True italic/sloped roman

Walking along the Mall we wondered who all those men were – tall hawk-featured men
perched on balconies and high places, scanning the city with heavy binoculars. What were
they seeking so earnestly? Who were they – so composed and steely-eyed? Timidly we
stopped a policeman to ask him. 'They are publishers' he said mildly. Publishers! Our hearts
stopped beating. 'They are on the look out for new talent.' Great God! It was for *us* they were
waiting and watching! Then the kindly policeman lowered his voice confidentially and said
in hollow and reverent tones: *'They are waiting for the new Trollope to be born!'* Do you
remember, at these words, how heavy our suitcases suddenly felt? How our blood slowed,
our footsteps lagged? Brother Ass, we had been bashfully thinking of a kind of illumination
such as Rimbaud dreamed of – a nagging poem which was not didactic or expository but

8 on 9pt

Walking along the Mall we wondered who all those men were – tall hawk-featured men
perched on balconies and high places, scanning the city with heavy binoculars. What were
they seeking so earnestly? Who were they – so composed and steely-eyed? Timidly we
stopped a policeman to ask him. 'They are publishers' he said mildly. Publishers! Our hearts
stopped beating. 'They are on the look out for new talent.' *Great God!* It was for *us* they were
waiting and watching! Then the kindly policeman lowered his voice confidentially and said
in hollow and reverent tones: *They are waiting for the new Trollope to be born!* Do you
remember, at these words, how heavy our suitcases suddenly felt? How our blood slowed,
our footsteps lagged? Brother Ass, we had been bashfully thinking of a kind of illumination

8 on 10.5pt

Walking along the Mall we wondered who all those men were – tall hawk-featured men perched on balconies and high places, scanning the city with heavy binoculars. What were they seeking so earnestly? Who were they – so composed and steely-eyed? Timidly we stopped a policeman to ask him. 'They are publishers' he said mildly. Publishers! Our hearts stopped beating. 'They are on the look out for new talent.' Great God! It was for *us* they were waiting and watching! Then the kindly policeman lowered his voice confidentially and said in hollow and reverent tones: *'They are waiting for the new Trollope to be born!'* Do you remember, at these words, how heavy our suitcases suddenly felt? How our blood slowed, our footsteps lagged? Brother Ass, we had been bashfully thinking of a kind of illumination such as Rimbaud dreamed of – a nagging poem which was not didactic or expository but which *infected* – was not simply a rationalised intuition, I mean, clothed in isinglass! We had come to the wrong shop, with the wrong change! A chill struck us as we saw the mist falling in Trafalgar Square, coiling around us its tendrils of ectoplasm! A million muffin-eating moralists were waiting, not for us, Brother Ass, but for the plucky and tedious Trollope! (If you are dissatisfied with your form, reach for the *curette*.) Now do you wonder if I laugh a little off-key? Do you ask yourself what has turned me into nature's bashful little aphorist? We who are, after all, simply poor

9 on 11pt

Walking along the Mall we wondered who all those men were – tall hawk-featured men perched on balconies and high places, scanning the city with heavy binoculars. What were they seeking so earnestly? Who were they – so composed and steely-eyed? Timidly we stopped a policeman to ask him. 'They are publishers' he said mildly. Publishers! Our hearts stopped beating. 'They are on the look out for new talent.' Great God! It was for *us* they were waiting and watching! Then the kindly policeman lowered his voice confidentially and said in hollow and reverent tones: *'They are waiting for the new Trollope to be born!'* Do you remember, at these words, how heavy our suitcases suddenly felt? How our blood slowed, our footsteps lagged? Brother Ass, we had been bashfully thinking of a kind of illumination such as Rimbaud dreamed of – a nagging poem which was not didactic or expository but which *infected* – was not simply a rationalised intuition, I mean, clothed in isinglass! We had come to the wrong shop, with the wrong change! A chill struck us as we saw the mist falling in Trafalgar Square, coiling around us its tendrils of ectoplasm! A million muffin-eating moralists were waiting, not for us, Brother Ass, but for the plucky and tedious Trollope! (If you are dissatisfied with your form, reach for the *curette*.) Now do you wonder if I laugh a little off-key? Do you ask yourself what has

9 on 12pt

Walking along the Mall we wondered who all those men were – tall hawk-featured men perched on balconies and high places, scanning the city with heavy binoculars. What were they seeking so earnestly? Who were they – so composed and steely-eyed? Timidly we stopped a policeman to ask him. 'They are publishers' he said mildly. Publishers! Our hearts stopped beating. 'They are on the look out for new talent.' Great God! It was for *us* they were waiting and watching! Then the kindly policeman lowered his voice confidentially and said in hollow and reverent tones: *'They are waiting for the new Trollope to be born!'* Do you remember, at these words, how heavy our suitcases suddenly felt? How our blood slowed, our footsteps lagged? Brother Ass, we had been bashfully thinking of a kind of illumination such as Rimbaud dreamed of – a nagging poem which was not didactic or expository but which *infected* – was not simply a rationalised intuition, I mean, clothed in isinglass! We had come to the wrong shop, with the wrong change! A chill struck us as we saw the mist falling in Trafalgar Square, coiling around us its tendrils of ectoplasm! A million muffin-eating moralists were waiting, not

10 on 12pt

Walking along the Mall we wondered who all those men were – tall hawk-featured men perched on balconies and high places, scanning the city with heavy binoculars. What were they seeking so earnestly? Who were they – so composed and steely-eyed? Timidly we stopped a policeman to ask him. 'They are publishers' he said mildly. Publishers! Our hearts stopped beating. 'They are on the look out for new talent.' Great God! It was for *us* they were waiting and watching! Then the kindly policeman lowered his voice confidentially and said in hollow and reverent tones: *'They are waiting for the new Trollope to be born!'* Do you remember, at these words, how heavy our suitcases suddenly felt? How our blood slowed, our footsteps lagged? Brother Ass, we had been bashfully thinking of a kind of illumination such as Rimbaud dreamed of – a nagging poem which was not didactic or expository but which *infected* – was not simply a rationalised intuition, I mean, clothed in isinglass! We had come to the wrong shop, with the wrong change! A chill struck us as we saw the mist falling in Trafalgar Square, coiling around us its

10 on 13.5pt

Walking along the Mall we wondered who all those men were – tall hawk-featured men perched on balconies and high places, scanning the city with heavy binoculars. What were they seeking so earnestly? Who were they – so composed and steely-eyed? Timidly we stopped a policeman to ask him. 'They are publishers' he said mildly. Publishers! Our hearts stopped beating. 'They are on the look out for new talent.' Great God! It was for *us* they were waiting and watching! Then the kindly policeman lowered his voice confidentially and said in hollow and reverent tones: *'They are waiting for the new Trollope to be born!'* Do you remember, at these words, how heavy our suitcases suddenly felt? How our blood slowed, our footsteps lagged? Brother Ass, we had been bashfully thinking of a kind of illumination such as Rimbaud dreamed of – a nagging poem which was not didactic or expository but which *infected* – was not simply a rationalised intuition, I mean, clothed in isinglass! We had come to the wrong shop,

11 on 13pt

Walking along the Mall we wondered who all those men were – tall hawk-featured men perched on balconies and high places, scanning the city with heavy binoculars. What were they seeking so earnestly? Who were they – so composed and steely-eyed? Timidly we stopped a policeman to ask him. 'They are publishers' he said mildly. Publishers! Our hearts stopped beating. 'They are on the look out for new talent.' Great God! It was for *us* they were waiting and watching! Then the kindly policeman lowered his voice confidentially and said in hollow and reverent tones: *'They are waiting for the new Trollope to be born!'* Do you remember, at these words, how heavy our suitcases suddenly felt? How our blood slowed, our footsteps lagged? Brother Ass, we had been bashfully thinking of a kind of illumination such as Rimbaud dreamed of – a nagging poem which was not didactic or expository but which *infected* – was not simply a rationalised intui-

11 on 14.5pt

Linotype **Berling**

roman (05589), **italic** (13589)
bold (07589)
Berlings Grafiska 1951 (Karl-Erik Forsberg)
Copyfitting code 128/118/128

Range also includes bold italic

ABCDEFGHIJKLMNOP
QRSTUVWXYZ abcdefg
hijklmnopqrstuvwxyz
1234567890 1234567890
fifl ()[]&£$.,;:-!?''

ABCDEFGHIJKLMNOP
QRSTUVWXYZ abcdefg
hijklmnopqrstuvwxyz
1234567890 1234567890
fifl ()[]&£$.,;:-!?''

ABCDEFGHIJKLMNOP
QRSTUVWXYZ abcdefg
hijklmnopqrstuvwxyz
1234567890 1234567890
fifl ()[]&£$.,;:-!?''

24 on 27pt

These examples show *normal* letterspacing and the effect of *reduced* letterspacing on roman setting *as well as on words in italic*: they also show the appearance of figures, for example 28 May 1964, within text. These & the ampersand are not included in the setting opposite.
Normal letterspacing

These examples show *normal* letterspacing and the effect of *reduced* letterspacing on roman setting *as well as on words in italic*: they also show the appearance of figures, for example 28 May 1964, within text. These & the ampersand are not included in the setting opposite.
Minus one unit spacing

These examples show *normal* letterspacing and the effect of *reduced* letterspacing on roman setting *as well as on words in italic*: they also show the appearance of figures, for example 28 May 1964, within text. These & the ampersand are not included in the setting opposite.
Minus two units spacing

WALKING ALONG THE MALL WE WONDERED WHO ALL
WALKING ALONG THE MALL WE WONDERED WHO
WALKING ALONG THE MALL WE WONDERED
Capitals: normal letterspacing/plus 4 units/plus 9 units

Walking along the Mall we wondered who all those men were – tall hawk-featured men perched on balconies and high places, scanning the CITY WITH HEAVY BINOCULARS. WHAT WERE they seeking so earnestly? Who were they – so composed and steely-eyed? Timidly we stopped a POLICEMAN TO ASK HIM. 'They are publishers' he said mildly. Publishers! Our hearts stopped beating. 'They are on the look out for new talent.' Great God! It was for *us* they were waiting and
Text with reduced caps normal letterspacing/plus 3 units

WALKING ALONG THE MALL we wondered who all those men were
WALKING ALONG THE MALL we wondered who all those men
True italic/sloped roman

Walking along the Mall we wondered who all those men were – tall hawk-featured men perched on balconies and high places, scanning the city with heavy binoculars. What were they seeking so earnestly? Who were they – so composed and steely-eyed? Timidly we stopped a policeman to ask him. 'They are publishers' he said mildly. Publishers! Our hearts stopped beating. 'They are on the look out for new talent.' Great God! It was for *us* they were waiting and watching! Then the kindly policeman lowered his voice confidentially and said in hollow and reverent tones: *'They are waiting for the new Trollope to be born!'* Do you remember, at these words, how heavy our suitcases suddenly felt? How our blood slowed, our footsteps lagged? Brother Ass, we had been bashfully thinking of a kind of illumination such as Rimbaud dreamed of – a nagging
8 on 9pt

Walking along the Mall we wondered who all those men were – tall hawk-featured men perched on balconies and high places, scanning the city with heavy binoculars. What were they seeking so earnestly? Who were they – so composed and steely-eyed? Timidly we stopped a policeman to ask him. 'They are publishers' he said mildly. Publishers! Our hearts stopped beating. 'They are on the look out for new talent.' Great God! It was for *us* they were waiting and watching! Then the kindly policeman lowered his voice confidentially and said in hollow and reverent tones: *'They are waiting for the new Trollope to be born!'* Do you remember, at these words, how heavy our suitcases suddenly felt? How our blood slowed, our footsteps lagged? Brother Ass, we had been
8 on 10.5pt

Walking along the Mall we wondered who all those men were – tall hawk-featured men perched on balconies and high places, scanning the city with heavy binoculars. What were they seeking so earnestly? Who were they – so composed and steely-eyed? Timidly we stopped a policeman to ask him. 'They are publishers' he said mildly. Publishers! Our hearts stopped beating. 'They are on the look out for new talent.' Great God! It was for *us* they were waiting and watching! Then the kindly policeman lowered his voice confidentially and said in hollow and reverent tones: *'They are waiting for the new Trollope to be born!'* Do you remember, at these words, how heavy our suitcases suddenly felt? How our blood slowed, our footsteps lagged? Brother Ass, we had been bashfully thinking of a kind of illumination such as Rimbaud dreamed of – a nagging poem which was not didactic or expository but which *infected* – was not simply a rationalised intuition, I mean, clothed in isinglass! We had come to the wrong shop, with the wrong change! A chill struck us as we saw the mist falling in Trafalgar Square, coiling round us its tendrils of ectoplasm! A million muffin-eating moralists were waiting, not for us, Brother Ass, but for the plucky and tedious Trollope! (If you are dissatisfied with your form, reach for the *curette*.) Now do you wonder if I laugh a little off-key? Do

9 on 11pt

Walking along the Mall we wondered who all those men were – tall hawk-featured men perched on balconies and high places, scanning the city with heavy binoculars. What were they seeking so earnestly? Who were they – so composed and steely-eyed? Timidly we stopped a policeman to ask him. 'They are publishers' he said mildly. Publishers! Our hearts stopped beating. 'They are on the look out for new talent.' Great God! It was for *us* they were waiting and watching! Then the kindly policeman lowered his voice confidentially and said in hollow and reverent tones: *'They are waiting for the new Trollope to be born!'* Do you remember, at these words, how heavy our suitcases suddenly felt? How our blood slowed, our footsteps lagged? Brother Ass, we had been bashfully thinking of a kind of illumination such as Rimbaud dreamed of – a nagging poem which was not didactic or expository but which *infected* – was not simply a rationalised intuition, I mean, clothed in isinglass! We had come to the wrong shop, with the wrong change! A chill struck us as we saw the mist falling in Trafalgar

10 on 12pt

Walking along the Mall we wondered who all those men were – tall hawk-featured men perched on balconies and high places, scanning the city with heavy binoculars. What were they seeking so earnestly? Who were they – so composed and steely-eyed? Timidly we stopped a policeman to ask him. 'They are publishers' he said mildly. Publishers! Our hearts stopped beating. 'They are on the look out for new talent.' Great God! It was for *us* they were waiting and watching! Then the kindly policeman lowered his voice confidentially and said in hollow and reverent tones: *'They are waiting for the new Trollope to be born!'* Do you remember, at these words, how heavy our suitcases suddenly felt? How our blood slowed, our footsteps lagged? Brother Ass, we had been bashfully thinking of a kind of illumination such as Rimbaud dreamed of – a nagging poem which was not didactic or expository but which *infected* – was not simply a rationalised

11 on 13pt

Walking along the Mall we wondered who all those men were – tall hawk-featured men perched on balconies and high places, scanning the city with heavy binoculars. What were they seeking so earnestly? Who were they – so composed and steely-eyed? Timidly we stopped a policeman to ask him. 'They are publishers' he said mildly. Publishers! Our hearts stopped beating. 'They are on the look out for new talent.' Great God! It was for *us* they were waiting and watching! Then the kindly policeman lowered his voice confidentially and said in hollow and reverent tones: *'They are waiting for the new Trollope to be born!'* Do you remember, at these words, how heavy our suitcases suddenly felt? How our blood slowed, our footsteps lagged? Brother Ass, we had been bashfully thinking of a kind of illumination such as Rimbaud dreamed of – a nagging poem which was not didactic or expository but which *infected* – was not simply a rationalised intuition, I mean, clothed in isinglass! We had come to the wrong shop, with the wrong

9 on 12pt

Walking along the Mall we wondered who all those men were – tall hawk-featured men perched on balconies and high places, scanning the city with heavy binoculars. What were they seeking so earnestly? Who were they – so composed and steely-eyed? Timidly we stopped a policeman to ask him. 'They are publishers' he said mildly. Publishers! Our hearts stopped beating. 'They are on the look out for new talent.' Great God! It was for *us* they were waiting and watching! Then the kindly policeman lowered his voice confidentially and said in hollow and reverent tones: *'They are waiting for the new Trollope to be born!'* Do you remember, at these words, how heavy our suitcases suddenly felt? How our blood slowed, our footsteps lagged? Brother Ass, we had been bashfully thinking of a kind of illumination such as Rimbaud dreamed of – a nagging poem which was not didactic or expository but which *infected* – was not simply a rationalised intuition, I mean, clothed in isinglass! We had come to the wrong shop, with the wrong

10 on 13.5pt

Walking along the Mall we wondered who all those men were – tall hawk-featured men perched on balconies and high places, scanning the city with heavy binoculars. What were they seeking so earnestly? Who were they – so composed and steely-eyed? Timidly we stopped a policeman to ask him. 'They are publishers' he said mildly. Publishers! Our hearts stopped beating. 'They are on the look out for new talent.' Great God! It was for *us* they were waiting and watching! Then the kindly policeman lowered his voice confidentially and said in hollow and reverent tones: *'They are waiting for the new Trollope to be born!'* Do you remember, at these words, how heavy our suitcases suddenly felt? How our blood slowed, our footsteps lagged? Brother Ass, we had been bashfully thinking of a kind of illumination such as Rimbaud dreamed of – a nagging poem which was not didactic

11 on 14.5pt

LINOTYPE BERLING

Monotype **Bodoni**

135 roman and italic
260 bold
Monotype 1921
Copyfitting factor 42.3/40.0/41.4

Related to Monotype Bodoni book 504, 529
bold condensed, 120 ultra bold

Linotype Bodoni is similar, but to a different
design by Morris F Benton, 1909. The roman
(copyfitting code 125) is slightly lighter, while
the italic (code 126) is considerably wider and
less tightly fitted

Based on M F Benton's 1907 design for ATF,
itself derived from a type in Bodoni's *Manuale
Tipografico* of 1818

ABCDEFGHIJKLMNOP
QRSTUVWXYZ abcdefg
hijklmnopqrstuvwxyz
1234567890
ff fi fl ffi ffl ()[]&£$.,;:-!?''

*ABCDEFGHIJKLMNOP
QRSTUVWXYZ abcdefg
hijklmnopqrstuvwxyz
1234567890
ff fi fl ffi ffl ( )[ ]&£$.,;:-!?''*

**ABCDEFGHIJKLMNOP
QRSTUVWXYZ abcdefg
hijklmnopqrstuvwxyz
1234567890
ff fi fl ffi ffl ()[]&£$.,;:-!?''**

24 on 27pt

These examples show *normal* letterspacing and the effect of *reduced*
letterspacing on roman setting *as well as on words in italic*: they also
show the appearance of figures, for example 28 May 1964, within text.
These & the ampersand are not included in the setting opposite.

Normal letterspacing

These examples show *normal* letterspacing and the effect of *reduced*
letterspacing on roman setting *as well as on words in italic*: they also
show the appearance of figures, for example 28 May 1964, within text.
These & the ampersand are not included in the setting opposite.

Minus one unit spacing

These examples show *normal* letterspacing and the effect of *reduced*
letterspacing on roman setting *as well as on words in italic*: they also
show the appearance of figures, for example 28 May 1964, within text.
These & the ampersand are not included in the setting opposite.

Minus two units spacing

WALKING ALONG THE MALL WE WONDERED WHO ALL
WALKING ALONG THE MALL WE WONDERED WHO
WALKING ALONG THE MALL WE WONDERED

Capitals: normal letterspacing/plus 9 units/plus 18 units

WALKING ALONG THE MALL WE WONDERED WHO ALL THOSE MEN WERE
WALKING ALONG THE MALL WE WONDERED WHO ALL THOSE MEN
WALKING ALONG THE MALL WE WONDERED WHO ALL THOSE

Small caps: normal letterspacing/plus 6 units/plus 12 units

WALKING ALONG THE MALL WE WONDERED WHO ALL THOSE MEN WERE
WALKING ALONG THE MALL WE WONDERED WHO ALL THOSE MEN WERE

True small caps/reduced capitals

*WALKING ALONG THE MALL we wondered who all those men were
WALKING ALONG THE MALL we wondered who all those men were*

True italic/sloped roman

Walking along the Mall we wondered who all those men were – tall hawk-featured men
perched on balconies and high places, scanning the city with heavy binoculars. What
were they seeking so earnestly? Who were they – so composed and steely-eyed? Timidly
we stopped a policeman to ask him. 'They are publishers' he said mildly. Publishers!
Our hearts stopped beating. 'They are on the look out for new talent.' Great God! It was
for *us* they were waiting and watching! Then the kindly policeman lowered his voice
confidentially and said in hollow and reverent tones: '*They are waiting for the new Trollope
to be born!*' Do you remember, at these words, how heavy our suitcases suddenly felt?
How our blood slowed, our footsteps lagged? Brother Ass, we had been bashfully thinking
of a kind of illumination such as Rimbaud dreamed of – a nagging poem which was not

8 on 9pt

WALKING ALONG THE MALL WE WONDERED WHO ALL THOSE MEN WERE – TALL
hawk-featured men perched on balconies and high places, scanning the city with heavy
binoculars. What were they seeking so earnestly? Who were they – so composed and
steely-eyed? Timidly we stopped a policeman to ask him. 'They are publishers' he said
mildly. Publishers! Our hearts stopped beating. 'They are on the look out for new talent.'
Great God! It was for *us* they were waiting and watching! Then the kindly policeman
lowered his voice confidentially and said in hollow and reverent tones: '*They are waiting
for the new Trollope to be born!*' Do you remember, at these words, how heavy our suitcases
suddenly felt? How our blood slowed, our footsteps lagged? Brother Ass, we had been

8 on 10.5pt

Walking along the Mall we wondered who all those men were – tall hawk-featured men perched on balconies and high places, scanning the city with heavy binoculars. What were they seeking so earnestly? Who were they – so composed and steely-eyed? Timidly we stopped a policeman to ask him. 'They are publishers' he said mildly. Publishers! Our hearts stopped beating. 'They are on the look out for new talent.' Great God! It was for *us* they were waiting and watching! Then the kindly policeman lowered his voice confidentially and said in hollow and reverent tones: *'They are waiting for the new Trollope to be born!'* Do you remember, at these words, how heavy our suitcases suddenly felt? How our blood slowed, our footsteps lagged? Brother Ass, we had been bashfully thinking of a kind of illumination such as Rimbaud dreamed of – a nagging poem which was not didactic or expository but which *infected* – was not simply a rationalised intuition, I mean, clothed in isinglass! We had come to the wrong shop, with the wrong change! A chill struck us as we saw the mist falling in Trafalgar Square, coiling around us its tendrils of ectoplasm! A million muffin-eating moralists were waiting, not for us, Brother Ass, but for the plucky and tedious Trollope! (If you are dissatisfied with your form, reach for the *curette*.) Now do you wonder if I laugh a little off-key? Do you ask yourself what has turned me into nature's bashful little aphorist? We who

9 on 11pt

Walking along the Mall we wondered who all those men were – tall hawk-featured men perched on balconies and high places, scanning the city with heavy binoculars. What were they seeking so earnestly? Who were they – so composed and steely-eyed? Timidly we stopped a policeman to ask him. 'They are publishers' he said mildly. Publishers! Our hearts stopped beating. 'They are on the look out for new talent.' Great God! It was for *us* they were waiting and watching! Then the kindly policeman lowered his voice confidentially and said in hollow and reverent tones: *'They are waiting for the new Trollope to be born!'* Do you remember, at these words, how heavy our suitcases suddenly felt? How our blood slowed, our footsteps lagged? Brother Ass, we had been bashfully thinking of a kind of illumination such as Rimbaud dreamed of – a nagging poem which was not didactic or expository but which *infected* – was not simply a rationalised intuition, I mean, clothed in isinglass! We had come to the wrong shop, with the wrong change! A chill struck us as we saw the mist falling in Trafalgar Square, coiling around us its tendrils of ectoplasm! A million

10 on 12pt

Walking along the Mall we wondered who all those men were – tall hawk-featured men perched on balconies and high places, scanning the city with heavy binoculars. What were they seeking so earnestly? Who were they – so composed and steely-eyed? Timidly we stopped a policeman to ask him. 'They are publishers' he said mildly. Publishers! Our hearts stopped beating. 'They are on the look out for new talent.' Great God! It was for *us* they were waiting and watching! Then the kindly policeman lowered his voice confidentially and said in hollow and reverent tones: *'They are waiting for the new Trollope to be born!'* Do you remember, at these words, how heavy our suitcases suddenly felt? How our blood slowed, our footsteps lagged? Brother Ass, we had been bashfully thinking of a kind of illumination such as Rimbaud dreamed of – a nagging poem which was not didactic or expository but which *infected* – was not simply a rationalised intuition, I mean, clothed in isinglass! We

11 on 13pt

WALKING ALONG THE MALL WE WONDERED WHO ALL THOSE MEN WERE – TALL hawk-featured men perched on balconies and high places, scanning the city with heavy binoculars. What were they seeking so earnestly? Who were they – so composed and steely-eyed? Timidly we stopped a policeman to ask him. 'They are publishers' he said mildly. Publishers! Our hearts stopped beating. 'They are on the look out for new talent.' Great God! It was for *us* they were waiting and watching! Then the kindly policeman lowered his voice confidentially and said in hollow and reverent tones: *'They are waiting for the new Trollope to be born!'* Do you remember, at these words, how heavy our suitcases suddenly felt? How our blood slowed, our footsteps lagged? Brother Ass, we had been bashfully thinking of a kind of illumination such as Rimbaud dreamed of – a nagging poem which was not didactic or expository but which *infected* – was not simply a rationalised intuition, I mean, clothed in isinglass! We had come to the wrong shop, with the wrong change! A chill struck us as we saw the mist falling in Trafalgar Square, coiling around us its tendrils of ectoplasm! A million muffin-eating moralists were waiting, not for us, Brother Ass, but for the plucky and tedious Trollope! (If you are dissatisfied with your form, reach for the *curette*.) Now do you wonder if I

9 on 12pt

WALKING ALONG THE MALL WE WONDERED WHO ALL THOSE MEN WERE – tall hawk-featured men perched on balconies and high places, scanning the city with heavy binoculars. What were they seeking so earnestly? Who were they – so composed and steely-eyed? Timidly we stopped a policeman to ask him. 'They are publishers' he said mildly. Publishers! Our hearts stopped beating. 'They are on the look out for new talent.' Great God! It was for *us* they were waiting and watching! Then the kindly policeman lowered his voice confidentially and said in hollow and rever-ent tones: *'They are waiting for the new Trollope to be born!'* Do you remem-ber, at these words, how heavy our suitcases suddenly felt? How our blood slowed, our footsteps lagged? Brother Ass, we had been bashfully thinking of a kind of illumination such as Rimbaud dreamed of – a nag-ging poem which was not didactic or expository but which *infected* – was not simply a rationalised intuition, I mean, clothed in isinglass! We had come to the wrong shop, with the wrong change! A chill struck us as we

10 on 13.5pt

WALKING ALONG THE MALL WE WONDERED WHO ALL THOSE MEN were – tall hawk-featured men perched on balconies and high places, scanning the city with heavy binoculars. What were they seeking so earnestly? Who were they – so composed and steely-eyed? Timidly we stopped a policeman to ask him. 'They are pub-lishers' he said mildly. Publishers! Our hearts stopped beating. 'They are on the look out for new talent.' Great God! It was for *us* they were waiting and watching! Then the kindly policeman low-ered his voice confidentially and said in hollow and reverent tones: *'They are waiting for the new Trollope to be born!'* Do you remember, at these words, how heavy our suitcases suddenly felt? How our blood slowed, our footsteps lagged? Brother Ass, we had been bashfully thinking of a kind of illumination such as Rimbaud dreamed of – a nagging poem which was not didactic or expository

11 on 14.5pt

MONOTYPE BODONI

Monotype Bodoni Book

504 book and book italic
135 roman
Monotype 1932 (135 roman: 1921)
Copyfitting factor 41.0/41.7/42.3

Related to Monotype Bodoni 260 bold, 529
bold condensed, 120 ultra bold

Linotype Bodoni book roman and italic
(copyfitting code 113/109), although a different
design by Morris F Benton, 1912, are very
similar. The roman is slightly lighter, the italic
slightly tighter

ABCDEFGHIJKLMNOP
QRSTUVWXYZ abcdefg
hijklmnopqrstuvwxyz
1234567890
ff fi fl ffi ffl ()[]&£$.,;:-!?''

ABCDEFGHIJKLMNOP
QRSTUVWXYZ abcdefg
hijklmnopqrstuvwxyz
1234567890
ff fi fl ffi ffl ( )[ ]&£$.,;:-!?''

ABCDEFGHIJKLMNOP
QRSTUVWXYZ abcdefg
hijklmnopqrstuvwxyz
1234567890
ff fi fl ffi ffl ()[]&£$.,;:-!?''

24 on 27pt

These examples show *normal* letterspacing and the effect of *reduced*
letterspacing on roman setting *as well as on words in italic*: they also
show the appearance of figures, for example 28 May 1964, within text.
These & the ampersand are not included in the setting opposite.

Normal letterspacing

These examples show *normal* letterspacing and the effect of *reduced*
letterspacing on roman setting *as well as on words in italic*: they also
show the appearance of figures, for example 28 May 1964, within text.
These & the ampersand are not included in the setting opposite.

Minus one unit spacing

These examples show *normal* letterspacing and the effect of *reduced*
letterspacing on roman setting *as well as on words in italic*: they also
show the appearance of figures, for example 28 May 1964, within text.
These & the ampersand are not included in the setting opposite.

Minus two units spacing

WALKING ALONG THE MALL WE WONDERED WHO ALL THOSE
WALKING ALONG THE MALL WE WONDERED WHO ALL
WALKING ALONG THE MALL WE WONDERED WHO

Capitals: normal letterspacing/plus 9 units/plus 18 units

WALKING ALONG THE MALL WE WONDERED WHO ALL THOSE MEN WERE
WALKING ALONG THE MALL WE WONDERED WHO ALL THOSE MEN WERE
WALKING ALONG THE MALL WE WONDERED WHO ALL THOSE MEN

Small caps: normal letterspacing/plus 6 units/plus 12 units

WALKING ALONG THE MALL WE WONDERED WHO ALL THOSE MEN WERE
WALKING ALONG THE MALL WE WONDERED WHO ALL THOSE MEN WERE

True small caps/reduced capitals

WALKING ALONG THE MALL we wondered who all those men were
WALKING ALONG THE MALL we wondered who all those men were

True italic/sloped roman

Walking along the Mall we wondered who all those men were – tall hawk-featured
men perched on balconies and high places, scanning the city with heavy binoculars. What
were they seeking so earnestly? Who were they – so composed and steely-eyed? Timidly we
stopped a policeman to ask him. 'They are publishers' he said mildly. Publishers! Our hearts
stopped beating. 'They are on the look out for new talent.' Great God! It was for *us* they
were waiting and watching! Then the kindly policeman lowered his voice confidentially and
said in hollow and reverent tones: *'They are waiting for the new Trollope to be born!'* Do
you remember, at these words, how heavy our suitcases suddenly felt? How our blood
slowed, our footsteps lagged? Brother Ass, we had been bashfully thinking of a kind of
illumination such as Rimbaud dreamed of – a nagging poem which was not didactic or

8 on 9pt

WALKING ALONG THE MALL WE WONDERED WHO ALL THOSE MEN WERE – TALL HAWK-
featured men perched on balconies and high places, scanning the city with heavy binoculars.
What were they seeking so earnestly? Who were they – so composed and steely-eyed?
Timidly we stopped a policeman to ask him. 'They are publishers' he said mildly.
Publishers! Our hearts stopped beating. 'They are on the look out for new talent.' Great
God! It was for *us* they were waiting and watching! Then the kindly policeman lowered his
voice confidentially and said in hollow and reverent tones: *'They are waiting for the new
Trollope to be born!'* Do you remember, at these words, how heavy our suitcases suddenly
felt? How our blood slowed, our footsteps lagged? Brother Ass, we had been bashfully

8 on 10.5pt

Walking along the Mall we wondered who all those men were – tall hawk-featured men perched on balconies and high places, scanning the city with heavy binoculars. What were they seeking so earnestly? Who were they – so composed and steely-eyed? Timidly we stopped a policeman to ask him. 'They are publishers' he said mildly. Publishers! Our hearts stopped beating. 'They are on the look out for new talent.' Great God! It was for *us* they were waiting and watching! Then the kindly policeman lowered his voice confidentially and said in hollow and reverent tones: *'They are waiting for the new Trollope to be born!'* Do you remember, at these words, how heavy our suitcases suddenly felt? How our blood slowed, our footsteps lagged? Brother Ass, we had been bashfully thinking of a kind of illumination such as Rimbaud dreamed of – a nagging poem which was not didactic or expository but which *infected* – was not simply a rationalised intuition, I mean, clothed in isinglass! We had come to the wrong shop, with the wrong change! A chill struck us as we saw the mist falling in Trafalgar Square, coiling around us its tendrils of ectoplasm! A million muffin-eating moralists were waiting, not for us, Brother Ass, but for the plucky and tedious Trollope! (If you are dissatisfied with your form, reach for the *curette*.) Now do you wonder if I laugh a little off-key? Do you ask yourself what has turned me into nature's bashful little aphorist? We who are, after all, simply poor

9 on 11pt

Walking along the Mall we wondered who all those men were – tall hawk-featured men perched on balconies and high places, scanning the city with heavy binoculars. What were they seeking so earnestly? Who were they – so composed and steely-eyed? Timidly we stopped a policeman to ask him. 'They are publishers' he said mildly. Publishers! Our hearts stopped beating. 'They are on the look out for new talent.' Great God! It was for *us* they were waiting and watching! Then the kindly policeman lowered his voice confidentially and said in hollow and reverent tones: *'They are waiting for the new Trollope to be born!'* Do you remember, at these words, how heavy our suitcases suddenly felt? How our blood slowed, our footsteps lagged? Brother Ass, we had been bashfully thinking of a kind of illumination such as Rimbaud dreamed of – a nagging poem which was not didactic or expository but which *infected* – was not simply a rationalised intuition, I mean, clothed in isinglass! We had come to the wrong shop, with the wrong change! A chill struck us as we saw the mist falling in Trafalgar Square, coiling around us its tendrils of ectoplasm! A million muffin-eating mor-

10 on 12pt

Walking along the Mall we wondered who all those men were – tall hawk-featured men perched on balconies and high places, scanning the city with heavy binoculars. What were they seeking so earnestly? Who were they – so composed and steely-eyed? Timidly we stopped a policeman to ask him. 'They are publishers' he said mildly. Publishers! Our hearts stopped beating. 'They are on the look out for new talent.' Great God! It was for *us* they were waiting and watching! Then the kindly policeman lowered his voice confidentially and said in hollow and reverent tones: *'They are waiting for the new Trollope to be born!'* Do you remember, at these words, how heavy our suitcases suddenly felt? How our blood slowed, our footsteps lagged? Brother Ass, we had been bashfully thinking of a kind of illumination such as Rimbaud dreamed of – a nagging poem which was not didactic or expository but which *infected* – was not simply a rationalised intuition, I mean, clothed in isinglass! We had come to the

11 on 13pt

WALKING ALONG THE MALL WE WONDERED WHO ALL THOSE MEN WERE – TALL hawk-featured men perched on balconies and high places, scanning the city with heavy binoculars. What were they seeking so earnestly? Who were they – so composed and steely-eyed? Timidly we stopped a policeman to ask him. 'They are publishers' he said mildly. Publishers! Our hearts stopped beating. 'They are on the look out for new talent.' Great God! It was for *us* they were waiting and watching! Then the kindly policeman lowered his voice confidentially and said in hollow and reverent tones: *'They are waiting for the new Trollope to be born!'* Do you remember, at these words, how heavy our suitcases suddenly felt? How our blood slowed, our footsteps lagged? Brother Ass, we had been bashfully thinking of a kind of illumination such as Rimbaud dreamed of – a nagging poem which was not didactic or expository but which *infected* – was not simply a rationalised intuition, I mean, clothed in isinglass! We had come to the wrong shop, with the wrong change! A chill struck us as we saw the mist falling in Trafalgar Square, coiling around us its tendrils of ectoplasm! A million muffin-eating moralists were waiting, not for us, Brother Ass, but for the plucky and tedious Trollope! (If you are dissatisfied with your form, reach for the *curette*.) Now do you wonder if I laugh a little off-key? Do you ask

9 on 12pt

WALKING ALONG THE MALL WE WONDERED WHO ALL THOSE MEN WERE – tall hawk-featured men perched on balconies and high places, scanning the city with heavy binoculars. What were they seeking so earnestly? Who were they – so composed and steely-eyed? Timidly we stopped a policeman to ask him. 'They are publishers' he said mildly. Publishers! Our hearts stopped beating. 'They are on the look out for new talent.' Great God! It was for *us* they were waiting and watching! Then the kindly policeman lowered his voice confidentially and said in hollow and reverent tones: *'They are waiting for the new Trollope to be born!'* Do you remember, at these words, how heavy our suitcases suddenly felt? How our blood slowed, our footsteps lagged? Brother Ass, we had been bashfully thinking of a kind of illumination such as Rimbaud dreamed of – a nagging poem which was not didactic or expository but which *infected* – was not simply a rationalised intuition, I mean, clothed in isinglass! We had come to the wrong shop, with the wrong change! A chill struck us as we saw the mist falling in Trafalgar Square,

10 on 13.5pt

WALKING ALONG THE MALL WE WONDERED WHO ALL THOSE MEN were – tall hawk-featured men perched on balconies and high places, scanning the city with heavy binoculars. What were they seeking so earnestly? Who were they – so composed and steely-eyed? Timidly we stopped a policeman to ask him. 'They are publishers' he said mildly. Publishers! Our hearts stopped beating. 'They are on the look out for new talent.' Great God! It was for *us* they were waiting and watching! Then the kindly policeman lowered his voice confidentially and said in hollow and reverent tones: *'They are waiting for the new Trollope to be born!'* Do you remember, at these words, how heavy our suitcases suddenly felt? How our blood slowed, our footsteps lagged? Brother Ass, we had been bashfully thinking of a kind of illumination such as Rimbaud dreamed of – a nagging poem which was not didactic or expository but which *infected* – was not

11 on 14.5pt

Linotype **Bauer Bodoni**

roman (05033), **italic** (13033)
bold (07033)
Bauer 1926 (Heinrich Jost)
Copyfitting code 126/125/137

Range also includes bold italic, bold
condensed, black, black italic, black condensed

ABCDEFGHIJKLMNOP
QRSTUVWXYZ abcdefg
hijklmnopqrstuvwxyz
1234567890 1234567890
fifl ()[]&£$.,;:-!?''

*ABCDEFGHIJKLMNOP
QRSTUVWXYZ abcdefg
hijklmnopqrstuvwxyz
1234567890 1234567890
fifl ()[]&£$.,;:-!?''*

**ABCDEFGHIJKLMNOP
QRSTUVWXYZ abcdefg
hijklmnopqrstuvwxyz
1234567890 1234567890
fifl ()[]&£$.,;:-!?''**

24 on 27pt

These examples show *normal* letterspacing and the effect of *reduced* letterspacing on roman setting *as well as on words in italic*: they also show the appearance of figures, for example 28 May 1964, within text. These & the ampersand are not included in the setting opposite.
Normal letterspacing

These examples show *normal* letterspacing and the effect of *reduced* letterspacing on roman setting *as well as on words in italic*: they also show the appearance of figures, for example 28 May 1964, within text. These & the ampersand are not included in the setting opposite.
Minus one unit spacing

These examples show *normal* letterspacing and the effect of *reduced* letterspacing on roman setting *as well as on words in italic*: they also show the appearance of figures, for example 28 May 1964, within text. These & the ampersand are not included in the setting opposite.
Minus two units spacing

WALKING ALONG THE MALL WE WONDERED WHO ALL
WALKING ALONG THE MALL WE WONDERED WHO ALL
WALKING ALONG THE MALL WE WONDERED
Capitals: normal letterspacing/plus 4 units/plus 9 units

WALKING ALONG THE MALL WE WONDERED WHO ALL THOSE MEN WERE
WALKING ALONG THE MALL WE WONDERED WHO ALL THOSE MEN
WALKING ALONG THE MALL WE WONDERED WHO ALL THOSE
Small caps: normal letterspacing/plus 3 units/plus 6 units

WALKING ALONG THE MALL WE WONDERED WHO ALL THOSE MEN WERE
WALKING ALONG THE MALL WE WONDERED WHO ALL THOSE MEN WERE
True small caps/reduced capitals

*WALKING ALONG THE MALL we wondered who all those men were
WALKING ALONG THE MALL we wondered who all those men we*
True italic/sloped roman

Walking along the Mall we wondered who all those men were – tall hawk-featured men perched on balconies and high places, scanning the city with heavy binoculars. What were they seeking so earnestly? Who were they – so composed and steely-eyed? Timidly we stopped a policeman to ask him. 'They are publishers' he said mildly. Publishers! Our hearts stopped beating. 'They are on the look out for new talent.' Great God! It was for *us* they were waiting and watching! Then the kindly policeman lowered his voice confidentially and said in hollow and reverent tones: *'They are waiting for the new Trollope to be born!'* Do you remember, at these words, how heavy our suitcases suddenly felt? How our blood slowed, our footsteps lagged? Brother Ass, we had been bashfully thinking of a kind of illumination such as Rimbaud dreamed of
8 on 9pt

WALKING ALONG THE MALL WE WONDERED WHO ALL THOSE MEN WERE – TALL HAWK-featured men perched on balconies and high places, scanning the city with heavy binoculars. What were they seeking so earnestly? Who were they – so composed and steely-eyed? Timidly we stopped a policeman to ask him. 'They are publishers' he said mildly. Publishers! Our hearts stopped beating. 'They are on the look out for new talent.' Great God! It was for *us* they were waiting and watching! Then the kindly policeman lowered his voice confidentially and said in hollow and reverent tones: *'They are waiting for the new Trollope to be born!'* Do you remember, at these words, how heavy our suitcases suddenly felt? How our blood slowed, our footsteps lagged? Brother Ass, we had been bashfully
8 on 10.5pt

102

Walking along the Mall we wondered who all those men were – tall
hawk-featured men perched on balconies and high places, scanning the city
with heavy binoculars. What were they seeking so earnestly? Who were they –
so composed and steely-eyed? Timidly we stopped a policeman to ask him.
'They are publishers' he said mildly. Publishers! Our hearts stopped beating.
'They are on the look out for new talent.' Great God! It was for *us* they were
waiting and watching! Then the kindly policeman lowered his voice confidentially and said in hollow and reverent tones: *'They are waiting for the new
Trollope to be born!'* Do you remember, at these words, how heavy our suitcases suddenly felt? How our blood slowed, our footsteps lagged? Brother Ass,
we had been bashfully thinking of a kind of illumination such as Rimbaud
dreamed of – a nagging poem which was not didactic or expository but which
infected – was not simply a rationalised intuition, I mean, clothed in isinglass!
We had come to the wrong shop, with the wrong change! A chill struck us as we
saw the mist falling in Trafalgar Square, coiling round us its tendrils of ectoplasm! A million muffin-eating moralists were waiting, not for us, Brother Ass,
but for the plucky and tedious Trollope! (If you are dissatisfied with your form,
reach for the *curette*.) Now do you wonder if I laugh a little off-key? Do you ask
9 on 11pt

Walking along the Mall we wondered who all those men were –
tall hawk-featured men perched on balconies and high places, scanning the city with heavy binoculars. What were they seeking so earnestly? Who were they – so composed and steely-eyed? Timidly we
stopped a policeman to ask him. 'They are publishers' he said mildly.
Publishers! Our hearts stopped beating. 'They are on the look out for
new talent.' Great God! It was for *us* they were waiting and watching!
Then the kindly policeman lowered his voice confidentially and said in
hollow and reverent tones: *'They are waiting for the new Trollope to
be born!'* Do you remember, at these words, how heavy our suitcases
suddenly felt? How our blood slowed, our footsteps lagged? Brother
Ass, we had been bashfully thinking of a kind of illumination such as
Rimbaud dreamed of – a nagging poem which was not didactic or
expository but which *infected* – was not simply a rationalised intuition,
I mean, clothed in isinglass! We had come to the wrong shop, with the
wrong change! A chill struck us as we saw the mist falling in Trafalgar
10 on 12pt

Walking along the Mall we wondered who all those men
were – tall hawk-featured men perched on balconies and high
places, scanning the city with heavy binoculars. What were they
seeking so earnestly? Who were they – so composed and steely-
eyed? Timidly we stopped a policeman to ask him. 'They are
publishers' he said mildly. Publishers! Our hearts stopped beating. 'They are on the look out for new talent.' Great God! It was
for *us* they were waiting and watching! Then the kindly policeman lowered his voice confidentially and said in hollow and
reverent tones: *'They are waiting for the new Trollope to be
born!'* Do you remember, at these words, how heavy our suitcases suddenly felt? How our blood slowed, our footsteps lagged?
Brother Ass, we had been bashfully thinking of a kind of illumination such as Rimbaud dreamed of – a nagging poem which
was not didactic or expository but which *infected* – was not
11 on 13pt

WALKING ALONG THE MALL WE WONDERED WHO ALL THOSE MEN WERE — TALL
hawk-featured men perched on balconies and high places, scanning the city
with heavy binoculars. What were they seeking so earnestly? Who were they –
so composed and steely-eyed? Timidly we stopped a policeman to ask him.
'They are publishers' he said mildly. Publishers! Our hearts stopped beating.
'They are on the look out for new talent.' Great God! It was for *us* they were
waiting and watching! Then the kindly policeman lowered his voice confidentially and said in hollow and reverent tones: *'They are waiting for the new
Trollope to be born!'* Do you remember, at these words, how heavy our suitcases suddenly felt? How our blood slowed, our footsteps lagged? Brother Ass,
we had been bashfully thinking of a kind of illumination such as Rimbaud
dreamed of – a nagging poem which was not didactic or expository but which
infected – was not simply a rationalised intuition, I mean, clothed in isinglass!
We had come to the wrong shop, with the wrong change! A chill struck us as we
saw the mist falling in Trafalgar Square, coiling round us its tendrils of ectoplasm! A million muffin-eating moralists were waiting, not for us, Brother Ass,
but for the plucky and tedious Trollope! (If you are dissatisfied with your form,
9 on 12pt

WALKING ALONG THE MALL WE WONDERED WHO ALL THOSE MEN WERE —
tall hawk-featured men perched on balconies and high places, scanning the city with heavy binoculars. What were they seeking so earnestly? Who were they – so composed and steely-eyed? Timidly we
stopped a policeman to ask him. 'They are publishers' he said mildly.
Publishers! Our hearts stopped beating. 'They are on the look out for
new talent.' Great God! It was for *us* they were waiting and watching!
Then the kindly policeman lowered his voice confidentially and said in
hollow and reverent tones: *'They are waiting for the new Trollope to
be born!'* Do you remember, at these words, how heavy our suitcases
suddenly felt? How our blood slowed, our footsteps lagged? Brother
Ass, we had been bashfully thinking of a kind of illumination such as
Rimbaud dreamed of – a nagging poem which was not didactic or
expository but which *infected* – was not simply a rationalised intuition,
I mean, clothed in isinglass! We had come to the wrong shop, with the
10 on 13.5pt

WALKING ALONG THE MALL WE WONDERED WHO ALL THOSE MEN WERE —
tall hawk-featured men perched on balconies and high places,
scanning the city with heavy binoculars. What were they seeking
so earnestly? Who were they – so composed and steely-eyed?
Timidly we stopped a policeman to ask him. 'They are publishers' he said mildly. Publishers! Our hearts stopped beating.
'They are on the look out for new talent.' Great God! It was for
us they were waiting and watching! Then the kindly policeman
lowered his voice confidentially and said in hollow and reverent
tones: *'They are waiting for the new Trollope to be born!'* Do
you remember, at these words, how heavy our suitcases suddenly felt? How our blood slowed, our footsteps lagged? Brother
Ass, we had been bashfully thinking of a kind of illumination
such as Rimbaud dreamed of – a nagging poem which was not
11 on 14.5pt

LINOTYPE BAUER BODONI

Linotype **Breughel**

roman 55 (05349), **italic 56** (13349)
bold 65 (07349)
Stempel 1981 (Adrian Frutiger)
Copyfitting code 130/123/134

Range also includes bold italic, black, black
italic

ABCDEFGHIJKLMNOP
QRSTUVWXYZ abcdefg
hijklmnopqrstuvwxyz
1234567890 1234567890
fifl ()[]&£$.,;:-!?"

ABCDEFGHIJKLMNOP
QRSTUVWXYZ abcdefg
hijklmnopqrstuvwxyz
1234567890 1234567890
fifl ()[] &£$.,;:-!?"

ABCDEFGHIJKLMNOP
QRSTUVWXYZ abcdefg
hijklmnopqrstuvwxyz
1234567890 1234567890
fifl ()[]&£$.,;:-!?"

24 on 27pt

These examples show *normal* letterspacing and the effect of *reduced* letterspacing on roman setting *as well as on words in italic*: they also show the appearance of figures, for example 28 May 1964, within text. These & the ampersand are not included in the setting opposite.
Normal letterspacing

These examples show *normal* letterspacing and the effect of *reduced* letterspacing on roman setting *as well as on words in italic*: they also show the appearance of figures, for example 28 May 1964, within text. These & the ampersand are not included in the setting opposite.
Minus one unit spacing

These examples show *normal* letterspacing and the effect of *reduced* letterspacing on roman setting *as well as on words in italic*: they also show the appearance of figures, for example 28 May 1964, within text. These & the ampersand are not included in the setting opposite.
Minus two units spacing

WALKING ALONG THE MALL WE WONDERED WHO ALL
WALKING ALONG THE MALL WE WONDERED WHO
WALKING ALONG THE MALL WE WONDERED
Capitals: normal letterspacing/plus 4 units/plus 9 units

WALKING ALONG THE MALL WE WONDERED WHO ALL THOSE MEN
WALKING ALONG THE MALL WE WONDERED WHO ALL THOSE
WALKING ALONG THE MALL WE WONDERED WHO ALL
Small caps: normal letterspacing/plus 3 units/plus 6 units

WALKING ALONG THE MALL WE WONDERED WHO ALL THOSE MEN
WALKING ALONG THE MALL WE WONDERED WHO ALL THOSE MEN WERE
True small caps/reduced capitals

WALKING ALONG THE MALL we wondered who all those men
WALKING ALONG THE MALL we wondered who all those men
True italic/sloped roman

Walking along the Mall we wondered who all those men were – tall hawk-featured men perched on balconies and high places, scanning the city with heavy binoculars. What were they seeking so earnestly? Who were they – so composed and steely-eyed? Timidly we stopped a policeman to ask him. 'They are publishers' he said mildly. Publishers! Our hearts stopped beating. 'They are on the look out for new talent.' Great God! It was for *us* they were waiting and watching! Then the kindly policeman lowered his voice confidentially and said in hollow and reverent tones: *'They are waiting for the new Trollope to be born!'* Do you remember, at these words, how heavy our suitcases suddenly felt? How our blood slowed, our footsteps lagged? Brother Ass, we had been bashfully thinking of a kind of illumination such as Rimbaud
8 on 9pt

WALKING ALONG THE MALL WE WONDERED WHO ALL THOSE MEN WERE – TALL hawk-featured men perched on balconies and high places, scanning the city with heavy binoculars. What were they seeking so earnestly? Who were they – so composed and steely-eyed? Timidly we stopped a policeman to ask him. 'They are publishers' he said mildly. Publishers! Our hearts stopped beating. 'They are on the look out for new talent.' Great God! It was for *us* they were waiting and watching! Then the kindly policeman lowered his voice confidentially and said in hollow and reverent tones: *'They are waiting for the new Trollope to be born!'* Do you remember, at these words, how heavy our suitcases suddenly felt? How our blood slowed, our
8 on 10.5pt

Walking along the Mall we wondered who all those men were – tall hawk-featured men perched on balconies and high places, scanning the city with heavy binoculars. What were they seeking so earnestly? Who were they – so composed and steely-eyed? Timidly we stopped a policeman to ask him. 'They are publishers' he said mildly. Publishers! Our hearts stopped beating. 'They are on the look out for new talent.' Great God! It was for *us* they were waiting and watching! Then the kindly policeman lowered his voice confidentially and said in hollow and reverent tones: *'They are waiting for the new Trollope to be born!'* Do you remember, at these words, how heavy our suitcases suddenly felt? How our blood slowed, our footsteps lagged? Brother Ass, we had been bashfully thinking of a kind of illumination such as Rimbaud dreamed of – a nagging poem which was not didactic or expository but which *infected* – was not simply a rationalised intuition, I mean, clothed in isinglass! We had come to the wrong shop, with the wrong change! A chill struck us as we saw the mist falling in Trafalgar Square, coiling round us its tendrils of ectoplasm! A million muffin-eating moralists were waiting, not for us, Brother Ass, but for the plucky and tedious Trollope! (If you are dissatisfied with your form, reach
9 on 11pt

Walking along the Mall we wondered who all those men were – tall hawk-featured men perched on balconies and high places, scanning the city with heavy binoculars. What were they seeking so earnestly? Who were they – so composed and steely-eyed? Timidly we stopped a policeman to ask him. 'They are publishers' he said mildly. Publishers! Our hearts stopped beating. 'They are on the look out for new talent.' Great God! It was for *us* they were waiting and watching! Then the kindly policeman lowered his voice confidentially and said in hollow and reverent tones: *'They are waiting for the new Trollope to be born!'* Do you remember, at these words, how heavy our suitcases suddenly felt? How our blood slowed, our footsteps lagged? Brother Ass, we had been bashfully thinking of a kind of illumination such as Rimbaud dreamed of – a nagging poem which was not didactic or expository but which *infected* – was not simply a rationalised intuition, I mean, clothed in isinglass! We had come to the wrong shop, with the wrong change! A chill struck us as
10 on 12pt

Walking along the Mall we wondered who all those men were – tall hawk-featured men perched on balconies and high places, scanning the city with heavy binoculars. What were they seeking so earnestly? Who were they – so composed and steely-eyed? Timidly we stopped a policeman to ask him. 'They are publishers' he said mildly. Publishers! Our hearts stopped beating. 'They are on the look out for new talent.' Great God! It was for *us* they were waiting and watching! Then the kindly policeman lowered his voice confidentially and said in hollow and reverent tones: *'They are waiting for the new Trollope to be born!'* Do you remember, at these words, how heavy our suitcases suddenly felt? How our blood slowed, our footsteps lagged? Brother Ass, we had been bashfully thinking of a kind of illumination such as Rimbaud dreamed of – a nagging poem which was not didactic or
11 on 13pt

WALKING ALONG THE MALL WE WONDERED WHO ALL THOSE MEN WERE – tall hawk-featured men perched on balconies and high places, scanning the city with heavy binoculars. What were they seeking so earnestly? Who were they – so composed and steely-eyed? Timidly we stopped a policeman to ask him. 'They are publishers' he said mildly. Publishers! Our hearts stopped beating. 'They are on the look out for new talent.' Great God! It was for *us* they were waiting and watching! Then the kindly policeman lowered his voice confidentially and said in hollow and reverent tones: *'They are waiting for the new Trollope to be born!'* Do you remember, at these words, how heavy our suitcases suddenly felt? How our blood slowed, our footsteps lagged? Brother Ass, we had been bashfully thinking of a kind of illumination such as Rimbaud dreamed of – a nagging poem which was not didactic or expository but which *infected* – was not simply a rationalised intuition, I mean, clothed in isinglass! We had come to the wrong shop, with the wrong change! A chill struck us as we saw the mist falling in Trafalgar Square, coiling round us its tendrils of ectoplasm! A million muffin-eating moralists were waiting, not for us, Brother Ass, but for the
9 on 12pt

WALKING ALONG THE MALL WE WONDERED WHO ALL THOSE MEN were – tall hawk-featured men perched on balconies and high places, scanning the city with heavy binoculars. What were they seeking so earnestly? Who were they – so composed and steely-eyed? Timidly we stopped a policeman to ask him. 'They are publishers' he said mildly. Publishers! Our hearts stopped beating. 'They are on the look out for new talent.' Great God! It was for *us* they were waiting and watching! Then the kindly policeman lowered his voice confidentially and said in hollow and reverent tones: *'They are waiting for the new Trollope to be born!'* Do you remember, at these words, how heavy our suitcases suddenly felt? How our blood slowed, our footsteps lagged? Brother Ass, we had been bashfully thinking of a kind of illumination such as Rimbaud dreamed of – a nagging poem which was not didactic or expository but which *infected* – was not simply a rationalised intuition, I mean, clothed in
10 on 13.5pt

WALKING ALONG THE MALL WE WONDERED WHO ALL THOSE men were – tall hawk-featured men perched on balconies and high places, scanning the city with heavy binoculars. What were they seeking so earnestly? Who were they – so composed and steely-eyed? Timidly we stopped a policeman to ask him. 'They are publishers' he said mildly. Publishers! Our hearts stopped beating. 'They are on the look out for new talent.' Great God! It was for *us* they were waiting and watching! Then the kindly policeman lowered his voice confidentially and said in hollow and reverent tones: *'They are waiting for the new Trollope to be born!'* Do you remember, at these words, how heavy our suitcases suddenly felt? How our blood slowed, our footsteps lagged? Brother Ass, we had been bashfully thinking of a kind of illumination such as Rimbaud
11 on 14.5pt

Linotype **Caledonia**

roman (05041), **italic** (13041)
bold (07041)
Linotype 1938-40 (William A Dwiggins)
Copyfitting code 124/125/126

Range also includes bold italic

Linotype New Caledonia roman and italic are
almost identical (copyfitting code 119/120), but
its wider range of weights is not comparable

Monotype Caledonia is very similar
(copyfitting factor 43.3/43.3/43.3)

Influenced by Scottish types of the early 19th
century, also by a type cut by William Martin
about 1790 and used by Bulmer

ABCDEFGHIJKLMNOP
QRSTUVWXYZ abcdefg
hijklmnopqrstuvwxyz
1234567890 1234567890
fifl ()[]&£$.,;:-!?"

ABCDEFGHIJKLMNOP
QRSTUVWXYZ abcdefg
hijklmnopqrstuvwxyz
1234567890 1234567890
fifl ()[]&£$.,;:-!?"

ABCDEFGHIJKLMNOP
QRSTUVWXYZ abcdefg
hijklmnopqrstuvwxyz
1234567890 1234567890
fifl ()[]&£$.,;:-!?"

24 on 27pt

These examples show *normal* letterspacing and the effect of *reduced*
letterspacing on roman setting *as well as on words in italic*: they also
show the appearance of figures, for example 28 May 1964, within text.
These & the ampersand are not included in the setting opposite.

Normal letterspacing

These examples show *normal* letterspacing and the effect of *reduced*
letterspacing on roman setting *as well as on words in italic*: they also
show the appearance of figures, for example 28 May 1964, within text.
These & the ampersand are not included in the setting opposite.

Minus one unit spacing

These examples show *normal* letterspacing and the effect of *reduced*
letterspacing on roman setting *as well as on words in italic*: they also
show the appearance of figures, for example 28 May 1964, within text.
These & the ampersand are not included in the setting opposite.

Minus two units spacing

WALKING ALONG THE MALL WE WONDERED WHO ALL
WALKING ALONG THE MALL WE WONDERED WHO
WALKING ALONG THE MALL WE WONDERED

Capitals: normal letterspacing/plus 4 units/plus 9 units

WALKING ALONG THE MALL WE WONDERED WHO ALL THOSE MEN
WALKING ALONG THE MALL WE WONDERED WHO ALL THOSE
WALKING ALONG THE MALL WE WONDERED WHO ALL

Small caps: normal letterspacing/plus 3 units/plus 6 units

WALKING ALONG THE MALL WE WONDERED WHO ALL THOSE MEN
WALKING ALONG THE MALL WE WONDERED WHO ALL THOSE MEN WERE

True small caps/reduced capitals

WALKING ALONG THE MALL we wondered who all those men were
WALKING ALONG THE MALL we wondered who all those men

True italic/sloped roman

Walking along the Mall we wondered who all those men were – tall hawk-featured men
perched on balconies and high places, scanning the city with heavy binoculars. What
were they seeking so earnestly? Who were they – so composed and steely-eyed? Timidly
we stopped a policeman to ask him. 'They are publishers' he said mildly. Publishers!
Our hearts stopped beating. 'They are on the look out for new talent.' Great God! It was
for *us* they were waiting and watching! Then the kindly policeman lowered his voice
confidentially and said in hollow and reverent tones: *'They are waiting for the new
Trollope to be born!'* Do you remember, at these words, how heavy our suitcases
suddenly felt? How our blood slowed, our footsteps lagged? Brother Ass, we had been
bashfully thinking of a kind of illumination such as Rimbaud dreamed of – a nagging

8 on 9pt

WALKING ALONG THE MALL WE WONDERED WHO ALL THOSE MEN WERE – TALL
hawk-featured men perched on balconies and high places, scanning the city with heavy
binoculars. What were they seeking so earnestly? Who were they – so composed and
steely-eyed? Timidly we stopped a policeman to ask him. 'They are publishers' he said
mildly. Publishers! Our hearts stopped beating. 'They are on the look out for new talent.'
Great God! It was for *us* they were waiting and watching! Then the kindly policeman
lowered his voice confidentially and said in hollow and reverent tones: *'They are waiting
for the new Trollope to be born!'* Do you remember, at these words, how heavy our
suitcases suddenly felt? How our blood slowed, our footsteps lagged? Brother Ass, we

8 on 10.5pt

Walking along the Mall we wondered who all those men were – tall hawk-featured men perched on balconies and high places, scanning the city with heavy binoculars. What were they seeking so earnestly? Who were they – so composed and steely-eyed? Timidly we stopped a policeman to ask him. 'They are publishers' he said mildly. Publishers! Our hearts stopped beating. 'They are on the look out for new talent.' Great God! It was for *us* they were waiting and watching! Then the kindly policeman lowered his voice confidentially and said in hollow and reverent tones: *'They are waiting for the new Trollope to be born!'* Do you remember, at these words, how heavy our suitcases suddenly felt? How our blood slowed, our footsteps lagged? Brother Ass, we had been bashfully thinking of a kind of illumination such as Rimbaud dreamed of – a nagging poem which was not didactic or expository but which *infected* – was not simply a rationalised intuition, I mean, clothed in isinglass! We had come to the wrong shop, with the wrong change! A chill struck us as we saw the mist falling in Trafalgar Square, coiling round us its tendrils of ectoplasm! A million muffin-eating moralists were waiting, not for us, Brother Ass, but for the plucky and tedious Trollope! (If you are dissatisfied with your form, reach for the *curette*.) Now do you wonder if I laugh a little off-key? Do you ask yourself

9 on 11pt

Walking along the Mall we wondered who all those men were – tall hawk-featured men perched on balconies and high places, scanning the city with heavy binoculars. What were they seeking so earnestly? Who were they – so composed and steely-eyed? Timidly we stopped a policeman to ask him. 'They are publishers' he said mildly. Publishers! Our hearts stopped beating. 'They are on the look out for new talent.' Great God! It was for *us* they were waiting and watching! Then the kindly policeman lowered his voice confidentially and said in hollow and reverent tones: *'They are waiting for the new Trollope to be born!'* Do you remember, at these words, how heavy our suitcases suddenly felt? How our blood slowed, our footsteps lagged? Brother Ass, we had been bashfully thinking of a kind of illumination such as Rimbaud dreamed of – a nagging poem which was not didactic or expository but which *infected* – was not simply a rationalised intuition, I mean, clothed in isinglass! We had come to the wrong shop, with the wrong

10 on 12pt

Walking along the Mall we wondered who all those men were – tall hawk-featured men perched on balconies and high places, scanning the city with heavy binoculars. What were they seeking so earnestly? Who were they – so composed and steely-eyed? Timidly we stopped a policeman to ask him. 'They are publishers' he said mildly. Publishers! Our hearts stopped beating. 'They are on the look out for new talent.' Great God! It was for *us* they were waiting and watching! Then the kindly policeman lowered his voice confidentially and said in hollow and reverent tones: *'They are waiting for the new Trollope to be born!'* Do you remember, at these words, how heavy our suitcases suddenly felt? How our blood slowed, our footsteps lagged? Brother Ass, we had been bashfully thinking of a kind of illumination such as Rimbaud dreamed of – a nagging poem which was not didactic or expository but which *infected* – was not simply a

11 on 13pt

WALKING ALONG THE MALL WE WONDERED WHO ALL THOSE MEN WERE – tall hawk-featured men perched on balconies and high places, scanning the city with heavy binoculars. What were they seeking so earnestly? Who were they – so composed and steely-eyed? Timidly we stopped a policeman to ask him. 'They are publishers' he said mildly. Publishers! Our hearts stopped beating. 'They are on the look out for new talent.' Great God! It was for *us* they were waiting and watching! Then the kindly policeman lowered his voice confidentially and said in hollow and reverent tones: *'They are waiting for the new Trollope to be born!'* Do you remember, at these words, how heavy our suitcases suddenly felt? How our blood slowed, our footsteps lagged? Brother Ass, we had been bashfully thinking of a kind of illumination such as Rimbaud dreamed of – a nagging poem which was not didactic or expository but which *infected* – was not simply a rationalised intuition, I mean, clothed in isinglass! We had come to the wrong shop, with the

9 on 12pt

WALKING ALONG THE MALL WE WONDERED WHO ALL THOSE MEN were – tall hawk-featured men perched on balconies and high places, scanning the city with heavy binoculars. What were they seeking so earnestly? Who were they – so composed and steely-eyed? Timidly we stopped a policeman to ask him. 'They are publishers' he said mildly. Publishers! Our hearts stopped beating. 'They are on the look out for new talent.' Great God! It was for *us* they were waiting and watching! Then the kindly policeman lowered his voice confidentially and said in hollow and reverent tones: *'They are waiting for the new Trollope to be born!'* Do you remember, at these words, how heavy our suitcases suddenly felt? How our blood slowed, our footsteps lagged? Brother Ass, we had been bashfully thinking of a kind of illumination such as Rimbaud dreamed of – a nagging poem which was not didactic or expository but which *infected* – was not simply a rationalised intuition, I mean, clothed in isinglass! We had come to the wrong shop, with the

10 on 13.5pt

WALKING ALONG THE MALL WE WONDERED WHO ALL THOSE men were – tall hawk-featured men perched on balconies and high places, scanning the city with heavy binoculars. What were they seeking so earnestly? Who were they – so composed and steely-eyed? Timidly we stopped a policeman to ask him. 'They are publishers' he said mildly. Publishers! Our hearts stopped beating. 'They are on the look out for new talent.' Great God! It was for *us* they were waiting and watching! Then the kindly policeman lowered his voice confidentially and said in hollow and reverent tones: *'They are waiting for the new Trollope to be born!'* Do you remember, at these words, how heavy our suitcases suddenly felt? How our blood slowed, our footsteps lagged? Brother Ass, we had been bashfully thinking of a kind of illumination such as Rimbaud dreamed of – a nagging poem which was

11 on 14.5pt

LINOTYPE CALEDONIA

Monotype **Calisto**

1160 roman and italic
1161 bold
Monotype 1988 (Ron Carpenter)
Copyfitting factor 42.4/38.4/43.8

Range also includes bold italic

ABCDEFGHIJKLMNOP
QRSTUVWXYZ abcdefg
hijklmnopqrstuvwxyz
1234567890 1234567890
ff fi fl ffi ffl ()[]&£$.,;:-!?''

ABCDEFGHIJKLMNOP
QRSTUVWXYZ abcdefg
hijklmnopqrstuvwxyz
1234567890 1234567890
ff fi fl ffi ffl ()[]&£$.,;:-!?''

ABCDEFGHIJKLMNOP
QRSTUVWXYZ abcdefg
hijklmnopqrstuvwxyz
1234567890
ff fi fl ffi ffl ()[]&£$.,;:-!?''

24 on 27pt

These examples show *normal* letterspacing and the effect of *reduced* letterspacing on roman setting *as well as on words in italic:* they also show the appearance of figures, for example 28 May 1964, within text. These & the ampersand are not included in the setting opposite.

Normal letterspacing

These examples show *normal* letterspacing and the effect of *reduced* letterspacing on roman setting *as well as on words in italic:* they also show the appearance of figures, for example 28 May 1964, within text. These & the ampersand are not included in the setting opposite.

Minus one unit spacing

These examples show *normal* letterspacing and the effect of *reduced* letterspacing on roman setting *as well as on words in italic:* they also show the appearance of figures, for example 28 May 1964, within text. These & the ampersand are not included in the setting opposite.

Minus two units spacing

WALKING ALONG THE MALL WE WONDERED WHO ALL
WALKING ALONG THE MALL WE WONDERED WHO
WALKING ALONG THE MALL WE WONDERED

Capitals: normal letterspacing/plus 9 units/plus 18 units

WALKING ALONG THE MALL WE WONDERED WHO ALL THOSE MEN WERE
WALKING ALONG THE MALL WE WONDERED WHO ALL THOSE MEN
WALKING ALONG THE MALL WE WONDERED WHO ALL THOSE

Small caps: normal letterspacing/plus 6 units/plus 12 units

WALKING ALONG THE MALL WE WONDERED WHO ALL THOSE MEN WERE
WALKING ALONG THE MALL WE WONDERED WHO ALL THOSE MEN WERE

True small caps/reduced capitals

WALKING ALONG THE MALL we wondered who all those men were
WALKING ALONG THE MALL we wondered who all those men

True italic/sloped roman

Walking along the Mall we wondered who all those men were – tall hawk-featured men perched on balconies and high places, scanning the city with heavy binoculars. What were they seeking so earnestly? Who were they – so composed and steely-eyed? Timidly we stopped a policeman to ask him. 'They are publishers' he said mildly. Publishers! Our hearts stopped beating. 'They are on the look out for new talent.' Great God! It was for *us* they were waiting and watching! Then the kindly policeman lowered his voice confidentially and said in hollow and reverent tones: *'They are waiting for the new Trollope to be born!'* Do you remember, at these words, how heavy our suitcases suddenly felt? How our blood slowed, our footsteps lagged? Brother Ass, we had been bashfully thinking of a kind of illumination such as Rimbaud dreamed of – a nagging poem which

8 on 9pt

WALKING ALONG THE MALL WE WONDERED WHO ALL THOSE MEN WERE – TALL HAWK -featured men perched on balconies and high places, scanning the city with heavy binoculars. What were they seeking so earnestly? Who were they – so composed and steely-eyed? Timidly we stopped a policeman to ask him. 'They are publishers' he said mildly. Publishers! Our hearts stopped beating. 'They are on the look out for new talent.' Great God! It was for *us* they were waiting and watching! Then the kindly policeman lowered his voice confidentially and said in hollow and reverent tones: *'They are waiting for the new Trollope to be born!'* Do you remember, at these words, how heavy our suitcases suddenly felt? How our blood slowed, our footsteps lagged? Brother Ass,

8 on 10.5pt

Walking along the Mall we wondered who all those men were – tall hawk-featured men perched on balconies and high places, scanning the city with heavy binoculars. What were they seeking so earnestly? Who were they – so composed and steely-eyed? Timidly we stopped a policeman to ask him. 'They are publishers' he said mildly. Publishers! Our hearts stopped beating. 'They are on the look out for new talent.' Great God! It was for *us* they were waiting and watching! Then the kindly policeman lowered his voice confidentially and said in hollow and reverent tones: *'They are waiting for the new Trollope to be born!'* Do you remember, at these words, how heavy our suitcases suddenly felt? How our blood slowed, our footsteps lagged? Brother Ass, we had been bashfully thinking of a kind of illumination such as Rimbaud dreamed of – a nagging poem which was not didactic or expository but which *infected* – was not simply a rationalised intuition, I mean, clothed in isinglass! We had come to the wrong shop, with the wrong change! A chill struck us as we saw the mist falling in Trafalgar Square, coiling around us its tendrils of ectoplasm! A million muffin-eating moralists were waiting, not for us, Brother Ass, but for the plucky and tedious Trollope! (If you are dissatisfied with your form, reach for the *curette*.) Now do you wonder if I laugh a little off-key? Do you ask yourself what has turned me into nature's

9 on 11pt

Walking along the Mall we wondered who all those men were – tall hawk-featured men perched on balconies and high places, scanning the city with heavy binoculars. What were they seeking so earnestly? Who were they – so composed and steely-eyed? Timidly we stopped a policeman to ask him. 'They are publishers' he said mildly. Publishers! Our hearts stopped beating. 'They are on the look out for new talent.' Great God! It was for *us* they were waiting and watching! Then the kindly policeman lowered his voice confidentially and said in hollow and reverent tones: *'They are waiting for the new Trollope to be born!'* Do you remember, at these words, how heavy our suitcases suddenly felt? How our blood slowed, our footsteps lagged? Brother Ass, we had been bashfully thinking of a kind of illumination such as Rimbaud dreamed of – a nagging poem which was not didactic or expository but which *infected* – was not simply a rationalised intuition, I mean, clothed in isinglass! We had come to the wrong shop, with the wrong change! A chill struck us as we saw the mist falling in Trafalgar Square, coiling around us its tendrils of ectoplasm! A million muffin-eating moralists were waiting, not for us, Brother Ass, but for the plucky and tedious Trollope! (If you are dissatisfied with your form, reach for the *curette*.) Now do you wonder if I

10 on 12pt

WALKING ALONG THE MALL WE WONDERED WHO ALL THOSE MEN WERE – TALL hawk-featured men perched on balconies and high places, scanning the city with heavy binoculars. What were they seeking so earnestly? Who were they – so composed and steely-eyed? Timidly we stopped a policeman to ask him. 'They are publishers' he said mildly. Publishers! Our hearts stopped beating. 'They are on the look out for new talent.' Great God! It was for *us* they were waiting and watching! Then the kindly policeman lowered his voice confidentially and said in hollow and reverent tones: *'They are waiting for the new Trollope to be born!'* Do you remember, at these words, how heavy our suitcases suddenly felt? How our blood slowed, our footsteps lagged? Brother Ass, we had been bashfully thinking of a kind of illumination such as Rimbaud dreamed of – a nagging poem which was not didactic or expository but which *infected* – was not simply a rationalised intuition, I mean, clothed in isinglass! We had come to the wrong shop, with the wrong change! A chill struck us as we saw the mist falling in Trafalgar Square, coiling around us its tendrils of ectoplasm! A million muffin-eating moralists were waiting, not for us, Brother Ass, but for the plucky and tedious Trollope! (If you are dissatisfied with your form, reach for the *curette*.) Now do you wonder if I

9 on 12pt

WALKING ALONG THE MALL WE WONDERED WHO ALL THOSE MEN WERE – tall hawk-featured men perched on balconies and high places, scanning the city with heavy binoculars. What were they seeking so earnestly? Who were they – so composed and steely-eyed? Timidly we stopped a policeman to ask him. 'They are publishers' he said mildly. Publishers! Our hearts stopped beating. 'They are on the look out for new talent.' Great God! It was for *us* they were waiting and watching! Then the kindly policeman lowered his voice confidentially and said in hollow and reverent tones: *'They are waiting for the new Trollope to be born!'* Do you remember, at these words, how heavy our suitcases suddenly felt? How our blood slowed, our footsteps lagged? Brother Ass, we had been bashfully thinking of a kind of illumination such as Rimbaud dreamed of – a nagging poem which was not didactic or expository but which *infected* – was not simply a rationalised intuition, I mean, clothed in isinglass! We had come to the wrong shop, with the wrong change! A chill struck us as

10 on 13.5pt

Walking along the Mall we wondered who all those men were – tall hawk-featured men perched on balconies and high places, scanning the city with heavy binoculars. What were they seeking so earnestly? Who were they – so composed and steely-eyed? Timidly we stopped a policeman to ask him. 'They are publishers' he said mildly. Publishers! Our hearts stopped beating. 'They are on the look out for new talent.' Great God! It was for *us* they were waiting and watching! Then the kindly policeman lowered his voice confidentially and said in hollow and reverent tones: *'They are waiting for the new Trollope to be born!'* Do you remember, at these words, how heavy our suitcases suddenly felt? How our blood slowed, our footsteps lagged? Brother Ass, we had been bashfully thinking of a kind of illumination such as Rimbaud dreamed of – a nagging poem which was not didactic or expository but which *infected* – was not simply a rationalised intuition, I mean, clothed in

11 on 13pt

WALKING ALONG THE MALL WE WONDERED WHO ALL THOSE MEN were – tall hawk-featured men perched on balconies and high places, scanning the city with heavy binoculars. What were they seeking so earnestly? Who were they – so composed and steely-eyed? Timidly we stopped a policeman to ask him. 'They are publishers' he said mildly. Publishers! Our hearts stopped beating. 'They are on the look out for new talent.' Great God! It was for *us* they were waiting and watching! Then the kindly policeman lowered his voice confidentially and said in hollow and reverent tones: *'They are waiting for the new Trollope to be born!'* Do you remember, at these words, how heavy our suitcases suddenly felt? How our blood slowed, our footsteps lagged? Brother Ass, we had been bashfully thinking of a kind of illumination such as Rimbaud dreamed of – a nagging poem which was not didactic or expository but which

11 on 14.5pt

MONOTYPE CALISTO

Monotype **Calvert**

806 light
808 bold
Monotype 1980 (Margaret Calvert)
Copyfitting factor 46.8/48.4

Range also includes medium

Derived from lettering designed for the sign
system on Tyne and Wear Metro

ABCDEFGHIJKLMNOP
QRSTUVWXYZ abcdefg
hijklmnopqrstuvwxyz
1234567890
ff fi fl ffi ffl ()[]&£$.,;:-!?''

ABCDEFGHIJKLMNOP
QRSTUVWXYZ abcdefg
hijklmnopqrstuvwxyz
1234567890
ff fi fl ffi ffl ()[]&£$.,;:-!?''

24 on 27pt

These examples show *normal* letterspacing and the effect of *reduced*
letterspacing on roman setting *as well as on words in italic:* they also
show the appearance of figures, for example 28 May 1964, within text.
These & the ampersand are not included in the setting opposite.

Normal letterspacing

These examples show *normal* letterspacing and the effect of *reduced*
letterspacing on roman setting *as well as on words in italic:* they also
show the appearance of figures, for example 28 May 1964, within text.
These & the ampersand are not included in the setting opposite.

Minus one unit spacing

These examples show *normal* letterspacing and the effect of *reduced*
letterspacing on roman setting *as well as on words in italic:* they also
show the appearance of figures, for example 28 May 1964, within text.
These & the ampersand are not included in the setting opposite.

Minus two units spacing

WALKING ALONG THE MALL WE WONDERED WHO ALL THOSE MEN
WALKING ALONG THE MALL WE WONDERED WHO ALL THOSE
WALKING ALONG THE MALL WE WONDERED WHO ALL

Capitals: normal letterspacing/plus 9 units/plus 18 units

Walking along the Mall we wondered who all those men were – tall
hawk-featured men perched on balconies and high places, scanning
THE CITY WITH HEAVY BINOCULARS. What were they seeking so earnestly?
Who were they – so composed and steely-eyed? Timidly we stopped a
policeman to ask him. 'THEY ARE PUBLISHERS' he said mildly.
Publishers! Our hearts stopped beating. 'They are on the look out for
new talent.' Great God! It was for *us* they were waiting and watching!

Text with reduced capitals normal letterspacing/plus 6 units

Walking along the Mall we wondered who all those men were – tall hawk-
featured men perched on balconies and high places, scanning the city with
heavy binoculars. What were they seeking so earnestly? Who were they – so
composed and steely-eyed? Timidly we stopped a policeman to ask him. 'They
are publishers' he said mildly. Publishers! Our hearts stopped beating. 'They
are on the look out for new talent.' Great God! It was for *us* they were waiting
and watching! Then the kindly policeman lowered his voice confidentially and
said in hollow and reverent tones: *'They are waiting for the new Trollope to be
born!'* Do you remember, at these words, how heavy our suitcases suddenly
felt? How our blood slowed, our footsteps lagged? Brother Ass, we had been

8 on 9pt

Walking along the Mall we wondered who all those men were – tall hawk-
featured men perched on balconies and high places, scanning the city with
heavy binoculars. What were they seeking so earnestly? Who were they – so
composed and steely-eyed? Timidly we stopped a policeman to ask him. 'They
are publishers' he said mildly. Publishers! Our hearts stopped beating. 'They
are on the look out for new talent.' Great God! It was for *us* they were waiting
and watching! Then the kindly policeman lowered his voice confidentially and
said in hollow and reverent tones: *'They are waiting for the new Trollope to be
born!'* Do you remember, at these words, how heavy our suitcases suddenly

8 on 10.5pt

Walking along the Mall we wondered who all those men were – tall hawk-featured men perched on balconies and high places, scanning the city with heavy binoculars. What were they seeking so earnestly? Who were they – so composed and steely-eyed? Timidly we stopped a policeman to ask him. 'They are publishers' he said mildly. Publishers! Our hearts stopped beating. 'They are on the look out for new talent.' Great God! It was for *us* they were waiting and watching! Then the kindly policeman lowered his voice confidentially and said in hollow and reverent tones: *'They are waiting for the new Trollope to be born!'* Do you remember, at these words, how heavy our suitcases suddenly felt? How our blood slowed, our footsteps lagged? Brother Ass, we had been bashfully thinking of a kind of illumination such as Rimbaud dreamed of – a nagging poem which was not didactic or expository but which *infected* – was not simply a rationalised intuition, I mean, clothed in isinglass! We had come to the wrong shop, with the wrong change! A chill struck us as we saw the mist falling in Trafalgar Square, coiling around us its tendrils of ectoplasm! A million muffin-eating moralists were waiting, not for us, Brother Ass, but for the plucky and tedious

9 on 11pt

Walking along the Mall we wondered who all those men were – tall hawk-featured men perched on balconies and high places, scanning the city with heavy binoculars. What were they seeking so earnestly? Who were they – so composed and steely-eyed? Timidly we stopped a policeman to ask him. 'They are publishers' he said mildly. Publishers! Our hearts stopped beating. 'They are on the look out for new talent.' Great God! It was for *us* they were waiting and watching! Then the kindly policeman lowered his voice confidentially and said in hollow and reverent tones: *'They are waiting for the new Trollope to be born!'* Do you remember, at these words, how heavy our suitcases suddenly felt? How our blood slowed, our footsteps lagged? Brother Ass, we had been bashfully thinking of a kind of illumination such as Rimbaud dreamed of – a nagging poem which was not didactic or expository but which *infected* – was not simply a rationalised intuition, I mean, clothed in isinglass! We had come to the wrong shop, with the wrong change! A chill struck us as we saw the mist falling in Trafalgar Square, coiling around us its tendrils of ectoplasm! A million muffin-eating moralists

9 on 12pt

Walking along the Mall we wondered who all those men were – tall hawk-featured men perched on balconies and high places, scanning the city with heavy binoculars. What were they seeking so earnestly? Who were they – so composed and steely-eyed? Timidly we stopped a policeman to ask him. 'They are publishers' he said mildly. Publishers! Our hearts stopped beating. 'They are on the look out for new talent.' Great God! It was for *us* they were waiting and watching! Then the kindly policeman lowered his voice confidentially and said in hollow and reverent tones: *'They are waiting for the new Trollope to be born!'* Do you remember, at these words, how heavy our suitcases suddenly felt? How our blood slowed, our footsteps lagged? Brother Ass, we had been bashfully thinking of a kind of illumination such as Rimbaud dreamed of – a nagging poem which was not didactic or expository but which *infected* – was not simply a rationalised intuition, I mean, clothed in isinglass! We had come to the wrong

10 on 12pt

Walking along the Mall we wondered who all those men were – tall hawk-featured men perched on balconies and high places, scanning the city with heavy binoculars. What were they seeking so earnestly? Who were they – so composed and steely-eyed? Timidly we stopped a policeman to ask him. 'They are publishers' he said mildly. Publishers! Our hearts stopped beating. 'They are on the look out for new talent.' Great God! It was for *us* they were waiting and watching! Then the kindly policeman lowered his voice confidentially and said in hollow and reverent tones: *'They are waiting for the new Trollope to be born!'* Do you remember, at these words, how heavy our suitcases suddenly felt? How our blood slowed, our footsteps lagged? Brother Ass, we had been bashfully thinking of a kind of illumination such as Rimbaud dreamed of – a nagging poem which was not didactic or expository but which *infected* – was not simply a rationalised

10 on 13.5pt

Walking along the Mall we wondered who all those men were – tall hawk-featured men perched on balconies and high places, scanning the city with heavy binoculars. What were they seeking so earnestly? Who were they – so composed and steely-eyed? Timidly we stopped a policeman to ask him. 'They are publishers' he said mildly. Publishers! Our hearts stopped beating. 'They are on the look out for new talent.' Great God! It was for *us* they were waiting and watching! Then the kindly policeman lowered his voice confidentially and said in hollow and reverent tones: *'They are waiting for the new Trollope to be born!'* Do you remember, at these words, how heavy our suitcases suddenly felt? How our blood slowed, our footsteps lagged? Brother Ass, we had been bashfully thinking of a kind of illumination such as Rimbaud dreamed of – a nagging

11 on 13pt

Walking along the Mall we wondered who all those men were – tall hawk-featured men perched on balconies and high places, scanning the city with heavy binoculars. What were they seeking so earnestly? Who were they – so composed and steely-eyed? Timidly we stopped a policeman to ask him. 'They are publishers' he said mildly. Publishers! Our hearts stopped beating. 'They are on the look out for new talent.' Great God! It was for *us* they were waiting and watching! Then the kindly policeman lowered his voice confidentially and said in hollow and reverent tones: *'They are waiting for the new Trollope to be born!'* Do you remember, at these words, how heavy our suitcases suddenly felt? How our blood slowed, our footsteps lagged? Brother Ass, we had been bashfully thinking of a kind of

11 on 14.5pt

Linotype CARTIER

roman (05043), **italic** (13043)
Designed by Carl Dair 1967
Copyfitting code 113/88

There are no italic capitals

ABCDEFGHIJKLMNOP
QRSTUVWXYZ abcdefg
hijklmnopqrstuvwxyz
1234567890
fifl ()[]&£$.,;:-!?''

ABCDEFGHIJKLMNOP
QRSTUVWXYZ *abcdefg*
hijklmnopqrstuvwxyz
1234567890
fifl ()[]&£$.,;:-!?''

24 on 27pt

These examples show *normal* letterspacing and the effect of *increased*
letterspacing on roman setting *as well as on words in italic*: they also
show the appearance of figures, for example 28 May 1964, within text.
These & the ampersand are not included in the setting opposite.
Normal letterspacing

These examples show *normal* letterspacing and the effect of *increased*
letterspacing on roman setting *as well as on words in italic*: they also
show the appearance of figures, for example 28 May 1964, within text.
These & the ampersand are not included in the setting opposite.
Plus one unit spacing

These examples show *normal* letterspacing and the effect of *increased*
letterspacing on roman setting *as well as on words in italic*: they also
show the appearance of figures, for example 28 May 1964, within text.
These & the ampersand are not included in the setting opposite.
Plus two units spacing

WALKING ALONG THE MALL WE WONDERED WHO ALL THOSE MEN
WALKING ALONG THE MALL WE WONDERED WHO ALL THOSE
WALKING ALONG THE MALL WE WONDERED WHO ALL
Capitals: normal letterspacing/plus 4 units/plus 9 units

Walking along the Mall we wondered who all those men were – tall hawk-
featured men perched on balconies and high places, scanning the city with
heavy binoculars. WHAT WERE THEY SEEKING SO EARNESTLY? Who were they – so
composed and steely-eyed? Timidly we stopped a policeman to ask him. 'They
are publishers' he said mildly. Publishers! OUR HEARTS STOPPED BEATING. 'They
are on the look out for new talent.' Great God! It was for *us* they were waiting
and watching! Then the kindly policeman lowered his voice confidentially and
Text with reduced caps normal letterspacing/plus 3 units

WALKING ALONG THE MALL *we wondered who all those men were*
WALKING ALONG THE MALL we wondered who all those men were
True italic/sloped roman

Walking along the Mall we wondered who all those men were – tall hawk-featured men perched
on balconies and high places, scanning the city with heavy binoculars. What were they seeking so
earnestly? Who were they – so composed and steely-eyed? Timidly we stopped a policeman to ask
him. 'They are publishers' he said mildly. Publishers! Our hearts stopped beating. 'They are on the
look out for new talent.' Great God! It was for *us* they were waiting and watching! Then the kindly
policeman lowered his voice confidentially and said in hollow and reverent tones: *'They are waiting*
for the new Trollope to be born!' Do you remember, at these words, how heavy our suitcases suddenly
felt? How our blood slowed, our footsteps lagged? Brother Ass, we had been bashfully thinking of
a kind of illumination such as Rimbaud dreamed of – a nagging poem which was not didactic or
expository but which *infected* – was not simply a rationalised intuition, I mean, clothed in isinglass!
8 on 9pt

Walking along the Mall we wondered who all those men were – tall hawk-featured men perched
on balconies and high places, scanning the city with heavy binoculars. What were they seeking so
earnestly? Who were they – so composed and steely-eyed? Timidly we stopped a policeman to ask
him. 'They are publishers' he said mildly. Publishers! Our hearts stopped beating. 'They are on the
look out for new talent.' Great God! It was for *us* they were waiting and watching! Then the kindly
policeman lowered his voice confidentially and said in hollow and reverent tones: *'They are waiting*
for the new Trollope to be born!' Do you remember, at these words, how heavy our suitcases suddenly
felt? How our blood slowed, our footsteps lagged? Brother Ass, we had been bashfully thinking of
a kind of illumination such as Rimbaud dreamed of – a nagging poem which was not didactic or
8 on 10.5pt

Walking along the Mall we wondered who all those men were – tall hawk-featured men perched on balconies and high places, scanning the city with heavy binoculars. What were they seeking so earnestly? Who were they – so composed and steely-eyed? Timidly we stopped a policeman to ask him. 'They are publishers' he said mildly. Publishers! Our hearts stopped beating. 'They are on the look out for new talent.' Great God! It was for *us* they were waiting and watching! Then the kindly policeman lowered his voice confidentially and said in hollow and reverent tones: *'They are waiting for the new Trollope to be born!'* Do you remember, at these words, how heavy our suitcases suddenly felt? How our blood slowed, our footsteps lagged? Brother Ass, we had been bashfully thinking of a kind of illumination such as Rimbaud dreamed of – a nagging poem which was not didactic or expository but which *infected* – was not simply a rationalised intuition, I mean, clothed in isinglass! We had come to the wrong shop, with the wrong change! A chill struck us as we saw the mist falling in Trafalgar Square, coiling round us its tendrils of ectoplasm! A million muffin-eating moralists were waiting, not for us, Brother Ass, but for the plucky and tedious Trollope! (If you are dissatisfied with your form, reach for the *curette*.) Now do you wonder if I laugh a little off-key? Do you ask yourself what has turned me into nature's bashful little aphorist? We who are, after all, simply poor co-workers in the psyche of our nation, what can we expect but the

9 on 11pt

Walking along the Mall we wondered who all those men were – tall hawk-featured men perched on balconies and high places, scanning the city with heavy binoculars. What were they seeking so earnestly? Who were they – so composed and steely-eyed? Timidly we stopped a policeman to ask him. 'They are publishers' he said mildly. Publishers! Our hearts stopped beating. 'They are on the look out for new talent.' Great God! It was for *us* they were waiting and watching! Then the kindly policeman lowered his voice confidentially and said in hollow and reverent tones: *'They are waiting for the new Trollope to be born!'* Do you remember, at these words, how heavy our suitcases suddenly felt? How our blood slowed, our footsteps lagged? Brother Ass, we had been bashfully thinking of a kind of illumination such as Rimbaud dreamed of – a nagging poem which was not didactic or expository but which *infected* – was not simply a rationalised intuition, I mean, clothed in isinglass! We had come to the wrong shop, with the wrong change! A chill struck us as we saw the mist falling in Trafalgar Square, coiling round us its tendrils of ectoplasm! A million muffin-eating moralists were waiting, not for us, Brother Ass, but for the plucky and tedious Trollope! (If you are dissatisfied with your form, reach for the *curette*.) Now do you wonder if I laugh a little off-key? Do you ask yourself what has turned me into nature's bashful little aphorist? We who are, after

9 on 12pt

Walking along the Mall we wondered who all those men were – tall hawk-featured men perched on balconies and high places, scanning the city with heavy binoculars. What were they seeking so earnestly? Who were they – so composed and steely-eyed? Timidly we stopped a policeman to ask him. 'They are publishers' he said mildly. Publishers! Our hearts stopped beating. 'They are on the look out for new talent.' Great God! It was for *us* they were waiting and watching! Then the kindly policeman lowered his voice confidentially and said in hollow and reverent tones: *'They are waiting for the new Trollope to be born!'* Do you remember, at these words, how heavy our suitcases suddenly felt? How our blood slowed, our footsteps lagged? Brother Ass, we had been bashfully thinking of a kind of illumination such as Rimbaud dreamed of – a nagging poem which was not didactic or expository but which *infected* – was not simply a rationalised intuition, I mean, clothed in isinglass! We had come to the wrong shop, with the wrong change! A chill struck us as we saw the mist falling in Trafalgar Square, coiling round us its tendrils of ectoplasm! A million muffin-eating moralists were waiting, not for us, Brother Ass, but for the plucky and

10 on 12pt

Walking along the Mall we wondered who all those men were – tall hawk-featured men perched on balconies and high places, scanning the city with heavy binoculars. What were they seeking so earnestly? Who were they – so composed and steely-eyed? Timidly we stopped a policeman to ask him. 'They are publishers' he said mildly. Publishers! Our hearts stopped beating. 'They are on the look out for new talent.' Great God! It was for *us* they were waiting and watching! Then the kindly policeman lowered his voice confidentially and said in hollow and reverent tones: *'They are waiting for the new Trollope to be born!'* Do you remember, at these words, how heavy our suitcases suddenly felt? How our blood slowed, our footsteps lagged? Brother Ass, we had been bashfully thinking of a kind of illumination such as Rimbaud dreamed of – a nagging poem which was not didactic or expository but which *infected* – was not simply a rationalised intuition, I mean, clothed in isinglass! We had come to the wrong shop, with the wrong change! A chill struck us as we saw the mist falling in Trafalgar Square, coiling round us its tendrils of ectoplasm! A million muffin-

10 on 13.5pt

Walking along the Mall we wondered who all those men were – tall hawk-featured men perched on balconies and high places, scanning the city with heavy binoculars. What were they seeking so earnestly? Who were they – so composed and steely-eyed? Timidly we stopped a police-man to ask him. 'They are publishers' he said mildly. Publishers! Our hearts stopped beating. 'They are on the look out for new talent.' Great God! It was for *us* they were waiting and watching! Then the kindly policeman lowered his voice confidentially and said in hollow and reverent tones: *'They are waiting for the new Trollope to be born!'* Do you remember, at these words, how heavy our suitcases suddenly felt? How our blood slowed, our footsteps lagged? Brother Ass, we had been bash-fully thinking of a kind of illumination such as Rimbaud dreamed of – a nagging poem which was not didactic or expository but which *infected* – was not simply a rationalised intuition, I mean, clothed in isinglass! We had come to the wrong shop, with the wrong change! A chill struck us

11 on 13pt

Walking along the Mall we wondered who all those men were – tall hawk-featured men perched on balconies and high places, scanning the city with heavy binoculars. What were they seeking so earnestly? Who were they – so composed and steely-eyed? Timidly we stopped a police-man to ask him. 'They are publishers' he said mildly. Publishers! Our hearts stopped beating. 'They are on the look out for new talent.' Great God! It was for *us* they were waiting and watching! Then the kindly policeman lowered his voice confidentially and said in hollow and reverent tones: *'They are waiting for the new Trollope to be born!'* Do you remember, at these words, how heavy our suitcases suddenly felt? How our blood slowed, our footsteps lagged? Brother Ass, we had been bash-fully thinking of a kind of illumination such as Rimbaud dreamed of – a nagging poem which was not didactic or expository but which *infected* – was not simply a rationalised intuition, I mean, clothed in isinglass! We

11 on 14.5pt

roman (05047), italic (13047)
ATF 1902
Copyfitting code 125/110

ABCDEFGHIJKLMNOP
QRSTUVWXYZ abcdefg
hijklmnopqrstuvwxyz
1234567890
fifl ()[]&£$.,;:-!?"

ABCDEFGHIJKLMNOP
QRSTUVWXYZ abcdefg
hijklmnopqrstuvwxyz
1234567890
fifl ()[]&£$.,;:-!?"

24 on 27pt

These examples show *normal* letterspacing and the effect of *reduced* letterspacing on roman setting *as well as on words in italic*: they also show the appearance of figures, for example 28 May 1964, within text. These & the ampersand are not included in the setting opposite.
Normal letterspacing

These examples show *normal* letterspacing and the effect of *reduced* letterspacing on roman setting *as well as on words in italic*: they also show the appearance of figures, for example 28 May 1964, within text. These & the ampersand are not included in the setting opposite.
Minus one unit spacing

These examples show *normal* letterspacing and the effect of *reduced* letterspacing on roman setting *as well as on words in italic*: they also show the appearance of figures, for example 28 May 1964, within text. These & the ampersand are not included in the setting opposite.
Minus two units spacing

WALKING ALONG THE MALL WE WONDERED WHO ALL
WALKING ALONG THE MALL WE WONDERED WHO
WALKING ALONG THE MALL WE WONDERED
Capitals: normal letterspacing/plus 4 units/plus 9 units

WALKING ALONG THE MALL WE WONDERED WHO ALL THOSE MEN WERE
WALKING ALONG THE MALL WE WONDERED WHO ALL THOSE MEN
WALKING ALONG THE MALL WE WONDERED WHO ALL THOSE
Small caps: normal letterspacing/plus 3 units/plus 6 units

WALKING ALONG THE MALL WE WONDERED WHO ALL THOSE MEN WERE
WALKING ALONG THE MALL WE WONDERED WHO ALL THOSE MEN WERE
True small caps/reduced capitals

WALKING ALONG THE MALL we wondered who all those men were
WALKING ALONG THE MALL we wondered who all those men
True italic/sloped roman

Walking along the Mall we wondered who all those men were – tall hawk-featured men perched on balconies and high places, scanning the city with heavy binoculars. What were they seeking so earnestly? Who were they – so composed and steely-eyed? Timidly we stopped a policeman to ask him. 'They are publishers' he said mildly. Publishers! Our hearts stopped beating. 'They are on the look out for new talent.' Great God! It was for *us* they were waiting and watching! Then the kindly policeman lowered his voice confidentially and said in hollow and reverent tones: *'They are waiting for the new Trollope to be born!'* Do you remember, at these words, how heavy our suitcases suddenly felt? How our blood slowed, our footsteps lagged? Brother Ass, we had been bashfully thinking of a kind of illumination such as Rimbaud dreamed of – a nagging poem
8 on 9pt

WALKING ALONG THE MALL WE WONDERED WHO ALL THOSE MEN WERE – TALL HAWK-featured men perched on balconies and high places, scanning the city with heavy binoculars. What were they seeking so earnestly? Who were they – so composed and steely-eyed? Timidly we stopped a policeman to ask him. 'They are publishers' he said mildly. Publishers! Our hearts stopped beating. 'They are on the look out for new talent.' Great God! It was for *us* they were waiting and watching! Then the kindly policeman lowered his voice confidentially and said in hollow and reverent tones: *'They are waiting for the new Trollope to be born!'* Do you remember, at these words, how heavy our suitcases suddenly felt? How our blood slowed, our footsteps lagged? Brother Ass,
8 on 10.5pt

114

Walking along the Mall we wondered who all those men were – tall hawk-featured men perched on balconies and high places, scanning the city with heavy binoculars. What were they seeking so earnestly? Who were they – so composed and steely-eyed? Timidly we stopped a policeman to ask him. 'They are publishers' he said mildly. Publishers! Our hearts stopped beating. 'They are on the look out for new talent.' Great God! It was for *us* they were waiting and watching! Then the kindly policeman lowered his voice confidentially and said in hollow and reverent tones: *'They are waiting for the new Trollope to be born!'* Do you remember, at these words, how heavy our suitcases suddenly felt? How our blood slowed, our footsteps lagged? Brother Ass, we had been bashfully thinking of a kind of illumination such as Rimbaud dreamed of – a nagging poem which was not didactic or expository but which *infected* – was not simply a rationalised intuition, I mean, clothed in isinglass! We had come to the wrong shop, with the wrong change! A chill struck us as we saw the mist falling in Trafalgar Square, coiling round us its tendrils of ectoplasm! A million muffin-eating moralists were waiting, not for us, Brother Ass, but for the plucky and tedious Trollope! (If you are dissatisfied with your form, reach for the *curette*.) Now do you wonder if I laugh a little off-key? Do you ask yourself

9 on 11pt

Walking along the Mall we wondered who all those men were – tall hawk-featured men perched on balconies and high places, scanning the city with heavy binoculars. What were they seeking so earnestly? Who were they – so composed and steely-eyed? Timidly we stopped a policeman to ask him. 'They are publishers' he said mildly. Publishers! Our hearts stopped beating. 'They are on the look out for new talent.' Great God! It was for *us* they were waiting and watching! Then the kindly policeman lowered his voice confidentially and said in hollow and reverent tones: *'They are waiting for the new Trollope to be born!'* Do you remember, at these words, how heavy our suitcases suddenly felt? How our blood slowed, our footsteps lagged? Brother Ass, we had been bashfully thinking of a kind of illumination such as Rimbaud dreamed of – a nagging poem which was not didactic or expository but which *infected* – was not simply a rationalised intuition, I mean, clothed in isinglass! We had come to the wrong shop, with the wrong change! A chill struck us as we saw the mist falling in Trafalgar Square, coiling round us its tendrils of ectoplasm! A million muffin-eating moralists were waiting, not for us, Brother Ass, but for the plucky and tedious Trollope! (If you are dissatisfied with your form, reach for

9 on 12pt

Walking along the Mall we wondered who all those men were – tall hawk-featured men perched on balconies and high places, scanning the city with heavy binoculars. What were they seeking so earnestly? Who were they – so composed and steely-eyed? Timidly we stopped a policeman to ask him. 'They are publishers' he said mildly. Publishers! Our hearts stopped beating. 'They are on the look out for new talent.' Great God! It was for *us* they were waiting and watching! Then the kindly policeman lowered his voice confidentially and said in hollow and reverent tones: *'They are waiting for the new Trollope to be born!'* Do you remember, at these words, how heavy our suitcases suddenly felt? How our blood slowed, our footsteps lagged? Brother Ass, we had been bashfully thinking of a kind of illumination such as Rimbaud dreamed of – a nagging poem which was not didactic or expository but which *infected* – was not simply a rationalised intuition, I mean, clothed in isinglass! We had come to the wrong shop, with the wrong change! A chill struck us as we saw the mist falling in Trafalgar Square, coiling

10 on 12pt

WALKING ALONG THE MALL WE WONDERED WHO ALL THOSE MEN WERE – tall hawk-featured men perched on balconies and high places, scanning the city with heavy binoculars. What were they seeking so earnestly? Who were they – so composed and steely-eyed? Timidly we stopped a policeman to ask him. 'They are publishers' he said mildly. Publishers! Our hearts stopped beating. 'They are on the look out for new talent.' Great God! It was for *us* they were waiting and watching! Then the kindly policeman lowered his voice confidentially and said in hollow and reverent tones: *'They are waiting for the new Trollope to be born!'* Do you remember, at these words, how heavy our suitcases suddenly felt? How our blood slowed, our footsteps lagged? Brother Ass, we had been bashfully thinking of a kind of illumination such as Rimbaud dreamed of – a nagging poem which was not didactic or expository but which *infected* – was not simply a rationalised intuition, I mean, clothed in isinglass! We had come to the wrong shop, with the wrong change!

10 on 13.5pt

Walking along the Mall we wondered who all those men were – tall hawk-featured men perched on balconies and high places, scanning the city with heavy binoculars. What were they seeking so earnestly? Who were they – so composed and steely-eyed? Timidly we stopped a policeman to ask him. 'They are publishers' he said mildly. Publishers! Our hearts stopped beating. 'They are on the look out for new talent.' Great God! It was for *us* they were waiting and watching! Then the kindly policeman lowered his voice confidentially and said in hollow and reverent tones: *'They are waiting for the new Trollope to be born!'* Do you remember, at these words, how heavy our suitcases suddenly felt? How our blood slowed, our footsteps lagged? Brother Ass, we had been bashfully thinking of a kind of illumination such as Rimbaud dreamed of – a nagging poem which was not didactic or expository but which *infected* – was not simply a rationalised

11 on 13pt

WALKING ALONG THE MALL WE WONDERED WHO ALL THOSE MEN were – tall hawk-featured men perched on balconies and high places, scanning the city with heavy binoculars. What were they seeking so earnestly? Who were they – so composed and steely-eyed? Timidly we stopped a policeman to ask him. 'They are publishers' he said mildly. Publishers! Our hearts stopped beating. 'They are on the look out for new talent.' Great God! It was for *us* they were waiting and watching! Then the kindly policeman lowered his voice confidentially and said in hollow and reverent tones: *'They are waiting for the new Trollope to be born!'* Do you remember, at these words, how heavy our suitcases suddenly felt? How our blood slowed, our footsteps lagged? Brother Ass, we had been bashfully thinking of a kind of illumination such as Rimbaud dreamed of – a nagging poem which was

11 on 14.5pt

Linotype **Century Expanded**

roman (05051), **italic** (13051)
bold (07050)
ATF 1894 (L B Benton)
(bold: 1905)
Copyfitting code 131/131

The Monotype version is rather different

ABCDEFGHIJKLMNOP
QRSTUVWXYZ abcdefg
hijklmnopqrstuvwxyz
1234567890
fifl ()[]&£$.,;:-!?"

ABCDEFGHIJKLMNOP
QRSTUVWXYZ abcdefg
hijklmnopqrstuvwxyz
1234567890
fifl ()[]&£$.,;:-!?"

ABCDEFGHIJKLMNOP
QRSTUVWXYZ abcdefg
hijklmnopqrstuvwxyz
1234567890
fifl ()[]&£$.,;:-!?"

24 on 27pt

These examples show *normal* letterspacing and the effect of *reduced* letterspacing on roman setting *as well as on words in italic*: they also show the appearance of figures, for example 28 May 1964, within text. These & the ampersand are not included in the setting opposite.

Normal letterspacing

These examples show *normal* letterspacing and the effect of *reduced* letterspacing on roman setting *as well as on words in italic*: they also show the appearance of figures, for example 28 May 1964, within text. These & the ampersand are not included in the setting opposite.

Minus one unit spacing

These examples show *normal* letterspacing and the effect of *reduced* letterspacing on roman setting *as well as on words in italic*: they also show the appearance of figures, for example 28 May 1964, within text. These & the ampersand are not included in the setting opposite.

Minus two units spacing

WALKING ALONG THE MALL WE WONDERED WHO ALL
WALKING ALONG THE MALL WE WONDERED WHO
WALKING ALONG THE MALL WE WONDERED

Capitals: normal letterspacing/plus 4 units/plus 9 units

WALKING ALONG THE MALL WE WONDERED WHO ALL THOSE MEN
WALKING ALONG THE MALL WE WONDERED WHO ALL THOSE
WALKING ALONG THE MALL WE WONDERED WHO ALL

Small caps: normal letterspacing/plus 3 units/plus 6 units

WALKING ALONG THE MALL WE WONDERED WHO ALL THOSE MEN
WALKING ALONG THE MALL WE WONDERED WHO ALL THOSE MEN WERE

True small caps/reduced capitals

WALKING ALONG THE MALL we wondered who all those men
WALKING ALONG THE MALL we wondered who all those men

True italic/sloped roman

Walking along the Mall we wondered who all those men were – tall hawk- featured men perched on balconies and high places, scanning the city with heavy binoculars. What were they seeking so earnestly? Who were they – so composed and steely-eyed? Timidly we stopped a policeman to ask him. 'They are publishers' he said mildly. Publishers! Our hearts stopped beating. 'They are on the look out for new talent.' Great God! It was for *us* they were waiting and watching! Then the kindly policeman lowered his voice confidentially and said in hollow and reverent tones: *'They are waiting for the new Trollope to be born!'* Do you remember, at these words, how heavy our suitcases suddenly felt? How our blood slowed, our footsteps lagged? Brother Ass, we had been bashfully thinking of a kind of illumination such as

8 on 9pt

WALKING ALONG THE MALL WE WONDERED WHO ALL THOSE MEN WERE – TALL hawk-featured men perched on balconies and high places, scanning the city with heavy binoculars. What were they seeking so earnestly? Who were they – so composed and steely-eyed? Timidly we stopped a policeman to ask him. 'They are publishers' he said mildly. Publishers! Our hearts stopped beating. 'They are on the look out for new talent.' Great God! It was for *us* they were waiting and watching! Then the kindly policeman lowered his voice confidentially and said in hollow and reverent tones: *'They are waiting for the new Trollope to be born!'* Do you remember, at these words, how heavy our suitcases suddenly felt? How our blood slowed, our

8 on 10.5pt

Walking along the Mall we wondered who all those men were – tall hawk-featured men perched on balconies and high places, scanning the city with heavy binoculars. What were they seeking so earnestly? Who were they – so composed and steely-eyed? Timidly we stopped a policeman to ask him. 'They are publishers' he said mildly. Publishers! Our hearts stopped beating. 'They are on the look out for new talent.' Great God! It was for *us* they were waiting and watching! Then the kindly policeman lowered his voice confidentially and said in hollow and reverent tones: *'They are waiting for the new Trollope to be born!'* Do you remember, at these words, how heavy our suitcases suddenly felt? How our blood slowed, our footsteps lagged? Brother Ass, we had been bashfully thinking of a kind of illumination such as Rimbaud dreamed of – a nagging poem which was not didactic or expository but which *infected* – was not simply a rationalised intuition, I mean, clothed in isinglass! We had come to the wrong shop, with the wrong change! A chill struck us as we saw the mist falling in Trafalgar Square, coiling round us its tendrils of ectoplasm! A million muffin-eating moralists were waiting, not for us, Brother Ass, but for the plucky and tedious Trollope! (If you are dissatisfied with your form, reach for the

9 on 11pt

Walking along the Mall we wondered who all those men were – tall hawk-featured men perched on balconies and high places, scanning the city with heavy binoculars. What were they seeking so earnestly? Who were they – so composed and steely-eyed? Timidly we stopped a policeman to ask him. 'They are publishers' he said mildly. Publishers! Our hearts stopped beating. 'They are on the look out for new talent.' Great God! It was for *us* they were waiting and watching! Then the kindly policeman lowered his voice confidentially and said in hollow and reverent tones: *'They are waiting for the new Trollope to be born!'* Do you remember, at these words, how heavy our suitcases suddenly felt? How our blood slowed, our footsteps lagged? Brother Ass, we had been bashfully thinking of a kind of illumination such as Rimbaud dreamed of – a nagging poem which was not didactic or expository but which *infected* – was not simply a rationalised intuition, I mean, clothed in isinglass! We had come to the wrong shop, with the wrong change! A chill struck us as

10 on 12pt

Walking along the Mall we wondered who all those men were – tall hawk-featured men perched on balconies and high places, scanning the city with heavy binoculars. What were they seeking so earnestly? Who were they – so composed and steely-eyed? Timidly we stopped a policeman to ask him. 'They are publishers' he said mildly. Publishers! Our hearts stopped beating. 'They are on the look out for new talent.' Great God! It was for *us* they were waiting and watching! Then the kindly policeman lowered his voice confidentially and said in hollow and reverent tones: *'They are waiting for the new Trollope to be born!'* Do you remember, at these words, how heavy our suitcases suddenly felt? How our blood slowed, our footsteps lagged? Brother Ass, we had been bashfully thinking of a kind of illumination such as Rimbaud dreamed of – a nagging poem which was not didactic or

11 on 13pt

WALKING ALONG THE MALL WE WONDERED WHO ALL THOSE MEN WERE – tall hawk-featured men perched on balconies and high places, scanning the city with heavy binoculars. What were they seeking so earnestly? Who were they – so composed and steely-eyed? Timidly we stopped a policeman to ask him. 'They are publishers' he said mildly. Publishers! Our hearts stopped beating. 'They are on the look out for new talent.' Great God! It was for *us* they were waiting and watching! Then the kindly policeman lowered his voice confidentially and said in hollow and reverent tones: *'They are waiting for the new Trollope to be born!'* Do you remember, at these words, how heavy our suitcases suddenly felt? How our blood slowed, our footsteps lagged? Brother Ass, we had been bashfully thinking of a kind of illumination such as Rimbaud dreamed of – a nagging poem which was not didactic or expository but which *infected* – was not simply a rationalised intuition, I mean, clothed in isinglass! We had come to the wrong shop, with the wrong change! A chill struck us as we saw the mist falling in Trafalgar Square, coiling round us its tendrils of ectoplasm! A million muffin-eating moralists were waiting, not for us, Brother Ass, but for the plucky and

9 on 12pt

WALKING ALONG THE MALL WE WONDERED WHO ALL THOSE MEN were – tall hawk-featured men perched on balconies and high places, scanning the city with heavy binoculars. What were they seeking so earnestly? Who were they – so composed and steely-eyed? Timidly we stopped a policeman to ask him. 'They are publishers' he said mildly. Publishers! Our hearts stopped beating. 'They are on the look out for new talent.' Great God! It was for *us* they were waiting and watching! Then the kindly policeman lowered his voice confidentially and said in hollow and reverent tones: *'They are waiting for the new Trollope to be born!'* Do you remember, at these words, how heavy our suitcases suddenly felt? How our blood slowed, our footsteps lagged? Brother Ass, we had been bashfully thinking of a kind of illumination such as Rimbaud dreamed of – a nagging poem which was not didactic or expository but which *infected* – was not simply a rationalised intuition, I mean, clothed in isinglass! We had

10 on 13.5pt

WALKING ALONG THE MALL WE WONDERED WHO ALL THOSE men were – tall hawk-featured men perched on balconies and high places, scanning the city with heavy binoculars. What were they seeking so earnestly? Who were they – so composed and steely-eyed? Timidly we stopped a policeman to ask him. 'They are publishers' he said mildly. Publishers! Our hearts stopped beating. 'They are on the look out for new talent.' Great God! It was for *us* they were waiting and watching! Then the kindly policeman lowered his voice confidentially and said in hollow and reverent tones: *'They are waiting for the new Trollope to be born!'* Do you remember, at these words, how heavy our suitcases suddenly felt? How our blood slowed, our footsteps lagged? Brother Ass, we had been bashfully thinking of a kind of illumination such as

11 on 14.5pt

LINOTYPE CENTURY EXPANDED

Monotype **Century Schoolbook**

227 **roman and italic**
477 **bold**
Monotype 1934
Copyfitting factor 46.2/45.0/50.4

Range also includes bold italic

Designed by M F Benton 1924 for ATF (based
on the original design of 1896 by L B Benton
for *Century* magazine)

Educational characters available

ABCDEFGHIJKLMNOP
QRSTUVWXYZ abcdefg
hijklmnopqrstuvwxyz
1234567890
ff fi fl ffi ffl ()[]&£$.,;:-!?''

ABCDEFGHIJKLMNOP
QRSTUVWXYZ abcdefg
hijklmnopqrstuvwxyz
1234567890
ff fi fl ffi ffl ()[]&£$.,;:-!?''

ABCDEFGHIJKLMNOP
QRSTUVWXYZ abcdefg
hijklmnopqrstuvwxyz
1234567890
ff fi fl ffi ffl ()[]&£$.,;:-!?''

24 on 27pt

These examples show *normal* letterspacing and the effect of *reduced* letterspacing on roman setting *as well as on words in italic*: they also show the appearance of figures, for example 28 May 1964, within text. These & the ampersand are not included in the setting opposite.

Normal letterspacing

These examples show *normal* letterspacing and the effect of *reduced* letterspacing on roman setting *as well as on words in italic*: they also show the appearance of figures, for example 28 May 1964, within text. These & the ampersand are not included in the setting opposite.

Minus one unit spacing

These examples show *normal* letterspacing and the effect of *reduced* letterspacing on roman setting *as well as on words in italic*: they also show the appearance of figures, for example 28 May 1964, within text. These & the ampersand are not included in the setting opposite.

Minus two units spacing

WALKING ALONG THE MALL WE WONDERED WHO ALL THOSE
WALKING ALONG THE MALL WE WONDERED WHO ALL
WALKING ALONG THE MALL WE WONDERED WHO

Capitals: normal letterspacing/plus 9 units/plus 18 units

WALKING ALONG THE MALL WE WONDERED WHO ALL THOSE MEN WERE
WALKING ALONG THE MALL WE WONDERED WHO ALL THOSE MEN WERE
WALKING ALONG THE MALL WE WONDERED WHO ALL THOSE MEN

Small caps: normal letterspacing/plus 6 units/plus 12 units

WALKING ALONG THE MALL WE WONDERED WHO ALL THOSE MEN WERE
WALKING ALONG THE MALL WE WONDERED WHO ALL THOSE MEN WERE

True small caps/reduced capitals

WALKING ALONG THE MALL we wondered who all those men were
WALKING ALONG THE MALL we wondered who all those men were

True italic/sloped roman

Walking along the Mall we wondered who all those men were – tall hawk-featured men perched on balconies and high places, scanning the city with heavy binoculars. What were they seeking so earnestly? Who were they – so composed and steely-eyed? Timidly we stopped a policeman to ask him. 'They are publishers' he said mildly. Publishers! Our hearts stopped beating. 'They are on the look out for new talent.' Great God! It was for *us* they were waiting and watching! Then the kindly policeman lowered his voice confidentially and said in hollow and reverent tones: *'They are waiting for the new Trollope to be born!'* Do you remember, at these words, how heavy our suitcases suddenly felt? How our blood slowed, our footsteps lagged? Brother Ass, we had been bashfully thinking

8 on 9pt

WALKING ALONG THE MALL WE WONDERED WHO ALL THOSE MEN WERE – TALL hawk-featured men perched on balconies and high places, scanning the city with heavy binoculars. What were they seeking so earnestly? Who were they – so composed and steely-eyed? Timidly we stopped a policeman to ask him. 'They are publishers' he said mildly. Publishers! Our hearts stopped beating. 'They are on the look out for new talent.' Great God! It was for *us* they were waiting and watching! Then the kindly policeman lowered his voice confidentially and said in hollow and reverent tones: *'They are waiting for the new Trollope to be born!'* Do you remember, at these words, how heavy our suitcases suddenly felt? How our

8 on 10.5pt

Walking along the Mall we wondered who all those men were – tall hawk-featured men perched on balconies and high places, scanning the city with heavy binoculars. What were they seeking so earnestly? Who were they – so composed and steely-eyed? Timidly we stopped a policeman to ask him. 'They are publishers' he said mildly. Publishers! Our hearts stopped beating. 'They are on the look out for new talent.' Great God! It was for *us* they were waiting and watching! Then the kindly policeman lowered his voice confidentially and said in hollow and reverent tones: *'They are waiting for the new Trollope to be born!'* Do you remember, at these words, how heavy our suitcases suddenly felt? How our blood slowed, our footsteps lagged? Brother Ass, we had been bashfully thinking of a kind of illumination such as Rimbaud dreamed of – a nagging poem which was not didactic or expository but which *infected* – was not simply a rationalised intuition, I mean, clothed in isinglass! We had come to the wrong shop, with the wrong change! A chill struck us as we saw the mist falling in Trafalgar Square, coiling around us its tendrils of ectoplasm! A million muffin-eating moralists were waiting, not for us, Brother Ass, but for the plucky and tedious Trollope! (If you are dissatisfied with your form,

9 on 11pt

Walking along the Mall we wondered who all those men were – tall hawk-featured men perched on balconies and high places, scanning the city with heavy binoculars. What were they seeking so earnestly? Who were they – so composed and steely-eyed? Timidly we stopped a policeman to ask him. 'They are publishers' he said mildly. Publishers! Our hearts stopped beating. 'They are on the look out for new talent.' Great God! It was for *us* they were waiting and watching! Then the kindly policeman lowered his voice confidentially and said in hollow and reverent tones: *'They are waiting for the new Trollope to be born!'* Do you remember, at these words, how heavy our suitcases suddenly felt? How our blood slowed, our footsteps lagged? Brother Ass, we had been bashfully thinking of a kind of illumination such as Rimbaud dreamed of – a nagging poem which was not didactic or expository but which *infected* – was not simply a rationalised intuition, I mean, clothed in isinglass! We had come to the wrong shop, with the wrong

10 on 12pt

Walking along the Mall we wondered who all those men were – tall hawk-featured men perched on balconies and high places, scanning the city with heavy binoculars. What were they seeking so earnestly? Who were they – so composed and steely-eyed? Timidly we stopped a policeman to ask him. 'They are publishers' he said mildly. Publishers! Our hearts stopped beating. 'They are on the look out for new talent.' Great God! It was for *us* they were waiting and watching! Then the kindly policeman lowered his voice confidentially and said in hollow and reverent tones: *'They are waiting for the new Trollope to be born!'* Do you remember, at these words, how heavy our suitcases suddenly felt? How our blood slowed, our footsteps lagged? Brother Ass, we had been bashfully thinking of a kind of illumination such as Rimbaud dreamed of – a nagging poem which was not

11 on 13pt

WALKING ALONG THE MALL WE WONDERED WHO ALL THOSE MEN WERE – tall hawk-featured men perched on balconies and high places, scanning the city with heavy binoculars. What were they seeking so earnestly? Who were they – so composed and steely-eyed? Timidly we stopped a policeman to ask him. 'They are publishers' he said mildly. Publishers! Our hearts stopped beating. 'They are on the look out for new talent.' Great God! It was for *us* they were waiting and watching! Then the kindly policeman lowered his voice confidentially and said in hollow and reverent tones: *'They are waiting for the new Trollope to be born!'* Do you remember, at these words, how heavy our suitcases suddenly felt? How our blood slowed, our footsteps lagged? Brother Ass, we had been bashfully thinking of a kind of illumination such as Rimbaud dreamed of – a nagging poem which was not didactic or expository but which *infected* – was not simply a rationalised intuition, I mean, clothed in isinglass! We had come to the wrong shop, with the wrong change! A chill struck us as we saw the mist falling in Trafalgar Square, coiling around us its tendrils of ectoplasm! A million muffin-eating moralists were waiting, not for us, Brother Ass, but

9 on 12pt

WALKING ALONG THE MALL WE WONDERED WHO ALL THOSE MEN were – tall hawk-featured men perched on balconies and high places, scanning the city with heavy binoculars. What were they seeking so earnestly? Who were they – so composed and steely-eyed? Timidly we stopped a policeman to ask him. 'They are publishers' he said mildly. Publishers! Our hearts stopped beating. 'They are on the look out for new talent.' Great God! It was for *us* they were waiting and watching! Then the kindly policeman lowered his voice confidentially and said in hollow and reverent tones: *'They are waiting for the new Trollope to be born!'* Do you remember, at these words, how heavy our suitcases suddenly felt? How our blood slowed, our footsteps lagged? Brother Ass, we had been bashfully thinking of a kind of illumination such as Rimbaud dreamed of – a nagging poem which was not didactic or expository but which *infected* – was not simply a rationalised intuition, I

10 on 13.5pt

WALKING ALONG THE MALL WE WONDERED WHO ALL THOSE men were – tall hawk-featured men perched on balconies and high places, scanning the city with heavy binoculars. What were they seeking so earnestly? Who were they – so composed and steely-eyed? Timidly we stopped a policeman to ask him. 'They are publishers' he said mildly. Publishers! Our hearts stopped beating. 'They are on the look out for new talent.' Great God! It was for *us* they were waiting and watching! Then the kindly policeman lowered his voice confidentially and said in hollow and reverent tones: *'They are waiting for the new Trollope to be born!'* Do you remember, at these words, how heavy our suitcases suddenly felt? How our blood slowed, our footsteps lagged? Brother Ass, we had been bashfully thinking of a kind of illumination such as

11 on 14.5pt

MONOTYPE CENTURY SCHOOLBOOK

Linotype **New Century Schoolbook**

roman (05497), **italic** (13497)
bold (07497)
Mergenthaler 1982
Copyfitting code 135/133/154

Range also includes semi-bold, semi-bold
italic, bold italic, black, black italic

Linotype Century Schoolbook roman and
italic are very similar but the roman is slightly
heavier (copyfitting code 134/133). There is
only one bold, with no bold italic

Derived from M F Benton's design of 1924 for
ATF (itself based on L B Benton's design of
1896 for *Century* magazine)

ABCDEFGHIJKLMNOP
QRSTUVWXYZ abcdefg
hijklmnopqrstuvwxyz
1234567890
fifl ()[]&£$.,;:-!?"

ABCDEFGHIJKLMNOP
QRSTUVWXYZ abcdefg
hijklmnopqrstuvwxyz
1234567890
fifl ()[]&£$.,;:-!?"

ABCDEFGHIJKLMNOP
QRSTUVWXYZ abcdefg
hijklmnopqrstuvwxyz
1234567890
fifl ()[]&£$.,;:-!?"

24 on 27pt

These examples show *normal* letterspacing and the effect of *reduced*
letterspacing on roman setting *as well as on words in italic*: they also
show the appearance of figures, for example 28 May 1964, within text.
These & the ampersand are not included in the setting opposite.
Normal letterspacing

These examples show *normal* letterspacing and the effect of *reduced*
letterspacing on roman setting *as well as on words in italic*: they also
show the appearance of figures, for example 28 May 1964, within text.
These & the ampersand are not included in the setting opposite.
Minus one unit spacing

These examples show *normal* letterspacing and the effect of *reduced*
letterspacing on roman setting *as well as on words in italic*: they also
show the appearance of figures, for example 28 May 1964, within text.
These & the ampersand are not included in the setting opposite.
Minus two units spacing

WALKING ALONG THE MALL WE WONDERED WHO ALL
WALKING ALONG THE MALL WE WONDERED WHO
WALKING ALONG THE MALL WE WONDERED
Capitals: normal letterspacing/plus 4 units/plus 9 units

WALKING ALONG THE MALL WE WONDERED WHO ALL THOSE MEN
WALKING ALONG THE MALL WE WONDERED WHO ALL THOSE
WALKING ALONG THE MALL WE WONDERED WHO ALL
Small caps: normal letterspacing/plus 3 units/plus 6 units

WALKING ALONG THE MALL WE WONDERED WHO ALL THOSE MEN
WALKING ALONG THE MALL WE WONDERED WHO ALL THOSE MEN WERE
True small caps/reduced capitals

WALKING ALONG THE MALL we wondered who all those men
WALKING ALONG THE MALL we wondered who all those men
True italic/sloped roman

Walking along the Mall we wondered who all those men were – tall hawk-
featured men perched on balconies and high places, scanning the city with heavy
binoculars. What were they seeking so earnestly? Who were they – so composed
and steely-eyed? Timidly we stopped a policeman to ask him. 'They are publishers'
he said mildly. Publishers! Our hearts stopped beating. 'They are on the look out
for new talent.' Great God! It was for *us* they were waiting and watching! Then the
kindly policeman lowered his voice confidentially and said in hollow and reverent
tones: *'They are waiting for the new Trollope to be born!'* Do you remember, at
these words, how heavy our suitcases suddenly felt? How our blood slowed, our
footsteps lagged? Brother Ass, we had been bashfully thinking of a kind of
8 on 9pt

WALKING ALONG THE MALL WE WONDERED WHO ALL THOSE MEN WERE – TALL
hawk-featured men perched on balconies and high places, scanning the city with
heavy binoculars. What were they seeking so earnestly? Who were they – so
composed and steely-eyed? Timidly we stopped a policeman to ask him. 'They are
publishers' he said mildly. Publishers! Our hearts stopped beating. 'They are on
the look out for new talent.' Great God! It was for *us* they were waiting and
watching! Then the kindly policeman lowered his voice confidentially and said in
hollow and reverent tones: *'They are waiting for the new Trollope to be born!'* Do
you remember, at these words, how heavy our suitcases suddenly felt? How our
8 on 10.5pt

Walking along the Mall we wondered who all those men were – tall hawk-featured men perched on balconies and high places, scanning the city with heavy binoculars. What were they seeking so earnestly? Who were they – so composed and steely-eyed? Timidly we stopped a policeman to ask him. 'They are publishers' he said mildly. Publishers! Our hearts stopped beating. 'They are on the look out for new talent.' Great God! It was for *us* they were waiting and watching! Then the kindly policeman lowered his voice confidentially and said in hollow and reverent tones: *'They are waiting for the new Trollope to be born!'* Do you remember, at these words, how heavy our suitcases suddenly felt? How our blood slowed, our footsteps lagged? Brother Ass, we had been bashfully thinking of a kind of illumination such as Rimbaud dreamed of – a nagging poem which was not didactic or expository but which *infected* – was not simply a rationalised intuition, I mean, clothed in isinglass! We had come to the wrong shop, with the wrong change! A chill struck us as we saw the mist falling in Trafalgar Square, coiling round us its tendrils of ectoplasm! A million muffin-eating moralists were waiting, not for us, Brother Ass, but for the plucky and tedious Trollope! (If you are dis-

9 on 11pt

Walking along the Mall we wondered who all those men were – tall hawk-featured men perched on balconies and high places, scanning the city with heavy binoculars. What were they seeking so earnestly? Who were they – so composed and steely-eyed? Timidly we stopped a policeman to ask him. 'They are publishers' he said mildly. Publishers! Our hearts stopped beating. 'They are on the look out for new talent.' Great God! It was for *us* they were waiting and watching! Then the kindly policeman lowered his voice confidentially and said in hollow and reverent tones: *'They are waiting for the new Trollope to be born!'* Do you remember, at these words, how heavy our suitcases suddenly felt? How our blood slowed, our footsteps lagged? Brother Ass, we had been bashfully thinking of a kind of illumination such as Rimbaud dreamed of – a nagging poem which was not didactic or expository but which *infected* – was not simply a rationalised intuition, I mean, clothed in isinglass! We had come to the wrong

10 on 12pt

Walking along the Mall we wondered who all those men were – tall hawk-featured men perched on balconies and high places, scanning the city with heavy binoculars. What were they seeking so earnestly? Who were they – so composed and steely-eyed? Timidly we stopped a policeman to ask him. 'They are publishers' he said mildly. Publishers! Our hearts stopped beating. 'They are on the look out for new talent.' Great God! It was for *us* they were waiting and watching! Then the kindly policeman lowered his voice confidentially and said in hollow and reverent tones: *'They are waiting for the new Trollope to be born!'* Do you remember, at these words, how heavy our suitcases suddenly felt? How our blood slowed, our footsteps lagged? Brother Ass, we had been bashfully thinking of a kind of illumination such as Rimbaud dreamed of – a nagging poem which was not

11 on 13pt

WALKING ALONG THE MALL WE WONDERED WHO ALL THOSE MEN WERE – tall hawk-featured men perched on balconies and high places, scanning the city with heavy binoculars. What were they seeking so earnestly? Who were they – so composed and steely-eyed? Timidly we stopped a policeman to ask him. 'They are publishers' he said mildly. Publishers! Our hearts stopped beating. 'They are on the look out for new talent.' Great God! It was for *us* they were waiting and watching! Then the kindly policeman lowered his voice confidentially and said in hollow and reverent tones: *'They are waiting for the new Trollope to be born!'* Do you remember, at these words, how heavy our suitcases suddenly felt? How our blood slowed, our footsteps lagged? Brother Ass, we had been bashfully thinking of a kind of illumination such as Rimbaud dreamed of – a nagging poem which was not didactic or expository but which *infected* – was not simply a rationalised intuition, I mean, clothed in isinglass! We had come to the wrong shop, with the wrong change! A chill struck us as we saw the mist falling in Trafalgar Square, coiling round us its tendrils of ectoplasm! A million muffin-eating moralists were waiting, not for us,

9 on 12pt

WALKING ALONG THE MALL WE WONDERED WHO ALL THOSE MEN were – tall hawk-featured men perched on balconies and high places, scanning the city with heavy binoculars. What were they seeking so earnestly? Who were they – so composed and steely-eyed? Timidly we stopped a policeman to ask him. 'They are publishers' he said mildly. Publishers! Our hearts stopped beating. 'They are on the look out for new talent.' Great God! It was for *us* they were waiting and watching! Then the kindly policeman lowered his voice confidentially and said in hollow and reverent tones: *'They are waiting for the new Trollope to be born!'* Do you remember, at these words, how heavy our suitcases suddenly felt? How our blood slowed, our footsteps lagged? Brother Ass, we had been bashfully thinking of a kind of illumination such as Rimbaud dreamed of – a nagging poem which was not didactic or expository but which *infected* – was not simply a rationalised

10 on 13.5pt

WALKING ALONG THE MALL WE WONDERED WHO ALL THOSE men were – tall hawk-featured men perched on balconies and high places, scanning the city with heavy binoculars. What were they seeking so earnestly? Who were they – so composed and steely-eyed? Timidly we stopped a policeman to ask him. 'They are publishers' he said mildly. Publishers! Our hearts stopped beating. 'They are on the look out for new talent.' Great God! It was for *us* they were waiting and watching! Then the kindly policeman lowered his voice confidentially and said in hollow and reverent tones: *'They are waiting for the new Trollope to be born!'* Do you remember, at these words, how heavy our suitcases suddenly felt? How our blood slowed, our footsteps lagged? Brother Ass, we had been bashfully thinking of a kind of illumination such as

11 on 14.5pt

Monotype **Clarion**

917 roman and italic
918 bold
Monotype 1983 (Robin Nicholas and Ron Carpenter)
Copyfitting factor 48.0/46.6/51.9

Designed as a newspaper type

ABCDEFGHIJKLMNOP
QRSTUVWXYZ abcdefg
hijklmnopqrstuvwxyz
1234567890
ff fi fl ffi ffl ()[]&£$.,;:-!?''

ABCDEFGHIJKLMNOP
QRSTUVWXYZ abcdefg
hijklmnopqrstuvwxyz
1234567890
ff fi fl ffi ffl ()[]&£$.,;:-!?''

ABCDEFGHIJKLMNOP
QRSTUVWXYZ abcdefg
hijklmnopqrstuvwxyz
1234567890
ff fi fl ffi ffl ()[]&£$.,;:-!?''

24 on 27pt

These examples show *normal* letterspacing and the effect of *reduced* letterspacing on roman setting *as well as on words in italic*: they also show the appearance of figures, for example 28 May 1964, within text. These & the ampersand are not included in the setting opposite.

Normal letterspacing

These examples show *normal* letterspacing and the effect of *reduced* letterspacing on roman setting *as well as on words in italic*: they also show the appearance of figures, for example 28 May 1964, within text. These & the ampersand are not included in the setting opposite.

Minus one unit spacing

These examples show *normal* letterspacing and the effect of *reduced* letterspacing on roman setting *as well as on words in italic*: they also show the appearance of figures, for example 28 May 1964, within text. These & the ampersand are not included in the setting opposite.

Minus two units spacing

WALKING ALONG THE MALL WE WONDERED WHO ALL THOSE
WALKING ALONG THE MALL WE WONDERED WHO ALL
WALKING ALONG THE MALL WE WONDERED WHO

Capitals: normal letterspacing/plus 9 units/plus 18 units

WALKING ALONG THE MALL WE WONDERED WHO ALL THOSE MEN WERE
WALKING ALONG THE MALL WE WONDERED WHO ALL THOSE MEN WERE
WALKING ALONG THE MALL WE WONDERED WHO ALL THOSE MEN

Small caps: normal letterspacing/plus 6 units/plus 12 units

WALKING ALONG THE MALL we wondered who all those men were
WALKING ALONG THE MALL we wondered who all those men were

True italic/sloped roman

WALKING ALONG THE MALL WE WONDERED WHO ALL THOSE MEN WERE
WALKING ALONG THE MALL WE WONDERED WHO ALL THOSE MEN WERE

True small caps/reduced capitals

Walking along the Mall we wondered who all those men were – tall hawk-featured men perched on balconies and high places, scanning the city with heavy binoculars. What were they seeking so earnestly? Who were they – so composed and steely-eyed? Timidly we stopped a policeman to ask him. 'They are publishers' he said mildly. Publishers! Our hearts stopped beating. 'They are on the look out for new talent.' Great God! It was for *us* they were waiting and watching! Then the kindly policeman lowered his voice confidentially and said in hollow and reverent tones: *'They are waiting for the new Trollope to be born!'* Do you remember, at these words, how heavy our suitcases suddenly felt? How our blood slowed, our footsteps lagged? Brother Ass, we

8 on 9pt

WALKING ALONG THE MALL WE WONDERED WHO ALL THOSE MEN WERE – TALL hawk-featured men perched on balconies and high places, scanning the city with heavy binoculars. What were they seeking so earnestly? Who were they – so composed and steely-eyed? Timidly we stopped a policeman to ask him. 'They are publishers' he said mildly. Publishers! Our hearts stopped beating. 'They are on the look out for new talent.' Great God! It was for *us* they were waiting and watching! Then the kindly policeman lowered his voice confidentially and said in hollow and reverent tones: *'They are waiting for the new Trollope to be born!'* Do you remember, at these words, how heavy our

8 on 10.5pt

Walking along the Mall we wondered who all those men were – tall hawk-featured men perched on balconies and high places, scanning the city with heavy binoculars. What were they seeking so earnestly? Who were they – so composed and steely-eyed? Timidly we stopped a policeman to ask him. 'They are publishers' he said mildly. Publishers! Our hearts stopped beating. 'They are on the look out for new talent.' Great God! It was for *us* they were waiting and watching! Then the kindly policeman lowered his voice confidentially and said in hollow and reverent tones: *'They are waiting for the new Trollope to be born!'* Do you remember, at these words, how heavy our suitcases suddenly felt? How our blood slowed, our footsteps lagged? Brother Ass, we had been bashfully thinking of a kind of illumination such as Rimbaud dreamed of – a nagging poem which was not didactic or expository but which *infected* – was not simply a rationalised intuition, I mean, clothed in isinglass! We had come to the wrong shop, with the wrong change! A chill struck us as we saw the mist falling in Trafalgar Square, coiling around us its tendrils of ectoplasm! A million muffin-eating moralists were waiting, not for us, Brother Ass, but for the

9 on 11pt

Walking along the Mall we wondered who all those men were – tall hawk-featured men perched on balconies and high places, scanning the city with heavy binoculars. What were they seeking so earnestly? Who were they – so composed and steely-eyed? Timidly we stopped a policeman to ask him. 'They are publishers' he said mildly. Publishers! Our hearts stopped beating. 'They are on the look out for new talent.' Great God! It was for *us* they were waiting and watching! Then the kindly policeman lowered his voice confidentially and said in hollow and reverent tones: *'They are waiting for the new Trollope to be born!'* Do you remember, at these words, how heavy our suitcases suddenly felt? How our blood slowed, our footsteps lagged? Brother Ass, we had been bashfully thinking of a kind of illumination such as Rimbaud dreamed of – a nagging poem which was not didactic or expository but which *infected* – was not simply a rationalised intuition, I mean, clothed in isinglass! We had come to the

10 on 12pt

Walking along the Mall we wondered who all those men were – tall hawk-featured men perched on balconies and high places, scanning the city with heavy binoculars. What were they seeking so earnestly? Who were they – so composed and steely-eyed? Timidly we stopped a policeman to ask him. 'They are publishers' he said mildly. Publishers! Our hearts stopped beating. 'They are on the look out for new talent.' Great God! It was for *us* they were waiting and watching! Then the kindly policeman lowered his voice confidentially and said in hollow and reverent tones: *'They are waiting for the new Trollope to be born!'* Do you remember, at these words, how heavy our suitcases suddenly felt? How our blood slowed, our footsteps lagged? Brother Ass, we had been bashfully thinking of a kind of illumination such as Rimbaud dreamed of

11 on 13pt

WALKING ALONG THE MALL WE WONDERED WHO ALL THOSE MEN WERE – tall hawk-featured men perched on balconies and high places, scanning the city with heavy binoculars. What were they seeking so earnestly? Who were they – so composed and steely-eyed? Timidly we stopped a policeman to ask him. 'They are publishers' he said mildly. Publishers! Our hearts stopped beating. 'They are on the look out for new talent.' Great God! It was for *us* they were waiting and watching! Then the kindly policeman lowered his voice confidentially and said in hollow and reverent tones: *'They are waiting for the new Trollope to be born!'* Do you remember, at these words, how heavy our suitcases suddenly felt? How our blood slowed, our footsteps lagged? Brother Ass, we had been bashfully thinking of a kind of illumination such as Rimbaud dreamed of – a nagging poem which was not didactic or expository but which *infected* – was not simply a rationalised intuition, I mean, clothed in isinglass! We had come to the wrong shop, with the wrong change! A chill struck us as we saw the mist falling in Trafalgar Square, coiling around us its tendrils of ectoplasm! A million muffin-

9 on 12pt

WALKING ALONG THE MALL WE WONDERED WHO ALL THOSE MEN were tall hawk-featured men perched on balconies and high places, scanning the city with heavy binoculars. What were they seeking so earnestly? Who were they – so composed and steely-eyed? Timidly we stopped a policeman to ask him. 'They are publishers' he said mildly. Publishers! Our hearts stopped beating. 'They are on the look out for new talent.' Great God! It was for *us* they were waiting and watching! Then the kindly policeman lowered his voice confidentially and said in hollow and reverent tones: *'They are waiting for the new Trollope to be born!'* Do you remember, at these words, how heavy our suitcases suddenly felt? How our blood slowed, our footsteps lagged? Brother Ass, we had been bashfully thinking of a kind of illumination such as Rimbaud dreamed of – a nagging poem which was not didactic or expository but which *infected* – was

10 on 13.5pt

WALKING ALONG THE MALL WE WONDERED WHO ALL THOSE men were – tall hawk-featured men perched on balconies and high places, scanning the city with heavy binoculars. What were they seeking so earnestly? Who were they – so composed and steely-eyed? Timidly we stopped a policeman to ask him. 'They are publishers' he said mildly. Publishers! Our hearts stopped beating. 'They are on the look out for new talent.' Great God! It was for *us* they were waiting and watching! Then the kindly policeman lowered his voice confidentially and said in hollow and reverent tones: *'They are waiting for the new Trollope to be born!'* Do you remember, at these words, how heavy our suitcases suddenly felt? How our blood slowed, our footsteps lagged? Brother Ass, we had been bashfully think-

11 on 14.5pt

MONOTYPE CLARION

Linotype **Concorde**

roman (05319), **italic** (13319)
bold (07319)
Berthold 1969 (Günter Gerhard Lange)
Copyfitting code 133/138/137

ABCDEFGHIJKLMNOP
QRSTUVWXYZ abcdefg
hijklmnopqrstuvwxyz
1234567890 1234567890
fifl ()[]&£$.,;:-!?"

ABCDEFGHIJKLMNOP
QRSTUVWXYZ abcdefg
hijklmnopqrstuvwxyz
1234567890
fifl ()[]&£$.,;:-!?"

ABCDEFGHIJKLMNOP
QRSTUVWXYZ abcdefg
hijklmnopqrstuvwxyz
1234567890
fifl ()[]&£$.,;:-!?"

24 on 27pt

These examples show *normal* letterspacing and the effect of *reduced* letterspacing on roman setting *as well as on words in italic*: they also show the appearance of figures, for example 28 May 1964, within text. These & the ampersand are not included in the setting opposite.
Normal letterspacing

These examples show *normal* letterspacing and the effect of *reduced* letterspacing on roman setting *as well as on words in italic*: they also show the appearance of figures, for example 28 May 1964, within text. These & the ampersand are not included in the setting opposite.
Minus one unit spacing

These examples show *normal* letterspacing and the effect of *reduced* letterspacing on roman setting *as well as on words in italic*: they also show the appearance of figures, for example 28 May 1964, within text. These & the ampersand are not included in the setting opposite.
Minus two units spacing

WALKING ALONG THE MALL WE WONDERED WHO ALL
WALKING ALONG THE MALL WE WONDERED WHO
WALKING ALONG THE MALL WE WONDERED
Capitals: normal letterspacing/plus 4 units/plus 9 units

WALKING ALONG THE MALL WE WONDERED WHO ALL THOSE MEN
WALKING ALONG THE MALL WE WONDERED WHO ALL THOSE
WALKING ALONG THE MALL WE WONDERED WHO ALL
Small caps: normal letterspacing/plus 3 units/plus 6 units

WALKING ALONG THE MALL WE WONDERED WHO ALL THOSE MEN
WALKING ALONG THE MALL WE WONDERED WHO ALL THOSE MEN WERE
True small caps/reduced capitals

WALKING ALONG THE MALL we wondered who all those
WALKING ALONG THE MALL we wondered who all those men
True italic/sloped roman

Walking along the Mall we wondered who all those men were – tall hawk-featured men perched on balconies and high places, scanning the city with heavy binoculars. What were they seeking so earnestly? Who were they – so composed and steely-eyed? Timidly we stopped a policeman to ask him. 'They are publishers' he said mildly. Publishers! Our hearts stopped beating. 'They are on the look out for new talent.' Great God! It was for *us* they were waiting and watching! Then the kindly policeman lowered his voice confidentially and said in hollow and reverent tones: *'They are waiting for the new Trollope to be born!'* Do you remember, at these words, how heavy our suitcases suddenly felt? How our blood slowed, our footsteps lagged? Brother Ass, we had been bashfully thinking of a kind of
8 on 9pt

WALKING ALONG THE MALL WE WONDERED WHO ALL THOSE MEN WERE – TALL HAWK-featured men perched on balconies and high places, scanning the city with heavy binoculars. What were they seeking so earnestly? Who were they – so composed and steely-eyed? Timidly we stopped a policeman to ask him. 'They are publishers' he said mildly. Publishers! Our hearts stopped beating. 'They are on the look out for new talent.' Great God! It was for *us* they were waiting and watching! Then the kindly policeman lowered his voice confidentially and said in hollow and reverent tones: *'They are waiting for the new Trollope to be born!'* Do you remember, at these words, how heavy our suitcases suddenly felt? How our blood slowed, our
8 on 10.5pt

Walking along the Mall we wondered who all those men were – tall hawk-featured men perched on balconies and high places, scanning the city with heavy binoculars. What were they seeking so earnestly? Who were they – so composed and steely-eyed? Timidly we stopped a policeman to ask him. 'They are publishers' he said mildly. Publishers! Our hearts stopped beating. 'They are on the look out for new talent.' Great God! It was for *us* they were waiting and watching! Then the kindly policeman lowered his voice confidentially and said in hollow and reverent tones: *'They are waiting for the new Trollope to be born!'* Do you remember, at these words, how heavy our suitcases suddenly felt? How our blood slowed, our footsteps lagged? Brother Ass, we had been bashfully thinking of a kind of illumination such as Rimbaud dreamed of – a nagging poem which was not didactic or expository but which *infected* – was not simply a rationalised intuition, I mean, clothed in isinglass! We had come to the wrong shop, with the wrong change! A chill struck us as we saw the mist falling in Trafalgar Square, coiling round us its tendrils of ectoplasm! A million muffin-eating moralists were waiting, not for us, Brother Ass, but for the plucky and tedious Trollope! (If you are dissatis-

9 on 11pt

Walking along the Mall we wondered who all those men were – tall hawk-featured men perched on balconies and high places, scanning the city with heavy binoculars. What were they seeking so earnestly? Who were they – so composed and steely-eyed? Timidly we stopped a policeman to ask him. 'They are publishers' he said mildly. Publishers! Our hearts stopped beating. 'They are on the look out for new talent.' Great God! It was for *us* they were waiting and watching! Then the kindly policeman lowered his voice confidentially and said in hollow and reverent tones: *'They are waiting for the new Trollope to be born!'* Do you remember, at these words, how heavy our suitcases suddenly felt? How our blood slowed, our footsteps lagged? Brother Ass, we had been bashfully thinking of a kind of illumination such as Rimbaud dreamed of – a nagging poem which was not didactic or expository but which *infected* – was not simply a rationalised intuition, I mean, clothed in isinglass! We had come to the wrong shop, with

10 on 12pt

Walking along the Mall we wondered who all those men were – tall hawk-featured men perched on balconies and high places, scanning the city with heavy binoculars. What were they seeking so earnestly? Who were they – so composed and steely-eyed? Timidly we stopped a policeman to ask him. 'They are publishers' he said mildly. Publishers! Our hearts stopped beating. 'They are on the look out for new talent.' Great God! It was for *us* they were waiting and watching! Then the kindly policeman lowered his voice confidentially and said in hollow and reverent tones: *'They are waiting for the new Trollope to be born!'* Do you remember, at these words, how heavy our suitcases suddenly felt? How our blood slowed, our footsteps lagged? Brother Ass, we had been bashfully thinking of a kind of illumination such as Rimbaud dreamed of – a nagging poem which was not

11 on 13pt

WALKING ALONG THE MALL WE WONDERED WHO ALL THOSE MEN WERE – tall hawk-featured men perched on balconies and high places, scanning the city with heavy binoculars. What were they seeking so earnestly? Who were they – so composed and steely-eyed? Timidly we stopped a policeman to ask him. 'They are publishers' he said mildly. Publishers! Our hearts stopped beating. 'They are on the look out for new talent.' Great God! It was for *us* they were waiting and watching! Then the kindly policeman lowered his voice confidentially and said in hollow and reverent tones: *'They are waiting for the new Trollope to be born!'* Do you remember, at these words, how heavy our suitcases suddenly felt? How our blood slowed, our footsteps lagged? Brother Ass, we had been bashfully thinking of a kind of illumination such as Rimbaud dreamed of – a nagging poem which was not didactic or expository but which *infected* – was not simply a rationalised intuition, I mean, clothed in isinglass! We had come to the wrong shop, with the wrong change! A chill struck us as we saw the mist falling in Trafalgar Square, coiling round us its tendrils of ectoplasm! A million muffin-eating moralists were waiting, not for us,

9 on 12pt

WALKING ALONG THE MALL WE WONDERED WHO ALL THOSE MEN were – tall hawk-featured men perched on balconies and high places, scanning the city with heavy binoculars. What were they seeking so earnestly? Who were they – so composed and steely-eyed? Timidly we stopped a policeman to ask him. 'They are publishers' he said mildly. Publishers! Our hearts stopped beating. 'They are on the look out for new talent.' Great God! It was for *us* they were waiting and watching! Then the kindly policeman lowered his voice confidentially and said in hollow and reverent tones: *'They are waiting for the new Trollope to be born!'* Do you remember, at these words, how heavy our suitcases suddenly felt? How our blood slowed, our footsteps lagged? Brother Ass, we had been bashfully thinking of a kind of illumination such as Rimbaud dreamed of – a nagging poem which was not didactic or expository but which *infected* – was not simply a rationalised intuition, I

10 on 13.5pt

WALKING ALONG THE MALL WE WONDERED WHO ALL THOSE men were – tall hawk-featured men perched on balconies and high places, scanning the city with heavy binoculars. What were they seeking so earnestly? Who were they – so composed and steely-eyed? Timidly we stopped a policeman to ask him. 'They are publishers' he said mildly. Publishers! Our hearts stopped beating. 'They are on the look out for new talent.' Great God! It was for *us* they were waiting and watching! Then the kindly policeman lowered his voice confidentially and said in hollow and reverent tones: *'They are waiting for the new Trollope to be born!'* Do you remember, at these words, how heavy our suitcases suddenly felt? How our blood slowed, our footsteps lagged? Brother Ass, we had been bashfully thinking of a kind of illumination such

11 on 14.5pt

LINOTYPE CONCORDE

Linotype **Egyptian 505**

roman (05081), **bold** (07081)
VGC 1965-66 (André Gürtler)
Copyfitting code 127/130

Range also includes light, medium. There is no
italic

ABCDEFGHIJKLMNOP
QRSTUVWXYZ abcdefg
hijklmnopqrstuvwxyz
1234567890
fifl ()[]&£$.,;:-!?`

ABCDEFGHIJKLMNOP
QRSTUVWXYZ abcdefg
hijklmnopqrstuvwxyz
1234567890
fifl ()[]&£$.,;:-!?`

24 on 27pt

These examples show *normal* letterspacing and the effect of *reduced*
letterspacing on roman setting *as well as on words in italic*: they also
show the appearance of figures, for example 28 May 1964, within text.
These & the ampersand are not included in the setting opposite.
Normal letterspacing

These examples show *normal* letterspacing and the effect of *reduced*
letterspacing on roman setting *as well as on words in italic*: they also
show the appearance of figures, for example 28 May 1964, within text.
These & the ampersand are not included in the setting opposite.
Minus one unit spacing

These examples show *normal* letterspacing and the effect of *reduced*
letterspacing on roman setting *as well as on words in italic*: they also
show the appearance of figures, for example 28 May 1964, within text.
These & the ampersand are not included in the setting opposite.
Minus two units spacing

WALKING ALONG THE MALL WE WONDERED WHO ALL THOSE
WALKING ALONG THE MALL WE WONDERED WHO ALL
WALKING ALONG THE MALL WE WONDERED WHO
Capitals: normal letterspacing/plus 4 units/plus 9 units

Walking along the Mall we wondered who all those men were – tall
hawk-featured men perched on balconies and high places, scanning
the city with heavy binoculars. WHAT WERE THEY SEEKING SO EARNESTLY?
Who were they – so composed and steely-eyed? Timidly we stopped a
policeman to ask him. 'THEY ARE PUBLISHERS' he said mildly.
Publishers! Our hearts stopped beating. 'They are on the look out for
new talent.' Great God! It was for *us* they were waiting and watching!
Text with reduced caps normal letterspacing/plus 3 units

Walking along the Mall we wondered who all those men were – tall hawk-featured
men perched on balconies and high places, scanning the city with heavy binoculars.
What were they seeking so earnestly? Who were they – so composed and steely-eyed?
Timidly we stopped a policeman to ask him. 'They are publishers' he said mildly.
Publishers! Our hearts stopped beating. 'They are on the look out for new talent.' Great
God! It was for *us* they were waiting and watching! Then the kindly policeman lowered
his voice confidentially and said in hollow and reverent tones: *'They are waiting for the
new Trollope to be born!'* Do you remember, at these words, how heavy our suitcases
suddenly felt? How our blood slowed, our footsteps lagged? Brother Ass, we had been
bashfully thinking of a kind of illumination such as Rimbaud dreamed of – a nagging
8 on 9pt

Walking along the Mall we wondered who all those men were – tall hawk-featured men
perched on balconies and high places, scanning the city with heavy binoculars. What
were they seeking so earnestly? Who were they – so composed and steely-eyed?
Timidly we stopped a policeman to ask him. 'They are publishers' he said mildly.
Publishers! Our hearts stopped beating. 'They are on the look out for new talent.' Great
God! It was for *us* they were waiting and watching! Then the kindly policeman lowered
his voice confidentially and said in hollow and reverent tones: *'They are waiting for the
new Trollope to be born!'* Do you remember, at these words, how heavy our suitcases
suddenly felt? How our blood slowed, our footsteps lagged? Brother Ass, we had been
8 on 10.5pt

Walking along the Mall we wondered who all those men were — tall hawk-featured men perched on balconies and high places, scanning the city with heavy binoculars. What were they seeking so earnestly? Who were they — so composed and steely-eyed? Timidly we stopped a policeman to ask him. 'They are publishers' he said mildly. Publishers! Our hearts stopped beating. 'They are on the look out for new talent.' Great God! It was for *us* they were waiting and watching! Then the kindly policeman lowered his voice confidentially and said in hollow and reverent tones: *'They are waiting for the new Trollope to be born!'* Do you remember, at these words, how heavy our suitcases suddenly felt? How our blood slowed, our footsteps lagged? Brother Ass, we had been bashfully thinking of a kind of illumination such as Rimbaud dreamed of — a nagging poem which was not didactic or expository but which *infected* — was not simply a rationalised intuition, I mean, clothed in isinglass! We had come to the wrong shop, with the wrong change! A chill struck us as we saw the mist falling in Trafalgar Square, coiling round us its tendrils of ectoplasm! A million muffin-eating moralists were waiting, not for us, Brother Ass, but for the plucky and tedious Trollope! (If you are dissatisfied with your form, reach for the *curette*.) Now do you wonder if I laugh a
9 on 11pt

Walking along the Mall we wondered who all those men were — tall hawk-featured men perched on balconies and high places, scanning the city with heavy binoculars. What were they seeking so earnestly? Who were they — so composed and steely-eyed? Timidly we stopped a policeman to ask him. 'They are publishers' he said mildly. Publishers! Our hearts stopped beating. 'They are on the look out for new talent.' Great God! It was for *us* they were waiting and watching! Then the kindly policeman lowered his voice confidentially and said in hollow and reverent tones: *'They are waiting for the new Trollope to be born!'* Do you remember, at these words, how heavy our suitcases suddenly felt? How our blood slowed, our footsteps lagged? Brother Ass, we had been bashfully thinking of a kind of illumination such as Rimbaud dreamed of — a nagging poem which was not didactic or expository but which *infected* — was not simply a rationalised intuition, I mean, clothed in isinglass! We had come to the wrong shop, with the wrong change! A chill struck us as we saw the mist falling in Trafalgar Square, coiling round us its tendrils of ectoplasm! A million muffin-eating moralists were waiting, not for us, Brother Ass, but for the plucky and tedious Trollope! (If you are dissatis-
9 on 12pt

Walking along the Mall we wondered who all those men were — tall hawk-featured men perched on balconies and high places, scanning the city with heavy binoculars. What were they seeking so earnestly? Who were they — so composed and steely-eyed? Timidly we stopped a policeman to ask him. 'They are publishers' he said mildly. Publishers! Our hearts stopped beating. 'They are on the look out for new talent.' Great God! It was for *us* they were waiting and watching! Then the kindly policeman lowered his voice confidentially and said in hollow and reverent tones: *'They are waiting for the new Trollope to be born!'* Do you remember, at these words, how heavy our suitcases suddenly felt? How our blood slowed, our footsteps lagged? Brother Ass, we had been bashfully thinking of a kind of illumination such as Rimbaud dreamed of — a nagging poem which was not didactic or expository but which *infected* — was not simply a rationalised intuition, I mean, clothed in isinglass! We had come to the wrong shop, with the wrong change! A chill struck us as we saw the mist falling in
10 on 12pt

Walking along the Mall we wondered who all those men were — tall hawk-featured men perched on balconies and high places, scanning the city with heavy binoculars. What were they seeking so earnestly? Who were they — so composed and steely-eyed? Timidly we stopped a policeman to ask him. 'They are publishers' he said mildly. Publishers! Our hearts stopped beating. 'They are on the look out for new talent.' Great God! It was for *us* they were waiting and watching! Then the kindly policeman lowered his voice confidentially and said in hollow and reverent tones: *'They are waiting for the new Trollope to be born!'* Do you remember, at these words, how heavy our suitcases suddenly felt? How our blood slowed, our footsteps lagged? Brother Ass, we had been bashfully thinking of a kind of illumination such as Rimbaud dreamed of — a nagging poem which was not didactic or expository but which *infected* — was not simply a rationalised intuition, I mean, clothed in isinglass! We had come to the wrong shop,
10 on 13.5pt

Walking along the Mall we wondered who all those men were — tall hawk-featured men perched on balconies and high places, scanning the city with heavy binoculars. What were they seeking so earnestly? Who were they — so composed and steely-eyed? Timidly we stopped a policeman to ask him. 'They are publishers' he said mildly. Publishers! Our hearts stopped beating. 'They are on the look out for new talent.' Great God! It was for *us* they were waiting and watching! Then the kindly policeman lowered his voice confidentially and said in hollow and reverent tones: *'They are waiting for the new Trollope to be born!'* Do you remember, at these words, how heavy our suitcases suddenly felt? How our blood slowed, our footsteps lagged? Brother Ass, we had been bashfully thinking of a kind of illumination such as Rimbaud dreamed of — a nagging poem which was not didactic or expository but which *infected* — was
11 on 13pt

Walking along the Mall we wondered who all those men were — tall hawk-featured men perched on balconies and high places, scanning the city with heavy binoculars. What were they seeking so earnestly? Who were they — so composed and steely-eyed? Timidly we stopped a policeman to ask him. 'They are publishers' he said mildly. Publishers! Our hearts stopped beating. 'They are on the look out for new talent.' Great God! It was for *us* they were waiting and watching! Then the kindly policeman lowered his voice confidentially and said in hollow and reverent tones: *'They are waiting for the new Trollope to be born!'* Do you remember, at these words, how heavy our suitcases suddenly felt? How our blood slowed, our footsteps lagged? Brother Ass, we had been bashfully thinking of a kind of illumination such as Rimbaud dreamed of — a nagging poem
11 on 14.5pt

Monotype **Ehrhardt**

453 roman and italic
573 semi-bold
Monotype 1938 (semi-bold: 1956)
Copyfitting factor 40.3/38.2/44.7

Range also includes semi-bold italic

A regularised version of a type of 1672 by
Nicholas Kis, Hungarian punch-cutter active in
Amsterdam

ABCDEFGHIJKLMNOP
QRSTUVWXYZ abcdefg
hijklmnopqrstuvwxyz
1234567890 1234567890
ff fi fl ffi ffl ()[]&£$.,;:-!?''

ABCDEFGHIJKLMNOP
QRSTUVWXYZ abcdefg
hijklmnopqrstuvwxyz
1234567890 1234567890
ff fi fl ffi ffl ()[]&£$.,;:-!?''

ABCDEFGHIJKLMNOP
QRSTUVWXYZ abcdefg
hijklmnopqrstuvwxyz
1234567890 1234567890
ff fi fl ffi ffl ()[]&£$.,;:-!?''

24 on 27pt

These examples show *normal* letterspacing and the effect of *reduced* letterspacing on roman setting *as well as on words in italic*: they also show the appearance of figures, for example 28 May 1964, within text. These & the ampersand are not included in the setting opposite.
Normal letterspacing

These examples show *normal* letterspacing and the effect of *reduced* letterspacing on roman setting *as well as on words in italic*: they also show the appearance of figures, for example 28 May 1964, within text. These & the ampersand are not included in the setting opposite.
Minus one unit spacing

These examples show *normal* letterspacing and the effect of *reduced* letterspacing on roman setting *as well as on words in italic*: they also show the appearance of figures, for example 28 May 1964, within text. These & the ampersand are not included in the setting opposite.
Minus two units spacing

WALKING ALONG THE MALL WE WONDERED WHO ALL
WALKING ALONG THE MALL WE WONDERED WHO
WALKING ALONG THE MALL WE WONDERED
Capitals: normal letterspacing/plus 9 units/plus 18 units

WALKING ALONG THE MALL WE WONDERED WHO ALL THOSE MEN WERE
WALKING ALONG THE MALL WE WONDERED WHO ALL THOSE MEN WERE
WALKING ALONG THE MALL WE WONDERED WHO ALL THOSE MEN
Small caps: normal letterspacing/plus 6 units/plus 12 units

WALKING ALONG THE MALL we wondered who all those men were
WALKING ALONG THE MALL we wondered who all those men were
True italic/sloped roman

WALKING ALONG THE MALL WE WONDERED WHO ALL THOSE MEN WERE
WALKING ALONG THE MALL WE WONDERED WHO ALL THOSE MEN WERE
True small caps/reduced capitals

Walking along the Mall we wondered who all those men were – tall hawk-featured men perched on balconies and high places, scanning the city with heavy binoculars. What were they seeking so earnestly? Who were they – so composed and steely-eyed? Timidly we stopped a policeman to ask him. 'They are publishers' he said mildly. Publishers! Our hearts stopped beating. 'They are on the look out for new talent.' Great God! It was for *us* they were waiting and watching! Then the kindly policeman lowered his voice confidentially and said in hollow and reverent tones: '*They are waiting for the new Trollope to be born!*' Do you remember, at these words, how heavy our suitcases suddenly felt? How our blood slowed, our footsteps lagged? Brother Ass, we had been bashfully thinking of a kind of illumination such as Rimbaud dreamed of – a nagging poem which was not didactic or expository but which
8 on 9pt

WALKING ALONG THE MALL WE WONDERED WHO ALL THOSE MEN WERE – TALL hawk-featured men perched on balconies and high places, scanning the city with heavy binoculars. What were they seeking so earnestly? Who were they – so composed and steely-eyed? Timidly we stopped a policeman to ask him. 'They are publishers' he said mildly. Publishers! Our hearts stopped beating. 'They are on the look out for new talent.' Great God! It was for *us* they were waiting and watching! Then the kindly policeman lowered his voice confidentially and said in hollow and reverent tones: '*They are waiting for the new Trollope to be born!*' Do you remember, at these words, how heavy our suitcases suddenly felt? How our blood slowed, our footsteps lagged? Brother Ass, we had been bashfully thinking of a kind of
8 on 10.5pt

Walking along the Mall we wondered who all those men were – tall hawk-featured men perched on balconies and high places, scanning the city with heavy binoculars. What were they seeking so earnestly? Who were they – so composed and steely-eyed? Timidly we stopped a policeman to ask him. 'They are publishers' he said mildly. Publishers! Our hearts stopped beating. 'They are on the look out for new talent.' Great God! It was for *us* they were waiting and watching! Then the kindly policeman lowered his voice confidentially and said in hollow and reverent tones: *'They are waiting for the new Trollope to be born!'* Do you remember, at these words, how heavy our suitcases suddenly felt? How our blood slowed, our footsteps lagged? Brother Ass, we had been bashfully thinking of a kind of illumination such as Rimbaud dreamed of – a nagging poem which was not didactic or expository but which *infected* – was not simply a rationalised intuition, I mean, clothed in isinglass! We had come to the wrong shop, with the wrong change! A chill struck us as we saw the mist falling in Trafalgar Square, coiling around us its tendrils of ectoplasm! A million muffin-eating moralists were waiting, not for us, Brother Ass, but for the plucky and tedious Trollope! (If you are dissatisfied with your form, reach for the *curette*.) Now do you wonder if I laugh a little off-key? Do you ask yourself what has turned me into nature's bashful little aphorist? We who are, after all, simply poor co-workers in the

9 on 11pt

Walking along the Mall we wondered who all those men were – tall hawk-featured men perched on balconies and high places, scanning the city with heavy binoculars. What were they seeking so earnestly? Who were they – so composed and steely-eyed? Timidly we stopped a policeman to ask him. 'They are publishers' he said mildly. Publishers! Our hearts stopped beating. 'They are on the look out for new talent.' Great God! It was for *us* they were waiting and watching! Then the kindly policeman lowered his voice confidentially and said in hollow and reverent tones: *'They are waiting for the new Trollope to be born!'* Do you remember, at these words, how heavy our suitcases suddenly felt? How our blood slowed, our footsteps lagged? Brother Ass, we had been bashfully thinking of a kind of illumination such as Rimbaud dreamed of – a nagging poem which was not didactic or expository but which *infected* – was not simply a rationalised intuition, I mean, clothed in isinglass! We had come to the wrong shop, with the wrong change! A chill struck us as we saw the mist falling in Trafalgar Square, coiling around us its tendrils of ectoplasm! A million muffin-eating moralists were waiting, not for

10 on 12pt

Walking along the Mall we wondered who all those men were – tall hawk-featured men perched on balconies and high places, scanning the city with heavy binoculars. What were they seeking so earnestly? Who were they – so composed and steely-eyed? Timidly we stopped a policeman to ask him. 'They are publishers' he said mildly. Publishers! Our hearts stopped beating. 'They are on the look out for new talent.' Great God! It was for *us* they were waiting and watching! Then the kindly policeman lowered his voice confidentially and said in hollow and reverent tones: *'They are waiting for the new Trollope to be born!'* Do you remember, at these words, how heavy our suitcases suddenly felt? How our blood slowed, our footsteps lagged? Brother Ass, we had been bashfully thinking of a kind of illumination such as Rimbaud dreamed of – a nagging poem which was not didactic or expository but which *infected* – was not simply a rationalised intuition, I mean, clothed in isinglass! We had come to the wrong shop, with the

11 on 13pt

WALKING ALONG THE MALL WE WONDERED WHO ALL THOSE MEN WERE – TALL hawk-featured men perched on balconies and high places, scanning the city with heavy binoculars. What were they seeking so earnestly? Who were they – so composed and steely-eyed? Timidly we stopped a policeman to ask him. 'They are publishers' he said mildly. Publishers! Our hearts stopped beating. 'They are on the look out for new talent.' Great God! It was for *us* they were waiting and watching! Then the kindly policeman lowered his voice confidentially and said in hollow and reverent tones: *'They are waiting for the new Trollope to be born!'* Do you remember, at these words, how heavy our suitcases suddenly felt? How our blood slowed, our footsteps lagged? Brother Ass, we had been bashfully thinking of a kind of illumination such as Rimbaud dreamed of – a nagging poem which was not didactic or expository but which *infected* – was not simply a rationalised intuition, I mean, clothed in isinglass! We had come to the wrong shop, with the wrong change! A chill struck us as we saw the mist falling in Trafalgar Square, coiling around us its tendrils of ectoplasm! A million muffin-eating moralists were waiting, not for us, Brother Ass, but for the plucky and tedious Trollope! (If you are dissatisfied with your form, reach for the *curette*.) Now do you wonder if I laugh a little off-key? Do you ask yourself what has turned me into

9 on 12pt

WALKING ALONG THE MALL WE WONDERED WHO ALL THOSE MEN WERE – tall hawk-featured men perched on balconies and high places, scanning the city with heavy binoculars. What were they seeking so earnestly? Who were they – so composed and steely-eyed? Timidly we stopped a policeman to ask him. 'They are publishers' he said mildly. Publishers! Our hearts stopped beating. 'They are on the look out for new talent.' Great God! It was for *us* they were waiting and watching! Then the kindly policeman lowered his voice confidentially and said in hollow and reverent tones: *'They are waiting for the new Trollope to be born!'* Do you remember, at these words, how heavy our suitcases suddenly felt? How our blood slowed, our footsteps lagged? Brother Ass, we had been bashfully thinking of a kind of illumination such as Rimbaud dreamed of – a nagging poem which was not didactic or expository but which *infected* – was not simply a rationalised intuition, I mean, clothed in isinglass! We had come to the wrong shop, with the wrong change! A chill struck us as we saw the mist falling in Trafalgar Square, coiling around us its

10 on 13.5pt

WALKING ALONG THE MALL WE WONDERED WHO ALL THOSE MEN were – tall hawk-featured men perched on balconies and high places, scanning the city with heavy binoculars. What were they seeking so earnestly? Who were they – so composed and steely-eyed? Timidly we stopped a policeman to ask him. 'They are publishers' he said mildly. Publishers! Our hearts stopped beating. 'They are on the look out for new talent.' Great God! It was for *us* they were waiting and watching! Then the kindly policeman lowered his voice confidentially and said in hollow and reverent tones: *'They are waiting for the new Trollope to be born!'* Do you remember, at these words, how heavy our suitcases suddenly felt? How our blood slowed, our footsteps lagged? Brother Ass, we had been bashfully thinking of a kind of illumination such as Rimbaud dreamed of – a nagging poem which was not didactic or expository but which *infected* – was not simply a rationalised intuition,

11 on 14.5pt

MONOTYPE EHRHARDT

Linotype **Ehrhardt**

roman (05371), **italic** (13371)
semi-bold (07371)
Monotype 1938 (semi-bold: 1956)
Copyfitting code 118/107/133

See Monotype Ehrhardt

ABCDEFGHIJKLMNOP
QRSTUVWXYZ abcdefg
hijklmnopqrstuvwxyz
1234567890 1234567890
fifl ()[]&£$.,;:-!?""

ABCDEFGHIJKLMNOP
QRSTUVWXYZ abcdefg
hijklmnopqrstuvwxyz
1234567890 1234567890
fifl ()[]&£$.,;:-!?""

ABCDEFGHIJKLMNOP
QRSTUVWXYZ abcdefg
hijklmnopqrstuvwxyz
1234567890 1234567890
fifl ()[]&£$.,;:-!?""

24 on 27pt

These examples show *normal* letterspacing and the effect of *reduced* letterspacing on roman setting *as well as on words in italic*: they also show the appearance of figures, for example 28 May 1964, within text. These & the ampersand are not included in the setting opposite.
Normal letterspacing

These examples show *normal* letterspacing and the effect of *reduced* letterspacing on roman setting *as well as on words in italic*: they also show the appearance of figures, for example 28 May 1964, within text. These & the ampersand are not included in the setting opposite.
Minus one unit spacing

These examples show *normal* letterspacing and the effect of *reduced* letterspacing on roman setting *as well as on words in italic*: they also show the appearance of figures, for example 28 May 1964, within text. These & the ampersand are not included in the setting opposite.
Minus two units spacing

WALKING ALONG THE MALL WE WONDERED WHO ALL
WALKING ALONG THE MALL WE WONDERED WHO
WALKING ALONG THE MALL WE WONDERED
Capitals: normal letterspacing/plus 4 units/plus 9 units

WALKING ALONG THE MALL WE WONDERED WHO ALL THOSE MEN WERE
WALKING ALONG THE MALL WE WONDERED WHO ALL THOSE MEN
WALKING ALONG THE MALL WE WONDERED WHO ALL THOSE
Small caps: normal letterspacing/plus 3 units/plus 6 units

WALKING ALONG THE MALL WE WONDERED WHO ALL THOSE MEN WERE
WALKING ALONG THE MALL WE WONDERED WHO ALL THOSE MEN WERE
True small caps/reduced capitals

WALKING ALONG THE MALL we wondered who all those men were
WALKING ALONG THE MALL we wondered who all those men
True italic/sloped roman

Walking along the Mall we wondered who all those men were – tall hawk-featured men perched on balconies and high places, scanning the city with heavy binoculars. What were they seeking so earnestly? Who were they – so composed and steely-eyed? Timidly we stopped a policeman to ask him. 'They are publishers' he said mildly. Publishers! Our hearts stopped beating. 'They are on the look out for new talent.' Great God! It was for *us* they were waiting and watching! Then the kindly policeman lowered his voice confidentially and said in hollow and reverent tones: *'They are waiting for the new Trollope to be born!'* Do you remember, at these words, how heavy our suitcases suddenly felt? How our blood slowed, our footsteps lagged? Brother Ass, we had been bashfully thinking of a kind of illumination such as Rimbaud dreamed of – a nagging poem which was not didactic or expository but

8 on 9pt

WALKING ALONG THE MALL WE WONDERED WHO ALL THOSE MEN WERE – TALL HAWK-featured men perched on balconies and high places, scanning the city with heavy binoculars. What were they seeking so earnestly? Who were they – so composed and steely-eyed? Timidly we stopped a policeman to ask him. 'They are publishers' he said mildly. Publishers! Our hearts stopped beating. 'They are on the look out for new talent.' Great God! It was for *us* they were waiting and watching! Then the kindly policeman lowered his voice confidentially and said in hollow and reverent tones: *'They are waiting for the new Trollope to be born!'* Do you remember, at these words, how heavy our suitcases suddenly felt? How our blood slowed, our footsteps lagged? Brother Ass, we had been bashfully thinking of

8 on 10.5pt

Walking along the Mall we wondered who all those men were – tall hawk-featured men perched on balconies and high places, scanning the city with heavy binoculars. What were they seeking so earnestly? Who were they – so composed and steely-eyed? Timidly we stopped a policeman to ask him. 'They are publishers' he said mildly. Publishers! Our hearts stopped beating. 'They are on the look out for new talent.' Great God! It was for *us* they were waiting and watching! Then the kindly policeman lowered his voice confidentially and said in hollow and reverent tones: *'They are waiting for the new Trollope to be born!'* Do you remember, at these words, how heavy our suitcases suddenly felt? How our blood slowed, our footsteps lagged? Brother Ass, we had been bashfully thinking of a kind of illumination such as Rimbaud dreamed of – a nagging poem which was not didactic or expository but which *infected* – was not simply a rationalised intuition, I mean, clothed in isinglass! We had come to the wrong shop, with the wrong change! A chill struck us as we saw the mist falling in Trafalgar Square, coiling round us its tendrils of ectoplasm! A million muffin-eating moralists were waiting, not for us, Brother Ass, but for the plucky and tedious Trollope! (If you are dissatisfied with your form, reach for the *curette*.) Now do you wonder if I laugh a little off-key? Do you ask yourself what has turned me into nature's bashful little aphorist? We who

9 on 11pt

Walking along the Mall we wondered who all those men were – tall hawk-featured men perched on balconies and high places, scanning the city with heavy binoculars. What were they seeking so earnestly? Who were they – so composed and steely-eyed? Timidly we stopped a policeman to ask him. 'They are publishers' he said mildly. Publishers! Our hearts stopped beating. 'They are on the look out for new talent.' Great God! It was for *us* they were waiting and watching! Then the kindly policeman lowered his voice confidentially and said in hollow and reverent tones: *'They are waiting for the new Trollope to be born!'* Do you remember, at these words, how heavy our suitcases suddenly felt? How our blood slowed, our footsteps lagged? Brother Ass, we had been bashfully thinking of a kind of illumination such as Rimbaud dreamed of – a nagging poem which was not didactic or expository but which *infected* – was not simply a rationalised intuition, I mean, clothed in isinglass! We had come to the wrong shop, with the wrong change! A chill struck us as we saw the mist falling in Trafalgar Square, coiling round us its tendrils of

10 on 12pt

Walking along the Mall we wondered who all those men were – tall hawk-featured men perched on balconies and high places, scanning the city with heavy binoculars. What were they seeking so earnestly? Who were they – so composed and steely-eyed? Timidly we stopped a policeman to ask him. 'They are publishers' he said mildly. Publishers! Our hearts stopped beating. 'They are on the look out for new talent.' Great God! It was for *us* they were waiting and watching! Then the kindly policeman lowered his voice confidentially and said in hollow and reverent tones: *'They are waiting for the new Trollope to be born!'* Do you remember, at these words, how heavy our suitcases suddenly felt? How our blood slowed, our footsteps lagged? Brother Ass, we had been bashfully thinking of a kind of illumination such as Rimbaud dreamed of – a nagging poem which was not didactic or expository but which *infected* – was not simply a rationalised intuition, I mean, clothed in isinglass! We

11 on 13pt

WALKING ALONG THE MALL WE WONDERED WHO ALL THOSE MEN WERE – TALL hawk-featured men perched on balconies and high places, scanning the city with heavy binoculars. What were they seeking so earnestly? Who were they – so composed and steely-eyed? Timidly we stopped a policeman to ask him. 'They are publishers' he said mildly. Publishers! Our hearts stopped beating. 'They are on the look out for new talent.' Great God! It was for *us* they were waiting and watching! Then the kindly policeman lowered his voice confidentially and said in hollow and reverent tones: *'They are waiting for the new Trollope to be born!'* Do you remember, at these words, how heavy our suitcases suddenly felt? How our blood slowed, our footsteps lagged? Brother Ass, we had been bashfully thinking of a kind of illumination such as Rimbaud dreamed of – a nagging poem which was not didactic or expository but which *infected* – was not simply a rationalised intuition, I mean, clothed in isinglass! We had come to the wrong shop, with the wrong change! A chill struck us as we saw the mist falling in Trafalgar Square, coiling round us its tendrils of ectoplasm! A million muffin-eating moralists were waiting, not for us, Brother Ass, but for the plucky and tedious Trollope! (If you are dissatisfied with your form, reach for the *curette*.) Now do you wonder if I

9 on 12pt

WALKING ALONG THE MALL WE WONDERED WHO ALL THOSE MEN WERE – tall hawk-featured men perched on balconies and high places, scanning the city with heavy binoculars. What were they seeking so earnestly? Who were they – so composed and steely-eyed? Timidly we stopped a policeman to ask him. 'They are publishers' he said mildly. Publishers! Our hearts stopped beating. 'They are on the look out for new talent.' Great God! It was for *us* they were waiting and watching! Then the kindly policeman lowered his voice confidentially and said in hollow and reverent tones: *'They are waiting for the new Trollope to be born!'* Do you remember, at these words, how heavy our suitcases suddenly felt? How our blood slowed, our footsteps lagged? Brother Ass, we had been bashfully thinking of a kind of illumination such as Rimbaud dreamed of – a nagging poem which was not didactic or expository but which *infected* – was not simply a rationalised intuition, I mean, clothed in isinglass! We had come to the wrong shop, with the wrong change! A chill struck us as we

10 on 13.5pt

WALKING ALONG THE MALL WE WONDERED WHO ALL THOSE MEN were – tall hawk-featured men perched on balconies and high places, scanning the city with heavy binoculars. What were they seeking so earnestly? Who were they – so composed and steely-eyed? Timidly we stopped a policeman to ask him. 'They are publishers' he said mildly. Publishers! Our hearts stopped beating. 'They are on the look out for new talent.' Great God! It was for *us* they were waiting and watching! Then the kindly policeman lowered his voice confidentially and said in hollow and reverent tones: *'They are waiting for the new Trollope to be born!'* Do you remember, at these words, how heavy our suitcases suddenly felt? How our blood slowed, our footsteps lagged? Brother Ass, we had been bashfully thinking of a kind of illumination such as Rimbaud dreamed of – a nagging poem which was not didactic or expository but which

11 on 14.5pt

LINOTYPE EHRHARDT

Monotype **Ellington**

1215 light and italic
1217 bold
Monotype 1990 (Michael Harvey)
Copyfitting factor 39.2/37.5/44.0

Range also includes roman, roman italic, bold
italic, extra bold, extra bold italic

ABCDEFGHIJKLMNOP
QRSTUVWXYZ abcdefg
hijklmnopqrstuvwxyz
1234567890 1234567890
ff fi fl ffi ffl () []&£$.,;:-!?''

ABCDEFGHIJKLMNOP
QRSTUVWXYZ abcdefg
hijklmnopqrstuvwxyz
1234567890 1234567890
ff fi fl ffi ffl ()[]&£$.,;:-!?''

ABCDEFGHIJKLMNOP
QRSTUVWXYZ abcdefg
hijklmnopqrstuvwxyz
1234567890 1234567890
ff fi fl ffi ffl ()[]&£$.,;:-!?''

24 on 27pt

These examples show *normal* letterspacing and the effect of *increased*
letterspacing on roman setting *as well as on words in italic:* they also
show the appearance of figures, for example 28 May 1964, within text.
These & the ampersand are not included in the setting opposite.

Normal letterspacing

These examples show *normal* letterspacing and the effect of *increased*
letterspacing on roman setting *as well as on words in italic:* they also
show the appearance of figures, for example 28 May 1964, within text.
These & the ampersand are not included in the setting opposite.

Plus one unit spacing

These examples show *normal* letterspacing and the effect of *increased*
letterspacing on roman setting *as well as on words in italic:* they also
show the appearance of figures, for example 28 May 1964, within text.
These & the ampersand are not included in the setting opposite.

Plus two unit spacing

WALKING ALONG THE MALL WE WONDERED WHO ALL THOSE MEN
WALKING ALONG THE MALL WE WONDERED WHO ALL THOSE
WALKING ALONG THE MALL WE WONDERED WHO ALL

Capitals: normal letterspacing/plus 9 units/plus 18 units

WALKING ALONG THE MALL WE WONDERED WHO ALL THOSE MEN WERE
WALKING ALONG THE MALL WE WONDERED WHO ALL THOSE MEN WERE
WALKING ALONG THE MALL WE WONDERED WHO ALL THOSE MEN

Small caps: normal letterspacing/plus 6 units/plus 12 units

WALKING ALONG THE MALL we wondered who all those men were
WALKING ALONG THE MALL we wondered who all those men were

True italic/sloped roman

WALKING ALONG THE MALL WE WONDERED WHO ALL THOSE MEN WERE
WALKING ALONG THE MALL WE WONDERED WHO ALL THOSE MEN WERE

True small caps/reduced capitals

Walking along the Mall we wondered who all those men were – tall hawk-featured
men perched on balconies and high places, scanning the city with heavy binoculars. What were
they seeking so earnestly? Who were they – so composed and steely-eyed? Timidly we stopped a
policeman to ask him. 'They are publishers' he said mildly. Publishers! Our hearts stopped
beating. 'They are on the look out for new talent.' Great God! It was for *us* they were waiting and
watching! Then the kindly policeman lowered his voice confidentially and said in hollow and
reverent tones: *'They are waiting for the new Trollope to be born!'* Do you remember, at these
words, how heavy our suitcases suddenly felt? How our blood slowed, our footsteps lagged?
Brother Ass, we had been bashfully thinking of a kind of illumination such as Rimbaud dreamed
of – a nagging poem which was not didactic or expository but which *infected* – was not simply a

8 on 9pt

WALKING ALONG THE MALL WE WONDERED WHO ALL THOSE MEN WERE – TALL
hawk-featured men perched on balconies and high places, scanning the city with heavy
binoculars. What were they seeking so earnestly? Who were they – so composed and steely-
eyed? Timidly we stopped a policeman to ask him. 'They are publishers' he said mildly.
Publishers! Our hearts stopped beating. 'They are on the look out for new talent.' Great God! It
was for *us* they were waiting and watching! Then the kindly policeman lowered his voice
confidentially and said in hollow and reverent tones: *'They are waiting for the new Trollope to be
born!'* Do you remember, at these words, how heavy our suitcases suddenly felt? How our blood
slowed, our footsteps lagged? Brother Ass, we had been bashfully thinking of a kind of

8 on 10.5pt

Walking along the Mall we wondered who all those men were – tall hawk-featured men perched on balconies and high places, scanning the city with heavy binoculars. What were they seeking so earnestly? Who were they – so composed and steely-eyed? Timidly we stopped a policeman to ask him. 'They are publishers' he said mildly. Publishers! Our hearts stopped beating. 'They are on the look out for new talent.' Great God! It was for *us* they were waiting and watching! Then the kindly policeman lowered his voice confidentially and said in hollow and reverent tones: *'They are waiting for the new Trollope to be born!'* Do you remember, at these words, how heavy our suitcases suddenly felt? How our blood slowed, our footsteps lagged? Brother Ass, we had been bashfully thinking of a kind of illumination such as Rimbaud dreamed of – a nagging poem which was not didactic or expository but which *infected* – was not simply a rationalised intuition, I mean, clothed in isinglass! We had come to the wrong shop, with the wrong change! A chill struck us as we saw the mist falling in Trafalgar Square, coiling around us its tendrils of ectoplasm! A million muffin-eating moralists were waiting, not for us, Brother Ass, but for the plucky and tedious Trollope! (If you are dissatisfied with your form, reach for the *curette*.) Now do you wonder if I laugh a little off-key? Do you ask yourself what has turned me into nature's bashful little aphorist? We who are, after all, simply poor co-workers in the psyche of our nation, what can we expect but the natural
9 on 11pt

Walking along the Mall we wondered who all those men were – tall hawk-featured men perched on balconies and high places, scanning the city with heavy binoculars. What were they seeking so earnestly? Who were they – so composed and steely-eyed? Timidly we stopped a policeman to ask him. 'They are publishers' he said mildly. Publishers! Our hearts stopped beating. 'They are on the look out for new talent.' Great God! It was for *us* they were waiting and watching! Then the kindly policeman lowered his voice confidentially and said in hollow and reverent tones: *'They are waiting for the new Trollope to be born!'* Do you remember, at these words, how heavy our suitcases suddenly felt? How our blood slowed, our footsteps lagged? Brother Ass, we had been bashfully thinking of a kind of illumination such as Rimbaud dreamed of – a nagging poem which was not didactic or expository but which *infected* – was not simply a rationalised intuition, I mean, clothed in isinglass! We had come to the wrong shop, with the wrong change! A chill struck us as we saw the mist falling in Trafalgar Square, coiling around us its tendrils of ectoplasm! A million muffin-eating moralists were waiting, not for us, Brother Ass, but for the plucky and
10 on 12pt

Walking along the Mall we wondered who all those men were – tall hawk-featured men perched on balconies and high places, scanning the city with heavy binoculars. What were they seeking so earnestly? Who were they – so composed and steely-eyed? Timidly we stopped a policeman to ask him. 'They are publishers' he said mildly. Publishers! Our hearts stopped beating. 'They are on the look out for new talent.' Great God! It was for *us* they were waiting and watching! Then the kindly policeman lowered his voice confidentially and said in hollow and reverent tones: *'They are waiting for the new Trollope to be born!'* Do you remember, at these words, how heavy our suitcases suddenly felt? How our blood slowed, our footsteps lagged? Brother Ass, we had been bashfully thinking of a kind of illumination such as Rimbaud dreamed of – a nagging poem which was not didactic or expository but which *infected* – was not simply a rationalised intuition, I mean, clothed in isinglass! We had come to the wrong shop, with the wrong change! A chill struck us as
11 on 13pt

WALKING ALONG THE MALL WE WONDERED WHO ALL THOSE MEN WERE – TALL HAWK-featured men perched on balconies and high places, scanning the city with heavy binoculars. What were they seeking so earnestly? Who were they – so composed and steely-eyed? Timidly we stopped a policeman to ask him. 'They are publishers' he said mildly. Publishers! Our hearts stopped beating. 'They are on the look out for new talent.' Great God! It was for *us* they were waiting and watching! Then the kindly policeman lowered his voice confidentially and said in hollow and reverent tones: *'They are waiting for the new Trollope to be born!'* Do you remember, at these words, how heavy our suitcases suddenly felt? How our blood slowed, our footsteps lagged? Brother Ass, we had been bashfully thinking of a kind of illumination such as Rimbaud dreamed of – a nagging poem which was not didactic or expository but which *infected* – was not simply a rationalised intuition, I mean, clothed in isinglass! We had come to the wrong shop, with the wrong change! A chill struck us as we saw the mist falling in Trafalgar Square, coiling around us its tendrils of ectoplasm! A million muffin-eating moralists were waiting, not for us, Brother Ass, but for the plucky and tedious Trollope! (If you are dissatisfied with your form, reach for the *curette*.) Now do you wonder if I laugh a little off-key? Do you ask yourself what has turned me into nature's bashful little aphorist? We who are, after all,
9 on 12pt

WALKING ALONG THE MALL WE WONDERED WHO ALL THOSE MEN WERE – tall hawk-featured men perched on balconies and high places, scanning the city with heavy binoculars. What were they seeking so earnestly? Who were they – so composed and steely-eyed? Timidly we stopped a policeman to ask him. 'They are publishers' he said mildly. Publishers! Our hearts stopped beating. 'They are on the look out for new talent.' Great God! It was for *us* they were waiting and watching! Then the kindly policeman lowered his voice confidentially and said in hollow and reverent tones: *'They are waiting for the new Trollope to be born!'* Do you remember, at these words, how heavy our suitcases suddenly felt? How our blood slowed, our footsteps lagged? Brother Ass, we had been bashfully thinking of a kind of illumination such as Rimbaud dreamed of – a nagging poem which was not didactic or expository but which *infected* – was not simply a rationalised intuition, I mean, clothed in isinglass! We had come to the wrong shop, with the wrong change! A chill struck us as we saw the mist falling in Trafalgar Square, coiling around us its tendrils of ectoplasm! A million
10 on 13.5pt

WALKING ALONG THE MALL WE WONDERED WHO ALL THOSE MEN were – tall hawk-featured men perched on balconies and high places, scanning the city with heavy binoculars. What were they seeking so earnestly? Who were they – so composed and steely-eyed? Timidly we stopped a policeman to ask him. 'They are publishers' he said mildly. Publishers! Our hearts stopped beating. 'They are on the look out for new talent.' Great God! It was for *us* they were waiting and watching! Then the kindly policeman lowered his voice confidentially and said in hollow and reverent tones: *'They are waiting for the new Trollope to be born!'* Do you remember, at these words, how heavy our suitcases suddenly felt? How our blood slowed, our footsteps lagged? Brother Ass, we had been bashfully thinking of a kind of illumination such as Rimbaud dreamed of – a nagging poem which was not didactic or expository but which *infected* – was not simply a rationalised intuition, I mean, clothed
11 on 14.5pt

Monotype FOURNIER

285 roman and italic
Monotype 1925
Copyfitting factor 37.6/35.7

This is the version with shortened capitals

The original hot metal design was a facsimile
of one of Fournier's medium text types
(St Augustin Ordinaire) in his *Manuel
Typographique* of 1764

ABCDEFGHIJKLMNOP
QRSTUVWXYZ abcdefg
hijklmnopqrstuvwxyz
1234567890 1234567890
ff fi fl ffi ffl ()[]&£$.,;:-!?''

*ABCDEFGHIJKLMNOP
QRSTUVWXYZ abcdefg
hijklmnopqrstuvwxyz
1234567890 1234567890
ff fi fl ffi ffl ()[]&£$.,;:-!?''*

24 on 27pt

These examples show *normal* letterspacing and the effect of *reduced*
letterspacing on roman setting *as well as on words in italic*: they also
show the appearance of figures, for example 28 May 1964, within text.
These & the ampersand are not included in the setting opposite.

Normal letterspacing

These examples show *normal* letterspacing and the effect of *reduced*
letterspacing on roman setting *as well as on words in italic*: they also
show the appearance of figures, for example 28 May 1964, within text.
These & the ampersand are not included in the setting opposite.

Minus one unit spacing

These examples show *normal* letterspacing and the effect of *reduced*
letterspacing on roman setting *as well as on words in italic*: they also
show the appearance of figures, for example 28 May 1964, within text.
These & the ampersand are not included in the setting opposite.

Minus two units spacing

WALKING ALONG THE MALL WE WONDERED WHO ALL THOSE
WALKING ALONG THE MALL WE WONDERED WHO ALL
WALKING ALONG THE MALL WE WONDERED WHO

Capitals: normal letterspacing/plus 9 units/plus 18 units

WALKING ALONG THE MALL WE WONDERED WHO ALL THOSE MEN WERE
WALKING ALONG THE MALL WE WONDERED WHO ALL THOSE MEN WERE
WALKING ALONG THE MALL WE WONDERED WHO ALL THOSE MEN

Small caps: normal letterspacing/plus 6 units/plus 12 units

*WALKING ALONG THE MALL we wondered who all those men were
WALKING ALONG THE MALL we wondered who all those men were*

True italic/sloped roman

WALKING ALONG THE MALL WE WONDERED WHO ALL THOSE MEN WERE
WALKING ALONG THE MALL WE WONDERED WHO ALL THOSE MEN WERE

True small caps/reduced capitals

Walking along the Mall we wondered who all those men were – tall hawk-featured men perched
on balconies and high places, scanning the city with heavy binoculars. What were they seeking so
earnestly? Who were they – so composed and steely-eyed? Timidly we stopped a policeman to ask
him. 'They are publishers' he said mildly. Publishers! Our hearts stopped beating. 'They are on the
look out for new talent.' Great God! It was for *us* they were waiting and watching! Then the kindly
policeman lowered his voice confidentially and said in hollow and reverent tones: *'They are waiting for
the new Trollope to be born!'* Do you remember, at these words, how heavy our suitcases suddenly felt?
How our blood slowed, our footsteps lagged? Brother Ass, we had been bashfully thinking of a kind
of illumination such as Rimbaud dreamed of – a nagging poem which was not didactic or expository
but which *infected* – was not simply a rationalised intuition, I mean, clothed in isinglass! We had

8 on 9pt

WALKING ALONG THE MALL WE WONDERED WHO ALL THOSE MEN WERE – TALL HAWK-FEATURED
men perched on balconies and high places, scanning the city with heavy binoculars. What were they
seeking so earnestly? Who were they – so composed and steely-eyed? Timidly we stopped a
policeman to ask him. 'They are publishers' he said mildly. Publishers! Our hearts stopped beating.
'They are on the look out for new talent.' Great God! It was for *us* they were waiting and watching!
Then the kindly policeman lowered his voice confidentially and said in hollow and reverent tones:
'They are waiting for the new Trollope to be born!' Do you remember, at these words, how heavy our
suitcases suddenly felt? How our blood slowed, our footsteps lagged? Brother Ass, we had been
bashfully thinking of a kind of illumination such as Rimbaud dreamed of – a nagging poem which

8 on 10.5pt

Walking along the Mall we wondered who all those men were – tall hawk-featured men perched on balconies and high places, scanning the city with heavy binoculars. What were they seeking so earnestly? Who were they – so composed and steely-eyed? Timidly we stopped a policeman to ask him. 'They are publishers' he said mildly. Publishers! Our hearts stopped beating. 'They are on the look out for new talent.' Great God! It was for *us* they were waiting and watching! Then the kindly policeman lowered his voice confidentially and said in hollow and reverent tones: *'They are waiting for the new Trollope to be born!'* Do you remember, at these words, how heavy our suitcases suddenly felt? How our blood slowed, our footsteps lagged? Brother Ass, we had been bashfully thinking of a kind of illumination such as Rimbaud dreamed of – a nagging poem which was not didactic or expository but which *infected* – was not simply a rationalised intuition, I mean, clothed in isinglass! We had come to the wrong shop, with the wrong change! A chill struck us as we saw the mist falling in Trafalgar Square, coiling around us its tendrils of ectoplasm! A million muffin-eating moralists were waiting, not for us, Brother Ass, but for the plucky and tedious Trollope! (If you are dissatisfied with your form, reach for the *curette*.) Now do you wonder if I laugh a little off-key? Do you ask yourself what has turned me into nature's bashful little aphorist? We who are, after all, simply poor co-workers in the psyche of our nation, what can we expect but the natural automatic rejection from a public which resents interference? And quite

9 on 11pt

Walking along the Mall we wondered who all those men were – tall hawk-featured men perched on balconies and high places, scanning the city with heavy binoculars. What were they seeking so earnestly? Who were they – so composed and steely-eyed? Timidly we stopped a policeman to ask him. 'They are publishers' he said mildly. Publishers! Our hearts stopped beating. 'They are on the look out for new talent.' Great God! It was for *us* they were waiting and watching! Then the kindly policeman lowered his voice confidentially and said in hollow and reverent tones: *'They are waiting for the new Trollope to be born!'* Do you remember, at these words, how heavy our suitcases suddenly felt? How our blood slowed, our footsteps lagged? Brother Ass, we had been bashfully thinking of a kind of illumination such as Rimbaud dreamed of – a nagging poem which was not didactic or expository but which *infected* – was not simply a rationalised intuition, I mean, clothed in isinglass! We had come to the wrong shop, with the wrong change! A chill struck us as we saw the mist falling in Trafalgar Square, coiling around us its tendrils of ectoplasm! A million muffin-eating moralists were waiting, not for us, Brother Ass, but for the plucky and tedious Trollope! (If you are dissatisfied with your form, reach for the

10 on 12pt

Walking along the Mall we wondered who all those men were – tall hawk-featured men perched on balconies and high places, scanning the city with heavy binoculars. What were they seeking so earnestly? Who were they – so composed and steely-eyed? Timidly we stopped a policeman to ask him. 'They are publishers' he said mildly. Publishers! Our hearts stopped beating. 'They are on the look out for new talent.' Great God! It was for *us* they were waiting and watching! Then the kindly policeman lowered his voice confidentially and said in hollow and reverent tones: *'They are waiting for the new Trollope to be born!'* Do you remember, at these words, how heavy our suitcases suddenly felt? How our blood slowed, our footsteps lagged? Brother Ass, we had been bashfully thinking of a kind of illumination such as Rimbaud dreamed of – a nagging poem which was not didactic or expository but which *infected* – was not simply a rationalised intuition, I mean, clothed in isinglass! We had come to the wrong shop, with the wrong change! A chill struck us as we saw the mist falling in Trafalgar Square,

11 on 13pt

WALKING ALONG THE MALL WE WONDERED WHO ALL THOSE MEN WERE — TALL HAWK-featured men perched on balconies and high places, scanning the city with heavy binoculars. What were they seeking so earnestly? Who were they — so composed and steely-eyed? Timidly we stopped a policeman to ask him. 'They are publishers' he said mildly. Publishers! Our hearts stopped beating. 'They are on the look out for new talent.' Great God! It was for *us* they were waiting and watching! Then the kindly policeman lowered his voice confidentially and said in hollow and reverent tones: *'They are waiting for the new Trollope to be born!'* Do you remember, at these words, how heavy our suitcases suddenly felt? How our blood slowed, our footsteps lagged? Brother Ass, we had been bashfully thinking of a kind of illumination such as Rimbaud dreamed of — a nagging poem which was not didactic or expository but which *infected* — was not simply a rationalised intuition, I mean, clothed in isinglass! We had come to the wrong shop, with the wrong change! A chill struck us as we saw the mist falling in Trafalgar Square, coiling around us its tendrils of ectoplasm! A million muffin-eating moralists were waiting, not for us, Brother Ass, but for the plucky and tedious Trollope! (If you are dissatisfied with your form, reach for the *curette*.) Now do you wonder if I laugh a little off-key? Do you ask yourself what has turned me into nature's bashful little aphorist? We who are, after all, simply poor co-workers in the psyche of our nation, what can

9 on 12pt

WALKING ALONG THE MALL WE WONDERED WHO ALL THOSE MEN WERE — TALL hawk-featured men perched on balconies and high places, scanning the city with heavy binoculars. What were they seeking so earnestly? Who were they — so composed and steely-eyed? Timidly we stopped a policeman to ask him. 'They are publishers' he said mildly. Publishers! Our hearts stopped beating. 'They are on the look out for new talent.' Great God! It was for *us* they were waiting and watching! Then the kindly policeman lowered his voice confidentially and said in hollow and reverent tones: *'They are waiting for the new Trollope to be born!'* Do you remember, at these words, how heavy our suitcases suddenly felt? How our blood slowed, our footsteps lagged? Brother Ass, we had been bashfully thinking of a kind of illumination such as Rimbaud dreamed of — a nagging poem which was not didactic or expository but which *infected* — was not simply a rationalised intuition, I mean, clothed in isinglass! We had come to the wrong shop, with the wrong change! A chill struck us as we saw the mist falling in Trafalgar Square, coiling around us its tendrils of ectoplasm! A million muffin-eating moralists were waiting, not for us,

10 on 13.5pt

WALKING ALONG THE MALL WE WONDERED WHO ALL THOSE MEN WERE — tall hawk-featured men perched on balconies and high places, scanning the city with heavy binoculars. What were they seeking so earnestly? Who were they — so composed and steely-eyed? Timidly we stopped a policeman to ask him. 'They are publishers' he said mildly. Publishers! Our hearts stopped beating. 'They are on the look out for new talent.' Great God! It was for *us* they were waiting and watching! Then the kindly policeman lowered his voice confidentially and said in hollow and reverent tones: *'They are waiting for the new Trollope to be born!'* Do you remember, at these words, how heavy our suitcases suddenly felt? How our blood slowed, our footsteps lagged? Brother Ass, we had been bashfully thinking of a kind of illumination such as Rimbaud dreamed of — a nagging poem which was not didactic or expository but which *infected* — was not simply a rationalised intuition, I mean, clothed in isinglass! We had come to the wrong shop, with the wrong

11 on 14.5pt

Linotype FOURNIER

roman (05452), **italic** (13452)
Monotype 1925
Copyfitting code 119/102

This version has the full-height capitals of
Monotype's original design

ABCDEFGHIJKLMNOP
QRSTUVWXYZ abcdefg
hijklmnopqrstuvwxyz
1234567890 1234567890
fifl ()[]&£$.,;:-!?''

ABCDEFGHIJKLMNOP
QRSTUVWXYZ abcdefg
hijklmnopqrstuvwxyz
1234567890 1234567890
fifl ()[]&£$.,;:-!?''

24 on 27pt

These examples show *normal* letterspacing and the effect of *reduced* letterspacing on roman setting *as well as on words in italic*: they also show the appearance of figures, for example 28 May 1964, within text. These & the ampersand are not included in the setting opposite.

These examples show *normal* letterspacing and the effect of *reduced* letterspacing on roman setting *as well as on words in italic*: they also show the appearance of figures, for example 28 May 1964, within text. These & the ampersand are not included in the setting opposite.

These examples show *normal* letterspacing and the effect of *reduced* letterspacing on roman setting *as well as on words in italic*: they also show the appearance of figures, for example 28 May 1964, within text. These & the ampersand are not included in the setting opposite.

WALKING ALONG THE MALL WE WONDERED WHO ALL
WALKING ALONG THE MALL WE WONDERED WHO ALL
WALKING ALONG THE MALL WE WONDERED

WALKING ALONG THE MALL WE WONDERED WHO ALL THOSE MEN WERE
WALKING ALONG THE MALL WE WONDERED WHO ALL THOSE MEN WERE
WALKING ALONG THE MALL WE WONDERED WHO ALL THOSE MEN

WALKING ALONG THE MALL WE WONDERED WHO ALL THOSE MEN WERE
WALKING ALONG THE MALL WE WONDERED WHO ALL THOSE MEN WERE

WALKING ALONG THE MALL we wondered who all those men were
WALKING ALONG THE MALL we wondered who all those men were

Walking along the Mall we wondered who all those men were – tall hawk-featured men perched on balconies and high places, scanning the city with heavy binoculars. What were they seeking so earnestly? Who were they – so composed and steely-eyed? Timidly we stopped a policeman to ask him. 'They are publishers' he said mildly. Publishers! Our hearts stopped beating. 'They are on the look out for new talent.' Great God! It was for *us* they were waiting and watching! Then the kindly policeman lowered his voice confidentially and said in hollow and reverent tones: *'They are waiting for the new Trollope to be born!'* Do you remember, at these words, how heavy our suitcases suddenly felt? How our blood slowed, our footsteps lagged? Brother Ass, we had been bashfully thinking of a kind of illumination such as Rimbaud dreamed of – a nagging poem which was not didactic or expository but which

WALKING ALONG THE MALL WE WONDERED WHO ALL THOSE MEN WERE – TALL HAWK-FEATURED men perched on balconies and high places, scanning the city with heavy binoculars. What were they seeking so earnestly? Who were they – so composed and steely-eyed? Timidly we stopped a policeman to ask him. 'They are publishers' he said mildly. Publishers! Our hearts stopped beating. 'They are on the look out for new talent.' Great God! It was for *us* they were waiting and watching! Then the kindly policeman lowered his voice confidentially and said in hollow and reverent tones: *'They are waiting for the new Trollope to be born!'* Do you remember, at these words, how heavy our suitcases suddenly felt? How our blood slowed, our footsteps lagged? Brother Ass, we had been bashfully thinking of a kind of illumination such as

Walking along the Mall we wondered who all those men were – tall hawk-featured men perched on balconies and high places, scanning the city with heavy binoculars. What were they seeking so earnestly? Who were they – so composed and steely-eyed? Timidly we stopped a policeman to ask him. 'They are publishers' he said mildly. Publishers! Our hearts stopped beating. 'They are on the look out for new talent.' Great God! It was for *us* they were waiting and watching! Then the kindly policeman lowered his voice confidentially and said in hollow and reverent tones: *'They are waiting for the new Trollope to be born!'* Do you remember, at these words, how heavy our suitcases suddenly felt? How our blood slowed, our footsteps lagged? Brother Ass, we had been bashfully thinking of a kind of illumination such as Rimbaud dreamed of – a nagging poem which was not didactic or expository but which *infected* – was not simply a rationalised intuition, I mean, clothed in isinglass! We had come to the wrong shop, with the wrong change! A chill struck us as we saw the mist falling in Trafalgar Square, coiling round us its tendrils of ectoplasm! A million muffin-eating moralists were waiting, not for us, Brother Ass, but for the plucky and tedious Trollope! (If you are dissatisfied with your form, reach for the *curette*.) Now do you wonder if I laugh a little off-key? Do you ask yourself what has turned me into nature's bashful little aphorist? We who are, after all, simply

9 on 11pt

Walking along the Mall we wondered who all those men were – tall hawk-featured men perched on balconies and high places, scanning the city with heavy binoculars. What were they seeking so earnestly? Who were they – so composed and steely-eyed? Timidly we stopped a policeman to ask him. 'They are publishers' he said mildly. Publishers! Our hearts stopped beating. 'They are on the look out for new talent.' Great God! It was for *us* they were waiting and watching! Then the kindly policeman lowered his voice confidentially and said in hollow and reverent tones: *They are waiting for the new Trollope to be born!'* Do you remember, at these words, how heavy our suitcases suddenly felt? How our blood slowed, our footsteps lagged? Brother Ass, we had been bashfully thinking of a kind of illumination such as Rimbaud dreamed of – a nagging poem which was not didactic or expository but which *infected* – was not simply a rationalised intuition, I mean, clothed in isinglass! We had come to the wrong shop, with the wrong change! A chill struck us as we saw the mist falling in Trafalgar Square, coiling round us its tendrils of ectoplasm! A million

10 on 12pt

Walking along the Mall we wondered who all those men were – tall hawk-featured men perched on balconies and high places, scanning the city with heavy binoculars. What were they seeking so earnestly? Who were they – so composed and steely-eyed? Timidly we stopped a policeman to ask him. 'They are publishers' he said mildly. Publishers! Our hearts stopped beating. 'They are on the look out for new talent.' Great God! It was for *us* they were waiting and watching! Then the kindly policeman lowered his voice confidentially and said in hollow and reverent tones: *They are waiting for the new Trollope to be born!'* Do you remember, at these words, how heavy our suitcases suddenly felt? How our blood slowed, our footsteps lagged? Brother Ass, we had been bashfully thinking of a kind of illumination such as Rimbaud dreamed of – a nagging poem which was not didactic or expository but which *infected* – was not simply a rationalised intuition, I mean, clothed in isinglass! We had

11 on 13pt

WALKING ALONG THE MALL WE WONDERED WHO ALL THOSE MEN WERE – TALL HAWK-featured men perched on balconies and high places, scanning the city with heavy binoculars. What were they seeking so earnestly? Who were they – so composed and steely-eyed? Timidly we stopped a policeman to ask him. 'They are publishers' he said mildly. Publishers! Our hearts stopped beating. 'They are on the look out for new talent.' Great God! It was for *us* they were waiting and watching! Then the kindly policeman lowered his voice confidentially and said in hollow and reverent tones: *'They are waiting for the new Trollope to be born!'* Do you remember, at these words, how heavy our suitcases suddenly felt? How our blood slowed, our footsteps lagged? Brother Ass, we had been bashfully thinking of a kind of illumination such as Rimbaud dreamed of – a nagging poem which was not didactic or expository but which *infected* – was not simply a rationalised intuition, I mean, clothed in isinglass! We had come to the wrong shop, with the wrong change! A chill struck us as we saw the mist falling in Trafalgar Square, coiling round us its tendrils of ectoplasm! A million muffin-eating moralists were waiting, not for us, Brother Ass, but for the plucky and tedious Trollope! (If you are dissatisfied with your form, reach for the *curette*.) Now do you wonder if I laugh a little off-key? Do you ask

9 on 12pt

WALKING ALONG THE MALL WE WONDERED WHO ALL THOSE MEN WERE – TALL hawk-featured men perched on balconies and high places, scanning the city with heavy binoculars. What were they seeking so earnestly? Who were they – so composed and steely-eyed? Timidly we stopped a policeman to ask him. 'They are publishers' he said mildly. Publishers! Our hearts stopped beating. 'They are on the look out for new talent.' Great God! It was for *us* they were waiting and watching! Then the kindly policeman lowered his voice confidentially and said in hollow and reverent tones: *They are waiting for the new Trollope to be born!'* Do you remember, at these words, how heavy our suitcases suddenly felt? How our blood slowed, our footsteps lagged? Brother Ass, we had been bashfully thinking of a kind of illumination such as Rimbaud dreamed of – a nagging poem which was not didactic or expository but which *infected* – was not simply a rationalised intuition, I mean, clothed in isinglass! We had come to the wrong shop, with the wrong change! A chill struck us as we saw the mist

10 on 13.5pt

WALKING ALONG THE MALL WE WONDERED WHO ALL THOSE MEN WERE – tall hawk-featured men perched on balconies and high places, scanning the city with heavy binoculars. What were they seeking so earnestly? Who were they – so composed and steely-eyed? Timidly we stopped a policeman to ask him. 'They are publishers' he said mildly. Publishers! Our hearts stopped beating. 'They are on the look out for new talent.' Great God! It was for *us* they were waiting and watching! Then the kindly policeman lowered his voice confidentially and said in hollow and reverent tones: *'They are waiting for the new Trollope to be born!'* Do you remember, at these words, how heavy our suitcases suddenly felt? How our blood slowed, our footsteps lagged? Brother Ass, we had been bashfully thinking of a kind of illumination such as Rimbaud dreamed of – a nagging poem which was not didactic or expository but which *infected* – was not

11 on 14.5pt

Monotype **Franklin Gothic**

1001 book and book italic
1003 demi-bold
ITC 1979 (Victor Caruso). Based on
M F Benton's design for ATF, 1904
Copyfitting factor 43.8/44.1/44.5

Range also includes medium, medium italic,
demi-bold italic, heavy, heavy italic, extra
condensed, extra condensed italic

The Linotype version is similar, although
slightly bolder, and the figures are slightly
tighter spaced. Copyfitting code 127/127/128

ABCDEFGHIJKLMNOP
QRSTUVWXYZ abcdefg
hijklmnopqrstuvwxyz
1234567890
ff fi fl ffi ffl ( ) [ ]&£$.,;:-!?''

ABCDEFGHIJKLMNOP
QRSTUVWXYZ abcdefg
hijklmnopqrstuvwxyz
1234567890
ff fi fl ffi ffl ( )[]&£$.,;:-!?''

ABCDEFGHIJKLMNOP
QRSTUVWXYZ abcdefg
hijklmnopqrstuvwxyz
1234567890
ff fi fl ffi ffl () [ ]&£$.,;:-!?''

24 on 27pt

These examples show *normal* letterspacing and the effect of *reduced*
letterspacing on roman setting *as well as on words in italic*: they also
show the appearance of figures, for example 28 May 1964, within text.
These & the ampersand are not included in the setting opposite.

Normal letterspacing

These examples show *normal* letterspacing and the effect of *reduced*
letterspacing on roman setting *as well as on words in italic*: they also
show the appearance of figures, for example 28 May 1964, within text.
These & the ampersand are not included in the setting opposite.

Minus one unit spacing

These examples show *normal* letterspacing and the effect of *reduced*
letterspacing on roman setting *as well as on words in italic*: they also
show the appearance of figures, for example 28 May 1964, within text.
These & the ampersand are not included in the setting opposite.

Minus two units spacing

WALKING ALONG THE MALL WE WONDERED WHO ALL THOSE MEN
WALKING ALONG THE MALL WE WONDERED WHO ALL THOSE
WALKING ALONG THE MALL WE WONDERED WHO ALL

Capitals: normal letterspacing/plus 9 units/plus 18 units

Walking along the Mall we wondered who all those men were – tall
hawk-featured men perched on balconies and high places, scanning
the city with heavy binoculars. WHAT WERE THEY SEEKING SO EARNESTLY?
Who were they – so composed and steely-eyed? Timidly we stopped
a policeman to ask him. 'They are publishers' he said mildly.
Publishers! OUR HEARTS STOPPED BEATING. 'They are on the look out
for new talent.' Great God! It was for *us* they were waiting and

Text with reduced capitals normal letterspacing/plus 6 units

WALKING ALONG THE MALL we wondered who all those men were
WALKING ALONG THE MALL we wondered who all those men were

True italic/sloped roman

Walking along the Mall we wondered who all those men were – tall hawk-featured
men perched on balconies and high places, scanning the city with heavy binoculars.
What were they seeking so earnestly? Who were they – so composed and steely-eyed?
Timidly we stopped a policeman to ask him. 'They are publishers' he said mildly.
Publishers! Our hearts stopped beating. 'They are on the look out for new talent.'
Great God! It was for *us* they were waiting and watching! Then the kindly policeman
lowered his voice confidentially and said in hollow and reverent tones: *'They are*
waiting for the new Trollope to be born!' Do you remember, at these words, how heavy
our suitcases suddenly felt? How our blood slowed, our footsteps lagged? Brother
Ass, we had been bashfully thinking of a kind of illumination such as Rimbaud

8 on 9pt

Walking along the Mall we wondered who all those men were – tall hawk-featured men
perched on balconies and high places, scanning the city with heavy binoculars. What
were they seeking so earnestly? Who were they – so composed and steely-eyed?
Timidly we stopped a policeman to ask him. 'They are publishers' he said mildly.
Publishers! Our hearts stopped beating. 'They are on the look out for new talent.'
Great God! It was for *us* they were waiting and watching! Then the kindly policeman
lowered his voice confidentially and said in hollow and reverent tones: *'They are*
waiting for the new Trollope to be born!' Do you remember, at these words, how heavy
our suitcases suddenly felt? How our blood slowed, our footsteps lagged? Brother

8 on 10.5pt

Walking along the Mall we wondered who all those men were – tall hawk-featured men perched on balconies and high places, scanning the city with heavy binoculars. What were they seeking so earnestly? Who were they – so composed and steely-eyed? Timidly we stopped a policeman to ask him. 'They are publishers' he said mildly. Publishers! Our hearts stopped beating. 'They are on the look out for new talent.' Great God! It was for *us* they were waiting and watching! Then the kindly policeman lowered his voice confidentially and said in hollow and reverent tones: *'They are waiting for the new Trollope to be born!'* Do you remember, at these words, how heavy our suitcases suddenly felt? How our blood slowed, our footsteps lagged? Brother Ass, we had been bashfully thinking of a kind of illumination such as Rimbaud dreamed of – a nagging poem which was not didactic or expository but which *infected* – was not simply a rationalised intuition, I mean, clothed in isinglass! We had come to the wrong shop, with the wrong change! A chill struck us as we saw the mist falling in Trafalgar Square, coiling around us its tendrils of ectoplasm! A million muffin-eating moralists were waiting, not for us, Brother Ass, but for the plucky and tedious Trollope! (If you are dissatisfied with your form, reach for the *curette*.) Now do you wonder if I laugh a little off-key? Do you ask yourself

9 on 11pt

Walking along the Mall we wondered who all those men were – tall hawk-featured men perched on balconies and high places, scanning the city with heavy binoculars. What were they seeking so earnestly? Who were they – so composed and steely-eyed? Timidly we stopped a policeman to ask him. 'They are publishers' he said mildly. Publishers! Our hearts stopped beating. 'They are on the look out for new talent.' Great God! It was for *us* they were waiting and watching! Then the kindly policeman lowered his voice confidentially and said in hollow and reverent tones: *'They are waiting for the new Trollope to be born!'* Do you remember, at these words, how heavy our suitcases suddenly felt? How our blood slowed, our footsteps lagged? Brother Ass, we had been bashfully thinking of a kind of illumination such as Rimbaud dreamed of – a nagging poem which was not didactic or expository but which *infected* – was not simply a rationalised intuition, I mean, clothed in isinglass! We had come to the wrong shop, with the wrong change! A chill struck us as we saw the mist falling in Trafalgar Square, coiling around us its tendrils of ectoplasm! A million muffin-eating moralists were waiting, not for us, Brother Ass, but for the plucky and tedious Trollope! (If you are dissatisfied with your form, reach for

9 on 12pt

Walking along the Mall we wondered who all those men were – tall hawk-featured men perched on balconies and high places, scanning the city with heavy binoculars. What were they seeking so earnestly? Who were they – so composed and steely-eyed? Timidly we stopped a policeman to ask him. 'They are publishers' he said mildly. Publishers! Our hearts stopped beating. 'They are on the look out for new talent.' Great God! It was for *us* they were waiting and watching! Then the kindly policeman lowered his voice confidentially and said in hollow and reverent tones: *'They are waiting for the new Trollope to be born!'* Do you remember, at these words, how heavy our suitcases suddenly felt? How our blood slowed, our footsteps lagged? Brother Ass, we had been bashfully thinking of a kind of illumination such as Rimbaud dreamed of – a nagging poem which was not didactic or expository but which *infected* – was not simply a rationalised intuition, I mean, clothed in isinglass! We had come to the wrong shop, with the wrong change! A chill struck us as we saw the mist falling in Trafalgar

10 on 12pt

Walking along the Mall we wondered who all those men were – tall hawk-featured men perched on balconies and high places, scanning the city with heavy binoculars. What were they seeking so earnestly? Who were they – so composed and steely-eyed? Timidly we stopped a policeman to ask him. 'They are publishers' he said mildly. Publishers! Our hearts stopped beating. 'They are on the look out for new talent.' Great God! It was for *us* they were waiting and watching! Then the kindly policeman lowered his voice confidentially and said in hollow and reverent tones: *'They are waiting for the new Trollope to be born!'* Do you remember, at these words, how heavy our suitcases suddenly felt? How our blood slowed, our footsteps lagged? Brother Ass, we had been bashfully thinking of a kind of illumination such as Rimbaud dreamed of – a nagging poem which was not didactic or expository but which *infected* – was not simply a rationalised intuition, I mean, clothed in isinglass! We had come to the wrong shop, with the wrong

10 on 13.5pt

Walking along the Mall we wondered who all those men were – tall hawk-featured men perched on balconies and high places, scanning the city with heavy binoculars. What were they seeking so earnestly? Who were they – so composed and steely-eyed? Timidly we stopped a policeman to ask him. 'They are publishers' he said mildly. Publishers! Our hearts stopped beating. 'They are on the look out for new talent.' Great God! It was for *us* they were waiting and watching! Then the kindly policeman lowered his voice confidentially and said in hollow and reverent tones: *'They are waiting for the new Trollope to be born!'* Do you remember, at these words, how heavy our suitcases suddenly felt? How our blood slowed, our footsteps lagged? Brother Ass, we had been bashfully thinking of a kind of illumination such as Rimbaud dreamed of – a nagging poem which was not didactic or expository but which *infected* – was not simply a rationalised

11 on 13pt

Walking along the Mall we wondered who all those men were – tall hawk-featured men perched on balconies and high places, scanning the city with heavy binoculars. What were they seeking so earnestly? Who were they – so composed and steely-eyed? Timidly we stopped a policeman to ask him. 'They are publishers' he said mildly. Publishers! Our hearts stopped beating. 'They are on the look out for new talent.' Great God! It was for *us* they were waiting and watching! Then the kindly policeman lowered his voice confidentially and said in hollow and reverent tones: *'They are waiting for the new Trollope to be born!'* Do you remember, at these words, how heavy our suitcases suddenly felt? How our blood slowed, our footsteps lagged? Brother Ass, we had been bashfully thinking of a kind of illumination such as Rimbaud dreamed of – a nagging poem which was not didactic

11 on 14.5pt

Monotype **Futura**

912 medium and medium italic
913 demi-bold
Bauer 1928-30 (Paul Renner)
Copyfitting factor 39.8/38.9/42.2

Range also includes light, book, quarter-bold,
demi-bold italic, bold, bold italic, extra bold,
black

Monotype's version differs considerably from
the Bauer original. Round letters such as a b c
d e are more geometric in construction,
lacking the subtlety of Renner's design.
Display sizes become rather uncouth

ABCDEFGHIJKLMNOP
QRSTUVWXYZ abcdefg
hijklmnopqrstuvwxyz
1234567890
ff fi fl ffi ffl ()[]&£$.,;:-!?"

ABCDEFGHIJKLMNOP
QRSTUVWXYZ abcdefg
hijklmnopqrstuvwxyz
1234567890
ff fi fl ffi ffl ()[]&£$.,;:-!?"

ABCDEFGHIJKLMNOP
QRSTUVWXYZ abcdefg
hijklmnopqrstuvwxyz
1234567890
ff fi fl ffi ffl ()[]&£$.,;:-!?"

24 on 27pt

These examples show *normal* letterspacing and the effect of *reduced*
letterspacing on roman setting *as well as on words in italic*: they also
show the appearance of figures, for example 28 May 1964, within text.
These & the ampersand are not included in the setting opposite.

Normal letterspacing

These examples show *normal* letterspacing and the effect of *reduced*
letterspacing on roman setting *as well as on words in italic*: they also
show the appearance of figures, for example 28 May 1964, within text.
These & the ampersand are not included in the setting opposite.

Minus one unit spacing

These examples show *normal* letterspacing and the effect of *reduced*
letterspacing on roman setting *as well as on words in italic*: they also
show the appearance of figures, for example 28 May 1964, within text.
These & the ampersand are not included in the setting opposite.

Minus two units spacing

WALKING ALONG THE MALL WE WONDERED WHO ALL THOSE MEN
WALKING ALONG THE MALL WE WONDERED WHO ALL THOSE
WALKING ALONG THE MALL WE WONDERED WHO ALL

Capitals: normal letterspacing/plus 9 units/plus 18 units

Walking along the Mall we wondered who all those men were – tall hawk-
featured men perched on balconies and high places, scanning the city with
heavy binoculars. WHAT WERE THEY SEEKING SO EARNESTLY? Who were they – so
composed and steely-eyed? Timidly we stopped a policeman to ask him.
'They are publishers' HE SAID MILDLY. PUBLISHERS! Our hearts stopped
beating. 'They are on the look out for new talent.' Great God! It was for *us*
they were waiting and watching! Then the kindly policeman lowered his

Text with reduced capitals normal letterspacing/plus 6 units

WALKING ALONG THE MALL we wondered who all those men were
WALKING ALONG THE MALL we wondered who all those men were

True italic/sloped roman

Walking along the Mall we wondered who all those men were – tall hawk-featured men
perched on balconies and high places, scanning the city with heavy binoculars. What were they
seeking so earnestly? Who were they – so composed and steely-eyed? Timidly we stopped a
policeman to ask him. 'They are publishers' he said mildly. Publishers! Our hearts stopped
beating. 'They are on the look out for new talent.' Great God! It was for *us* they were waiting
and watching! Then the kindly policeman lowered his voice confidentially and said in hollow
and reverent tones: *'They are waiting for the new Trollope to be born!'* Do you remember, at
these words, how heavy our suitcases suddenly felt? How our blood slowed, our footsteps
lagged? Brother Ass, we had been bashfully thinking of a kind of illumination such as Rimbaud
dreamed of – a nagging poem which was not didactic or expository but which *infected* – was

8 on 9pt

Walking along the Mall we wondered who all those men were – tall hawk-featured men
perched on balconies and high places, scanning the city with heavy binoculars. What were they
seeking so earnestly? Who were they – so composed and steely-eyed? Timidly we stopped a
policeman to ask him. 'They are publishers' he said mildly. Publishers! Our hearts stopped
beating. 'They are on the look out for new talent.' Great God! It was for *us* they were waiting
and watching! Then the kindly policeman lowered his voice confidentially and said in hollow
and reverent tones: *'They are waiting for the new Trollope to be born!'* Do you remember, at
these words, how heavy our suitcases suddenly felt? How our blood slowed, our footsteps
lagged? Brother Ass, we had been bashfully thinking of a kind of illumination such as Rimbaud

8 on 10.5pt

Walking along the Mall we wondered who all those men were — tall hawk-featured men perched on balconies and high places, scanning the city with heavy binoculars. What were they seeking so earnestly? Who were they — so composed and steely-eyed? Timidly we stopped a policeman to ask him. 'They are publishers' he said mildly. Publishers! Our hearts stopped beating. 'They are on the look out for new talent.' Great God! It was for *us* they were waiting and watching! Then the kindly policeman lowered his voice confidentially and said in hollow and reverent tones: *'They are waiting for the new Trollope to be born!'* Do you remember, at these words, how heavy our suitcases suddenly felt? How our blood slowed, our footsteps lagged? Brother Ass, we had been bashfully thinking of a kind of illumination such as Rimbaud dreamed of — a nagging poem which was not didactic or expository but which *infected* — was not simply a rationalised intuition, I mean, clothed in isinglass! We had come to the wrong shop, with the wrong change! A chill struck us as we saw the mist falling in Trafalgar Square, coiling around us its tendrils of ectoplasm! A million muffin-eating moralists were waiting, not for us, Brother Ass, but for the plucky and tedious Trollope! (If you are dissatisfied with your form, reach for the *curette*.) Now do you wonder if I laugh a little off-key? Do you ask yourself what has turned me into nature's bashful little aphorist? We who are, after all, simply poor co-workers in the psyche of our nation,
9 on 11pt

Walking along the Mall we wondered who all those men were — tall hawk-featured men perched on balconies and high places, scanning the city with heavy binoculars. What were they seeking so earnestly? Who were they — so composed and steely-eyed? Timidly we stopped a policeman to ask him. 'They are publishers' he said mildly. Publishers! Our hearts stopped beating. 'They are on the look out for new talent.' Great God! It was for *us* they were waiting and watching! Then the kindly policeman lowered his voice confidentially and said in hollow and reverent tones: *'They are waiting for the new Trollope to be born!'* Do you remember, at these words, how heavy our suitcases suddenly felt? How our blood slowed, our footsteps lagged? Brother Ass, we had been bashfully thinking of a kind of illumination such as Rimbaud dreamed of — a nagging poem which was not didactic or expository but which *infected* — was not simply a rationalised intuition, I mean, clothed in isinglass! We had come to the wrong shop, with the wrong change! A chill struck us as we saw the mist falling in Trafalgar Square, coiling around us its tendrils of ectoplasm! A million muffin-eating moralists were waiting, not for us, Brother Ass, but for the plucky and tedious Trollope! (If you are dissatisfied with your form, reach for the *curette*.) Now do you wonder if I laugh a little off-key? Do you ask yourself what has turned me into nature's bashful little aphorist?
9 on 12pt

Walking along the Mall we wondered who all those men were — tall hawk-featured men perched on balconies and high places, scanning the city with heavy binoculars. What were they seeking so earnestly? Who were they — so composed and steely-eyed? Timidly we stopped a policeman to ask him. 'They are publishers' he said mildly. Publishers! Our hearts stopped beating. 'They are on the look out for new talent.' Great God! It was for *us* they were waiting and watching! Then the kindly policeman lowered his voice confidentially and said in hollow and reverent tones: *'They are waiting for the new Trollope to be born!'* Do you remember, at these words, how heavy our suitcases suddenly felt? How our blood slowed, our footsteps lagged? Brother Ass, we had been bashfully thinking of a kind of illumination such as Rimbaud dreamed of — a nagging poem which was not didactic or expository but which *infected* — was not simply a rationalised intuition, I mean, clothed in isinglass! We had come to the wrong shop, with the wrong change! A chill struck us as we saw the mist falling in Trafalgar Square, coiling around us its tendrils of ectoplasm! A million muffin-eating moralists were waiting, not for us, Brother
10 on 12pt

Walking along the Mall we wondered who all those men were — tall hawk-featured men perched on balconies and high places, scanning the city with heavy binoculars. What were they seeking so earnestly? Who were they — so composed and steely-eyed? Timidly we stopped a policeman to ask him. 'They are publishers' he said mildly. Publishers! Our hearts stopped beating. 'They are on the look out for new talent.' Great God! It was for *us* they were waiting and watching! Then the kindly policeman lowered his voice confidentially and said in hollow and reverent tones: *'They are waiting for the new Trollope to be born!'* Do you remember, at these words, how heavy our suitcases suddenly felt? How our blood slowed, our footsteps lagged? Brother Ass, we had been bashfully thinking of a kind of illumination such as Rimbaud dreamed of — a nagging poem which was not didactic or expository but which *infected* — was not simply a rationalised intuition, I mean, clothed in isinglass! We had come to the wrong shop, with the wrong change! A chill struck us as we saw the mist falling in Trafalgar Square, coiling around us its tendrils of ectoplasm! A million
10 on 13.5pt

Walking along the Mall we wondered who all those men were — tall hawk-featured men perched on balconies and high places, scanning the city with heavy binoculars. What were they seeking so earnestly? Who were they — so composed and steely-eyed? Timidly we stopped a policeman to ask him. 'They are publishers' he said mildly. Publishers! Our hearts stopped beating. 'They are on the look out for new talent.' Great God! It was for *us* they were waiting and watching! Then the kindly policeman lowered his voice confidentially and said in hollow and reverent tones: *'They are waiting for the new Trollope to be born!'* Do you remember, at these words, how heavy our suitcases suddenly felt? How our blood slowed, our footsteps lagged? Brother Ass, we had been bashfully thinking of a kind of illumination such as Rimbaud dreamed of — a nagging poem which was not didactic or expository but which *infected* — was not simply a rationalised intuition, I mean, clothed in isinglass! We had come to the wrong shop, with the wrong
11 on 13pt

Walking along the Mall we wondered who all those men were — tall hawk-featured men perched on balconies and high places, scanning the city with heavy binoculars. What were they seeking so earnestly? Who were they — so composed and steely-eyed? Timidly we stopped a policeman to ask him. 'They are publishers' he said mildly. Publishers! Our hearts stopped beating. 'They are on the look out for new talent.' Great God! It was for *us* they were waiting and watching! Then the kindly policeman lowered his voice confidentially and said in hollow and reverent tones: *'They are waiting for the new Trollope to be born!'* Do you remember, at these words, how heavy our suitcases suddenly felt? How our blood slowed, our footsteps lagged? Brother Ass, we had been bashfully thinking of a kind of illumination such as Rimbaud dreamed of — a nagging poem which was not didactic or expository but which *infected* — was not simply a rationalised intuition, I mean,
11 on 14.5pt

MONOTYPE FUTURA

Linotype **Futura**

medium (07105), **medium italic** (14105)
bold (09105)
Bauer 1928-30 (Paul Renner)
Copyfitting code 125/122/166

There is a very extensive range of weights and variations

The Linotype version closely follows the Bauer original in its subtly ungeometric round letters, although letterspacing is tighter

Educational characters available

ABCDEFGHIJKLMNOP
QRSTUVWXYZ abcdefg
hijklmnopqrstuvwxyz
1234567890
fifl ()[]&£$.,;:-!?"

ABCDEFGHIJKLMNOP
QRSTUVWXYZ abcdefg
hijklmnopqrstuvwxyz
1234567890
fifl ()[]&£$.,;:-!?"

ABCDEFGHIJKLMNOP
QRSTUVWXYZ abcdefg
ghijklmnopqrstuvwxyz
1234567890
fifl ()[]&£$.,;:-!?"

24 on 27pt

These examples show *normal* letterspacing and the effect of *reduced* letterspacing on roman setting *as well as on words in italic*: they also show the appearance of figures, for example 28 May 1964, within text. These & the ampersand are not included in the setting opposite.
Normal letterspacing

These examples show *normal* letterspacing and the effect of *reduced* letterspacing on roman setting *as well as on words in italic*: they also show the appearance of figures, for example 28 May 1964, within text. These & the ampersand are not included in the setting opposite.
Minus one unit spacing

These examples show *normal* letterspacing and the effect of *reduced* letterspacing on roman setting *as well as on words in italic*: they also show the appearance of figures, for example 28 May 1964, within text. These & the ampersand are not included in the setting opposite.
Minus two units spacing

WALKING ALONG THE MALL WE WONDERED WHO ALL THOSE
WALKING ALONG THE MALL WE WONDERED WHO ALL
WALKING ALONG THE MALL WE WONDERED WHO
Capitals: normal letterspacing/plus 4 units/plus 9 units

Walking along the Mall we wondered who all those men were – tall hawk-featured men perched on balconies and high places, scanning the city with heavy binoculars. WHAT WERE THEY SEEKING SO EARNESTLY? Who were they – so composed and steely-eyed? Timidly we stopped a policeman to ask him. 'They are publishers' HE SAID MILDLY. Publishers! Our hearts stopped beating. 'They are on the look out for new talent.' Great God! It was for *us* they were waiting and watching!
Text with reduced caps normal letterspacing/plus 3 units

WALKING ALONG THE MALL we wondered who all those men were
WALKING ALONG THE MALL we wondered who all those men were
True italic/sloped roman

Walking along the Mall we wondered who all those men were – tall hawk-featured men perched on balconies and high places, scanning the city with heavy binoculars. What were they seeking so earnestly? Who were they – so composed and steely-eyed? Timidly we stopped a policeman to ask him. 'They are publishers' he said mildly. Publishers! Our hearts stopped beating. 'They are on the look out for new talent.' Great God! It was for *us* they were waiting and watching! Then the kindly policeman lowered his voice confidentially and said in hollow and reverent tones: *'They are waiting for the new Trollope to be born!'* Do you remember, at these words, how heavy our suitcases suddenly felt? How our blood slowed, our footsteps lagged? Brother Ass, we had been bashfully thinking of a kind of illumination such as Rimbaud dreamed of – a
8 on 9pt

Walking along the Mall we wondered who all those men were – tall hawk-featured men perched on balconies and high places, scanning the city with heavy binoculars. What were they seeking so earnestly? Who were they – so composed and steely-eyed? Timidly we stopped a policeman to ask him. 'They are publishers' he said mildly. Publishers! Our hearts stopped beating. 'They are on the look out for new talent.' Great God! It was for *us* they were waiting and watching! Then the kindly policeman lowered his voice confidentially and said in hollow and reverent tones: *'They are waiting for the new Trollope to be born!'* Do you remember, at these words, how heavy our suitcases suddenly felt? How our blood slowed, our footsteps lagged? Brother Ass, we had been
8 on 10.5pt

Walking along the Mall we wondered who all those men were — tall hawk-featured men perched on balconies and high places, scanning the city with heavy binoculars. What were they seeking so earnestly? Who were they — so composed and steely-eyed? Timidly we stopped a policeman to ask him. 'They are publishers' he said mildly. Publishers! Our hearts stopped beating. 'They are on the look out for new talent.' Great God! It was for *us* they were waiting and watching! Then the kindly policeman lowered his voice confidentially and said in hollow and reverent tones: *'They are waiting for the new Trollope to be born!'* Do you remember, at these words, how heavy our suitcases suddenly felt? How our blood slowed, our footsteps lagged? Brother Ass, we had been bashfully thinking of a kind of illumination such as Rimbaud dreamed of — a nagging poem which was not didactic or expository but which *infected* — was not simply a rationalised intuition, I mean, clothed in isinglass! We had come to the wrong shop, with the wrong change! A chill struck us as we saw the mist falling in Trafalgar Square, coiling round us its tendrils of ectoplasm! A million muffin-eating moralists were waiting, not for us, Brother Ass, but for the plucky and tedious Trollope! (If you are dissatisfied with your form, reach for the *curette*.) Now do you wonder if I laugh a little
9 on 11pt

Walking along the Mall we wondered who all those men were — tall hawk-featured men perched on balconies and high places, scanning the city with heavy binoculars. What were they seeking so earnestly? Who were they — so composed and steely-eyed? Timidly we stopped a policeman to ask him. 'They are publishers' he said mildly. Publishers! Our hearts stopped beating. 'They are on the look out for new talent.' Great God! It was for *us* they were waiting and watching! Then the kindly policeman lowered his voice confidentially and said in hollow and reverent tones: *'They are waiting for the new Trollope to be born!'* Do you remember, at these words, how heavy our suitcases suddenly felt? How our blood slowed, our footsteps lagged? Brother Ass, we had been bashfully thinking of a kind of illumination such as Rimbaud dreamed of — a nagging poem which was not didactic or expository but which *infected* — was not simply a rationalised intuition, I mean, clothed in isinglass! We had come to the wrong shop, with the wrong change! A chill struck us as we saw the
10 on 12pt

Walking along the Mall we wondered who all those men were — tall hawk-featured men perched on balconies and high places, scanning the city with heavy binoculars. What were they seeking so earnestly? Who were they — so composed and steely-eyed? Timidly we stopped a policeman to ask him. 'They are publishers' he said mildly. Publishers! Our hearts stopped beating. 'They are on the look out for new talent.' Great God! It was for *us* they were waiting and watching! Then the kindly policeman lowered his voice confidentially and said in hollow and reverent tones: *'They are waiting for the new Trollope to be born!'* Do you remember, at these words, how heavy our suitcases suddenly felt? How our blood slowed, our footsteps lagged? Brother Ass, we had been bashfully thinking of a kind of illumination such as Rimbaud dreamed of — a nagging poem which was not didactic or expository but which
11 on 13pt

Walking along the Mall we wondered who all those men were — tall hawk-featured men perched on balconies and high places, scanning the city with heavy binoculars. What were they seeking so earnestly? Who were they — so composed and steely-eyed? Timidly we stopped a policeman to ask him. 'They are publishers' he said mildly. Publishers! Our hearts stopped beating. 'They are on the look out for new talent.' Great God! It was for *us* they were waiting and watching! Then the kindly policeman lowered his voice confidentially and said in hollow and reverent tones: *'They are waiting for the new Trollope to be born!'* Do you remember, at these words, how heavy our suitcases suddenly felt? How our blood slowed, our footsteps lagged? Brother Ass, we had been bashfully thinking of a kind of illumination such as Rimbaud dreamed of — a nagging poem which was not didactic or expository but which *infected* — was not simply a rationalised intuition, I mean, clothed in isinglass! We had come to the wrong shop, with the wrong change! A chill struck us as we saw the mist falling in Trafalgar Square, coiling round us its tendrils of ectoplasm! A million muffin-eating moralists were waiting, not for us, Brother Ass, but for the plucky and tedious Trollope! (If you are dissatisfied with your form, reach for the
9 on 12pt

Walking along the Mall we wondered who all those men were — tall hawk-featured men perched on balconies and high places, scanning the city with heavy binoculars. What were they seeking so earnestly? Who were they — so composed and steely-eyed? Timidly we stopped a policeman to ask him. 'They are publishers' he said mildly. Publishers! Our hearts stopped beating. 'They are on the look out for new talent.' Great God! It was for *us* they were waiting and watching! Then the kindly policeman lowered his voice confidentially and said in hollow and reverent tones: *'They are waiting for the new Trollope to be born!'* Do you remember, at these words, how heavy our suitcases suddenly felt? How our blood slowed, our footsteps lagged? Brother Ass, we had been bashfully thinking of a kind of illumination such as Rimbaud dreamed of — a nagging poem which was not didactic or expository but which *infected* — was not simply a rationalised intuition, I mean, clothed in isinglass! We had come to the wrong shop, with the wrong
10 on 13.5pt

Walking along the Mall we wondered who all those men were — tall hawk-featured men perched on balconies and high places, scanning the city with heavy binoculars. What were they seeking so earnestly? Who were they — so composed and steely-eyed? Timidly we stopped a policeman to ask him. 'They are publishers' he said mildly. Publishers! Our hearts stopped beating. 'They are on the look out for new talent.' Great God! It was for *us* they were waiting and watching! Then the kindly policeman lowered his voice confidentially and said in hollow and reverent tones: *'They are waiting for the new Trollope to be born!'* Do you remember, at these words, how heavy our suitcases suddenly felt? How our blood slowed, our footsteps lagged? Brother Ass, we had been bashfully thinking of a kind of illumination such as Rimbaud dreamed of — a nagging poem
11 on 14.5pt

Monotype **Galliard**

1105 roman and italic
1106 bold
ITC 1978 (Matthew Carter)
(Originally designed for Mergenthaler
Linotype)
Copyfitting factor 38.5/37.3/40.6

Range also includes bold italic, black, black
italic, ultra, ultra italic

A free interpretation of Granjon's types.
Designed at the height of the fashion in some
quarters for extra tight spacing, this type is
greatly improved by increasing the
letterspacing by one or even two units

ABCDEFGHIJKLMNOP
QRSTUVWXYZ abcdefg
hijklmnopqrstuvwxyz
1234567890
ff fi fl ffi ffl ( )[ ]&£$.,;:-!?''

ABCDEFGHIJKLMNOP
QRSTUVWXYZ abcdefg
hijklmnopqrstuvwxyz
1234567890
ff fi fl ffi ffl ( )[ ]&£$.,;:-!?''

ABCDEFGHIJKLMNOP
QRSTUVWXYZ abcdefg
hijklmnopqrstuvwxyz
1234567890
ff fi fl ffi ffl ( )[ ]&£$.,;:-!?''

24 on 27pt

These examples show *normal* letterspacing and the effect of *increased* letterspacing on roman setting *as well as on words in italic*: they also show the appearance of figures, for example 28 May 1964, within text. These & the ampersand are not included in the setting opposite.

Normal letterspacing

These examples show *normal* letterspacing and the effect of *increased* letterspacing on roman setting *as well as on words in italic*: they also show the appearance of figures, for example 28 May 1964, within text. These & the ampersand are not included in the setting opposite.

Plus one unit spacing

These examples show *normal* letterspacing and the effect of *increased* letterspacing on roman setting *as well as on words in italic*: they also show the appearance of figures, for example 28 May 1964, within text. These & the ampersand are not included in the setting opposite.

Plus two units spacing

WALKING ALONG THE MALL WE WONDERED WHO ALL THOSE
WALKING ALONG THE MALL WE WONDERED WHO ALL
WALKING ALONG THE MALL WE WONDERED WHO

Capitals: normal letterspacing/plus 9 units/plus 18 units

Walking along the Mall we wondered who all those men were – tall hawk-featured men perched on balconies and high places, scanning the city with heavy binoculars. WHAT WERE THEY SEEKING SO EARNESTLY? Who were they – so composed and steely-eyed? Timidly we stopped a policeman to ask him. 'They are publishers' HE SAID MILDLY. PUBLISHERS! Our hearts stopped beating. 'They are on the look out for new talent.' Great God! It was for *us* they were waiting and watching! Then the kindly policeman lowered his voice

Text with reduced capitals normal letterspacing/plus 6 units

WALKING ALONG THE MALL we wondered who all those men were
WALKING ALONG THE MALL we wondered who all those men were

True italic/sloped roman

Walking along the Mall we wondered who all those men were – tall hawk-featured men perched on balconies and high places, scanning the city with heavy binoculars. What were they seeking so earnestly? Who were they – so composed and steely-eyed? Timidly we stopped a policeman to ask him. 'They are publishers' he said mildly. Publishers! Our hearts stopped beating. 'They are on the look out for new talent.' Great God! It was for *us* they were waiting and watching! Then the kindly policeman lowered his voice confidentially and said in hollow and reverent tones: *'They are waiting for the new Trollope to be born!'* Do you remember, at these words, how heavy our suitcases suddenly felt? How our blood slowed, our footsteps lagged? Brother Ass, we had been bashfully thinking of a kind of illumination such as Rimbaud dreamed of – a nagging poem which was not didactic or expository but which *infected* – was not simply a

8 on 9pt

Walking along the Mall we wondered who all those men were – tall hawk-featured men perched on balconies and high places, scanning the city with heavy binoculars. What were they seeking so earnestly? Who were they – so composed and steely-eyed? Timidly we stopped a policeman to ask him. 'They are publishers' he said mildly. Publishers! Our hearts stopped beating. 'They are on the look out for new talent.' Great God! It was for *us* they were waiting and watching! Then the kindly policeman lowered his voice confidentially and said in hollow and reverent tones: *'They are waiting for the new Trollope to be born!'* Do you remember, at these words, how heavy our suitcases suddenly felt? How our blood slowed, our footsteps lagged? Brother Ass, we had been bashfully thinking of a kind of illumination such as Rimbaud dreamed of – a nagging poem

8 on 10.5pt

Walking along the Mall we wondered who all those men were – tall hawk-featured men perched on balconies and high places, scanning the city with heavy binoculars. What were they seeking so earnestly? Who were they – so composed and steely-eyed? Timidly we stopped a policeman to ask him. 'They are publishers' he said mildly. Publishers! Our hearts stopped beating. 'They are on the look out for new talent.' Great God! It was for *us* they were waiting and watching! Then the kindly policeman lowered his voice confidentially and said in hollow and reverent tones: *'They are waiting for the new Trollope to be born!'* Do you remember, at these words, how heavy our suitcases suddenly felt? How our blood slowed, our footsteps lagged? Brother Ass, we had been bashfully thinking of a kind of illumination such as Rimbaud dreamed of – a nagging poem which was not didactic or expository but which *infected* – was not simply a rationalised intuition, I mean, clothed in isinglass! We had come to the wrong shop, with the wrong change! A chill struck us as we saw the mist falling in Trafalgar Square, coiling around us its tendrils of ectoplasm! A million muffin-eating moralists were waiting, not for us, Brother Ass, but for the plucky and tedious Trollope! (If you are dissatisfied with your form, reach for the *curette*.) Now do you wonder if I laugh a little off-key? Do you ask yourself what has turned me into nature's bashful little aphorist? We who are, after all, simply poor co-workers in the psyche of our nation, what can we expect but the natural automatic

9 on 11pt

Walking along the Mall we wondered who all those men were – tall hawk- featured men perched on balconies and high places, scanning the city with heavy binoculars. What were they seeking so earnestly? Who were they – so composed and steely-eyed? Timidly we stopped a policeman to ask him. 'They are publishers' he said mildly. Publishers! Our hearts stopped beating. 'They are on the look out for new talent.' Great God! It was for *us* they were waiting and watching! Then the kindly policeman lowered his voice confidentially and said in hollow and reverent tones: *'They are waiting for the new Trollope to be born!'* Do you remember, at these words, how heavy our suitcases suddenly felt? How our blood slowed, our footsteps lagged? Brother Ass, we had been bashfully thinking of a kind of illumination such as Rimbaud dreamed of – a nagging poem which was not didactic or expository but which *infected* – was not simply a rationalised intuition, I mean, clothed in isinglass! We had come to the wrong shop, with the wrong change! A chill struck us as we saw the mist falling in Trafalgar Square, coiling around us its tendrils of ectoplasm! A million muffin-eating moralists were waiting, not for us, Brother Ass, but for the plucky and tedious Trollope! (If you

10 on 12pt

Walking along the Mall we wondered who all those men were – tall hawk-featured men perched on balconies and high places, scanning the city with heavy binoculars. What were they seeking so earnestly? Who were they – so composed and steely-eyed? Timidly we stopped a policeman to ask him. 'They are publishers' he said mildly. Publishers! Our hearts stopped beating. 'They are on the look out for new talent.' Great God! It was for *us* they were waiting and watching! Then the kindly policeman lowered his voice confidentially and said in hollow and reverent tones: *'They are waiting for the new Trollope to be born!'* Do you remember, at these words, how heavy our suitcases suddenly felt? How our blood slowed, our footsteps lagged? Brother Ass, we had been bashfully thinking of a kind of illumination such as Rimbaud dreamed of – a nagging poem which was not didactic or expository but which *infected* – was not simply a rationalised intuition, I mean, clothed in isinglass! We had come to the wrong shop, with the wrong change! A chill struck us as we

11 on 13pt

Walking along the Mall we wondered who all those men were – tall hawk-featured men perched on balconies and high places, scanning the city with heavy binoculars. What were they seeking so earnestly? Who were they – so composed and steely-eyed? Timidly we stopped a policeman to ask him. 'They are publishers' he said mildly. Publishers! Our hearts stopped beating. 'They are on the look out for new talent.' Great God! It was for *us* they were waiting and watching! Then the kindly policeman lowered his voice confidentially and said in hollow and reverent tones: *'They are waiting for the new Trollope to be born!'* Do you remember, at these words, how heavy our suitcases suddenly felt? How our blood slowed, our footsteps lagged? Brother Ass, we had been bashfully thinking of a kind of illumination such as Rimbaud dreamed of – a nagging poem which was not didactic or expository but which *infected* – was not simply a rationalised intuition, I mean, clothed in isinglass! We had come to the wrong shop, with the wrong change! A chill struck us as we saw the mist falling in Trafalgar Square, coiling around us its tendrils of ectoplasm! A million muffin-eating moralists were

9 on 12pt

Walking along the Mall we wondered who all those men were – tall hawk-featured men perched on balconies and high places, scanning the city with heavy binoculars. What were they seeking so earnestly? Who were they – so composed and steely-eyed? Timidly we stopped a policeman to ask him. 'They are publishers' he said mildly. Publishers! Our hearts stopped beating. 'They are on the look out for new talent.' Great God! It was for *us* they were waiting and watching! Then the kindly policeman lowered his voice confidentially and said in hollow and reverent tones: *'They are waiting for the new Trollope to be born!'* Do you remember, at these words, how heavy our suitcases suddenly felt? How our blood slowed, our footsteps lagged? Brother Ass, we had been bashfully thinking of a kind of illumination such as Rimbaud dreamed of – a nagging poem which was not didactic or expository but which *infected* – was not simply a rationalised intuition, I mean, clothed in isinglass! We had come to the wrong shop, with the wrong change! A chill struck us as we saw the mist falling in Trafalgar Square, coiling around us its tendrils of ectoplasm! A million muffin-eating moralists were

10 on 13.5pt

Walking along the Mall we wondered who all those men were – tall hawk-featured men perched on balconies and high places, scanning the city with heavy binoculars. What were they seeking so earnestly? Who were they – so composed and steely-eyed? Timidly we stopped a policeman to ask him. 'They are publishers' he said mildly. Publishers! Our hearts stopped beating. 'They are on the look out for new talent.' Great God! It was for *us* they were waiting and watching! Then the kindly policeman lowered his voice confidentially and said in hollow and reverent tones: *'They are waiting for the new Trollope to be born!'* Do you remember, at these words, how heavy our suitcases suddenly felt? How our blood slowed, our footsteps lagged? Brother Ass, we had been bashfully thinking of a kind of illumination such as Rimbaud dreamed of – a nagging poem which was not didactic or expository but which *infected* – was not simply a rationalised intuition, I mean, clothed in isinglass! We had

11 on 14.5pt

Linotype **Galliard**

roman (05520), **italic** (13520)
bold (07520)
ITC 1978 (Matthew Carter)
(Originally designed for Mergenthaler
Linotype)
Copyfitting code 124/112/132

Range also includes bold italic, black, black
italic, ultra, ultra italic

A free interpretation of Granjon's types.
Designed at the height of the fashion in some
quarters for extra tight spacing, this type is
greatly improved by increasing the letter
spacing by one unit

ABCDEFGHIJKLMNOP
QRSTUVWXYZ abcdefg
hijklmnopqrstuvwxyz
1234567890 1234567890
fifl ()[]&£$.,;:-!?''

ABCDEFGHIJKLMNOP
QRSTUVWXYZ abcdefg
hijklmnopqrstuvwxyz
1234567890 1234567890
fifl () [] &£$.,;:-!?''

ABCDEFGHIJKLMNOP
QRSTUVWXYZ abcdefg
hijklmnopqrstuvwxyz
1234567890 1234567890
fifl ()[]&£$.,;:-!?''

24 on 27pt

146

These examples show *normal* letterspacing and the effect of *increased* letterspacing on roman setting *as well as on words in italic*: they also show the appearance of figures, for example 28 May 1964 within text. These & the ampersand are not included in the setting opposite.
Normal letterspacing

These examples show *normal* letterspacing and the effect of *increased* letterspacing on roman setting *as well as on words in italic*: they also show the appearance of figures, for example 28 May 1964 within text. These & the ampersand are not included in the setting opposite.
Plus one unit spacing

These examples show *normal* letterspacing and the effect of *increased* letterspacing on roman setting *as well as on words in italic*: they also show the appearance of figures, for example 28 May 1964 within text. These & the ampersand are not included in the setting opposite.
Plus two units spacing

WALKING ALONG THE MALL WE WONDERED WHO ALL
WALKING ALONG THE MALL WE WONDERED WHO
WALKING ALONG THE MALL WE WONDERED
Capitals: normal letterspacing/plus 4 units/plus 9 units

WALKING ALONG THE MALL WE WONDERED WHO ALL THOSE MEN
WALKING ALONG THE MALL WE WONDERED WHO ALL THOSE
WALKING ALONG THE MALL WE WONDERED WHO ALL
Small caps: normal letterspacing/plus 3 units/plus 6 units

WALKING ALONG THE MALL WE WONDERED WHO ALL THOSE MEN
WALKING ALONG THE MALL WE WONDERED WHO ALL THOSE MEN WERE
True small caps/reduced capitals

WALKING ALONG THE MALL we wondered who all those men were
WALKING ALONG THE MALL we wondered who all those men
True italic/sloped roman

Walking along the Mall we wondered who all those men were – tall hawk-featured men perched on balconies and high places, scanning the city with heavy binoculars. What were they seeking so earnestly? Who were they – so composed and steely-eyed? Timidly we stopped a policeman to ask him. 'They are publishers' he said mildly. Publishers! Our hearts stopped beating. 'They are on the look out for new talent.' Great God! It was for *us* they were waiting and watching! Then the kindly policeman lowered his voice confidentially and said in hollow and reverent tones: *'They are waiting for the new Trollope to be born!'* Do you remember, at these words, how heavy our suitcases suddenly felt? How our blood slowed, our footsteps lagged? Brother Ass, we had been bashfully thinking of a kind of illumination such as Rimbaud dreamed of – a nagging poem
8 on 9pt

WALKING ALONG THE MALL WE WONDERED WHO ALL THOSE MEN WERE – TALL hawk-featured men perched on balconies and high places, scanning the city with heavy binoculars. What were they seeking so earnestly? Who were they – so composed and steely-eyed? Timidly we stopped a policeman to ask him. 'They are publishers' he said mildly. Publishers! Our hearts stopped beating. 'They are on the look out for new talent.' Great God! It was for *us* they were waiting and watching! Then the kindly policeman lowered his voice confidentially and said in hollow and reverent tones: *'They are waiting for the new Trollope to be born!'* Do you remember, at these words, how heavy our suitcases suddenly felt? How our blood slowed, our footsteps lagged? Brother Ass, we had been
8 on 10.5pt

Walking along the Mall we wondered who all those men were – tall hawk-featured men perched on balconies and high places, scanning the city with heavy binoculars. What were they seeking so earnestly? Who were they – so composed and steely-eyed? Timidly we stopped a policeman to ask him. 'They are publishers' he said mildly. Publishers! Our hearts stopped beating. 'They are on the look out for new talent.' Great God! It was for *us* they were waiting and watching! Then the kindly policeman lowered his voice confidentially and said in hollow and reverent tones: *'They are waiting for the new Trollope to be born!'* Do you remember, at these words, how heavy our suitcases suddenly felt? How our blood slowed, our footsteps lagged? Brother Ass, we had been bashfully thinking of a kind of illumination such as Rimbaud dreamed of – a nagging poem which was not didactic or expository but which *infected* – was not simply a rationalised intuition, I mean, clothed in isinglass! We had come to the wrong shop, with the wrong change! A chill struck us as we saw the mist falling in Trafalgar Square, coiling round us its tendrils of ectoplasm! A million muffin-eating moralists were waiting, not for us, Brother Ass, but for the plucky and tedious Trollope! (If you are dissatisfied with your form, reach for the *curette*.) Now do you wonder if I laugh a little off-key? Do you ask yourself what has

9 on 11pt

Walking along the Mall we wondered who all those men were – tall hawk-featured men perched on balconies and high places, scanning the city with heavy binoculars. What were they seeking so earnestly? Who were they – so composed and steely-eyed? Timidly we stopped a policeman to ask him. 'They are publishers' he said mildly. Publishers! Our hearts stopped beating. 'They are on the look out for new talent.' Great God! It was for *us* they were waiting and watching! Then the kindly policeman lowered his voice confidentially and said in hollow and reverent tones: *'They are waiting for the new Trollope to be born!'* Do you remember, at these words, how heavy our suitcases suddenly felt? How our blood slowed, our footsteps lagged? Brother Ass, we had been bashfully thinking of a kind of illumination such as Rimbaud dreamed of – a nagging poem which was not didactic or expository but which *infected* – was not simply a rationalised intuition, I mean, clothed in isinglass! We had come to the wrong shop, with the wrong change! A chill struck us as we saw the mist falling in Trafalgar Square, coiling

10 on 12pt

Walking along the Mall we wondered who all those men were – tall hawk-featured men perched on balconies and high places, scanning the city with heavy binoculars. What were they seeking so earnestly? Who were they – so composed and steely-eyed? Timidly we stopped a policeman to ask him. 'They are publishers' he said mildly. Publishers! Our hearts stopped beating. 'They are on the look out for new talent.' Great God! It was for *us* they were waiting and watching! Then the kindly policeman lowered his voice confidentially and said in hollow and reverent tones: *'They are waiting for the new Trollope to be born!'* Do you remember, at these words, how heavy our suitcases suddenly felt? How our blood slowed, our footsteps lagged? Brother Ass, we had been bashfully thinking of a kind of illumination such as Rimbaud dreamed of – a nagging poem which was not didactic or expository but which *infected* – was not

11 on 13pt

WALKING ALONG THE MALL WE WONDERED WHO ALL THOSE MEN WERE – tall hawk-featured men perched on balconies and high places, scanning the city with heavy binoculars. What were they seeking so earnestly? Who were they – so composed and steely-eyed? Timidly we stopped a policeman to ask him. 'They are publishers' he said mildly. Publishers! Our hearts stopped beating. 'They are on the look out for new talent.' Great God! It was for *us* they were waiting and watching! Then the kindly policeman lowered his voice confidentially and said in hollow and reverent tones: *'They are waiting for the new Trollope to be born!'* Do you remember, at these words, how heavy our suitcases suddenly felt? How our blood slowed, our footsteps lagged? Brother Ass, we had been bashfully thinking of a kind of illumination such as Rimbaud dreamed of – a nagging poem which was not didactic or expository but which *infected* – was not simply a rationalised intuition, I mean, clothed in isinglass! We had come to the wrong shop, with the wrong change! A chill struck us as we saw the mist falling in Trafalgar Square, coiling round us its tendrils of ectoplasm! A million muffin-eating moralists were waiting, not for us, Brother Ass, but for the plucky and tedious Trollope! (If you are dissatisfied with your form, reach for the

9 on 12pt

WALKING ALONG THE MALL WE WONDERED WHO ALL THOSE MEN were – tall hawk-featured men perched on balconies and high places, scanning the city with heavy binoculars. What were they seeking so earnestly? Who were they – so composed and steely-eyed? Timidly we stopped a policeman to ask him. 'They are publishers' he said mildly. Publishers! Our hearts stopped beating. 'They are on the look out for new talent.' Great God! It was for *us* they were waiting and watching! Then the kindly policeman lowered his voice confidentially and said in hollow and reverent tones: *'They are waiting for the new Trollope to be born!'* Do you remember, at these words, how heavy our suitcases suddenly felt? How our blood slowed, our footsteps lagged? Brother Ass, we had been bashfully thinking of a kind of illumination such as Rimbaud dreamed of – a nagging poem which was not didactic or expository but which *infected* – was not simply a rationalised intuition, I mean, clothed in isinglass! We had come to the wrong shop, with the

10 on 13.5pt

WALKING ALONG THE MALL WE WONDERED WHO ALL THOSE men were – tall hawk-featured men perched on balconies and high places, scanning the city with heavy binoculars. What were they seeking so earnestly? Who were they – so composed and steely-eyed? Timidly we stopped a policeman to ask him. 'They are publishers' he said mildly. Publishers! Our hearts stopped beating. 'They are on the look out for new talent.' Great God! It was for *us* they were waiting and watching! Then the kindly policeman lowered his voice confidentially and said in hollow and reverent tones: *'They are waiting for the new Trollope to be born!'* Do you remember, at these words, how heavy our suitcases suddenly felt? How our blood slowed, our footsteps lagged? Brother Ass, we had been bashfully thinking of a kind of illumination such as Rimbaud dreamed of – a nagging poem which

11 on 14.5pt

Monotype **Garamond**

156 roman and italic
201 bold
Monotype 1922
Copyfitting factor 40.8/35.8/43.9

Range also includes bold italic

Stanley Morison's first revival for Monotype. Based on punches from the Imprimerie Royale, then attributed to Garamond but now known to be cut by Jannon about 1620. The italic is from a fount of Granjon, c.1550

Display sizes are about the same weight as the original hot metal version (although the letters are wider and the serifs lighter) but when reduced to text sizes the design is too light. This once-popular type deserves a strengthened version for text sizes to make up for the ink squash missing from today's printing techniques. The actual letterforms have been faithfully recreated, although serifs seem slightly under-emphasised

ABCDEFGHIJKLMNOP
QRSTUVWXYZ abcdefg
hijklmnopqrstuvwxyz
1234567890 1234567890
ff fi fl ffi ffl ()[]&£$.,;:-!?''

ABCDEFGHIJKLMNOP
QRSTUVWXYZ abcdefg
hijklmnopqrstuvwxyz
1234567890 1234567890
ff fi fl ffi ffl ( )[ ]&£$.,;:-!?''

ABCDEFGHIJKLMNOP
QRSTUVWXYZ abcdefg
hijklmnopqrstuvwxyz
1234567890 1234567890
ff fi fl ffi ffl ()[]&£$.,;:-!?''

24 on 27pt

These examples show *normal* letterspacing and the effect of *reduced* letterspacing on roman setting *as well as on words in italic*: they also show the appearance of figures, for example 28 May 1964, within text. These & the ampersand are not included in the setting opposite.

Normal letterspacing

These examples show *normal* letterspacing and the effect of *reduced* letterspacing on roman setting *as well as on words in italic*: they also show the appearance of figures, for example 28 May 1964, within text. These & the ampersand are not included in the setting opposite.

Minus one unit spacing

These examples show *normal* letterspacing and the effect of *reduced* letterspacing on roman setting *as well as on words in italic*: they also show the appearance of figures, for example 28 May 1964, within text. These & the ampersand are not included in the setting opposite.

Minus two units spacing

WALKING ALONG THE MALL WE WONDERED WHO ALL
WALKING ALONG THE MALL WE WONDERED WHO
WALKING ALONG THE MALL WE WONDERED

Capitals: normal letterspacing/plus 9 units/plus 18 units

WALKING ALONG THE MALL WE WONDERED WHO ALL THOSE MEN WERE
WALKING ALONG THE MALL WE WONDERED WHO ALL THOSE MEN
WALKING ALONG THE MALL WE WONDERED WHO ALL THOSE

Small caps: normal letterspacing/plus 6 units/plus 12 units

WALKING ALONG THE MALL we wondered who all those men were
WALKING ALONG THE MALL we wondered who all those men were

True italic/sloped roman

WALKING ALONG THE MALL WE WONDERED WHO ALL THOSE MEN WERE
WALKING ALONG THE MALL WE WONDERED WHO ALL THOSE MEN WERE

True small caps/reduced capitals

Walking along the Mall we wondered who all those men were – tall hawk-featured men perched on balconies and high places, scanning the city with heavy binoculars. What were they seeking so earnestly? Who were they – so composed and steely-eyed? Timidly we stopped a policeman to ask him. 'They are publishers' he said mildly. Publishers! Our hearts stopped beating. 'They are on the look out for new talent.' Great God! It was for *us* they were waiting and watching! Then the kindly policeman lowered his voice confidentially and said in hollow and reverent tones: '*They are waiting for the new Trollope to be born!*' Do you remember, at these words, how heavy our suitcases suddenly felt? How our blood slowed, our footsteps lagged? Brother Ass, we had been bashfully thinking of a kind of illumination such as Rimbaud dreamed of – a nagging poem which was not didactic or expository but

8 on 9pt

WALKING ALONG THE MALL WE WONDERED WHO ALL THOSE MEN WERE – TALL hawk-featured men perched on balconies and high places, scanning the city with heavy binoculars. What were they seeking so earnestly? Who were they – so composed and steely-eyed? Timidly we stopped a policeman to ask him. 'They are publishers' he said mildly. Publishers! Our hearts stopped beating. 'They are on the look out for new talent.' Great God! It was for *us* they were waiting and watching! Then the kindly policeman lowered his voice confidentially and said in hollow and reverent tones: '*They are waiting for the new Trollope to be born!*' Do you remember, at these words, how heavy our suitcases suddenly felt? How our blood slowed, our footsteps lagged? Brother Ass, we had been bashfully thinking of a

8 on 10.5pt

Walking along the Mall we wondered who all those men were – tall hawk-featured men perched on balconies and high places, scanning the city with heavy binoculars. What were they seeking so earnestly? Who were they – so composed and steely-eyed? Timidly we stopped a policeman to ask him. 'They are publishers' he said mildly. Publishers! Our hearts stopped beating. 'They are on the look out for new talent.' Great God! It was for *us* they were waiting and watching! Then the kindly policeman lowered his voice confidentially and said in hollow and reverent tones: *'They are waiting for the new Trollope to be born!'* Do you remember, at these words, how heavy our suitcases suddenly felt? How our blood slowed, our footsteps lagged? Brother Ass, we had been bashfully thinking of a kind of illumination such as Rimbaud dreamed of – a nagging poem which was not didactic or expository but which *infected* – was not simply a rationalised intuition, I mean, clothed in isinglass! We had come to the wrong shop, with the wrong change! A chill struck us as we saw the mist falling in Trafalgar Square, coiling around us its tendrils of ectoplasm! A million muffin-eating moralists were waiting, not for us, Brother Ass, but for the plucky and tedious Trollope! (If you are dissatisfied with your form, reach for the *curette*.) Now do you wonder if I laugh a little off-key? Do you ask yourself what has turned me into nature's bashful little aphorist? We who are, after all, simply poor

9 on 11pt

Walking along the Mall we wondered who all those men were – tall hawk-featured men perched on balconies and high places, scanning the city with heavy binoculars. What were they seeking so earnestly? Who were they – so composed and steely-eyed? Timidly we stopped a policeman to ask him. 'They are publishers' he said mildly. Publishers! Our hearts stopped beating. 'They are on the look out for new talent.' Great God! It was for *us* they were waiting and watching! Then the kindly policeman lowered his voice confidentially and said in hollow and reverent tones: *'They are waiting for the new Trollope to be born!'* Do you remember, at these words, how heavy our suitcases suddenly felt? How our blood slowed, our footsteps lagged? Brother Ass, we had been bashfully thinking of a kind of illumination such as Rimbaud dreamed of – a nagging poem which was not didactic or expository but which *infected* – was not simply a rationalised intuition, I mean, clothed in isinglass! We had come to the wrong shop, with the wrong change! A chill struck us as we saw the mist falling in Trafalgar Square, coiling around us its tendrils of ectoplasm! A million muffin-eating moralists were waiting, not

10 on 12pt

Walking along the Mall we wondered who all those men were – tall hawk-featured men perched on balconies and high places, scanning the city with heavy binoculars. What were they seeking so earnestly? Who were they – so composed and steely-eyed? Timidly we stopped a policeman to ask him. 'They are publishers' he said mildly. Publishers! Our hearts stopped beating. 'They are on the look out for new talent.' Great God! It was for *us* they were waiting and watching! Then the kindly policeman lowered his voice confidentially and said in hollow and reverent tones: *'They are waiting for the new Trollope to be born!'* Do you remember, at these words, how heavy our suitcases suddenly felt? How our blood slowed, our footsteps lagged? Brother Ass, we had been bashfully thinking of a kind of illumination such as Rimbaud dreamed of – a nagging poem which was not didactic or expository but which *infected* – was not simply a rationalised intuition, I mean, clothed in isinglass! We had come to the wrong shop, with the

11 on 13pt

WALKING ALONG THE MALL WE WONDERED WHO ALL THOSE MEN WERE – TALL hawk-featured men perched on balconies and high places, scanning the city with heavy binoculars. What were they seeking so earnestly? Who were they – so composed and steely-eyed? Timidly we stopped a policeman to ask him. 'They are publishers' he said mildly. Publishers! Our hearts stopped beating. 'They are on the look out for new talent.' Great God! It was for *us* they were waiting and watching! Then the kindly policeman lowered his voice confidentially and said in hollow and reverent tones: *'They are waiting for the new Trollope to be born!'* Do you remember, at these words, how heavy our suitcases suddenly felt? How our blood slowed, our footsteps lagged? Brother Ass, we had been bashfully thinking of a kind of illumination such as Rimbaud dreamed of – a nagging poem which was not didactic or expository but which *infected* – was not simply a rationalised intuition, I mean, clothed in isinglass! We had come to the wrong shop, with the wrong change! A chill struck us as we saw the mist falling in Trafalgar Square, coiling around us its tendrils of ectoplasm! A million muffin-eating moralists were waiting, not for us, Brother Ass, but for the plucky and tedious Trollope! (If you are dissatisfied with your form, reach for the *curette*.) Now do you wonder if I laugh a little off-key? Do you ask yourself what has

9 on 12pt

WALKING ALONG THE MALL WE WONDERED WHO ALL THOSE MEN WERE – tall hawk-featured men perched on balconies and high places, scanning the city with heavy binoculars. What were they seeking so earnestly? Who were they – so composed and steely-eyed? Timidly we stopped a policeman to ask him. 'They are publishers' he said mildly. Publishers! Our hearts stopped beating. 'They are on the look out for new talent.' Great God! It was for *us* they were waiting and watching! Then the kindly policeman lowered his voice confidentially and said in hollow and reverent tones: *'They are waiting for the new Trollope to be born!'* Do you remember, at these words, how heavy our suitcases suddenly felt? How our blood slowed, our footsteps lagged? Brother Ass, we had been bashfully thinking of a kind of illumination such as Rimbaud dreamed of – a nagging poem which was not didactic or expository but which *infected* – was not simply a rationalised intuition, I mean, clothed in isinglass! We had come to the wrong shop, with the wrong change! A chill struck us as we saw the mist falling in Trafalgar Square, coiling around us its

10 on 13.5pt

WALKING ALONG THE MALL WE WONDERED WHO ALL THOSE MEN were – tall hawk-featured men perched on balconies and high places, scanning the city with heavy binoculars. What were they seeking so earnestly? Who were they – so composed and steely-eyed? Timidly we stopped a policeman to ask him. 'They are publishers' he said mildly. Publishers! Our hearts stopped beating. 'They are on the look out for new talent.' Great God! It was for *us* they were waiting and watching! Then the kindly policeman lowered his voice confidentially and said in hollow and reverent tones: *'They are waiting for the new Trollope to be born!'* Do you remember, at these words, how heavy our suitcases suddenly felt? How our blood slowed, our footsteps lagged? Brother Ass, we had been bashfully thinking of a kind of illumination such as Rimbaud dreamed of – a nagging poem which was not didactic or expository but which *infected* – was not simply a rationalised intuition,

11 on 14.5pt

MONOTYPE GARAMOND

Monotype **Garamond (Simoncini)**

1224 roman and italic
1226 bold
Neufville 1958-61 (Francesco Simoncini and
W Bilz)
Copyfitting factor 38.4/35.9/38.9

Range also includes demi-bold

The Linotype version is effectively similar in
design and fit, and includes small caps and
non-lining figures. Sizes are visually
approximately one size larger (copyfitting
code 121/116/122). Our settings of *Linotype
Garamond (Stempel)* give a good indication of
these sizes

ABCDEFGHIJKLMNOP
QRSTUVWXYZ abcdefg
hijklmnopqrstuvwxyz
1234567890
ff fi fl ffi ffl ( )[ ]&£$.,;:-!?''

*ABCDEFGHIJKLMNOP
QRSTUVWXYZ abcdefg
hijklmnopqrstuvwxyz
1234567890
ff fi fl ffi ffl ( )[ ]&£$.,;:-!?''*

**ABCDEFGHIJKLMNOP
QRSTUVWXYZ abcdefg
hijklmnopqrstuvwxyz
1234567890
ff fi fl ffi ffl ( )[ ]&£$.,;:-!?''**

24 on 27pt

These examples show *normal* letterspacing and the effect of *reduced*
letterspacing on roman setting *as well as on words in italic*: they also
show the appearance of figures, for example 28 May 1964, within text.
These & the ampersand are not included in the setting opposite.

Normal letterspacing

These examples show *normal* letterspacing and the effect of *reduced*
letterspacing on roman setting *as well as on words in italic*: they also
show the appearance of figures, for example 28 May 1964, within text.
These & the ampersand are not included in the setting opposite.

Minus one unit spacing

These examples show *normal* letterspacing and the effect of *reduced*
letterspacing on roman setting *as well as on words in italic*: they also
show the appearance of figures, for example 28 May 1964, within text.
These & the ampersand are not included in the setting opposite.

Minus two units spacing

WALKING ALONG THE MALL WE WONDERED WHO ALL THOSE
WALKING ALONG THE MALL WE WONDERED WHO ALL
WALKING ALONG THE MALL WE WONDERED WHO

Capitals: normal letterspacing/plus 9 units/plus 18 units

Walking along the Mall we wondered who all those men were – tall hawk-
featured men perched on balconies and high places, scanning the city with
heavy binoculars. WHAT WERE THEY SEEKING SO EARNESTLY? Who were they
– so composed and steely-eyed? Timidly we stopped a policeman to ask him.
'They are publishers' HE SAID MILDLY. PUBLISHERS! Our hearts stopped
beating. 'They are on the look out for new talent.' Great God! It was for *us*
they were waiting and watching! Then the kindly policeman lowered his voice

Text with reduced capitals normal letterspacing/plus 6 units

*WALKING ALONG THE MALL we wondered who all those men were
WALKING ALONG THE MALL we wondered who all those men were*

True italic/sloped roman

Walking along the Mall we wondered who all those men were – tall hawk-featured men
perched on balconies and high places, scanning the city with heavy binoculars. What were they
seeking so earnestly? Who were they – so composed and steely-eyed? Timidly we stopped a
policeman to ask him. 'They are publishers' he said mildly. Publishers! Our hearts stopped beating.
'They are on the look out for new talent.' Great God! It was for *us* they were waiting and watching!
Then the kindly policeman lowered his voice confidentially and said in hollow and reverent tones:
'They are waiting for the new Trollope to be born!' Do you remember, at these words, how heavy our
suitcases suddenly felt? How our blood slowed, our footsteps lagged? Brother Ass, we had been
bashfully thinking of a kind of illumination such as Rimbaud dreamed of – a nagging poem which
was not didactic or expository but which *infected* – was not simply a rationalised intuition, I mean,

8 on 9pt

Walking along the Mall we wondered who all those men were – tall hawk-featured men perched
on balconies and high places, scanning the city with heavy binoculars. What were they seeking so
earnestly? Who were they – so composed and steely-eyed? Timidly we stopped a policeman to ask
him. 'They are publishers' he said mildly. Publishers! Our hearts stopped beating. 'They are on the
look out for new talent.' Great God! It was for *us* they were waiting and watching! Then the kindly
policeman lowered his voice confidentially and said in hollow and reverent tones: *'They are waiting
for the new Trollope to be born!'* Do you remember, at these words, how heavy our suitcases
suddenly felt? How our blood slowed, our footsteps lagged? Brother Ass, we had been bashfully
thinking of a kind of illumination such as Rimbaud dreamed of – a nagging poem which was not

8 on 10.5pt

Walking along the Mall we wondered who all those men were – tall hawk-featured men perched on balconies and high places, scanning the city with heavy binoculars. What were they seeking so earnestly? Who were they – so composed and steely-eyed? Timidly we stopped a policeman to ask him. 'They are publishers' he said mildly. Publishers! Our hearts stopped beating. 'They are on the look out for new talent.' Great God! It was for *us* they were waiting and watching! Then the kindly policeman lowered his voice confidentially and said in hollow and reverent tones: *'They are waiting for the new Trollope to be born!'* Do you remember, at these words, how heavy our suitcases suddenly felt? How our blood slowed, our footsteps lagged? Brother Ass, we had been bashfully thinking of a kind of illumination such as Rimbaud dreamed of – a nagging poem which was not didactic or expository but which *infected* – was not simply a rationalised intuition, I mean, clothed in isinglass! We had come to the wrong shop, with the wrong change! A chill struck us as we saw the mist falling in Trafalgar Square, coiling around us its tendrils of ectoplasm! A million muffin-eating moralists were waiting, not for us, Brother Ass, but for the plucky and tedious Trollope! (If you are dissatisfied with your form, reach for the *curette*.) Now do you wonder if I laugh a little off-key? Do you ask yourself what has turned me into nature's bashful little aphorist? We who are, after all, simply poor co-workers in the psyche of our nation, what can we expect but the natural automatic rejection from a public which resents

9 on 11pt

Walking along the Mall we wondered who all those men were – tall hawk- featured men perched on balconies and high places, scanning the city with heavy binoculars. What were they seeking so earnestly? Who were they – so composed and steely-eyed? Timidly we stopped a policeman to ask him. 'They are publishers' he said mildly. Publishers! Our hearts stopped beating. 'They are on the look out for new talent.' Great God! It was for *us* they were waiting and watching! Then the kindly policeman lowered his voice confidentially and said in hollow and reverent tones: *'They are waiting for the new Trollope to be born!'* Do you remember, at these words, how heavy our suitcases suddenly felt? How our blood slowed, our footsteps lagged? Brother Ass, we had been bashfully thinking of a kind of illumination such as Rimbaud dreamed of – a nagging poem which was not didactic or expository but which *infected* – was not simply a rationalised intuition, I mean, clothed in isinglass! We had come to the wrong shop, with the wrong change! A chill struck us as we saw the mist falling in Trafalgar Square, coiling around us its tendrils of ectoplasm! A million muffin-eating moralists were waiting, not for us, Brother Ass, but for the plucky and tedious Trollope! (If you

10 on 12pt

Walking along the Mall we wondered who all those men were – tall hawk-featured men perched on balconies and high places, scanning the city with heavy binoculars. What were they seeking so earnestly? Who were they – so composed and steely-eyed? Timidly we stopped a policeman to ask him. 'They are publishers' he said mildly. Publishers! Our hearts stopped beating. 'They are on the look out for new talent.' Great God! It was for *us* they were waiting and watching! Then the kindly policeman lowered his voice confidentially and said in hollow and reverent tones: *'They are waiting for the new Trollope to be born!'* Do you remember, at these words, how heavy our suitcases suddenly felt? How our blood slowed, our footsteps lagged? Brother Ass, we had been bashfully thinking of a kind of illumination such as Rimbaud dreamed of – a nagging poem which was not didactic or expository but which *infected* – was not simply a rationalised intuition, I mean, clothed in isinglass! We had come to the wrong shop, with the wrong change! A chill struck us as we saw the mist

11 on 13pt

Walking along the Mall we wondered who all those men were – tall hawk-featured men perched on balconies and high places, scanning the city with heavy binoculars. What were they seeking so earnestly? Who were they – so composed and steely-eyed? Timidly we stopped a policeman to ask him. 'They are publishers' he said mildly. Publishers! Our hearts stopped beating. 'They are on the look out for new talent.' Great God! It was for *us* they were waiting and watching! Then the kindly policeman lowered his voice confidentially and said in hollow and reverent tones: *'They are waiting for the new Trollope to be born!'* Do you remember, at these words, how heavy our suitcases suddenly felt? How our blood slowed, our footsteps lagged? Brother Ass, we had been bashfully thinking of a kind of illumination such as Rimbaud dreamed of – a nagging poem which was not didactic or expository but which *infected* – was not simply a rationalised intuition, I mean, clothed in isinglass! We had come to the wrong shop, with the wrong change! A chill struck us as we saw the mist falling in Trafalgar Square, coiling around us its tendrils of ectoplasm! A million muffin-eating moralists were waiting, not for us,

10 on 13.5pt

Walking along the Mall we wondered who all those men were – tall hawk-featured men perched on balconies and high places, scanning the city with heavy binoculars. What were they seeking so earnestly? Who were they – so composed and steely-eyed? Timidly we stopped a policeman to ask him. 'They are publishers' he said mildly. Publishers! Our hearts stopped beating. 'They are on the look out for new talent.' Great God! It was for *us* they were waiting and watching! Then the kindly policeman lowered his voice confidentially and said in hollow and reverent tones: *'They are waiting for the new Trollope to be born!'* Do you remember, at these words, how heavy our suitcases suddenly felt? How our blood slowed, our footsteps lagged? Brother Ass, we had been bashfully thinking of a kind of illumination such as Rimbaud dreamed of – a nagging poem which was not didactic or expository but which *infected* – was not simply a rationalised intuition, I mean, clothed in isinglass! We had come to the wrong shop, with the

11 on 14.5pt

roman (05108), **italic** (13108)
bold (07108)
Stempel 1925-27
Copyfitting code 127/126/133

The range also includes light, light italic, bold italic, black, black italic, and condensed versions of all weights. There is an extensive range of swash letters

The Monotype version is effectively similar in design and fit, but has no small caps or non-lining figures, and is available only in roman, italic and bold. Sizes are visually approximately one size smaller (copyfitting factor 38.1/37.2/38.9). Our settings of *Monotype Garamond (Simoncini)* give a good indication of these sizes

ABCDEFGHIJKLMNOP
QRSTUVWXYZ abcdefg
hijklmnopqrstuvwxyz
1234567890 1234567890
fifl ()[]&£$.,;:-!?""

ABCDEFGHIJKLMNOP
QRSTUVWXYZ abcdefg
hijklmnopqrstuvwxyz
1234567890 1234567890
fifl ()[]&£$.,;:-!?""

ABCDEFGHIJKLMNOP
QRSTUVWXYZ abcdefg
hijklmnopqrstuvwxyz
1234567890 1234567890
fifl ()[]&£$.,;:-!?""

24 on 27pt

These examples show *normal* letterspacing and the effect of *reduced* letterspacing on roman setting *as well as on words in italic*: they also show the appearance of figures, for example 28 May 1964, within text. These & the ampersand are not included in the setting opposite.
Normal letterspacing

These examples show *normal* letterspacing and the effect of *reduced* letterspacing on roman setting *as well as on words in italic*: they also show the appearance of figures, for example 28 May 1964, within text. These & the ampersand are not included in the setting opposite.
Minus one unit spacing

These examples show *normal* letterspacing and the effect of *reduced* letterspacing on roman setting *as well as on words in italic*: they also show the appearance of figures, for example 28 May 1964, within text. These & the ampersand are not included in the setting opposite.
Minus two units spacing

WALKING ALONG THE MALL WE WONDERED WHO ALL
WALKING ALONG THE MALL WE WONDERED WHO
WALKING ALONG THE MALL WE WONDERED
Capitals: normal letterspacing/plus 4 units/plus 9 units

WALKING ALONG THE MALL WE WONDERED WHO ALL THOSE MEN WERE
WALKING ALONG THE MALL WE WONDERED WHO ALL THOSE MEN
WALKING ALONG THE MALL WE WONDERED WHO ALL THOSE
Small caps: normal letterspacing/plus 3 units/plus 6 units

WALKING ALONG THE MALL WE WONDERED WHO ALL THOSE MEN WERE
WALKING ALONG THE MALL WE WONDERED WHO ALL THOSE MEN WERE
True small caps/reduced capitals

WALKING ALONG THE MALL we wondered who all those men
WALKING ALONG THE MALL we wondered who all those men
True italic/sloped roman

Walking along the Mall we wondered who all those men were – tall hawk-featured men perched on balconies and high places, scanning the city with heavy binoculars. What were they seeking so earnestly? Who were they – so composed and steely-eyed? Timidly we stopped a policeman to ask him. 'They are publishers' he said mildly. Publishers! Our hearts stopped beating. 'They are on the look out for new talent.' Great God! It was for *us* they were waiting and watching! Then the kindly policeman lowered his voice confidentially and said in hollow and reverent tones: *'They are waiting for the new Trollope to be born!'* Do you remember, at these words, how heavy our suitcases suddenly felt? How our blood slowed, our footsteps lagged? Brother Ass, we had been bashfully thinking of a kind of illumination such as Rimbaud dreamed of – a nagging
8 on 9pt

WALKING ALONG THE MALL WE WONDERED WHO ALL THOSE MEN WERE – TALL HAWK-featured men perched on balconies and high places, scanning the city with heavy binoculars. What were they seeking so earnestly? Who were they – so composed and steely-eyed? Timidly we stopped a policeman to ask him. 'They are publishers' he said mildly. Publishers! Our hearts stopped beating. 'They are on the look out for new talent.' Great God! It was for *us* they were waiting and watching! Then the kindly policeman lowered his voice confidentially and said in hollow and reverent tones: *'They are waiting for the new Trollope to be born!'* Do you remember, at these words, how heavy our suitcases suddenly felt? How our blood slowed, our footsteps lagged?
8 on 10.5pt

Walking along the Mall we wondered who all those men were – tall hawk-featured men perched on balconies and high places, scanning the city with heavy binoculars. What were they seeking so earnestly? Who were they – so composed and steely-eyed? Timidly we stopped a policeman to ask him. 'They are publishers' he said mildly. Publishers! Our hearts stopped beating. 'They are on the look out for new talent.' Great God! It was for *us* they were waiting and watching! Then the kindly policeman lowered his voice confidentially and said in hollow and reverent tones: *'They are waiting for the new Trollope to be born!'* Do you remember, at these words, how heavy our suitcases suddenly felt? How our blood slowed, our footsteps lagged? Brother Ass, we had been bashfully thinking of a kind of illumination such as Rimbaud dreamed of – a nagging poem which was not didactic or expository but which *infected* – was not simply a rationalised intuition, I mean, clothed in isinglass! We had come to the wrong shop, with the wrong change! A chill struck us as we saw the mist falling in Trafalgar Square, coiling round us its tendrils of ectoplasm! A million muffin-eating moralists were waiting, not for us, Brother Ass, but for the plucky and tedious Trollope! (If you are dissatisfied with your form, reach for the *curette*.) Now do you wonder if I laugh a little off-key? Do you ask your-

9 on 11pt

Walking along the Mall we wondered who all those men were – tall hawk-featured men perched on balconies and high places, scanning the city with heavy binoculars. What were they seeking so earnestly? Who were they – so composed and steely-eyed? Timidly we stopped a policeman to ask him. 'They are publishers' he said mildly. Publishers! Our hearts stopped beating. 'They are on the look out for new talent.' Great God! It was for *us* they were waiting and watching! Then the kindly policeman lowered his voice confidentially and said in hollow and reverent tones: *'They are waiting for the new Trollope to be born!'* Do you remember, at these words, how heavy our suitcases suddenly felt? How our blood slowed, our footsteps lagged? Brother Ass, we had been bashfully thinking of a kind of illumination such as Rimbaud dreamed of – a nagging poem which was not didactic or expository but which *infected* – was not simply a rationalised intuition, I mean, clothed in isinglass! We had come to the wrong shop, with the wrong change! A chill struck us as we saw the mist falling in Trafalgar Square, coiling

10 on 12pt

Walking along the Mall we wondered who all those men were – tall hawk-featured men perched on balconies and high places, scanning the city with heavy binoculars. What were they seeking so earnestly? Who were they – so composed and steely-eyed? Timidly we stopped a policeman to ask him. 'They are publishers' he said mildly. Publishers! Our hearts stopped beating. 'They are on the look out for new talent.' Great God! It was for *us* they were waiting and watching! Then the kindly policeman lowered his voice confidentially and said in hollow and reverent tones: *'They are waiting for the new Trollope to be born!'* Do you remember, at these words, how heavy our suitcases suddenly felt? How our blood slowed, our footsteps lagged? Brother Ass, we had been bashfully thinking of a kind of illumination such as Rimbaud dreamed of – a nagging poem which was not didactic or expository but which *infected* – was

11 on 13pt

WALKING ALONG THE MALL WE WONDERED WHO ALL THOSE MEN WERE – tall hawk-featured men perched on balconies and high places, scanning the city with heavy binoculars. What were they seeking so earnestly? Who were they – so composed and steely-eyed? Timidly we stopped a policeman to ask him. 'They are publishers' he said mildly. Publishers! Our hearts stopped beating. 'They are on the look out for new talent.' Great God! It was for *us* they were waiting and watching! Then the kindly policeman lowered his voice confidentially and said in hollow and reverent tones: *'They are waiting for the new Trollope to be born!'* Do you remember, at these words, how heavy our suitcases suddenly felt? How our blood slowed, our footsteps lagged? Brother Ass, we had been bashfully thinking of a kind of illumination such as Rimbaud dreamed of – a nagging poem which was not didactic or expository but which *infected* – was not simply a rationalised intuition, I mean, clothed in isinglass! We had come to the wrong shop, with the wrong change! A chill struck us as we saw the mist falling in Trafalgar Square, coiling round us its tendrils of ectoplasm! A million muffin-eating moralists were waiting, not for us, Brother Ass, but for the plucky and tedious Trollope! (If you are dissatisfied with your

9 on 12pt

WALKING ALONG THE MALL WE WONDERED WHO ALL THOSE MEN were – tall hawk-featured men perched on balconies and high places, scanning the city with heavy binoculars. What were they seeking so earnestly? Who were they – so composed and steely-eyed? Timidly we stopped a policeman to ask him. 'They are publishers' he said mildly. Publishers! Our hearts stopped beating. 'They are on the look out for new talent.' Great God! It was for *us* they were waiting and watching! Then the kindly policeman lowered his voice confidentially and said in hollow and reverent tones: *'They are waiting for the new Trollope to be born!'* Do you remember, at these words, how heavy our suitcases suddenly felt? How our blood slowed, our footsteps lagged? Brother Ass, we had been bashfully thinking of a kind of illumination such as Rimbaud dreamed of – a nagging poem which was not didactic or expository but which *infected* – was not simply a rationalised intuition, I mean, clothed in isinglass! We had come to the wrong shop, with the

10 on 13.5pt

WALKING ALONG THE MALL WE WONDERED WHO ALL THOSE men were – tall hawk-featured men perched on balconies and high places, scanning the city with heavy binoculars. What were they seeking so earnestly? Who were they – so composed and steely-eyed? Timidly we stopped a policeman to ask him. 'They are publishers' he said mildly. Publishers! Our hearts stopped beating. 'They are on the look out for new talent.' Great God! It was for *us* they were waiting and watching! Then the kindly policeman lowered his voice confidentially and said in hollow and reverent tones: *'They are waiting for the new Trollope to be born!'* Do you remember, at these words, how heavy our suitcases suddenly felt? How our blood slowed, our footsteps lagged? Brother Ass, we had been bashfully thinking of a kind of illumination such as Rimbaud dreamed of – a nagging poem

11 on 14.5pt

LINOTYPE GARAMOND (STEMPEL)

Monotype **Gill Sans**

262 roman and italic
275 bold
Monotype 1928 onwards (Eric Gill)
Copyfitting factor 43.9/41.1/48.8

Range also includes light, light italic, bold italic, extra bold, ultra bold, condensed, bold condensed, ultra bold condensed, shadow

The Linotype design (copyfitting code 115/108/135), although basically identical is more tightly fitted (too tight?). The normal Monotype setting, however, is perhaps slightly loose. It is also slightly bolder than the original

In both Lino and Mono, c and o are not now purely geometrical, and the construction of d, p and q differs from that of display sizes of the original

Gill modelled his design on Edward Johnston's London Transport Railway type, much improving it and emphasizing its classical proportions

Educational characters available

ABCDEFGHIJKLMNOP
QRSTUVWXYZ abcdefg
hijklmnopqrstuvwxyz
1234567890
ff fi fl ffi ffl ()[]&£$.,;:-!?''

ABCDEFGHIJKLMNOP
QRSTUVWXYZ abcdefg
hijklmnopqrstuvwxyz
1234567890
ff fi fl ffi ffl ()[]&£$.,;:-!?''

ABCDEFGHIJKLMNOP
QRSTUVWXYZ abcdefg
hijklmnopqrstuvwxyz
1234567890
ff fi fl ffi ffl ()[]&£$.,;:-!?''

24 on 27pt

These examples show *normal* letterspacing and the effect of *reduced* letterspacing on roman setting *as well as on words in italic*: they also show the appearance of figures, for example 28 May 1964, within text. These & the ampersand are not included in the setting opposite.

Normal letterspacing

These examples show *normal* letterspacing and the effect of *reduced* letterspacing on roman setting *as well as on words in italic*: they also show the appearance of figures, for example 28 May 1964, within text. These & the ampersand are not included in the setting opposite.

Minus one unit spacing

These examples show *normal* letterspacing and the effect of *reduced* letterspacing on roman setting *as well as on words in italic*: they also show the appearance of figures, for example 28 May 1964, within text. These & the ampersand are not included in the setting opposite.

Minus two units spacing

WALKING ALONG THE MALL WE WONDERED WHO ALL THOSE
WALKING ALONG THE MALL WE WONDERED WHO ALL
WALKING ALONG THE MALL WE WONDERED WHO

Capitals: normal letterspacing/plus 9 units/plus 18 units

Walking along the Mall we wondered who all those men were – tall hawk-featured men perched on balconies and high places, scanning the city with heavy binoculars. WHAT WERE THEY SEEKING SO EARNESTLY? Who were they – so composed and steely-eyed? Timidly we stopped a policeman to ask him. 'They are publishers' he said mildly. Publishers! OUR HEARTS STOPPED BEATING. 'They are on the look out for new talent.' Great God! It was for *us* they were waiting

Text with reduced capitals normal letterspacing/plus 6 units

WALKING ALONG THE MALL we wondered who all those men were
WALKING ALONG THE MALL we wondered who all those men

True italic/sloped roman

Walking along the Mall we wondered who all those men were – tall hawk-featured men perched on balconies and high places, scanning the city with heavy binoculars. What were they seeking so earnestly? Who were they – so composed and steely-eyed? Timidly we stopped a policeman to ask him. 'They are publishers' he said mildly. Publishers! Our hearts stopped beating. 'They are on the look out for new talent.' Great God! It was for *us* they were waiting and watching! Then the kindly policeman lowered his voice confidentially and said in hollow and reverent tones: *'They are waiting for the new Trollope to be born!'* Do you remember, at these words, how heavy our suitcases suddenly felt? How our blood slowed, our footsteps lagged? Brother Ass, we had been bashfully thinking of a kind of illumination such as Rimbaud

8 on 9pt

Walking along the Mall we wondered who all those men were – tall hawk-featured men perched on balconies and high places, scanning the city with heavy binoculars. What were they seeking so earnestly? Who were they – so composed and steely-eyed? Timidly we stopped a policeman to ask him. 'They are publishers' he said mildly. Publishers! Our hearts stopped beating. 'They are on the look out for new talent.' Great God! It was for *us* they were waiting and watching! Then the kindly policeman lowered his voice confidentially and said in hollow and reverent tones: *'They are waiting for the new Trollope to be born!'* Do you remember, at these words, how heavy our suitcases suddenly felt? How our blood slowed, our footsteps lagged? Brother Ass,

8 on 10.5pt

Walking along the Mall we wondered who all those men were – tall hawk-featured men perched on balconies and high places, scanning the city with heavy binoculars. What were they seeking so earnestly? Who were they – so composed and steely-eyed? Timidly we stopped a policeman to ask him. 'They are publishers' he said mildly. Publishers! Our hearts stopped beating. 'They are on the look out for new talent.' Great God! It was for *us* they were waiting and watching! Then the kindly policeman lowered his voice confidentially and said in hollow and reverent tones: *'They are waiting for the new Trollope to be born!'* Do you remember, at these words, how heavy our suitcases suddenly felt? How our blood slowed, our footsteps lagged? Brother Ass, we had been bashfully thinking of a kind of illumination such as Rimbaud dreamed of – a nagging poem which was not didactic or expository but which *infected* – was not simply a rationalised intuition, I mean, clothed in isinglass! We had come to the wrong shop, with the wrong change! A chill struck us as we saw the mist falling in Trafalgar Square, coiling around us its tendrils of ectoplasm! A million muffin-eating moralists were waiting, not for us, Brother Ass, but for the plucky and tedious Trollope! (If you are dissatisfied with your form, reach for the *curette*.) Now do you wonder if I laugh a little off-key? Do you ask
9 on 11pt

Walking along the Mall we wondered who all those men were – tall hawk-featured men perched on balconies and high places, scanning the city with heavy binoculars. What were they seeking so earnestly? Who were they – so composed and steely-eyed? Timidly we stopped a policeman to ask him. 'They are publishers' he said mildly. Publishers! Our hearts stopped beating. 'They are on the look out for new talent.' Great God! It was for *us* they were waiting and watching! Then the kindly policeman lowered his voice confidentially and said in hollow and reverent tones: *'They are waiting for the new Trollope to be born!'* Do you remember, at these words, how heavy our suitcases suddenly felt? How our blood slowed, our footsteps lagged? Brother Ass, we had been bashfully thinking of a kind of illumination such as Rimbaud dreamed of – a nagging poem which was not didactic or expository but which *infected* – was not simply a rationalised intuition, I mean, clothed in isinglass! We had come to the wrong shop, with the wrong change! A chill struck us as we saw the mist falling in Trafalgar Square,
10 on 12pt

Walking along the Mall we wondered who all those men were – tall hawk-featured men perched on balconies and high places, scanning the city with heavy binoculars. What were they seeking so earnestly? Who were they – so composed and steely-eyed? Timidly we stopped a policeman to ask him. 'They are publishers' he said mildly. Publishers! Our hearts stopped beating. 'They are on the look out for new talent.' Great God! It was for *us* they were waiting and watching! Then the kindly policeman lowered his voice confidentially and said in hollow and reverent tones: *'They are waiting for the new Trollope to be born!'* Do you remember, at these words, how heavy our suitcases suddenly felt? How our blood slowed, our footsteps lagged? Brother Ass, we had been bashfully thinking of a kind of illumination such as Rimbaud dreamed of – a nagging poem which was not didactic or expository but which *infected* – was not simply a
11 on 13pt

Walking along the Mall we wondered who all those men were – tall hawk-featured men perched on balconies and high places, scanning the city with heavy binoculars. What were they seeking so earnestly? Who were they – so composed and steely-eyed? Timidly we stopped a policeman to ask him. 'They are publishers' he said mildly. Publishers! Our hearts stopped beating. 'They are on the look out for new talent.' Great God! It was for *us* they were waiting and watching! Then the kindly policeman lowered his voice confidentially and said in hollow and reverent tones: *'They are waiting for the new Trollope to be born!'* Do you remember, at these words, how heavy our suitcases suddenly felt? How our blood slowed, our footsteps lagged? Brother Ass, we had been bashfully thinking of a kind of illumination such as Rimbaud dreamed of – a nagging poem which was not didactic or expository but which *infected* – was not simply a rationalised intuition, I mean, clothed in isinglass! We had come to the wrong shop, with the wrong change! A chill struck us as we saw the mist falling in Trafalgar Square, coiling around us its tendrils of ectoplasm! A million muffin-eating moralists were waiting, not for us, Brother Ass, but for the plucky and tedious Trollope! (If you are dissatisfied with your form, reach for
9 on 12pt

Walking along the Mall we wondered who all those men were – tall hawk-featured men perched on balconies and high places, scanning the city with heavy binoculars. What were they seeking so earnestly? Who were they – so composed and steely-eyed? Timidly we stopped a policeman to ask him. 'They are publishers' he said mildly. Publishers! Our hearts stopped beating. 'They are on the look out for new talent.' Great God! It was for *us* they were waiting and watching! Then the kindly policeman lowered his voice confidentially and said in hollow and reverent tones: *'They are waiting for the new Trollope to be born!'* Do you remember, at these words, how heavy our suitcases suddenly felt? How our blood slowed, our footsteps lagged? Brother Ass, we had been bashfully thinking of a kind of illumination such as Rimbaud dreamed of – a nagging poem which was not didactic or expository but which *infected* – was not simply a rationalised intuition, I mean, clothed in isinglass! We had come to the wrong shop, with the wrong
10 on 13.5pt

Walking along the Mall we wondered who all those men were – tall hawk-featured men perched on balconies and high places, scanning the city with heavy binoculars. What were they seeking so earnestly? Who were they – so composed and steely-eyed? Timidly we stopped a policeman to ask him. 'They are publishers' he said mildly. Publishers! Our hearts stopped beating. 'They are on the look out for new talent.' Great God! It was for *us* they were waiting and watching! Then the kindly policeman lowered his voice confidentially and said in hollow and reverent tones: *'They are waiting for the new Trollope to be born!'* Do you remember, at these words, how heavy our suitcases suddenly felt? How our blood slowed, our footsteps lagged? Brother Ass, we had been bashfully thinking of a kind of illumination such as Rimbaud dreamed of – a nagging poem which was not didactic or
11 on 14.5pt

MONOTYPE GILL SANS

Linotype **Glypha**

roman 55 (05115), **italic 56** (13115)
black 75 (09115)
Stempel 1977 (Adrian Frutiger)
Copyfitting code 140/140/154

Range also includes thin, thin italic, light, light
italic, bold, bold italic, black italic

ABCDEFGHIJKLMNOP
QRSTUVWXYZ abcdefg
hijklmnopqrstuvwxyz
1234567890
fifl ()[]&£$.,;:-!?''

ABCDEFGHIJKLMNOP
QRSTUVWXYZ abcdefg
hijklmnopqrstuvwxyz
1234567890
fifl ()[]&£$.,;:-!?''

ABCDEFGHIJKLMNOP
QRSTUVWXYZ abcdefg
hijklmnopqrstuvwxyz
1234567890
fifl ()[]&£$.,;:-!?''

24 on 27pt

These examples show *normal* letterspacing and the effect of *reduced*
letterspacing on roman setting *as well as on words in italic*: they also
show the appearance of figures, for example 28 May 1964, within text.
These & the ampersand are not included in the setting opposite.
Normal letterspacing

These examples show *normal* letterspacing and the effect of *reduced*
letterspacing on roman setting *as well as on words in italic*: they also
show the appearance of figures, for example 28 May 1964, within text.
These & the ampersand are not included in the setting opposite.
Minus one unit spacing

These examples show *normal* letterspacing and the effect of *reduced*
letterspacing on roman setting *as well as on words in italic*: they also
show the appearance of figures, for example 28 May 1964, within text.
These & the ampersand are not included in the setting opposite.
Minus two units spacing

WALKING ALONG THE MALL WE WONDERED WHO ALL THOSE
WALKING ALONG THE MALL WE WONDERED WHO ALL
WALKING ALONG THE MALL WE WONDERED WHO
Capitals: normal letterspacing/plus 4 units/plus 9 units

Walking along the Mall we wondered who all those men were – tall
hawk-featured men perched on balconies and high places, scanning
the city with heavy binoculars. WHAT WERE THEY SEEKING SO EARNESTLY?
Who were they – so composed and steely-eyed? Timidly we stopped a
policeman to ask him. 'THEY ARE PUBLISHERS' he said mildly. Publishers!
Our hearts stopped beating. 'They are on the look out for new talent.'
Great God! It was for *us* they were waiting and watching! Then the
Text with reduced caps normal letterspacing/plus 3 units

WALKING ALONG THE MALL we wondered who all those men were
WALKING ALONG THE MALL we wondered who all those men were
True italic/sloped roman

Walking along the Mall we wondered who all those men were – tall hawk-
featured men perched on balconies and high places, scanning the city with
heavy binoculars. What were they seeking so earnestly? Who were they – so
composed and steely-eyed? Timidly we stopped a policeman to ask him. 'They
are publishers' he said mildly. Publishers! Our hearts stopped beating. 'They are
on the look out for new talent.' Great God! It was for *us* they were waiting and
watching! Then the kindly policeman lowered his voice confidentially and said
in hollow and reverent tones: *'They are waiting for the new Trollope to be born!'*
Do you remember, at these words, how heavy our suitcases suddenly felt? How
our blood slowed, our footsteps lagged? Brother Ass, we had been bashfully
8 on 9pt

Walking along the Mall we wondered who all those men were – tall hawk-
featured men perched on balconies and high places, scanning the city with
heavy binoculars. What were they seeking so earnestly? Who were they – so
composed and steely-eyed? Timidly we stopped a policeman to ask him. 'They
are publishers' he said mildly. Publishers! Our hearts stopped beating. 'They are
on the look out for new talent.' Great God! It was for *us* they were waiting and
watching! Then the kindly policeman lowered his voice confidentially and said
in hollow and reverent tones: *'They are waiting for the new Trollope to be born!'*
Do you remember, at these words, how heavy our suitcases suddenly felt? How
8 on 10.5pt

Walking along the Mall we wondered who all those men were –
tall hawk-featured men perched on balconies and high places, scanning
the city with heavy binoculars. What were they seeking so earnestly?
Who were they – so composed and steely-eyed? Timidly we stopped a
policeman to ask him. 'They are publishers' he said mildly. Publishers!
Our hearts stopped beating. 'They are on the look out for new talent.'
Great God! It was for *us* they were waiting and watching! Then the
kindly policeman lowered his voice confidentially and said in hollow
and reverent tones: *'They are waiting for the new Trollope to be born!'*
Do you remember, at these words, how heavy our suitcases suddenly
felt? How our blood slowed, our footsteps lagged? Brother Ass, we had
been bashfully thinking of a kind of illumination such as Rimbaud
dreamed of – a nagging poem which was not didactic or expository
but which *infected* – was not simply a rationalised intuition, I mean,
clothed in isinglass! We had come to the wrong shop, with the wrong
change! A chill struck us as we saw the mist falling in Trafalgar Square,
coiling round us its tendrils of ectoplasm! A million muffin-eating
moralists were waiting, not for us, Brother Ass, but for the plucky and
9 on 11pt

Walking along the Mall we wondered who all those men were – tall
hawk-featured men perched on balconies and high places, scanning
the city with heavy binoculars. What were they seeking so earnestly?
Who were they – so composed and steely-eyed? Timidly we stopped a
policeman to ask him. 'They are publishers' he said mildly. Publishers!
Our hearts stopped beating. 'They are on the look out for new talent.'
Great God! It was for *us* they were waiting and watching! Then the
kindly policeman lowered his voice confidentially and said in hollow
and reverent tones: *'They are waiting for the new Trollope to be born!'*
Do you remember, at these words, how heavy our suitcases suddenly
felt? How our blood slowed, our footsteps lagged? Brother Ass, we had
been bashfully thinking of a kind of illumination such as Rimbaud
dreamed of – a nagging poem which was not didactic or expository but
which *infected* – was not simply a rationalised intuition, I mean, clothed
in isinglass! We had come to the wrong shop, with the wrong change!
A chill struck us as we saw the mist falling in Trafalgar Square, coiling
round us its tendrils of ectoplasm! A million muffin-eating moralists
9 on 12pt

Walking along the Mall we wondered who all those men
were – tall hawk-featured men perched on balconies and high
places, scanning the city with heavy binoculars. What were
they seeking so earnestly? Who were they – so composed and
steely-eyed? Timidly we stopped a policeman to ask him. 'They
are publishers' he said mildly. Publishers! Our hearts stopped
beating. 'They are on the look out for new talent.' Great God! It
was for *us* they were waiting and watching! Then the kindly
policeman lowered his voice confidentially and said in hollow
and reverent tones: *'They are waiting for the new Trollope to
be born!'* Do you remember, at these words, how heavy our
suitcases suddenly felt? How our blood slowed, our footsteps
lagged? Brother Ass, we had been bashfully thinking of a kind
of illumination such as Rimbaud dreamed of – a nagging poem
which was not didactic or expository but which *infected* – was
not simply a rationalised intuition, I mean, clothed in isinglass!
10 on 12pt

Walking along the Mall we wondered who all those men were –
tall hawk-featured men perched on balconies and high places,
scanning the city with heavy binoculars. What were they seeking so earnestly? Who were they – so composed and steely-
eyed? Timidly we stopped a policeman to ask him. 'They are
publishers' he said mildly. Publishers! Our hearts stopped beating. 'They are on the look out for new talent.' Great God! It was
for *us* they were waiting and watching! Then the kindly policeman lowered his voice confidentially and said in hollow and
reverent tones: *'They are waiting for the new Trollope to be
born!'* Do you remember, at these words, how heavy our suitcases suddenly felt? How our blood slowed, our footsteps
lagged? Brother Ass, we had been bashfully thinking of a kind
of illumination such as Rimbaud dreamed of – a nagging poem
which was not didactic or expository but which *infected* – was
10 on 13.5pt

Walking along the Mall we wondered who all those
men were – tall hawk-featured men perched on balconies
and high places, scanning the city with heavy binoculars.
What were they seeking so earnestly? Who were they – so
composed and steely-eyed? Timidly we stopped a policeman to ask him. 'They are publishers' he said mildly.
Publishers! Our hearts stopped beating. 'They are on the
look out for new talent.' Great God! It was for *us* they
were waiting and watching! Then the kindly policeman
lowered his voice confidentially and said in hollow and
reverent tones: *'They are waiting for the new Trollope to
be born!'* Do you remember, at these words, how heavy
our suitcases suddenly felt? How our blood slowed, our
footsteps lagged? Brother Ass, we had been bashfully
thinking of a kind of illumination such as Rimbaud
11 on 13pt

Walking along the Mall we wondered who all those men
were – tall hawk-featured men perched on balconies and
high places, scanning the city with heavy binoculars.
What were they seeking so earnestly? Who were they – so
composed and steely-eyed? Timidly we stopped a policeman to ask him. 'They are publishers' he said mildly. Publishers! Our hearts stopped beating. 'They are on the look
out for new talent.' Great God! It was for *us* they were
waiting and watching! Then the kindly policeman lowered
his voice confidentially and said in hollow and reverent
tones: *'They are waiting for the new Trollope to be born!'*
Do you remember, at these words, how heavy our suitcases suddenly felt? How our blood slowed, our footsteps
lagged? Brother Ass, we had been bashfully thinking of a
11 on 14.5pt

LINOTYPE GLYPHA

Monotype **Goudy Old Style**

291 roman and italic
441 bold
Monotype 1929. Adapted from the design by
F W Goudy, 1915, for ATF
Copyfitting factor 43.1/39.7/44.6

Range also includes extra bold

The Linotype version (copyfitting code
117/107/121) is substantially similar but slightly
lighter; some characters vary a little. Serifs are
less sculptured, letter stems straight and more
mechanical. The bold is considerably narrower

The capitals were based on Renaissance
lettering and an Aldine letter was the basis for
the italic

Alternative figures:

4 7

ABCDEFGHIJKLMNOP
QRSTUVWXYZ abcdefg
hijklmnopqrstuvwxyz
1234567890
ff fi fl ffi ffl ()[]&£$.,;:-!?''

ABCDEFGHIJKLMNOP
QRSTUVWXYZ abcdefg
hijklmnopqrstuvwxyz
1234567890 1234567890
ff fi fl ffi ffl () [] &£$.,;:-!?''

ABCDEFGHIJKLMNOP
QRSTUVWXYZ abcdefg
hijklmnopqrstuvwxyz
1234567890
ff fi fl ffi ffl ()[]&£$.,;:-!?''

24 on 27pt

These examples show *normal* letterspacing and the effect of *reduced*
letterspacing on roman setting *as well as on words in italic*: they also
show the appearance of figures, for example 28 May 1964, within text.
These & the ampersand are not included in the setting opposite.
Normal letterspacing

These examples show *normal* letterspacing and the effect of *reduced*
letterspacing on roman setting *as well as on words in italic*: they also
show the appearance of figures, for example 28 May 1964, within text.
These & the ampersand are not included in the setting opposite.
Minus one unit spacing

These examples show *normal* letterspacing and the effect of *reduced*
letterspacing on roman setting *as well as on words in italic*: they also
show the appearance of figures, for example 28 May 1964, within text.
These & the ampersand are not included in the setting opposite.
Minus two units spacing

WALKING ALONG THE MALL WE WONDERED WHO ALL
WALKING ALONG THE MALL WE WONDERED WHO
WALKING ALONG THE MALL WE WONDERED
Capitals: normal letterspacing/plus 9 units/plus 18 units

WALKING ALONG THE MALL WE WONDERED WHO ALL THOSE MEN WERE
WALKING ALONG THE MALL WE WONDERED WHO ALL THOSE MEN
WALKING ALONG THE MALL WE WONDERED WHO ALL THOSE
Small caps: normal letterspacing/plus 6 units/plus 12 units

WALKING ALONG THE MALL we wondered who all those men were
WALKING ALONG THE MALL we wondered who all those men
True italic/sloped roman

WALKING ALONG THE MALL WE WONDERED WHO ALL THOSE MEN WERE
WALKING ALONG THE MALL WE WONDERED WHO ALL THOSE MEN WERE
True small caps/reduced capitals

Walking along the Mall we wondered who all those men were – tall hawk-featured
men perched on balconies and high places, scanning the city with heavy binoculars.
What were they seeking so earnestly? Who were they – so composed and steely-eyed?
Timidly we stopped a policeman to ask him. 'They are publishers' he said mildly.
Publishers! Our hearts stopped beating. 'They are on the look out for new talent.' Great
God! It was for *us* they were waiting and watching! Then the kindly policeman lowered
his voice confidentially and said in hollow and reverent tones: *'They are waiting for the
new Trollope to be born!'* Do you remember, at these words, how heavy our suitcases
suddenly felt? How our blood slowed, our footsteps lagged? Brother Ass, we had been
bashfully thinking of a kind of illumination such as Rimbaud dreamed of – a nagging
8 on 9pt

WALKING ALONG THE MALL WE WONDERED WHO ALL THOSE MEN WERE – TALL
hawk-featured men perched on balconies and high places, scanning the city with heavy
binoculars. What were they seeking so earnestly? Who were they – so composed and
steely-eyed? Timidly we stopped a policeman to ask him. 'They are publishers' he said
mildly. Publishers! Our hearts stopped beating. 'They are on the look out for new
talent.' Great God! It was for *us* they were waiting and watching! Then the kindly
policeman lowered his voice confidentially and said in hollow and reverent tones: *'They
are waiting for the new Trollope to be born!'* Do you remember, at these words, how heavy
our suitcases suddenly felt? How our blood slowed, our footsteps lagged? Brother Ass,
8 on 10.5pt

Walking along the Mall we wondered who all those men were – tall hawk-featured men perched on balconies and high places, scanning the city with heavy binoculars. What were they seeking so earnestly? Who were they – so composed and steely-eyed? Timidly we stopped a policeman to ask him. 'They are publishers' he said mildly. Publishers! Our hearts stopped beating. 'They are on the look out for new talent.' Great God! It was for *us* they were waiting and watching! Then the kindly policeman lowered his voice confidentially and said in hollow and reverent tones: *'They are waiting for the new Trollope to be born!'* Do you remember, at these words, how heavy our suitcases suddenly felt? How our blood slowed, our footsteps lagged? Brother Ass, we had been bashfully thinking of a kind of illumination such as Rimbaud dreamed of – a nagging poem which was not didactic or expository but which *infected* – was not simply a rationalised intuition, I mean, clothed in isinglass! We had come to the wrong shop, with the wrong change! A chill struck us as we saw the mist falling in Trafalgar Square, coiling around us its tendrils of ectoplasm! A million muffin-eating moralists were waiting, not for us, Brother Ass, but for the plucky and tedious Trollope! (If you are dissatisfied with your form, reach for the *curette*.) Now do you wonder if I laugh a little off-key? Do you ask yourself what

9 on 11pt

Walking along the Mall we wondered who all those men were – tall hawk-featured men perched on balconies and high places, scanning the city with heavy binoculars. What were they seeking so earnestly? Who were they – so composed and steely-eyed? Timidly we stopped a police-man to ask him. 'They are publishers' he said mildly. Publishers! Our hearts stopped beating. 'They are on the look out for new talent.' Great God! It was for *us* they were waiting and watching! Then the kindly policeman lowered his voice confidentially and said in hollow and reverent tones: *'They are waiting for the new Trollope to be born!'* Do you remember, at these words, how heavy our suitcases suddenly felt? How our blood slowed, our footsteps lagged? Brother Ass, we had been bashfully thinking of a kind of illumination such as Rimbaud dreamed of – a nagging poem which was not didactic or expository but which *infected* – was not simply a rationalised intuition, I mean, clothed in isinglass! We had come to the wrong shop, with the wrong change! A chill struck us as we saw the mist falling in Trafalgar Square, coiling around us its tendrils

10 on 12pt

Walking along the Mall we wondered who all those men were – tall hawk-featured men perched on balconies and high places, scanning the city with heavy binoculars. What were they seeking so earnestly? Who were they – so composed and steely-eyed? Timidly we stopped a policeman to ask him. 'They are pub-lishers' he said mildly. Publishers! Our hearts stopped beating. 'They are on the look out for new talent.' Great God! It was for *us* they were waiting and watching! Then the kindly policeman low-ered his voice confidentially and said in hollow and reverent tones: *'They are waiting for the new Trollope to be born!'* Do you remember, at these words, how heavy our suitcases suddenly felt? How our blood slowed, our footsteps lagged? Brother Ass, we had been bashfully thinking of a kind of illumination such as Rimbaud dreamed of – a nagging poem which was not didactic or expository but which *infected* – was not simply a rationalised

11 on 13pt

WALKING ALONG THE MALL WE WONDERED WHO ALL THOSE MEN WERE – TALL hawk-featured men perched on balconies and high places, scanning the city with heavy binoculars. What were they seeking so earnestly? Who were they – so composed and steely-eyed? Timidly we stopped a policeman to ask him. 'They are publishers' he said mildly. Publishers! Our hearts stopped beating. 'They are on the look out for new talent.' Great God! It was for *us* they were waiting and watching! Then the kindly policeman lowered his voice confidentially and said in hollow and reverent tones: *'They are waiting for the new Trollope to be born!'* Do you remember, at these words, how heavy our suitcases suddenly felt? How our blood slowed, our footsteps lagged? Brother Ass, we had been bashfully think-ing of a kind of illumination such as Rimbaud dreamed of – a nagging poem which was not didactic or expository but which *infected* – was not simply a rationalised intuition, I mean, clothed in isinglass! We had come to the wrong shop, with the wrong change! A chill struck us as we saw the mist falling in Trafalgar Square, coiling around us its tendrils of ectoplasm! A million muffin-eating moralists were waiting, not for us, Brother Ass, but for the plucky and tedious Trollope! (If you are dissatisfied with your form, reach for the

9 on 12pt

WALKING ALONG THE MALL WE WONDERED WHO ALL THOSE MEN were – tall hawk-featured men perched on balconies and high places, scanning the city with heavy binoculars. What were they seeking so earnestly? Who were they – so composed and steely-eyed? Timidly we stopped a policeman to ask him. 'They are publishers' he said mildly. Publishers! Our hearts stopped beating. 'They are on the look out for new talent.' Great God! It was for *us* they were waiting and watching! Then the kindly policeman lowered his voice confidentially and said in hollow and reverent tones: *'They are waiting for the new Trollope to be born!'* Do you remember, at these words, how heavy our suitcases sud-denly felt? How our blood slowed, our footsteps lagged? Brother Ass, we had been bashfully thinking of a kind of illumination such as Rim-baud dreamed of – a nagging poem which was not didactic or expository but which *infected* – was not simply a rationalised intuition, I mean, clothed in isinglass! We had come to the wrong shop, with the wrong

10 on 13.5pt

WALKING ALONG THE MALL WE WONDERED WHO ALL THOSE men were – tall hawk-featured men perched on balconies and high places, scanning the city with heavy binoculars. What were they seeking so earnestly? Who were they – so composed and steely-eyed? Timidly we stopped a policeman to ask him. 'They are publishers' he said mildly. Publishers! Our hearts stopped beating. 'They are on the look out for new talent.' Great God! It was for *us* they were waiting and watching! Then the kindly policeman lowered his voice confidentially and said in hollow and reverent tones: *'They are waiting for the new Trollope to be born!'* Do you remember, at these words, how heavy our suitcases suddenly felt? How our blood slowed, our footsteps lagged? Bro-ther Ass, we had been bashfully thinking of a kind of illumination such as Rimbaud dreamed of – a nagging poem which was not

11 on 14.5pt

Linotype **Granjon**

roman (05493), **italic** (13493)
bold (07493)
Linotype 1928 (G W Jones)
(bold: 1930, C H Griffith)
Copyfitting code 117/107/117

Based on a 16th-century Paris book perhaps
printed by Garamond. It has been called the
best reproduction of a Garamond type today

ABCDEFGHIJKLMNOP
QRSTUVWXYZ abcdefg
hijklmnopqrstuvwxyz
1234567890 1234567890
fifl ()[]&£$.,;:-!?""

ABCDEFGHIJKLMNOP
QRSTUVWXYZ abcdefg
hijklmnopqrstuvwxyz
1234567890 1234567890
fifl ()[]&£$.,;:-!?""

ABCDEFGHIJKLMNOP
QRSTUVWXYZ abcdefg
hijklmnopqrstuvwxyz
1234567890 1234567890
fifl () []&£$.,;:-!?""

24 on 27pt

160

These examples show *normal* letterspacing and the effect of *reduced*
letterspacing on roman setting *as well as on words in italic*: they also
show the appearance of figures, for example 28 May 1964, within text.
These & the ampersand are not included in the setting opposite.

Normal letterspacing

These examples show *normal* letterspacing and the effect of *reduced*
letterspacing on roman setting *as well as on words in italic*: they also
show the appearance of figures, for example 28 May 1964, within text.
These & the ampersand are not included in the setting opposite.

Minus one unit spacing

These examples show *normal* letterspacing and the effect of *reduced*
letterspacing on roman setting *as well as on words in italic*: they also
show the appearance of figures, for example 28 May 1964, within text.
These & the ampersand are not included in the setting opposite.

Minus two units spacing

WALKING ALONG THE MALL WE WONDERED WHO ALL
WALKING ALONG THE MALL WE WONDERED WHO
WALKING ALONG THE MALL WE WONDERED

Capitals: normal letterspacing/plus 4 units/plus 9 units

WALKING ALONG THE MALL WE WONDERED WHO ALL THOSE MEN WERE
WALKING ALONG THE MALL WE WONDERED WHO ALL THOSE MEN WERE
WALKING ALONG THE MALL WE WONDERED WHO ALL THOSE MEN

Small caps: normal letterspacing/plus 3 units/plus 6 units

WALKING ALONG THE MALL WE WONDERED WHO ALL THOSE MEN WERE
WALKING ALONG THE MALL WE WONDERED WHO ALL THOSE MEN WERE

True small caps/reduced capitals

WALKING ALONG THE MALL we wondered who all those men were
WALKING ALONG THE MALL we wondered who all those men were

True italic/sloped roman

Walking along the Mall we wondered who all those men were – tall hawk-featured men
perched on balconies and high places, scanning the city with heavy binoculars. What were they
seeking so earnestly? Who were they – so composed and steely-eyed? Timidly we stopped a
policeman to ask him. 'They are publishers' he said mildly. Publishers! Our hearts stopped
beating. 'They are on the look out for new talent.' Great God! It was for *us* they were waiting
and watching! Then the kindly policeman lowered his voice confidentially and said in hollow
and reverent tones: *'They are waiting for the new Trollope to be born!'* Do you remember, at these
words, how heavy our suitcases suddenly felt? How our blood slowed, our footsteps lagged?
Brother Ass, we had been bashfully thinking of a kind of illumination such as Rimbaud
dreamed of – a nagging poem which was not didactic or expository but which *infected*

8 on 9pt

WALKING ALONG THE MALL WE WONDERED WHO ALL THOSE MEN WERE – TALL HAWK-FEATURED
men perched on balconies and high places, scanning the city with heavy binoculars. What were
they seeking so earnestly? Who were they – so composed and steely-eyed? Timidly we stopped a
policeman to ask him. 'They are publishers' he said mildly. Publishers! Our hearts stopped
beating. 'They are on the look out for new talent.' Great God! It was for *us* they were waiting
and watching! Then the kindly policeman lowered his voice confidentially and said in hollow
and reverent tones: *'They are waiting for the new Trollope to be born!'* Do you remember, at these
words, how heavy our suitcases suddenly felt? How our blood slowed, our footsteps lagged?
Brother Ass, we had been bashfully thinking of a kind of illumination such as Rimbaud

8 on 10.5pt

Walking along the Mall we wondered who all those men were – tall hawk-featured men perched on balconies and high places, scanning the city with heavy binoculars. What were they seeking so earnestly? Who were they – so composed and steely-eyed? Timidly we stopped a policeman to ask him. 'They are publishers' he said mildly. Publishers! Our hearts stopped beating. 'They are on the look out for new talent.' Great God! It was for *us* they were waiting and watching! Then the kindly policeman lowered his voice confidentially and said in hollow and reverent tones: *'They are waiting for the new Trollope to be born!'* Do you remember, at these words, how heavy our suitcases suddenly felt? How our blood slowed, our footsteps lagged? Brother Ass, we had been bashfully thinking of a kind of illumination such as Rimbaud dreamed of – a nagging poem which was not didactic or expository but which *infected* – was not simply a rationalised intuition, I mean, clothed in isinglass! We had come to the wrong shop, with the wrong change! A chill struck us as we saw the mist falling in Trafalgar Square, coiling round us its tendrils of ectoplasm! A million muffin-eating moralists were waiting, not for us, Brother Ass, but for the plucky and tedious Trollope! (If you are dissatisfied with your form, reach for the *curette*.) Now do you wonder if I laugh a little off-key? Do you ask yourself what has turned me into nature's bashful little aphorist? We who are, after all, simply poor co-workers in the

9 on 11pt

Walking along the Mall we wondered who all those men were – tall hawk-featured men perched on balconies and high places, scanning the city with heavy binoculars. What were they seeking so earnestly? Who were they – so composed and steely-eyed? Timidly we stopped a policeman to ask him. 'They are publishers' he said mildly. Publishers! Our hearts stopped beating. 'They are on the look out for new talent.' Great God! It was for *us* they were waiting and watching! Then the kindly policeman lowered his voice confidentially and said in hollow and reverent tones: *'They are waiting for the new Trollope to be born!'* Do you remember, at these words, how heavy our suitcases suddenly felt? How our blood slowed, our footsteps lagged? Brother Ass, we had been bashfully thinking of a kind of illumination such as Rimbaud dreamed of – a nagging poem which was not didactic or expository but which *infected* – was not simply a rationalised intuition, I mean, clothed in isinglass! We had come to the wrong shop, with the wrong change! A chill struck us as we saw the mist falling in Trafalgar Square, coiling round us its tendrils of ectoplasm! A million muffin-eating moralists were waiting, not

10 on 12pt

Walking along the Mall we wondered who all those men were – tall hawk-featured men perched on balconies and high places, scanning the city with heavy binoculars. What were they seeking so earnestly? Who were they – so composed and steely-eyed? Timidly we stopped a policeman to ask him. 'They are publishers' he said mildly. Publishers! Our hearts stopped beating. 'They are on the look out for new talent.' Great God! It was for *us* they were waiting and watching! Then the kindly policeman lowered his voice confidentially and said in hollow and reverent tones: *'They are waiting for the new Trollope to be born!'* Do you remember, at these words, how heavy our suitcases suddenly felt? How our blood slowed, our footsteps lagged? Brother Ass, we had been bashfully thinking of a kind of illumination such as Rimbaud dreamed of – a nagging poem which was not didactic or expository but which *infected* – was not simply a rationalised intuition, I mean, clothed in isinglass! We had come to the wrong shop, with the wrong

11 on 13pt

WALKING ALONG THE MALL WE WONDERED WHO ALL THOSE MEN WERE – TALL HAWK-featured men perched on balconies and high places, scanning the city with heavy binoculars. What were they seeking so earnestly? Who were they – so composed and steely-eyed? Timidly we stopped a policeman to ask him. 'They are publishers' he said mildly. Publishers! Our hearts stopped beating. 'They are on the look out for new talent.' Great God! It was for *us* they were waiting and watching! Then the kindly policeman lowered his voice confidentially and said in hollow and reverent tones: *'They are waiting for the new Trollope to be born!'* Do you remember, at these words, how heavy our suitcases suddenly felt? How our blood slowed, our footsteps lagged? Brother Ass, we had been bashfully thinking of a kind of illumination such as Rimbaud dreamed of – a nagging poem which was not didactic or expository but which *infected* – was not simply a rationalised intuition, I mean, clothed in isinglass! We had come to the wrong shop, with the wrong change! A chill struck us as we saw the mist falling in Trafalgar Square, coiling round us its tendrils of ectoplasm! A million muffin-eating moralists were waiting, not for us, Brother Ass, but for the plucky and tedious Trollope! (If you are dissatisfied with your form, reach for the *curette*.) Now do you wonder if I laugh a little off-key? Do you ask yourself what has

9 on 12pt

WALKING ALONG THE MALL WE WONDERED WHO ALL THOSE MEN WERE – TALL hawk-featured men perched on balconies and high places, scanning the city with heavy binoculars. What were they seeking so earnestly? Who were they – so composed and steely-eyed? Timidly we stopped a policeman to ask him. 'They are publishers' he said mildly. Publishers! Our hearts stopped beating. 'They are on the look out for new talent.' Great God! It was for *us* they were waiting and watching! Then the kindly policeman lowered his voice confidentially and said in hollow and reverent tones: *'They are waiting for the new Trollope to be born!'* Do you remember, at these words, how heavy our suitcases suddenly felt? How our blood slowed, our footsteps lagged? Brother Ass, we had been bashfully thinking of a kind of illumination such as Rimbaud dreamed of – a nagging poem which was not didactic or expository but which *infected* – was not simply a rationalised intuition, I mean, clothed in isinglass! We had come to the wrong shop, with the wrong change! A chill struck us as we saw the mist falling in Trafalgar Square, coiling round us its

10 on 13.5pt

WALKING ALONG THE MALL WE WONDERED WHO ALL THOSE MEN WERE – tall hawk-featured men perched on balconies and high places, scanning the city with heavy binoculars. What were they seeking so earnestly? Who were they – so composed and steely-eyed? Timidly we stopped a policeman to ask him. 'They are publishers' he said mildly. Publishers! Our hearts stopped beating. 'They are on the look out for new talent.' Great God! It was for *us* they were waiting and watching! Then the kindly policeman lowered his voice confidentially and said in hollow and reverent tones: *'They are waiting for the new Trollope to be born!'* Do you remember, at these words, how heavy our suitcases suddenly felt? How our blood slowed, our footsteps lagged? Brother Ass, we had been bashfully thinking of a kind of illumination such as Rimbaud dreamed of – a nagging poem which was not didactic or expository but which *infected* – was not simply a rationalised intuition,

11 on 14.5pt

LINOTYPE GRANJON

Monotype **Grotesque**

215 roman and italic
216 bold
Monotype 1926
Copyfitting factor 45.9/43.8/50.3

Range also includes light, light italic

The Linotype version is apparently very
similar, although it is slightly tighter set.
Copyfitting code 130/127/144

ABCDEFGHIJKLMNOP
QRSTUVWXYZ abcdefg
hijklmnopqrstuvwxyz
1234567890
ff fi fl ffi ffl ()[]&£$.,;:-!?''

ABCDEFGHIJKLMNOP
QRSTUVWXYZ abcdefg
hijklmnopqrstuvwxyz
1234567890
ff fi fl ffi ffl ()[]&£$.,;:-!?''

ABCDEFGHIJKLMNOP
QRSTUVWXYZ abcdefg
hijklmnopqrstuvwxyz
1234567890
ff fi fl ffi ffl ()[]&£$.,;:-!?''

24 on 27pt

These examples show *normal* letterspacing and the effect of *reduced* letterspacing on roman setting *as well as on words in italic*: they also show the appearance of figures, for example 28 May 1964, within text. These & the ampersand are not included in the setting opposite.

Normal letterspacing

These examples show *normal* letterspacing and the effect of *reduced* letterspacing on roman setting *as well as on words in italic*: they also show the appearance of figures, for example 28 May 1964, within text. These & the ampersand are not included in the setting opposite.

Minus one unit spacing

These examples show *normal* letterspacing and the effect of *reduced* letterspacing on roman setting *as well as on words in italic*: they also show the appearance of figures, for example 28 May 1964, within text. These & the ampersand are not included in the setting opposite.

Minus two units spacing

WALKING ALONG THE MALL WE WONDERED WHO ALL THOSE
WALKING ALONG THE MALL WE WONDERED WHO ALL
WALKING ALONG THE MALL WE WONDERED WHO

Capitals: normal letterspacing/plus 9 units/plus 18 units

Walking along the Mall we wondered who all those men were – tall hawk-featured men perched on balconies and high places, scanning the city with heavy binoculars. WHAT WERE THEY SEEKING SO EARNESTLY? Who were they – so composed and steely-eyed? Timidly we stopped a policeman to ask him. 'They are publishers' he said mildly. Publishers! OUR HEARTS STOPPED BEATING. 'They are on the look out for new talent.' Great God! It was for *us*

Text with reduced capitals normal letterspacing/plus 6 units

WALKING ALONG THE MALL we wondered who all those men were
WALKING ALONG THE MALL we wondered who all those men were

True italic/sloped roman

Walking along the Mall we wondered who all those men were – tall hawk-featured men perched on balconies and high places, scanning the city with heavy binoculars. What were they seeking so earnestly? Who were they – so composed and steely-eyed? Timidly we stopped a policeman to ask him. 'They are publishers' he said mildly. Publishers! Our hearts stopped beating. 'They are on the look out for new talent.' Great God! It was for *us* they were waiting and watching! Then the kindly policeman lowered his voice confidentially and said in hollow and reverent tones: *'They are waiting for the new Trollope to be born!'* Do you remember, at these words, how heavy our suitcases suddenly felt? How our blood slowed, our footsteps lagged? Brother Ass, we had been bashfully thinking

8 on 9pt

Walking along the Mall we wondered who all those men were – tall hawk-featured men perched on balconies and high places, scanning the city with heavy bin-oculars. What were they seeking so earnestly? Who were they – so composed and steely-eyed? Timidly we stopped a policeman to ask him. 'They are publishers' he said mildly. Publishers! Our hearts stopped beating. 'They are on the look out for new talent.' Great God! It was for *us* they were waiting and watching! Then the kindly policeman lowered his voice confidentially and said in hollow and reverent tones: *'They are waiting for the new Trollope to be born!'* Do you remember, at these words, how heavy our suitcases suddenly felt? How our blood slowed, our

8 on 10.5pt

Walking along the Mall we wondered who all those men were – tall hawk-featured men perched on balconies and high places, scanning the city with heavy binoculars. What were they seeking so earnestly? Who were they – so composed and steely-eyed? Timidly we stopped a policeman to ask him. 'They are publishers' he said mildly. Publishers! Our hearts stopped beating. 'They are on the look out for new talent.' Great God! It was for *us* they were waiting and watching! Then the kindly policeman lowered his voice confidentially and said in hollow and reverent tones: *'They are waiting for the new Trollope to be born!'* Do you remember, at these words, how heavy our suitcases suddenly felt? How our blood slowed, our footsteps lagged? Brother Ass, we had been bashfully thinking of a kind of illumination such as Rimbaud dreamed of – a nagging poem which was not didactic or expository but which *infected* – was not simply a rationalised intuition, I mean, clothed in isinglass! We had come to the wrong shop, with the wrong change! A chill struck us as we saw the mist falling in Trafalgar Square, coiling around us its tendrils of ectoplasm! A million muffin-eating moralists were waiting, not for us, Brother Ass, but for the plucky and tedious Trollope! (If you are dissatisfied with your form, reach

9 on 11pt

Walking along the Mall we wondered who all those men were – tall hawk-featured men perched on balconies and high places, scanning the city with heavy binoculars. What were they seeking so earnestly? Who were they – so composed and steely-eyed? Timidly we stopped a policeman to ask him. 'They are publishers' he said mildly. Publishers! Our hearts stopped beating. 'They are on the look out for new talent.' Great God! It was for *us* they were waiting and watching! Then the kindly policeman lowered his voice confidentially and said in hollow and reverent tones: *'They are waiting for the new Trollope to be born!'* Do you remember, at these words, how heavy our suitcases suddenly felt? How our blood slowed, our footsteps lagged? Brother Ass, we had been bashfully thinking of a kind of illumination such as Rimbaud dreamed of – a nagging poem which was not didactic or expository but which *infected* – was not simply a rationalised intuition, I mean, clothed in isinglass! We had come to the wrong shop, with the wrong change! A chill struck us as we saw the mist falling in Trafalgar Square, coiling around us its tendrils of ectoplasm! A million muffin-eating moralists were waiting, not for us, Brother Ass, but for the

9 on 12pt

Walking along the Mall we wondered who all those men were – tall hawk-featured men perched on balconies and high places, scanning the city with heavy binoculars. What were they seeking so earnestly? Who were they – so composed and steely-eyed? Timidly we stopped a policeman to ask him. 'They are publishers' he said mildly. Publishers! Our hearts stopped beating. 'They are on the look out for new talent.' Great God! It was for *us* they were waiting and watching! Then the kindly policeman lowered his voice confidentially and said in hollow and reverent tones: *'They are waiting for the new Trollope to be born!'* Do you remember, at these words, how heavy our suitcases suddenly felt? How our blood slowed, our footsteps lagged? Brother Ass, we had been bashfully thinking of a kind of illumination such as Rimbaud dreamed of – a nagging poem which was not didactic or expository but which *infected* – was not simply a rationalised intuition, I mean, clothed in isinglass! We had come to the wrong shop, with the wrong change! A chill struck us

10 on 12pt

Walking along the Mall we wondered who all those men were – tall hawk-featured men perched on balconies and high places, scanning the city with heavy binoculars. What were they seeking so earnestly? Who were they – so composed and steely-eyed? Timidly we stopped a policeman to ask him. 'They are publishers' he said mildly. Publishers! Our hearts stopped beating. 'They are on the look out for new talent.' Great God! It was for *us* they were waiting and watching! Then the kindly policeman lowered his voice confidentially and said in hollow and reverent tones: *'They are waiting for the new Trollope to be born!'* Do you remember, at these words, how heavy our suitcases suddenly felt? How our blood slowed, our footsteps lagged? Brother Ass, we had been bashfully thinking of a kind of illumination such as Rimbaud dreamed of – a nagging poem which was not didactic or expository but which *infected* – was not simply a rationalised intuition, I mean, clothed in isinglass! We had

10 on 13.5pt

Walking along the Mall we wondered who all those men were – tall hawk-featured men perched on balconies and high places, scanning the city with heavy binoculars. What were they seeking so earnestly? Who were they – so composed and steely-eyed? Timidly we stopped a policeman to ask him. 'They are publishers' he said mildly. Publishers! Our hearts stopped beating. 'They are on the look out for new talent.' Great God! It was for *us* they were waiting and watching! Then the kindly policeman lowered his voice confidentially and said in hollow and reverent tones: *'They are waiting for the new Trollope to be born!'* Do you remember, at these words, how heavy our suitcases suddenly felt? How our blood slowed, our footsteps lagged? Brother Ass, we had been bashfully thinking of a kind of illumination such as Rimbaud dreamed of – a nagging poem which was not didactic or

11 on 13pt

Walking along the Mall we wondered who all those men were – tall hawk-featured men perched on balconies and high places, scanning the city with heavy binoculars. What were they seeking so earnestly? Who were they – so composed and steely-eyed? Timidly we stopped a policeman to ask him. 'They are publishers' he said mildly. Publishers! Our hearts stopped beating. 'They are on the look out for new talent.' Great God! It was for *us* they were waiting and watching! Then the kindly policeman lowered his voice confidentially and said in hollow and reverent tones: *'They are waiting for the new Trollope to be born!'* Do you remember, at these words, how heavy our suitcases suddenly felt? How our blood slowed, our footsteps lagged? Brother Ass, we had been bashfully thinking of a kind of illumination such as Rimbaud

11 on 14.5pt

MONOTYPE GROTESQUE

Linotype **Guardi**

roman 55 (05551), **italic 56** (13551)
bold 75 (07551)
Linotype 1986 (Reinhard Haus)
Copyfitting code 130/114/141

Range also includes bold italic, black, black
italic

ABCDEFGHIJKLMNOP
QRSTUVWXYZ abcdefg
hijklmnopqrstuvwxyz
1234567890 1234567890
fifl ()[]&£$.,;:-!?''

ABCDEFGHIJKLMNOP
QRSTUVWXYZ abcdefg
hijklmnopqrstuvwxyz
1234567890 1234567890
fifl ()[]&£$.,;:-!?''

ABCDEFGHIJKLMNOP
QRSTUVWXYZ abcdefg
hijklmnopqrstuvwxyz
1234567890 1234567890
fifl ()[]&£$.,;:-!?''

24 on 27pt

These examples show *normal* letterspacing and the effect of *reduced*
letterspacing on roman setting *as well as on words in italic*: they also
show the appearance of figures, for example 28 May 1964, within text.
These & the ampersand are not included in the setting opposite.
Normal letterspacing

These examples show *normal* letterspacing and the effect of *reduced*
letterspacing on roman setting *as well as on words in italic*: they also
show the appearance of figures, for example 28 May 1964, within text.
These & the ampersand are not included in the setting opposite.
Minus one unit spacing

These examples show *normal* letterspacing and the effect of *reduced*
letterspacing on roman setting *as well as on words in italic*: they also
show the appearance of figures, for example 28 May 1964, within text.
These & the ampersand are not included in the setting opposite.
Minus two units spacing

WALKING ALONG THE MALL WE WONDERED WHO ALL
WALKING ALONG THE MALL WE WONDERED WHO
WALKING ALONG THE MALL WE WONDERED
Capitals: normal letterspacing/plus 4 units/plus 9 units

WALKING ALONG THE MALL WE WONDERED WHO ALL THOSE MEN
WALKING ALONG THE MALL WE WONDERED WHO ALL THOSE
WALKING ALONG THE MALL WE WONDERED WHO ALL
Small caps: normal letterspacing/plus 3 units/plus 6 units

WALKING ALONG THE MALL WE WONDERED WHO ALL THOSE MEN
WALKING ALONG THE MALL WE WONDERED WHO ALL THOSE MEN WERE
True small caps/reduced capitals

WALKING ALONG THE MALL we wondered who all those men were
WALKING ALONG THE MALL we wondered who all those men
True italic/sloped roman

Walking along the Mall we wondered who all those men were – tall hawk-
featured men perched on balconies and high places, scanning the city with heavy
binoculars. What were they seeking so earnestly? Who were they – so composed and
steely-eyed? Timidly we stopped a policeman to ask him. 'They are publishers' he
said mildly. Publishers! Our hearts stopped beating. 'They are on the look out for
new talent.' Great God! It was for *us* they were waiting and watching! Then the kindly
policeman lowered his voice confidentially and said in hollow and reverent tones:
'They are waiting for the new Trollope to be born!' Do you remember, at these words, how
heavy our suitcases suddenly felt? How our blood slowed, our footsteps lagged?
Brother Ass, we had been bashfully thinking of a kind of illumination such as
8 on 9pt

WALKING ALONG THE MALL WE WONDERED WHO ALL THOSE MEN WERE – TALL
hawk-featured men perched on balconies and high places, scanning the city with
heavy binoculars. What were they seeking so earnestly? Who were they – so
composed and steely-eyed? Timidly we stopped a policeman to ask him. 'They are
publishers' he said mildly. Publishers! Our hearts stopped beating. 'They are on the
look out for new talent.' Great God! It was for *us* they were waiting and watching!
Then the kindly policeman lowered his voice confidentially and said in hollow and
reverent tones: *'They are waiting for the new Trollope to be born!'* Do you remember, at
these words, how heavy our suitcases suddenly felt? How our blood slowed, our
8 on 10.5pt

Walking along the Mall we wondered who all those men were – tall hawk-featured men perched on balconies and high places, scanning the city with heavy binoculars. What were they seeking so earnestly? Who were they – so composed and steely-eyed? Timidly we stopped a policeman to ask him. 'They are publishers' he said mildly. Publishers! Our hearts stopped beating. 'They are on the look out for new talent.' Great God! It was for *us* they were waiting and watching! Then the kindly policeman lowered his voice confidentially and said in hollow and reverent tones: *'They are waiting for the new Trollope to be born!'* Do you remember, at these words, how heavy our suitcases suddenly felt? How our blood slowed, our footsteps lagged? Brother Ass, we had been bashfully thinking of a kind of illumination such as Rimbaud dreamed of – a nagging poem which was not didactic or expository but which *infected* – was not simply a rationalised intuition, I mean, clothed in isinglass! We had come to the wrong shop, with the wrong change! A chill struck us as we saw the mist falling in Trafalgar Square, coiling round us its tendrils of ectoplasm! A million muffin-eating moralists were waiting, not for us, Brother Ass, but for the plucky and tedious Trollope! (If you are dissatisfied with your form, reach for the *curette*.) Now

9 on 11pt

Walking along the Mall we wondered who all those men were – hawk-featured men perched on balconies and high places, scanning the city with heavy binoculars. What were they seeking so earnestly? Who were they – so composed and steely-eyed? Timidly we stopped a policeman to ask him. 'They are publishers' he said mildly. Publishers! Our hearts stopped beating. 'They are on the look out for new talent.' Great God! It was for *us* they were waiting and watching! Then the kindly policeman lowered his voice confidentially and said in hollow and reverent tones: *'They are waiting for the new Trollope to be born!'* Do you remember, at these words, how heavy our suitcases suddenly felt? How our blood slowed, our footsteps lagged? Brother had been bashfully thinking of a kind of illumination such as Rimbaud dreamed of – a nagging poem which was not didactic or expository but which *infected* – was not simply a rationalised intuition, I mean, clothed in isinglass! We had come to the wrong shop, with the wrong change! A chill struck us as we saw the mist

10 on 12pt

Walking along the Mall we wondered who all those men were – tall hawk-featured men perched on balconies and high places, scanning the city with heavy binoculars. What were they seeking so earnestly? Who were they – so composed and steely-eyed? Timidly we stopped a policeman to ask him. 'They are publishers' he said mildly. Publishers! Our hearts stopped beating. 'They are on the look out for new talent.' Great God! It was for *us* they were waiting and watching! Then the kindly policeman lowered his voice confidentially and said in hollow and reverent tones: *'They are waiting for the new Trollope to be born!'* Do you remember, at these words, how heavy our suitcases suddenly felt? How our blood slowed, our footsteps lagged? Brother Ass, we had been bashfully thinking of a kind of illumination such as Rimbaud dreamed of – a nagging poem which was not didactic or expository but

11 on 13pt

WALKING ALONG THE MALL WE WONDERED WHO ALL THOSE MEN WERE – tall hawk-featured men perched on balconies and high places, scanning the city with heavy binoculars. What were they seeking so earnestly? Who were they – so composed and steely-eyed? Timidly we stopped a policeman to ask him. 'They are publishers' he said mildly. Publishers! Our hearts stopped beating. 'They are on the look out for new talent.' Great God! It was for *us* they were waiting and watching! Then the kindly policeman lowered his voice confidentially and said in hollow and reverent tones: *'They are waiting for the new Trollope to be born!'* Do you remember, at these words, how heavy our suitcases suddenly felt? How our blood slowed, our footsteps lagged? Brother Ass, we had been bashfully thinking of a kind of illumination such as Rimbaud dreamed of – a nagging poem which was not didactic or expository but which *infected* – was not simply a rationalised intuition, I mean, clothed in isinglass! We had come to the wrong shop, with the wrong change! A chill struck us as we saw the mist falling in Trafalgar Square, coiling round us its tendrils of ectoplasm! A million muffin-eating moralists were waiting, not for us, Brother Ass, but for the plucky and tedious

9 on 12pt

WALKING ALONG THE MALL WE WONDERED WHO ALL THOSE MEN were – tall hawk-featured men perched on balconies and high places, scanning the city with heavy binoculars. What were they seeking so earnestly? Who were they – so composed and steely-eyed? Timidly we stopped a policeman to ask him. 'They are publishers' he said mildly. Publishers! Our hearts stopped beating. 'They are on the look out for new talent.' Great God! It was for *us* they were waiting and watching! Then the kindly policeman lowered his voice confidentially and said in hollow and reverent tones: *'They are waiting for the new Trollope to be born!'* Do you remember, at these words, how heavy our suitcases suddenly felt? How our blood slowed, our footsteps lagged? Brother Ass, we had been bashfully thinking of a kind of illumination such as Rimbaud dreamed of – a nagging poem which was not didactic or expository but which *infected* – was not simply a rationalised intuition, I mean, clothed in

10 on 13.5pt

WALKING ALONG THE MALL WE WONDERED WHO ALL THOSE men were – tall hawk-featured men perched on balconies and high places, scanning the city with heavy binoculars. What were they seeking so earnestly? Who were they – so composed and steely-eyed? Timidly we stopped a policeman to ask him. 'They are publishers' he said mildly. Publishers! Our hearts stopped beating. 'They are on the look out for new talent.' Great God! It was for *us* they were waiting and watching! Then the kindly policeman lowered his voice confidentially and said in hollow and reverent tones: *'They are waiting for the new Trollope to be born!'* Do you remember, at these words, how heavy our suitcases suddenly felt? How our blood slowed, our footsteps lagged? Brother Ass, we had been bashfully thinking of a kind of illumination such as Rimbaud

11 on 14.5pt

LINOTYPE GUARDI

Monotype **Helvetica**

765 roman and italic
766 medium
Haas 1957 (Max Meidinger)
Copyfitting factor 44.4/44.4/44.4

There is a very extensive range of weights and variations

Linotype Helvetica (copyfitting code 127/131/140) more closely resembles Neue Helvetica in size, fit and design. It also includes small caps

Strongly influenced by early twentieth-century German grotesques such as Akzidenz-Grotesk. It is more monoline than Univers

Educational characters available

ABCDEFGHIJKLMNOP
QRSTUVWXYZ abcdefg
hijklmnopqrstuvwxyz
1234567890
()[]&£$.,;:-!?''

ABCDEFGHIJKLMNOP
QRSTUVWXYZ abcdefg
hijklmnopqrstuvwxyz
1234567890
()[]&£$.,;:-!?''

ABCDEFGHIJKLMNOP
QRSTUVWXYZ abcdefg
hijklmnopqrstuvwxyz
1234567890
()[]&£$.,;:-!?''

24 on 27pt

166

These examples show *normal* letterspacing and the effect of *reduced* letterspacing on roman setting *as well as on words in italic*: they also show the appearance of figures, for example 28 May 1964, within text. These & the ampersand are not included in the setting opposite.
Normal letterspacing

These examples show *normal* letterspacing and the effect of *reduced* letterspacing on roman setting *as well as on words in italic*: they also show the appearance of figures, for example 28 May 1964, within text. These & the ampersand are not included in the setting opposite.
Minus one unit spacing

These examples show *normal* letterspacing and the effect of *reduced* letterspacing on roman setting *as well as on words in italic*: they also show the appearance of figures, for example 28 May 1964, within text. These & the ampersand are not included in the setting opposite.
Minus two units spacing

WALKING ALONG THE MALL WE WONDERED WHO ALL THOSE MEN
WALKING ALONG THE MALL WE WONDERED WHO ALL
WALKING ALONG THE MALL WE WONDERED WHO
Capitals: normal letterspacing/plus 9 units/plus 18 units

Walking along the Mall we wondered who all those men were – tall hawk-featured men perched on balconies and high places, scanning the city with heavy binoculars. WHAT WERE THEY SEEKING SO EARNESTLY? Who were they – so composed and steely-eyed? Timidly we stopped a policeman to ask him. 'They are publishers' he said mildly. Publishers! OUR HEARTS STOPPED BEATING. 'They are on the look out for new talent.' Great God! It was for *us* they were waiting
Text with reduced capitals normal letterspacing/plus 6 units

WALKING ALONG THE MALL we wondered who all those men were
WALKING ALONG THE MALL we wondered who all those men were
True italic/sloped roman

Walking along the Mall we wondered who all those men were – tall hawk-featured men perched on balconies and high places, scanning the city with heavy binoculars. What were they seeking so earnestly? Who were they – so composed and steely-eyed? Timidly we stopped a policeman to ask him. 'They are publishers' he said mildly. Publishers! Our hearts stopped beating. 'They are on the look out for new talent.' Great God! It was for *us* they were waiting and watching! Then the kindly policeman lowered his voice confidentially and said in hollow and reverent tones: *'They are waiting for the new Trollope to be born!'* Do you remember, at these words, how heavy our suitcases suddenly felt? How our blood slowed, our footsteps lagged? Brother Ass, we had been bashfully thinking of a kind of illumination such
8 on 9pt

Walking along the Mall we wondered who all those men were – tall hawk-featured men perched on balconies and high places, scanning the city with heavy binoculars. What were they seeking so earnestly? Who were they – so composed and steely-eyed? Timidly we stopped a policeman to ask him. 'They are publishers' he said mildly. Publishers! Our hearts stopped beating. 'They are on the look out for new talent.' Great God! It was for *us* they were waiting and watching! Then the kindly policeman lowered his voice confidentially and said in hollow and reverent tones: *'They are waiting for the new Trollope to be born!'* Do you remember, at these words, how heavy our suitcases suddenly felt? How our blood slowed, our footsteps
8 on 10.5pt

Walking along the Mall we wondered who all those men were – tall hawk-featured men perched on balconies and high places, scanning the city with heavy binoculars. What were they seeking so earnestly? Who were they – so composed and steely-eyed? Timidly we stopped a policeman to ask him. 'They are publishers' he said mildly. Publishers! Our hearts stopped beating. 'They are on the look out for new talent.' Great God! It was for *us* they were waiting and watching! Then the kindly policeman lowered his voice confidentially and said in hollow and reverent tones: *'They are waiting for the new Trollope to be born!'* Do you remember, at these words, how heavy our suitcases suddenly felt? How our blood slowed, our footsteps lagged? Brother Ass, we had been bashfully thinking of a kind of illumination such as Rimbaud dreamed of – a nagging poem which was not didactic or expository but which *infected* – was not simply a rationalised intuition, I mean, clothed in isinglass! We had come to the wrong shop, with the wrong change! A chill struck us as we saw the mist falling in Trafalgar Square, coiling around us its tendrils of ectoplasm! A million muffin-eating moralists were waiting, not for us, Brother Ass, but for the plucky and tedious Trollope! (If you are dissatisfied with your form, reach for the *curette*.) Now do you wonder if I laugh a little off-key? Do
9 on 11pt

Walking along the Mall we wondered who all those men were – tall hawk-featured men perched on balconies and high places, scanning the city with heavy binoculars. What were they seeking so earnestly? Who were they – so composed and steely-eyed? Timidly we stopped a policeman to ask him. 'They are publishers' he said mildly. Publishers! Our hearts stopped beating. 'They are on the look out for new talent.' Great God! It was for *us* they were waiting and watching! Then the kindly policeman lowered his voice confidentially and said in hollow and reverent tones: *'They are waiting for the new Trollope to be born!'* Do you remember, at these words, how heavy our suitcases suddenly felt? How our blood slowed, our footsteps lagged? Brother Ass, we had been bashfully thinking of a kind of illumination such as Rimbaud dreamed of – a nagging poem which was not didactic or expository but which *infected* – was not simply a rationalised intuition, I mean, clothed in isinglass! We had come to the wrong shop, with the wrong change! A chill struck us as we saw the mist falling in Trafalgar Square, coiling around us its tendrils of ectoplasm! A million muffin-eating moralists were waiting, not for us, Brother Ass, but for the plucky and tedious Trollope! (If you are dissatisfied with your
9 on 12pt

Walking along the Mall we wondered who all those men were – tall hawk-featured men perched on balconies and high places, scanning the city with heavy binoculars. What were they seeking so earnestly? Who were they – so composed and steely-eyed? Timidly we stopped a policeman to ask him. 'They are publishers' he said mildly. Publishers! Our hearts stopped beating. 'They are on the look out for new talent.' Great God! It was for *us* they were waiting and watching! Then the kindly policeman lowered his voice confidentially and said in hollow and reverent tones: *'They are waiting for the new Trollope to be born!'* Do you remember, at these words, how heavy our suitcases suddenly felt? How our blood slowed, our footsteps lagged? Brother Ass, we had been bashfully thinking of a kind of illumination such as Rimbaud dreamed of – a nagging poem which was not didactic or expository but which *infected* – was not simply a rationalised intuition, I mean, clothed in isinglass! We had come to the wrong shop, with the wrong change! A chill struck us as we saw the mist falling in
10 on 12pt

Walking along the Mall we wondered who all those men were – tall hawk-featured men perched on balconies and high places, scanning the city with heavy binoculars. What were they seeking so earnestly? Who were they – so composed and steely-eyed? Timidly we stopped a policeman to ask him. 'They are publishers' he said mildly. Publishers! Our hearts stopped beating. 'They are on the look out for new talent.' Great God! It was for *us* they were waiting and watching! Then the kindly policeman lowered his voice confidentially and said in hollow and reverent tones: *'They are waiting for the new Trollope to be born!'* Do you remember, at these words, how heavy our suitcases suddenly felt? How our blood slowed, our footsteps lagged? Brother Ass, we had been bashfully thinking of a kind of illumination such as Rimbaud dreamed of – a nagging poem which was not didactic or expository but which *infected* – was not simply a rationalised intuition, I mean, clothed in isinglass! We had come to the wrong shop,
10 on 13.5pt

Walking along the Mall we wondered who all those men were – tall hawk-featured men perched on balconies and high places, scanning the city with heavy binoculars. What were they seeking so earnestly? Who were they – so composed and steely-eyed? Timidly we stopped a policeman to ask him. 'They are publishers' he said mildly. Publishers! Our hearts stopped beating. 'They are on the look out for new talent.' Great God! It was for *us* they were waiting and watching! Then the kindly policeman lowered his voice confidentially and said in hollow and reverent tones: *'They are waiting for the new Trollope to be born!'* Do you remember, at these words, how heavy our suitcases suddenly felt? How our blood slowed, our footsteps lagged? Brother Ass, we had been bashfully thinking of a kind of illumination such as Rimbaud dreamed of – a nagging poem which was not didactic or expository but which *infected* – was
11 on 13pt

Walking along the Mall we wondered who all those men were – tall hawk-featured men perched on balconies and high places, scanning the city with heavy binoculars. What were they seeking so earnestly? Who were they – so composed and steely-eyed? Timidly we stopped a policeman to ask him. 'They are publishers' he said mildly. Publishers! Our hearts stopped beating. 'They are on the look out for new talent.' Great God! It was for *us* they were waiting and watching! Then the kindly policeman lowered his voice confidentially and said in hollow and reverent tones: *'They are waiting for the new Trollope to be born!'* Do you remember, at these words, how heavy our suitcases suddenly felt? How our blood slowed, our footsteps lagged? Brother Ass, we had been bashfully thinking of a kind of illumination such as Rimbaud dreamed of – a nagging poem
11 on 14.5pt

Linotype **Neue Helvetica**

roman 55 (05472), **italic 45** (13472)
bold 75 (07472)
Stempel 1983
Copyfitting code 130/128/139

There is an enormous range of weights and
variations

ABCDEFGHIJKLMNOP
QRSTUVWXYZ abcdefg
hijklmnopqrstuvwxyz
1234567890
fifl ()[]&£$.,;:-!?''

ABCDEFGHIJKLMNOP
QRSTUVWXYZ abcdefg
hijklmnopqrstuvwxyz
1234567890
fifl ()[]&£$.,;:-!?''

ABCDEFGHIJKLMNOP
QRSTUVWXYZ abcdefg
hijklmnopqrstuvwxyz
1234567890
fifl ()[]&£$.,;:-!?''

24 on 27pt

These examples show *normal* letterspacing and the effect of *reduced* letterspacing on roman setting *as well as on words in italic*: they also show the appearance of figures, for example 28 May 1964, within text. These & the ampersand are not included in the setting opposite.

Normal letterspacing

These examples show *normal* letterspacing and the effect of *reduced* letterspacing on roman setting *as well as on words in italic*: they also show the appearance of figures, for example 28 May 1964, within text. These & the ampersand are not included in the setting opposite.

Minus one unit spacing

These examples show *normal* letterspacing and the effect of *reduced* letterspacing on roman setting *as well as on words in italic*: they also show the appearance of figures, for example 28 May 1964, within text. These & the ampersand are not included in the setting opposite.

Minus two units spacing

WALKING ALONG THE MALL WE WONDERED WHO ALL THOSE
WALKING ALONG THE MALL WE WONDERED WHO ALL
WALKING ALONG THE MALL WE WONDERED WHO

Capitals: normal letterspacing/plus 4 units/plus 9 units

Walking along the Mall we wondered who all those men were – tall hawk-featured men perched on balconies and high places, scanning the city with heavy binoculars. WHAT WERE THEY SEEKING SO EARNESTLY? Who were they – so composed and steely-eyed? Timidly we stopped a policeman to ask him. 'THEY ARE PUBLISHERS' he said mildly. Publishers! Our hearts stopped beating. 'They are on the look out for new talent.' Great God! It was for *us* they were waiting

Text with reduced caps normal letterspacing/plus 3 units

WALKING ALONG THE MALL we wondered who all those men were
WALKING ALONG THE MALL we wondered who all those men were

True italic/sloped roman

Walking along the Mall we wondered who all those men were – tall hawk-
featured men perched on balconies and high places, scanning the city with heavy binoculars. What were they seeking so earnestly? Who were they – so composed and steely-eyed? Timidly we stopped a policeman to ask him. 'They are publishers' he said mildly. Publishers! Our hearts stopped beating. 'They are on the look out for new talent.' Great God! It was for *us* they were waiting and watching! Then the kindly policeman lowered his voice confidentially and said in hollow and reverent tones: *'They are waiting for the new Trollope to be born!'* Do you remember, at these words, how heavy our suitcases suddenly felt? How our blood slowed, our footsteps lagged? Brother Ass, we had been bashfully thinking of a kind of illumination

8 on 9pt

Walking along the Mall we wondered who all those men were – tall hawk-featured men perched on balconies and high places, scanning the city with heavy binoculars. What were they seeking so earnestly? Who were they – so composed and steely-eyed? Timidly we stopped a policeman to ask him. 'They are publishers' he said mildly. Publishers! Our hearts stopped beating. 'They are on the look out for new talent.' Great God! It was for *us* they were waiting and watching! Then the kindly policeman lowered his voice confidentially and said in hollow and reverent tones: *'They are waiting for the new Trollope to be born!'* Do you remember, at these words, how heavy our suitcases suddenly felt? How our blood slowed, our footsteps

8 on 10.5pt

Walking along the Mall we wondered who all those men were – tall hawk-featured men perched on balconies and high places, scanning the city with heavy binoculars. What were they seeking so earnestly? Who were they – so composed and steely-eyed? Timidly we stopped a policeman to ask him. 'They are publishers' he said mildly. Publishers! Our hearts stopped beating. 'They are on the look out for new talent.' Great God! It was for *us* they were waiting and watching! Then the kindly policeman lowered his voice confidentially and said in hollow and reverent tones: *'They are waiting for the new Trollope to be born!'* Do you remember, at these words, how heavy our suitcases suddenly felt? How our blood slowed, our footsteps lagged? Brother Ass, we had been bashfully thinking of a kind of illumination such as Rimbaud dreamed of – a nagging poem which was not didactic or expository but which *infected* – was not simply a rationalised intuition, I mean, clothed in isinglass! We had come to the wrong shop, with the wrong change! A chill struck us as we saw the mist falling in Trafalgar Square, coiling round us its tendrils of ectoplasm! A million muffin-eating moralists were waiting, not for us, Brother Ass, but for the plucky and tedious Trollope! (If you are dissatisfied with your form, reach for the *curette*.) Now
9 on 11pt

Walking along the Mall we wondered who all those men were – tall hawk-featured men perched on balconies and high places, scanning the city with heavy binoculars. What were they seeking so earnestly? Who were they – so composed and steely-eyed? Timidly we stopped a policeman to ask him. 'They are publishers' he said mildly. Publishers! Our hearts stopped beating. 'They are on the look out for new talent.' Great God! It was for *us* they were waiting and watching! Then the kindly policeman lowered his voice confidentially and said in hollow and reverent tones: *'They are waiting for the new Trollope to be born!'* Do you remember, at these words, how heavy our suitcases suddenly felt? How our blood slowed, our footsteps lagged? Brother Ass, we had been bashfully thinking of a kind of illumination such as Rimbaud dreamed of – a nagging poem which was not didactic or expository but which *infected* – was not simply a rationalised intuition, I mean, clothed in isinglass! We had come to the wrong shop, with the wrong change! A chill struck us as
10 on 12pt

Walking along the Mall we wondered who all those men were – tall hawk-featured men perched on balconies and high places, scanning the city with heavy binoculars. What were they seeking so earnestly? Who were they – so composed and steely-eyed? Timidly we stopped a policeman to ask him. 'They are publishers' he said mildly. Publishers! Our hearts stopped beating. 'They are on the look out for new talent.' Great God! It was for *us* they were waiting and watching! Then the kindly policeman lowered his voice confidentially and said in hollow and reverent tones: *'They are waiting for the new Trollope to be born!'* Do you remember, at these words, how heavy our suitcases suddenly felt? How our blood slowed, our footsteps lagged? Brother Ass, we had been bashfully thinking of a kind of illumination such as Rimbaud dreamed of – a nagging poem which was not didactic or expository but
11 on 13pt

Walking along the Mall we wondered who all those men were – tall hawk-featured men perched on balconies and high places, scanning the city with heavy binoculars. What were they seeking so earnestly? Who were they – so composed and steely-eyed? Timidly we stopped a policeman to ask him. 'They are publishers' he said mildly. Publishers! Our hearts stopped beating. 'They are on the look out for new talent.' Great God! It was for *us* they were waiting and watching! Then the kindly policeman lowered his voice confidentially and said in hollow and reverent tones: *'They are waiting for the new Trollope to be born!'* Do you remember, at these words, how heavy our suitcases suddenly felt? How our blood slowed, our footsteps lagged? Brother Ass, we had been bashfully thinking of a kind of illumination such as Rimbaud dreamed of – a nagging poem which was not didactic or expository but which *infected* – was not simply a rationalised intuition, I mean, clothed in isinglass! We had come to the
9 on 12pt

Walking along the Mall we wondered who all those men were – tall hawk-featured men perched on balconies and high places, scanning the city with heavy binoculars. What were they seeking so earnestly? Who were they – so composed and steely-eyed? Timidly we stopped a policeman to ask him. 'They are publishers' he said mildly. Publishers! Our hearts stopped beating. 'They are on the look out for new talent.' Great God! It was for *us* they were waiting and watching! Then the kindly policeman lowered his voice confidentially and said in hollow and reverent tones: *'They are waiting for the new Trollope to be born!'* Do you remember, at these words, how heavy our suitcases suddenly felt? How our blood slowed, our footsteps lagged? Brother Ass, we had been bashfully thinking of a kind of illumination such as Rimbaud dreamed of – a nagging poem which was not didactic or expository but which *infected* – was not simply a rationalised intuition, I mean, clothed in isinglass! We had come to the
10 on 13.5pt

Walking along the Mall we wondered who all those men were – tall hawk-featured men perched on balconies and high places, scanning the city with heavy binoculars. What were they seeking so earnestly? Who were they – so composed and steely-eyed? Timidly we stopped a policeman to ask him. 'They are publishers' he said mildly. Publishers! Our hearts stopped beating. 'They are on the look out for new talent.' Great God! It was for *us* they were waiting and watching! Then the kindly policeman lowered his voice confidentially and said in hollow and reverent tones: *'They are waiting for the new Trollope to be born!'* Do you remember, at these words, how heavy our suitcases suddenly felt? How our blood slowed, our footsteps lagged? Brother Ass, we had been bashfully thinking of a kind of illumination such as Rimbaud dreamed of
11 on 14.5pt

199 roman and italic
261 bold
Monotype 1925
Copyfitting factor 41.6/39.3/45.2

Range also includes light, light italic, semi-bold, semi-bold italic, bold italic

Linotype's adaptation varies considerably

ABCDEFGHIJKLMNOP
QRSTUVWXYZ abcdefg
hijklmnopqrstuvwxyz
1234567890
ff fi fl ffi ffl ()[]&£$.,;:-!?''

ABCDEFGHIJKLMNOP
QRSTUVWXYZ abcdefg
hijklmnopqrstuvwxyz
1234567890
ff fi fl ffi ffl ()[]&£$.,;:-!?''

ABCDEFGHIJKLMNOP
QRSTUVWXYZ abcdefg
hijklmnopqrstuvwxyz
1234567890
ff fi fl ffi ffl ()[]&£$.,;:-!?''

24 on 27pt

These examples show *normal* letterspacing and the effect of *reduced* letterspacing on roman setting *as well as on words in italic*: they also show the appearance of figures, for example 28 May 1964, within text. These & the ampersand are not included in the setting opposite.

Normal letterspacing

These examples show *normal* letterspacing and the effect of *reduced* letterspacing on roman setting *as well as on words in italic*: they also show the appearance of figures, for example 28 May 1964, within text. These & the ampersand are not included in the setting opposite.

Minus one unit spacing

These examples show *normal* letterspacing and the effect of *reduced* letterspacing on roman setting *as well as on words in italic*: they also show the appearance of figures, for example 28 May 1964, within text. These & the ampersand are not included in the setting opposite.

Minus two units spacing

WALKING ALONG THE MALL WE WONDERED WHO ALL
WALKING ALONG THE MALL WE WONDERED WHO
WALKING ALONG THE MALL WE WONDERED

Capitals: normal letterspacing/plus 9 units/plus 18 units

Walking along the Mall we wondered who all those men were – tall hawk-featured men perched on balconies and high places, scanning the city with heavy binoculars. WHAT WERE THEY SEEKING SO EARNESTLY? Who were they – so composed and steely-eyed? Timidly we stopped a policeman to ask him. 'THEY ARE PUBLISHERS' he said mildly. Publishers! Our hearts stopped beating. 'They are on the look out for new talent.' Great God! It was for *us* they were waiting and watching!

Text with reduced capitals normal letterspacing/plus 6 units

WALKING ALONG THE MALL we wondered who all those men were
WALKING ALONG THE MALL we wondered who all those men

True italic/sloped roman

Walking along the Mall we wondered who all those men were – tall hawk-featured men perched on balconies and high places, scanning the city with heavy binoculars. What were they seeking so earnestly? Who were they – so composed and steely-eyed? Timidly we stopped a policeman to ask him. 'They are publishers' he said mildly. Publishers! Our hearts stopped beating. 'They are on the look out for new talent.' Great God! It was for *us* they were waiting and watching! Then the kindly policeman lowered his voice confidentially and said in hollow and reverent tones: '*They are waiting for the new Trollope to be born!*' Do you remember, at these words, how heavy our suitcases suddenly felt? How our blood slowed, our footsteps lagged? Brother Ass, we had been bashfully thinking of a kind of illumination such as Rimbaud dreamed of – a nagging poem which was not

8 on 9pt

Walking along the Mall we wondered who all those men were – tall hawk-featured men perched on balconies and high places, scanning the city with heavy binoculars. What were they seeking so earnestly? Who were they – so composed and steely-eyed? Timidly we stopped a policeman to ask him. 'They are publishers' he said mildly. Publishers! Our hearts stopped beating. 'They are on the look out for new talent.' Great God! It was for *us* they were waiting and watching! Then the kindly policeman lowered his voice confidentially and said in hollow and reverent tones: '*They are waiting for the new Trollope to be born!*' Do you remember, at these words, how heavy our suitcases suddenly felt? How our blood slowed, our footsteps lagged? Brother Ass, we had been bashfully thinking of a

8 on 10.5pt

Walking along the Mall we wondered who all those men were – tall hawk-featured men perched on balconies and high places, scanning the city with heavy binoculars. What were they seeking so earnestly? Who were they – so composed and steely-eyed? Timidly we stopped a policeman to ask him. 'They are publishers' he said mildly. Publishers! Our hearts stopped beating. 'They are on the look out for new talent.' Great God! It was for *us* they were waiting and watching! Then the kindly policeman lowered his voice confidentially and said in hollow and reverent tones: *'They are waiting for the new Trollope to be born!'* Do you remember, at these words, how heavy our suitcases suddenly felt? How our blood slowed, our footsteps lagged? Brother Ass, we had been bashfully thinking of a kind of illumination such as Rimbaud dreamed of – a nagging poem which was not didactic or expository but which *infected* – was not simply a rationalised intuition, I mean, clothed in isinglass! We had come to the wrong shop, with the wrong change! A chill struck us as we saw the mist falling in Trafalgar Square, coiling around us its tendrils of ectoplasm! A million muffin-eating moralists were waiting, not for us, Brother Ass, but for the plucky and tedious Trollope! (If you are dissatisfied with your form, reach for the *curette*.) Now do you wonder if I laugh a little off-key? Do you ask yourself what has turned me into nature's bashful little aphorist? We who are, after all, simply poor

9 on 11pt

Walking along the Mall we wondered who all those men were – tall
hawk-featured men perched on balconies and high places, scanning the city with heavy binoculars. What were they seeking so earnestly? Who were they – so composed and steely-eyed? Timidly we stopped a policeman to ask him. 'They are publishers' he said mildly. Publishers! Our hearts stopped beating. 'They are on the look out for new talent.' Great God! It was for *us* they were waiting and watching! Then the kindly policeman lowered his voice confidentially and said in hollow and reverent tones: *'They are waiting for the new Trollope to be born!'* Do you remember, at these words, how heavy our suitcases suddenly felt? How our blood slowed, our footsteps lagged? Brother Ass, we had been bashfully thinking of a kind of illumination such as Rimbaud dreamed of – a nagging poem which was not didactic or expository but which *infected* – was not simply a rationalised intuition, I mean, clothed in isinglass! We had come to the wrong shop, with the wrong change! A chill struck us as we saw the mist falling in Trafalgar Square, coiling around us its tendrils of ectoplasm! A million

10 on 12pt

Walking along the Mall we wondered who all those men were
– tall hawk-featured men perched on balconies and high places, scanning the city with heavy binoculars. What were they seeking so earnestly? Who were they – so composed and steely-eyed? Timidly we stopped a policeman to ask him. 'They are publishers' he said mildly. Publishers! Our hearts stopped beating. 'They are on the look out for new talent.' Great God! It was for *us* they were waiting and watching! Then the kindly policeman lowered his voice confidentially and said in hollow and reverent tones: *'They are waiting for the new Trollope to be born!'* Do you remember, at these words, how heavy our suitcases suddenly felt? How our blood slowed, our footsteps lagged? Brother Ass, we had been bashfully thinking of a kind of illumination such as Rimbaud dreamed of – a nagging poem which was not didactic or expository but which *infected* – was not simply a rationalised intuition, I mean, clothed in isinglass! We had

11 on 13pt

Walking along the Mall we wondered who all those men were – tall hawk-featured men perched on balconies and high places, scanning the city with heavy binoculars. What were they seeking so earnestly? Who were they – so composed and steely-eyed? Timidly we stopped a policeman to ask him. 'They are publishers' he said mildly. Publishers! Our hearts stopped beating. 'They are on the look out for new talent.' Great God! It was for *us* they were waiting and watching! Then the kindly policeman lowered his voice confidentially and said in hollow and reverent tones: *'They are waiting for the new Trollope to be born!'* Do you remember, at these words, how heavy our suitcases suddenly felt? How our blood slowed, our footsteps lagged? Brother Ass, we had been bashfully thinking of a kind of illumination such as Rimbaud dreamed of – a nagging poem which was not didactic or expository but which *infected* – was not simply a rationalised intuition, I mean, clothed in isinglass! We had come to the wrong shop, with the wrong change! A chill struck us as we saw the mist falling in Trafalgar Square, coiling around us its tendrils of ectoplasm! A million muffin-eating moralists were waiting, not for us, Brother Ass, but for the plucky and tedious Trollope! (If you are dissatisfied with your form, reach for the *curette*.) Now do you wonder if I laugh a little off-key? Do you ask yourself what has

9 on 12pt

'They are publishers' he said mildly. Publishers! Our hearts stopped beating. 'They are on the look out for new talent.' Great God! It was for *us* they were waiting and watching! Then the kindly policeman lowered his voice confidentially and said in hollow and reverent tones: *'They are waiting for the new Trollope to be born!'* Do you remember, at these words, how heavy our suitcases suddenly felt? How our blood slowed, our footsteps lagged? Brother Ass, we had been bashfully thinking of a kind of illumination such as Rimbaud dreamed of – a nagging poem which was not didactic or expository but which *infected* – was not simply a rationalised intuition, I mean, clothed in isinglass! We had come to the wrong shop, with the wrong change! A chill struck us as we saw the mist falling in Trafalgar Square, coiling around us its tendrils of ectoplasm! A million muffin-eating moralists were waiting, not for us, Brother Ass, but for the plucky and tedious Trollope! (If you are dissatisfied with your form, reach for the *curette*.) Now do you wonder if I laugh a little off-key? Do you ask yourself

10 on 13.5pt

Walking along the Mall we wondered who all those men were – tall hawk-featured men perched on balconies and high places, scanning the city with heavy binoculars. What were they seeking so earnestly? Who were they – so composed and steely-eyed? Timidly we stopped a policeman to ask him. 'They are publishers' he said mildly. Publishers! Our hearts stopped beating. 'They are on the look out for new talent.' Great God! It was for *us* they were waiting and watching! Then the kindly policeman lowered his voice confidentially and said in hollow and reverent tones: *'They are waiting for the new Trollope to be born!'* Do you remember, at these words, how heavy our suitcases suddenly felt? How our blood slowed, our footsteps lagged? Brother Ass, we had been bashfully thinking of a kind of illumination such as Rimbaud dreamed of – a nagging poem which was not didactic or expository but which

11 on 14.5pt

Monotype **Imprint**

101 roman and italic
410 bold
Monotype 1912 (with assistance from Edward Johnston and J H Mason)
Copyfitting factor 43.8/41.6/48.7

Range also includes bold italic

Derived from late 18th-century types, including Caslon's. The first original book type designed for machine composition, it was cut for Gerard Meynell and his magazine *The Imprint*

Slightly thinner and less rich, especially in text sizes, than the original hot-metal designs. Looser fit. Italic opened out. General effect more spidery

Educational characters available

ABCDEFGHIJKLMNOP
QRSTUVWXYZ abcdefg
hijklmnopqrstuvwxyz
1234567890 1234567890
ff fi fl ffi ffl ()[]&£$.,;:-!?''

ABCDEFGHIJKLMNOP
QRSTUVWXYZ abcdefg
hijklmnopqrstuvwxyz
1234567890 1234567890
ff fi fl ffi ffl ( ) [ ] & £ $.,;:-!?''

ABCDEFGHIJKLMNOP
QRSTUVWXYZ abcdefg
hijklmnopqrstuvwxyz
1234567890 1234567890
ff fi fl ffi ffl ()[]&£$.,;:-!?''

24 on 27pt

These examples show *normal* letterspacing and the effect of *reduced* letterspacing on roman setting *as well as on words in italic*: they also show the appearance of figures, for example 28 May 1964, within text. These & the ampersand are not included in the setting opposite.

Normal letterspacing

These examples show *normal* letterspacing and the effect of *reduced* letterspacing on roman setting *as well as on words in italic*: they also show the appearance of figures, for example 28 May 1964, within text. These & the ampersand are not included in the setting opposite.

Minus one unit spacing

These examples show *normal* letterspacing and the effect of *reduced* letterspacing on roman setting *as well as on words in italic*: they also show the appearance of figures, for example 28 May 1964, within text. These & the ampersand are not included in the setting opposite.

Minus two units spacing

WALKING ALONG THE MALL WE WONDERED WHO ALL
WALKING ALONG THE MALL WE WONDERED WHO
WALKING ALONG THE MALL WE WONDERED

Capitals: normal letterspacing/plus 9 units/plus 18 units

WALKING ALONG THE MALL WE WONDERED WHO ALL THOSE MEN WERE
WALKING ALONG THE MALL WE WONDERED WHO ALL THOSE MEN
WALKING ALONG THE MALL WE WONDERED WHO ALL THOSE

Small caps: normal letterspacing/plus 6 units/plus 12 units

WALKING ALONG THE MALL we wondered who all those men were
WALKING ALONG THE MALL we wondered who all those men

True italic/sloped roman

WALKING ALONG THE MALL WE WONDERED WHO ALL THOSE MEN WERE
WALKING ALONG THE MALL WE WONDERED WHO ALL THOSE MEN WERE

True small caps/reduced capitals

Walking along the Mall we wondered who all those men were – tall hawk- featured men perched on balconies and high places, scanning the city with heavy binoculars. What were they seeking so earnestly? Who were they – so composed and steely-eyed? Timidly we stopped a policeman to ask him. 'They are publishers' he said mildly. Publishers! Our hearts stopped beating. 'They are on the look out for new talent.' Great God! It was for *us* they were waiting and watching! Then the kindly policeman lowered his voice confidentially and said in hollow and reverent tones: '*They are waiting for the new Trollope to be born!*' Do you remember, at these words, how heavy our suitcases suddenly felt? How our blood slowed, our footsteps lagged? Brother Ass, we had been bashfully thinking of a kind of illumination such as

8 on 9pt

WALKING ALONG THE MALL WE WONDERED WHO ALL THOSE MEN WERE – TALL hawk-featured men perched on balconies and high places, scanning the city with heavy binoculars. What were they seeking so earnestly? Who were they – so composed and steely-eyed? Timidly we stopped a policeman to ask him. 'They are publishers' he said mildly. Publishers! Our hearts stopped beating. 'They are on the look out for new talent.' Great God! It was for *us* they were waiting and watching! Then the kindly policeman lowered his voice confidentially and said in hollow and reverent tones: '*They are waiting for the new Trollope to be born!*' Do you remember, at these words, how heavy our suitcases suddenly felt? How our blood slowed, our footsteps

8 on 10.5pt

Walking along the Mall we wondered who all those men were – tall hawk-featured men perched on balconies and high places, scanning the city with heavy binoculars. What were they seeking so earnestly? Who were they – so composed and steely-eyed? Timidly we stopped a policeman to ask him. 'They are publishers' he said mildly. Publishers! Our hearts stopped beating. 'They are on the look out for new talent.' Great God! It was for *us* they were waiting and watching! Then the kindly policeman lowered his voice confidentially and said in hollow and reverent tones: *'They are waiting for the new Trollope to be born!'* Do you remember, at these words, how heavy our suitcases suddenly felt? How our blood slowed, our footsteps lagged? Brother Ass, we had been bashfully thinking of a kind of illumination such as Rimbaud dreamed of – a nagging poem which was not didactic or expository but which *infected* – was not simply a rationalised intuition, I mean, clothed in isinglass! We had come to the wrong shop, with the wrong change! A chill struck us as we saw the mist falling in Trafalgar Square, coiling around us its tendrils of ectoplasm! A million muffin-eating moralists were waiting, not for us, Brother Ass, but for the plucky and tedious Trollope! (If you are dissatisfied with your form, reach for the *curette*.) Now do you wonder if I laugh a little off-key? Do

9 on 11pt

Walking along the Mall we wondered who all those men were – tall hawk-featured men perched on balconies and high places, scanning the city with heavy binoculars. What were they seeking so earnestly? Who were they – so composed and steely-eyed? Timidly we stopped a policeman to ask him. 'They are publishers' he said mildly. Publishers! Our hearts stopped beating. 'They are on the look out for new talent.' Great God! It was for *us* they were waiting and watching! Then the kindly policeman lowered his voice confidentially and said in hollow and reverent tones: *'They are waiting for the new Trollope to be born!'* Do you remember, at these words, how heavy our suitcases suddenly felt? How our blood slowed, our footsteps lagged? Brother Ass, we had been bashfully thinking of a kind of illumination such as Rimbaud dreamed of – a nagging poem which was not didactic or expository but which *infected* – was not simply a rationalised intuition, I mean, clothed in isinglass! We had come to the wrong shop, with the wrong change! A chill struck us as we saw the mist falling in Trafalgar

10 on 12pt

Walking along the Mall we wondered who all those men were – tall hawk-featured men perched on balconies and high places, scanning the city with heavy binoculars. What were they seeking so earnestly? Who were they – so composed and steely-eyed? Timidly we stopped a policeman to ask him. 'They are publishers' he said mildly. Publishers! Our hearts stopped beating. 'They are on the look out for new talent.' Great God! It was for *us* they were waiting and watching! Then the kindly policeman lowered his voice confidentially and said in hollow and reverent tones: *'They are waiting for the new Trollope to be born!'* Do you remember, at these words, how heavy our suitcases suddenly felt? How our blood slowed, our footsteps lagged? Brother Ass, we had been bashfully thinking of a kind of illumination such as Rimbaud dreamed of – a nagging poem which was not didactic or expository but which *infected* – was not simply a

11 on 13pt

WALKING ALONG THE MALL WE WONDERED WHO ALL THOSE MEN WERE – tall hawk-featured men perched on balconies and high places, scanning the city with heavy binoculars. What were they seeking so earnestly? Who were they – so composed and steely-eyed? Timidly we stopped a policeman to ask him. 'They are publishers' he said mildly. Publishers! Our hearts stopped beating. 'They are on the look out for new talent.' Great God! It was for *us* they were waiting and watching! Then the kindly policeman lowered his voice confidentially and said in hollow and reverent tones: *'They are waiting for the new Trollope to be born!'* Do you remember, at these words, how heavy our suitcases suddenly felt? How our blood slowed, our footsteps lagged? Brother Ass, we had been bashfully thinking of a kind of illumination such as Rimbaud dreamed of – a nagging poem which was not didactic or expository but which *infected* – was not simply a rationalised intuition, I mean, clothed in isinglass! We had come to the wrong shop, with the wrong change! A chill struck us as we saw the mist falling in Trafalgar Square, coiling around us its tendrils of ectoplasm! A million muffin-eating moralists were waiting, not for us, Brother Ass, but for the plucky and tedious Trollope! (If you are dissatisfied with your

9 on 12pt

WALKING ALONG THE MALL WE WONDERED WHO ALL THOSE MEN were – tall hawk-featured men perched on balconies and high places, scanning the city with heavy binoculars. What were they seeking so earnestly? Who were they – so composed and steely-eyed? Timidly we stopped a policeman to ask him. 'They are publishers' he said mildly. Publishers! Our hearts stopped beating. 'They are on the look out for new talent.' Great God! It was for *us* they were waiting and watching! Then the kindly policeman lowered his voice confidentially and said in hollow and reverent tones: *'They are waiting for the new Trollope to be born!'* Do you remember, at these words, how heavy our suitcases suddenly felt? How our blood slowed, our footsteps lagged? Brother Ass, we had been bashfully thinking of a kind of illumination such as Rimbaud dreamed of – a nagging poem which was not didactic or expository but which *infected* – was not simply a rationalised intuition, I mean, clothed in isinglass! We had come to the wrong shop, with the

10 on 13.5pt

WALKING ALONG THE MALL WE WONDERED WHO ALL THOSE men were – tall hawk-featured men perched on balconies and high places, scanning the city with heavy binoculars. What were they seeking so earnestly? Who were they – so composed and steely-eyed? Timidly we stopped a policeman to ask him. 'They are publishers' he said mildly. Publishers! Our hearts stopped beating. 'They are on the look out for new talent.' Great God! It was for *us* they were waiting and watching! Then the kindly policeman lowered his voice confidentially and said in hollow and reverent tones: *'They are waiting for the new Trollope to be born!'* Do you remember, at these words, how heavy our suitcases suddenly felt? How our blood slowed, our footsteps lagged? Brother Ass, we had been bashfully thinking of a kind of illumination such as Rimbaud dreamed of – a nagging poem

11 on 14.5pt

Linotype **Imprint**

roman (05135), **italic** (13135)
bold (07135)
Monotype 1912
Copyfitting code 125/123/142

Educational characters available

see Monotype Imprint

ABCDEFGHIJKLMNOP
QRSTUVWXYZ abcdefg
hijklmnopqrstuvwxyz
1234567890 1234567890
fifl ()[]&£$.,;:-!?"

ABCDEFGHIJKLMNOP
QRSTUVWXYZ abcdefg
hijklmnopqrstuvwxyz
1234567890 1234567890
fifl ()[]&£$.,;:-!?"

ABCDEFGHIJKLMNOP
QRSTUVWXYZ abcdefg
hijklmnopqrstuvwxyz
1234567890 1234567890
fifl ()[]&£$.,;:-!?"

24 on 27pt

These examples show *normal* letterspacing and the effect of *reduced* letterspacing on roman setting *as well as on words in italic*: they also show the appearance of figures, for example 28 May 1964, within text. These & the ampersand are not included in the setting opposite.
Normal letterspacing

These examples show *normal* letterspacing and the effect of *reduced* letterspacing on roman setting *as well as on words in italic*: they also show the appearance of figures, for example 28 May 1964, within text. These & the ampersand are not included in the setting opposite.
Minus one unit spacing

These examples show *normal* letterspacing and the effect of *reduced* letterspacing on roman setting *as well as on words in italic*: they also show the appearance of figures, for example 28 May 1964, within text. These & the ampersand are not included in the setting opposite.
Minus two units spacing

WALKING ALONG THE MALL WE WONDERED WHO ALL
WALKING ALONG THE MALL WE WONDERED WHO
WALKING ALONG THE MALL WE WONDERED
Capitals: normal letterspacing/plus 4 units/plus 9 units

WALKING ALONG THE MALL WE WONDERED WHO ALL THOSE MEN WERE
WALKING ALONG THE MALL WE WONDERED WHO ALL THOSE MEN
WALKING ALONG THE MALL WE WONDERED WHO ALL THOSE
Small caps: normal letterspacing/plus 3 units/plus 6 units

WALKING ALONG THE MALL WE WONDERED WHO ALL THOSE MEN WERE
WALKING ALONG THE MALL WE WONDERED WHO ALL THOSE MEN WERE
True small caps/reduced capitals

WALKING ALONG THE MALL we wondered who all those men were
WALKING ALONG THE MALL we wondered who all those men
True italic/sloped roman

Walking along the Mall we wondered who all those men were – tall hawk-featured men perched on balconies and high places, scanning the city with heavy binoculars. What were they seeking so earnestly? Who were they – so composed and steely-eyed? Timidly we stopped a policeman to ask him. 'They are publishers' he said mildly. Publishers! Our hearts stopped beating. 'They are on the look out for new talent.' Great God! It was for *us* they were waiting and watching! Then the kindly policeman lowered his voice confidentially and said in hollow and reverent tones: *'They are waiting for the new Trollope to be born!'* Do you remember, at these words, how heavy our suitcases suddenly felt? How our blood slowed, our footsteps lagged? Brother Ass, we had been bashfully thinking of a kind of illumination such as Rimbaud dreamed of – a
8 on 9pt

WALKING ALONG THE MALL WE WONDERED WHO ALL THOSE MEN WERE – TALL HAWK-featured men perched on balconies and high places, scanning the city with heavy binoculars. What were they seeking so earnestly? Who were they – so composed and steely-eyed? Timidly we stopped a policeman to ask him. 'They are publishers' he said mildly. Publishers! Our hearts stopped beating. 'They are on the look out for new talent.' Great God! It was for *us* they were waiting and watching! Then the kindly policeman lowered his voice confidentially and said in hollow and reverent tones: *'They are waiting for the new Trollope to be born!'* Do you remember, at these words, how heavy our suitcases suddenly felt? How our blood slowed, our footsteps lagged? Brother Ass, we
8 on 10.5pt

Walking along the Mall we wondered who all those men were – tall hawk-featured men perched on balconies and high places, scanning the city with heavy binoculars. What were they seeking so earnestly? Who were they – so composed and steely-eyed? Timidly we stopped a policeman to ask him. 'They are publishers' he said mildly. Publishers! Our hearts stopped beating. 'They are on the look out for new talent.' Great God! It was for *us* they were waiting and watching! Then the kindly policeman lowered his voice confidentially and said in hollow and reverent tones: *'They are waiting for the new Trollope to be born!'* Do you remember, at these words, how heavy our suitcases suddenly felt? How our blood slowed, our footsteps lagged? Brother Ass, we had been bashfully thinking of a kind of illumination such as Rimbaud dreamed of – a nagging poem which was not didactic or expository but which *infected* – was not simply a rationalised intuition, I mean, clothed in isinglass! We had come to the wrong shop, with the wrong change! A chill struck us as we saw the mist falling in Trafalgar Square, coiling round us its tendrils of ectoplasm! A million muffin-eating moralists were waiting, not for us, Brother Ass, but for the plucky and tedious Trollope! (If you are dissatisfied with your form, reach for the *curette*.) Now do you wonder if I laugh a little off-key? Do you ask your-

9 on 11pt

Walking along the Mall we wondered who all those men were – tall hawk-featured men perched on balconies and high places, scanning the city with heavy binoculars. What were they seeking so earnestly? Who were they – so composed and steely-eyed? Timidly we stopped a policeman to ask him. 'They are publishers' he said mildly. Publishers! Our hearts stopped beating. 'They are on the look out for new talent.' Great God! It was for *us* they were waiting and watching! Then the kindly policeman lowered his voice confidentially and said in hollow and reverent tones: *'They are waiting for the new Trollope to be born!'* Do you remember, at these words, how heavy our suitcases suddenly felt? How our blood slowed, our footsteps lagged? Brother Ass, we had been bashfully thinking of a kind of illumination such as Rimbaud dreamed of – a nagging poem which was not didactic or expository but which *infected* – was not simply a rationalised intuition, I mean, clothed in isinglass! We had come to the wrong shop, with the wrong change! A chill struck us as we saw the mist falling in Trafalgar Square, coiling

10 on 12pt

Walking along the Mall we wondered who all those men were – tall hawk-featured men perched on balconies and high places, scanning the city with heavy binoculars. What were they seeking so earnestly? Who were they – so composed and steely-eyed? Timidly we stopped a policeman to ask him. 'They are publishers' he said mildly. Publishers! Our hearts stopped beating. 'They are on the look out for new talent.' Great God! It was for *us* they were waiting and watching! Then the kindly policeman lowered his voice confidentially and said in hollow and reverent tones: *'They are waiting for the new Trollope to be born!'* Do you remember, at these words, how heavy our suitcases suddenly felt? How our blood slowed, our footsteps lagged? Brother Ass, we had been bashfully thinking of a kind of illumination such as Rimbaud dreamed of – a nagging poem which was not didactic or expository but which *infected* – was not simply a

11 on 13pt

WALKING ALONG THE MALL WE WONDERED WHO ALL THOSE MEN WERE – TALL hawk-featured men perched on balconies and high places, scanning the city with heavy binoculars. What were they seeking so earnestly? Who were they – so composed and steely-eyed? Timidly we stopped a policeman to ask him. 'They are publishers' he said mildly. Publishers! Our hearts stopped beating. 'They are on the look out for new talent.' Great God! It was for *us* they were waiting and watching! Then the kindly policeman lowered his voice confidentially and said in hollow and reverent tones: *'They are waiting for the new Trollope to be born!'* Do you remember, at these words, how heavy our suitcases suddenly felt? How our blood slowed, our footsteps lagged? Brother Ass, we had been bashfully thinking of a kind of illumination such as Rimbaud dreamed of – a nagging poem which was not didactic or expository but which *infected* – was not simply a rationalised intuition, I mean, clothed in isinglass! We had come to the wrong shop, with the wrong change! A chill struck us as we saw the mist falling in Trafalgar Square, coiling round us its tendrils of ectoplasm! A million muffin-eating moralists were waiting, not for us, Brother Ass, but for the plucky and tedious Trollope! (If you are dissatisfied with your form, reach

9 on 12pt

WALKING ALONG THE MALL WE WONDERED WHO ALL THOSE MEN WERE – tall hawk-featured men perched on balconies and high places, scanning the city with heavy binoculars. What were they seeking so earnestly? Who were they – so composed and steely-eyed? Timidly we stopped a policeman to ask him. 'They are publishers' he said mildly. Publishers! Our hearts stopped beating. 'They are on the look out for new talent.' Great God! It was for *us* they were waiting and watching! Then the kindly policeman lowered his voice confidentially and said in hollow and reverent tones: *'They are waiting for the new Trollope to be born!'* Do you remember, at these words, how heavy our suitcases suddenly felt? How our blood slowed, our footsteps lagged? Brother Ass, we had been bashfully thinking of a kind of illumination such as Rimbaud dreamed of – a nagging poem which was not didactic or expository but which *infected* – was not simply a rationalised intuition, I mean, clothed in isinglass! We had come to the wrong shop, with the

10 on 13.5pt

WALKING ALONG THE MALL WE WONDERED WHO ALL THOSE MEN were – tall hawk-featured men perched on balconies and high places, scanning the city with heavy binoculars. What were they seeking so earnestly? Who were they – so composed and steely-eyed? Timidly we stopped a policeman to ask him. 'They are publishers' he said mildly. Publishers! Our hearts stopped beating. 'They are on the look out for new talent.' Great God! It was for *us* they were waiting and watching! Then the kindly policeman lowered his voice confidentially and said in hollow and reverent tones: *'They are waiting for the new Trollope to be born!'* Do you remember, at these words, how heavy our suitcases suddenly felt? How our blood slowed, our footsteps lagged? Brother Ass, we had been bashfully thinking of a kind of illumination such as Rimbaud dreamed of – a nagging poem which was

11 on 14.5pt

LINOTYPE IMPRINT

Monotype **Ionic**

342 roman and italic
1137 bold
Monotype 1932 (bold: 1985)
Copyfitting factor 51.8/48.4/48.5

ABCDEFGHIJKLMNOP
QRSTUVWXYZ abcdefg
hijklmnopqrstuvwxyz
1234567890
ff fi fl ffi ffl ()[]&£$.,;:-!?''

ABCDEFGHIJKLMNOP
QRSTUVWXYZ abcdefg
hijklmnopqrstuvwxyz
1234567890
ff fi fl ffi ffl ()[]&£$.,;:-!?''

ABCDEFGHIJKLMNOP
QRSTUVWXYZ abcdefg
hijklmnopqrstuvwxyz
1234567890
ff fi fl ffi ffl ()[]&£$.,;:-!?''

24 on 27pt

These examples show *normal* letterspacing and the effect of *reduced* letterspacing on roman setting *as well as on words in italic*: they also show the appearance of figures, for example 28 May 1964, within text. These & the ampersand are not included in the setting opposite.

Normal letterspacing

These examples show *normal* letterspacing and the effect of *reduced* letterspacing on roman setting *as well as on words in italic*: they also show the appearance of figures, for example 28 May 1964, within text. These & the ampersand are not included in the setting opposite.

Minus one unit spacing

These examples show *normal* letterspacing and the effect of *reduced* letterspacing on roman setting *as well as on words in italic*: they also show the appearance of figures, for example 28 May 1964, within text. These & the ampersand are not included in the setting opposite.

Minus two units spacing

WALKING ALONG THE MALL WE WONDERED WHO ALL
WALKING ALONG THE MALL WE WONDERED WHO
WALKING ALONG THE MALL WE WONDERED

Capitals: normal letterspacing/plus 9 units/plus 18 units

Walking along the Mall we wondered who all those men were – tall hawk-featured men perched on balconies and high places, SCANNING THE CITY with heavy binoculars. What were they seeking so earnestly? Who were they – so composed and steely-eyed? TIMIDLY WE STOPPED A POLICEMAN to ask him. 'They are publishers' he said mildly. Publishers! Our hearts stopped beating. 'They are on the look out for new talent.' Great God! It was for *us* they were waiting and watching! Then

Text with reduced capitals normal letterspacing/plus 6 units

WALKING ALONG THE MALL we wondered who all those men were
WALKING ALONG THE MALL we wondered who all those men

True italic/sloped roman

Walking along the Mall we wondered who all those men were – tall hawk-featured men perched on balconies and high places, scanning the city with heavy binoculars. What were they seeking so earnestly? Who were they – so composed and steely-eyed? Timidly we stopped a policeman to ask him. 'They are publishers' he said mildly. Publishers! Our hearts stopped beating. 'They are on the look out for new talent.' Great God! It was for *us* they were waiting and watching! Then the kindly policeman lowered his voice confidentially and said in hollow and reverent tones: *'They are waiting for the new Trollope to be born!'* Do you remember, at these words, how heavy our suitcases suddenly felt? How our blood

8 on 9pt

Walking along the Mall we wondered who all those men were – tall hawk-featured men perched on balconies and high places, scanning the city with heavy binoculars. What were they seeking so earnestly? Who were they – so composed and steely-eyed? Timidly we stopped a policeman to ask him. 'They are publishers' he said mildly. Publishers! Our hearts stopped beating. 'They are on the look out for new talent.' Great God! It was for *us* they were waiting and watching! Then the kindly policeman lowered his voice confidentially and said in hollow and reverent tones: *'They are waiting for the new Trollope to be born!'*

8 on 10.5pt

Walking along the Mall we wondered who all those men were – tall hawk-featured men perched on balconies and high places, scanning the city with heavy binoculars. What were they seeking so earnestly? Who were they – so composed and steely-eyed? Timidly we stopped a policeman to ask him. 'They are publishers' he said mildly. Publishers! Our hearts stopped beating. 'They are on the look out for new talent.' Great God! It was for *us* they were waiting and watching! Then the kindly policeman lowered his voice confidentially and said in hollow and reverent tones: *'They are waiting for the new Trollope to be born!'* Do you remember, at these words, how heavy our suitcases suddenly felt? How our blood slowed, our footsteps lagged? Brother Ass, we had been bashfully thinking of a kind of illumination such as Rimbaud dreamed of – a nagging poem which was not didactic or expository but which *infected* – was not simply a rationalised intuition, I mean, clothed in isinglass! We had come to the wrong shop, with the wrong change! A chill struck us as we saw the mist falling in Trafalgar Square, coiling around us its tendrils of ectoplasm! A

9 on 11pt

Walking along the Mall we wondered who all those men were – tall hawk-featured men perched on balconies and high places, scanning the city with heavy binoculars. What were they seeking so earnestly? Who were they – so composed and steely-eyed? Timidly we stopped a policeman to ask him. 'They are publishers' he said mildly. Publishers! Our hearts stopped beating. 'They are on the look out for new talent.' Great God! It was for *us* they were waiting and watching! Then the kindly policeman lowered his voice confidentially and said in hollow and reverent tones: *'They are waiting for the new Trollope to be born!'* Do you remember, at these words, how heavy our suitcases suddenly felt? How our blood slowed, our footsteps lagged? Brother Ass, we had been bashfully thinking of a kind of illumination such as Rimbaud dreamed of – a nagging poem which was not didactic or expository but which *infected* – was not

10 on 12pt

Walking along the Mall we wondered who all those men were – tall hawk-featured men perched on balconies and high places, scanning the city with heavy binoculars. What were they seeking so earnestly? Who were they – so composed and steely-eyed? Timidly we stopped a policeman to ask him. 'They are publishers' he said mildly. Publishers! Our hearts stopped beating. 'They are on the look out for new talent.' Great God! It was for *us* they were waiting and watching! Then the kindly policeman lowered his voice confidentially and said in hollow and reverent tones: *'They are waiting for the new Trollope to be born!'* Do you remember, at these words, how heavy our suitcases suddenly felt? How our blood slowed, our footsteps lagged? Brother Ass, we had been bashfully thinking

11 on 13pt

Walking along the Mall we wondered who all those men were – tall hawk-featured men perched on balconies and high places, scanning the city with heavy binoculars. What were they seeking so earnestly? Who were they – so composed and steely-eyed? Timidly we stopped a policeman to ask him. 'They are publishers' he said mildly. Publishers! Our hearts stopped beating. 'They are on the look out for new talent.' Great God! It was for *us* they were waiting and watching! Then the kindly policeman lowered his voice confidentially and said in hollow and reverent tones: *'They are waiting for the new Trollope to be born!'* Do you remember, at these words, how heavy our suitcases suddenly felt? How our blood slowed, our footsteps lagged? Brother Ass, we had been bashfully thinking of a kind of illumination such as Rimbaud dreamed of – a nagging poem which was not didactic or expository but which *infected* – was not simply a rationalised intuition, I mean, clothed in isinglass! We had come to the wrong shop, with the wrong change! A chill struck us as we saw the mist falling in

9 on 12pt

Walking along the Mall we wondered who all those men were – tall hawk-featured men perched on balconies and high places, scanning the city with heavy binoculars. What were they seeking so earnestly? Who were they – so composed and steely-eyed? Timidly we stopped a policeman to ask him. 'They are publishers' he said mildly. Publishers! Our hearts stopped beating. 'They are on the look out for new talent.' Great God! It was for *us* they were waiting and watching! Then the kindly policeman lowered his voice confidentially and said in hollow and reverent tones: *'They are waiting for the new Trollope to be born!'* Do you remember, at these words, how heavy our suitcases suddenly felt? How our blood slowed, our footsteps lagged? Brother Ass, we had been bashfully thinking of a kind of illumination such as Rimbaud dreamed of – a nagging poem which was

10 on 13.5pt

Walking along the Mall we wondered who all those men were – tall hawk-featured men perched on balconies and high places, scanning the city with heavy binoculars. What were they seeking so earnestly? Who were they – so composed and steely-eyed? Timidly we stopped a policeman to ask him. 'They are publishers' he said mildly. Publishers! Our hearts stopped beating. 'They are on the look out for new talent.' Great God! It was for *us* they were waiting and watching! Then the kindly policeman lowered his voice confidentially and said in hollow and reverent tones: *'They are waiting for the new Trollope to be born!'* Do you remember, at these words, how heavy our suitcases suddenly felt? How our blood slowed, our

11 on 14.5pt

Linotype **Iridium**

roman (05137), **italic** (13137)
bold (07137)
Stempel 1972 (Adrian Frutiger)
Copyfitting code 135/132/137

ABCDEFGHIJKLMNOP
QRSTUVWXYZ abcdefg
hijklmnopqrstuvwxyz
1234567890
fifl ()[]&£$.,;:-!?"

ABCDEFGHIJKLMNOP
QRSTUVWXYZ abcdefg
hijklmnopqrstuvwxyz
1234567890
fifl ()[]&£$.,;:-!?"

ABCDEFGHIJKLMNOP
QRSTUVWXYZ abcdefg
hijklmnopqrstuvwxyz
1234567890
fifl ()[]&£$.,;:-!?"

24 on 27pt

These examples show *normal* letterspacing and the effect of *reduced* letterspacing on roman setting *as well as on words in italic*: they also show the appearance of figures, for example 28 May 1964, within text. These & the ampersand are not included in the setting opposite.
Normal letterspacing

These examples show *normal* letterspacing and the effect of *reduced* letterspacing on roman setting *as well as on words in italic*: they also show the appearance of figures, for example 28 May 1964, within text. These & the ampersand are not included in the setting opposite.
Minus one unit spacing

These examples show *normal* letterspacing and the effect of *reduced* letterspacing on roman setting *as well as on words in italic*: they also show the appearance of figures, for example 28 May 1964, within text. These & the ampersand are not included in the setting opposite.
Minus two units spacing

WALKING ALONG THE MALL WE WONDERED WHO ALL THOSE
WALKING ALONG THE MALL WE WONDERED WHO ALL
WALKING ALONG THE MALL WE WONDERED WHO
Capitals: normal letterspacing/plus 4 units/plus 9 units

Walking along the Mall we wondered who all those men were – tall hawk-featured men perched on balconies and high places, scanning the city with heavy binoculars. WHAT WERE THEY SEEKING SO EARNESTLY? Who were they – so composed and steely-eyed? Timidly we stopped a policeman to ask him. 'THEY ARE PUBLISHERS' he said mildly. Publishers! Our hearts stopped beating. 'They are on the look out for new talent.' Great God! It was for *us* they were waiting and watching! Then the kindly policeman
Text with reduced caps normal letterspacing/plus 3 units

WALKING ALONG THE MALL we wondered who all those men were
WALKING ALONG THE MALL we wondered who all those men were
True italic/sloped roman

Walking along the Mall we wondered who all those men were – tall hawk-featured men perched on balconies and high places, scanning the city with heavy binoculars. What were they seeking so earnestly? Who were they – so composed and steely-eyed? Timidly we stopped a policeman to ask him. 'They are publishers' he said mildly. Publishers! Our hearts stopped beating. 'They are on the look out for new talent.' Great God! It was for *us* they were waiting and watching! Then the kindly policeman lowered his voice confidentially and said in hollow and reverent tones: *'They are waiting for the new Trollope to be born!'* Do you remember, at these words, how heavy our suitcases suddenly felt? How our blood slowed, our footsteps lagged? Brother Ass, we had been bashfully thinking of a kind of
8 on 9pt

Walking along the Mall we wondered who all those men were – tall hawk-featured men perched on balconies and high places, scanning the city with heavy binoculars. What were they seeking so earnestly? Who were they – so composed and steely-eyed? Timidly we stopped a policeman to ask him. 'They are publishers' he said mildly. Publishers! Our hearts stopped beating. 'They are on the look out for new talent.' Great God! It was for *us* they were waiting and watching! Then the kindly policeman lowered his voice confidentially and said in hollow and reverent tones: *'They are waiting for the new Trollope to be born!'* Do you remember, at these words, how heavy our suitcases suddenly felt? How our blood slowed, our
8 on 10.5pt

Walking along the Mall we wondered who all those men were – tall hawk-featured men perched on balconies and high places, scanning the city with heavy binoculars. What were they seeking so earnestly? Who were they – so composed and steely-eyed? Timidly we stopped a policeman to ask him. 'They are publishers' he said mildly. Publishers! Our hearts stopped beating. 'They are on the look out for new talent.' Great God! It was for *us* they were waiting and watching! Then the kindly policeman lowered his voice confidentially and said in hollow and reverent tones: *'They are waiting for the new Trollope to be born!'* Do you remember, at these words, how heavy our suitcases suddenly felt? How our blood slowed, our footsteps lagged? Brother Ass, we had been bashfully thinking of a kind of illumination such as Rimbaud dreamed of – a nagging poem which was not didactic or expository but which *infected* – was not simply a rationalised intuition, I mean, clothed in isinglass! We had come to the wrong shop, with the wrong change! A chill struck us as we saw the mist falling in Trafalgar Square, coiling round us its tendrils of ectoplasm! A million muffin-eating moralists were waiting, not for us, Brother Ass, but for the plucky and tedious Trollope! (If you are dis-
9 on 11pt

Walking along the Mall we wondered who all those men were – tall hawk-featured men perched on balconies and high places, scanning the city with heavy binoculars. What were they seeking so earnestly? Who were they – so composed and steely-eyed? Timidly we stopped a policeman to ask him. 'They are publishers' he said mildly. Publishers! Our hearts stopped beating. 'They are on the look out for new talent.' Great God! It was for *us* they were waiting and watching! Then the kindly policeman lowered his voice confidentially and said in hollow and reverent tones: *'They are waiting for the new Trollope to be born!'* Do you remember, at these words, how heavy our suitcases suddenly felt? How our blood slowed, our footsteps lagged? Brother Ass, we had been bashfully thinking of a kind of illumination such as Rimbaud dreamed of – a nagging poem which was not didactic or expository but which *infected* – was not simply a rationalised intuition, I mean, clothed in isinglass! We had come to the wrong shop, with
10 on 12pt

Walking along the Mall we wondered who all those men were – tall hawk-featured men perched on balconies and high places, scanning the city with heavy binoculars. What were they seeking so earnestly? Who were they – so composed and steely-eyed? Timidly we stopped a policeman to ask him. 'They are publishers' he said mildly. Publishers! Our hearts stopped beating. 'They are on the look out for new talent.' Great God! It was for *us* they were waiting and watching! Then the kindly policeman lowered his voice confidentially and said in hollow and reverent tones: *'They are waiting for the new Trollope to be born!'* Do you remember, at these words, how heavy our suitcases suddenly felt? How our blood slowed, our footsteps lagged? Brother Ass, we had been bashfully thinking of a kind of illumination such as Rimbaud dreamed of – a nagging poem which was not
11 on 13pt

Walking along the Mall we wondered who all those men were – tall hawk-featured men perched on balconies and high places, scanning the city with heavy binoculars. What were they seeking so earnestly? Who were they – so composed and steely-eyed? Timidly we stopped a policeman to ask him. 'They are publishers' he said mildly. Publishers! Our hearts stopped beating. 'They are on the look out for new talent.' Great God! It was for *us* they were waiting and watching! Then the kindly policeman lowered his voice confidentially and said in hollow and reverent tones: *'They are waiting for the new Trollope to be born!'* Do you remember, at these words, how heavy our suitcases suddenly felt? How our blood slowed, our footsteps lagged? Brother Ass, we had been bashfully thinking of a kind of illumination such as Rimbaud dreamed of – a nagging poem which was not didactic or expository but which *infected* – was not simply a rationalised intuition,
10 on 13.5pt

Walking along the Mall we wondered who all those men were – tall hawk-featured men perched on balconies and high places, scanning the city with heavy binoculars. What were they seeking so earnestly? Who were they – so composed and steely-eyed? Timidly we stopped a policeman to ask him. 'They are publishers' he said mildly. Publishers! Our hearts stopped beating. 'They are on the look out for new talent.' Great God! It was for *us* they were waiting and watching! Then the kindly policeman lowered his voice confidentially and said in hollow and reverent tones: *'They are waiting for the new Trollope to be born!'* Do you remember, at these words, how heavy our suitcases suddenly felt? How our blood slowed, our footsteps lagged? Brother Ass, we had been bashfully thinking of a kind of illumination such
11 on 14.5pt

Monotype **Italian Old Style**

108 roman and italic
149 bold
Monotype 1911
Copyfitting factor 41.5/37.9/45.4

Range also includes bold italic

The design reflects types of Nicholas Jenson
and his Venetian contemporaries of the 1470s

ABCDEFGHIJKLMNOP
QRSTUVWXYZ abcdefg
hijklmnopqrstuvwxyz
1234567890
ff fi fl ffi ffl ()[]&£$.,;:-!?''

ABCDEFGHIJKLMNOP
QRSTUVWXYZ abcdefg
hijklmnopqrstuvwxyz
1234567890
ff fi fl ffi ffl ()[]&£$.,;:-!?''

ABCDEFGHIJKLMNOP
QRSTUVWXYZ abcdefg
hijklmnopqrstuvwxyz
1234567890
ff fi fl ffi ffl ()[]&£$.,;:-!?''

24 on 27pt

These examples show *normal* letterspacing and the effect of *reduced*
letterspacing on roman setting *as well as on words in italic*: they also
show the appearance of figures, for example 28 May 1964, within text.
These & the ampersand are not included in the setting opposite.

Normal letterspacing

These examples show *normal* letterspacing and the effect of *reduced*
letterspacing on roman setting *as well as on words in italic*: they also
show the appearance of figures, for example 28 May 1964, within text.
These & the ampersand are not included in the setting opposite.

Minus one unit spacing

These examples show *normal* letterspacing and the effect of *reduced*
letterspacing on roman setting *as well as on words in italic*: they also
show the appearance of figures, for example 28 May 1964, within text.
These & the ampersand are not included in the setting opposite.

Minus two units spacing

WALKING ALONG THE MALL WE WONDERED WHO ALL
WALKING ALONG THE MALL WE WONDERED WHO
WALKING ALONG THE MALL WE WONDERED

Capitals: normal letterspacing/plus 9 units/plus 18 units

WALKING ALONG THE MALL WE WONDERED WHO ALL THOSE MEN WERE
WALKING ALONG THE MALL WE WONDERED WHO ALL THOSE MEN
WALKING ALONG THE MALL WE WONDERED WHO ALL THOSE

Small caps: normal letterspacing/plus 6 units/plus 12 units

WALKING ALONG THE MALL we wondered who all those men were
WALKING ALONG THE MALL we wondered who all those men

True italic/sloped roman

WALKING ALONG THE MALL WE WONDERED WHO ALL THOSE MEN WERE
WALKING ALONG THE MALL WE WONDERED WHO ALL THOSE MEN WERE

True small caps/reduced capitals

Walking along the Mall we wondered who all those men were – tall hawk-featured
men perched on balconies and high places, scanning the city with heavy binoculars. What
were they seeking so earnestly? Who were they – so composed and steely-eyed? Timidly
we stopped a policeman to ask him. 'They are publishers' he said mildly. Publishers!
Our hearts stopped beating. 'They are on the look out for new talent.' Great God! It
was for *us* they were waiting and watching! Then the kindly policeman lowered his voice
confidentially and said in hollow and reverent tones: *'They are waiting for the new Trollope*
to be born!' Do you remember, at these words, how heavy our suitcases suddenly felt?
How our blood slowed, our footsteps lagged? Brother Ass, we had been bashfully
thinking of a kind of illumination such as Rimbaud dreamed of – a nagging poem

8 on 9pt

WALKING ALONG THE MALL WE WONDERED WHO ALL THOSE MEN WERE – TALL HAWK-
featured perched on balconies and high places, scanning the city with heavy binoculars.
What were they seeking so earnestly? Who were they – so composed and steely-eyed?
Timidly we stopped a policeman to ask him. 'They are publishers' he said mildly.
Publishers! Our hearts stopped beating. 'They are on the look out for new talent.' Great
God! It was for *us* they were waiting and watching! Then the kindly policeman lowered
his voice confidentially and said in hollow and reverent tones: *'They are waiting for the new*
Trollope to be born!' Do you remember, at these words, how heavy our suitcases suddenly
felt? How our blood slowed, our footsteps lagged? Brother Ass, we had been bashfully

8 on 10.5pt

Walking along the Mall we wondered who all those men were – tall hawk-featured men perched on balconies and high places, scanning the city with heavy binoculars. What were they seeking so earnestly? Who were they – so composed and steely-eyed? Timidly we stopped a policeman to ask him. 'They are publishers' he said mildly. Publishers! Our hearts stopped beating. 'They are on the look out for new talent.' Great God! It was for *us* they were waiting and watching! Then the kindly policeman lowered his voice confidentially and said in hollow and reverent tones: *'They are waiting for the new Trollope to be born!'* Do you remember, at these words, how heavy our suitcases suddenly felt? How our blood slowed, our footsteps lagged? Brother Ass, we had been bashfully thinking of a kind of illumination such as Rimbaud dreamed of – a nagging poem which was not didactic or expository but which *infected* – was not simply a rationalised intuition, I mean, clothed in isinglass! We had come to the wrong shop, with the wrong change! A chill struck us as we saw the mist falling in Trafalgar Square, coiling around us its tendrils of ectoplasm! A million muffin-eating moralists were waiting, not for us, Brother Ass, but for the plucky and tedious Trollope! (If you are dissatisfied with your form, reach for the *curette*.) Now do you wonder if I laugh a little off-key? Do you ask yourself what has turned me into nature's bashful little

9 on 11pt

Walking along the Mall we wondered who all those men were – tall hawk-featured men perched on balconies and high places, scanning the city with heavy binoculars. What were they seeking so earnestly? Who were they – so composed and steely-eyed? Timidly we stopped a police-man to ask him. 'They are publishers' he said mildly. Publishers! Our hearts stopped beating. 'They are on the look out for new talent.' Great God! It was for *us* they were waiting and watching! Then the kindly policeman lowered his voice confidentially and said in hollow and reverent tones: *'They are waiting for the new Trollope to be born!'* Do you remember, at these words, how heavy our suitcases suddenly felt? How our blood slowed, our footsteps lagged? Brother Ass, we had been bashfully thinking of a kind of illumination such as Rimbaud dreamed of – a nagging poem which was not didactic or expository but which *infected* – was not simply a rationalised intuition, I mean, clothed in isinglass! We had come to the wrong shop, with the wrong change! A chill struck us as we saw the mist falling in Trafalgar Square, coiling around us its tendrils of

10 on 12pt

Walking along the Mall we wondered who all those men were – tall hawk-featured men perched on balconies and high places, scanning the city with heavy binoculars. What were they seeking so earnestly? Who were they – so composed and steely-eyed? Timidly we stopped a policeman to ask him. 'They are publishers' he said mildly. Publishers! Our hearts stopped beating. 'They are on the look out for new talent.' Great God! It was for *us* they were waiting and watching! Then the kindly policeman lowered his voice confidentially and said in hollow and reverent tones: *'They are waiting for the new Trollope to be born!'* Do you remember, at these words, how heavy our suitcases suddenly felt? How our blood slowed, our footsteps lagged? Brother Ass, we had been bashfully thinking of a kind of illumination such as Rimbaud dreamed of – a nagging poem which was not didactic or expository but which *infected* – was not simply a rationalised intuition, I mean, clothed in isinglass! We

11 on 13pt

WALKING ALONG THE MALL WE WONDERED WHO ALL THOSE MEN WERE – TALL hawk-featured men perched on balconies and high places, scanning the city with heavy binoculars. What were they seeking so earnestly? Who were they – so composed and steely-eyed? Timidly we stopped a policeman to ask him. 'They are publishers' he said mildly. Publishers! Our hearts stopped beating. 'They are on the look out for new talent.' Great God! It was for *us* they were waiting and watching! Then the kindly policeman lowered his voice confidentially and said in hollow and reverent tones: *'They are waiting for the new Trollope to be born!'* Do you remember, at these words, how heavy our suitcases suddenly felt? How our blood slowed, our footsteps lagged? Brother Ass, we had been bashfully thinking of a kind of illumination such as Rimbaud dreamed of – a nagging poem which was not didactic or expository but which *infected* – was not simply a rationalised intuition, I mean, clothed in isinglass! We had come to the wrong shop, with the wrong change! A chill struck us as we saw the mist falling in Trafalgar Square, coiling around us its tendrils of ectoplasm! A million muffin-eating moralists were waiting, not for us, Brother Ass, but for the plucky and tedious Trollope! (If you are dissatisfied with your form, reach for the *curette*.) Now do you wonder if I laugh a

9 on 12pt

WALKING ALONG THE MALL WE WONDERED WHO ALL THOSE MEN WERE – tall hawk-featured men perched on balconies and high places, scanning the city with heavy binoculars. What were they seeking so earnestly? Who were they – so composed and steely-eyed? Timidly we stopped a police-man to ask him. 'They are publishers' he said mildly. Publishers! Our hearts stopped beating. 'They are on the look out for new talent.' Great God! It was for *us* they were waiting and watching! Then the kindly policeman lowered his voice confidentially and said in hollow and rever-ent tones: *'They are waiting for the new Trollope to be born!'* Do you remem-ber, at these words, how heavy our suitcases suddenly felt? How our blood slowed, our footsteps lagged? Brother Ass, we had been bashfully thinking of a kind of illumination such as Rimbaud dreamed of – a nag-ging poem which was not didactic or expository but which *infected* – was not simply a rationalised intuition, I mean, clothed in isinglass! We had come to the wrong shop, with the wrong change! A chill struck us as we

10 on 13.5pt

WALKING ALONG THE MALL WE WONDERED WHO ALL THOSE MEN were – tall hawk-featured men perched on balconies and high places, scanning the city with heavy binoculars. What were they seeking so earnestly? Who were they – so composed and steely-eyed? Timidly we stopped a policeman to ask him. 'They are pub-lishers' he said mildly. Publishers! Our hearts stopped beating. 'They are on the look out for new talent.' Great God! It was for *us* they were waiting and watching! Then the kindly policeman low-ered his voice confidentially and said in hollow and reverent tones: *'They are waiting for the new Trollope to be born!'* Do you remember, at these words, how heavy our suitcases suddenly felt? How our blood slowed, our footsteps lagged? Brother Ass, we had been bashfully thinking of a kind of illumination such as Rimbaud dreamed of – a nagging poem which was not didactic or expository

11 on 14.5pt

Monotype **Janson**

1173 roman and italic
1174 bold
Monotype 1986
Copyfitting factor 40.2/35.4/42.4

Range also includes bold italic

Derived from designs of 1720

ABCDEFGHIJKLMNOP
QRSTUVWXYZ abcdefg
hijklmnopqrstuvwxyz
1234567890 1234567890
ff fi fl ffi ffl () [] &£$.,;:-!?"

ABCDEFGHIJKLMNOP
QRSTUVWXYZ abcdefg
hijklmnopqrstuvwxyz
1234567890 1234567890
ff fi fl ffi ffl () [] &£$.,;:-!?"

ABCDEFGHIJKLMNOP
QRSTUVWXYZ abcdefg
hijklmnopqrstuvwxyz
1234567890 1234567890
ff fi fl ffi ffl () [] &£$.,;:-!?"

24 on 27pt

These examples show *normal* letterspacing and the effect of *reduced* letterspacing on roman setting *as well as on words in italic:* they also show the appearance of figures, for example 28 May 1964, within text. These & the ampersand are not included in the setting opposite.

Normal letterspacing

These examples show *normal* letterspacing and the effect of *reduced* letterspacing on roman setting *as well as on words in italic:* they also show the appearance of figures, for example 28 May 1964, within text. These & the ampersand are not included in the setting opposite.

Minus one unit spacing

These examples show *normal* letterspacing and the effect of *reduced* letterspacing on roman setting *as well as on words in italic:* they also show the appearance of figures, for example 28 May 1964, within text. These & the ampersand are not included in the setting opposite.

Minus two units spacing

WALKING ALONG THE MALL WE WONDERED WHO ALL THOSE
WALKING ALONG THE MALL WE WONDERED WHO ALL
WALKING ALONG THE MALL WE WONDERED WHO

Capitals: normal letterspacing/plus 9 units/plus 18 units

Walking along the Mall we wondered who all those men were – tall hawk-featured men perched on balconies and high places, scanning the city with heavy binoculars. WHAT WERE THEY SEEKING SO EARNESTLY? Who were they – so composed and steely-eyed? Timidly we stopped a policeman to ask him. 'THEY ARE PUBLISHERS' he said mildly. Publishers! Our hearts stopped beating. 'They are on the look out for new talent.' Great God! It was for *us* they were waiting and watching! Then the kindly policeman

Text with reduced capitals normal letterspacing/plus 6 units

WALKING ALONG THE MALL we wondered who all those men were
WALKING ALONG THE MALL we wondered who all those men were

True italic/sloped roman

Walking along the Mall we wondered who all those men were – tall hawk-featured men perched on balconies and high places, scanning the city with heavy binoculars. What were they seeking so earnestly? Who were they – so composed and steely-eyed? Timidly we stopped a policeman to ask him. 'They are publishers' he said mildly. Publishers! Our hearts stopped beating. 'They are on the look out for new talent.' Great God! It was for *us* they were waiting and watching! Then the kindly policeman lowered his voice confidentially and said in hollow and reverent tones: *'They are waiting for the new Trollope to be born!'* Do you remember, at these words, how heavy our suitcases suddenly felt? How our blood slowed, our footsteps lagged? Brother Ass, we had been bashfully thinking of a kind of illumination such as Rimbaud dreamed of – a nagging poem which was not didactic or expository but which *infected* – was

8 on 9pt

Walking along the Mall we wondered who all those men were – tall hawk-featured men perched on balconies and high places, scanning the city with heavy binoculars. What were they seeking so earnestly? Who were they – so composed and steely-eyed? Timidly we stopped a policeman to ask him. 'They are publishers' he said mildly. Publishers! Our hearts stopped beating. 'They are on the look out for new talent.' Great God! It was for *us* they were waiting and watching! Then the kindly policeman lowered his voice confidentially and said in hollow and reverent tones: *'They are waiting for the new Trollope to be born!'* Do you remember, at these words, how heavy our suitcases suddenly felt? How our blood slowed, our footsteps lagged? Brother Ass, we had been bashfully thinking of a kind of illumination such as

8 on 10.5pt

Walking along the Mall we wondered who all those men were – tall hawk-featured men perched on balconies and high places, scanning the city with heavy binoculars. What were they seeking so earnestly? Who were they – so composed and steely-eyed? Timidly we stopped a policeman to ask him. 'They are publishers' he said mildly. Publishers! Our hearts stopped beating. 'They are on the look out for new talent.' Great God! It was for *us* they were waiting and watching! Then the kindly policeman lowered his voice confidentially and said in hollow and reverent tones: *'They are waiting for the new Trollope to be born!'* Do you remember, at these words, how heavy our suitcases suddenly felt? How our blood slowed, our footsteps lagged? Brother Ass, we had been bashfully thinking of a kind of illumination such as Rimbaud dreamed of – a nagging poem which was not didactic or expository but which *infected* – was not simply a rationalised intuition, I mean, clothed in isinglass! We had come to the wrong shop, with the wrong change! A chill struck us as we saw the mist falling in Trafalgar Square, coiling around us its tendrils of ectoplasm! A million muffin-eating moralists were waiting, not for us, Brother Ass, but for the plucky and tedious Trollope! (If you are dissatisfied with your form, reach for the *curette*.) Now do you wonder if I laugh a little off-key? Do you ask yourself what has turned me into nature's bashful little aphorist? We who are, after all, simply poor co-workers in the psyche of our

9 on 11pt

Walking along the Mall we wondered who all those men were – tall hawk-featured men perched on balconies and high places, scanning the city with heavy binoculars. What were they seeking so earnestly? Who were they – so composed and steely-eyed? Timidly we stopped a policeman to ask him. 'They are publishers' he said mildly. Publishers! Our hearts stopped beating. 'They are on the look out for new talent.' Great God! It was for *us* they were waiting and watching! Then the kindly policeman lowered his voice confidentially and said in hollow and reverent tones: *'They are waiting for the new Trollope to be born!'* Do you remember, at these words, how heavy our suitcases suddenly felt? How our blood slowed, our footsteps lagged? Brother Ass, we had been bashfully thinking of a kind of illumination such as Rimbaud dreamed of – a nagging poem which was not didactic or expository but which *infected* – was not simply a rationalised intuition, I mean, clothed in isinglass! We had come to the wrong shop, with the wrong change! A chill struck us as we saw the mist falling in Trafalgar Square, coiling around us its tendrils of ectoplasm! A million muffin-eating moralists were waiting, not for us, Brother Ass, but for the plucky and tedious Trollope! (If you are dissatisfied with your form, reach for the *curette*.) Now do you wonder if I laugh a little off-key? Do you ask yourself what has turned me into nature's bashful little aphorist?

9 on 12pt

Walking along the Mall we wondered who all those men were – tall hawk-featured men perched on balconies and high places, scanning the city with heavy binoculars. What were they seeking so earnestly? Who were they – so composed and steely-eyed? Timidly we stopped a policeman to ask him. 'They are publishers' he said mildly. Publishers! Our hearts stopped beating. 'They are on the look out for new talent.' Great God! It was for *us* they were waiting and watching! Then the kindly policeman lowered his voice confidentially and said in hollow and reverent tones: *'They are waiting for the new Trollope to be born!'* Do you remember, at these words, how heavy our suitcases suddenly felt? How our blood slowed, our footsteps lagged? Brother Ass, we had been bashfully thinking of a kind of illumination such as Rimbaud dreamed of – a nagging poem which was not didactic or expository but which *infected* – was not simply a rationalised intuition, I mean, clothed in isinglass! We had come to the wrong shop, with the wrong change! A chill struck us as we saw the mist falling in Trafalgar Square, coiling around us its tendrils of ectoplasm! A million muffin-eating moralists were waiting, not for us, Brother

10 on 12pt

Walking along the Mall we wondered who all those men were – tall hawk-featured men perched on balconies and high places, scanning the city with heavy binoculars. What were they seeking so earnestly? Who were they – so composed and steely-eyed? Timidly we stopped a policeman to ask him. 'They are publishers' he said mildly. Publishers! Our hearts stopped beating. 'They are on the look out for new talent.' Great God! It was for *us* they were waiting and watching! Then the kindly policeman lowered his voice confidentially and said in hollow and reverent tones: *'They are waiting for the new Trollope to be born!'* Do you remember, at these words, how heavy our suitcases suddenly felt? How our blood slowed, our footsteps lagged? Brother Ass, we had been bashfully thinking of a kind of illumination such as Rimbaud dreamed of – a nagging poem which was not didactic or expository but which *infected* – was not simply a rationalised intuition, I mean, clothed in isinglass! We had come to the wrong shop, with the wrong change! A chill struck us as we saw the mist falling in Trafalgar Square, coiling around us its tendrils of

10 on 13.5pt

Walking along the Mall we wondered who all those men were – tall hawk-featured men perched on balconies and high places, scanning the city with heavy binoculars. What were they seeking so earnestly? Who were they – so composed and steely-eyed? Timidly we stopped a policeman to ask him. 'They are publishers' he said mildly. Publishers! Our hearts stopped beating. 'They are on the look out for new talent.' Great God! It was for *us* they were waiting and watching! Then the kindly policeman lowered his voice confidentially and said in hollow and reverent tones: *'They are waiting for the new Trollope to be born!'* Do you remember, at these words, how heavy our suitcases suddenly felt? How our blood slowed, our footsteps lagged? Brother Ass, we had been bashfully thinking of a kind of illumination such as Rimbaud dreamed of – a nagging poem which was not didactic or expository but which *infected* – was not simply a rationalised intuition, I mean, clothed in isinglass! We had come to the wrong shop, with the wrong change! A

11 on 13pt

Walking along the Mall we wondered who all those men were – tall hawk-featured men perched on balconies and high places, scanning the city with heavy binoculars. What were they seeking so earnestly? Who were they – so composed and steely-eyed? Timidly we stopped a policeman to ask him. 'They are publishers' he said mildly. Publishers! Our hearts stopped beating. 'They are on the look out for new talent.' Great God! It was for *us* they were waiting and watching! Then the kindly policeman lowered his voice confidentially and said in hollow and reverent tones: *'They are waiting for the new Trollope to be born!'* Do you remember, at these words, how heavy our suitcases suddenly felt? How our blood slowed, our footsteps lagged? Brother Ass, we had been bashfully thinking of a kind of illumination such as Rimbaud dreamed of – a nagging poem which was not didactic or expository but which *infected* – was not simply a rationalised intuition, I mean, clothed in

11 on 14.5pt

MONOTYPE JANSON

Linotype JANSON

roman (05139), **italic** (13139)
Linotype 1930 (C H Griffith)
Copyfitting code 126/110

Based on an original of 1670-90, cut by
Nicholas Kis of Amsterdam

ABCDEFGHIJKLMNOP
QRSTUVWXYZ abcdefg
hijklmnopqrstuvwxyz
1234567890 1234567890
fifl ()[]&£$.,;:-!?"

ABCDEFGHIJKLMNOP
QRSTUVWXYZ abcdefg
hijklmnopqrstuvwxyz
1234567890 1234567890
fifl ()[]&£$.,;:-!?"

24 on 27pt

These examples show *normal* letterspacing and the effect of *reduced* letterspacing on roman setting *as well as on words in italic*: they also show the appearance of figures, for example 28 May 1964, within text. These & the ampersand are not included in the setting opposite.

Normal letterspacing

These examples show *normal* letterspacing and the effect of *reduced* letterspacing on roman setting *as well as on words in italic*: they also show the appearance of figures, for example 28 May 1964, within text. These & the ampersand are not included in the setting opposite.

Minus one unit spacing

These examples show *normal* letterspacing and the effect of *reduced* letterspacing on roman setting *as well as on words in italic*: they also show the appearance of figures, for example 28 May 1964, within text. These & the ampersand are not included in the setting opposite.

Minus two units spacing

WALKING ALONG THE MALL WE WONDERED WHO ALL
WALKING ALONG THE MALL WE WONDERED WHO
WALKING ALONG THE MALL WE WONDERED

Capitals: normal letterspacing/plus 4 units/plus 9 units

WALKING ALONG THE MALL WE WONDERED WHO ALL THOSE MEN WERE
WALKING ALONG THE MALL WE WONDERED WHO ALL THOSE MEN
WALKING ALONG THE MALL WE WONDERED WHO ALL THOSE

Small caps: normal letterspacing/plus 3 units/plus 6 units

WALKING ALONG THE MALL WE WONDERED WHO ALL THOSE MEN WERE
WALKING ALONG THE MALL WE WONDERED WHO ALL THOSE MEN WERE

True small caps/reduced capitals

WALKING ALONG THE MALL we wondered who all those men were
WALKING ALONG THE MALL we wondered who all those men

True italic/sloped roman

Walking along the Mall we wondered who all those men were – tall hawk-featured men perched on balconies and high places, scanning the city with heavy binoculars. What were they seeking so earnestly? Who were they – so composed and steely-eyed? Timidly we stopped a policeman to ask him. 'They are publishers' he said mildly. Publishers! Our hearts stopped beating. 'They are on the look out for new talent.' Great God! It was for *us* they were waiting and watching! Then the kindly policeman lowered his voice confidentially and said in hollow and reverent tones: *'They are waiting for the new Trollope to be born!'* Do you remember, at these words, how heavy our suitcases suddenly felt? How our blood slowed, our footsteps lagged? Brother Ass, we had been bashfully thinking of a kind of illumination such as Rimbaud dreamed of – a nagging poem which was not

8 on 9pt

WALKING ALONG THE MALL WE WONDERED WHO ALL THOSE MEN WERE – TALL HAWK-featured men perched on balconies and high places, scanning the city with heavy binoculars. What were they seeking so earnestly? Who were they – so composed and steely-eyed? Timidly we stopped a policeman to ask him. 'They are publishers' he said mildly. Publishers! Our hearts stopped beating. 'They are on the look out for new talent.' Great God! It was for *us* they were waiting and watching! Then the kindly policeman lowered his voice confidentially and said in hollow and reverent tones: *'They are waiting for the new Trollope to be born!'* Do you remember, at these words, how heavy our suitcases suddenly felt? How our blood slowed, our footsteps lagged? Brother Ass, we had been

8 on 10.5pt

Walking along the Mall we wondered who all those men were – tall hawk-featured men perched on balconies and high places, scanning the city with heavy binoculars. What were they seeking so earnestly? Who were they – so composed and steely-eyed? Timidly we stopped a policeman to ask him. 'They are publishers' he said mildly. Publishers! Our hearts stopped beating. 'They are on the look out for new talent.' Great God! It was for *us* they were waiting and watching! Then the kindly policeman lowered his voice confidentially and said in hollow and reverent tones: *'They are waiting for the new Trollope to be born!'* Do you remember, at these words, how heavy our suitcases suddenly felt? How our blood slowed, our footsteps lagged? Brother Ass, we had been bashfully thinking of a kind of illumination such as Rimbaud dreamed of – a nagging poem which was not didactic or expository but which *infected* – was not simply a rationalised intuition, I mean, clothed in isinglass! We had come to the wrong shop, with the wrong change! A chill struck us as we saw the mist falling in Trafalgar Square, coiling round us its tendrils of ectoplasm! A million muffin-eating moralists were waiting, not for us, Brother Ass, but for the plucky and tedious Trollope! (If you are dissatisfied with your form, reach for the *curette*.) Now do you wonder if I laugh a little off-key? Do you ask yourself what has

9 on 11pt

Walking along the Mall we wondered who all those men were – tall hawk-featured men perched on balconies and high places, scanning the city with heavy binoculars. What were they seeking so earnestly? Who were they – so composed and steely-eyed? Timidly we stopped a policeman to ask him. 'They are publishers' he said mildly. Publishers! Our hearts stopped beating. 'They are on the look out for new talent.' Great God! It was for *us* they were waiting and watching! Then the kindly policeman lowered his voice confidentially and said in hollow and reverent tones: *'They are waiting for the new Trollope to be born!'* Do you remember, at these words, how heavy our suitcases suddenly felt? How our blood slowed, our footsteps lagged? Brother Ass, we had been bashfully thinking of a kind of illumination such as Rimbaud dreamed of – a nagging poem which was not didactic or expository but which *infected* – was not simply a rationalised intuition, I mean, clothed in isinglass! We had come to the wrong shop, with the wrong change! A chill struck us as we saw the mist falling in Trafalgar Square, coiling

10 on 12pt

Walking along the Mall we wondered who all those men were – tall hawk-featured men perched on balconies and high places, scanning the city with heavy binoculars. What were they seeking so earnestly? Who were they – so composed and steely-eyed? Timidly we stopped a policeman to ask him. 'They are publishers' he said mildly. Publishers! Our hearts stopped beating. 'They are on the look out for new talent.' Great God! It was for *us* they were waiting and watching! Then the kindly policeman lowered his voice confidentially and said in hollow and reverent tones: *'They are waiting for the new Trollope to be born!'* Do you remember, at these words, how heavy our suitcases suddenly felt? How our blood slowed, our footsteps lagged? Brother Ass, we had been bashfully thinking of a kind of illumination such as Rimbaud dreamed of – a nagging poem which was not didactic or expository but which *infected* – was not simply a rationalised

11 on 13pt

WALKING ALONG THE MALL WE WONDERED WHO ALL THOSE MEN WERE – TALL hawk-featured men perched on balconies and high places, scanning the city with heavy binoculars. What were they seeking so earnestly? Who were they – so composed and steely-eyed? Timidly we stopped a policeman to ask him. 'They are publishers' he said mildly. Publishers! Our hearts stopped beating. 'They are on the look out for new talent.' Great God! It was for *us* they were waiting and watching! Then the kindly policeman lowered his voice confidentially and said in hollow and reverent tones: *'They are waiting for the new Trollope to be born!'* Do you remember, at these words, how heavy our suitcases suddenly felt? How our blood slowed, our footsteps lagged? Brother Ass, we had been bashfully thinking of a kind of illumination such as Rimbaud dreamed of – a nagging poem which was not didactic or expository but which *infected* – was not simply a rationalised intuition, I mean, clothed in isinglass! We had come to the wrong shop, with the wrong change! A chill struck us as we saw the mist falling in Trafalgar Square, coiling round us its tendrils of ectoplasm! A million muffin-eating moralists were waiting, not for us, Brother Ass, but for the plucky and tedious Trollope! (If you are dissatisfied with your form, reach for the

9 on 12pt

WALKING ALONG THE MALL WE WONDERED WHO ALL THOSE MEN WERE – tall hawk-featured men perched on balconies and high places, scanning the city with heavy binoculars. What were they seeking so earnestly? Who were they – so composed and steely-eyed? Timidly we stopped a policeman to ask him. 'They are publishers' he said mildly. Publishers! Our hearts stopped beating. 'They are on the look out for new talent.' Great God! It was for *us* they were waiting and watching! Then the kindly policeman lowered his voice confidentially and said in hollow and reverent tones: *'They are waiting for the new Trollope to be born!'* Do you remember, at these words, how heavy our suitcases suddenly felt? How our blood slowed, our footsteps lagged? Brother Ass, we had been bashfully thinking of a kind of illumination such as Rimbaud dreamed of – a nagging poem which was not didactic or expository but which *infected* – was not simply a rationalised intuition, I mean, clothed in isinglass! We had come to the wrong shop, with the wrong change!

10 on 13.5pt

WALKING ALONG THE MALL WE WONDERED WHO ALL THOSE MEN were – tall hawk-featured men perched on balconies and high places, scanning the city with heavy binoculars. What were they seeking so earnestly? Who were they – so composed and steely-eyed? Timidly we stopped a policeman to ask him. 'They are publishers' he said mildly. Publishers! Our hearts stopped beating. 'They are on the look out for new talent.' Great God! It was for *us* they were waiting and watching! Then the kindly policeman lowered his voice confidentially and said in hollow and reverent tones: *'They are waiting for the new Trollope to be born!'* Do you remember, at these words, how heavy our suitcases suddenly felt? How our blood slowed, our footsteps lagged? Brother Ass, we had been bashfully thinking of a kind of illumination such as Rimbaud dreamed of – a nagging poem which was not didactic

11 on 14.5pt

LINOTYPE JANSON

Linotype **Janson Text**

roman 55 (05563), **italic 56** (13563)
bold 75 (07563)
Linotype 1985
Copyfitting code 122/112/132

Range also includes bold italic, black, black
italic

Derived from types of 1690 by Nicholas Kis

ABCDEFGHIJKLMNOP
QRSTUVWXYZ abcdefg
hijklmnopqrstuvwxyz
1234567890 1234567890
fifl ()[]&£$.,;:-!?""

ABCDEFGHIJKLMNOP
QRSTUVWXYZ abcdefg
hijklmnopqrstuvwxyz
1234567890 1234567890
fifl ()[]&£$.,;:-!?""

ABCDEFGHIJKLMNOP
QRSTUVWXYZ abcdefg
hijklmnopqrstuvwxyz
1234567890 1234567890
fifl ()[]&£$.,;:-!?""

24 on 27pt

These examples show *normal* letterspacing and the effect of *reduced*
letterspacing on roman setting *as well as on words in italic*: they also
show the appearance of figures, for example 28 May 1964, within text.
These & the ampersand are not included in the setting opposite.

Normal letterspacing

These examples show *normal* letterspacing and the effect of *reduced*
letterspacing on roman setting *as well as on words in italic*: they also
show the appearance of figures, for example 28 May 1964, within text.
These & the ampersand are not included in the setting opposite.

Minus one unit spacing

These examples show *normal* letterspacing and the effect of *reduced*
letterspacing on roman setting *as well as on words in italic*: they also
show the appearance of figures, for example 28 May 1964, within text.
These & the ampersand are not included in the setting opposite.

Minus two units spacing

WALKING ALONG THE MALL WE WONDERED WHO ALL
WALKING ALONG THE MALL WE WONDERED WHO
WALKING ALONG THE MALL WE WONDERED

Capitals: normal letterspacing/plus 4 units/plus 9 units

WALKING ALONG THE MALL WE WONDERED WHO ALL THOSE MEN
WALKING ALONG THE MALL WE WONDERED WHO ALL THOSE
WALKING ALONG THE MALL WE WONDERED WHO ALL

Small caps: normal letterspacing/plus 3 units/plus 6 units

WALKING ALONG THE MALL WE WONDERED WHO ALL THOSE MEN
WALKING ALONG THE MALL WE WONDERED WHO ALL THOSE MEN WERE

True small caps/reduced capitals

WALKING ALONG THE MALL we wondered who all those men were
WALKING ALONG THE MALL we wondered who all those men

True italic/sloped roman

Walking along the Mall we wondered who all those men were – tall hawk-featured
men perched on balconies and high places, scanning the city with heavy binoculars. What
were they seeking so earnestly? Who were they – so composed and steely-eyed? Timidly
we stopped a policeman to ask him. 'They are publishers' he said mildly. Publishers! Our
hearts stopped beating. 'They are on the look out for new talent.' Great God! It was for
us they were waiting and watching! Then the kindly policeman lowered his voice
confidentially and said in hollow and reverent tones: *'They are waiting for the new Trollope*
to be born!' Do you remember, at these words, how heavy our suitcases suddenly felt? How
our blood slowed, our footsteps lagged? Brother Ass, we had been bashfully thinking of a
kind of illumination such as Rimbaud dreamed of – a nagging poem which was not

8 on 9pt

WALKING ALONG THE MALL WE WONDERED WHO ALL THOSE MEN WERE – TALL HAWK-
featured men perched on balconies and high places, scanning the city with heavy
binoculars. What were they seeking so earnestly? Who were they – so composed and
steely-eyed? Timidly we stopped a policeman to ask him. 'They are publishers' he said
mildly. Publishers! Our hearts stopped beating. 'They are on the look out for new talent.'
Great God! It was for *us* they were waiting and watching! Then the kindly policeman
lowered his voice confidentially and said in hollow and reverent tones: *'They are waiting*
for the new Trollope to be born!' Do you remember, at these words, how heavy our suitcases
suddenly felt? How our blood slowed, our footsteps lagged? Brother Ass, we had been

8 on 10.5pt

Walking along the Mall we wondered who all those men were – tall hawk-featured men perched on balconies and high places, scanning the city with heavy binoculars. What were they seeking so earnestly? Who were they – so composed and steely-eyed? Timidly we stopped a policeman to ask him. 'They are publishers' he said mildly. Publishers! Our hearts stopped beating. 'They are on the look out for new talent.' Great God! It was for *us* they were waiting and watching! Then the kindly policeman lowered his voice confidentially and said in hollow and reverent tones: *'They are waiting for the new Trollope to be born!'* Do you remember, at these words, how heavy our suitcases suddenly felt? How our blood slowed, our footsteps lagged? Brother Ass, we had been bashfully thinking of a kind of illumination such as Rimbaud dreamed of – a nagging poem which was not didactic or expository but which *infected* – was not simply a rationalised intuition, I mean, clothed in isinglass! We had come to the wrong shop, with the wrong change! A chill struck us as we saw the mist falling in Trafalgar Square, coiling round us its tendrils of ectoplasm! A million muffin-eating moralists were waiting, not for us, Brother Ass, but for the plucky and tedious Trollope! (If you are dissatisfied with your form, reach for the *curette*.) Now do you wonder if I laugh a little off-key? Do you ask yourself what has turned me

9 on 11pt

Walking along the Mall we wondered who all those men were – tall hawk-featured men perched on balconies and high places, scanning the city with heavy binoculars. What were they seeking so earnestly? Who were they – so composed and steely-eyed? Timidly we stopped a policeman to ask him. 'They are publishers' he said mildly. Publishers! Our hearts stopped beating. 'They are on the look out for new talent.' Great God! It was for *us* they were waiting and watching! Then the kindly policeman lowered his voice confidentially and said in hollow and reverent tones: *'They are waiting for the new Trollope to be born!'* Do you remember, at these words, how heavy our suitcases suddenly felt? How our blood slowed, our footsteps lagged? Brother Ass, we had been bashfully thinking of a kind of illumination such as Rimbaud dreamed of – a nagging poem which was not didactic or expository but which *infected* – was not simply a rationalised intuition, I mean, clothed in isinglass! We had come to the wrong shop, with the wrong change! A chill struck us as we saw the mist falling in Trafalgar Square, coiling

10 on 12pt

Walking along the Mall we wondered who all those men were – tall hawk-featured men perched on balconies and high places, scanning the city with heavy binoculars. What were they seeking so earnestly? Who were they – so composed and steely-eyed? Timidly we stopped a policeman to ask him. 'They are publishers' he said mildly. Publishers! Our hearts stopped beating. 'They are on the look out for new talent.' Great God! It was for *us* they were waiting and watching! Then the kindly policeman lowered his voice confidentially and said in hollow and reverent tones: *'They are waiting for the new Trollope to be born!'* Do you remember, at these words, how heavy our suitcases suddenly felt? How our blood slowed, our footsteps lagged? Brother Ass, we had been bashfully thinking of a kind of illumination such as Rimbaud dreamed of – a nagging poem which was not didactic or expository but which *infected* – was not simply a ration-

11 on 13pt

WALKING ALONG THE MALL WE WONDERED WHO ALL THOSE MEN WERE – TALL hawk-featured men perched on balconies and high places, scanning the city with heavy binoculars. What were they seeking so earnestly? Who were they – so composed and steely-eyed? Timidly we stopped a policeman to ask him. 'They are publishers' he said mildly. Publishers! Our hearts stopped beating. 'They are on the look out for new talent.' Great God! It was for *us* they were waiting and watching! Then the kindly policeman lowered his voice confidentially and said in hollow and reverent tones: *'They are waiting for the new Trollope to be born!'* Do you remember, at these words, how heavy our suitcases suddenly felt? How our blood slowed, our footsteps lagged? Brother Ass, we had been bashfully thinking of a kind of illumination such as Rimbaud dreamed of – a nagging poem which was not didactic or expository but which *infected* – was not simply a rationalised intuition, I mean, clothed in isinglass! We had come to the wrong shop, with the wrong change! A chill struck us as we saw the mist falling in Trafalgar Square, coiling round us its tendrils of ectoplasm! A million muffin-eating moralists were waiting, not for us, Brother Ass, but for the plucky and tedious Trollope! (If you are dissatisfied with your form, reach for the *curette*.)

9 on 12pt

WALKING ALONG THE MALL WE WONDERED WHO ALL THOSE MEN WERE – tall hawk-featured men perched on balconies and high places, scanning the city with heavy binoculars. What were they seeking so earnestly? Who were they – so composed and steely-eyed? Timidly we stopped a policeman to ask him. 'They are publishers' he said mildly. Publishers! Our hearts stopped beating. 'They are on the look out for new talent.' Great God! It was for *us* they were waiting and watching! Then the kindly policeman lowered his voice confidentially and said in hollow and reverent tones: *'They are waiting for the new Trollope to be born!'* Do you remember, at these words, how heavy our suitcases suddenly felt? How our blood slowed, our footsteps lagged? Brother Ass, we had been bashfully thinking of a kind of illumination such as Rimbaud dreamed of – a nagging poem which was not didactic or expository but which *infected* – was not simply a rationalised intuition, I mean, clothed in isinglass! We had come to the wrong shop, with the wrong change!

10 on 13.5pt

WALKING ALONG THE MALL WE WONDERED WHO ALL THOSE MEN were – tall hawk-featured men perched on balconies and high places, scanning the city with heavy binoculars. What were they seeking so earnestly? Who were they – so composed and steely-eyed? Timidly we stopped a policeman to ask him. 'They are publishers' he said mildly. Publishers! Our hearts stopped beating. 'They are on the look out for new talent.' Great God! It was for *us* they were waiting and watching! Then the kindly police-man lowered his voice confidentially and said in hollow and reverent tones: *'They are waiting for the new Trollope to be born!'* Do you remember, at these words, how heavy our suitcases suddenly felt? How our blood slowed, our footsteps lagged? Brother Ass, we had been bashfully thinking of a kind of illumination such as Rimbaud dreamed of – a nagging poem which was not

11 on 14.5pt

LINOTYPE JANSON TEXT

Monotype **Joanna**

478 **roman and italic**
541 **bold**
Designed by Eric Gill 1930, recut by
Monotype 1937 for J M Dent; made generally
available 1958
Copyfitting factor 40.0/31.9/42.2

Range also includes semi-bold, semi-bold
italic, bold italic

ABCDEFGHIJKLMNOP
QRSTUVWXYZ abcdefg
hijklmnopqrstuvwxyz
1234567890 1234567890
ff fi fl ffi ffl () []&£$.,;:-!?''

*ABCDEFGHIJKLMNOP
QRSTUVWXYZ abcdefg
hijklmnopqrstuvwxyz
1234567890 1234567890
ff fi fl ffi ffl () []&£$.,;:-!?''*

**ABCDEFGHIJKLMNOP
QRSTUVWXYZ abcdefg
hijklmnopqrstuvwxyz
1234567890 1234567890
ff fi fl ffi ffl () []&£$.,;:-!?''**

24 on 27pt

These examples show *normal* letterspacing and the effect of *reduced*
letterspacing on roman setting *as well as on words in italic:* they also
show the appearance of figures, for example 28 May 1964, within text.
These & the ampersand are not included in the setting opposite.

Normal letterspacing

These examples show *normal* letterspacing and the effect of *reduced*
letterspacing on roman setting *as well as on words in italic:* they also
show the appearance of figures, for example 28 May 1964, within text.
These & the ampersand are not included in the setting opposite.

Minus one unit spacing

These examples show *normal* letterspacing and the effect of *reduced*
letterspacing on roman setting *as well as on words in italic:* they also
show the appearance of figures, for example 28 May 1964, within text.
These & the ampersand are not included in the setting opposite.

Minus two units spacing

WALKING ALONG THE MALL WE WONDERED WHO ALL THOSE MEN
WALKING ALONG THE MALL WE WONDERED WHO ALL THOSE
WALKING ALONG THE MALL WE WONDERED WHO ALL

Capitals: normal letterspacing/plus 9 units/plus 18 units

WALKING ALONG THE MALL WE WONDERED WHO ALL THOSE MEN WERE
WALKING ALONG THE MALL WE WONDERED WHO ALL THOSE MEN WERE
WALKING ALONG THE MALL WE WONDERED WHO ALL THOSE MEN

Small caps: normal letterspacing/plus 6 units/plus 12 units

WALKING ALONG THE MALL we wondered who all those men were
WALKING ALONG THE MALL we wondered who all those men were

True italic/sloped roman

WALKING ALONG THE MALL WE WONDERED WHO ALL THOSE MEN WERE
WALKING ALONG THE MALL WE WONDERED WHO ALL THOSE MEN WERE

True small caps/reduced capitals

Walking along the Mall we wondered who all those men were – tall hawk-featured
men perched on balconies and high places, scanning the city with heavy binoculars. What were
they seeking so earnestly? Who were they – so composed and steely-eyed? Timidly we stopped
a policeman to ask him. 'They are publishers' he said mildly. Publishers! Our hearts stopped
beating. 'They are on the look out for new talent.' Great God! It was for *us* they were waiting
and watching! Then the kindly policeman lowered his voice confidentially and said in hollow
and reverent tones: *'They are waiting for the new Trollope to be born!'* Do you remember, at these
words, how heavy our suitcases suddenly felt? How our blood slowed, our footsteps lagged?
Brother Ass, we had been bashfully thinking of a kind of illumination such as Rimbaud
dreamed of – a nagging poem which was not didactic or expository but which *infected* – was

8 on 9pt

WALKING ALONG THE MALL WE WONDERED WHO ALL THOSE MEN WERE – TALL HAWK-
featured men perched on balconies and high places, scanning the city with heavy binoculars.
What were they seeking so earnestly? Who were they – so composed and steely-eyed? Timidly
we stopped a policeman to ask him. 'They are publishers' he said mildly. Publishers! Our hearts
stopped beating. 'They are on the look out for new talent.' Great God! It was for *us* they were
waiting and watching! Then the kindly policeman lowered his voice confidentially and said in
hollow and reverent tones: *'They are waiting for the new Trollope to be born!'* Do you remember, at
these words, how heavy our suitcases suddenly felt? How our blood slowed, our footsteps
lagged? Brother Ass, we had been bashfully thinking of a kind of illumination such as Rimbaud

8 on 10.5pt

Walking along the Mall we wondered who all those men were – tall hawk-featured men perched on balconies and high places, scanning the city with heavy binoculars. What were they seeking so earnestly? Who were they – so composed and steely-eyed? Timidly we stopped a policeman to ask him. 'They are publishers' he said mildly. Publishers! Our hearts stopped beating. 'They are on the look out for new talent.' Great God! It was for *us* they were waiting and watching! Then the kindly policeman lowered his voice confidentially and said in hollow and reverent tones: *'They are waiting for the new Trollope to be born!'* Do you remember, at these words, how heavy our suitcases suddenly felt? How our blood slowed, our footsteps lagged? Brother Ass, we had been bashfully thinking of a kind of illumination such as Rimbaud dreamed of – a nagging poem which was not didactic or expository but which *infected* – was not simply a rationalised intuition, I mean, clothed in isinglass! We had come to the wrong shop, with the wrong change! A chill struck us as we saw the mist falling in Trafalgar Square, coiling around us its tendrils of ectoplasm! A million muffin-eating moralists were waiting, not for us, Brother Ass, but for the plucky and tedious Trollope! (If you are dissatisfied with your form, reach for the *curette*.) Now do you wonder if I laugh a little off-key? Do you ask yourself what has turned me into nature's bashful little aphorist? We who are, after all, simply poor co-workers in the psyche of our nation, what can we

9 on 11pt

Walking along the Mall we wondered who all those men were – tall hawk-featured men perched on balconies and high places, scanning the city with heavy binoculars. What were they seeking so earnestly? Who were they – so composed and steely-eyed? Timidly we stopped a policeman to ask him. 'They are publishers' he said mildly. Publishers! Our hearts stopped beating. 'They are on the look out for new talent.' Great God! It was for *us* they were waiting and watching! Then the kindly policeman lowered his voice confidentially and said in hollow and reverent tones: *'They are waiting for the new Trollope to be born!'* Do you remember, at these words, how heavy our suitcases suddenly felt? How our blood slowed, our footsteps lagged? Brother Ass, we had been bashfully thinking of a kind of illumination such as Rimbaud dreamed of – a nagging poem which was not didactic or expository but which *infected* – was not simply a rationalised intuition, I mean, clothed in isinglass! We had come to the wrong shop, with the wrong change! A chill struck us as we saw the mist falling in Trafalgar Square, coiling around us its tendrils of ectoplasm! A million muffin-eating moralists were waiting, not for us, Brother Ass, but for the plucky and tedious Trollope! (If you are dissatisfied with your form, reach for the *curette*.) Now do you wonder if I laugh a little off-key? Do you ask yourself what has turned me into nature's bashful little aphorist?

9 on 12pt

Walking along the Mall we wondered who all those men were – tall hawk-featured men perched on balconies and high places, scanning the city with heavy binoculars. What were they seeking so earnestly? Who were they – so composed and steely-eyed? Timidly we stopped a policeman to ask him. 'They are publishers' he said mildly. Publishers! Our hearts stopped beating. 'They are on the look out for new talent.' Great God! It was for *us* they were waiting and watching! Then the kindly policeman lowered his voice confidentially and said in hollow and reverent tones: *'They are waiting for the new Trollope to be born!'* Do you remember, at these words, how heavy our suitcases suddenly felt? How our blood slowed, our footsteps lagged? Brother Ass, we had been bashfully thinking of a kind of illumination such as Rimbaud dreamed of – a nagging poem which was not didactic or expository but which *infected* – was not simply a rationalised intuition, I mean, clothed in isinglass! We had come to the wrong shop, with the wrong change! A chill struck us as we saw the mist falling in Trafalgar Square, coiling around us its tendrils of ectoplasm! A million muffin-eating moralists were waiting, not for us, Brother Ass, but for

10 on 12pt

Walking along the Mall we wondered who all those men were – tall hawk-featured men perched on balconies and high places, scanning the city with heavy binoculars. What were they seeking so earnestly? Who were they – so composed and steely-eyed? Timidly we stopped a policeman to ask him. 'They are publishers' he said mildly. Publishers! Our hearts stopped beating. 'They are on the look out for new talent.' Great God! It was for *us* they were waiting and watching! Then the kindly policeman lowered his voice confidentially and said in hollow and reverent tones: *'They are waiting for the new Trollope to be born!'* Do you remember, at these words, how heavy our suitcases suddenly felt? How our blood slowed, our footsteps lagged? Brother Ass, we had been bashfully thinking of a kind of illumination such as Rimbaud dreamed of – a nagging poem which was not didactic or expository but which *infected* – was not simply a rationalised intuition, I mean, clothed in isinglass! We had come to the wrong shop, with the wrong change! A chill struck us as we saw the mist falling in Trafalgar Square, coiling around us its tendrils of ectoplasm! A

10 on 13.5pt

Walking along the Mall we wondered who all those men were – tall hawk-featured men perched on balconies and high places, scanning the city with heavy binoculars. What were they seeking so earnestly? Who were they – so composed and steely-eyed? Timidly we stopped a policeman to ask him. 'They are publishers' he said mildly. Publishers! Our hearts stopped beating. 'They are on the look out for new talent.' Great God! It was for *us* they were waiting and watching! Then the kindly policeman lowered his voice confidentially and said in hollow and reverent tones: *'They are waiting for the new Trollope to be born!'* Do you remember, at these words, how heavy our suitcases suddenly felt? How our blood slowed, our footsteps lagged? Brother Ass, we had been bashfully thinking of a kind of illumination such as Rimbaud dreamed of – a nagging poem which was not didactic or expository but which *infected* – was not simply a rationalised intuition, I mean, clothed in isinglass! We had come to the wrong shop, with the wrong change!

11 on 13pt

Walking along the Mall we wondered who all those men were – tall hawk-featured men perched on balconies and high places, scanning the city with heavy binoculars. What were they seeking so earnestly? Who were they – so composed and steely-eyed? Timidly we stopped a policeman to ask him. 'They are publishers' he said mildly. Publishers! Our hearts stopped beating. 'They are on the look out for new talent.' Great God! It was for *us* they were waiting and watching! Then the kindly policeman lowered his voice confidentially and said in hollow and reverent tones: *'They are waiting for the new Trollope to be born!'* Do you remember, at these words, how heavy our suitcases suddenly felt? How our blood slowed, our footsteps lagged? Brother Ass, we had been bashfully thinking of a kind of illumination such as Rimbaud dreamed of – a nagging poem which was not didactic or expository but which *infected* – was not simply a rationalised intuition, I mean, clothed

11 on 14.5pt

Linotype **Joanna**

roman (05465), **italic** (13465)
bold (07465)
Designed by Eric Gill 1930, recut by
Monotype 1937 for J M Dent; made generally
available 1958
Copyfitting code 133/105/146

Range also includes extra bold

This Linotype version must be leaded at least
1½ pts in 8 pt, to at least 2½ pts in 12 pt, to avoid
descenders and ascenders clashing

ABCDEFGHIJKLMNOP
QRSTUVWXYZ abcdefg
hijklmnopqrstuvwxyz
1234567890 1234567890
fifl ()[]&£$.,;:-!?"

ABCDEFGHIJKLMNOP
QRSTUVWXYZ abcdefg
hijklmnopqrstuvwxyz
1234567890
fifl ()[]&£$.,;:-!?"

ABCDEFGHIJKLMNOP
QRSTUVWXYZ abcdefg
hijklmnopqrstuvwxyz
1234567890
fifl ()[]&£$.,;:-!?"

24 on 27pt

These examples show *normal* letterspacing and the effect of *reduced*
letterspacing on roman setting *as well as on words in italic:* they also
show the appearance of figures, for example 28 May 1964, within text.
These & the ampersand are not included in the setting opposite.
Normal letterspacing

These examples show *normal* letterspacing and the effect of *reduced*
letterspacing on roman setting *as well as on words in italic:* they also
show the appearance of figures, for example 28 May 1964, within text.
These & the ampersand are not included in the setting opposite.
Minus one unit spacing

These examples show *normal* letterspacing and the effect of *reduced*
letterspacing on roman setting *as well as on words in italic:* they also
show the appearance of figures, for example 28 May 1964, within text.
These & the ampersand are not included in the setting opposite.
Minus two units spacing

WALKING ALONG THE MALL WE WONDERED WHO ALL
WALKING ALONG THE MALL WE WONDERED WHO
WALKING ALONG THE MALL WE WONDERED
Capitals: normal letterspacing/plus 4 units/plus 9 units

WALKING ALONG THE MALL WE WONDERED WHO ALL THOSE MEN
WALKING ALONG THE MALL WE WONDERED WHO ALL THOSE
WALKING ALONG THE MALL WE WONDERED WHO ALL
Small caps: normal letterspacing/plus 3 units/plus 6 units

WALKING ALONG THE MALL WE WONDERED WHO ALL THOSE MEN WE
WALKING ALONG THE MALL WE WONDERED WHO ALL THOSE MEN WERE
True small caps/reduced capitals

WALKING ALONG THE MALL we wondered who all those men were
WALKING ALONG THE MALL we wondered who all those men
True italic/sloped roman

Walking along the Mall we wondered who all those men were – tall hawk-
featured men perched on balconies and high places, scanning the city with heavy
binoculars. What were they seeking so earnestly? Who were they – so composed
and steely-eyed? Timidly we stopped a policeman to ask him. 'They are publishers'
he said mildly. Publishers! Our hearts stopped beating. 'They are on the look out for
new talent.' Great God! It was for *us* they were waiting and watching! Then the kindly
policeman lowered his voice confidentially and said in hollow and reverent tones:
'They are waiting for the new Trollope to be born!' Do you remember, at these words, how
heavy our suitcases suddenly felt? How our blood slowed, our footsteps lagged?
Brother Ass, we had been bashfully thinking of a kind of illumination such as
8 on 9pt

WALKING ALONG THE MALL WE WONDERED WHO ALL THOSE MEN WERE – TALL HAWK-
featured men perched on balconies and high places, scanning the city with heavy
binoculars. What were they seeking so earnestly? Who were they – so composed
and steely-eyed? Timidly we stopped a policeman to ask him. 'They are publishers'
he said mildly. Publishers! Our hearts stopped beating. 'They are on the look out for
new talent.' Great God! It was for *us* they were waiting and watching! Then the kindly
policeman lowered his voice confidentially and said in hollow and reverent tones:
'They are waiting for the new Trollope to be born!' Do you remember, at these words, how
heavy our suitcases suddenly felt? How our blood slowed, our footsteps lagged?
8 on 10.5pt

Walking along the Mall we wondered who all those men were – tall hawk-featured men perched on balconies and high places, scanning the city with heavy binoculars. What were they seeking so earnestly? Who were they – so composed and steely-eyed? Timidly we stopped a policeman to ask him. 'They are publishers' he said mildly. Publishers! Our hearts stopped beating. 'They are on the look out for new talent.' Great God! It was for *us* they were waiting and watching! Then the kindly policeman lowered his voice confidentially and said in hollow and reverent tones: *'They are waiting for the new Trollope to be born!'* Do you remember, at these words, how heavy our suitcases suddenly felt? How our blood slowed, our footsteps lagged? Brother Ass, we had been bashfully thinking of a kind of illumination such as Rimbaud dreamed of – a nagging poem which was not didactic or expository but which *infected* – was not simply a rationalised intuition, I mean, clothed in isinglass! We had come to the wrong shop, with the wrong change! A chill struck us as we saw the mist falling in Trafalgar Square, coiling round us its tendrils of ectoplasm! A million muffin-eating moralists were waiting, not for us, Brother Ass, but for the plucky and tedious Trollope! (If you are dissatisfied with your form, reach for the

9 on 11pt

Walking along the Mall we wondered who all those men were – tall hawk-featured men perched on balconies and high places, scanning the city with heavy binoculars. What were they seeking so earnestly? Who were they – so composed and steely-eyed? Timidly we stopped a policeman to ask him. 'They are publishers' he said mildly. Publishers! Our hearts stopped beating. 'They are on the look out for new talent.' Great God! It was for *us* they were waiting and watching! Then the kindly policeman lowered his voice confidentially and said in hollow and reverent tones: *'They are waiting for the new Trollope to be born!'* Do you remember, at these words, how heavy our suitcases suddenly felt? How our blood slowed, our footsteps lagged? Brother Ass, we had been bashfully thinking of a kind of illumination such as Rimbaud dreamed of – a nagging poem which was not didactic or expository but which *infected* – was not simply a rationalised intuition, I mean, clothed in isinglass! We had come to the wrong shop, with the wrong change! A chill struck

10 on 12pt

Walking along the Mall we wondered who all those men were – tall hawk-featured men perched on balconies and high places, scanning the city with heavy binoculars. What were they seeking so earnestly? Who were they – so composed and steely-eyed? Timidly we stopped a policeman to ask him. 'They are publishers' he said mildly. Publishers! Our hearts stopped beating. 'They are on the look out for new talent.' Great God! It was for *us* they were waiting and watching! Then the kindly policeman lowered his voice confidentially and said in hollow and reverent tones: *'They are waiting for the new Trollope to be born!'* Do you remember, at these words, how heavy our suitcases suddenly felt? How our blood slowed, our footsteps lagged? Brother Ass, we had been bashfully thinking of a kind of illumination such as Rimbaud dreamed of – a nagging poem which was not didactic or

11 on 13pt

WALKING ALONG THE MALL WE WONDERED WHO ALL THOSE MEN WERE – tall hawk-featured men perched on balconies and high places, scanning the city with heavy binoculars. What were they seeking so earnestly? Who were they – so composed and steely-eyed? Timidly we stopped a policeman to ask him. 'They are publishers' he said mildly. Publishers! Our hearts stopped beating. 'They are on the look out for new talent.' Great God! It was for *us* they were waiting and watching! Then the kindly policeman lowered his voice confidentially and said in hollow and reverent tones: *'They are waiting for the new Trollope to be born!'* Do you remember, at these words, how heavy our suitcases suddenly felt? How our blood slowed, our footsteps lagged? Brother Ass, we had been bashfully thinking of a kind of illumination such as Rimbaud dreamed of – a nagging poem which was not didactic or expository but which *infected* – was not simply a rationalised intuition, I mean, clothed in isinglass! We had come to the wrong shop, with the wrong change! A chill struck us as we saw the mist falling in Trafalgar Square, coiling round us its tendrils of ectoplasm! A million muffin-eating moralists were waiting, not for us, Brother Ass, but for the plucky

9 on 12pt

WALKING ALONG THE MALL WE WONDERED WHO ALL THOSE MEN were – tall hawk-featured men perched on balconies and high places, scanning the city with heavy binoculars. What were they seeking so earnestly? Who were they – so composed and steely-eyed? Timidly we stopped a policeman to ask him. 'They are publishers' he said mildly. Publishers! Our hearts stopped beating. 'They are on the look out for new talent.' Great God! It was for *us* they were waiting and watching! Then the kindly policeman lowered his voice confidentially and said in hollow and reverent tones: *'They are waiting for the new Trollope to be born!'* Do you remember, at these words, how heavy our suitcases suddenly felt? How our blood slowed, our footsteps lagged? Brother Ass, we had been bashfully thinking of a kind of illumination such as Rimbaud dreamed of – a nagging poem which was not didactic or expository but which *infected* – was not simply a rationalised intuition, I mean, clothed in isinglass! We had

10 on 13.5pt

WALKING ALONG THE MALL WE WONDERED WHO ALL THOSE men were – tall hawk-featured men perched on balconies and high places, scanning the city with heavy binoculars. What were they seeking so earnestly? Who were they – so composed and steely-eyed? Timidly we stopped a policeman to ask him. 'They are publishers' he said mildly. Publishers! Our hearts stopped beating. 'They are on the look out for new talent.' Great God! It was for *us* they were waiting and watching! Then the kindly policeman lowered his voice confidentially and said in hollow and reverent tones: *'They are waiting for the new Trollope to be born!'* Do you remember, at these words, how heavy our suitcases suddenly felt? How our blood slowed, our footsteps lagged? Brother Ass, we had been bashfully thinking of a kind of illumination such as Rimbaud

11 on 14.5pt

LINOTYPE JOANNA

Linotype **Kennerley**

roman (05408), **italic** (13408)
bold (07408)
Stempel 1982, based on types by Frederic W
Goudy of 1911-24
Copyfitting code 123/119/135

Range also includes bold italic

Goudy's design was possibly based upon
Jenson's *Eusebius* type of 1470

ABCDEFGHIJKLMNOP
QRSTUVWXYZ abcdefg
hijklmnopqrstuvwxyz
1234567890 1234567890
fifl ()[]&£$.,;:-!?"

*ABCDEFGHIJKLMNOP
QRSTUVWXYZ abcdefg
hijklmnopqrstuvwxyz
1234567890 1234567890
fifl ()[]&£$.,;:-!?"*

**ABCDEFGHIJKLMNOP
QRSTUVWXYZ abcdefg
hijklmnopqrstuvwxyz
1234567890 1234567890
fifl ()[]&£$.,;:-!?"**

24 on 27pt

These examples show *normal* letterspacing and the effect of *reduced* letterspacing on roman setting *as well as on words in italic*: they also show the appearance of figures, for example 28 May 1964, within text. These & the ampersand are not included in the setting opposite.

Normal letterspacing

These examples show *normal* letterspacing and the effect of *reduced* letterspacing on roman setting *as well as on words in italic*: they also show the appearance of figures, for example 28 May 1964, within text. These & the ampersand are not included in the setting opposite.

Minus one unit spacing

These examples show *normal* letterspacing and the effect of *reduced* letterspacing on roman setting *as well as on words in italic*: they also show the appearance of figures, for example 28 May 1964, within text. These & the ampersand are not included in the setting opposite.

Minus two units spacing

WALKING ALONG THE MALL WE WONDERED WHO ALL
WALKING ALONG THE MALL WE WONDERED WHO
WALKING ALONG THE MALL WE WONDERED

Capitals: normal letterspacing/plus 4 units/plus 9 units

WALKING ALONG THE MALL WE WONDERED WHO ALL THOSE MEN
WALKING ALONG THE MALL WE WONDERED WHO ALL THOSE MEN
WALKING ALONG THE MALL WE WONDERED WHO ALL THOSE

Small caps: normal letterspacing/plus 3 units/plus 6 units

WALKING ALONG THE MALL WE WONDERED WHO ALL THOSE MEN
WALKING ALONG THE MALL WE WONDERED WHO ALL THOSE MEN WERE

True small caps/reduced capitals

*WALKING ALONG THE MALL we wondered who all those men
WALKING ALONG THE MALL we wondered who all those men*

True italic/sloped roman

Walking along the Mall we wondered who all those men were – tall hawk-featured men perched on balconies and high places, scanning the city with heavy binoculars. What were they seeking so earnestly? Who were they – so composed and steely-eyed? Timidly we stopped a policeman to ask him. 'They are publishers' he said mildly. Publishers! Our hearts stopped beating. 'They are on the look out for new talent.' Great God! It was for *us* they were waiting and watching! Then the kindly policeman lowered his voice confidentially and said in hollow and reverent tones: *'They are waiting for the new Trollope to be born!'* Do you remember, at these words, how heavy our suitcases suddenly felt? How our blood slowed, our footsteps lagged? Brother Ass, we had been bashfully thinking of a kind of illumination such as Rimbaud dreamed of – a nagging poem which was not

8 on 9pt

WALKING ALONG THE MALL WE WONDERED WHO ALL THOSE MEN WERE – TALL HAWK-featured men perched on balconies and high places, scanning the city with heavy binoculars. What were they seeking so earnestly? Who were they – so composed and steely-eyed? Timidly we stopped a policeman to ask him. 'They are publishers' he said mildly. Publishers! Our hearts stopped beating. 'They are on the look out for new talent.' Great God! It was for *us* they were waiting and watching! Then the kindly policeman lowered his voice confidentially and said in hollow and reverent tones: *'They are waiting for the new Trollope to be born!'* Do you remember, at these words, how heavy our suitcases suddenly felt? How our blood slowed, our footsteps lagged? Brother Ass,

8 on 10.5pt

Walking along the Mall we wondered who all those men were – tall hawk-featured men perched on balconies and high places, scanning the city with heavy binoculars. What were they seeking so earnestly? Who were they – so composed and steely-eyed? Timidly we stopped a policeman to ask him. 'They are publishers' he said mildly. Publishers! Our hearts stopped beating. 'They are on the look out for new talent.' Great God! It was for *us* they were waiting and watching! Then the kindly policeman lowered his voice confidentially and said in hollow and reverent tones: *'They are waiting for the new Trollope to be born!'* Do you remember, at these words, how heavy our suitcases suddenly felt? How our blood slowed, our footsteps lagged? Brother Ass, we had been bashfully thinking of a kind of illumination such as Rimbaud dreamed of – a nagging poem which was not didactic or expository but which *infected* – was not simply a rationalised intuition, I mean, clothed in isinglass! We had come to the wrong shop, with the wrong change! A chill struck us as we saw the mist falling in Trafalgar Square, coiling round us its tendrils of ectoplasm! A million muffin-eating moralists were waiting, not for us, Brother Ass, but for the plucky and tedious Trollope! (If you are dissatisfied with your form, reach for the *curette*.) Now do you wonder if I laugh a little off-key? Do you ask yourself what has

9 on 11pt

Walking along the Mall we wondered who all those men were – tall hawk-featured men perched on balconies and high places, scanning the city with heavy binoculars. What were they seeking so earnestly? Who were they – so composed and steely-eyed? Timidly we stopped a policeman to ask him. 'They are publishers' he said mildly. Publishers! Our hearts stopped beating. 'They are on the look out for new talent.' Great God! It was for *us* they were waiting and watching! Then the kindly policeman lowered his voice confidentially and said in hollow and reverent tones: *'They are waiting for the new Trollope to be born!'* Do you remember, at these words, how heavy our suitcases suddenly felt? How our blood slowed, our footsteps lagged? Brother Ass, we had been bashfully thinking of a kind of illumination such as Rimbaud dreamed of – a nagging poem which was not didactic or expository but which *infected* – was not simply a rationalised intuition, I mean, clothed in isinglass! We had come to the wrong shop, with the wrong change! A chill struck us as we saw the mist falling in Trafalgar Square, coiling

10 on 12pt

Walking along the Mall we wondered who all those men were – tall hawk-featured men perched on balconies and high places, scanning the city with heavy binoculars. What were they seeking so earnestly? Who were they – so composed and steely-eyed? Timidly we stopped a policeman to ask him. 'They are publishers' he said mildly. Publishers! Our hearts stopped beating. 'They are on the look out for new talent.' Great God! It was for *us* they were waiting and watching! Then the kindly policeman lowered his voice confidentially and said in hollow and reverent tones: *'They are waiting for the new Trollope to be born!'* Do you remember, at these words, how heavy our suitcases suddenly felt? How our blood slowed, our footsteps lagged? Brother Ass, we had been bashfully thinking of a kind of illumination such as Rimbaud dreamed of – a nagging poem which was not didactic or expository but which *infected* – was not simply a rationalised

11 on 13pt

WALKING ALONG THE MALL WE WONDERED WHO ALL THOSE MEN WERE – TALL hawk-featured men perched on balconies and high places, scanning the city with heavy binoculars. What were they seeking so earnestly? Who were they – so composed and steely-eyed? Timidly we stopped a policeman to ask him. 'They are publishers' he said mildly. Publishers! Our hearts stopped beating. 'They are on the look out for new talent.' Great God! It was for *us* they were waiting and watching! Then the kindly policeman lowered his voice confidentially and said in hollow and reverent tones: *'They are waiting for the new Trollope to be born!'* Do you remember, at these words, how heavy our suitcases suddenly felt? How our blood slowed, our footsteps lagged? Brother Ass, we had been bashfully thinking of a kind of illumination such as Rimbaud dreamed of – a nagging poem which was not didactic or expository but which *infected* – was not simply a rationalised intuition, I mean, clothed in isinglass! We had come to the wrong shop, with the wrong change! A chill struck us as we saw the mist falling in Trafalgar Square, coiling round us its tendrils of ectoplasm! A million muffin-eating moralists were waiting, not for us, Brother Ass, but for the plucky and tedious Trollope! (If you are dissatisfied with your form, reach for the *curette*.)

9 on 12pt

WALKING ALONG THE MALL WE WONDERED WHO ALL THOSE MEN WERE – tall hawk-featured men perched on balconies and high places, scanning the city with heavy binoculars. What were they seeking so earnestly? Who were they – so composed and steely-eyed? Timidly we stopped a policeman to ask him. 'They are publishers' he said mildly. Publishers! Our hearts stopped beating. 'They are on the look out for new talent.' Great God! It was for *us* they were waiting and watching! Then the kindly policeman lowered his voice confidentially and said in hollow and reverent tones: *'They are waiting for the new Trollope to be born!'* Do you remember, at these words, how heavy our suitcases suddenly felt? How our blood slowed, our footsteps lagged? Brother Ass, we had been bashfully thinking of a kind of illumination such as Rimbaud dreamed of – a nagging poem which was not didactic or expository but which *infected* – was not simply a rationalised intuition, I mean, clothed in isinglass! We had come to the wrong shop, with the wrong change!

10 on 13.5pt

WALKING ALONG THE MALL WE WONDERED WHO ALL THOSE MEN were – tall hawk-featured men perched on balconies and high places, scanning the city with heavy binoculars. What were they seeking so earnestly? Who were they – so composed and steely-eyed? Timidly we stopped a policeman to ask him. 'They are publishers' he said mildly. Publishers! Our hearts stopped beating. 'They are on the look out for new talent.' Great God! It was for *us* they were waiting and watching! Then the kindly policeman lowered his voice confidentially and said in hollow and reverent tones: *'They are waiting for the new Trollope to be born!'* Do you remember, at these words, how heavy our suitcases suddenly felt? How our blood slowed, our footsteps lagged? Brother Ass, we had been bashfully thinking of a kind of illumination such as Rimbaud dreamed of – a nagging poem which was not didactic or

11 on 14.5pt

LINOTYPE KENNERLEY

Linotype Lectura

roman (05610), **italic** (13610)
bold (07610)
Tetterode 1969 (Dick Dooijes)
Copyfitting code 123/119/124

Range also includes black condensed

ABCDEFGHIJKLMNOP
QRSTUVWXYZ abcdefg
hijklmnopqrstuvwxyz
1234567890
fifl ()[]&£$.,;:-!?''

ABCDEFGHIJKLMNOP
QRSTUVWXYZ abcdefg
hijklmnopqrstuvwxyz
1234567890
fifl ()[]&£$.,;:-!?''

ABCDEFGHIJKLMNOP
QRSTUVWXYZ abcdefg
hijklmnopqrstuvwxyz
1234567890
fifl ()[]&£$.,;:-!?''

24 on 27pt

These examples show *normal* letterspacing and the effect of *reduced* letterspacing on roman setting *as well as on words in italic*: they also show the appearance of figures, for example 28 May 1964, within text. These & the ampersand are not included in the setting opposite.

Normal letterspacing

These examples show *normal* letterspacing and the effect of *reduced* letterspacing on roman setting *as well as on words in italic*: they also show the appearance of figures, for example 28 May 1964, within text. These & the ampersand are not included in the setting opposite.

Minus one unit spacing

These examples show *normal* letterspacing and the effect of *reduced* letterspacing on roman setting *as well as on words in italic*: they also show the appearance of figures, for example 28 May 1964, within text. These & the ampersand are not included in the setting opposite.

Minus two units spacing

WALKING ALONG THE MALL WE WONDERED WHO ALL THOSE
WALKING ALONG THE MALL WE WONDERED WHO ALL
WALKING ALONG THE MALL WE WONDERED WHO

Capitals: normal letterspacing/plus 4 units/plus 9 units

Walking along the Mall we wondered who all those men were – tall hawk-featured men perched on balconies and high places, scanning the city with heavy binoculars. WHAT WERE THEY SEEKING SO EARNESTLY? Who were they – so composed and steely-eyed? Timidly we stopped a policeman to ask him. 'THEY ARE PUBLISHERS' he said mildly. Publishers! Our hearts stopped beating. 'They are on the look out for new talent.' Great God! It was for *us* they were waiting and watching!

Text with reduced caps normal letterspacing/plus 3 units

WALKING ALONG THE MALL we wondered who all those men were
WALKING ALONG THE MALL we wondered who all those men were

True italic/sloped roman

Walking along the Mall we wondered who all those men were – tall hawk-featured men perched on balconies and high places, scanning the city with heavy binoculars. What were they seeking so earnestly? Who were they – so composed and steely-eyed? Timidly we stopped a policeman to ask him. 'They are publishers' he said mildly. Publishers! Our hearts stopped beating. 'They are on the look out for new talent.' Great God! It was for *us* they were waiting and watching! Then the kindly policeman lowered his voice confidentially and said in hollow and reverent tones: *'They are waiting for the new Trollope to be born!'* Do you remember, at these words, how heavy our suitcases suddenly felt? How our blood slowed, our footsteps lagged? Brother Ass, we had been bashfully thinking of a kind of illumination such as Rimbaud dreamed of – a nagging poem which was not

8 on 9pt

Walking along the Mall we wondered who all those men were – tall hawk-featured men perched on balconies and high places, scanning the city with heavy binoculars. What were they seeking so earnestly? Who were they – so composed and steely-eyed? Timidly we stopped a policeman to ask him. 'They are publishers' he said mildly. Publishers! Our hearts stopped beating. 'They are on the look out for new talent.' Great God! It was for *us* they were waiting and watching! Then the kindly policeman lowered his voice confidentially and said in hollow and reverent tones: *'They are waiting for the new Trollope to be born!'* Do you remember, at these words, how heavy our suitcases suddenly felt? How our blood slowed, our footsteps lagged? Brother Ass, we had been bashfully

8 on 10.5pt

Walking along the Mall we wondered who all those men were – tall hawk-featured men perched on balconies and high places, scanning the city with heavy binoculars. What were they seeking so earnestly? Who were they – so composed and steely-eyed? Timidly we stopped a policeman to ask him. 'They are publishers' he said mildly. Publishers! Our hearts stopped beating. 'They are on the look out for new talent.' Great God! It was for *us* they were waiting and watching! Then the kindly policeman lowered his voice confidentially and said in hollow and reverent tones: *'They are waiting for the new Trollope to be born!'* Do you remember, at these words, how heavy our suitcases suddenly felt? How our blood slowed, our footsteps lagged? Brother Ass, we had been bashfully thinking of a kind of illumination such as Rimbaud dreamed of – a nagging poem which was not didactic or expository but which *infected* – was not simply a rationalised intuition, I mean, clothed in isinglass! We had come to the wrong shop, with the wrong change! A chill struck us as we saw the mist falling in Trafalgar Square, coiling round us its tendrils of ectoplasm! A million muffin-eating moralists were waiting, not for us, Brother Ass, but for the plucky and tedious Trollope! (If you are dissatisfied with your form, reach for the *curette*.) Now do you wonder if I laugh a little off-key? Do you ask yourself what has
9 on 11pt

Walking along the Mall we wondered who all those men were – tall hawk-featured men perched on balconies and high places, scanning the city with heavy binoculars. What were they seeking so earnestly? Who were they – so composed and steely-eyed? Timidly we stopped a policeman to ask him. 'They are publishers' he said mildly. Publishers! Our hearts stopped beating. 'They are on the look out for new talent.' Great God! It was for *us* they were waiting and watching! Then the kindly policeman lowered his voice confidentially and said in hollow and reverent tones: *'They are waiting for the new Trollope to be born!'* Do you remember, at these words, how heavy our suitcases suddenly felt? How our blood slowed, our footsteps lagged? Brother Ass, we had been bashfully thinking of a kind of illumination such as Rimbaud dreamed of – a nagging poem which was not didactic or expository but which *infected* – was not simply a rationalised intuition, I mean, clothed in isinglass! We had come to the wrong shop, with the wrong change! A chill struck us as we saw the mist falling in Trafalgar Square, coiling round us its tendrils of ectoplasm! A million muffin-eating moralists were waiting, not for us, Brother Ass, but for the plucky and tedious Trollope! (If you are dissatisfied with your form, reach for the *curette*.)
9 on 12pt

Walking along the Mall we wondered who all those men were – tall hawk-featured men perched on balconies and high places, scanning the city with heavy binoculars. What were they seeking so earnestly? Who were they – so composed and steely-eyed? Timidly we stopped a police-man to ask him. 'They are publishers' he said mildly. Publishers! Our hearts stopped beating. 'They are on the look out for new talent.' Great God! It was for *us* they were waiting and watching! Then the kindly policeman lowered his voice confidentially and said in hollow and reverent tones: *'They are waiting for the new Trollope to be born!'* Do you remember, at these words, how heavy our suitcases suddenly felt? How our blood slowed, our footsteps lagged? Brother Ass, we had been bash-fully thinking of a kind of illumination such as Rimbaud dreamed of – a nagging poem which was not didactic or expository but which *infected* – was not simply a rationalised intuition, I mean, clothed in isinglass! We had come to the wrong shop, with the wrong change! A chill struck us as we saw the mist falling in Trafalgar Square, coiling round us its
10 on 12pt

Walking along the Mall we wondered who all those men were – tall hawk-featured men perched on balconies and high places, scanning the city with heavy binoculars. What were they seeking so earnestly? Who were they – so composed and steely-eyed? Timidly we stopped a police-man to ask him. 'They are publishers' he said mildly. Publishers! Our hearts stopped beating. 'They are on the look out for new talent.' Great God! It was for *us* they were waiting and watching! Then the kindly policeman lowered his voicc confidentially and said in hollow and rever-ent tones: *'They are waiting for the new Trollope to be born!'* Do you remember, at these words, how heavy our suitcases suddenly felt? How our blood slowed, our footsteps lagged? Brother Ass, we had been bash-fully thinking of a kind of illumination such as Rimbaud dreamed of – a nagging poem which was not didactic or expository but which *infected* – was not simply a rationalised intuition, I mean, clothed in isinglass! We had come to the wrong shop, with the wrong change! A chill struck us
10 on 13.5pt

Walking along the Mall we wondered who all those men were – tall hawk-featured men perched on balconies and high places, scanning the city with heavy binoculars. What were they seeking so earnestly? Who were they – so composed and steely-eyed? Timidly we stopped a policeman to ask him. 'They are publishers' he said mildly. Publishers! Our hearts stopped beating. 'They are on the look out for new talent.' Great God! It was for *us* they were waiting and watching! Then the kindly policeman lowered his voice confidentially and said in hollow and reverent tones: *'They are waiting for the new Trollope to be born!'* Do you remember, at these words, how heavy our suitcases suddenly felt? How our blood slowed, our footsteps lagged? Brother Ass, we had been bashfully thinking of a kind of illumination such as Rimbaud dreamed of – a nagging poem which was not didactic or expository but which *infected* – was not simply a rationalised intuition, I
11 on 13pt

Walking along the Mall we wondered who all those men were – tall hawk-featured men perched on balconies and high places, scanning the city with heavy binoculars. What were they seeking so earnestly? Who were they – so composed and steely-eyed? Timidly we stopped a policeman to ask him. 'They are publishers' he said mildly. Publishers! Our hearts stopped beating. 'They are on the look out for new talent.' Great God! It was for *us* they were waiting and watching! Then the kindly policeman lowered his voice confidentially and said in hollow and reverent tones: *'They are waiting for the new Trollope to be born!'* Do you remember, at these words, how heavy our suitcases suddenly felt? How our blood slowed, our footsteps lagged? Brother Ass, we had been bashfully thinking of a kind of illumination such as Rimbaud dreamed of – a nagging poem which was not didactic or exposi-
11 on 14.5pt

LINOTYPE LECTURA

Monotype **Melior**

720 roman and italic
730 semi-bold
Stempel 1952 (Hermann Zapf)
Copyfitting factor 43.1/43.1/43.1

See Linotype Melior

ABCDEFGHIJKLMNOP
QRSTUVWXYZ abcdefg
hijklmnopqrstuvwxyz
1234567890
ff fi fl ffi ffl ()[]&£$.,;:-!?''

ABCDEFGHIJKLMNOP
QRSTUVWXYZ abcdefg
hijklmnopqrstuvwxyz
1234567890
ff fi fl ffi ffl ()[]&£$.,;:-!?''

ABCDEFGHIJKLMNOP
QRSTUVWXYZ abcdefg
hijklmnopqrstuvwxyz
1234567890
ff fi fl ffi ffl ()[]&£$.,;:-!?''

24 on 27pt

These examples show *normal* letterspacing and the effect of *reduced* letterspacing on roman setting *as well as on words in italic*: they also show the appearance of figures, for example 28 May 1964, within text. These & the ampersand are not included in the setting opposite.

Normal letterspacing

These examples show *normal* letterspacing and the effect of *reduced* letterspacing on roman setting *as well as on words in italic*: they also show the appearance of figures, for example 28 May 1964, within text. These & the ampersand are not included in the setting opposite.

Minus one unit spacing

These examples show *normal* letterspacing and the effect of *reduced* letterspacing on roman setting *as well as on words in italic*: they also show the appearance of figures, for example 28 May 1964, within text. These & the ampersand are not included in the setting opposite.

Minus two units spacing

WALKING ALONG THE MALL WE WONDERED WHO ALL THOSE
WALKING ALONG THE MALL WE WONDERED WHO ALL
WALKING ALONG THE MALL WE WONDERED WHO

Capitals: normal letterspacing/plus 9 units/plus 18 units

Walking along the Mall we wondered who all those men were – tall hawk-featured men perched on balconies and high places, scanning the city with heavy binoculars. WHAT WERE THEY SEEKING SO EARNESTLY? Who were they – so composed and steely-eyed? Timidly we stopped a policeman to ask him. 'They are publishers' he said mildly. Publishers! OUR HEARTS STOPPED BEATING. 'They are on the look out for new talent.' Great God! It was for us they were waiting

Text with reduced capitals normal letterspacing/plus 6 units

WALKING ALONG THE MALL we wondered who all those men were
WALKING ALONG THE MALL we wondered who all those men were

True italic/sloped roman

Walking along the Mall we wondered who all those men were – tall hawk-featured men perched on balconies and high places, scanning the city with heavy binoculars. What were they seeking so earnestly? Who were they – so composed and steely-eyed? Timidly we stopped a policeman to ask him. 'They are publishers' he said mildly. Publishers! Our hearts stopped beating. 'They are on the look out for new talent.' Great God! It was for us they were waiting and watching! Then the kindly policeman lowered his voice confidentially and said in hollow and reverent tones: *'They are waiting for the new Trollope to be born!'* Do you remember, at these words, how heavy our suitcases suddenly felt? How our blood slowed, our footsteps lagged? Brother Ass, we had been bashfully thinking of a kind of illumination such as Rimbaud dreamed of – a nagging

8 on 9pt

Walking along the Mall we wondered who all those men were – tall hawk-featured men perched on balconies and high places, scanning the city with heavy binoculars. What were they seeking so earnestly? Who were they – so composed and steely-eyed? Timidly we stopped a policeman to ask him. 'They are publishers' he said mildly. Publishers! Our hearts stopped beating. 'They are on the look out for new talent.' Great God! It was for us they were waiting and watching! Then the kindly policeman lowered his voice confidentially and said in hollow and reverent tones: *'They are waiting for the new Trollope to be born!'* Do you remember, at these words, how heavy our suitcases suddenly felt? How our blood slowed, our footsteps lagged? Brother Ass, we had been

8 on 10.5pt

Walking along the Mall we wondered who all those men were – tall hawk-featured men perched on balconies and high places, scanning the city with heavy binoculars. What were they seeking so earnestly? Who were they – so composed and steely-eyed? Timidly we stopped a policeman to ask him. 'They are publishers' he said mildly. Publishers! Our hearts stopped beating. 'They are on the look out for new talent.' Great God! It was for us they were waiting and watching! Then the kindly policeman lowered his voice confidentially and said in hollow and reverent tones: *They are waiting for the new Trollope to be born!*' Do you remember, at these words, how heavy our suitcases suddenly felt? How our blood slowed, our footsteps lagged? Brother Ass, we had been bashfully thinking of a kind of illumination such as Rimbaud dreamed of – a nagging poem which was not didactic or expository but which *infected* – was not simply a rationalised intuition, I mean, clothed in isinglass! We had come to the wrong shop, with the wrong change! A chill struck us as we saw the mist falling in Trafalgar Square, coiling around us its tendrils of ectoplasm! A million muffin-eating moralists were waiting, not for us, Brother Ass, but for the plucky and tedious Trollope! (If you are dissatisfied with your form, reach for the *curette*.) Now do you wonder if I laugh a little off-key? Do you ask yourself what

9 on 11pt

Walking along the Mall we wondered who all those men were – tall hawk-featured men perched on balconies and high places, scanning the city with heavy binoculars. What were they seeking so earnestly? Who were they – so composed and steely-eyed? Timidly we stopped a policeman to ask him. 'They are publishers' he said mildly. Publishers! Our hearts stopped beating. 'They are on the look out for new talent.' Great God! It was for us they were waiting and watching! Then the kindly policeman lowered his voice confidentially and said in hollow and reverent tones: *They are waiting for the new Trollope to be born!*' Do you remember, at these words, how heavy our suitcases suddenly felt? How our blood slowed, our footsteps lagged? Brother Ass, we had been bashfully thinking of a kind of illumination such as Rimbaud dreamed of – a nagging poem which was not didactic or expository but which *infected* – was not simply a rationalised intuition, I mean, clothed in isinglass! We had come to the wrong shop, with the wrong change! A chill struck us as we saw the mist falling in Trafalgar Square, coiling around us its tendrils of ectoplasm! A million muffin-eating moralists were waiting, not for us, Brother Ass, but for the plucky and tedious Trollope! (If you are dissatisfied with your form, reach for the

9 on 12pt

Walking along the Mall we wondered who all those men were – tall hawk-featured men perched on balconies and high places, scanning the city with heavy binoculars. What were they seeking so earnestly? Who were they – so composed and steely-eyed? Timidly we stopped a police-man to ask him. 'They are publishers' he said mildly. Publishers! Our hearts stopped beating. 'They are on the look out for new talent.' Great God! It was for us they were waiting and watching! Then the kindly policeman lowered his voice confidentially and said in hollow and rever-ent tones: *They are waiting for the new Trollope to be born!*' Do you remember, at these words, how heavy our suitcases suddenly felt? How our blood slowed, our footsteps lagged? Brother Ass, we had been bash-fully thinking of a kind of illumination such as Rimbaud dreamed of – a nagging poem which was not didactic or expository but which *infected* – was not simply a rationalised intuition, I mean, clothed in isinglass! We had come to the wrong shop, with the wrong change! A chill struck us as we saw the mist falling in Trafalgar Square, coiling around us its

10 on 12pt

Walking along the Mall we wondered who all those men were – tall hawk-featured men perched on balconies and high places, scanning the city with heavy binoculars. What were they seeking so earnestly? Who were they – so composed and steely-eyed? Timidly we stopped a police-man to ask him. 'They are publishers' he said mildly. Publishers! Our hearts stopped beating. 'They are on the look out for new talent.' Great God! It was for us they were waiting and watching! Then the kindly policeman lowered his voice confidentially and said in hollow and rever-ent tones: *They are waiting for the new Trollope to be born!*' Do you remember, at these words, how heavy our suitcases suddenly felt? How our blood slowed, our footsteps lagged? Brother Ass, we had been bash-fully thinking of a kind of illumination such as Rimbaud dreamed of – a nagging poem which was not didactic or expository but which *infected* – was not simply a rationalised intuition, I mean, clothed in isinglass! We had come to the wrong shop, with the wrong change! A chill struck

10 on 13.5pt

Walking along the Mall we wondered who all those men were – tall hawk-featured men perched on balconies and high places, scanning the city with heavy binoculars. What were they seeking so earnestly? Who were they – so composed and steely-eyed? Timidly we stopped a policeman to ask him. 'They are publishers' he said mildly. Publishers! Our hearts stopped beating. 'They are on the look out for new talent.' Great God! It was for us they were waiting and watching! Then the kindly policeman lowered his voice confidentially and said in hollow and reverent tones: *They are waiting for the new Trollope to be born!*' Do you remember, at these words, how heavy our suitcases suddenly felt? How our blood slowed, our footsteps lagged? Brother Ass, we had been bashfully thinking of a kind of illumination such as Rimbaud dreamed of – a nagging poem which was not didactic or expository but which *infected* – was not simply a rationalised intuition,

11 on 13pt

Walking along the Mall we wondered who all those men were – tall hawk-featured men perched on balconies and high places, scanning the city with heavy binoculars. What were they seeking so earnestly? Who were they – so composed and steely-eyed? Timidly we stopped a policeman to ask him. 'They are publishers' he said mildly. Publishers! Our hearts stopped beating. 'They are on the look out for new talent.' Great God! It was for us they were waiting and watching! Then the kindly policeman lowered his voice confidentially and said in hollow and reverent tones: *They are waiting for the new Trollope to be born!*' Do you remember, at these words, how heavy our suitcases suddenly felt? How our blood slowed, our footsteps lagged? Brother Ass, we had been bashfully thinking of a kind of illumination such as Rimbaud dreamed of – a nagging poem which was not didactic or exposi-

11 on 14.5pt

MONOTYPE MELIOR

Linotype **Melior**

roman (05170), **italic** (13170)
bold (07170)
Stempel 1952 (Hermann Zapf)
Copyfitting code 135/136/138

Range also includes medium, medium italic,
bold italic, black, black italic

Designed as a newspaper face and first used
by *Hannoversche Presse*

Educational characters available

ABCDEFGHIJKLMNOP
QRSTUVWXYZ abcdefg
hijklmnopqrstuvwxyz
1234567890 1234567890
fifl ()[]&£$.,;:-!?''

ABCDEFGHIJKLMNOP
QRSTUVWXYZ abcdefg
hijklmnopqrstuvwxyz
1234567890 1234567890
fifl ()[]&£$.,;:-!?''

ABCDEFGHIJKLMNOP
QRSTUVWXYZ abcdefg
hijklmnopqrstuvwxyz
1234567890 1234567890
fifl ()[]&£$.,;:-!?''

24 on 27pt

These examples show *normal* letterspacing and the effect of *reduced* letterspacing on roman setting *as well as on words in italic*: they also show the appearance of figures, for example 28 May 1964, within text. These & the ampersand are not included in the setting opposite.
Normal letterspacing

These examples show *normal* letterspacing and the effect of *reduced* letterspacing on roman setting *as well as on words in italic*: they also show the appearance of figures, for example 28 May 1964, within text. These & the ampersand are not included in the setting opposite.
Minus one unit spacing

These examples show *normal* letterspacing and the effect of *reduced* letterspacing on roman setting *as well as on words in italic*: they also show the appearance of figures, for example 28 May 1964, within text. These & the ampersand are not included in the setting opposite.
Minus two units spacing

WALKING ALONG THE MALL WE WONDERED WHO ALL
WALKING ALONG THE MALL WE WONDERED WHO
WALKING ALONG THE MALL WE WONDERED
Capitals: normal letterspacing/plus 4 units/plus 9 units

WALKING ALONG THE MALL WE WONDERED WHO ALL THOSE MEN
WALKING ALONG THE MALL WE WONDERED WHO ALL THOSE
WALKING ALONG THE MALL WE WONDERED WHO ALL
Small caps: normal letterspacing/plus 3 units/plus 6 units

WALKING ALONG THE MALL WE WONDERED WHO ALL THOSE MEN
WALKING ALONG THE MALL WE WONDERED WHO ALL THOSE MEN WERE
True small caps/reduced capitals

WALKING ALONG THE MALL we wondered who all those men
WALKING ALONG THE MALL we wondered who all those men
True italic/sloped roman

Walking along the Mall we wondered who all those men were – tall hawk-featured men perched on balconies and high places, scanning the city with heavy binoculars. What were they seeking so earnestly? Who were they – so composed and steely-eyed? Timidly we stopped a policeman to ask him. 'They are publishers' he said mildly. Publishers! Our hearts stopped beating. 'They are on the look out for new talent.' Great God! It was for us they were waiting and watching! Then the kindly policeman lowered his voice confidentially and said in hollow and reverent tones: '*They are waiting for the new Trollope to be born!*' Do you remember, at these words, how heavy our suitcases suddenly felt? How our blood slowed, our footsteps lagged? Brother Ass, we had been bashfully thinking

8 on 9pt

WALKING ALONG THE MALL WE WONDERED WHO ALL THOSE MEN WERE – TALL hawk-featured men perched on balconies and high places, scanning the city with heavy binoculars. What were they seeking so earnestly? Who were they – so composed and steely-eyed? Timidly we stopped a policeman to ask him. 'They are publishers' he said mildly. Publishers! Our hearts stopped beating. 'They are on the look out for new talent.' Great God! It was for *us* they were waiting and watching! Then the kindly policeman lowered his voice confidentially and said in hollow and reverent tones: '*They are waiting for the new Trollope to be born!*' Do you remember, at these words, how heavy our suitcases suddenly felt? How our

8 on 10.5pt

Walking along the Mall we wondered who all those men were – tall hawk-featured men perched on balconies and high places, scanning the city with heavy binoculars. What were they seeking so earnestly? Who were they – so composed and steely-eyed? Timidly we stopped a policeman to ask him. 'They are publishers' he said mildly. Publishers! Our hearts stopped beating. 'They are on the look out for new talent.' Great God! It was for *us* they were waiting and watching! Then the kindly policeman lowered his voice confidentially and said in hollow and reverent tones: *'They are waiting for the new Trollope to be born!'* Do you remember, at these words, how heavy our suitcases suddenly felt? How our blood slowed, our footsteps lagged? Brother Ass, we had been bashfully thinking of a kind of illumination such as Rimbaud dreamed of – a nagging poem which was not didactic or expository but which *infected* – was not simply a rationalised intuition, I mean, clothed in isinglass! We had come to the wrong shop, with the wrong change! A chill struck us as we saw the mist falling in Trafalgar Square, coiling round us its tendrils of ectoplasm! A million muffin-eating moralists were waiting, not for us, Brother Ass, but for the plucky and tedious Trollope! (If you are dis-

9 on 11pt

Walking along the Mall we wondered who all those men were – tall hawk-featured men perched on balconies and high places, scanning the city with heavy binoculars. What were they seeking so earnestly? Who were they – so composed and steely-eyed? Timidly we stopped a policeman to ask him. 'They are publishers' he said mildly. Publishers! Our hearts stopped beating. 'They are on the look out for new talent.' Great God! It was for *us* they were waiting and watching! Then the kindly policeman lowered his voice confidentially and said in hollow and reverent tones: *'They are waiting for the new Trollope to be born!'* Do you remember, at these words, how heavy our suitcases suddenly felt? How our blood slowed, our footsteps lagged? Brother Ass, we had been bashfully thinking of a kind of illumination such as Rimbaud dreamed of – a nagging poem which was not didactic or expository but which *infected* – was not simply a rationalised intuition, I mean, clothed in isinglass! We had come to the wrong shop, with

10 on 12pt

Walking along the Mall we wondered who all those men were – tall hawk-featured men perched on balconies and high places, scanning the city with heavy binoculars. What were they seeking so earnestly? Who were they – so composed and steely-eyed? Timidly we stopped a policeman to ask him. 'They are publishers' he said mildly. Publishers! Our hearts stopped beating. 'They are on the look out for new talent.' Great God! It was for *us* they were waiting and watching! Then the kindly policeman lowered his voice confidentially and said in hollow and reverent tones: *'They are waiting for the new Trollope to be born!'* Do you remember, at these words, how heavy our suitcases suddenly felt? How our blood slowed, our footsteps lagged? Brother Ass, we had been bashfully thinking of a kind of illumination such as Rimbaud dreamed of – a nagging poem which was

11 on 13pt

WALKING ALONG THE MALL WE WONDERED WHO ALL THOSE MEN WERE – tall hawk-featured men perched on balconies and high places, scanning the city with heavy binoculars. What were they seeking so earnestly? Who were they – so composed and steely-eyed? Timidly we stopped a policeman to ask him. 'They are publishers' he said mildly. Publishers! Our hearts stopped beating. 'They are on the look out for new talent.' Great God! It was for *us* they were waiting and watching! Then the kindly policeman lowered his voice confidentially and said in hollow and reverent tones: *'They are waiting for the new Trollope to be born!'* Do you remember, at these words, how heavy our suitcases suddenly felt? How our blood slowed, our footsteps lagged? Brother Ass, we had been bashfully thinking of a kind of illumination such as Rimbaud dreamed of – a nagging poem which was not didactic or expository but which *infected* – was not simply a rationalised intuition, I mean, clothed in isinglass! We had come to the wrong shop, with the wrong change! A chill struck us as we saw the mist falling in Trafalgar Square, coiling round us its tendrils of ectoplasm! A million muffin-eating moralists were waiting, not for us,

9 on 12pt

WALKING ALONG THE MALL WE WONDERED WHO ALL THOSE MEN were – tall hawk-featured men perched on balconies and high places, scanning the city with heavy binoculars. What were they seeking so earnestly? Who were they – so composed and steely-eyed? Timidly we stopped a policeman to ask him. 'They are publishers' he said mildly. Publishers! Our hearts stopped beating. 'They are on the look out for new talent.' Great God! It was for *us* they were waiting and watching! Then the kindly policeman lowered his voice confidentially and said in hollow and reverent tones: *'They are waiting for the new Trollope to be born!'* Do you remember, at these words, how heavy our suitcases suddenly felt? How our blood slowed, our footsteps lagged? Brother Ass, we had been bashfully thinking of a kind of illumination such as Rimbaud dreamed of – a nagging poem which was not didactic or expository but which *infected* – was not simply a rationalised intuition,

10 on 13.5pt

WALKING ALONG THE MALL WE WONDERED WHO ALL THOSE men were – tall hawk-featured men perched on balconies and high places, scanning the city with heavy binoculars. What were they seeking so earnestly? Who were they – so composed and steely-eyed? Timidly we stopped a policeman to ask him. 'They are publishers' he said mildly. Publishers! Our hearts stopped beating. 'They are on the look out for new talent.' Great God! It was for *us* they were waiting and watching! Then the kindly policeman lowered his voice confidentially and said in hollow and reverent tones: *'They are waiting for the new Trollope to be born!'* Do you remember, at these words, how heavy our suitcases suddenly felt? How our blood slowed, our footsteps lagged? Brother Ass, we had been bashfully thinking of a kind of illumination

11 on 14.5pt

LINOTYPE MELIOR

Monotype **Meridien**

930 roman and italic
932 bold
Deberney & Peignot 1957 (Adrian Frutiger)
Copyfitting factor 49.4/45.1/44.7

Range also includes bold italic

The Linotype version is similar (copyfitting
code 131/116/149)

ABCDEFGHIJKLMNOP
QRSTUVWXYZ abcdefg
hijklmnopqrstuvwxyz
1234567890
ff fi fl ffi ffi ffl () [] &£$.,;:-!?''

ABCDEFGHIJKLMNOP
QRSTUVWXYZ abcdefg
hijklmnopqrstuvwxyz
1234567890
ff fi fl ffi ffi ffl () [] &£$.,;:-!?''

ABCDEFGHIJKLMNOP
QRSTUVWXYZ abcdefg
hijklmnopqrstuvwxyz
1234567890
ff fi fl ffi ffi ffl () [] &£$.,;:-!?''

24 on 27pt

200

These examples show *normal* letterspacing and the effect of *reduced*
letterspacing on roman setting *as well as on words in italic*: they also
show the appearance of figures, for example 28 May 1964, within text.
These & the ampersand are not included in the setting opposite.

Normal letterspacing

These examples show *normal* letterspacing and the effect of *reduced*
letterspacing on roman setting *as well as on words in italic*: they also
show the appearance of figures, for example 28 May 1964, within text.
These & the ampersand are not included in the setting opposite.

Minus one unit spacing

These examples show *normal* letterspacing and the effect of *reduced*
letterspacing on roman setting *as well as on words in italic*: they also
show the appearance of figures, for example 28 May 1964, within text.
These & the ampersand are not included in the setting opposite.

Minus two units spacing

WALKING ALONG THE MALL WE WONDERED WHO ALL THOSE
WALKING ALONG THE MALL WE WONDERED WHO ALL
WALKING ALONG THE MALL WE WONDERED WHO

Capitals: normal letterspacing/plus 9 units/plus 18 units

Walking along the Mall we wondered who all those men were –
tall hawk-featured men perched on balconies and high places,
scanning the city with heavy binoculars. WHAT WERE THEY SEEKING
SO EARNESTLY? Who were they – so composed and steely-eyed?
Timidly we stopped a policeman to ask him. 'They are
publishers' HE SAID MILDLY. PUBLISHERS! Our hearts stopped
beating. 'They are on the look out for new talent.' Great God! It

Text with reduced capitals normal letterspacing/plus 6 units

WALKING ALONG THE MALL we wondered who all those men were
WALKING ALONG THE MALL we wondered who all those men were

True italic/sloped roman

Walking along the Mall we wondered who all those men were – tall hawk-
featured men perched on balconies and high places, scanning the city with heavy
binoculars. What were they seeking so earnestly? Who were they – so composed and
steely-eyed? Timidly we stopped a policeman to ask him. 'They are publishers' he
said mildly. Publishers! Our hearts stopped beating. 'They are on the look out for
new talent.' Great God! It was for *us* they were waiting and watching! Then the
kindly policeman lowered his voice confidentially and said in hollow and reverent
tones: *'They are waiting for the new Trollope to be born!'* Do you remember, at these
words, how heavy our suitcases suddenly felt? How our blood slowed, our footsteps
lagged? Brother Ass, we had been bashfully thinking of a kind of illumination such

8 on 9pt

Walking along the Mall we wondered who all those men were – tall hawk-featured
men perched on balconies and high places, scanning the city with heavy binoculars.
What were they seeking so earnestly? Who were they – so composed and steely-
eyed? Timidly we stopped a policeman to ask him. 'They are publishers' he said
mildly. Publishers! Our hearts stopped beating. 'They are on the look out for new
talent.' Great God! It was for *us* they were waiting and watching! Then the kindly
policeman lowered his voice confidentially and said in hollow and reverent tones:
'They are waiting for the new Trollope to be born!' Do you remember, at these words, how
heavy our suitcases suddenly felt? How our blood slowed, our footsteps lagged?

8 on 10.5pt

Walking along the Mall we wondered who all those men were – tall hawk-featured men perched on balconies and high places, scanning the city with heavy binoculars. What were they seeking so earnestly? Who were they – so composed and steely-eyed? Timidly we stopped a policeman to ask him. 'They are publishers' he said mildly. Publishers! Our hearts stopped beating. 'They are on the look out for new talent.' Great God! It was for *us* they were waiting and watching! Then the kindly policeman lowered his voice confidentially and said in hollow and reverent tones: *'They are waiting for the new Trollope to be born!'* Do you remember, at these words, how heavy our suitcases suddenly felt? How our blood slowed, our footsteps lagged? Brother Ass, we had been bashfully thinking of a kind of illumination such as Rimbaud dreamed of – a nagging poem which was not didactic or expository but which *infected* – was not simply a rationalised intuition, I mean, clothed in isinglass! We had come to the wrong shop, with the wrong change! A chill struck us as we saw the mist falling in Trafalgar Square, coiling around us its tendrils of ectoplasm! A million muffin-eating moralists were waiting, not for us, Brother Ass, but for the plucky and tedious Trollope! (If you are dissatisfied with your form, reach for the *curette*.) Now do you wonder if I laugh a little off-key?

9 on 11pt

Walking along the Mall we wondered who all those men were – tall hawk-featured men perched on balconies and high places, scanning the city with heavy binoculars. What were they seeking so earnestly? Who were they – so composed and steely-eyed? Timidly we stopped a policeman to ask him. 'They are publishers' he said mildly. Publishers! Our hearts stopped beating. 'They are on the look out for new talent.' Great God! It was for *us* they were waiting and watching! Then the kindly policeman lowered his voice confidentially and said in hollow and reverent tones: *'They are waiting for the new Trollope to be born!'* Do you remember, at these words, how heavy our suitcases suddenly felt? How our blood slowed, our footsteps lagged? Brother Ass, we had been bashfully thinking of a kind of illumination such as Rimbaud dreamed of – a nagging poem which was not didactic or expository but which *infected* – was not simply a rationalised intuition, I mean, clothed in isinglass! We had come to the wrong shop, with the wrong change! A chill struck us as we saw the mist falling in

10 on 12pt

Walking along the Mall we wondered who all those men were – tall hawk-featured men perched on balconies and high places, scanning the city with heavy binoculars. What were they seeking so earnestly? Who were they – so composed and steely-eyed? Timidly we stopped a policeman to ask him. 'They are publishers' he said mildly. Publishers! Our hearts stopped beating. 'They are on the look out for new talent.' Great God! It was for *us* they were waiting and watching! Then the kindly policeman lowered his voice confidentially and said in hollow and reverent tones: *'They are waiting for the new Trollope to be born!'* Do you remember, at these words, how heavy our suitcases suddenly felt? How our blood slowed, our footsteps lagged? Brother Ass, we had been bashfully thinking of a kind of illumination such as Rimbaud dreamed of – a nagging poem which was not didactic or expository but which *infected* – was

11 on 13pt

Walking along the Mall we wondered who all those men were – tall hawk-featured men perched on balconies and high places, scanning the city with heavy binoculars. What were they seeking so earnestly? Who were they – so composed and steely-eyed? Timidly we stopped a policeman to ask him. 'They are publishers' he said mildly. Publishers! Our hearts stopped beating. 'They are on the look out for new talent.' Great God! It was for *us* they were waiting and watching! Then the kindly policeman lowered his voice confidentially and said in hollow and reverent tones: *'They are waiting for the new Trollope to be born!'* Do you remember, at these words, how heavy our suitcases suddenly felt? How our blood slowed, our footsteps lagged? Brother Ass, we had been bashfully thinking of a kind of illumination such as Rimbaud dreamed of – a nagging poem which was not didactic or expository but which *infected* – was not simply a rationalised intuition, I mean, clothed in isinglass! We had come to the wrong shop,

10 on 13.5pt

Walking along the Mall we wondered who all those men were – tall hawk-featured men perched on balconies and high places, scanning the city with heavy binoculars. What were they seeking so earnestly? Who were they – so composed and steely-eyed? Timidly we stopped a policeman to ask him. 'They are publishers' he said mildly. Publishers! Our hearts stopped beating. 'They are on the look out for new talent.' Great God! It was for *us* they were waiting and watching! Then the kindly policeman lowered his voice confidentially and said in hollow and reverent tones: *'They are waiting for the new Trollope to be born!'* Do you remember, at these words, how heavy our suitcases suddenly felt? How our blood slowed, our footsteps lagged? Brother Ass, we had been bashfully thinking of a kind of illumination such as Rimbaud dreamed of – a nagging poem

11 on 14.5pt

Monotype **Modern Extended**

7 roman and italic
570 bold
Monotype 1902 (bold 1954)
Copyfitting factor 43.9/41.4/43.0

Range also includes bold italic. Monotype
Clarendon 12 is a useful alternative bold

From a Miller & Richard face (possibly cut by
Richard Austin) which was used by *The Times*.
One of the first types made for mechanical
composition

ABCDEFGHIJKLMNOP
QRSTUVWXYZ abcdefg
hijklmnopqrstuvwxyz
1234567890
ff fi fl ffi ffl ()[]&£$.,;:-!?''

ABCDEFGHIJKLMNOP
QRSTUVWXYZ abcdefg
hijklmnopqrstuvwxyz
1234567890
ff fi fl ffi ffl ( ) [ ] & £ $.,;:-!?''

ABCDEFGHIJKLMNOP
QRSTUVWXYZ abcdefg
hijklmnopqrstuvwxyz
1234567890
ff fi fl ffi ffl ()[]&£$.,;:-!?''

24 on 27pt

These examples show *normal* letterspacing and the effect of *reduced*
letterspacing on roman setting *as well as on words in italic*: they also
show the appearance of figures, for example 28 May 1964, within text.
These & the ampersand are not included in the setting opposite.

Normal letterspacing

These examples show *normal* letterspacing and the effect of *reduced*
letterspacing on roman setting *as well as on words in italic*: they also
show the appearance of figures, for example 28 May 1964, within text.
These & the ampersand are not included in the setting opposite.

Minus one unit spacing

These examples show *normal* letterspacing and the effect of *reduced*
letterspacing on roman setting *as well as on words in italic*: they also
show the appearance of figures, for example 28 May 1964, within text.
These & the ampersand are not included in the setting opposite.

Minus two units spacing

WALKING ALONG THE MALL WE WONDERED WHO ALL
WALKING ALONG THE MALL WE WONDERED WHO
WALKING ALONG THE MALL WE WONDERED

Capitals: normal letterspacing/plus 9 units/plus 18 units

WALKING ALONG THE MALL WE WONDERED WHO ALL THOSE MEN WERE
WALKING ALONG THE MALL WE WONDERED WHO ALL THOSE MEN
WALKING ALONG THE MALL WE WONDERED WHO ALL THOSE

Small caps: normal letterspacing/plus 6 units/plus 12 units

WALKING ALONG THE MALL we wondered who all those men were
WALKING ALONG THE MALL we wondered who all those men

True italic/sloped roman

WALKING ALONG THE MALL WE WONDERED WHO ALL THOSE MEN WERE
WALKING ALONG THE MALL WE WONDERED WHO ALL THOSE MEN WERE

True small caps/reduced capitals

Walking along the Mall we wondered who all those men were – tall hawk-featured
men perched on balconies and high places, scanning the city with heavy binoculars.
What were they seeking so earnestly? Who were they – so composed and steely-eyed?
Timidly we stopped a policeman to ask him. 'They are publishers' he said mildly.
Publishers! Our hearts stopped beating. 'They are on the look out for new talent.'
Great God! It was for *us* they were waiting and watching! Then the kindly policeman
lowered his voice confidentially and said in hollow and reverent tones: *'They are*
waiting for the new Trollope to be born!' Do you remember, at these words, how heavy
our suitcases suddenly felt? How our blood slowed, our footsteps lagged? Brother Ass,
we had been bashfully thinking of a kind of illumination such as Rimbaud dreamed of

8 on 9pt

WALKING ALONG THE MALL WE WONDERED WHO ALL THOSE MEN WERE – TALL
hawk-featured men perched on balconies and high places, scanning the city with
heavy binoculars. What were they seeking so earnestly? Who were they – so composed
and steely-eyed? Timidly we stopped a policeman to ask him. 'They are publishers' he
said mildly. Publishers! Our hearts stopped beating. 'They are on the look out for new
talent.' Great God! It was for *us* they were waiting and watching! Then the kindly
policeman lowered his voice confidentially and said in hollow and reverent tones:
'They are waiting for the new Trollope to be born!' Do you remember, at these words,
how heavy our suitcases suddenly felt? How our blood slowed, our footsteps lagged?

8 on 10.5pt

Walking along the Mall we wondered who all those men were – tall hawk-featured men perched on balconies and high places, scanning the city with heavy binoculars. What were they seeking so earnestly? Who were they – so composed and steely-eyed? Timidly we stopped a policeman to ask him. 'They are publishers' he said mildly. Publishers! Our hearts stopped beating. 'They are on the look out for new talent.' Great God! It was for *us* they were waiting and watching! Then the kindly policeman lowered his voice confidentially and said in hollow and reverent tones: *'They are waiting for the new Trollope to be born!'* Do you remember, at these words, how heavy our suitcases suddenly felt? How our blood slowed, our footsteps lagged? Brother Ass, we had been bashfully thinking of a kind of illumination such as Rimbaud dreamed of – a nagging poem which was not didactic or expository but which *infected* – was not simply a rationalised intuition, I mean, clothed in isinglass! We had come to the wrong shop, with the wrong change! A chill struck us as we saw the mist falling in Trafalgar Square, coiling around us its tendrils of ectoplasm! A million muffin-eating moralists were waiting, not for us, Brother Ass, but for the plucky and tedious Trollope! (If you are dissatisfied with your form, reach for the *curette*.) Now do you wonder if I laugh a little off-key? Do you ask yourself

9 on 11pt

Walking along the Mall we wondered who all those men were – tall hawk-featured men perched on balconies and high places, scanning the city with heavy binoculars. What were they seeking so earnestly? Who were they – so composed and steely-eyed? Timidly we stopped a policeman to ask him. 'They are publishers' he said mildly. Publishers! Our hearts stopped beating. 'They are on the look out for new talent.' Great God! It was for *us* they were waiting and watching! Then the kindly policeman lowered his voice confidentially and said in hollow and reverent tones: *'They are waiting for the new Trollope to be born!'* Do you remember, at these words, how heavy our suitcases suddenly felt? How our blood slowed, our footsteps lagged? Brother Ass, we had been bashfully thinking of a kind of illumination such as Rimbaud dreamed of – a nagging poem which was not didactic or expository but which *infected* – was not simply a rationalised intuition, I mean, clothed in isinglass! We had come to the wrong shop, with the wrong change! A chill struck us as we saw the mist falling in Trafalgar Square, coiling

10 on 12pt

Walking along the Mall we wondered who all those men were – tall hawk-featured men perched on balconies and high places, scanning the city with heavy binoculars. What were they seeking so earnestly? Who were they – so composed and steely-eyed? Timidly we stopped a policeman to ask him. 'They are publishers' he said mildly. Publishers! Our hearts stopped beating. 'They are on the look out for new talent.' Great God! It was for *us* they were waiting and watching! Then the kindly policeman lowered his voice confidentially and said in hollow and reverent tones: *'They are waiting for the new Trollope to be born!'* Do you remember, at these words, how heavy our suitcases suddenly felt? How our blood slowed, our footsteps lagged? Brother Ass, we had been bashfully thinking of a kind of illumination such as Rimbaud dreamed of – a nagging poem which was not didactic or expository but which *infected* – was not simply a rationalised

11 on 13pt

WALKING ALONG THE MALL WE WONDERED WHO ALL THOSE MEN WERE – tall hawk-featured men perched on balconies and high places, scanning the city with heavy binoculars. What were they seeking so earnestly? Who were they – so composed and steely-eyed? Timidly we stopped a policeman to ask him. 'They are publishers' he said mildly. Publishers! Our hearts stopped beating. 'They are on the look out for new talent.' Great God! It was for *us* they were waiting and watching! Then the kindly policeman lowered his voice confidentially and said in hollow and reverent tones: *'They are waiting for the new Trollope to be born!'* Do you remember, at these words, how heavy our suitcases suddenly felt? How our blood slowed, our footsteps lagged? Brother Ass, we had been bashfully thinking of a kind of illumination such as Rimbaud dreamed of – a nagging poem which was not didactic or expository but which *infected* – was not simply a rationalised intuition, I mean, clothed in isinglass! We had come to the wrong shop, with the wrong change! A chill struck us as we saw the mist falling in Trafalgar Square, coiling around us its tendrils of ectoplasm! A million muffin-eating moralists were waiting, not for us, Brother Ass, but for the plucky and tedious Trollope! (If you are dissatisfied with your

9 on 12pt

WALKING ALONG THE MALL WE WONDERED WHO ALL THOSE MEN were – tall hawk-featured men perched on balconies and high places, scanning the city with heavy binoculars. What were they seeking so earnestly? Who were they – so composed and steely-eyed? Timidly we stopped a policeman to ask him. 'They are publishers' he said mildly. Publishers! Our hearts stopped beating. 'They are on the look out for new talent.' Great God! It was for *us* they were waiting and watching! Then the kindly policeman lowered his voice confidentially and said in hollow and reverent tones: *'They are waiting for the new Trollope to be born!'* Do you remember, at these words, how heavy our suitcases suddenly felt? How our blood slowed, our footsteps lagged? Brother Ass, we had been bashfully thinking of a kind of illumination such as Rimbaud dreamed of – a nagging poem which was not didactic or expository but which *infected* – was not simply a rationalised intuition, I mean, clothed in isinglass! We had come to the wrong shop, with the

10 on 13.5pt

WALKING ALONG THE MALL WE WONDERED WHO ALL THOSE men were – tall hawk-featured men perched on balconies and high places, scanning the city with heavy binoculars. What were they seeking so earnestly? Who were they – so composed and steely-eyed? Timidly we stopped a policeman to ask him. 'They are publishers' he said mildly. Publishers! Our hearts stopped beating. 'They are on the look out for new talent.' Great God! It was for *us* they were waiting and watching! Then the kindly policeman lowered his voice confidentially and said in hollow and reverent tones: *'They are waiting for the new Trollope to be born!'* Do you remember, at these words, how heavy our suitcases suddenly felt? How our blood slowed, our footsteps lagged? Brother Ass, we had been bashfully thinking of a kind of illumination such as Rimbaud dreamed of – a nagging poem

11 on 14.5pt

Monotype MODERN WIDE

16 roman and italic
Monotype 1903
Copyfitting factor 50.0/47.1

Based on a Miller & Richard typeface

ABCDEFGHIJK
LMNOPQRSTUVW
XYZ
abcdefghijklmn
opqrstuvwxyz
1234567890
ff fi fl ffi ffl ( )[ ]&£$.,;:-!?''

ABCDEFGHIJK
LMNOPQRSTUVW
XYZ
abcdefghijklmn
opqrstuvwxyz
1234567890
ff fi fl ffi ffl ( )[ ]&£$.,;:-!?''

24 on 27pt

These examples show *normal* letterspacing and the effect of *reduced* letterspacing on roman setting *as well as on words in italic*: they also show the appearance of figures, for example 28 May 1964, within text. These & the ampersand are not included in the setting opposite.
Normal letterspacing

These examples show *normal* letterspacing and the effect of *reduced* letterspacing on roman setting *as well as on words in italic*: they also show the appearance of figures, for example 28 May 1964, within text. These & the ampersand are not included in the setting opposite.
Minus one unit spacing

These examples show *normal* letterspacing and the effect of *reduced* letterspacing on roman setting *as well as on words in italic*: they also show the appearance of figures, for example 28 May 1964, within text. These & the ampersand are not included in the setting opposite.
Minus two units spacing

WALKING ALONG THE MALL WE WONDERED WHO ALL
WALKING ALONG THE MALL WE WONDERED WHO
WALKING ALONG THE MALL WE WONDERED
Capitals: normal letterspacing/plus 9 units/plus 18 units

Walking along the Mall we wondered who all those men were – tall hawk-featured men perched on balconies and high places, scanning the city with heavy binoculars. WHAT WERE THEY SEEKING SO EARNESTLY? Who were they – so composed and steely-eyed? Timidly we stopped a policeman to ask him. 'They are publishers' HE SAID MILDLY. PUBLISHERS! our hearts stopped beating. 'They are on the look out for new talent.' Great God! It
Text with reduced capitals normal letterspacing/plus 6 units

WALKING ALONG THE MALL we wondered who all those men
WALKING ALONG THE MALL we wondered who all those men
True italic/sloped roman

Walking along the Mall we wondered who all those men were – tall hawk-featured men perched on balconies and high places, scanning the city with heavy binoculars. What were they seeking so earnestly? Who were they – so composed and steely-eyed? Timidly we stopped a policeman to ask him. 'They are publishers' he said mildly. Publishers! Our hearts stopped beating. 'They are on the look out for new talent.' Great God! It was for *us* they were waiting and watching! Then the kindly policeman lowered his voice confidentially and said in hollow and reverent tones: '*They are waiting for the new Trollope to be born!*' Do you remember, at these words, how heavy our suitcases suddenly felt? How our blood slowed, our
8 on 9pt

Walking along the Mall we wondered who all those men were – tall hawk-featured men perched on balconies and high places, scanning the city with heavy binoculars. What were they seeking so earnestly? Who were they – so composed and steely-eyed? Timidly we stopped a policeman to ask him. 'They are publishers' he said mildly. Publishers! Our hearts stopped beating. 'They are on the look out for new talent.' Great God! It was for *us* they were waiting and watching! Then the kindly policeman lowered his voice confidentially and said in hollow and reverent tones: '*They are waiting for the new Trollope to be born!*' Do you remember, at these words,
8 on 10.5pt

Walking along the Mall we wondered who all those men were – tall hawk-featured men perched on balconies and high places, scanning the city with heavy binoculars. What were they seeking so earnestly? Who were they – so composed and steely-eyed? Timidly we stopped a policeman to ask him. 'They are publishers' he said mildly. Publishers! Our hearts stopped beating. 'They are on the look out for new talent.' Great God! It was for *us* they were waiting and watching! Then the kindly policeman lowered his voice confidentially and said in hollow and reverent tones: '*They are waiting for the new Trollope to be born!*' Do you remember, at these words, how heavy our suitcases suddenly felt? How our blood slowed, our footsteps lagged? Brother Ass, we had been bashfully thinking of a kind of illumination such as Rimbaud dreamed of – a nagging poem which was not didactic or expository but which *infected* – was not simply a rationalised intuition, I mean, clothed in isinglass! We had come to the wrong shop, with the wrong change! A chill struck us as we saw the mist falling in Trafalgar Square, coiling around us its tendrils of ectoplasm! A million muffin-eating moralists were wait-

9 on 11pt

Walking along the Mall we wondered who all those men were – tall hawk-featured men perched on balconies and high places, scanning the city with heavy binoculars. What were they seeking so earnestly? Who were they – so composed and steely-eyed? Timidly we stopped a policeman to ask him. 'They are publishers' he said mildly. Publishers! Our hearts stopped beating. 'They are on the look out for new talent.' Great God! It was for *us* they were waiting and watching! Then the kindly policeman lowered his voice confidentially and said in hollow and reverent tones: '*They are waiting for the new Trollope to be born!*' Do you remember, at these words, how heavy our suitcases suddenly felt? How our blood slowed, our footsteps lagged? Brother Ass, we had been bashfully thinking of a kind of illumination such as Rimbaud dreamed of – a nagging poem which was not didactic or expository but which *infected* – was not simply a rationalised intuition, I mean, clothed in isinglass! We had come to the wrong shop, with the wrong change! A chill struck us as we saw the mist falling in Trafalgar Square, coiling around us its

9 on 12pt

Walking along the Mall we wondered who all those men were – tall hawk-featured men perched on balconies and high places, scanning the city with heavy binoculars. What were they seeking so earnestly? Who were they – so composed and steely-eyed? Timidly we stopped a policeman to ask him. 'They are publishers' he said mildly. Publishers! Our hearts stopped beating. 'They are on the look out for new talent.' Great God! It was for *us* they were waiting and watching! Then the kindly policeman lowered his voice confidentially and said in hollow and reverent tones: '*They are waiting for the new Trollope to be born!*' Do you remember, at these words, how heavy our suitcases suddenly felt? How our blood slowed, our footsteps lagged? Brother Ass, we had been bashfully thinking of a kind of illumination such as Rimbaud dreamed of – a nagging poem which was not didactic or expository but which *infected* – was not simply a rationalised

10 on 12pt

Walking along the Mall we wondered who all those men were – tall hawk-featured men perched on balconies and high places, scanning the city with heavy binoculars. What were they seeking so earnestly? Who were they – so composed and steely-eyed? Timidly we stopped a policeman to ask him. 'They are publishers' he said mildly. Publishers! Our hearts stopped beating. 'They are on the look out for new talent.' Great God! It was for *us* they were waiting and watching! Then the kindly policeman lowered his voice confidentially and said in hollow and reverent tones: '*They are waiting for the new Trollope to be born!*' Do you remember, at these words, how heavy our suitcases suddenly felt? How our blood slowed, our footsteps lagged? Brother Ass, we had been bashfully thinking of a kind of illumination such as Rimbaud dreamed of – a nagging poem which was not didactic or

10 on 13.5pt

Walking along the Mall we wondered who all those men were – tall hawk-featured men perched on balconies and high places, scanning the city with heavy binoculars. What were they seeking so earnestly? Who were they – so composed and steely-eyed? Timidly we stopped a policeman to ask him. 'They are publishers' he said mildly. Publishers! Our hearts stopped beating. 'They are on the look out for new talent.' Great God! It was for *us* they were waiting and watching! Then the kindly policeman lowered his voice confidentially and said in hollow and reverent tones: '*They are waiting for the new Trollope to be born!*' Do you remember, at these words, how heavy our suitcases suddenly felt? How our blood slowed, our footsteps lagged? Brother Ass, we had been bashfully thinking of a kind of illumination such as

11 on 13pt

Walking along the Mall we wondered who all those men were – tall hawk-featured men perched on balconies and high places, scanning the city with heavy binoculars. What were they seeking so earnestly? Who were they – so composed and steely-eyed? Timidly we stopped a policeman to ask him. 'They are publishers' he said mildly. Publishers! Our hearts stopped beating. 'They are on the look out for new talent.' Great God! It was for *us* they were waiting and watching! Then the kindly policeman lowered his voice confidentially and said in hollow and reverent tones: '*They are waiting for the new Trollope to be born!*' Do you remember, at these words, how heavy our suitcases suddenly felt? How our blood slowed, our footsteps lagged? Brother Ass, we had been

11 on 14.5pt

603 roman and italic
Monotype 1963 (Will Carter and David
Kindersley)
Modified for phototypesetting 1975
Copyfitting factor 37.0/36.7

ABCDEFGHIJKLMNOP
QRSTUVWXYZ abcdefg
hijklmnopqrstuvwxyz
1234567890
ff fi fl ffi ffl ()[]&£$.,;:-!?''

ABCDEFGHIJKLMNOP
QRSTUVWXYZ abcdefg
hijklmnopqrstuvwxyz
1234567890
fffi fl ffi ffl ()[]&£$.,;:-!?''

24 on 27pt

These examples show *normal* letterspacing and the effect of *reduced*
letterspacing on roman setting *as well as on words in italic*: they also
show the appearance of figures, for example 28 May 1964, within text.
These & the ampersand are not included in the setting opposite.

Normal letterspacing

These examples show *normal* letterspacing and the effect of *reduced*
letterspacing on roman setting *as well as on words in italic*: they also
show the appearance of figures, for example 28 May 1964, within text.
These & the ampersand are not included in the setting opposite.

Minus one unit spacing

These examples show *normal* letterspacing and the effect of *reduced*
letterspacing on roman setting *as well as on words in italic*: they also
show the appearance of figures, for example 28 May 1964, within text.
These & the ampersand are not included in the setting opposite.

Minus two units spacing

WALKING ALONG THE MALL WE WONDERED WHO ALL THOSE MEN WERE
WALKING ALONG THE MALL WE WONDERED WHO ALL THOSE
WALKING ALONG THE MALL WE WONDERED WHO ALL

Capitals: normal letterspacing/plus 9 units/plus 18 units

WALKING ALONG THE MALL WE WONDERED WHO ALL THOSE MEN WERE
WALKING ALONG THE MALL WE WONDERED WHO ALL THOSE MEN WERE
WALKING ALONG THE MALL WE WONDERED WHO ALL THOSE MEN

Small caps: normal letterspacing/plus 6 units/plus 12 units

WALKING ALONG THE MALL we wondered who all those men were
WALKING ALONG THE MALL we wondered who all those men were

True italic/sloped roman

WALKING ALONG THE MALL WE WONDERED WHO ALL THOSE MEN WERE
WALKING ALONG THE MALL WE WONDERED WHO ALL THOSE MEN WERE

True small caps/reduced capitals

Walking along the Mall we wondered who all those men were – tall hawk-featured men perched on
balconies and high places, scanning the city with heavy binoculars. What were they seeking so
earnestly? Who were they – so composed and steely-eyed? Timidly we stopped a policeman to ask him.
'They are publishers' he said mildly. Publishers! Our hearts stopped beating. 'They are on the look out
for new talent.' Great God! It was for *us* they were waiting and watching! Then the kindly policeman
lowered his voice confidentially and said in hollow and reverent tones: *'They are waiting for the new*
Trollope to be born!' Do you remember, at these words, how heavy our suitcases suddenly felt? How
our blood slowed, our footsteps lagged? Brother Ass, we had been bashfully thinking of a kind of
illumination such as Rimbaud dreamed of – a nagging poem which was not didactic or expository but
which *infected* – was not simply a rationalised intuition, I mean, clothed in isinglass! We had come to

8 on 9pt

WALKING ALONG THE MALL WE WONDERED WHO ALL THOSE MEN WERE – TALL HAWK-
featured men perched on balconies and high places, scanning the city with heavy binoculars. What
were they seeking so earnestly? Who were they – so composed and steely-eyed? Timidly we stopped a
policeman to ask him. 'They are publishers' he said mildly. Publishers! Our hearts stopped beating.
'They are on the look out for new talent.' Great God! It was for *us* they were waiting and watching!
Then the kindly policeman lowered his voice confidentially and said in hollow and reverent tones:
'They are waiting for the new Trollope to be born!' Do you remember, at these words, how heavy our
suitcases suddenly felt? How our blood slowed, our footsteps lagged? Brother Ass, we had been
bashfully thinking of a kind of illumination such as Rimbaud dreamed of – a nagging poem which

8 on 10.5pt

Walking along the Mall we wondered who all those men were – tall hawk-featured men perched on balconies and high places, scanning the city with heavy binoculars. What were they seeking so earnestly? Who were they – so composed and steely-eyed? Timidly we stopped a policeman to ask him. 'They are publishers' he said mildly. Publishers! Our hearts stopped beating. 'They are on the look out for new talent.' Great God! It was for *us* they were waiting and watching! Then the kindly policeman lowered his voice confidentially and said in hollow and reverent tones: *'They are waiting for the new Trollope to be born!'* Do you remember, at these words, how heavy our suitcases suddenly felt? How our blood slowed, our footsteps lagged? Brother Ass, we had been bashfully thinking of a kind of illumination such as Rimbaud dreamed of – a nagging poem which was not didactic or expository but which *infected* – was not simply a rationalised intuition, I mean, clothed in isinglass! We had come to the wrong shop, with the wrong change! A chill struck us as we saw the mist falling in Trafalgar Square, coiling around us its tendrils of ectoplasm! A million muffin-eating moralists were waiting, not for us, Brother Ass, but for the plucky and tedious Trollope! (If you are dissatisfied with your form, reach for the *curette*.) Now do you wonder if I laugh a little off-key? Do you ask yourself what has turned me into nature's bashful little aphorist? We who are, after all, simply poor co-workers in the psyche of our nation, what can we expect but the natural automatic rejection from a public which resents interference? And quite right too. There is no injustice in the matter,

9 on 11pt

Walking along the Mall we wondered who all those men were – tall hawk-featured men perched on balconies and high places, scanning the city with heavy binoculars. What were they seeking so earnestly? Who were they – so composed and steely-eyed? Timidly we stopped a policeman to ask him. 'They are publishers' he said mildly. Publishers! Our hearts stopped beating. 'They are on the look out for new talent.' Great God! It was for *us* they were waiting and watching! Then the kindly policeman lowered his voice confidentially and said in hollow and reverent tones: *'They are waiting for the new Trollope to be born!'* Do you remember, at these words, how heavy our suitcases suddenly felt? How our blood slowed, our footsteps lagged? Brother Ass, we had been bashfully thinking of a kind of illumination such as Rimbaud dreamed of – a nagging poem which was not didactic or expository but which *infected* – was not simply a rationalised intuition, I mean, clothed in isinglass! We had come to the wrong shop, with the wrong change! A chill struck us as we saw the mist falling in Trafalgar Square, coiling around us its tendrils of ectoplasm! A million muffin-eating moralists were waiting, not for us, Brother Ass, but for the plucky and tedious Trollope! (If you are dissatisfied with your form, reach for the *curette*.) Now do you wonder if I laugh a little off-key? Do you ask yourself what has turned me into nature's bashful little aphorist? We who are, after all, simply poor co-workers in the psyche of our nation, what can we expect but the natural

9 on 12pt

Walking along the Mall we wondered who all those men were – tall hawk-featured men perched on balconies and high places, scanning the city with heavy binoculars. What were they seeking so earnestly? Who were they – so composed and steely-eyed? Timidly we stopped a policeman to ask him. 'They are publishers' he said mildly. Publishers! Our hearts stopped beating. 'They are on the look out for new talent.' Great God! It was for *us* they were waiting and watching! Then the kindly policeman lowered his voice confidentially and said in hollow and reverent tones: *'They are waiting for the new Trollope to be born!'* Do you remember, at these words, how heavy our suitcases suddenly felt? How our blood slowed, our footsteps lagged? Brother Ass, we had been bashfully thinking of a kind of illumination such as Rimbaud dreamed of – a nagging poem which was not didactic or expository but which *infected* – was not simply a rationalised intuition, I mean, clothed in isinglass! We had come to the wrong shop, with the wrong change! A chill struck us as we saw the mist falling in Trafalgar Square, coiling around us its tendrils of ectoplasm! A million muffin-eating moralists were waiting, not for us, Brother Ass, but for the plucky and tedious Trollope! (If you are dissatisfied with your form, reach for the

10 on 12pt

WALKING ALONG THE MALL WE WONDERED WHO ALL THOSE MEN WERE – TALL HAWK-featured men perched on balconies and high places, scanning the city with heavy binoculars. What were they seeking so earnestly? Who were they – so composed and steely-eyed? Timidly we stopped a policeman to ask him. 'They are publishers' he said mildly. Publishers! Our hearts stopped beating. 'They are on the look out for new talent.' Great God! It was for *us* they were waiting and watching! Then the kindly policeman lowered his voice confidentially and said in hollow and reverent tones: *'They are waiting for the new Trollope to be born!'* Do you remember, at these words, how heavy our suitcases suddenly felt? How our blood slowed, our footsteps lagged? Brother Ass, we had been bashfully thinking of a kind of illumination such as Rimbaud dreamed of – a nagging poem which was not didactic or expository but which *infected* – was not simply a rationalised intuition, I mean, clothed in isinglass! We had come to the wrong shop, with the wrong change! A chill struck us as we saw the mist falling in Trafalgar Square, coiling around us its tendrils of ectoplasm! A million muffin-eating moralists were waiting, not for us, Brother Ass,

10 on 13.5pt

WALKING ALONG THE MALL WE WONDERED WHO ALL THOSE MEN WERE – TALL hawk-featured men perched on balconies and high places, scanning the city with heavy binoculars. What were they seeking so earnestly? Who were they – so composed and steely-eyed? Timidly we stopped a policeman to ask him. 'They are publishers' he said mildly. Publishers! Our hearts stopped beating. 'They are on the look out for new talent.' Great God! It was for *us* they were waiting and watching! Then the kindly policeman lowered his voice confidentially and said in hollow and reverent tones: *'They are waiting for the new Trollope to be born!'* Do you remember, at these words, how heavy our suitcases suddenly felt? How our blood slowed, our footsteps lagged? Brother Ass, we had been bashfully thinking of a kind of illumination such as Rimbaud dreamed of – a nagging poem which was not didactic or expository but which *infected* – was not simply a rationalised intuition, I mean, clothed in isinglass! We had come to the wrong shop, with the wrong change! A chill struck us as we saw the mist falling in Trafalgar Square, coiling around us its tendrils of ectoplasm! A million muffin-eating moralists were waiting, not for us, Brother Ass,

11 on 13pt

WALKING ALONG THE MALL WE WONDERED WHO ALL THOSE MEN WERE – tall hawk-featured men perched on balconies and high places, scanning the city with heavy binoculars. What were they seeking so earnestly? Who were they – so composed and steely-eyed? Timidly we stopped a policeman to ask him. 'They are publishers' he said mildly. Publishers! Our hearts stopped beating. 'They are on the look out for new talent.' Great God! It was for *us* they were waiting and watching! Then the kindly policeman lowered his voice confidentially and said in hollow and reverent tones: *'They are waiting for the new Trollope to be born!'* Do you remember, at these words, how heavy our suitcases suddenly felt? How our blood slowed, our footsteps lagged? Brother Ass, we had been bashfully thinking of a kind of illumination such as Rimbaud dreamed of – a nagging poem which was not didactic or expository but which *infected* – was not simply a rationalised intuition, I mean, clothed in isinglass! We had come to the wrong shop, with the wrong change! A chill

11 on 14.5pt

MONOTYPE OCTAVIAN

Monotype **Old Style**

2 roman and italic
53 bold
Monotype 1901 (bold: 1911)
Copyfitting factor 43.9/41.4/48.4

Range also includes bold italic

A derivation of Miller & Richards' Old Style of 1852, cut by Alexander Phemister

Slightly stronger than hot metal original – to its advantage

ABCDEFGHIJKLMNOP
QRSTUVWXYZ abcdefg
hijklmnopqrstuvwxyz
1234567890
ff fi fl ffi ffl () [] &£$.,;:-!?''

ABCDEFGHIJKLMNOP
QRSTUVWXYZ abcdefg
hijklmnopqrstuvwxyz
1234567890 1234567890
ff fi fl ffi ffl () [] &£$.,;:-!?''

ABCDEFGHIJKLMNOP
QRSTUVWXYZ abcdefg
hijklmnopqrstuvwxyz
1234567890 1234567890
ff fi fl ffi ffl () [] &£$.,;:-!?''

24 on 27pt

These examples show *normal* letterspacing and the effect of *reduced* letterspacing on roman setting *as well as on words in italic*: they also show the appearance of figures, for example 28 May 1964, within text. These & the ampersand are not included in the setting opposite.

Normal letterspacing

These examples show *normal* letterspacing and the effect of *reduced* letterspacing on roman setting *as well as on words in italic*: they also show the appearance of figures, for example 28 May 1964, within text. These & the ampersand are not included in the setting opposite.

Minus one unit spacing

These examples show *normal* letterspacing and the effect of *reduced* letterspacing on roman setting *as well as on words in italic*: they also show the appearance of figures, for example 28 May 1964, within text. These & the ampersand are not included in the setting opposite.

Minus two units spacing

WALKING ALONG THE MALL WE WONDERED WHO ALL
WALKING ALONG THE MALL WE WONDERED WHO
WALKING ALONG THE MALL WE WONDERED

Capitals: normal letterspacing/plus 9 units/plus 18 units

WALKING ALONG THE MALL WE WONDERED WHO ALL THOSE MEN WERE
WALKING ALONG THE MALL WE WONDERED WHO ALL THOSE MEN
WALKING ALONG THE MALL WE WONDERED WHO ALL THOSE

Small caps: normal letterspacing/plus 6 units/plus 12 units

WALKING ALONG THE MALL we wondered who all those men were
WALKING ALONG THE MALL we wondered who all those men were

True italic/sloped roman

WALKING ALONG THE MALL WE WONDERED WHO ALL THOSE MEN WERE
WALKING ALONG THE MALL WE WONDERED WHO ALL THOSE MEN WERE

True small caps/reduced capitals

Walking along the Mall we wondered who all those men were – tall hawk-featured men perched on balconies and high places, scanning the city with heavy binoculars. What were they seeking so earnestly? Who were they – so composed and steely-eyed? Timidly we stopped a policeman to ask him. 'They are publishers' he said mildly. Publishers! Our hearts stopped beating. 'They are on the look out for new talent.' Great God! It was for *us* they were waiting and watching! Then the kindly policeman lowered his voice confidentially and said in hollow and reverent tones: *'They are waiting for the new Trollope to be born!'* Do you remember, at these words, how heavy our suitcases suddenly felt? How our blood slowed, our footsteps lagged? Brother Ass, we had been bashfully thinking of a kind of illumination such as

8 on 9pt

WALKING ALONG THE MALL WE WONDERED WHO ALL THOSE MEN WERE – TALL hawk-featured men perched on balconies and high places, scanning the city with heavy binoculars. What were they seeking so earnestly? Who were they – so composed and steely-eyed? Timidly we stopped a policeman to ask him. 'They are publishers' he said mildly. Publishers! Our hearts stopped beating. 'They are on the look out for new talent.' Great God! It was for *us* they were waiting and watching! Then the kindly policeman lowered his voice confidentially and said in hollow and reverent tones: *'They are waiting for the new Trollope to be born!'* Do you remember, at these words, how heavy our suitcases suddenly felt? How our blood slowed, our footsteps lagged?

8 on 10.5pt

Walking along the Mall we wondered who all those men were – tall hawk-featured men perched on balconies and high places, scanning the city with heavy binoculars. What were they seeking so earnestly? Who were they – so composed and steely-eyed? Timidly we stopped a policeman to ask him. 'They are publishers' he said mildly. Publishers! Our hearts stopped beating. 'They are on the look out for new talent.' Great God! It was for *us* they were waiting and watching! Then the kindly policeman lowered his voice confidentially and said in hollow and reverent tones: *'They are waiting for the new Trollope to be born!'* Do you remember, at these words, how heavy our suitcases suddenly felt? How our blood slowed, our footsteps lagged? Brother Ass, we had been bashfully thinking of a kind of illumination such as Rimbaud dreamed of – a nagging poem which was not didactic or expository but which *infected* – was not simply a rationalised intuition, I mean, clothed in isinglass! We had come to the wrong shop, with the wrong change! A chill struck us as we saw the mist falling in Trafalgar Square, coiling around us its tendrils of ectoplasm! A million muffin-eating moralists were waiting, not for us, Brother Ass, but for the plucky and tedious Trollope! (If you are dissatisfied with your form, reach for the *curette*.) Now do you wonder if I laugh a little off-key? Do

9 on 11pt

Walking along the Mall we wondered who all those men were – tall hawk-featured men perched on balconies and high places, scanning the city with heavy binoculars. What were they seeking so earnestly? Who were they – so composed and steely-eyed? Timidly we stopped a policeman to ask him. 'They are publishers' he said mildly. Publishers! Our hearts stopped beating. 'They are on the look out for new talent.' Great God! It was for *us* they were waiting and watching! Then the kindly policeman lowered his voice confidentially and said in hollow and reverent tones: *'They are waiting for the new Trollope to be born!'* Do you remember, at these words, how heavy our suitcases suddenly felt? How our blood slowed, our footsteps lagged? Brother Ass, we had been bashfully thinking of a kind of illumination such as Rimbaud dreamed of – a nagging poem which was not didactic or expository but which *infected* – was not simply a rationalised intuition, I mean, clothed in isinglass! We had come to the wrong shop, with the wrong change! A chill struck us as we saw the mist falling in Trafalgar Square, coiling around us its tendrils of ectoplasm! A million muffin-eating moralists were waiting, not for us, Brother Ass, but for the plucky and tedious Trollope! (If you are dissatisfied with your

9 on 12pt

Walking along the Mall we wondered who all those men were – tall hawk-featured men perched on balconies and high places, scanning the city with heavy binoculars. What were they seeking so earnestly? Who were they – so composed and steely-eyed? Timidly we stopped a policeman to ask him. 'They are publishers' he said mildly. Publishers! Our hearts stopped beating. 'They are on the look out for new talent.' Great God! It was for *us* they were waiting and watching! Then the kindly policeman lowered his voice confidentially and said in hollow and reverent tones: *'They are waiting for the new Trollope to be born!'* Do you remember, at these words, how heavy our suitcases suddenly felt? How our blood slowed, our footsteps lagged? Brother Ass, we had been bashfully thinking of a kind of illumination such as Rimbaud dreamed of – a nagging poem which was not didactic or expository but which *infected* – was not simply a rationalised intuition, I mean, clothed in isinglass! We had come to the wrong shop, with the

10 on 12pt

WALKING ALONG THE MALL WE WONDERED WHO ALL THOSE MEN were – tall hawk-featured men perched on balconies and high places, scanning the city with heavy binoculars. What were they seeking so earnestly? Who were they – so composed and steely-eyed? Timidly we stopped a policeman to ask him. 'They are publishers' he said mildly. Publishers! Our hearts stopped beating. 'They are on the look out for new talent.' Great God! It was for *us* they were waiting and watching! Then the kindly policeman lowered his voice confidentially and said in hollow and reverent tones: *'They are waiting for the new Trollope to be born!'* Do you remember, at these words, how heavy our suitcases suddenly felt? How our blood slowed, our footsteps lagged? Brother Ass, we had been bashfully thinking of a kind of illumination such as Rimbaud dreamed of – a nagging poem which was not didactic or expository but which *infected* – was not simply a rationalised intuition, I mean, clothed in isinglass! We had come to the wrong shop, with the

10 on 13.5pt

Walking along the Mall we wondered who all those men were – tall hawk-featured men perched on balconies and high places, scanning the city with heavy binoculars. What were they seeking so earnestly? Who were they – so composed and steely-eyed? Timidly we stopped a policeman to ask him. 'They are publishers' he said mildly. Publishers! Our hearts stopped beating. 'They are on the look out for new talent.' Great God! It was for *us* they were waiting and watching! Then the kindly policeman lowered his voice confidentially and said in hollow and reverent tones: *'They are waiting for the new Trollope to be born!'* Do you remember, at these words, how heavy our suitcases suddenly felt? How our blood slowed, our footsteps lagged? Brother Ass, we had been bashfully thinking of a kind of illumination such as Rimbaud dreamed of – a nagging poem which was not didactic or expository but which *infected* – was not simply a

11 on 13pt

WALKING ALONG THE MALL WE WONDERED WHO ALL THOSE men were – tall hawk-featured men perched on balconies and high places, scanning the city with heavy binoculars. What were they seeking so earnestly? Who were they – so composed and steely-eyed? Timidly we stopped a policeman to ask him. 'They are publishers' he said mildly. Publishers! Our hearts stopped beating. 'They are on the look out for new talent.' Great God! It was for *us* they were waiting and watching! Then the kindly policeman lowered his voice confidentially and said in hollow and reverent tones: *'They are waiting for the new Trollope to be born!'* Do you remember, at these words, how heavy our suitcases suddenly felt? How our blood slowed, our footsteps lagged? Brother Ass, we had been bashfully thinking of a kind of illumination such as Rimbaud dreamed of – a nagging poem

11 on 14.5pt

MONOTYPE OLD STYLE

Linotype **Old Style S**

roman (05522), **italic** (13522)
bold (07522)
Stempel 1982
Copyfitting code 130/121/133

ABCDEFGHIJKLMNOP
QRSTUVWXYZ abcdefg
hijklmnopqrstuvwxyz
1234567890
fifl ()[]&£$.,;:-!?''

*ABCDEFGHIJKLMNOP
QRSTUVWXYZ abcdefg
hijklmnopqrstuvwxyz
1234567890
fifl ()[]&£$.,;:-!?''*

**ABCDEFGHIJKLMNOP
QRSTUVWXYZ abcdefg
hijklmnopqrstuvwxyz
1234567890
fifl ()[]&£$.,;:-!?''**

24 on 27pt

These examples show *normal* letterspacing and the effect of *reduced* letterspacing on roman setting *as well as on words in italic*: they also show the appearance of figures, for example 28 May 1964, within text. These & the ampersand are not included in the setting opposite.

Normal letterspacing

These examples show *normal* letterspacing and the effect of *reduced* letterspacing on roman setting *as well as on words in italic*: they also show the appearance of figures, for example 28 May 1964, within text. These & the ampersand are not included in the setting opposite.

Minus one unit spacing

These examples show *normal* letterspacing and the effect of *reduced* letterspacing on roman setting *as well as on words in italic*: they also show the appearance of figures, for example 28 May 1964, within text. These & the ampersand are not included in the setting opposite.

Minus two units spacing

WALKING ALONG THE MALL WE WONDERED WHO ALL
WALKING ALONG THE MALL WE WONDERED WHO
WALKING ALONG THE MALL WE WONDERED

Capitals: normal letterspacing/plus 4 units/plus 9 units

WALKING ALONG THE MALL WE WONDERED WHO ALL THOSE MEN WERE
WALKING ALONG THE MALL WE WONDERED WHO ALL THOSE MEN
WALKING ALONG THE MALL WE WONDERED WHO ALL THOSE

Small caps: normal letterspacing/plus 3 units/plus 6 units

WALKING ALONG THE MALL WE WONDERED WHO ALL THOSE MEN WERE
WALKING ALONG THE MALL WE WONDERED WHO ALL THOSE MEN WERE

True small caps/reduced capitals

*WALKING ALONG THE MALL we wondered who all those men were
WALKING ALONG THE MALL we wondered who all those men*

True italic/sloped roman

Walking along the Mall we wondered who all those men were – tall hawk-featured men perched on balconies and high places, scanning the city with heavy binoculars. What were they seeking so earnestly? Who were they – so composed and steely-eyed? Timidly we stopped a policeman to ask him. 'They are publishers' he said mildly. Publishers! Our hearts stopped beating. 'They are on the look out for new talent.' Great God! It was for *us* they were waiting and watching! Then the kindly policeman lowered his voice confidentially and said in hollow and reverent tones: *'They are waiting for the new Trollope to be born!'* Do you remember, at these words, how heavy our suitcases suddenly felt? How our blood slowed, our footsteps lagged? Brother Ass, we had been bashfully thinking of a kind of illumination such as Rimbaud

8 on 9pt

WALKING ALONG THE MALL WE WONDERED WHO ALL THOSE MEN WERE – TALL HAWK-featured men perched on balconies and high places, scanning the city with heavy binoculars. What were they seeking so earnestly? Who were they – so composed and steely-eyed? Timidly we stopped a policeman to ask him. 'They are publishers' he said mildly. Publishers! Our hearts stopped beating. 'They are on the look out for new talent.' Great God! It was for *us* they were waiting and watching! Then the kindly policeman lowered his voice confidentially and said in hollow and reverent tones: *'They are waiting for the new Trollope to be born!'* Do you remember, at these words, how heavy our suitcases suddenly felt? How our blood slowed, our footsteps lagged?

8 on 10.5pt

Walking along the Mall we wondered who all those men were – tall hawk-featured men perched on balconies and high places, scanning the city with heavy binoculars. What were they seeking so earnestly? Who were they – so composed and steely-eyed? Timidly we stopped a policeman to ask him. 'They are publishers' he said mildly. Publishers! Our hearts stopped beating. 'They are on the look out for new talent.' Great God! It was for *us* they were waiting and watching! Then the kindly policeman lowered his voice confidentially and said in hollow and reverent tones: *'They are waiting for the new Trollope to be born!'* Do you remember, at these words, how heavy our suitcases suddenly felt? How our blood slowed, our footsteps lagged? Brother Ass, we had been bashfully thinking of a kind of illumination such as Rimbaud dreamed of – a nagging poem which was not didactic or expository but which *infected* – was not simply a rationalised intuition, I mean, clothed in isinglass! We had come to the wrong shop, with the wrong change! A chill struck us as we saw the mist falling in Trafalgar Square, coiling round us its tendrils of ectoplasm! A million muffin-eating moralists were waiting, not for us, Brother Ass, but for the plucky and tedious Trollope! (If you are dissatisfied with your form, reach for the *curette*.) Now do you wonder if I
9 on 11pt

Walking along the Mall we wondered who all those men were – tall hawk-featured men perched on balconies and high places, scanning the city with heavy binoculars. What were they seeking so earnestly? Who were they – so composed and steely-eyed? Timidly we stopped a policeman to ask him. 'They are publishers' he said mildly. Publishers! Our hearts stopped beating. 'They are on the look out for new talent.' Great God! It was for *us* they were waiting and watching! Then the kindly policeman lowered his voice confidentially and said in hollow and reverent tones: *'They are waiting for the new Trollope to be born!'* Do you remember, at these words, how heavy our suitcases suddenly felt? How our blood slowed, our footsteps lagged? Brother Ass, we had been bashfully thinking of a kind of illumination such as Rimbaud dreamed of – a nagging poem which was not didactic or expository but which *infected* – was not simply a rationalised intuition, I mean, clothed in isinglass! We had come to the wrong shop, with the wrong change! A chill struck us as we saw the mist falling in Trafalgar Square, coiling round us its tendrils of ectoplasm! A million muffin-eating moralists were waiting, not for us, Brother Ass, but for the plucky and tedious Trollope! (If you are
9 on 12pt

Walking along the Mall we wondered who all those men were – tall hawk-featured men perched on balconies and high places, scanning the city with heavy binoculars. What were they seeking so earnestly? Who were they – so composed and steely-eyed? Timidly we stopped a policeman to ask him. 'They are publishers' he said mildly. Publishers! Our hearts stopped beating. 'They are on the look out for new talent.' Great God! It was for *us* they were waiting and watching! Then the kindly policeman lowered his voice confidentially and said in hollow and reverent tones: *'They are waiting for the new Trollope to be born!'* Do you remember, at these words, how heavy our suitcases suddenly felt? How our blood slowed, our footsteps lagged? Brother Ass, we had been bashfully thinking of a kind of illumination such as Rimbaud dreamed of – a nagging poem which was not didactic or expository but which *infected* – was not simply a rationalised intuition, I mean, clothed in isinglass! We had come to the wrong shop, with the wrong change! A chill struck us as we saw the mist
10 on 12pt

Walking along the Mall we wondered who all those men were – tall hawk-featured men perched on balconies and high places, scanning the city with heavy binoculars. What were they seeking so earnestly? Who were they – so composed and steely-eyed? Timidly we stopped a policeman to ask him. 'They are publishers' he said mildly. Publishers! Our hearts stopped beating. 'They are on the look out for new talent.' Great God! It was for *us* they were waiting and watching! Then the kindly policeman lowered his voice confidentially and said in hollow and reverent tones: *'They are waiting for the new Trollope to be born!'* Do you remember, at these words, how heavy our suitcases suddenly felt? How our blood slowed, our footsteps lagged? Brother Ass, we had been bashfully thinking of a kind of illumination such as Rimbaud dreamed of – a nagging poem which was not didactic or expository but which *infected* – was not simply a rationalised intuition, I mean, clothed in isinglass! We had come to
10 on 13.5pt

Walking along the Mall we wondered who all those men were – tall hawk-featured men perched on balconies and high places, scanning the city with heavy binoculars. What were they seeking so earnestly? Who were they – so composed and steely-eyed? Timidly we stopped a policeman to ask him. 'They are publishers' he said mildly. Publishers! Our hearts stopped beating. 'They are on the look out for new talent.' Great God! It was for *us* they were waiting and watching! Then the kindly policeman lowered his voice confidentially and said in hollow and reverent tones: *'They are waiting for the new Trollope to be born!'* Do you remember, at these words, how heavy our suitcases suddenly felt? How our blood slowed, our footsteps lagged? Brother Ass, we had been bashfully thinking of a kind of illumination such as Rimbaud dreamed of – a nagging poem which was not didactic or expository but which *infected*
11 on 13pt

Walking along the Mall we wondered who all those men were – tall hawk-featured men perched on balconies and high places, scanning the city with heavy binoculars. What were they seeking so earnestly? Who were they – so composed and steely-eyed? Timidly we stopped a policeman to ask him. 'They are publishers' he said mildly. Publishers! Our hearts stopped beating. 'They are on the look out for new talent.' Great God! It was for *us* they were waiting and watching! Then the kindly policeman lowered his voice confidentially and said in hollow and reverent tones: *'They are waiting for the new Trollope to be born!'* Do you remember, at these words, how heavy our suitcases suddenly felt? How our blood slowed, our footsteps lagged? Brother Ass, we had been bashfully thinking of a kind of illumination such as Rimbaud dreamed of – a nagging
11 on 14.5pt

Monotype **Optima**

722 roman and italic
732 semi-bold
Stempel 1958 (Hermann Zapf)
Copyfitting factor 40.5/39.5/40.8

Range also includes semi-bold italic

The Linotype version is fractionally bolder, appears rather larger (9, 10 and 11 pt Lino approximate to 10, 11 and 12 pt Mono), and includes small caps and non-lining figures. Roman and italic copyfitting code 126/125. The wider range of weights is not comparable

A serif-less roman influenced by Italian inscriptional lettering of the quattrocento

Educational characters available

ABCDEFGHIJKLMNOP
QRSTUVWXYZ abcdefg
hijklmnopqrstuvwxyz
1234567890
ff fi fl ffi ffl ()[]&£$.,;:-!?"

ABCDEFGHIJKLMNOP
QRSTUVWXYZ abcdefg
hijklmnopqrstuvwxyz
1234567890
ff fi fl ffi ffl ()[]&£$.,;:-!?"

ABCDEFGHIJKLMNOP
QRSTUVWXYZ abcdefg
hijklmnopqrstuvwxyz
1234567890
ff fi fl ffi ffl ()[]&£$.,;:-!?"

24 on 27pt

These examples show *normal* letterspacing and the effect of *reduced* letterspacing on roman setting *as well as on words in italic*: they also show the appearance of figures, for example 28 May 1964, within text. These & the ampersand are not included in the setting opposite.

Normal letterspacing

These examples show *normal* letterspacing and the effect of *reduced* letterspacing on roman setting *as well as on words in italic*: they also show the appearance of figures, for example 28 May 1964, within text. These & the ampersand are not included in the setting opposite.

Minus one unit spacing

These examples show *normal* letterspacing and the effect of *reduced* letterspacing on roman setting *as well as on words in italic*: they also show the appearance of figures, for example 28 May 1964, within text. These & the ampersand are not included in the setting opposite.

Minus two units spacing

WALKING ALONG THE MALL WE WONDERED WHO ALL THOSE MEN
WALKING ALONG THE MALL WE WONDERED WHO ALL THOSE
WALKING ALONG THE MALL WE WONDERED WHO ALL

Capitals: normal letterspacing/plus 9 units/plus 18 units

Walking along the Mall we wondered who all those men were – tall hawk-featured men perched on balconies and high places, scanning the city with heavy binoculars. WHAT WERE THEY SEEKING SO EARNESTLY? Who were they – so composed and steely-eyed? Timidly we stopped a policeman to ask him. 'They are publishers' HE SAID MILDLY. PUBLISHERS! Our hearts stopped beating. 'They are on the look out for new talent.' Great God! It was for *us* they were waiting and watching! Then the kindly policeman lowered his

Text with reduced capitals normal letterspacing/plus 6 units

WALKING ALONG THE MALL we wondered who all those men were
WALKING ALONG THE MALL we wondered who all those men were

True italic/sloped roman

Walking along the Mall we wondered who all those men were – tall hawk-featured men perched on balconies and high places, scanning the city with heavy binoculars. What were they seeking so earnestly? Who were they – so composed and steely-eyed? Timidly we stopped a policeman to ask him. 'They are publishers' he said mildly. Publishers! Our hearts stopped beating. 'They are on the look out for new talent.' Great God! It was for *us* they were waiting and watching! Then the kindly policeman lowered his voice confidentially and said in hollow and reverent tones: *'They are waiting for the new Trollope to be born!'* Do you remember, at these words, how heavy our suitcases suddenly felt? How our blood slowed, our footsteps lagged? Brother Ass, we had been bashfully thinking of a kind of illumination such as Rimbaud dreamed of – a nagging poem which was not didactic or expository but which

8 on 9pt

Walking along the Mall we wondered who all those men were – tall hawk-featured men perched on balconies and high places, scanning the city with heavy binoculars. What were they seeking so earnestly? Who were they – so composed and steely-eyed? Timidly we stopped a policeman to ask him. 'They are publishers' he said mildly. Publishers! Our hearts stopped beating. 'They are on the look out for new talent.' Great God! It was for *us* they were waiting and watching! Then the kindly policeman lowered his voice confidentially and said in hollow and reverent tones: *'They are waiting for the new Trollope to be born!'* Do you remember, at these words, how heavy our suitcases suddenly felt? How our blood slowed, our footsteps lagged? Brother Ass, we had been bashfully thinking of a kind of illumination such as

8 on 10.5pt

Walking along the Mall we wondered who all those men were – tall hawk-featured
men perched on balconies and high places, scanning the city with heavy binoculars.
What were they seeking so earnestly? Who were they – so composed and steely-
eyed? Timidly we stopped a policeman to ask him. 'They are publishers' he said mildly.
Publishers! Our hearts stopped beating. 'They are on the look out for new talent.'
Great God! It was for *us* they were waiting and watching! Then the kindly policeman
lowered his voice confidentially and said in hollow and reverent tones: *'They are*
waiting for the new Trollope to be born!' Do you remember, at these words, how heavy
our suitcases suddenly felt? How our blood slowed, our footsteps lagged? Brother Ass,
we had been bashfully thinking of a kind of illumination such as Rimbaud dreamed of
– a nagging poem which was not didactic or expository but which *infected* – was not
simply a rationalised intuition, I mean, clothed in isinglass! We had come to the wrong
shop, with the wrong change! A chill struck us as we saw the mist falling in Trafalgar
Square, coiling around us its tendrils of ectoplasm! A million muffin-eating moralists
were waiting, not for us, Brother Ass, but for the plucky and tedious Trollope! (If you
are dissatisfied with your form, reach for the *curette*.) Now do you wonder if I laugh a
little off-key? Do you ask yourself what has turned me into nature's bashful little
aphorist? We who are, after all, simply poor co-workers in the psyche of our nation,
9 on 11pt

Walking along the Mall we wondered who all those men were – tall hawk-featured
men perched on balconies and high places, scanning the city with heavy binoculars.
What were they seeking so earnestly? Who were they – so composed and steely-
eyed? Timidly we stopped a policeman to ask him. 'They are publishers' he said mildly.
Publishers! Our hearts stopped beating. 'They are on the look out for new talent.'
Great God! It was for *us* they were waiting and watching! Then the kindly policeman
lowered his voice confidentially and said in hollow and reverent tones: *'They are*
waiting for the new Trollope to be born!' Do you remember, at these words, how heavy
our suitcases suddenly felt? How our blood slowed, our footsteps lagged? Brother Ass,
we had been bashfully thinking of a kind of illumination such as Rimbaud dreamed of
– a nagging poem which was not didactic or expository but which *infected* – was not
simply a rationalised intuition, I mean, clothed in isinglass! We had come to the wrong
shop, with the wrong change! A chill struck us as we saw the mist falling in Trafalgar
Square, coiling around us its tendrils of ectoplasm! A million muffin-eating moralists
were waiting, not for us, Brother Ass, but for the plucky and tedious Trollope! (If you
are dissatisfied with your form, reach for the *curette*.) Now do you wonder if I laugh a
little off-key? Do you ask yourself what has turned me into nature's bashful little
9 on 12pt

Walking along the Mall we wondered who all those men were – tall hawk-
featured men perched on balconies and high places, scanning the city with
heavy binoculars. What were they seeking so earnestly? Who were they – so
composed and steely-eyed? Timidly we stopped a policeman to ask him.
'They are publishers' he said mildly. Publishers! Our hearts stopped beating.
'They are on the look out for new talent.' Great God! It was for *us* they were
waiting and watching! Then the kindly policeman lowered his voice confidentially and said in hollow and reverent tones: *'They are waiting for the new*
Trollope to be born!' Do you remember, at these words, how heavy our
suitcases suddenly felt? How our blood slowed, our footsteps lagged? Brother
Ass, we had been bashfully thinking of a kind of illumination such as Rimbaud
dreamed of – a nagging poem which was not didactic or expository but
which *infected* – was not simply a rationalised intuition, I mean, clothed in
isinglass! We had come to the wrong shop, with the wrong change! A chill
struck us as we saw the mist falling in Trafalgar Square, coiling around us its
tendrils of ectoplasm! A million muffin-eating moralists were waiting, not for
10 on 12pt

Walking along the Mall we wondered who all those men were – tall hawk-
featured men perched on balconies and high places, scanning the city with
heavy binoculars. What were they seeking so earnestly? Who were they – so
composed and steely-eyed? Timidly we stopped a policeman to ask him.
'They are publishers' he said mildly. Publishers! Our hearts stopped beating.
'They are on the look out for new talent.' Great God! It was for *us* they were
waiting and watching! Then the kindly policeman lowered his voice confidentially and said in hollow and reverent tones: *'They are waiting for the new*
Trollope to be born!' Do you remember, at these words, how heavy our
suitcases suddenly felt? How our blood slowed, our footsteps lagged? Brother
Ass, we had been bashfully thinking of a kind of illumination such as Rimbaud
dreamed of – a nagging poem which was not didactic or expository but
which *infected* – was not simply a rationalised intuition, I mean, clothed in
isinglass! We had come to the wrong shop, with the wrong change! A chill
struck us as we saw the mist falling in Trafalgar Square, coiling around us its
10 on 13.5pt

Walking along the Mall we wondered who all those men were – tall
hawk-featured men perched on balconies and high places, scanning
the city with heavy binoculars. What were they seeking so earnestly?
Who were they – so composed and steely-eyed? Timidly we stopped a
policeman to ask him. 'They are publishers' he said mildly. Publishers!
Our hearts stopped beating. 'They are on the look out for new talent.'
Great God! It was for *us* they were waiting and watching! Then the
kindly policeman lowered his voice confidentially and said in hollow
and reverent tones: *'They are waiting for the new Trollope to be born!'*
Do you remember, at these words, how heavy our suitcases suddenly
felt? How our blood slowed, our footsteps lagged? Brother Ass, we had
been bashfully thinking of a kind of illumination such as Rimbaud
dreamed of – a nagging poem which was not didactic or expository
but which *infected* – was not simply a rationalised intuition, I mean,
clothed in isinglass! We had come to the wrong shop, with the wrong
11 on 13pt

Walking along the Mall we wondered who all those men were – tall
hawk-featured men perched on balconies and high places, scanning
the city with heavy binoculars. What were they seeking so earnestly?
Who were they – so composed and steely-eyed? Timidly we stopped a
policeman to ask him. 'They are publishers' he said mildly. Publishers!
Our hearts stopped beating. 'They are on the look out for new talent.'
Great God! It was for *us* they were waiting and watching! Then the
kindly policeman lowered his voice confidentially and said in hollow
and reverent tones: *'They are waiting for the new Trollope to be born!'*
Do you remember, at these words, how heavy our suitcases suddenly
felt? How our blood slowed, our footsteps lagged? Brother Ass, we had
been bashfully thinking of a kind of illumination such as Rimbaud
dreamed of – a nagging poem which was not didactic or expository
but which *infected* – was not simply a rationalised intuition, I mean,
11 on 14.5pt

Linotype ORION

roman (05204), **italic** (13204)
Linotype 1974 (Hermann Zapf)
Copyfitting code 128/128

ABCDEFGHIJKLMNOP
QRSTUVWXYZ abcdefg
hijklmnopqrstuvwxyz
1234567890
fifl ()[]&£$.,;:-!?''

ABCDEFGHIJKLMNOP
QRSTUVWXYZ abcdefg
hijklmnopqrstuvwxyz
1234567890
fifl ()[]&£$.,;:-!?''

24 on 27pt

These examples show *normal* letterspacing and the effect of *reduced* letterspacing on roman setting *as well as on words in italic*: they also show the appearance of figures, for example 28 May 1964, within text. These & the ampersand are not included in the setting opposite.
Normal letterspacing

These examples show *normal* letterspacing and the effect of *reduced* letterspacing on roman setting *as well as on words in italic*: they also show the appearance of figures, for example 28 May 1964, within text. These & the ampersand are not included in the setting opposite.
Minus one unit spacing

These examples show *normal* letterspacing and the effect of *reduced* letterspacing on roman setting *as well as on words in italic*: they also show the appearance of figures, for example 28 May 1964, within text. These & the ampersand are not included in the setting opposite.
Minus two units spacing

WALKING ALONG THE MALL WE WONDERED WHO ALL
WALKING ALONG THE MALL WE WONDERED WHO
WALKING ALONG THE MALL WE WONDERED
Capitals: normal letterspacing/plus 4 units/plus 9 units

Walking along the Mall we wondered who all those men were – tall hawk-featured men perched on balconies and high places, scanning the city with heavy binoculars. WHAT WERE THEY SEEKING SO EARNESTLY? Who were they – so composed and steely-eyed? Timidly we stopped a policeman to ask him. 'THEY ARE PUBLISHERS' he said mildly. Publishers! Our hearts stopped beating. 'They are on the look out for new talent.' Great God! It was for *us* they were waiting
Text with reduced caps normal letterspacing/plus 3 units

WALKING ALONG THE MALL we wondered who all those men
WALKING ALONG THE MALL we wondered who all those men
True italic/sloped roman

Walking along the Mall we wondered who all those men were – tall hawk-featured men perched on balconies and high places, scanning the city with heavy binoculars. What were they seeking so earnestly? Who were they – so composed and steely-eyed? Timidly we stopped a policeman to ask him. 'They are publishers' he said mildly. Publishers! Our hearts stopped beating. 'They are on the look out for new talent.' Great God! It was for *us* they were waiting and watching! Then the kindly policeman lowered his voice confidentially and said in hollow and reverent tones: *'They are waiting for the new Trollope to be born!'* Do you remember, at these words, how heavy our suitcases suddenly felt? How our blood slowed, our footsteps lagged? Brother Ass, we had been bashfully thinking of a kind of illumination such as
8 on 9pt

Walking along the Mall we wondered who all those men were – tall hawk-featured men perched on balconies and high places, scanning the city with heavy binoculars. What were they seeking so earnestly? Who were they – so composed and steely-eyed? Timidly we stopped a policeman to ask him. 'They are publishers' he said mildly. Publishers! Our hearts stopped beating. 'They are on the look out for new talent.' Great God! It was for *us* they were waiting and watching! Then the kindly policeman lowered his voice confidentially and said in hollow and reverent tones: *'They are waiting for the new Trollope to be born!'* Do you remember, at these words, how heavy our suitcases suddenly felt? How our blood slowed, our footsteps lagged?
8 on 10.5pt

Walking along the Mall we wondered who all those men were – tall hawk-featured men perched on balconies and high places, scanning the city with heavy binoculars. What were they seeking so earnestly? Who were they – so composed and steely-eyed? Timidly we stopped a policeman to ask him. 'They are publishers' he said mildly. Publishers! Our hearts stopped beating. 'They are on the look out for new talent.' Great God! It was for *us* they were waiting and watching! Then the kindly policeman lowered his voice confidentially and said in hollow and reverent tones: *'They are waiting for the new Trollope to be born!'* Do you remember, at these words, how heavy our suitcases suddenly felt? How our blood slowed, our footsteps lagged? Brother Ass, we had been bashfully thinking of a kind of illumination such as Rimbaud dreamed of – a nagging poem which was not didactic or expository but which *infected* – was not simply a rationalised intuition, I mean, clothed in isinglass! We had come to the wrong shop, with the wrong change! A chill struck us as we saw the mist falling in Trafalgar Square, coiling round us its tendrils of ectoplasm! A million muffin-eating moralists were waiting, not for us, Brother Ass, but for the plucky and tedious Trollope! (If you are dissatisfied with your form, reach for the *curette.*) Now do you wonder if I laugh a

9 on 11pt

Walking along the Mall we wondered who all those men were – tall hawk-featured men perched on balconies and high places, scanning the city with heavy binoculars. What were they seeking so earnestly? Who were they – so composed and steely-eyed? Timidly we stopped a policeman to ask him. 'They are publishers' he said mildly. Publishers! Our hearts stopped beating. 'They are on the look out for new talent.' Great God! It was for *us* they were waiting and watching! Then the kindly policeman lowered his voice confidentially and said in hollow and reverent tones: *'They are waiting for the new Trollope to be born!'* Do you remember, at these words, how heavy our suitcases suddenly felt? How our blood slowed, our footsteps lagged? Brother Ass, we had been bashfully thinking of a kind of illumination such as Rimbaud dreamed of – a nagging poem which was not didactic or expository but which *infected* – was not simply a rationalised intuition, I mean, clothed in isinglass! We had come to the wrong shop, with the wrong change! A chill struck us as we saw the mist falling in Trafalgar Square, coiling round us its tendrils of ectoplasm! A million muffin-eating moralists were waiting, not for us, Brother Ass, but for the plucky and tedious Trollope! (If you are

9 on 12pt

Walking along the Mall we wondered who all those men were – tall hawk-featured men perched on balconies and high places, scanning the city with heavy binoculars. What were they seeking so earnestly? Who were they – so composed and steely-eyed? Timidly we stopped a policeman to ask him. 'They are publishers' he said mildly. Publishers! Our hearts stopped beating. 'They are on the look out for new talent.' Great God! It was for *us* they were waiting and watching! Then the kindly policeman lowered his voice confidentially and said in hollow and reverent tones: *'They are waiting for the new Trollope to be born!'* Do you remember, at these words, how heavy our suitcases suddenly felt? How our blood slowed, our footsteps lagged? Brother Ass, we had been bashfully thinking of a kind of illumination such as Rimbaud dreamed of – a nagging poem which was not didactic or expository but which *infected* – was not simply a rationalised intuition, I mean, clothed in isinglass! We had come to the wrong shop, with the wrong change! A chill struck us as we saw

10 on 12pt

Walking along the Mall we wondered who all those men were – tall hawk-featured men perched on balconies and high places, scanning the city with heavy binoculars. What were they seeking so earnestly? Who were they – so composed and steely-eyed? Timidly we stopped a policeman to ask him. 'They are publishers' he said mildly. Publishers! Our hearts stopped beating. 'They are on the look out for new talent.' Great God! It was for *us* they were waiting and watching! Then the kindly policeman lowered his voice confidentially and said in hollow and reverent tones: *'They are waiting for the new Trollope to be born!'* Do you remember, at these words, how heavy our suitcases suddenly felt? How our blood slowed, our footsteps lagged? Brother Ass, we had been bashfully thinking of a kind of illumination such as Rimbaud dreamed of – a nagging poem which was not didactic or expository but which *infected* – was not simply a rationalised intuition, I mean, clothed in isinglass! We had come to

10 on 13.5pt

Walking along the Mall we wondered who all those men were – tall hawk-featured men perched on balconies and high places, scanning the city with heavy binoculars. What were they seeking so earnestly? Who were they – so composed and steely-eyed? Timidly we stopped a policeman to ask him. 'They are publishers' he said mildly. Publishers! Our hearts stopped beating. 'They are on the look out for new talent.' Great God! It was for *us* they were waiting and watching! Then the kindly policeman lowered his voice confidentially and said in hollow and reverent tones: *'They are waiting for the new Trollope to be born!'* Do you remember, at these words, how heavy our suitcases suddenly felt? How our blood slowed, our footsteps lagged? Brother Ass, we had been bashfully thinking of a kind of illumination such as Rimbaud dreamed of – a nagging poem which was not didactic or

11 on 13pt

Walking along the Mall we wondered who all those men were – tall hawk-featured men perched on balconies and high places, scanning the city with heavy binoculars. What were they seeking so earnestly? Who were they – so composed and steely-eyed? Timidly we stopped a policeman to ask him. 'They are publishers' he said mildly. Publishers! Our hearts stopped beating. 'They are on the look out for new talent.' Great God! It was for *us* they were waiting and watching! Then the kindly policeman lowered his voice confidentially and said in hollow and reverent tones: *'They are waiting for the new Trollope to be born!'* Do you remember, at these words, how heavy our suitcases suddenly felt? How our blood slowed, our footsteps lagged? Brother Ass, we had been bashfully thinking of a kind of illumination such as Rimbaud

11 on 14.5pt

Monotype **Palatino**

853 roman and italic
854 bold
Stempel 1950 (Herman Zapf)
Copyfitting factor 38.7/35.5/41.7

Range also includes bold italic

The design of the Monotype digitised version,
supervised by Zapf, more closely follows the
original design for Stempel (with its smaller
x-height) than later Linotype versions. Bembo
figures are used for non-lining bold

ABCDEFGHIJKLMNOP
QRSTUVWXYZ abcdefg
hijklmnopqrstuvwxyz
1234567890 1234567890
ff fi fl ffi ffl ()[]&£$.,;:-!?"

ABCDEFGHIJKLMNOP
QRSTUVWXYZ abcdefg
hijklmnopqrstuvwxyz
1234567890 1234567890
ff fi fl ffi ffl ()[]&£$.,;:-!?"

ABCDEFGHIJKLMNOP
QRSTUVWXYZ abcdefg
hijklmnopqrstuvwxyz
1234567890 1234567890
ff fi fl ffi ffl ()[]&£$.,;:-!?"

24 on 27pt

These examples show *normal* letterspacing and the effect of *reduced*
letterspacing on roman setting *as well as on words in italic*: they also
show the appearance of figures, for example 28 May 1964, within text.
These & the ampersand are not included in the setting opposite.

Normal letterspacing

These examples show *normal* letterspacing and the effect of *reduced*
letterspacing on roman setting *as well as on words in italic*: they also
show the appearance of figures, for example 28 May 1964, within text.
These & the ampersand are not included in the setting opposite.

Minus one unit spacing

These examples show *normal* letterspacing and the effect of *reduced*
letterspacing on roman setting *as well as on words in italic*: they also
show the appearance of figures, for example 28 May 1964, within text.
These & the ampersand are not included in the setting opposite.

Minus two units spacing

WALKING ALONG THE MALL WE WONDERED WHO ALL THOSE MEN
WALKING ALONG THE MALL WE WONDERED WHO ALL
WALKING ALONG THE MALL WE WONDERED WHO

Capitals: normal letterspacing/plus 9 units/plus 18 units

WALKING ALONG THE MALL WE WONDERED WHO ALL THOSE MEN WERE
WALKING ALONG THE MALL WE WONDERED WHO ALL THOSE MEN WERE
WALKING ALONG THE MALL WE WONDERED WHO ALL THOSE MEN

Small caps: normal letterspacing/plus 6 units/plus 12 units

WALKING ALONG THE MALL we wondered who all those men were
WALKING ALONG THE MALL we wondered who all those men were

True italic/sloped roman

WALKING ALONG THE MALL WE WONDERED WHO ALL THOSE MEN WERE
WALKING ALONG THE MALL WE WONDERED WHO ALL THOSE MEN WERE

True small caps/reduced capitals

Walking along the Mall we wondered who all those men were – tall hawk-featured
men perched on balconies and high places, scanning the city with heavy binoculars. What were
they seeking so earnestly? Who were they – so composed and steely-eyed? Timidly we stopped a
policeman to ask him. 'They are publishers' he said mildly. Publishers! Our hearts stopped beating.
'They are on the look out for new talent.' Great God! It was for *us* they were waiting and
watching! Then the kindly policeman lowered his voice confidentially and said in hollow and
reverent tones: *'They are waiting for the new Trollope to be born!'* Do you remember, at these words,
how heavy our suitcases suddenly felt? How our blood slowed, our footsteps lagged? Brother Ass,
we had been bashfully thinking of a kind of illumination such as Rimbaud dreamed of – a nagging
poem which was not didactic or expository but which *infected* – was not simply a rationalised

8 on 9pt

WALKING ALONG THE MALL WE WONDERED WHO ALL THOSE MEN WERE – TALL HAWK-FEATURED MEN
perched on balconies and high places, scanning the city with heavy binoculars. What were they
seeking so earnestly? Who were they – so composed and steely-eyed? Timidly we stopped a
policeman to ask him. 'They are publishers' he said mildly. Publishers! Our hearts stopped beating.
'They are on the look out for new talent.' Great God! It was for *us* they were waiting and
watching! Then the kindly policeman lowered his voice confidentially and said in hollow and
reverent tones: *'They are waiting for the new Trollope to be born!'* Do you remember, at these words,
how heavy our suitcases suddenly felt? How our blood slowed, our footsteps lagged? Brother Ass,
we had been bashfully thinking of a kind of illumination such as Rimbaud dreamed of – a nagging

8 on 10.5pt

Walking along the Mall we wondered who all those men were – tall hawk-featured men perched on balconies and high places, scanning the city with heavy binoculars. What were they seeking so earnestly? Who were they – so composed and steely-eyed? Timidly we stopped a policeman to ask him. 'They are publishers' he said mildly. Publishers! Our hearts stopped beating. 'They are on the look out for new talent.' Great God! It was for *us* they were waiting and watching! Then the kindly policeman lowered his voice confidentially and said in hollow and reverent tones: *'They are waiting for the new Trollope to be born!'* Do you remember, at these words, how heavy our suitcases suddenly felt? How our blood slowed, our footsteps lagged? Brother Ass, we had been bashfully thinking of a kind of illumination such as Rimbaud dreamed of – a nagging poem which was not didactic or expository but which *infected* – was not simply a rationalised intuition, I mean, clothed in isinglass! We had come to the wrong shop, with the wrong change! A chill struck us as we saw the mist falling in Trafalgar Square, coiling around us its tendrils of ectoplasm! A million muffin-eating moralists were waiting, not for us, Brother Ass, but for the plucky and tedious Trollope! (If you are dissatisfied with your form, reach for the *curette*.) Now do you wonder if I laugh a little off-key? Do you ask yourself what has turned me into nature's bashful little aphorist? We who are, after all, simply poor co-workers in the psyche of our nation, what can we expect but the natural automatic rejection from a public which resents

9 on 11pt

Walking along the Mall we wondered who all those men were – tall hawk- featured men perched on balconies and high places, scanning the city with heavy binoculars. What were they seeking so earnestly? Who were they – so composed and steely-eyed? Timidly we stopped a policeman to ask him. 'They are publishers' he said mildly. Publishers! Our hearts stopped beating. 'They are on the look out for new talent.' Great God! It was for *us* they were waiting and watching! Then the kindly policeman lowered his voice confidentially and said in hollow and reverent tones: *'They are waiting for the new Trollope to be born!'* Do you remember, at these words, how heavy our suitcases suddenly felt? How our blood slowed, our footsteps lagged? Brother Ass, we had been bashfully thinking of a kind of illumination such as Rimbaud dreamed of – a nagging poem which was not didactic or expository but which *infected* – was not simply a rationalised intuition, I mean, clothed in isinglass! We had come to the wrong shop, with the wrong change! A chill struck us as we saw the mist falling in Trafalgar Square, coiling around us its tendrils of ectoplasm! A million muffin-eating moralists were waiting, not for us, Brother Ass, but for the plucky and tedious Trollope! (If you

10 on 12pt

Walking along the Mall we wondered who all those men were – tall hawk-featured men perched on balconies and high places, scanning the city with heavy binoculars. What were they seeking so earnestly? Who were they – so composed and steely-eyed? Timidly we stopped a policeman to ask him. 'They are publishers' he said mildly. Publishers! Our hearts stopped beating. 'They are on the look out for new talent.' Great God! It was for *us* they were waiting and watching! Then the kindly policeman lowered his voice confidentially and said in hollow and reverent tones: *'They are waiting for the new Trollope to be born!'* Do you remember, at these words, how heavy our suitcases suddenly felt? How our blood slowed, our footsteps lagged? Brother Ass, we had been bashfully thinking of a kind of illumination such as Rimbaud dreamed of – a nagging poem which was not didactic or expository but which *infected* – was not simply a rationalised intuition, I mean, clothed in isinglass! We had come to the wrong shop, with the wrong change! A chill struck us as we saw the

11 on 13pt

WALKING ALONG THE MALL WE WONDERED WHO ALL THOSE MEN WERE — TALL HAWK-featured men perched on balconies and high places, scanning the city with heavy binoculars. What were they seeking so earnestly? Who were they — so composed and steely-eyed? Timidly we stopped a policeman to ask him. 'They are publishers' he said mildly. Publishers! Our hearts stopped beating. 'They are on the look out for new talent.' Great God! It was for *us* they were waiting and watching! Then the kindly policeman lowered his voice confidentially and said in hollow and reverent tones: *'They are waiting for the new Trollope to be born!'* Do you remember, at these words, how heavy our suitcases suddenly felt? How our blood slowed, our footsteps lagged? Brother Ass, we had been bashfully thinking of a kind of illumination such as Rimbaud dreamed of — a nagging poem which was not didactic or expository but which *infected* — was not simply a rationalised intuition, I mean, clothed in isinglass! We had come to the wrong shop, with the wrong change! A chill struck us as we saw the mist falling in Trafalgar Square, coiling around us its tendrils of ectoplasm! A million muffin-eating moralists were waiting, not for us, Brother Ass, but for the plucky and tedious Trollope! (If you are dissatisfied with your form, reach for the *curette*.) Now do you wonder if I laugh a little off-key? Do you ask yourself what has turned me into nature's bashful little aphorist? We who are, after all, simply poor co-

9 on 12pt

WALKING ALONG THE MALL WE WONDERED WHO ALL THOSE MEN WERE — tall hawk-featured men perched on balconies and high places, scanning the city with heavy binoculars. What were they seeking so earnestly? Who were they — so composed and steely-eyed? Timidly we stopped a policeman to ask him. 'They are publishers' he said mildly. Publishers! Our hearts stopped beating. 'They are on the look out for new talent.' Great God! It was for *us* they were waiting and watching! Then the kindly policeman lowered his voice confidentially and said in hollow and reverent tones: *'They are waiting for the new Trollope to be born!'* Do you remember, at these words, how heavy our suitcases suddenly felt? How our blood slowed, our footsteps lagged? Brother Ass, we had been bashfully thinking of a kind of illumination such as Rimbaud dreamed of — a nagging poem which was not didactic or expository but which *infected* — was not simply a rationalised intuition, I mean, clothed in isinglass! We had come to the wrong shop, with the wrong change! A chill struck us as we saw the mist falling in Trafalgar Square, coiling around us its tendrils of ectoplasm! A million muffin-eating moralists were

10 on 13.5pt

WALKING ALONG THE MALL WE WONDERED WHO ALL THOSE MEN WERE — tall hawk-featured men perched on balconies and high places, scanning the city with heavy binoculars. What were they seeking so earnestly? Who were they — so composed and steely-eyed? Timidly we stopped a policeman to ask him. 'They are publishers' he said mildly. Publishers! Our hearts stopped beating. 'They are on the look out for new talent.' Great God! It was for *us* they were waiting and watching! Then the kindly policeman lowered his voice confidentially and said in hollow and rever-ent tones: *'They are waiting for the new Trollope to be born!'* Do you remem-ber, at these words, how heavy our suitcases suddenly felt? How our blood slowed, our footsteps lagged? Brother Ass, we had been bashfully thinking of a kind of illumination such as Rimbaud dreamed of — a nagging poem which was not didactic or expository but which *infected* — was not simply a rationalised intuition, I mean, clothed in isinglass! We had come

11 on 14.5pt

Linotype **Palatino**

roman (05206), **italic** (13206)
bold (07206)
Stempel 1950 (Hermann Zapf)
Copyfitting code 134/118/138

Range also includes light, light italic, medium,
medium italic, bold italic, black, black italic

This version differs considerably from the
original Stempel design. Linotype Palatino
1950, based on this, has a smaller x-height and
somewhat resembles the Monotype version.
Copyfitting code 134/117/132

ABCDEFGHIJKLMNOP
QRSTUVWXYZ abcdefg
hijklmnopqrstuvwxyz
1234567890 1234567890
fifl ()[]&£$.,;:-!?"

*ABCDEFGHIJKLMNOP
QRSTUVWXYZ abcdefg
hijklmnopqrstuvwxyz
1234567890 1234567890
fifl ()[]&£$.,;:-!?"*

**ABCDEFGHIJKLMNOP
QRSTUVWXYZ abcdefg
hijklmnopqrstuvwxyz
1234567890 1234567890
fifl ()[]&£$.,;:-!?"**

24 on 27pt

218

These examples show *normal* letterspacing and the effect of *reduced*
letterspacing on roman setting *as well as on words in italic*: they also
show the appearance of figures, for example 28 May 1964, within text.
These & the ampersand are not included in the setting opposite.
Normal letterspacing

These examples show *normal* letterspacing and the effect of *reduced*
letterspacing on roman setting *as well as on words in italic*: they also
show the appearance of figures, for example 28 May 1964, within text.
These & the ampersand are not included in the setting opposite.
Minus one unit spacing

These examples show *normal* letterspacing and the effect of *reduced*
letterspacing on roman setting *as well as on words in italic*: they also
show the appearance of figures, for example 28 May 1964, within text.
These & the ampersand are not included in the setting opposite.
Minus two units spacing

WALKING ALONG THE MALL WE WONDERED WHO ALL
WALKING ALONG THE MALL WE WONDERED WHO
WALKING ALONG THE MALL WE WONDERED
Capitals: normal letterspacing/plus 4 units/plus 9 units

WALKING ALONG THE MALL WE WONDERED WHO ALL THOSE MEN
WALKING ALONG THE MALL WE WONDERED WHO ALL THOSE
WALKING ALONG THE MALL WE WONDERED WHO ALL
Small caps: normal letterspacing/plus 3 units/plus 6 units

WALKING ALONG THE MALL WE WONDERED WHO ALL THOSE MEN
WALKING ALONG THE MALL WE WONDERED WHO ALL THOSE MEN WERE
True small caps/reduced capitals

*WALKING ALONG THE MALL we wondered who all those men were
WALKING ALONG THE MALL we wondered who all those men*
True italic/sloped roman

Walking along the Mall we wondered who all those men were – tall hawk-featured
men perched on balconies and high places, scanning the city with heavy binoculars.
What were they seeking so earnestly? Who were they – so composed and steely-
eyed? Timidly we stopped a policeman to ask him. 'They are publishers' he said
mildly. Publishers! Our hearts stopped beating. 'They are on the look out for new
talent.' Great God! It was for *us* they were waiting and watching! Then the kindly
policeman lowered his voice confidentially and said in hollow and reverent tones:
'They are waiting for the new Trollope to be born!' Do you remember, at these words,
how heavy our suitcases suddenly felt? How our blood slowed, our footsteps
lagged? Brother Ass, we had been bashfully thinking of a kind of illumination
8 on 9pt

WALKING ALONG THE MALL WE WONDERED WHO ALL THOSE MEN WERE – TALL HAWK-
featured men perched on balconies and high places, scanning the city with heavy
binoculars. What were they seeking so earnestly? Who were they – so composed
and steely-eyed? Timidly we stopped a policeman to ask him. 'They are publishers'
he said mildly. Publishers! Our hearts stopped beating. 'They are on the look out for
new talent.' Great God! It was for *us* they were waiting and watching! Then the
kindly policeman lowered his voice confidentially and said in hollow and reverent
tones: *'They are waiting for the new Trollope to be born!'* Do you remember, at these
words, how heavy our suitcases suddenly felt? How our blood slowed, our
8 on 10.5pt

Walking along the Mall we wondered who all those men were – tall hawk-featured men perched on balconies and high places, scanning the city with heavy binoculars. What were they seeking so earnestly? Who were they – so composed and steely-eyed? Timidly we stopped a policeman to ask him. 'They are publishers' he said mildly. Publishers! Our hearts stopped beating. 'They are on the look out for new talent.' Great God! It was for *us* they were waiting and watching! Then the kindly policeman lowered his voice confidentially and said in hollow and reverent tones: *'They are waiting for the new Trollope to be born!'* Do you remember, at these words, how heavy our suitcases suddenly felt? How our blood slowed, our footsteps lagged? Brother Ass, we had been bashfully thinking of a kind of illumination such as Rimbaud dreamed of – a nagging poem which was not didactic or expository but which *infected* – was not simply a rationalised intuition, I mean, clothed in isinglass! We had come to the wrong shop, with the wrong change! A chill struck us as we saw the mist falling in Trafalgar Square, coiling round us its tendrils of ectoplasm! A million muffin-eating moralists were waiting, not for us, Brother Ass, but for the plucky and tedious Trollope! (If you are dissatisfied with your

9 on 11pt

Walking along the Mall we wondered who all those men were – tall hawk-featured men perched on balconies and high places, scanning the city with heavy binoculars. What were they seeking so earnestly? Who were they – so composed and steely-eyed? Timidly we stopped a policeman to ask him. 'They are publishers' he said mildly. Publishers! Our hearts stopped beating. 'They are on the look out for new talent.' Great God! It was for *us* they were waiting and watching! Then the kindly policeman lowered his voice confidentially and said in hollow and reverent tones: *'They are waiting for the new Trollope to be born!'* Do you remember, at these words, how heavy our suitcases suddenly felt? How our blood slowed, our footsteps lagged? Brother Ass, we had been bashfully thinking of a kind of illumination such as Rimbaud dreamed of – a nagging poem which was not didactic or expository but which *infected* – was not simply a rationalised intuition, I mean, clothed in isinglass! We had come to the wrong shop, with the wrong change!

10 on 12pt

Walking along the Mall we wondered who all those men were – tall hawk-featured men perched on balconies and high places, scanning the city with heavy binoculars. What were they seeking so earnestly? Who were they – so composed and steely-eyed? Timidly we stopped a policeman to ask him. 'They are publishers' he said mildly. Publishers! Our hearts stopped beating. 'They are on the look out for new talent.' Great God! It was for *us* they were waiting and watching! Then the kindly policeman lowered his voice confidentially and said in hollow and reverent tones: *'They are waiting for the new Trollope to be born!'* Do you remember, at these words, how heavy our suitcases suddenly felt? How our blood slowed, our footsteps lagged? Brother Ass, we had been bashfully thinking of a kind of illumination such as Rimbaud dreamed of – a nagging poem which was not

11 on 13pt

tall hawk-featured men perched on balconies and high places, scanning the city with heavy binoculars. What were they seeking so earnestly? Who were they – so composed and steely-eyed? Timidly we stopped a policeman to ask him. 'They are publishers' he said mildly. Publishers! Our hearts stopped beating. 'They are on the look out for new talent.' Great God! It was for *us* they were waiting and watching! Then the kindly policeman lowered his voice confidentially and said in hollow and reverent tones: *'They are waiting for the new Trollope to be born!'* Do you remember, at these words, how heavy our suitcases suddenly felt? How our blood slowed, our footsteps lagged? Brother Ass, we had been bashfully thinking of a kind of illumination such as Rimbaud dreamed of – a nagging poem which was not didactic or expository but which *infected* – was not simply a rationalised intuition, I mean, clothed in isinglass! We had come to the wrong shop, with the wrong change! A chill struck us as we saw the mist falling in Trafalgar Square, coiling round us its tendrils of ectoplasm! A million muffin-eating moralists were waiting, not for us, Brother Ass,

9 on 12pt

were – tall hawk-featured men perched on balconies and high places, scanning the city with heavy binoculars. What were they seeking so earnestly? Who were they – so composed and steely-eyed? Timidly we stopped a policeman to ask him. 'They are publishers' he said mildly. Publishers! Our hearts stopped beating. 'They are on the look out for new talent.' Great God! It was for *us* they were waiting and watching! Then the kindly policeman lowered his voice confidentially and said in hollow and reverent tones: *'They are waiting for the new Trollope to be born!'* Do you remember, at these words, how heavy our suitcases suddenly felt? How our blood slowed, our footsteps lagged? Brother Ass, we had been bashfully thinking of a kind of illumination such as Rimbaud dreamed of – a nagging poem which was not for us, Brother Ass, but for the plucky and tedious Trollope! (If you are dissatisfied

10 on 13.5pt

men were – tall hawk-featured men perched on balconies and high places, scanning the city with heavy binoculars. What were they seeking so earnestly? Who were they – so composed and steely-eyed? Timidly we stopped a policeman to ask him. 'They are publishers' he said mildly. Publishers! Our hearts stopped beating. 'They are on the look out for new talent.' Great God! It was for *us* they were waiting and watching! Then the kindly policeman lowered his voice confidentially and said in hollow and reverent tones: *'They are waiting for the new Trollope to be born!'* Do you remember, at these words, how heavy our suitcases suddenly felt? How our blood slowed, our footsteps lagged? Brother Ass, we had been bashfully thinking of a kind of illumination such as

11 on 14.5pt

LINOTYPE PALATINO

Linotype **Pegasus**

roman (05530), **italic** (13530)
bold (07530)
Monotype 1937 (Berthold Wolpe)
Copyfitting code 115/99/118

ABCDEFGHIJKLMNOP
QRSTUVWXYZ abcdefg
hijklmnopqrstuvwxyz
1234567890
fifl ()[]&£$.,;:-!?''

ABCDEFGHIJKLMNOP
QRSTUVWXYZ abcdefg
hijklmnopqrstuvwxyz
1234567890
fifl ()[]&£$.,;:-!?''

ABCDEFGHIJKLMNOP
QRSTUVWXYZ abcdefg
hijklmnopqrstuvwxyz
1234567890
fifl ()[]&£$.,;:-!?''

24 on 27pt

These examples show *normal* letterspacing and the effect of *reduced* letterspacing on roman setting *as well as on words in italic*: they also show the appearance of figures, for example 28 May 1964, within text. These & the ampersand are not included in the setting opposite.
Normal letterspacing

These examples show *normal* letterspacing and the effect of *reduced* letterspacing on roman setting *as well as on words in italic*: they also show the appearance of figures, for example 28 May 1964, within text. These & the ampersand are not included in the setting opposite.
Minus one unit spacing

These examples show *normal* letterspacing and the effect of *reduced* letterspacing on roman setting *as well as on words in italic*: they also show the appearance of figures, for example 28 May 1964, within text. These & the ampersand are not included in the setting opposite.
Minus two units spacing

WALKING ALONG THE MALL WE WONDERED WHO ALL THOSE
WALKING ALONG THE MALL WE WONDERED WHO ALL
WALKING ALONG THE MALL WE WONDERED WHO
Capitals: normal letterspacing/plus 4 units/plus 9 units

Walking along the Mall we wondered who all those men were – tall hawk-featured men perched on balconies and high places, scanning the city with heavy binoculars. WHAT WERE THEY SEEKING SO EARNESTLY? Who were they – so composed and steely-eyed? Timidly we stopped a policeman to ask him. 'THEY ARE PUBLISHERS' he said mildly. Publishers! Our hearts stopped beating. 'They are on the look out for new talent.' Great God! It was for *us* they were waiting and watching! Then the kindly policeman lowered his
Text with reduced caps normal letterspacing/plus 3 units

WALKING ALONG THE MALL we wondered who all those men were
WALKING ALONG THE MALL we wondered who all those men were
True italic/sloped roman

Walking along the Mall we wondered who all those men were – tall hawk-featured men perched on balconies and high places, scanning the city with heavy binoculars. What were they seeking so earnestly? Who were they – so composed and steely-eyed? Timidly we stopped a policeman to ask him. 'They are publishers' he said mildly. Publishers! Our hearts stopped beating. 'They are on the look out for new talent.' Great God! It was for *us* they were waiting and watching! Then the kindly policeman lowered his voice confidentially and said in hollow and reverent tones: *'They are waiting for the new Trollope to be born!'* Do you remember, at these words, how heavy our suitcases suddenly felt? How our blood slowed, our footsteps lagged? Brother Ass, we had been bashfully thinking of a kind of illumination such as Rimbaud dreamed of – a nagging poem which was not didactic or expository but which *infected*
8 on 9pt

Walking along the Mall we wondered who all those men were – tall hawk-featured men perched on balconies and high places, scanning the city with heavy binoculars. What were they seeking so earnestly? Who were they – so composed and steely-eyed? Timidly we stopped a policeman to ask him. 'They are publishers' he said mildly. Publishers! Our hearts stopped beating. 'They are on the look out for new talent.' Great God! It was for *us* they were waiting and watching! Then the kindly policeman lowered his voice confidentially and said in hollow and reverent tones: *'They are waiting for the new Trollope to be born!'* Do you remember, at these words, how heavy our suitcases suddenly felt? How our blood slowed, our footsteps lagged? Brother Ass, we had been bashfully thinking of a kind of illumination such as Rimbaud
8 on 10.5pt

Walking along the Mall we wondered who all those men were – tall hawk-featured men perched on balconies and high places, scanning the city with heavy binoculars. What were they seeking so earnestly? Who were they – so composed and steely-eyed? Timidly we stopped a policeman to ask him. 'They are publishers' he said mildly. Publishers! Our hearts stopped beating. 'They are on the look out for new talent.' Great God! It was for *us* they were waiting and watching! Then the kindly policeman lowered his voice confidentially and said in hollow and reverent tones: *'They are waiting for the new Trollope to be born!'* Do you remember, at these words, how heavy our suitcases suddenly felt? How our blood slowed, our footsteps lagged? Brother Ass, we had been bashfully thinking of a kind of illumination such as Rimbaud dreamed of – a nagging poem which was not didactic or expository but which *infected* – was not simply a rationalised intuition, I mean, clothed in isinglass! We had come to the wrong shop, with the wrong change! A chill struck us as we saw the mist falling in Trafalgar Square, coiling round us its tendrils of ectoplasm! A million muffin-eating moralists were waiting, not for us, Brother Ass, but for the plucky and tedious Trollope! (If you are dissatisfied with your form, reach for the *curette*.) Now do you wonder if I laugh a little off-key? Do you ask yourself what has turned me into nature's bashful little aphorist? We who are, after all, simply poor

9 on 11pt

Walking along the Mall we wondered who all those men were – tall hawk-featured men perched on balconies and high places, scanning the city with heavy binoculars. What were they seeking so earnestly? Who were they – so composed and steely-eyed? Timidly we stopped a policeman to ask him. 'They are publishers' he said mildly. Publishers! Our hearts stopped beating. 'They are on the look out for new talent.' Great God! It was for *us* they were waiting and watching! Then the kindly policeman lowered his voice confidentially and said in hollow and reverent tones: *'They are waiting for the new Trollope to be born!'* Do you remember, at these words, how heavy our suitcases suddenly felt? How our blood slowed, our footsteps lagged? Brother Ass, we had been bashfully thinking of a kind of illumination such as Rimbaud dreamed of – a nagging poem which was not didactic or expository but which *infected* – was not simply a rationalised intuition, I mean, clothed in isinglass! We had come to the wrong shop, with the wrong change! A chill struck us as we saw the mist falling in Trafalgar Square, coiling round us its tendrils of ectoplasm! A million muffin-eating moralists were waiting, not for us, Brother Ass, but for the plucky and tedious Trollope! (If you are dissatisfied with your form, reach for the *curette*.) Now do you wonder if I laugh a little off-key? Do you ask yourself what has turned me into

9 on 12pt

Walking along the Mall we wondered who all those men were – tall hawk-featured men perched on balconies and high places, scanning the city with heavy binoculars. What were they seeking so earnestly? Who were they – so composed and steely-eyed? Timidly we stopped a policeman to ask him. 'They are publishers' he said mildly. Publishers! Our hearts stopped beating. 'They are on the look out for new talent.' Great God! It was for *us* they were waiting and watching! Then the kindly policeman lowered his voice confidentially and said in hollow and reverent tones: *'They are waiting for the new Trollope to be born!'* Do you remember, at these words, how heavy our suitcases suddenly felt? How our blood slowed, our footsteps lagged? Brother Ass, we had been bashfully thinking of a kind of illumination such as Rimbaud dreamed of – a nagging poem which was not didactic or expository but which *infected* – was not simply a rationalised intuition, I mean, clothed in isinglass! We had come to the wrong shop, with the wrong change! A chill struck us as we saw the mist falling in Trafalgar Square, coiling round us its tendrils of ectoplasm! A million muffin-eating moralists were waiting, not for us, Brother Ass, but for the plucky and tedious Trollope! (If you are

10 on 12pt

Walking along the Mall we wondered who all those men were – tall hawk-featured men perched on balconies and high places, scanning the city with heavy binoculars. What were they seeking so earnestly? Who were they – so composed and steely-eyed? Timidly we stopped a policeman to ask him. 'They are publishers' he said mildly. Publishers! Our hearts stopped beating. 'They are on the look out for new talent.' Great God! It was for *us* they were waiting and watching! Then the kindly policeman lowered his voice confidentially and said in hollow and reverent tones: *'They are waiting for the new Trollope to be born!'* Do you remember, at these words, how heavy our suitcases suddenly felt? How our blood slowed, our footsteps lagged? Brother Ass, we had been bashfully thinking of a kind of illumination such as Rimbaud dreamed of – a nagging poem which was not didactic or expository but which *infected* – was not simply a rationalised intuition, I mean, clothed in isinglass! We had come to the wrong shop, with the wrong change! A chill struck us as we saw the mist falling in Trafalgar Square,

10 on 13.5pt

Walking along the Mall we wondered who all those men were – tall hawk-featured men perched on balconies and high places, scanning the city with heavy binoculars. What were they seeking so earnestly? Who were they – so composed and steely-eyed? Timidly we stopped a policeman to ask him. 'They are publishers' he said mildly. Publishers! Our hearts stopped beating. 'They are on the look out for new talent.' Great God! It was for *us* they were waiting and watching! Then the kindly policeman lowered his voice confidentially and said in hollow and reverent tones: *'They are waiting for the new Trollope to be born!'* Do you remember, at these words, how heavy our suitcases suddenly felt? How our blood slowed, our footsteps lagged? Brother Ass, we had been bashfully thinking of a kind of illumination such as Rimbaud dreamed of – a nagging poem which was not didactic or expository but which *infected* – was not simply a rationalised intuition, I mean, clothed in isinglass! We had come to the wrong shop, with

11 on 13pt

Walking along the Mall we wondered who all those men were – tall hawk-featured men perched on balconies and high places, scanning the city with heavy binoculars. What were they seeking so earnestly? Who were they – so composed and steely-eyed? Timidly we stopped a policeman to ask him. 'They are publishers' he said mildly. Publishers! Our hearts stopped beating. 'They are on the look out for new talent.' Great God! It was for *us* they were waiting and watching! Then the kindly policeman lowered his voice confidentially and said in hollow and reverent tones: *'They are waiting for the new Trollope to be born!'* Do you remember, at these words, how heavy our suitcases suddenly felt? How our blood slowed, our footsteps lagged? Brother Ass, we had been bashfully thinking of a kind of illumination such as Rimbaud dreamed of – a nagging poem which was not didactic or expository but which *infected* – was not simply a rational-

11 on 14.5pt

Monotype **Perpetua**

239 roman and italic
461 bold
Monotype 1929 (Eric Gill)
Copyfitting factor 38.1/34.1/43.6

Range also includes bold italic

The Linotype version is similar, but does not
include small caps. Copyfitting code
104/88/124

Gill's design was originally cut by Charles
Malin of Paris; the final drawings were done
from pulls of the resulting type, considerably
modified and regularised. The italic was
originally named Felicity

ABCDEFGHIJKLMNOP
QRSTUVWXYZ abcdefg
hijklmnopqrstuvwxyz
1234567890 1234567890
ff fi fl ffi ffl ()[]&£$.,;:-!?''

ABCDEFGHIJKLMNOP
QRSTUVWXYZ abcdefg
hijklmnopqrstuvwxyz
1234567890 1234567890
ff fi fl ffi ffl ()[]& £$.,;:-!?''

ABCDEFGHIJKLMNOP
QRSTUVWXYZ abcdefg
hijklmnopqrstuvwxyz
1234567890 1234567890
ff fi fl ffi ffl ()[]&£$.,;:-!?''

24 on 27pt

These examples show *normal* letterspacing and the effect of *reduced*
letterspacing on roman setting *as well as on words in italic*: they also
show the appearance of figures, for example 28 May 1964, within text.
These & the ampersand are not included in the setting opposite.

Normal letterspacing

These examples show *normal* letterspacing and the effect of *reduced*
letterspacing on roman setting *as well as on words in italic*: they also
show the appearance of figures, for example 28 May 1964, within text.
These & the ampersand are not included in the setting opposite.

Minus one unit spacing

These examples show *normal* letterspacing and the effect of *reduced*
letterspacing on roman setting *as well as on words in italic*: they also
show the appearance of figures, for example 28 May 1964, within text.
These & the ampersand are not included in the setting opposite.

Minus two units spacing

WALKING ALONG THE MALL WE WONDERED WHO ALL THOSE MEN
WALKING ALONG THE MALL WE WONDERED WHO ALL THOSE
WALKING ALONG THE MALL WE WONDERED WHO ALL

Capitals: normal letterspacing/plus 9 units/plus 18 units

WALKING ALONG THE MALL WE WONDERED WHO ALL THOSE MEN WERE
WALKING ALONG THE MALL WE WONDERED WHO ALL THOSE MEN WERE
WALKING ALONG THE MALL WE WONDERED WHO ALL THOSE MEN

Small caps: normal letterspacing/plus 6 units/plus 12 units

WALKING ALONG THE MALL we wondered who all those men were
WALKING ALONG THE MALL we wondered who all those men were

True italic/sloped roman

WALKING ALONG THE MALL WE WONDERED WHO ALL THOSE MEN WERE
WALKING ALONG THE MALL WE WONDERED WHO ALL THOSE MEN WERE

True small caps/reduced capitals

Walking along the Mall we wondered who all those men were – tall hawk-featured
men perched on balconies and high places, scanning the city with heavy binoculars. What were
they seeking so earnestly? Who were they – so composed and steely-eyed? Timidly we stopped a
policeman to ask him. 'They are publishers' he said mildly. Publishers! Our hearts stopped beating.
'They are on the look out for new talent.' Great God! It was for *us* they were waiting and watching!
Then the kindly policeman lowered his voice confidentially and said in hollow and reverent tones:
'They are waiting for the new Trollope to be born!' Do you remember, at these words, how heavy our
suitcases suddenly felt? How our blood slowed, our footsteps lagged? Brother Ass, we had been
bashfully thinking of a kind of illumination such as Rimbaud dreamed of – a nagging poem which
was not didactic or expository but which *infected* – was not simply a rationalised intuition, I mean,

8 on 9pt

WALKING ALONG THE MALL WE WONDERED WHO ALL THOSE MEN WERE – TALL HAWK-
featured men perched on balconies and high places, scanning the city with heavy binoculars. What
were they seeking so earnestly? Who were they – so composed and steely-eyed? Timidly we stopped
a policeman to ask him. 'They are publishers' he said mildly. Publishers! Our hearts stopped
beating. 'They are on the look out for new talent.' Great God! It was for *us* they were waiting
and watching! Then the kindly policeman lowered his voice confidentially and said in hollow and
reverent tones: *'They are waiting for the new Trollope to be born!'* Do you remember, at these words,
how heavy our suitcases suddenly felt? How our blood slowed, our footsteps lagged? Brother Ass, we
had been bashfully thinking of a kind of illumination such as Rimbaud dreamed of – a nagging poem

8 on 10.5pt

Walking along the Mall we wondered who all those men were – tall hawk-
featured men perched on balconies and high places, scanning the city with heavy binoculars. What were they seeking so earnestly? Who were they – so composed and steely-eyed? Timidly we stopped a policeman to ask him. 'They are publishers' he said mildly. Publishers! Our hearts stopped beating. 'They are on the look out for new talent.' Great God! It was for *us* they were waiting and watching! Then the kindly policeman lowered his voice confidentially and said in hollow and reverent tones: *'They are waiting for the new Trollope to be born!'* Do you remember, at these words, how heavy our suitcases suddenly felt? How our blood slowed, our footsteps lagged? Brother Ass, we had been bashfully thinking of a kind of illumination such as Rimbaud dreamed of – a nagging poem which was not didactic or expository but which *infected* – was not simply a rationalised intuition, I mean, clothed in isinglass! We had come to the wrong shop, with the wrong change! A chill struck us as we saw the mist falling in Trafalgar Square, coiling around us its tendrils of ectoplasm! A million muffin-eating moralists were waiting, not for us, Brother Ass, but for the plucky and tedious Trollope! (If you are dissatisfied with your form, reach for the *curette*.) Now do you wonder if I laugh a little off-key? Do you ask yourself what has turned me into nature's bashful little aphorist? We who are, after all, simply poor co-workers in the psyche of our nation, what can we expect but the natural automatic rejection from a public which resents

9 on 11pt

WALKING ALONG THE MALL WE WONDERED WHO ALL THOSE MEN WERE – TALL HAWK-
featured men perched on balconies and high places, scanning the city with heavy binoculars. What were they seeking so earnestly? Who were they – so composed and steely-eyed? Timidly we stopped a policeman to ask him. 'They are publishers' he said mildly. Publishers! Our hearts stopped beating. 'They are on the look out for new talent.' Great God! It was for *us* they were waiting and watching! Then the kindly policeman lowered his voice confidentially and said in hollow and reverent tones: *'They are waiting for the new Trollope to be born!'* Do you remember, at these words, how heavy our suitcases suddenly felt? How our blood slowed, our footsteps lagged? Brother Ass, we had been bashfully thinking of a kind of illumination such as Rimbaud dreamed of – a nagging poem which was not didactic or expository but which *infected* – was not simply a rationalised intuition, I mean, clothed in isinglass! We had come to the wrong shop, with the wrong change! A chill struck us as we saw the mist falling in Trafalgar Square, coiling around us its tendrils of ectoplasm! A million muffin-eating moralists were waiting, not for us, Brother Ass, but for the plucky and tedious Trollope! (If you are dissatisfied with your form, reach for the *curette*.) Now do you wonder if I laugh a little off-key? Do you ask yourself what has turned me into nature's bashful little aphorist? We who are, after all, simply poor co-workers in the psyche of our

9 on 12pt

Walking along the Mall we wondered who all those men were – tall
hawk-featured men perched on balconies and high places, scanning the city with heavy binoculars. What were they seeking so earnestly? Who were they – so composed and steely-eyed? Timidly we stopped a policeman to ask him. 'They are publishers' he said mildly. Publishers! Our hearts stopped beating. 'They are on the look out for new talent.' Great God! It was for *us* they were waiting and watching! Then the kindly policeman lowered his voice confidentially and said in hollow and reverent tones: *'They are waiting for the new Trollope to be born!'* Do you remember, at these words, how heavy our suitcases suddenly felt? How our blood slowed, our footsteps lagged? Brother Ass, we had been bashfully thinking of a kind of illumination such as Rimbaud dreamed of – a nagging poem which was not didactic or expository but which *infected* – was not simply a rationalised intuition, I mean, clothed in isinglass! We had come to the wrong shop, with the wrong change! A chill struck us as we saw the mist falling in Trafalgar Square, coiling around us its tendrils of ectoplasm! A million muffin-eating moralists were waiting, not for us, Brother Ass, but for the plucky and tedious Trollope! (If you are

10 on 12pt

WALKING ALONG THE MALL WE WONDERED WHO ALL THOSE MEN WERE – TALL
hawk-featured men perched on balconies and high places, scanning the city with heavy binoculars. What were they seeking so earnestly? Who were they – so composed and steely-eyed? Timidly we stopped a policeman to ask him. 'They are publishers' he said mildly. Publishers! Our hearts stopped beating. 'They are on the look out for new talent.' Great God! It was for *us* they were waiting and watching! Then the kindly policeman lowered his voice confidentially and said in hollow and reverent tones: *'They are waiting for the new Trollope to be born!'* Do you remember, at these words, how heavy our suitcases suddenly felt? How our blood slowed, our footsteps lagged? Brother Ass, we had been bashfully thinking of a kind of illumination such as Rimbaud dreamed of – a nagging poem which was not didactic or expository but which *infected* – was not simply a rationalised intuition, I mean, clothed in isinglass! We had come to the wrong shop, with the wrong change! A chill struck us as we saw the mist falling in Trafalgar Square, coiling around us its tendrils of ectoplasm! A million muffin-eating moralists were wait-

10 on 13.5pt

Walking along the Mall we wondered who all those men were
– tall hawk-featured men perched on balconies and high places, scanning the city with heavy binoculars. What were they seeking so earnestly? Who were they – so composed and steely-eyed? Timidly we stopped a policeman to ask him. 'They are publishers' he said mildly. Publishers! Our hearts stopped beating. 'They are on the look out for new talent.' Great God! It was for *us* they were waiting and watching! Then the kindly policeman lowered his voice confidentially and said in hollow and reverent tones: *'They are waiting for the new Trollope to be born!'* Do you remember, at these words, how heavy our suitcases suddenly felt? How our blood slowed, our footsteps lagged? Brother Ass, we had been bashfully thinking of a kind of illumination such as Rimbaud dreamed of – a nagging poem which was not didactic or expository but which *infected* – was not simply a rationalised intuition, I mean, clothed in isinglass! We had come to the wrong shop, with the wrong change! A chill struck us as we saw the mist falling in

11 on 13pt

WALKING ALONG THE MALL WE WONDERED WHO ALL THOSE MEN WERE
– tall hawk-featured men perched on balconies and high places, scanning the city with heavy binoculars. What were they seeking so earnestly? Who were they – so composed and steely-eyed? Timidly we stopped a policeman to ask him. 'They are publishers' he said mildly. Publishers! Our hearts stopped beating. 'They are on the look out for new talent.' Great God! It was for *us* they were waiting and watching! Then the kindly policeman lowered his voice confidentially and said in hollow and reverent tones: *'They are waiting for the new Trollope to be born!'* Do you remember, at these words, how heavy our suitcases suddenly felt? How our blood slowed, our footsteps lagged? Brother Ass, we had been bashfully thinking of a kind of illumination such as Rimbaud dreamed of – a nagging poem which was not didactic or expository but which *infected* – was not simply a rationalised intuition, I mean, clothed in isinglass! We had come to the wrong shop,

11 on 14.5pt

MONOTYPE PERPETUA

Monotype **Photina**

747 roman and italic
748 semi-bold
Monotype 1971 (José Mendoza)
Copyfitting factor 42.6/39.5/42.7

Range also includes semi-bold italic, bold, bold
italic, ultra bold, ultra bold italic

ABCDEFGHIJKLMNOP
QRSTUVWXYZ abcdefg
hijklmnopqrstuvwxyz
1234567890 1234567890
ff fi fl ffi ffl ()[]&£$.,;:-!?''

ABCDEFGHIJKLMNOP
QRSTUVWXYZ abcdefg
hijklmnopqrstuvwxyz
1234567890 1234567890
ff fi fl ffi ffl ()[]&£$.,;:-!?''

ABCDEFGHIJKLMNOP
QRSTUVWXYZ abcdefg
hijklmnopqrstuvwxyz
1234567890 1234567890
ff fi fl ffi ffl ()[]&£$.,;:-!?''

24 on 27pt

These examples show *normal* letterspacing and the effect of *reduced* letterspacing on roman setting *as well as on words in italic*: they also show the appearance of figures, for example 28 May 1964, within text. These & the ampersand are not included in the setting opposite.

Normal letterspacing

These examples show *normal* letterspacing and the effect of *reduced* letterspacing on roman setting *as well as on words in italic*: they also show the appearance of figures, for example 28 May 1964, within text. These & the ampersand are not included in the setting opposite.

Minus one unit spacing

These examples show *normal* letterspacing and the effect of *reduced* letterspacing on roman setting *as well as on words in italic*: they also show the appearance of figures, for example 28 May 1964, within text. These & the ampersand are not included in the setting opposite.

Minus two units spacing

WALKING ALONG THE MALL WE WONDERED WHO ALL THOSE MEN
WALKING ALONG THE MALL WE WONDERED WHO ALL
WALKING ALONG THE MALL WE WONDERED WHO

Capitals: normal letterspacing/plus 9 units/plus 18 units

WALKING ALONG THE MALL WE WONDERED WHO ALL THOSE MEN WERE
WALKING ALONG THE MALL WE WONDERED WHO ALL THOSE MEN WERE
WALKING ALONG THE MALL WE WONDERED WHO ALL THOSE MEN

Small caps: normal letterspacing/plus 6 units/plus 12 units

WALKING ALONG THE MALL we wondered who all those men were
WALKING ALONG THE MALL we wondered who all those men were

True italic/sloped roman

WALKING ALONG THE MALL WE WONDERED WHO ALL THOSE MEN WERE
WALKING ALONG THE MALL WE WONDERED WHO ALL THOSE MEN WERE

True small caps/reduced capitals

Walking along the Mall we wondered who all those men were – tall hawk-featured men perched on balconies and high places, scanning the city with heavy binoculars. What were they seeking so earnestly? Who were they – so composed and steely-eyed? Timidly we stopped a policeman to ask him. 'They are publishers' he said mildly. Publishers! Our hearts stopped beating. 'They are on the look out for new talent.' Great God! It was for *us* they were waiting and watching! Then the kindly policeman lowered his voice confidentially and said in hollow and reverent tones: *'They are waiting for the new Trollope to be born!'* Do you remember, at these words, how heavy our suitcases suddenly felt? How our blood slowed, our footsteps lagged? Brother Ass, we had been bashfully thinking of a kind of illumination such as Rimbaud dreamed of – a nagging

8 on 9pt

WALKING ALONG THE MALL WE WONDERED WHO ALL THOSE MEN WERE – TALL HAWK-featured men perched on balconies and high places, scanning the city with heavy binoculars. What were they seeking so earnestly? Who were they – so composed and steely-eyed? Timidly we stopped a policeman to ask him. 'They are publishers' he said mildly. Publishers! Our hearts stopped beating. 'They are on the look out for new talent.' Great God! It was for *us* they were waiting and watching! Then the kindly policeman lowered his voice confidentially and said in hollow and reverent tones: *'They are waiting for the new Trollope to be born!'* Do you remember, at these words, how heavy our suitcases suddenly felt? How our blood slowed, our footsteps lagged? Brother Ass, we

8 on 10.5pt

Walking along the Mall we wondered who all those men were – tall hawk-featured men perched on balconies and high places, scanning the city with heavy binoculars. What were they seeking so earnestly? Who were they – so composed and steely-eyed? Timidly we stopped a policeman to ask him. 'They are publishers' he said mildly. Publishers! Our hearts stopped beating. 'They are on the look out for new talent.' Great God! It was for *us* they were waiting and watching! Then the kindly policeman lowered his voice confidentially and said in hollow and reverent tones: *'They are waiting for the new Trollope to be born!'* Do you remember, at these words, how heavy our suitcases suddenly felt? How our blood slowed, our footsteps lagged? Brother Ass, we had been bashfully thinking of a kind of illumination such as Rimbaud dreamed of – a nagging poem which was not didactic or expository but which *infected* – was not simply a rationalised intuition, I mean, clothed in isinglass! We had come to the wrong shop, with the wrong change! A chill struck us as we saw the mist falling in Trafalgar Square, coiling around us its tendrils of ectoplasm! A million muffin-eating moralists were waiting, not for us, Brother Ass, but for the plucky and tedious Trollope! (If you are dissatisfied with your form, reach for the *curette*.) Now do you wonder if I laugh a little off-key? Do you ask yourself what has turned me into nature's

9 on 11pt

Walking along the Mall we wondered who all those men were – tall hawk-featured men perched on balconies and high places, scanning the city with heavy binoculars. What were they seeking so earnestly? Who were they – so composed and steely-eyed? Timidly we stopped a policeman to ask him. 'They are publishers' he said mildly. Publishers! Our hearts stopped beating. 'They are on the look out for new talent.' Great God! It was for *us* they were waiting and watching! Then the kindly policeman lowered his voice confidentially and said in hollow and reverent tones: *'They are waiting for the new Trollope to be born!'* Do you remember, at these words, how heavy our suitcases suddenly felt? How our blood slowed, our footsteps lagged? Brother Ass, we had been bashfully thinking of a kind of illumination such as Rimbaud dreamed of – a nagging poem which was not didactic or expository but which *infected* – was not simply a rationalised intuition, I mean, clothed in isinglass! We had come to the wrong shop, with the wrong change! A chill struck us as we saw the mist falling in Trafalgar Square, coiling around us its tendrils of

10 on 12pt

Walking along the Mall we wondered who all those men were – tall hawk-featured men perched on balconies and high places, scanning the city with heavy binoculars. What were they seeking so earnestly? Who were they – so composed and steely-eyed? Timidly we stopped a policeman to ask him. 'They are publishers' he said mildly. Publishers! Our hearts stopped beating. 'They are on the look out for new talent.' Great God! It was for *us* they were waiting and watching! Then the kindly policeman lowered his voice confidentially and said in hollow and reverent tones: *'They are waiting for the new Trollope to be born!'* Do you remember, at these words, how heavy our suitcases suddenly felt? How our blood slowed, our footsteps lagged? Brother Ass, we had been bashfully thinking of a kind of illumination such as Rimbaud dreamed of – a nagging poem which was not didactic or expository but which *infected* – was not simply a rationalised intuition, I

11 on 13pt

WALKING ALONG THE MALL WE WONDERED WHO ALL THOSE MEN WERE – TALL hawk-featured men perched on balconies and high places, scanning the city with heavy binoculars. What were they seeking so earnestly? Who were they – so composed and steely-eyed? Timidly we stopped a policeman to ask him. 'They are publishers' he said mildly. Publishers! Our hearts stopped beating. 'They are on the look out for new talent.' Great God! It was for *us* they were waiting and watching! Then the kindly policeman lowered his voice confidentially and said in hollow and reverent tones: *'They are waiting for the new Trollope to be born!'* Do you remember, at these words, how heavy our suitcases suddenly felt? How our blood slowed, our footsteps lagged? Brother Ass, we had been bashfully thinking of a kind of illumination such as Rimbaud dreamed of – a nagging poem which was not didactic or expository but which *infected* – was not simply a rationalised intuition, I mean, clothed in isinglass! We had come to the wrong shop, with the wrong change! A chill struck us as we saw the mist falling in Trafalgar Square, coiling around us its tendrils of ectoplasm! A million muffin-eating moralists were waiting, not for us, Brother Ass, but for the plucky and tedious Trollope! (If you are dissatisfied with your form, reach for the *curette*.) Now do you wonder if I

9 on 12pt

WALKING ALONG THE MALL WE WONDERED WHO ALL THOSE MEN WERE – tall hawk-featured men perched on balconies and high places, scanning the city with heavy binoculars. What were they seeking so earnestly? Who were they – so composed and steely-eyed? Timidly we stopped a policeman to ask him. 'They are publishers' he said mildly. Publishers! Our hearts stopped beating. 'They are on the look out for new talent.' Great God! It was for *us* they were waiting and watching! Then the kindly policeman lowered his voice confidentially and said in hollow and reverent tones: *'They are waiting for the new Trollope to be born!'* Do you remember, at these words, how heavy our suitcases suddenly felt? How our blood slowed, our footsteps lagged? Brother Ass, we had been bashfully thinking of a kind of illumination such as Rimbaud dreamed of – a nagging poem which was not didactic or expository but which *infected* – was not simply a rationalised intuition, I mean, clothed in isinglass! We had come to the wrong shop, with the wrong change! A chill struck us as we

10 on 13.5pt

WALKING ALONG THE MALL WE WONDERED WHO ALL THOSE MEN were – tall hawk-featured men perched on balconies and high places, scanning the city with heavy binoculars. What were they seeking so earnestly? Who were they – so composed and steely-eyed? Timidly we stopped a policeman to ask him. 'They are publishers' he said mildly. Publishers! Our hearts stopped beating. 'They are on the look out for new talent.' Great God! It was for *us* they were waiting and watching! Then the kindly policeman lowered his voice confidentially and said in hollow and reverent tones: *'They are waiting for the new Trollope to be born!'* Do you remember, at these words, how heavy our suitcases suddenly felt? How our blood slowed, our footsteps lagged? Brother Ass, we had been bashfully thinking of a kind of illumination such as Rimbaud dreamed of – a nagging poem which was not didactic or exposi-

11 on 14.5pt

MONOTYPE PHOTINA

Linotype PILGRIM

roman (05214), **italic** (13214)
Designed by Eric Gill 1934 for Limited
Editions Club of New York (and called
Bunyan), recut by Linotype 1953
Copyfitting code 136/137

ABCDEFGHIJKLMNOP
QRSTUVWXYZ abcdefg
hijklmnopqrstuvwxyz
1234567890
fifl ()[]&£$.,;:-!?''

*ABCDEFGHIJKLMNOP
QRSTUVWXYZ abcdefg
hijklmnopqrstuvwxyz
1234567890
fifl ()[]&£$.,;:-!?''*

24 on 27pt

These examples show *normal* letterspacing and the effect of *reduced* letterspacing on roman setting *as well as on words in italic*: they also show the appearance of figures, for example 28 May 1964, within text. These & the ampersand are not included in the setting opposite.
Normal letterspacing

These examples show *normal* letterspacing and the effect of *reduced* letterspacing on roman setting *as well as on words in italic*: they also show the appearance of figures, for example 28 May 1964, within text. These & the ampersand are not included in the setting opposite.
Minus one unit spacing

These examples show *normal* letterspacing and the effect of *reduced* letterspacing on roman setting *as well as on words in italic*: they also show the appearance of figures, for example 28 May 1964, within text. These & the ampersand are not included in the setting opposite.
Minus two units spacing

WALKING ALONG THE MALL WE WONDERED WHO ALL THOSE
WALKING ALONG THE MALL WE WONDERED WHO ALL
WALKING ALONG THE MALL WE WONDERED WHO ALL
Capitals: normal letterspacing/plus 4 units/plus 9 units

Walking along the Mall we wondered who all those men were – tall hawk-featured men perched on balconies and high places, scanning the city with heavy binoculars. WHAT WERE THEY SEEKING SO EARNESTLY? Who were they – so composed and steely-eyed? Timidly we stopped a policeman to ask him. 'THEY ARE PUBLISHERS' he said mildly. Publishers! Our hearts stopped beating. 'They are on the look out for new talent.' Great God! It was for *us* they were waiting and watching! Then the
Text with reduced caps normal letterspacing/plus 3 units

WALKING ALONG THE MALL we wondered who all those men were
WALKING ALONG THE MALL we wondered who all those men were
True italic/sloped roman

Walking along the Mall we wondered who all those men were – tall hawk-featured men perched on balconies and high places, scanning the city with heavy binoculars. What were they seeking so earnestly? Who were they – so composed and steely-eyed? Timidly we stopped a policeman to ask him. 'They are publishers' he said mildly. Publishers! Our hearts stopped beating. 'They are on the look out for new talent.' Great God! It was for *us* they were waiting and watching! Then the kindly policeman lowered his voice confidentially and said in hollow and reverent tones: *'They are waiting for the new Trollope to be born!'* Do you remember, at these words, how heavy our suitcases suddenly felt? How our blood slowed, our footsteps lagged? Brother Ass, we had been bashfully thinking of a kind of
8 on 9pt

Walking along the Mall we wondered who all those men were – tall hawk-featured men perched on balconies and high places, scanning the city with heavy binoculars. What were they seeking so earnestly? Who were they – so composed and steely-eyed? Timidly we stopped a policeman to ask him. 'They are publishers' he said mildly. Publishers! Our hearts stopped beating. 'They are on the look out for new talent.' Great God! It was for *us* they were waiting and watching! Then the kindly policeman lowered his voice confidentially and said in hollow and reverent tones: *'They are waiting for the new Trollope to be born!'* Do you remember, at these words, how heavy our suitcases suddenly felt? How our blood slowed, our
8 on 10.5pt

Walking along the Mall we wondered who all those men were – tall hawk-featured men perched on balconies and high places, scanning the city with heavy binoculars. What were they seeking so earnestly? Who were they – so composed and steely-eyed? Timidly we stopped a policeman to ask him. 'They are publishers' he said mildly. Publishers! Our hearts stopped beating. 'They are on the look out for new talent.' Great God! It was for *us* they were waiting and watching! Then the kindly policeman lowered his voice confidentially and said in hollow and reverent tones: '*They are waiting for the new Trollope to be born!*' Do you remember, at these words, how heavy our suitcases suddenly felt? How our blood slowed, our footsteps lagged? Brother Ass, we had been bashfully thinking of a kind of illumination such as Rimbaud dreamed of – a nagging poem which was not didactic or expository but which *infected* – was not simply a rationalised intuition, I mean, clothed in isinglass! We had come to the wrong shop, with the wrong change! A chill struck us as we saw the mist falling in Trafalgar Square, coiling round us its tendrils of ectoplasm! A million muffin-eating moralists were waiting, not for us, Brother Ass, but for the plucky and tedious Trollope! (If you are dis-
9 on 11pt

Walking along the Mall we wondered who all those men were – tall hawk-featured men perched on balconies and high places, scanning the city with heavy binoculars. What were they seeking so earnestly? Who were they – so composed and steely-eyed? Timidly we stopped a policeman to ask him. 'They are publishers' he said mildly. Publishers! Our hearts stopped beating. 'They are on the look out for new talent.' Great God! It was for *us* they were waiting and watching! Then the kindly policeman lowered his voice confidentially and said in hollow and reverent tones: '*They are waiting for the new Trollope to be born!*' Do you remember, at these words, how heavy our suitcases suddenly felt? How our blood slowed, our footsteps lagged? Brother Ass, we had been bashfully thinking of a kind of illumination such as Rimbaud dreamed of – a nagging poem which was not didactic or expository but which *infected* – was not simply a rationalised intuition, I mean, clothed in isinglass! We had come to the wrong shop, with the wrong change! A chill struck us as we saw the mist falling in Trafalgar Square, coiling round us its tendrils of ectoplasm! A million muffin-eating moralists were waiting, not for us,
9 on 12pt

Walking along the Mall we wondered who all those men were – tall hawk-featured men perched on balconies and high places, scanning the city with heavy binoculars. What were they seeking so earnestly? Who were they – so composed and steely-eyed? Timidly we stopped a policeman to ask him. 'They are publishers' he said mildly. Publishers! Our hearts stopped beating. 'They are on the look out for new talent.' Great God! It was for *us* they were waiting and watching! Then the kindly policeman lowered his voice confidentially and said in hollow and reverent tones: '*They are waiting for the new Trollope to be born!*' Do you remember, at these words, how heavy our suitcases suddenly felt? How our blood slowed, our footsteps lagged? Brother Ass, we had been bashfully thinking of a kind of illumination such as Rimbaud dreamed of – a nagging poem which was not didactic or expository but which *infected* – was not simply a rationalised intuition, I mean, clothed in isinglass! We had come to the wrong shop,
10 on 12pt

Walking along the Mall we wondered who all those men were – tall hawk-featured men perched on balconies and high places, scanning the city with heavy binoculars. What were they seeking so earnestly? Who were they – so composed and steely-eyed? Timidly we stopped a policeman to ask him. 'They are publishers' he said mildly. Publishers! Our hearts stopped beating. 'They are on the look out for new talent.' Great God! It was for *us* they were waiting and watching! Then the kindly policeman lowered his voice confidentially and said in hollow and reverent tones: '*They are waiting for the new Trollope to be born!*' Do you remember, at these words, how heavy our suitcases suddenly felt? How our blood slowed, our footsteps lagged? Brother Ass, we had been bashfully thinking of a kind of illumination such as Rimbaud dreamed of – a nagging poem which was not didactic or expository but which *infected* – was not simply a rationalised intuition,
10 on 13.5pt

Walking along the Mall we wondered who all those men were – tall hawk-featured men perched on balconies and high places, scanning the city with heavy binoculars. What were they seeking so earnestly? Who were they – so composed and steely-eyed? Timidly we stopped a policeman to ask him. 'They are publishers' he said mildly. Publishers! Our hearts stopped beating. 'They are on the look out for new talent.' Great God! It was for *us* they were waiting and watching! Then the kindly policeman lowered his voice confidentially and said in hollow and reverent tones: '*They are waiting for the new Trollope to be born!*' Do you remember, at these words, how heavy our suitcases suddenly felt? How our blood slowed, our footsteps lagged? Brother Ass, we had been bashfully thinking of a kind of illumination such as Rimbaud dreamed of – a nagging poem which
11 on 13pt

Walking along the Mall we wondered who all those men were – tall hawk-featured men perched on balconies and high places, scanning the city with heavy binoculars. What were they seeking so earnestly? Who were they – so composed and steely-eyed? Timidly we stopped a policeman to ask him. 'They are publishers' he said mildly. Publishers! Our hearts stopped beating. 'They are on the look out for new talent.' Great God! It was for *us* they were waiting and watching! Then the kindly policeman lowered his voice confidentially and said in hollow and reverent tones: '*They are waiting for the new Trollope to be born!*' Do you remember, at these words, how heavy our suitcases suddenly felt? How our blood slowed, our footsteps lagged? Brother Ass, we had been bashfully thinking of a kind of illumi-
11 on 14.5pt

Monotype **Plantin**

110 roman and italic
194 bold
Monotype 1913 (Frank Pierpont)
Copyfitting factor 43.8/41.6/49.0

Range also includes light, light italic, semi-bold, semi-bold italic, bold italic, bold condensed

Derived from a Granjon face used by successors of the Antwerp printer Christopher Plantin, working during the 16th century. It was also used in Frankfurt and Basle about 1570

The first type designed for art paper

Educational characters available

ABCDEFGHIJKLMNOP
QRSTUVWXYZ abcdefg
hijklmnopqrstuvwxyz
1234567890 1234567890
ff fi fl ffi ffl ()[]&£$.,;:-!?''

ABCDEFGHIJKLMNOP
QRSTUVWXYZ abcdefg
hijklmnopqrstuvwxyz
1234567890 1234567890
ff fi fl ffi ffl ( ) [ ] & £ $.,; :-!?''

ABCDEFGHIJKLMNOP
QRSTUVWXYZ abcdefg
hijklmnopqrstuvwxyz
1234567890 1234567890
ff fi fl ffi ffl ()[]&£$.,;:-!?''

24 on 27pt

These examples show *normal* letterspacing and the effect of *reduced* letterspacing on roman setting *as well as on words in italic*: they also show the appearance of figures, for example 28 May 1964, within text. These & the ampersand are not included in the setting opposite.

Normal letterspacing

These examples show *normal* letterspacing and the effect of *reduced* letterspacing on roman setting *as well as on words in italic*: they also show the appearance of figures, for example 28 May 1964, within text. These & the ampersand are not included in the setting opposite.

Minus one unit spacing

These examples show *normal* letterspacing and the effect of *reduced* letterspacing on roman setting *as well as on words in italic*: they also show the appearance of figures, for example 28 May 1964, within text. These & the ampersand are not included in the setting opposite.

Minus two units spacing

WALKING ALONG THE MALL WE WONDERED WHO ALL
WALKING ALONG THE MALL WE WONDERED WHO
WALKING ALONG THE MALL WE WONDERED

Capitals: normal letterspacing/plus 9 units/plus 18 units

WALKING ALONG THE MALL WE WONDERED WHO ALL THOSE MEN WERE
WALKING ALONG THE MALL WE WONDERED WHO ALL THOSE MEN
WALKING ALONG THE MALL WE WONDERED WHO ALL THOSE

Small caps: normal letterspacing/plus 6 units/plus 12 units

WALKING ALONG THE MALL we wondered who all those men were
WALKING ALONG THE MALL we wondered who all those men

True italic/sloped roman

WALKING ALONG THE MALL WE WONDERED WHO ALL THOSE MEN WERE
WALKING ALONG THE MALL WE WONDERED WHO ALL THOSE MEN

True small caps/reduced capitals

Walking along the Mall we wondered who all those men were – tall hawk-featured men perched on balconies and high places, scanning the city with heavy binoculars. What were they seeking so earnestly? Who were they – so composed and steely-eyed? Timidly we stopped a policeman to ask him. 'They are publishers' he said mildly. Publishers! Our hearts stopped beating. 'They are on the look out for new talent.' Great God! It was for *us* they were waiting and watching! Then the kindly policeman lowered his voice confidentially and said in hollow and reverent tones: '*They are waiting for the new Trollope to be born!*' Do you remember, at these words, how heavy our suitcases suddenly felt? How our blood slowed, our footsteps lagged? Brother Ass, we had been bashfully thinking of a kind of illumination such as

8 on 9pt

WALKING ALONG THE MALL WE WONDERED WHO ALL THOSE MEN WERE – TALL hawk-featured men perched on balconies and high places, scanning the city with heavy binoculars. What were they seeking so earnestly? Who were they – so composed and steely-eyed? Timidly we stopped a policeman to ask him. 'They are publishers' he said mildly. Publishers! Our hearts stopped beating. 'They are on the look out for new talent.' Great God! It was for *us* they were waiting and watching! Then the kindly policeman lowered his voice confidentially and said in hollow and reverent tones: '*They are waiting for the new Trollope to be born!*' Do you remember, at these words, how heavy our suitcases suddenly felt? How our blood slowed, our footsteps lagged?

8 on 10.5pt

Walking along the Mall we wondered who all those men were – tall hawk-featured men perched on balconies and high places, scanning the city with heavy binoculars. What were they seeking so earnestly? Who were they – so composed and steely-eyed? Timidly we stopped a policeman to ask him. 'They are publishers' he said mildly. Publishers! Our hearts stopped beating. 'They are on the look out for new talent.' Great God! It was for *us* they were waiting and watching! Then the kindly policeman lowered his voice confidentially and said in hollow and reverent tones: '*They are waiting for the new Trollope to be born!*' Do you remember, at these words, how heavy our suitcases suddenly felt? How our blood slowed, our footsteps lagged? Brother Ass, we had been bashfully thinking of a kind of illumination such as Rimbaud dreamed of – a nagging poem which was not didactic or expository but which *infected* – was not simply a rationalised intuition, I mean, clothed in isinglass! We had come to the wrong shop, with the wrong change! A chill struck us as we saw the mist falling in Trafalgar Square, coiling around us its tendrils of ectoplasm! A million muffin-eating moralists were waiting, not for us, Brother Ass, but for the plucky and tedious Trollope! (If you are dissatisfied with your form, reach for the *curette*.) Now do you wonder if I laugh a little off-key? Do

9 on 11pt

Walking along the Mall we wondered who all those men were – tall hawk-featured men perched on balconies and high places, scanning the city with heavy binoculars. What were they seeking so earnestly? Who were they – so composed and steely-eyed? Timidly we stopped a policeman to ask him. 'They are publishers' he said mildly. Publishers! Our hearts stopped beating. 'They are on the look out for new talent.' Great God! It was for *us* they were waiting and watching! Then the kindly policeman lowered his voice confidentially and said in hollow and reverent tones: '*They are waiting for the new Trollope to be born!*' Do you remember, at these words, how heavy our suitcases suddenly felt? How our blood slowed, our footsteps lagged? Brother Ass, we had been bashfully thinking of a kind of illumination such as Rimbaud dreamed of – a nagging poem which was not didactic or expository but which *infected* – was not simply a rationalised intuition, I mean, clothed in isinglass! We had come to the wrong shop, with the

10 on 12pt

Walking along the Mall we wondered who all those men were – tall hawk-featured men perched on balconies and high places, scanning the city with heavy binoculars. What were they seeking so earnestly? Who were they – so composed and steely-eyed? Timidly we stopped a policeman to ask him. 'They are publishers' he said mildly. Publishers! Our hearts stopped beating. 'They are on the look out for new talent.' Great God! It was for *us* they were waiting and watching! Then the kindly policeman lowered his voice confidentially and said in hollow and reverent tones: '*They are waiting for the new Trollope to be born!*' Do you remember, at these words, how heavy our suitcases suddenly felt? How our blood slowed, our footsteps lagged? Brother Ass, we had been bashfully thinking of a kind of illumination such as Rimbaud dreamed of – a nagging poem which was not didactic or expository but which *infected* – was not simply a

11 on 13pt

WALKING ALONG THE MALL WE WONDERED WHO ALL THOSE MEN WERE – tall hawk-featured men perched on balconies and high places, scanning the city with heavy binoculars. What were they seeking so earnestly? Who were they – so composed and steely-eyed? Timidly we stopped a policeman to ask him. 'They are publishers' he said mildly. Publishers! Our hearts stopped beating. 'They are on the look out for new talent.' Great God! It was for *us* they were waiting and watching! Then the kindly policeman lowered his voice confidentially and said in hollow and reverent tones: '*They are waiting for the new Trollope to be born!*' Do you remember, at these words, how heavy our suitcases suddenly felt? How our blood slowed, our footsteps lagged? Brother Ass, we had been bashfully thinking of a kind of illumination such as Rimbaud dreamed of – a nagging poem which was not didactic or expository but which *infected* – was not simply a rationalised intuition, I mean, clothed in isinglass! We had come to the wrong shop, with the wrong change! A chill struck us as we saw the mist falling in Trafalgar Square, coiling around us its tendrils of ectoplasm! A million muffin-eating moralists were waiting, not for us, Brother Ass, but for the plucky and tedious Trollope! (If you are dissatisfied with your

9 on 12pt

WALKING ALONG THE MALL WE WONDERED WHO ALL THOSE MEN were – tall hawk-featured men perched on balconies and high places, scanning the city with heavy binoculars. What were they seeking so earnestly? Who were they – so composed and steely-eyed? Timidly we stopped a policeman to ask him. 'They are publishers' he said mildly. Publishers! Our hearts stopped beating. 'They are on the look out for new talent.' Great God! It was for *us* they were waiting and watching! Then the kindly policeman lowered his voice confidentially and said in hollow and reverent tones: '*They are waiting for the new Trollope to be born!*' Do you remember, at these words, how heavy our suitcases suddenly felt? How our blood slowed, our footsteps lagged? Brother Ass, we had been bashfully thinking of a kind of illumination such as Rimbaud dreamed of – a nagging poem which was not didactic or expository but which *infected* – was not simply a rationalised intuition, I mean, clothed in isinglass! We had come to the wrong shop, with the

10 on 13.5pt

WALKING ALONG THE MALL WE WONDERED WHO ALL THOSE men were – tall hawk-featured men perched on balconies and high places, scanning the city with heavy binoculars. What were they seeking so earnestly? Who were they – so composed and steely-eyed? Timidly we stopped a policeman to ask him. 'They are publishers' he said mildly. Publishers! Our hearts stopped beating. 'They are on the look out for new talent.' Great God! It was for *us* they were waiting and watching! Then the kindly policeman lowered his voice confidentially and said in hollow and reverent tones: '*They are waiting for the new Trollope to be born!*' Do you remember, at these words, how heavy our suitcases suddenly felt? How our blood slowed, our footsteps lagged? Brother Ass, we had been bashfully thinking of a kind of illumination such as Rimbaud dreamed of – a nagging poem

11 on 14.5pt

Monotype **Plantin Light**

113 light and light italic
663 semi-bold
Monotype 1914
Copyfitting factor 43.8/41.6/49.0

Range also includes roman, italic, semi-bold
italic, bold, bold italic, bold condensed

ABCDEFGHIJKLMNOP
QRSTUVWXYZ abcdefg
hijklmnopqrstuvwxyz
1234567890 1234567890
ff fi fl ffi ffl ()[]&£$.,;:-!?''

ABCDEFGHIJKLMNOP
QRSTUVWXYZ abcdefg
hijklmnopqrstuvwxyz
1234567890 1234567890
ff fi fl ffi ffl ( ) [ ] & £ $.,;:-!?''

ABCDEFGHIJKLMNOP
QRSTUVWXYZ abcdefg
hijklmnopqrstuvwxyz
1234567890 1234567890
ff fi fl ffi ffl ()[]&£$.,;:-!?''

24 on 27pt

These examples show *normal* letterspacing and the effect of *reduced* letterspacing on roman setting *as well as on words in italic*: they also show the appearance of figures, for example 28 May 1964, within text. These & the ampersand are not included in the setting opposite.

Normal letterspacing

These examples show *normal* letterspacing and the effect of *reduced* letterspacing on roman setting *as well as on words in italic*: they also show the appearance of figures, for example 28 May 1964, within text. These & the ampersand are not included in the setting opposite.

Minus one unit spacing

These examples show *normal* letterspacing and the effect of *reduced* letterspacing on roman setting *as well as on words in italic*: they also show the appearance of figures, for example 28 May 1964, within text. These & the ampersand are not included in the setting opposite.

Minus two units spacing

WALKING ALONG THE MALL WE WONDERED WHO ALL
WALKING ALONG THE MALL WE WONDERED WHO
WALKING ALONG THE MALL WE WONDERED

Capitals: normal letterspacing/plus 9 units/plus 18 units

WALKING ALONG THE MALL WE WONDERED WHO ALL THOSE MEN WERE
WALKING ALONG THE MALL WE WONDERED WHO ALL THOSE MEN
WALKING ALONG THE MALL WE WONDERED WHO ALL THOSE

Small caps: normal letterspacing/plus 6 units/plus 12 units

WALKING ALONG THE MALL we wondered who all those men were
WALKING ALONG THE MALL we wondered who all those men

True italic/sloped roman

WALKING ALONG THE MALL WE WONDERED WHO ALL THOSE MEN WERE
WALKING ALONG THE MALL WE WONDERED WHO ALL THOSE MEN WERE

True small caps/reduced capitals

Walking along the Mall we wondered who all those men were – tall hawk-featured men perched on balconies and high places, scanning the city with heavy binoculars. What were they seeking so earnestly? Who were they – so composed and steely-eyed? Timidly we stopped a policeman to ask him. 'They are publishers' he said mildly. Publishers! Our hearts stopped beating. 'They are on the look out for new talent.' Great God! It was for *us* they were waiting and watching! Then the kindly policeman lowered his voice confidentially and said in hollow and reverent tones: *'They are waiting for the new Trollope to be born!'* Do you remember, at these words, how heavy our suitcases suddenly felt? How our blood slowed, our footsteps lagged? Brother Ass, we had been bashfully thinking of a kind of illumination such as

8 on 9pt

WALKING ALONG THE MALL WE WONDERED WHO ALL THOSE MEN WERE – TALL hawk-featured men perched on balconies and high places, scanning the city with heavy binoculars. What were they seeking so earnestly? Who were they – so composed and steely-eyed? Timidly we stopped a policeman to ask him. 'They are publishers' he said mildly. Publishers! Our hearts stopped beating. 'They are on the look out for new talent.' Great God! It was for *us* they were waiting and watching! Then the kindly policeman lowered his voice confidentially and said in hollow and reverent tones: *'They are waiting for the new Trollope to be born!'* Do you remember, at these words, how heavy our suitcases suddenly felt? How our blood slowed, our footsteps lagged?

8 on 10.5pt

Walking along the Mall we wondered who all those men were – tall hawk-featured men perched on balconies and high places, scanning the city with heavy binoculars. What were they seeking so earnestly? Who were they – so composed and steely-eyed? Timidly we stopped a policeman to ask him. 'They are publishers' he said mildly. Publishers! Our hearts stopped beating. 'They are on the look out for new talent.' Great God! It was for *us* they were waiting and watching! Then the kindly policeman lowered his voice confidentially and said in hollow and reverent tones: *'They are waiting for the new Trollope to be born!'* Do you remember, at these words, how heavy our suitcases suddenly felt? How our blood slowed, our footsteps lagged? Brother Ass, we had been bashfully thinking of a kind of illumination such as Rimbaud dreamed of – a nagging poem which was not didactic or expository but which *infected* – was not simply a rationalised intuition, I mean, clothed in isinglass! We had come to the wrong shop, with the wrong change! A chill struck us as we saw the mist falling in Trafalgar Square, coiling around us its tendrils of ectoplasm! A million muffin-eating moralists were waiting, not for us, Brother Ass, but for the plucky and tedious Trollope! (If you are dissatisfied with your form, reach for the *curette*.) Now do you wonder if I laugh a little off-key? Do

9 on 11pt

Walking along the Mall we wondered who all those men were – tall hawk-featured men perched on balconies and high places, scanning the city with heavy binoculars. What were they seeking so earnestly? Who were they – so composed and steely-eyed? Timidly we stopped a policeman to ask him. 'They are publishers' he said mildly. Publishers! Our hearts stopped beating. 'They are on the look out for new talent.' Great God! It was for *us* they were waiting and watching! Then the kindly policeman lowered his voice confidentially and said in hollow and reverent tones: *'They are waiting for the new Trollope to be born!'* Do you remember, at these words, how heavy our suitcases suddenly felt? How our blood slowed, our footsteps lagged? Brother Ass, we had been bashfully thinking of a kind of illumination such as Rimbaud dreamed of – a nagging poem which was not didactic or expository but which *infected* – was not simply a rationalised intuition, I mean, clothed in isinglass! We had come to the wrong shop, with the wrong change! A chill struck us as we saw the mist falling in Trafalgar Square, coiling around us its tendrils of ectoplasm! A million muffin-eating moralists were waiting, not for us, Brother Ass, but for the plucky and tedious Trollope! (If you are dissatisfied with your

9 on 12pt

Walking along the Mall we wondered who all those men were – tall hawk-featured men perched on balconies and high places, scanning the city with heavy binoculars. What were they seeking so earnestly? Who were they – so composed and steely-eyed? Timidly we stopped a policeman to ask him. 'They are publishers' he said mildly. Publishers! Our hearts stopped beating. 'They are on the look out for new talent.' Great God! It was for *us* they were waiting and watching! Then the kindly policeman lowered his voice confidentially and said in hollow and reverent tones: *'They are waiting for the new Trollope to be born!'* Do you remember, at these words, how heavy our suitcases suddenly felt? How our blood slowed, our footsteps lagged? Brother Ass, we had been bashfully thinking of a kind of illumination such as Rimbaud dreamed of – a nagging poem which was not didactic or expository but which *infected* – was not simply a rationalised intuition, I mean, clothed in isinglass! We had come to the wrong shop, with the wrong change! A chill struck us as we saw the mist falling in Trafalgar

10 on 12pt

WALKING ALONG THE MALL WE WONDERED WHO ALL THOSE MEN were – tall hawk-featured men perched on balconies and high places, scanning the city with heavy binoculars. What were they seeking so earnestly? Who were they – so composed and steely-eyed? Timidly we stopped a policeman to ask him. 'They are publishers' he said mildly. Publishers! Our hearts stopped beating. 'They are on the look out for new talent.' Great God! It was for *us* they were waiting and watching! Then the kindly policeman lowered his voice confidentially and said in hollow and reverent tones: *'They are waiting for the new Trollope to be born!'* Do you remember, at these words, how heavy our suitcases suddenly felt? How our blood slowed, our footsteps lagged? Brother Ass, we had been bashfully thinking of a kind of illumination such as Rimbaud dreamed of – a nagging poem which was not didactic or expository but which *infected* – was not simply a rationalised intuition, I mean, clothed in isinglass! We had come to the wrong shop, with the

10 on 13.5pt

Walking along the Mall we wondered who all those men were – tall hawk-featured men perched on balconies and high places, scanning the city with heavy binoculars. What were they seeking so earnestly? Who were they – so composed and steely-eyed? Timidly we stopped a policeman to ask him. 'They are publishers' he said mildly. Publishers! Our hearts stopped beating. 'They are on the look out for new talent.' Great God! It was for *us* they were waiting and watching! Then the kindly policeman lowered his voice confidentially and said in hollow and reverent tones: *'They are waiting for the new Trollope to be born!'* Do you remember, at these words, how heavy our suitcases suddenly felt? How our blood slowed, our footsteps lagged? Brother Ass, we had been bashfully thinking of a kind of illumination such as Rimbaud dreamed of – a nagging poem which was not didactic or expository but which *infected* – was not simply a

11 on 13pt

WALKING ALONG THE MALL WE WONDERED WHO ALL THOSE men were – tall hawk-featured men perched on balconies and high places, scanning the city with heavy binoculars. What were they seeking so earnestly? Who were they – so composed and steely-eyed? Timidly we stopped a policeman to ask him. 'They are publishers' he said mildly. Publishers! Our hearts stopped beating. 'They are on the look out for new talent.' Great God! It was for *us* they were waiting and watching! Then the kindly policeman lowered his voice confidentially and said in hollow and reverent tones: *'They are waiting for the new Trollope to be born!'* Do you remember, at these words, how heavy our suitcases suddenly felt? How our blood slowed, our footsteps lagged? Brother Ass, we had been bashfully thinking of a kind of illumination such as Rimbaud dreamed of – a nagging poem

11 on 14.5pt

MONOTYPE PLANTIN LIGHT

Linotype **Plantin**

roman (05215), **italic** (13215)
bold (07215)
Monotype 1913 (Frank Pierpont)
Copyfitting code 125/115/127

Range also includes light, light italic, bold
italic, bold condensed

Educational characters available

See Monotype Plantin

ABCDEFGHIJKLMNOP
QRSTUVWXYZ abcdefg
hijklmnopqrstuvwxyz
1234567890 1234567890
fifl ()[]&£$.,;:-!?''

ABCDEFGHIJKLMNOP
QRSTUVWXYZ abcdefg
hijklmnopqrstuvwxyz
1234567890 1234567890
fifl ()[]&£$.,;:-!?''

ABCDEFGHIJKLMNOP
QRSTUVWXYZ abcdefg
hijklmnopqrstuvwxyz
1234567890 1234567890
fifl ()[]&£$.,;:-!?''

24 on 27pt

These examples show *normal* letterspacing and the effect of *reduced*
letterspacing on roman setting *as well as on words in italic*: they also
show the appearance of figures, for example 28 May 1964, within text.
These & the ampersand are not included in the setting opposite.
Normal letterspacing

These examples show *normal* letterspacing and the effect of *reduced*
letterspacing on roman setting *as well as on words in italic*: they also
show the appearance of figures, for example 28 May 1964, within text.
These & the ampersand are not included in the setting opposite.
Minus one unit spacing

These examples show *normal* letterspacing and the effect of *reduced*
letterspacing on roman setting *as well as on words in italic*: they also
show the appearance of figures, for example 28 May 1964, within text.
These & the ampersand are not included in the setting opposite.
Minus two units spacing

WALKING ALONG THE MALL WE WONDERED WHO ALL
WALKING ALONG THE MALL WE WONDERED WHO
WALKING ALONG THE MALL WE WONDERED
Capitals: normal letterspacing/plus 4 units/plus 9 units

WALKING ALONG THE MALL WE WONDERED WHO ALL THOSE MEN WERE
WALKING ALONG THE MALL WE WONDERED WHO ALL THOSE MEN
WALKING ALONG THE MALL WE WONDERED WHO ALL THOSE
Small caps: normal letterspacing/plus 3 units/plus 6 units

WALKING ALONG THE MALL WE WONDERED WHO ALL THOSE MEN WERE
WALKING ALONG THE MALL WE WONDERED WHO ALL THOSE MEN WERE
True small caps/reduced capitals

WALKING ALONG THE MALL we wondered who all those men were
WALKING ALONG THE MALL we wondered who all those men
True italic/sloped roman

Walking along the Mall we wondered who all those men were – tall hawk-featured men
perched on balconies and high places, scanning the city with heavy binoculars. What
were they seeking so earnestly? Who were they – so composed and steely-eyed? Timidly
we stopped a policeman to ask him. 'They are publishers' he said mildly. Publishers!
Our hearts stopped beating. 'They are on the look out for new talent.' Great God! It was
for *us* they were waiting and watching! Then the kindly policeman lowered his voice
confidentially and said in hollow and reverent tones: *'They are waiting for the new Trollope
to be born!'* Do you remember, at these words, how heavy our suitcases suddenly felt?
How our blood slowed, our footsteps lagged? Brother Ass, we had been bashfully
thinking of a kind of illumination such as Rimbaud dreamed of – a nagging poem
8 on 9pt

WALKING ALONG THE MALL WE WONDERED WHO ALL THOSE MEN WERE – TALL HAWK-
featured men perched on balconies and high places, scanning the city with heavy
binoculars. What were they seeking so earnestly? Who were they – so composed and
steely-eyed? Timidly we stopped a policeman to ask him. 'They are publishers' he said
mildly. Publishers! Our hearts stopped beating. 'They are on the look out for new talent.'
Great God! It was for *us* they were waiting and watching! Then the kindly policeman
lowered his voice confidentially and said in hollow and reverent tones: *'They are waiting
for the new Trollope to be born!'* Do you remember, at these words, how heavy our
suitcases suddenly felt? How our blood slowed, our footsteps lagged? Brother Ass
8 on 10.5pt

Walking along the Mall we wondered who all those men were – tall hawk-featured men perched on balconies and high places, scanning the city with heavy binoculars. What were they seeking so earnestly? Who were they – so composed and steely-eyed? Timidly we stopped a policeman to ask him. 'They are publishers' he said mildly. Publishers! Our hearts stopped beating. 'They are on the look out for new talent.' Great God! It was for *us* they were waiting and watching! Then the kindly policeman lowered his voice confidentially and said in hollow and reverent tones: *'They are waiting for the new Trollope to be born!'* Do you remember, at these words, how heavy our suitcases suddenly felt? How our blood slowed, our footsteps lagged? Brother Ass, we had been bashfully thinking of a kind of illumination such as Rimbaud dreamed of – a nagging poem which was not didactic or expository but which *infected* – was not simply a rationalised intuition, I mean, clothed in isinglass! We had come to the wrong shop, with the wrong change! A chill struck us as we saw the mist falling in Trafalgar Square, coiling round us its tendrils of ectoplasm! A million muffin-eating moralists were waiting, not for us, Brother Ass, but for the plucky and tedious Trollope! (If you are dissatisfied with your form, reach for the *curette*.) Now do you wonder if I laugh a little off-key? Do you ask yourself what

9 on 11pt

Walking along the Mall we wondered who all those men were – tall hawk-featured men perched on balconies and high places, scanning the city with heavy binoculars. What were they seeking so earnestly? Who were they – so composed and steely-eyed? Timidly we stopped a policeman to ask him. 'They are publishers' he said mildly. Publishers! Our hearts stopped beating. 'They are on the look out for new talent.' Great God! It was for *us* they were waiting and watching! Then the kindly policeman lowered his voice confidentially and said in hollow and reverent tones: *'They are waiting for the new Trollope to be born!'* Do you remember, at these words, how heavy our suitcases suddenly felt? How our blood slowed, our footsteps lagged? Brother Ass, we had been bashfully thinking of a kind of illumination such as Rimbaud dreamed of – a nagging poem which was not didactic or expository but which *infected* – was not simply a rationalised intuition, I mean, clothed in isinglass! We had come to the wrong shop, with the wrong change! A chill struck us as we saw the mist falling in Trafalgar Square, coiling round us its

10 on 12pt

Walking along the Mall we wondered who all those men were – tall hawk-featured men perched on balconies and high places, scanning the city with heavy binoculars. What were they seeking so earnestly? Who were they – so composed and steely-eyed? Timidly we stopped a policeman to ask him. 'They are publishers' he said mildly. Publishers! Our hearts stopped beating. 'They are on the look out for new talent.' Great God! It was for *us* they were waiting and watching! Then the kindly policeman lowered his voice confidentially and said in hollow and reverent tones: *'They are waiting for the new Trollope to be born!'* Do you remember, at these words, how heavy our suitcases suddenly felt? How our blood slowed, our footsteps lagged? Brother Ass, we had been bashfully thinking of a kind of illumination such as Rimbaud dreamed of – a nagging poem which was not didactic or expository but which *infected* – was not simply a rationalised

11 on 13pt

WALKING ALONG THE MALL WE WONDERED WHO ALL THOSE MEN WERE – TALL hawk-featured men perched on balconies and high places, scanning the city with heavy binoculars. What were they seeking so earnestly? Who were they – so composed and steely-eyed? Timidly we stopped a policeman to ask him. 'They are publishers' he said mildly. Publishers! Our hearts stopped beating. 'They are on the look out for new talent.' Great God! It was for *us* they were waiting and watching! Then the kindly policeman lowered his voice confidentially and said in hollow and reverent tones: *'They are waiting for the new Trollope to be born!'* Do you remember, at these words, how heavy our suitcases suddenly felt? How our blood slowed, our footsteps lagged? Brother Ass, we had been bashfully thinking of a kind of illumination such as Rimbaud dreamed of – a nagging poem which was not didactic or expository but which *infected* – was not simply a rationalised intuition, I mean, clothed in isinglass! We had come to the wrong shop, with the wrong change! A chill struck us as we saw the mist falling in Trafalgar Square, coiling round us its tendrils of ectoplasm! A million muffin-eating moralists were waiting, not for us, Brother Ass, but for the plucky and tedious Trollope! (If you are dissatisfied with your form, reach for

9 on 12pt

WALKING ALONG THE MALL WE WONDERED WHO ALL THOSE MEN WERE – tall hawk-featured men perched on balconies and high places, scanning the city with heavy binoculars. What were they seeking so earnestly? Who were they – so composed and steely-eyed? Timidly we stopped a policeman to ask him. 'They are publishers' he said mildly. Publishers! Our hearts stopped beating. 'They are on the look out for new talent.' Great God! It was for *us* they were waiting and watching! Then the kindly policeman lowered his voice confidentially and said in hollow and reverent tones: *'They are waiting for the new Trollope to be born!'* Do you remember, at these words, how heavy our suitcases suddenly felt? How our blood slowed, our footsteps lagged? Brother Ass, we had been bashfully thinking of a kind of illumination such as Rimbaud dreamed of – a nagging poem which was not didactic or expository but which *infected* – was not simply a rationalised intuition, I mean, clothed in isinglass! We had come to the wrong shop, with the wrong change!

10 on 13.5pt

WALKING ALONG THE MALL WE WONDERED WHO ALL THOSE MEN were – tall hawk-featured men perched on balconies and high places, scanning the city with heavy binoculars. What were they seeking so earnestly? Who were they – so composed and steely-eyed? Timidly we stopped a policeman to ask him. 'They are publishers' he said mildly. Publishers! Our hearts stopped beating. 'They are on the look out for new talent.' Great God! It was for *us* they were waiting and watching! Then the kindly policeman lowered his voice confidentially and said in hollow and reverent tones: *'They are waiting for the new Trollope to be born!'* Do you remember, at these words, how heavy our suitcases suddenly felt? How our blood slowed, our footsteps lagged? Brother Ass, we had been bashfully thinking of a kind of illumination such as Rimbaud dreamed of – a nagging poem which was not didactic or

11 on 14.5pt

LINOTYPE PLANTIN

Linotype PLANTIN LIGHT

light (02215), **light italic** (11215)
Monotype 1914
Copyfitting code 125/114

Range also includes roman, italic, bold, bold
italic, bold condensed

ABCDEFGHIJKLMNOP
QRSTUVWXYZ abcdefg
hijklmnopqrstuvwxyz
1234567890 1234567890
fifl ()[]&£$.,;:-!?"

ABCDEFGHIJKLMNOP
QRSTUVWXYZ abcdefg
hijklmnopqrstuvwxyz
1234567890 1234567890
fifl () [] &£$.,;:-!?"

24 on 27pt

These examples show *normal* letterspacing and the effect of *reduced*
letterspacing on roman setting *as well as on words in italic*: they also
show the appearance of figures, for example 28 May 1964, within text.
These & the ampersand are not included in the setting opposite.
Normal letterspacing

These examples show *normal* letterspacing and the effect of *reduced*
letterspacing on roman setting *as well as on words in italic*: they also
show the appearance of figures, for example 28 May 1964, within text.
These & the ampersand are not included in the setting opposite.
Minus one unit spacing

These examples show *normal* letterspacing and the effect of *reduced*
letterspacing on roman setting *as well as on words in italic*: they also
show the appearance of figures, for example 28 May 1964, within text.
These & the ampersand are not included in the setting opposite.
Minus two units spacing

WALKING ALONG THE MALL WE WONDERED WHO ALL
WALKING ALONG THE MALL WE WONDERED WHO
WALKING ALONG THE MALL WE WONDERED
Capitals: normal letterspacing/plus 4 units/plus 9 units

WALKING ALONG THE MALL WE WONDERED WHO ALL THOSE MEN WERE
WALKING ALONG THE MALL WE WONDERED WHO ALL THOSE MEN
WALKING ALONG THE MALL WE WONDERED WHO ALL THOSE
Small caps: normal letterspacing/plus 3 units/plus 6 units

WALKING ALONG THE MALL WE WONDERED WHO ALL THOSE MEN WERE
WALKING ALONG THE MALL WE WONDERED WHO ALL THOSE MEN WERE
True small caps/reduced capitals

WALKING ALONG THE MALL we wondered who all those men were
WALKING ALONG THE MALL we wondered who all those men
True italic/sloped roman

Walking along the Mall we wondered who all those men were – tall hawk-featured men
perched on balconies and high places, scanning the city with heavy binoculars. What were
they seeking so earnestly? Who were they – so composed and steely-eyed? Timidly we
stopped a policeman to ask him. 'They are publishers' he said mildly. Publishers! Our
hearts stopped beating. 'They are on the look out for new talent.' Great God! It was
for *us* they were waiting and watching! Then the kindly policeman lowered his voice
confidentially and said in hollow and reverent tones: *'They are waiting for the new Trollope
to be born!'* Do you remember, at these words, how heavy our suitcases suddenly felt?
How our blood slowed, our footsteps lagged? Brother Ass, we had been bashfully
thinking of a kind of illumination such as Rimbaud dreamed of – a nagging poem
8 on 9pt

WALKING ALONG THE MALL WE WONDERED WHO ALL THOSE MEN WERE – TALL HAWK-featured men perched on balconies and high places, scanning the city with heavy
binoculars. What were they seeking so earnestly? Who were they – so composed and
steely-eyed? Timidly we stopped a policeman to ask him. 'They are publishers' he said
mildly. Publishers! Our hearts stopped beating. 'They are on the look out for new talent.'
Great God! It was for *us* they were waiting and watching! Then the kindly policeman
lowered his voice confidentially and said in hollow and reverent tones: *'They are waiting
for the new Trollope to be born!'* Do you remember, at these words, how heavy our suitcases
suddenly felt? How our blood slowed, our footsteps lagged? Brother Ass, we had been
8 on 10.5pt

Walking along the Mall we wondered who all those men were – tall hawk-featured men perched on balconies and high places, scanning the city with heavy binoculars. What were they seeking so earnestly? Who were they – so composed and steely-eyed? Timidly we stopped a policeman to ask him. 'They are publishers' he said mildly. Publishers! Our hearts stopped beating. 'They are on the look out for new talent.' Great God! It was for *us* they were waiting and watching! Then the kindly policeman lowered his voice confidentially and said in hollow and reverent tones: *'They are waiting for the new Trollope to be born!'* Do you remember, at these words, how heavy our suitcases suddenly felt? How our blood slowed, our footsteps lagged? Brother Ass, we had been bashfully thinking of a kind of illumination such as Rimbaud dreamed of – a nagging poem which was not didactic or expository but which *infected* – was not simply a rationalised intuition, I mean, clothed in isinglass! We had come to the wrong shop, with the wrong change! A chill struck us as we saw the mist falling in Trafalgar Square, coiling round us its tendrils of ectoplasm! A million muffin-eating moralists were waiting, not for us, Brother Ass, but for the plucky and tedious Trollope! (If you are dissatisfied with your form, reach for the *curette*.) Now do you wonder if I laugh a little off-key? Do you ask yourself what has

9 on 11pt

Walking along the Mall we wondered who all those men were – tall hawk-featured men perched on balconies and high places, scanning the city with heavy binoculars. What were they seeking so earnestly? Who were they – so composed and steely-eyed? Timidly we stopped a policeman to ask him. 'They are publishers' he said mildly. Publishers! Our hearts stopped beating. 'They are on the look out for new talent.' Great God! It was for *us* they were waiting and watching! Then the kindly policeman lowered his voice confidentially and said in hollow and reverent tones: *'They are waiting for the new Trollope to be born!'* Do you remember, at these words, how heavy our suitcases suddenly felt? How our blood slowed, our footsteps lagged? Brother Ass, we had been bashfully thinking of a kind of illumination such as Rimbaud dreamed of – a nagging poem which was not didactic or expository but which *infected* – was not simply a rationalised intuition, I mean, clothed in isinglass! We had come to the wrong shop, with the wrong change! A chill struck us as we saw the mist falling in Trafalgar Square, coiling round us its

10 on 12pt

Walking along the Mall we wondered who all those men were – tall hawk-featured men perched on balconies and high places, scanning the city with heavy binoculars. What were they seeking so earnestly? Who were they – so composed and steely-eyed? Timidly we stopped a policeman to ask him. 'They are publishers' he said mildly. Publishers! Our hearts stopped beating. 'They are on the look out for new talent.' Great God! It was for *us* they were waiting and watching! Then the kindly policeman lowered his voice confidentially and said in hollow and reverent tones: *'They are waiting for the new Trollope to be born!'* Do you remember, at these words, how heavy our suitcases suddenly felt? How our blood slowed, our footsteps lagged? Brother Ass, we had been bashfully thinking of a kind of illumination such as Rimbaud dreamed of – a nagging poem which was not didactic or expository but which *infected* – was not simply a rationalised intuition,

11 on 13pt

WALKING ALONG THE MALL WE WONDERED WHO ALL THOSE MEN WERE – TALL hawk-featured men perched on balconies and high places, scanning the city with heavy binoculars. What were they seeking so earnestly? Who were they – so composed and steely-eyed? Timidly we stopped a policeman to ask him. 'They are publishers' he said mildly. Publishers! Our hearts stopped beating. 'They are on the look out for new talent.' Great God! It was for *us* they were waiting and watching! Then the kindly policeman lowered his voice confidentially and said in hollow and reverent tones: *'They are waiting for the new Trollope to be born!'* Do you remember, at these words, how heavy our suitcases suddenly felt? How our blood slowed, our footsteps lagged? Brother Ass, we had been bashfully thinking of a kind of illumination such as Rimbaud dreamed of – a nagging poem which was not didactic or expository but which *infected* – was not simply a rationalised intuition, I mean, clothed in isinglass! We had come to the wrong shop, with the wrong change! A chill struck us as we saw the mist falling in Trafalgar Square, coiling round us its tendrils of ectoplasm! A million muffin-eating moralists were waiting, not for us, Brother Ass, but for the plucky and tedious Trollope! (If you are dissatisfied with your form, reach for

9 on 12pt

WALKING ALONG THE MALL WE WONDERED WHO ALL THOSE MEN WERE – tall hawk-featured men perched on balconies and high places, scanning the city with heavy binoculars. What were they seeking so earnestly? Who were they – so composed and steely-eyed? Timidly we stopped a policeman to ask him. 'They are publishers' he said mildly. Publishers! Our hearts stopped beating. 'They are on the look out for new talent.' Great God! It was for *us* they were waiting and watching! Then the kindly policeman lowered his voice confidentially and said in hollow and reverent tones: *'They are waiting for the new Trollope to be born!'* Do you remember, at these words, how heavy our suitcases suddenly felt? How our blood slowed, our footsteps lagged? Brother Ass, we had been bashfully thinking of a kind of illumination such as Rimbaud dreamed of – a nagging poem which was not didactic or expository but which *infected* – was not simply a rationalised intuition, I mean, clothed in isinglass! We had come to the wrong shop, with the wrong change!

10 on 13.5pt

WALKING ALONG THE MALL WE WONDERED WHO ALL THOSE MEN were – tall hawk-featured men perched on balconies and high places, scanning the city with heavy binoculars. What were they seeking so earnestly? Who were they – so composed and steely-eyed? Timidly we stopped a policeman to ask him. 'They are publishers' he said mildly. Publishers! Our hearts stopped beating. 'They are on the look out for new talent.' Great God! It was for *us* they were waiting and watching! Then the kindly policeman lowered his voice confidentially and said in hollow and reverent tones: *'They are waiting for the new Trollope to be born!'* Do you remember, at these words, how heavy our suitcases suddenly felt? How our blood slowed, our footsteps lagged? Brother Ass, we had been bashfully thinking of a kind of illumination such as Rimbaud dreamed of – a nagging poem which was not didactic or

11 on 14.5pt

Monotype POLIPHILUS / BLADO

170 roman, 119 Blado italic
Monotype 1923
Copyfitting factor 36.4/32.1

Derived from Aldus's roman of 1499. The original 1923 cutting was a facsimile revival, retaining all irregularities

Blado italic is based on letters designed by Arrighi in 1526, and used by Antonio Blado, printer to the Vatican

Slightly bolder than hot metal version. The italic appears (in display sizes) to have been roughened up somewhat, to match the irregularities of the roman

ABCDEFGHIJKLMNOP
QRSTUVWXYZ abcdefg
hijklmnopqrstuvwxyz
1234567890 1234567890
ffffiflffiffl ()[]&£$.,;:-!?"

ABCDEFGHIJKLMNOP
QRSTUVWXYZ abcdefg
hijklmnopqrstuvwxyz
1234567890 1234567890
ffffiflffiffl ()[]&£$.,;:-!?"

24 on 27pt

These examples show *normal* letterspacing and the effect of *reduced* letterspacing on roman setting *as well as on words in italic*: they also show the appearance of figures, for example 28 May 1964, within text. These & the ampersand are not included in the setting opposite.

Normal letterspacing

These examples show *normal* letterspacing and the effect of *reduced* letterspacing on roman setting *as well as on words in italic*: they also show the appearance of figures, for example 28 May 1964, within text. These & the ampersand are not included in the setting opposite.

Minus one unit spacing

These examples show *normal* letterspacing and the effect of *reduced* letterspacing on roman setting *as well as on words in italic*: they also show the appearance of figures, for example 28 May 1964, within text. These & the ampersand are not included in the setting opposite.

Minus two units spacing

WALKING ALONG THE MALL WE WONDERED WHO ALL
WALKING ALONG THE MALL WE WONDERED WHO
WALKING ALONG THE MALL WE WONDERED

Capitals: normal letterspacing/plus 9 units/plus 18 units

WALKING ALONG THE MALL WE WONDERED WHO ALL THOSE MEN WERE
WALKING ALONG THE MALL WE WONDERED WHO ALL THOSE MEN WERE
WALKING ALONG THE MALL WE WONDERED WHO ALL THOSE MEN

Small caps: normal letterspacing/plus 6 units/plus 12 units

WALKING ALONG THE MALL we wondered who all those men were
WALKING ALONG THE MALL we wondered who all those men were

True italic/sloped roman

WALKING ALONG THE MALL WE WONDERED WHO ALL THOSE MEN WERE
WALKING ALONG THE MALL WE WONDERED WHO ALL THOSE MEN WERE

True small caps/reduced capitals

Walking along the Mall we wondered who all those men were – tall hawk-featured men perched on balconies and high places, scanning the city with heavy binoculars. What were they seeking so earnestly? Who were they – so composed and steely-eyed? Timidly we stopped a policeman to ask him. 'They are publishers' he said mildly. Publishers! Our hearts stopped beating. 'They are on the look out for new talent.' Great God! It was for *us* they were waiting and watching! Then the kindly policeman lowered his voice confidentially and said in hollow and reverent tones: *'They are waiting for the new Trollope to be born!'* Do you remember, at these words, how heavy our suitcases suddenly felt? How our blood slowed, our footsteps lagged? Brother Ass, we had been bashfully thinking of a kind of illumination such as Rimbaud dreamed of – a nagging poem which was not didactic or expository but which *infected* – was not simply a rationalised intuition, I mean, clothed in isinglass! We had come to the wrong shop, with

8 on 9pt

WALKING ALONG THE MALL WE WONDERED WHO ALL THOSE MEN WERE – TALL HAWK-featured men perched on balconies and high places, scanning the city with heavy binoculars. What were they seeking so earnestly? Who were they – so composed and steely-eyed? Timidly we stopped a policeman to ask him. 'They are publishers' he said mildly. Publishers! Our hearts stopped beating. 'They are on the look out for new talent.' Great God! It was for *us* they were waiting and watching! Then the kindly policeman lowered his voice confidentially and said in hollow and reverent tones: *'They are waiting for the new Trollope to be born!'* Do you remember, at these words, how heavy our suitcases suddenly felt? How our blood slowed, our footsteps lagged? Brother Ass, we had been bashfully thinking of a kind of illumination such as Rimbaud dreamed of – a nagging poem which was not didactic or

8 on 10.5pt

Walking along the Mall we wondered who all those men were – tall hawk-featured men perched on balconies and high places, scanning the city with heavy binoculars. What were they seeking so earnestly? Who were they – so composed and steely-eyed? Timidly we stopped a policeman to ask him. 'They are publishers' he said mildly. Publishers! Our hearts stopped beating. 'They are on the look out for new talent.' Great God! It was for *us* they were waiting and watching! Then the kindly policeman lowered his voice confidentially and said in hollow and reverent tones: *'They are waiting for the new Trollope to be born!'* Do you remember, at these words, how heavy our suitcases suddenly felt? How our blood slowed, our footsteps lagged? Brother Ass, we had been bashfully thinking of a kind of illumination such as Rimbaud dreamed of – a nagging poem which was not didactic or expository but which *infected* – was not simply a rationalised intuition, I mean, clothed in isinglass! We had come to the wrong shop, with the wrong change! A chill struck us as we saw the mist falling in Trafalgar Square, coiling around us its tendrils of ectoplasm! A million muffin-eating moralists were waiting, not for us, Brother Ass, but for the plucky and tedious Trollope! (If you are dissatisfied with your form, reach for the *curette*.) Now do you wonder if I laugh a little off-key? Do you ask yourself what has turned me into nature's bashful little aphorist? We who are, after all, simply poor co-workers in the psyche of our nation, what can we expect but the natural automatic rejection from a public which resents interference? And quite right too. There is no injustice in the matter, for I also resent

9 on 11pt

Walking along the Mall we wondered who all those men were – tall hawk-featured men perched on balconies and high places, scanning the city with heavy binoculars. What were they seeking so earnestly? Who were they – so composed and steely-eyed? Timidly we stopped a policeman to ask him. 'They are publishers' he said mildly. Publishers! Our hearts stopped beating. 'They are on the look out for new talent.' Great God! It was for *us* they were waiting and watching! Then the kindly policeman lowered his voice confidentially and said in hollow and reverent tones: *'They are waiting for the new Trollope to be born!'* Do you remember, at these words, how heavy our suitcases suddenly felt? How our blood slowed, our footsteps lagged? Brother Ass, we had been bashfully thinking of a kind of illumination such as Rimbaud dreamed of – a nagging poem which was not didactic or expository but which *infected* – was not simply a rationalised intuition, I mean, clothed in isinglass! We had come to the wrong shop, with the wrong change! A chill struck us as we saw the mist falling in Trafalgar Square, coiling around us its tendrils of ectoplasm! A million muffin-eating moralists were waiting, not for us, Brother Ass, but for the plucky and tedious Trollope! (If you

10 on 12pt

Walking along the Mall we wondered who all those men were – tall hawk-featured men perched on balconies and high places, scanning the city with heavy binoculars. What were they seeking so earnestly? Who were they – so composed and steely-eyed? Timidly we stopped a policeman to ask him. 'They are publishers' he said mildly. Publishers! Our hearts stopped beating. 'They are on the look out for new talent.' Great God! It was for *us* they were waiting and watching! Then the kindly policeman lowered his voice confidentially and said in hollow and reverent tones: *'They are waiting for the new Trollope to be born!'* Do you remember, at these words, how heavy our suitcases suddenly felt? How our blood slowed, our footsteps lagged? Brother Ass, we had been bashfully thinking of a kind of illumination such as Rimbaud dreamed of – a nagging poem which was not didactic or expository but which *infected* – was not simply a rationalised intuition, I mean, clothed in isinglass! We had come to the wrong shop, with the wrong change! A chill struck us as we saw the mist falling in Trafalgar Square, coiling around us its tendrils of ectoplasm! A

11 on 13pt

WALKING ALONG THE MALL WE WONDERED WHO ALL THOSE MEN WERE — TALL hawk-featured men perched on balconies and high places, scanning the city with heavy binoculars. What were they seeking so earnestly? Who were they – so composed and steely-eyed? Timidly we stopped a policeman to ask him. 'They are publishers' he said mildly. Publishers! Our hearts stopped beating. 'They are on the look out for new talent.' Great God! It was for *us* they were waiting and watching! Then the kindly policeman lowered his voice confidentially and said in hollow and reverent tones: *'They are waiting for the new Trollope to be born!'* Do you remember, at these words, how heavy our suitcases suddenly felt? How our blood slowed, our footsteps lagged? Brother Ass, we had been bashfully thinking of a kind of illumination such as Rimbaud dreamed of – a nagging poem which was not didactic or expository but which *infected* – was not simply a rationalised intuition, I mean, clothed in isinglass! We had come to the wrong shop, with the wrong change! A chill struck us as we saw the mist falling in Trafalgar Square, coiling around us its tendrils of ectoplasm! A million muffin-eating moralists were waiting, not for us, Brother Ass, but for the plucky and tedious Trollope! (If you are dissatisfied with your form, reach for the *curette*.) Now do you wonder if I laugh a little off-key? Do you ask yourself what has turned me into nature's bashful little aphorist? We who are, after all, simply poor co-workers in the psyche of our nation, what can we expect but the natural automatic

9 on 12pt

WALKING ALONG THE MALL WE WONDERED WHO ALL THOSE MEN WERE — tall hawk-featured men perched on balconies and high places, scanning the city with heavy binoculars. What were they seeking so earnestly? Who were they – so composed and steely-eyed? Timidly we stopped a policeman to ask him. 'They are publishers' he said mildly. Publishers! Our hearts stopped beating. 'They are on the look out for new talent.' Great God! It was for *us* they were waiting and watching! Then the kindly policeman lowered his voice confidentially and said in hollow and reverent tones: *'They are waiting for the new Trollope to be born!'* Do you remember, at these words, how heavy our suitcases suddenly felt? How our blood slowed, our footsteps lagged? Brother Ass, we had been bashfully thinking of a kind of illumination such as Rimbaud dreamed of – a nagging poem which was not didactic or expository but which *infected* – was not simply a rationalised intuition, I mean, clothed in isinglass! We had come to the wrong shop, with the wrong change! A chill struck us as we saw the mist falling in Trafalgar Square, coiling around us its tendrils of ectoplasm! A million muffin-eating moralists were waiting, not for us, Brother Ass, but for the plucky and tedious Trollope! (If you

10 on 13.5pt

WALKING ALONG THE MALL WE WONDERED WHO ALL THOSE MEN were – tall hawk-featured men perched on balconies and high places, scanning the city with heavy binoculars. What were they seeking so earnestly? Who were they – so composed and steely-eyed? Timidly we stopped a policeman to ask him. 'They are publishers' he said mildly. Publishers! Our hearts stopped beating. 'They are on the look out for new talent.' Great God! It was for *us* they were waiting and watching! Then the kindly policeman lowered his voice confidentially and said in hollow and reverent tones: *'They are waiting for the new Trollope to be born!'* Do you remember, at these words, how heavy our suitcases suddenly felt? How our blood slowed, our footsteps lagged? Brother Ass, we had been bashfully thinking of a kind of illumination such as Rimbaud dreamed of – a nagging poem which was not didactic or expository but which *infected* – was not simply a rationalised intuition, I mean, clothed in isinglass! We had come to the wrong shop, with the wrong change! A chill struck us as

11 on 14.5pt

Monotype **Rockwell**

390 light and italic
371 roman
Monotype 1933
Copyfitting factor 46.6/46.4/46.4

Range also includes roman italic, bold, bold italic, extra bold, condensed, bold condensed

The Linotype design is slightly narrower; combined with slightly narrower serifs, this allows a tighter fit. These differences are particularly noticeable in the bold. Letters are a little larger on the body. Copyfitting code 128/129/129

ABCDEFGHIJKLMNOP
QRSTUVWXYZ abcdefg
hijklmnopqrstuvwxyz
1234567890
ff fi fl ffi ffl ()[]&£$.,;:-!?''

ABCDEFGHIJKLMNOP
QRSTUVWXYZ abcdefg
hijklmnopqrstuvwxyz
1234567890
ff fi fl ffi ffl ()[]&£$.,;:-!?''

ABCDEFGHIJKLMNOP
QRSTUVWXYZ abcdefg
hijklmnopqrstuvwxyz
1234567890
ff fi fl ffi ffl ()[]&£$.,;:-!?''

24 on 27pt

These examples show *normal* letterspacing and the effect of *reduced* letterspacing on roman setting *as well as on words in italic:* they also show the appearance of figures, for example 28 May 1964, within text. These & the ampersand are not included in the setting opposite.

Normal letterspacing

These examples show *normal* letterspacing and the effect of *reduced* letterspacing on roman setting *as well as on words in italic:* they also show the appearance of figures, for example 28 May 1964, within text. These & the ampersand are not included in the setting opposite.

Minus one unit spacing

These examples show *normal* letterspacing and the effect of *reduced* letterspacing on roman setting *as well as on words in italic:* they also show the appearance of figures, for example 28 May 1964, within text. These & the ampersand are not included in the setting opposite.

Minus two units spacing

WALKING ALONG THE MALL WE WONDERED WHO ALL THOSE
WALKING ALONG THE MALL WE WONDERED WHO ALL
WALKING ALONG THE MALL WE WONDERED WHO

Capitals: normal letterspacing/plus 9 units/plus 18 units

Walking along the Mall we wondered who all those men were – tall hawk-featured men perched on balconies and high places, scanning the city with heavy binoculars. WHAT WERE THEY SEEKING SO EARNESTLY? Who were they – so composed and steely-eyed? Timidly we stopped a policeman to ask him. 'They are publishers' he said mildly. Publishers! OUR HEARTS STOPPED BEATING. 'They are on the look out for new talent.' Great God! It was for *us* they were waiting and watching! Then the

Text with reduced capitals normal letterspacing/plus 6 units

WALKING ALONG THE MALL we wondered who all those men were
WALKING ALONG THE MALL we wondered who all those men were

True italic/sloped roman

Walking along the Mall we wondered who all those men were – tall hawk-featured men perched on balconies and high places, scanning the city with heavy binoculars. What were they seeking so earnestly? Who were they – so composed and steely-eyed? Timidly we stopped a policeman to ask him. 'They are publishers' he said mildly. Publishers! Our hearts stopped beating. 'They are on the look out for new talent.' Great God! It was for *us* they were waiting and watching! Then the kindly policeman lowered his voice confidentially and said in hollow and reverent tones: *'They are waiting for the new Trollope to be born!'* Do you remember, at these words, how heavy our suitcases suddenly felt? How our blood slowed, our footsteps lagged? Brother Ass, we had been bashfully

8 on 9pt

Walking along the Mall we wondered who all those men were – tall hawk-featured men perched on balconies and high places, scanning the city with heavy binoculars. What were they seeking so earnestly? Who were they – so composed and steely-eyed? Timidly we stopped a policeman to ask him. 'They are publishers' he said mildly. Publishers! Our hearts stopped beating. 'They are on the look out for new talent.' Great God! It was for *us* they were waiting and watching! Then the kindly policeman lowered his voice confidentially and said in hollow and reverent tones: *'They are waiting for the new Trollope to be born!'* Do you remember, at these words, how heavy our suitcases suddenly felt? How

8 on 10.5pt

Walking along the Mall we wondered who all those men were – tall hawk-featured men perched on balconies and high places, scanning the city with heavy binoculars. What were they seeking so earnestly? Who were they – so composed and steely-eyed? Timidly we stopped a policeman to ask him. 'They are publishers' he said mildly. Publishers! Our hearts stopped beating. 'They are on the look out for new talent.' Great God! It was for *us* they were waiting and watching! Then the kindly policeman lowered his voice confidentially and said in hollow and reverent tones: *'They are waiting for the new Trollope to be born!'* Do you remember, at these words, how heavy our suitcases suddenly felt? How our blood slowed, our footsteps lagged? Brother Ass, we had been bashfully thinking of a kind of illumination such as Rimbaud dreamed of – a nagging poem which was not didactic or expository but which *infected* – was not simply a rationalised intuition, I mean, clothed in isinglass! We had come to the wrong shop, with the wrong change! A chill struck us as we saw the mist falling in Trafalgar Square, coiling around us its tendrils of ectoplasm! A million muffin-eating moralists were waiting, not for us, Brother Ass, but for the plucky and tedious Trollope! (If you are dissatisfied

9 on 11pt

Walking along the Mall we wondered who all those men were – tall hawk-featured men perched on balconies and high places, scanning the city with heavy binoculars. What were they seeking so earnestly? Who were they – so composed and steely-eyed? Timidly we stopped a policeman to ask him. 'They are publishers' he said mildly. Publishers! Our hearts stopped beating. 'They are on the look out for new talent.' Great God! It was for *us* they were waiting and watching! Then the kindly policeman lowered his voice confidentially and said in hollow and reverent tones: *'They are waiting for the new Trollope to be born!'* Do you remember, at these words, how heavy our suitcases suddenly felt? How our blood slowed, our footsteps lagged? Brother Ass, we had been bashfully thinking of a kind of illumination such as Rimbaud dreamed of – a nagging poem which was not didactic or expository but which *infected* – was not simply a rationalised intuition, I mean, clothed in isinglass! We had come to the wrong shop, with the wrong change! A chill struck us as we saw the mist falling in Trafalgar Square, coiling around us its tendrils of ectoplasm! A million muffin-eating moralists were waiting, not for us, Bro-

9 on 12pt

Walking along the Mall we wondered who all those men were – tall hawk-featured men perched on balconies and high places, scanning the city with heavy binoculars. What were they seeking so earnestly? Who were they – so composed and steely-eyed? Timidly we stopped a policeman to ask him. 'They are publishers' he said mildly. Publishers! Our hearts stopped beating. 'They are on the look out for new talent.' Great God! It was for *us* they were waiting and watching! Then the kindly policeman lowered his voice confidentially and said in hollow and reverent tones: *'They are waiting for the new Trollope to be born!'* Do you remember, at these words, how heavy our suitcases suddenly felt? How our blood slowed, our footsteps lagged? Brother Ass, we had been bashfully thinking of a kind of illumination such as Rimbaud dreamed of – a nagging poem which was not didactic or expository but which *infected* – was not simply a rationalised intuition, I mean, clothed in isinglass! We had come to the wrong shop, with

10 on 12pt

Walking along the Mall we wondered who all those men were – tall hawk-featured men perched on balconies and high places, scanning the city with heavy binoculars. What were they seeking so earnestly? Who were they – so composed and steely-eyed? Timidly we stopped a policeman to ask him. 'They are publishers' he said mildly. Publishers! Our hearts stopped beating. 'They are on the look out for new talent.' Great God! It was for *us* they were waiting and watching! Then the kindly policeman lowered his voice confidentially and said in hollow and reverent tones: *'They are waiting for the new Trollope to be born!'* Do you remember, at these words, how heavy our suitcases suddenly felt? How our blood slowed, our footsteps lagged? Brother Ass, we had been bashfully thinking of a kind of illumination such as Rimbaud dreamed of – a nagging poem which was not didactic or expository but which *infected* – was not simply a rationalised intuition, I

10 on 13.5pt

Walking along the Mall we wondered who all those men were – tall hawk-featured men perched on balconies and high places, scanning the city with heavy binoculars. What were they seeking so earnestly? Who were they – so composed and steely-eyed? Timidly we stopped a policeman to ask him. 'They are publishers' he said mildly. Publishers! Our hearts stopped beating. 'They are on the look out for new talent.' Great God! It was for *us* they were waiting and watching! Then the kindly policeman lowered his voice confidentially and said in hollow and reverent tones: *'They are waiting for the new Trollope to be born!'* Do you remember, at these words, how heavy our suitcases suddenly felt? How our blood slowed, our footsteps lagged? Brother Ass, we had been bashfully thinking of a kind of illumination such as Rimbaud dreamed of – a nagging poem which was not

11 on 13pt

Walking along the Mall we wondered who all those men were – tall hawk-featured men perched on balconies and high places, scanning the city with heavy binoculars. What were they seeking so earnestly? Who were they – so composed and steely-eyed? Timidly we stopped a policeman to ask him. 'They are publishers' he said mildly. Publishers! Our hearts stopped beating. 'They are on the look out for new talent.' Great God! It was for *us* they were waiting and watching! Then the kindly policeman lowered his voice confidentially and said in hollow and reverent tones: *'They are waiting for the new Trollope to be born!'* Do you remember, at these words, how heavy our suitcases suddenly felt? How our blood slowed, our footsteps lagged? Brother Ass, we had been bashfully thinking of a kind of illumination such

11 on 14.5pt

MONOTYPE ROCKWELL

Linotype **Rotation**

roman (05229), **italic** (13229)
bold (07229)
Stempel 1971 (Arthur Ritzel)
Copyfitting code 130/130/130

ABCDEFGHIJKLMNOP
QRSTUVWXYZ abcdefg
hijklmnopqrstuvwxyz
1234567890
fifl ()[]&£$.,;:-!?""

*ABCDEFGHIJKLMNOP
QRSTUVWXYZ abcdefg
hijklmnopqrstuvwxyz
1234567890
fifl ()[]&£$.,;:-!?""*

**ABCDEFGHIJKLMNOP
QRSTUVWXYZ abcdefg
hijklmnopqrstuvwxyz
1234567890
fifl ()[]&£$.,;:-!?""**

24 on 27pt

These examples show *normal* letterspacing and the effect of *reduced* letterspacing on roman setting *as well as on words in italic*: they also show the appearance of figures, for example 28 May 1964, within text. These & the ampersand are not included in the setting opposite.

Normal letterspacing

These examples show *normal* letterspacing and the effect of *reduced* letterspacing on roman setting *as well as on words in italic*: they also show the appearance of figures, for example 28 May 1964, within text. These & the ampersand are not included in the setting opposite.

Minus one unit spacing

These examples show *normal* letterspacing and the effect of *reduced* letterspacing on roman setting *as well as on words in italic*: they also show the appearance of figures, for example 28 May 1964, within text. These & the ampersand are not included in the setting opposite.

Minus two units spacing

WALKING ALONG THE MALL WE WONDERED WHO ALL
WALKING ALONG THE MALL WE WONDERED WHO
WALKING ALONG THE MALL WE WONDERED

Capitals: normal letterspacing/plus 4 units/plus 9 units

Walking along the Mall we wondered who all those men were – tall hawk-featured men perched on balconies and high places, scanning the city with heavy binoculars. WHAT WERE THEY SEEKING SO EARNESTLY? Who were they – so composed and steely-eyed? Timidly we stopped a policeman to ask him. 'THEY ARE PUBLISHERS' he said mildly. Publishers! Our hearts stopped beating. 'They are on the look out for new talent.' Great God! It was for *us* they were waiting and

Text with reduced caps normal letterspacing/plus 3 units

*WALKING ALONG THE MALL we wondered who all those men
WALKING ALONG THE MALL we wondered who all those men*

True italic/sloped roman

Walking along the Mall we wondered who all those men were – tall hawk-featured men perched on balconies and high places, scanning the city with heavy binoculars. What were they seeking so earnestly? Who were they – so composed and steely-eyed? Timidly we stopped a policeman to ask him. 'They are publishers' he said mildly. Publishers! Our hearts stopped beating. 'They are on the look out for new talent.' Great God! It was for *us* they were waiting and watching! Then the kindly policeman lowered his voice confidentially and said in hollow and reverent tones: *'They are waiting for the new Trollope to be born!'* Do you remember, at these words, how heavy our suitcases suddenly felt? How our blood slowed, our footsteps lagged? Brother Ass, we had been bashfully thinking of a kind of illumination such as

8 on 9pt

Walking along the Mall we wondered who all those men were – tall hawk-featured men perched on balconies and high places, scanning the city with heavy binoculars. What were they seeking so earnestly? Who were they – so composed and steely-eyed? Timidly we stopped a policeman to ask him. 'They are publishers' he said mildly. Publishers! Our hearts stopped beating. 'They are on the look out for new talent.' Great God! It was for *us* they were waiting and watching! Then the kindly policeman lowered his voice confidentially and said in hollow and reverent tones: *'They are waiting for the new Trollope to be born!'* Do you remember, at these words, how heavy our suitcases suddenly felt? How our blood slowed, our footsteps lagged?

8 on 10.5pt

Walking along the Mall we wondered who all those men were – tall hawk-featured men perched on balconies and high places, scanning the city with heavy binoculars. What were they seeking so earnestly? Who were they – so composed and steely-eyed? Timidly we stopped a policeman to ask him. 'They are publishers' he said mildly. Publishers! Our hearts stopped beating. 'They are on the look out for new talent.' Great God! It was for *us* they were waiting and watching! Then the kindly policeman lowered his voice confidentially and said in hollow and reverent tones: *'They are waiting for the new Trollope to be born!'* Do you remember, at these words, how heavy our suitcases suddenly felt? How our blood slowed, our footsteps lagged? Brother Ass, we had been bashfully thinking of a kind of illumination such as Rimbaud dreamed of – a nagging poem which was not didactic or expository but which *infected* – was not simply a rationalised intuition, I mean, clothed in isinglass! We had come to the wrong shop, with the wrong change! A chill struck us as we saw the mist falling in Trafalgar Square, coiling round us its tendrils of ectoplasm! A million muffin-eating moralists were waiting, not for us, Brother Ass, but for the plucky and tedious Trollope! (If you are dissatisfied with your form, reach for the *curette*.) Now do you wonder if I laugh a

9 on 11pt

Walking along the Mall we wondered who all those men were – tall hawk-featured men perched on balconies and high places, scanning the city with heavy binoculars. What were they seeking so earnestly? Who were they – so composed and steely-eyed? Timidly we stopped a policeman to ask him. 'They are publishers' he said mildly. Publishers! Our hearts stopped beating. 'They are on the look out for new talent.' Great God! It was for *us* they were waiting and watching! Then the kindly policeman lowered his voice confidentially and said in hollow and reverent tones: *'They are waiting for the new Trollope to be born!'* Do you remember, at these words, how heavy our suitcases suddenly felt? How our blood slowed, our footsteps lagged? Brother Ass, we had been bashfully thinking of a kind of illumination such as Rimbaud dreamed of – a nagging poem which was not didactic or expository but which *infected* – was not simply a rationalised intuition, I mean, clothed in isinglass! We had come to the wrong shop, with the wrong change! A chill struck us as we saw the mist falling in Trafalgar Square, coiling round us its tendrils of ectoplasm! A million muffin-eating moralists were waiting, not for us, Brother Ass, but for the plucky and tedious Trollope! (If you are dissatisfied with

9 on 12pt

Walking along the Mall we wondered who all those men were – tall hawk-featured men perched on balconies and high places, scanning the city with heavy binoculars. What were they seeking so earnestly? Who were they – so composed and steely-eyed? Timidly we stopped a policeman to ask him. 'They are publishers' he said mildly. Publishers! Our hearts stopped beating. 'They are on the look out for new talent.' Great God! It was for *us* they were waiting and watching! Then the kindly policeman lowered his voice confidentially and said in hollow and reverent tones: *'They are waiting for the new Trollope to be born!'* Do you remember, at these words, how heavy our suitcases suddenly felt? How our blood slowed, our footsteps lagged? Brother Ass, we had been bashfully thinking of a kind of illumination such as Rimbaud dreamed of – a nagging poem which was not didactic or expository but which *infected* – was not simply a rationalised intuition, I mean, clothed in isinglass! We had come to the wrong shop, with the wrong change! A chill struck us as we saw the mist

10 on 12pt

Walking along the Mall we wondered who all those men were – tall hawk-featured men perched on balconies and high places, scanning the city with heavy binoculars. What were they seeking so earnestly? Who were they – so composed and steely-eyed? Timidly we stopped a policeman to ask him. 'They are publishers' he said mildly. Publishers! Our hearts stopped beating. 'They are on the look out for new talent.' Great God! It was for *us* they were waiting and watching! Then the kindly policeman lowered his voice confidentially and said in hollow and reverent tones: *'They are waiting for the new Trollope to be born!'* Do you remember, at these words, how heavy our suitcases suddenly felt? How our blood slowed, our footsteps lagged? Brother Ass, we had been bashfully thinking of a kind of illumination such as Rimbaud dreamed of – a nagging poem which was not didactic or expository but which *infected* – was not simply a rationalised intuition, I mean, clothed in isinglass! We had come to the wrong

10 on 13.5pt

Walking along the Mall we wondered who all those men were – tall hawk-featured men perched on balconies and high places, scanning the city with heavy binoculars. What were they seeking so earnestly? Who were they – so composed and steely-eyed? Timidly we stopped a policeman to ask him. 'They are publishers' he said mildly. Publishers! Our hearts stopped beating. 'They are on the look out for new talent.' Great God! It was for *us* they were waiting and watching! Then the kindly policeman lowered his voice confidentially and said in hollow and reverent tones: *'They are waiting for the new Trollope to be born!'* Do you remember, at these words, how heavy our suitcases suddenly felt? How our blood slowed, our footsteps lagged? Brother Ass, we had been bashfully thinking of a kind of illumination such as Rimbaud dreamed of – a nagging poem which was not didactic or expository but which *infected* – was

11 on 13pt

Walking along the Mall we wondered who all those men were – tall hawk-featured men perched on balconies and high places, scanning the city with heavy binoculars. What were they seeking so earnestly? Who were they – so composed and steely-eyed? Timidly we stopped a policeman to ask him. 'They are publishers' he said mildly. Publishers! Our hearts stopped beating. 'They are on the look out for new talent.' Great God! It was for *us* they were waiting and watching! Then the kindly policeman lowered his voice confidentially and said in hollow and reverent tones: *'They are waiting for the new Trollope to be born!'* Do you remember, at these words, how heavy our suitcases suddenly felt? How our blood slowed, our footsteps lagged? Brother Ass, we had been bashfully thinking of a kind of illumination such as Rimbaud dreamed of – a nagging poem

11 on 14.5pt

LINOTYPE ROTATION

Monotype **Sabon**

669 roman and italic
673 semi-bold
Designed by Jan Tschichold 1967 for Stempel,
Linotype and Monotype
Copyfitting code 41.8/41.8/41.8

Derived from Garamond's types, the original
design was a considerable technical
achievement, combining the requirements
(and restrictions) of two machine setting
systems with those of the founder's type to
produce interchangeable results. The present
letterforms of Lino and Mono are similar, but
sizes differ. Both forms differ slightly from the
original Stempel founder's type

ABCDEFGHIJKLMNOP
QRSTUVWXYZ abcdefg
hijklmnopqrstuvwxyz
1234567890 1234567890
ff fi fl ffi ffl () [] & £$.,;:-!?''

ABCDEFGHIJKLMNOP
QRSTUVWXYZ abcdefg
hijklmnopqrstuvwxyz
1234567890 1234567890
ff fi fl ffi ffl () [] & £$.,;:-!?''

ABCDEFGHIJKLMNOP
QRSTUVWXYZ abcdefg
hijklmnopqrstuvwxyz
1234567890 1234567890
ff fi fl ffi ffl () [] & £$.,;:-!?''

24 on 27pt

These examples show *normal* letterspacing and the effect of *reduced* letterspacing on roman setting *as well as on words in italic*: they also show the appearance of figures, for example 28 May 1964, within text. These & the ampersand are not included in the setting opposite.

Normal letterspacing

These examples show *normal* letterspacing and the effect of *reduced* letterspacing on roman setting *as well as on words in italic*: they also show the appearance of figures, for example 28 May 1964, within text. These & the ampersand are not included in the setting opposite.

Minus one unit spacing

These examples show *normal* letterspacing and the effect of *reduced* letterspacing on roman setting *as well as on words in italic*: they also show the appearance of figures, for example 28 May 1964, within text. These & the ampersand are not included in the setting opposite.

Minus two units spacing

WALKING ALONG THE MALL WE WONDERED WHO ALL THOSE
WALKING ALONG THE MALL WE WONDERED WHO ALL
WALKING ALONG THE MALL WE WONDERED WHO

Capitals: normal letterspacing/plus 9 units/plus 18 units

WALKING ALONG THE MALL WE WONDERED WHO ALL THOSE MEN WERE
WALKING ALONG THE MALL WE WONDERED WHO ALL THOSE MEN
WALKING ALONG THE MALL WE WONDERED WHO ALL THOSE

Small caps: normal letterspacing/plus 6 units/plus 12 units

WALKING ALONG THE MALL we wondered who all those men were
WALKING ALONG THE MALL we wondered who all those men were

True italic/sloped roman

WALKING ALONG THE MALL WE WONDERED WHO ALL THOSE MEN WERE
WALKING ALONG THE MALL WE WONDERED WHO ALL THOSE MEN WERE

True small caps/reduced capitals

Walking along the Mall we wondered who all those men were – tall hawk-featured men perched on balconies and high places, scanning the city with heavy binoculars. What were they seeking so earnestly? Who were they – so composed and steely-eyed? Timidly we stopped a policeman to ask him. 'They are publishers' he said mildly. Publishers! Our hearts stopped beating. 'They are on the look out for new talent.' Great God! It was for *us* they were waiting and watching! Then the kindly policeman lowered his voice confidentially and said in hollow and reverent tones: *'They are waiting for the new Trollope to be born!'* Do you remember, at these words, how heavy our suitcases suddenly felt? How our blood slowed, our footsteps lagged? Brother Ass, we had been bashfully thinking of a kind of illumination such as Rimbaud dreamed of – a nagging poem which

8 on 9pt

WALKING ALONG THE MALL WE WONDERED WHO ALL THOSE MEN WERE – TALL hawk-featured men perched on balconies and high places, scanning the city with heavy binoculars. What were they seeking so earnestly? Who were they – so composed and steely-eyed? Timidly we stopped a policeman to ask him. 'They are publishers' he said mildly. Publishers! Our hearts stopped beating. 'They are on the look out for new talent.' Great God! It was for *us* they were waiting and watching! Then the kindly policeman lowered his voice confidentially and said in hollow and reverent tones: *'They are waiting for the new Trollope to be born!'* Do you remember, at these words, how heavy our suitcases suddenly felt? How our blood slowed, our footsteps lagged? Brother Ass, we

8 on 10.5pt

Walking along the Mall we wondered who all those men were – tall hawk-featured men perched on balconies and high places, scanning the city with heavy binoculars. What were they seeking so earnestly? Who were they – so composed and steely-eyed? Timidly we stopped a policeman to ask him. 'They are publishers' he said mildly. Publishers! Our hearts stopped beating. 'They are on the look out for new talent.' Great God! It was for *us* they were waiting and watching! Then the kindly policeman lowered his voice confidentially and said in hollow and reverent tones: *'They are waiting for the new Trollope to be born!'* Do you remember, at these words, how heavy our suitcases suddenly felt? How our blood slowed, our footsteps lagged? Brother Ass, we had been bashfully thinking of a kind of illumination such as Rimbaud dreamed of – a nagging poem which was not didactic or expository but which *infected* – was not simply a rationalised intuition, I mean, clothed in isinglass! We had come to the wrong shop, with the wrong change! A chill struck us as we saw the mist falling in Trafalgar Square, coiling around us its tendrils of ectoplasm! A million muffin-eating moralists were waiting, not for us, Brother Ass, but for the plucky and tedious Trollope! (If you are dissatisfied with your form, reach for the *curette*.) Now do you wonder if I laugh a little off-key? Do you ask yourself what has turned me into nature's bashful little aphorist? We who are, after

9 on 11pt

Walking along the Mall we wondered who all those men were – tall hawk-featured men perched on balconies and high places, scanning the city with heavy binoculars. What were they seeking so earnestly? Who were they – so composed and steely-eyed? Timidly we stopped a policeman to ask him. 'They are publishers' he said mildly. Publishers! Our hearts stopped beating. 'They are on the look out for new talent.' Great God! It was for *us* they were waiting and watching! Then the kindly policeman lowered his voice confidentially and said in hollow and reverent tones: *'They are waiting for the new Trollope to be born!'* Do you remember, at these words, how heavy our suitcases suddenly felt? How our blood slowed, our footsteps lagged? Brother Ass, we had been bashfully thinking of a kind of illumination such as Rimbaud dreamed of – a nagging poem which was not didactic or expository but which *infected* – was not simply a rationalised intuition, I mean, clothed in isinglass! We had come to the wrong shop, with the wrong change! A chill struck us as we saw the mist falling in Trafalgar Square, coiling around us its tendrils of ectoplasm! A million

10 on 12pt

Walking along the Mall we wondered who all those men were – tall hawk-featured men perched on balconies and high places, scanning the city with heavy binoculars. What were they seeking so earnestly? Who were they – so composed and steely-eyed? Timidly we stopped a policeman to ask him. 'They are publishers' he said mildly. Publishers! Our hearts stopped beating. 'They are on the look out for new talent.' Great God! It was for *us* they were waiting and watching! Then the kindly policeman lowered his voice confidentially and said in hollow and reverent tones: *'They are waiting for the new Trollope to be born!'* Do you remember, at these words, how heavy our suitcases suddenly felt? How our blood slowed, our footsteps lagged? Brother Ass, we had been bashfully thinking of a kind of illumination such as Rimbaud dreamed of – a nagging poem which was not didactic or expository but which *infected* – was not simply a rationalised intuition, I mean, clothed in isinglass! We had

11 on 13pt

WALKING ALONG THE MALL WE WONDERED WHO ALL THOSE MEN WERE – TALL hawk-featured men perched on balconies and high places, scanning the city with heavy binoculars. What were they seeking so earnestly? Who were they – so composed and steely-eyed? Timidly we stopped a policeman to ask him. 'They are publishers' he said mildly. Publishers! Our hearts stopped beating. 'They are on the look out for new talent.' Great God! It was for *us* they were waiting and watching! Then the kindly policeman lowered his voice confidentially and said in hollow and reverent tones: *'They are waiting for the new Trollope to be born!'* Do you remember, at these words, how heavy our suitcases suddenly felt? How our blood slowed, our footsteps lagged? Brother Ass, we had been bashfully thinking of a kind of illumination such as Rimbaud dreamed of – a nagging poem which was not didactic or expository but which *infected* – was not simply a rationalised intuition, I mean, clothed in isinglass! We had come to the wrong shop, with the wrong change! A chill struck us as we saw the mist falling in Trafalgar Square, coiling around us its tendrils of ectoplasm! A million muffin-eating moralists were waiting, not for us, Brother Ass, but for the plucky and tedious Trollope! (If you are dissatisfied with your form, reach for the *curette*.) Now do you wonder if I laugh a

9 on 12pt

WALKING ALONG THE MALL WE WONDERED WHO ALL THOSE MEN WERE – tall hawk-featured men perched on balconies and high places, scanning the city with heavy binoculars. What were they seeking so earnestly? Who were they – so composed and steely-eyed? Timidly we stopped a policeman to ask him. 'They are publishers' he said mildly. Publishers! Our hearts stopped beating. 'They are on the look out for new talent.' Great God! It was for *us* they were waiting and watching! Then the kindly policeman lowered his voice confidentially and said in hollow and reverent tones: *'They are waiting for the new Trollope to be born!'* Do you remember, at these words, how heavy our suitcases suddenly felt? How our blood slowed, our footsteps lagged? Brother Ass, we had been bashfully thinking of a kind of illumination such as Rimbaud dreamed of – a nagging poem which was not didactic or expository but which *infected* – was not simply a rationalised intuition, I mean, clothed in isinglass! We had come to the wrong shop, with the wrong change! A chill struck us as we saw the mist

10 on 13.5pt

WALKING ALONG THE MALL WE WONDERED WHO ALL THOSE MEN were – tall hawk-featured men perched on balconies and high places, scanning the city with heavy binoculars. What were they seeking so earnestly? Who were they – so composed and steely-eyed? Timidly we stopped a policeman to ask him. 'They are publishers' he said mildly. Publishers! Our hearts stopped beating. 'They are on the look out for new talent.' Great God! It was for *us* they were waiting and watching! Then the kindly policeman lowered his voice confidentially and said in hollow and reverent tones: *'They are waiting for the new Trollope to be born!'* Do you remember, at these words, how heavy our suitcases suddenly felt? How our blood slowed, our footsteps lagged? Brother Ass, we had been bashfully thinking of a kind of illumination such as Rimbaud dreamed of – a nagging poem which was not didactic or expository

11 on 14.5pt

MONOTYPE SABON

Linotype **Sabon**

roman (05232), **italic** (13232)
bold (07232)
Designed by Jan Tschichold 1967 for Stempel,
Linotype and Monotype
Copyfitting code 127/127/127

Range also includes bold italic

The letterform is similar to Monotype Sabon,
but sizes are very different

See Monotype Sabon

ABCDEFGHIJKLMNOP
QRSTUVWXYZ abcdefg
hijklmnopqrstuvwxyz
1234567890 1234567890
fifl ()[]&£$.,;:-!?"

ABCDEFGHIJKLMNOP
QRSTUVWXYZ abcdefg
hijklmnopqrstuvwxyz
1234567890 1234567890
fifl ()[]&£$.,;:-!?"

ABCDEFGHIJKLMNOP
QRSTUVWXYZ abcdefg
hijklmnopqrstuvwxyz
1234567890 1234567890
fifl ()[]&£$.,;:-!?"

24 on 27pt

244

These examples show *normal* letterspacing and the effect of *reduced* letterspacing on roman setting *as well as on words in italic*: they also show the appearance of figures, for example 28 May 1964, within text. These & the ampersand are not included in the setting opposite.
Normal letterspacing

These examples show *normal* letterspacing and the effect of *reduced* letterspacing on roman setting *as well as on words in italic*: they also show the appearance of figures, for example 28 May 1964, within text. These & the ampersand are not included in the setting opposite.
Minus one unit spacing

These examples show *normal* letterspacing and the effect of *reduced* letterspacing on roman setting *as well as on words in italic*: they also show the appearance of figures, for example 28 May 1964, within text. These & the ampersand are not included in the setting opposite.
Minus two units spacing

WALKING ALONG THE MALL WE WONDERED WHO ALL
WALKING ALONG THE MALL WE WONDERED WHO
WALKING ALONG THE MALL WE WONDERED
Capitals: normal letterspacing/plus 4 units/plus 9 units

WALKING ALONG THE MALL WE WONDERED WHO ALL THOSE MEN
WALKING ALONG THE MALL WE WONDERED WHO ALL THOSE
WALKING ALONG THE MALL WE WONDERED WHO ALL
Small caps: normal letterspacing/plus 3 units/plus 6 units

WALKING ALONG THE MALL WE WONDERED WHO ALL THOSE MEN
WALKING ALONG THE MALL WE WONDERED WHO ALL THOSE MEN WERE
True small caps/reduced capitals

WALKING ALONG THE MALL we wondered who all those men
WALKING ALONG THE MALL we wondered who all those men
True italic/sloped roman

Walking along the Mall we wondered who all those men were – tall hawk-featured men perched on balconies and high places, scanning the city with heavy binoculars. What were they seeking so earnestly? Who were they – so composed and steely-eyed? Timidly we stopped a policeman to ask him. 'They are publishers' he said mildly. Publishers! Our hearts stopped beating. 'They are on the look out for new talent.' Great God! It was for *us* they were waiting and watching! Then the kindly policeman lowered his voice confidentially and said in hollow and reverent tones: *'They are waiting for the new Trollope to be born!'* Do you remember, at these words, how heavy our suitcases suddenly felt? How our blood slowed, our footsteps lagged? Brother Ass, we had been bashfully thinking of a kind of illumination such as Rimbaud dreamed of – a nagging
8 on 9pt

WALKING ALONG THE MALL WE WONDERED WHO ALL THOSE MEN WERE – TALL HAWK-featured men perched on balconies and high places, scanning the city with heavy binoculars. What were they seeking so earnestly? Who were they – so composed and steely-eyed? Timidly we stopped a policeman to ask him. 'They are publishers' he said mildly. Publishers! Our hearts stopped beating. 'They are on the look out for new talent.' Great God! It was for *us* they were waiting and watching! Then the kindly policeman lowered his voice confidentially and said in hollow and reverent tones: *'They are waiting for the new Trollope to be born!'* Do you remember, at these words, how heavy our suitcases suddenly felt? How our blood slowed, our footsteps lagged?
8 on 10.5pt

Walking along the Mall we wondered who all those men were – tall hawk-featured men perched on balconies and high places, scanning the city with heavy binoculars. What were they seeking so earnestly? Who were they – so composed and steely-eyed? Timidly we stopped a policeman to ask him. 'They are publishers' he said mildly. Publishers! Our hearts stopped beating. 'They are on the look out for new talent.' Great God! It was for *us* they were waiting and watching! Then the kindly policeman lowered his voice confidentially and said in hollow and reverent tones: *'They are waiting for the new Trollope to be born!'* Do you remember, at these words, how heavy our suitcases suddenly felt? How our blood slowed, our footsteps lagged? Brother Ass, we had been bashfully thinking of a kind of illumination such as Rimbaud dreamed of – a nagging poem which was not didactic or expository but which *infected* – was not simply a rationalised intuition, I mean, clothed in isinglass! We had come to the wrong shop, with the wrong change! A chill struck us as we saw the mist falling in Trafalgar Square, coiling round us its tendrils of ectoplasm! A million muffin-eating moralists were waiting, not for us, Brother Ass, but for the plucky and tedious Trollope! (If you are dissatisfied with your form, reach for the *curette*.) Now do you wonder if I laugh a little off-key? Do you ask

9 on 11pt

Walking along the Mall we wondered who all those men were – tall hawk-featured men perched on balconies and high places, scanning the city with heavy binoculars. What were they seeking so earnestly? Who were they – so composed and steely-eyed? Timidly we stopped a policeman to ask him. 'They are publishers' he said mildly. Publishers! Our hearts stopped beating. 'They are on the look out for new talent.' Great God! It was for *us* they were waiting and watching! Then the kindly policeman lowered his voice confidentially and said in hollow and reverent tones: *'They are waiting for the new Trollope to be born!'* Do you remember, at these words, how heavy our suitcases suddenly felt? How our blood slowed, our footsteps lagged? Brother Ass, we had been bashfully thinking of a kind of illumination such as Rimbaud dreamed of – a nagging poem which was not didactic or expository but which *infected* – was not simply a rationalised intuition, I mean, clothed in isinglass! We had come to the wrong shop, with the wrong change! A chill struck us as we saw the mist falling in Trafalgar

10 on 12pt

Walking along the Mall we wondered who all those men were – tall hawk-featured men perched on balconies and high places, scanning the city with heavy binoculars. What were they seeking so earnestly? Who were they – so composed and steely-eyed? Timidly we stopped a policeman to ask him. 'They are publishers' he said mildly. Publishers! Our hearts stopped beating. 'They are on the look out for new talent.' Great God! It was for *us* they were waiting and watching! Then the kindly policeman lowered his voice confidentially and said in hollow and reverent tones: *'They are waiting for the new Trollope to be born!'* Do you remember, at these words, how heavy our suitcases suddenly felt? How our blood slowed, our footsteps lagged? Brother Ass, we had been bashfully thinking of a kind of illumination such as Rimbaud dreamed of – a nagging poem which was not didactic or expository but which *infected* – was not simply a rationalised

11 on 13pt

WALKING ALONG THE MALL WE WONDERED WHO ALL THOSE MEN WERE – tall hawk-featured men perched on balconies and high places, scanning the city with heavy binoculars. What were they seeking so earnestly? Who were they – so composed and steely-eyed? Timidly we stopped a policeman to ask him. 'They are publishers' he said mildly. Publishers! Our hearts stopped beating. 'They are on the look out for new talent.' Great God! It was for *us* they were waiting and watching! Then the kindly policeman lowered his voice confidentially and said in hollow and reverent tones: *'They are waiting for the new Trollope to be born!'* Do you remember, at these words, how heavy our suitcases suddenly felt? How our blood slowed, our footsteps lagged? Brother Ass, we had been bashfully thinking of a kind of illumination such as Rimbaud dreamed of – a nagging poem which was not didactic or expository but which *infected* – was not simply a rationalised intuition, I mean, clothed in isinglass! We had come to the wrong shop, with the wrong change! A chill struck us as we saw the mist falling in Trafalgar Square, coiling round us its tendrils of ectoplasm! A million muffin-eating moralists were waiting, not for us, Brother Ass, but for the plucky and tedious Trollope! (If you are dissatisfied

9 on 12pt

WALKING ALONG THE MALL WE WONDERED WHO ALL THOSE MEN were – tall hawk-featured men perched on balconies and high places, scanning the city with heavy binoculars. What were they seeking so earnestly? Who were they – so composed and steely-eyed? Timidly we stopped a policeman to ask him. 'They are publishers' he said mildly. Publishers! Our hearts stopped beating. 'They are on the look out for new talent.' Great God! It was for *us* they were waiting and watching! Then the kindly policeman lowered his voice confidentially and said in hollow and reverent tones: *'They are waiting for the new Trollope to be born!'* Do you remember, at these words, how heavy our suitcases suddenly felt? How our blood slowed, our footsteps lagged? Brother Ass, we had been bashfully thinking of a kind of illumination such as Rimbaud dreamed of – a nagging poem which was not didactic or expository but which *infected* – was not simply a rationalised intuition, I mean, clothed in isinglass! We had come to the wrong shop, with the

10 on 13.5pt

WALKING ALONG THE MALL WE WONDERED WHO ALL THOSE men were – tall hawk-featured men perched on balconies and high places, scanning the city with heavy binoculars. What were they seeking so earnestly? Who were they – so composed and steely-eyed? Timidly we stopped a policeman to ask him. 'They are publishers' he said mildly. Publishers! Our hearts stopped beating. 'They are on the look out for new talent.' Great God! It was for *us* they were waiting and watching! Then the kindly policeman lowered his voice confidentially and said in hollow and reverent tones: *'They are waiting for the new Trollope to be born!'* Do you remember, at these words, how heavy our suitcases suddenly felt? How our blood slowed, our footsteps lagged? Brother Ass, we had been bashfully thinking of a kind of illumination such as Rimbaud dreamed of – a nagging poem

11 on 14.5pt

LINOTYPE SABON

Monotype SCOTCH ROMAN

46 roman and italic
Monotype 1907
Copyfitting factor 44.3/41.8

Was originally produced for the printers
R & R Clark as an accurate recutting of Miller
& Richard types of 1810

ABCDEFGHIJKLMNOP
QRSTUVWXYZ abcdefg
hijklmnopqrstuvwxyz
1234567890
ff fi fl ffi ffl ( )[ ]&£$.,;:-!?''

ABCDEFGHIJKLMNOP
QRSTUVWXYZ abcdefg
hijklmnopqrstuvwxyz
1234567890
ff fi fl ffi ffl ( )[ ]&£$.,;:-!?''

24 on 27pt

These examples show *normal* letterspacing and the effect of *reduced* letterspacing on roman setting *as well as on words in italic*: they also show the appearance of figures, for example 28 May 1964, within text. These & the ampersand are not included in the setting opposite.

Normal letterspacing

These examples show *normal* letterspacing and the effect of *reduced* letterspacing on roman setting *as well as on words in italic*: they also show the appearance of figures, for example 28 May 1964, within text. These & the ampersand are not included in the setting opposite.

Minus one unit spacing

These examples show *normal* letterspacing and the effect of *reduced* letterspacing on roman setting *as well as on words in italic*: they also show the appearance of figures, for example 28 May 1964, within text. These & the ampersand are not included in the setting opposite.

Minus two units spacing

WALKING ALONG THE MALL WE WONDERED WHO ALL
WALKING ALONG THE MALL WE WONDERED WHO
WALKING ALONG THE MALL WE WONDERED

Capitals: normal letterspacing/plus 9 units/plus 18 units

Walking along the Mall we wondered who all those men were – tall hawk-featured men perched on balconies and high places, scanning the city with heavy binoculars. WHAT WERE THEY SEEKING SO EARNESTLY? Who were they – so composed and steely-eyed? Timidly we stopped a policeman to ask him. 'They are publishers' he said mildly. Publishers! OUR HEARTS STOPPED BEATING. 'They are on the look out for new talent.' Great God! It was for *us* they

Text with reduced capitals normal letterspacing/plus 6 units

WALKING ALONG THE MALL we wondered who all those men were
WALKING ALONG THE MALL we wondered who all those men

True italic/sloped roman

Walking along the Mall we wondered who all those men were – tall hawk-featured men perched on balconies and high places, scanning the city with heavy binoculars. What were they seeking so earnestly? Who were they – so composed and steely-eyed? Timidly we stopped a policeman to ask him. 'They are publishers' he said mildly. Publishers! Our hearts stopped beating. 'They are on the look out for new talent.' Great God! It was for *us* they were waiting and watching! Then the kindly policeman lowered his voice confidentially and said in hollow and reverent tones: *'They are waiting for the new Trollope to be born!'* Do you remember, at these words, how heavy our suitcases suddenly felt? How our blood slowed, our footsteps lagged? Brother Ass, we had been bashfully thinking of a kind of illumination such as Rimbaud

8 on 9pt

Walking along the Mall we wondered who all those men were – tall hawk-featured men perched on balconies and high places, scanning the city with heavy binoculars. What were they seeking so earnestly? Who were they – so composed and steely-eyed? Timidly we stopped a policeman to ask him. 'They are publishers' he said mildly. Publishers! Our hearts stopped beating. 'They are on the look out for new talent.' Great God! It was for *us* they were waiting and watching! Then the kindly policeman lowered his voice confidentially and said in hollow and reverent tones: *'They are waiting for the new Trollope to be born!'* Do you remember, at these words, how heavy our suitcases suddenly felt? How our blood slowed, our footsteps lagged? Brother

8 on 10.5pt

Walking along the Mall we wondered who all those men were – tall hawk-featured men perched on balconies and high places, scanning the city with heavy binoculars. What were they seeking so earnestly? Who were they – so composed and steely-eyed? Timidly we stopped a policeman to ask him. 'They are publishers' he said mildly. Publishers! Our hearts stopped beating. 'They are on the look out for new talent.' Great God! It was for *us* they were waiting and watching! Then the kindly policeman lowered his voice confidentially and said in hollow and reverent tones: *'They are waiting for the new Trollope to be born!'* Do you remember, at these words, how heavy our suitcases suddenly felt? How our blood slowed, our footsteps lagged? Brother Ass, we had been bashfully thinking of a kind of illumination such as Rimbaud dreamed of – a nagging poem which was not didactic or expository but which *infected* – was not simply a rationalised intuition, I mean, clothed in isinglass! We had come to the wrong shop, with the wrong change! A chill struck us as we saw the mist falling in Trafalgar Square, coiling around us its tendrils of ectoplasm! A million muffin-eating moralists were waiting, not for us, Brother Ass, but for the plucky and tedious Trollope! (If you are dissatisfied with your form, reach for the *curette*.) Now do you wonder if I laugh a

9 on 11pt

Walking along the Mall we wondered who all those men were – tall hawk-featured men perched on balconies and high places, scanning the city with heavy binoculars. What were they seeking so earnestly? Who were they – so composed and steely-eyed? Timidly we stopped a policeman to ask him. 'They are publishers' he said mildly. Publishers! Our hearts stopped beating. 'They are on the look out for new talent.' Great God! It was for *us* they were waiting and watching! Then the kindly policeman lowered his voice confidentially and said in hollow and reverent tones: *'They are waiting for the new Trollope to be born!'* Do you remember, at these words, how heavy our suitcases suddenly felt? How our blood slowed, our footsteps lagged? Brother Ass, we had been bashfully thinking of a kind of illumination such as Rimbaud dreamed of – a nagging poem which was not didactic or expository but which *infected* – was not simply a rationalised intuition, I mean, clothed in isinglass! We had come to the wrong shop, with the wrong change! A chill struck us as we saw the mist falling in Trafalgar Square, coiling around us its tendrils of ectoplasm! A million muffin-eating moralists were waiting, not for us, Brother Ass, but for the plucky and tedious Trollope! (If you are dissa-

9 on 12pt

Walking along the Mall we wondered who all those men were – tall hawk-featured men perched on balconies and high places, scanning the city with heavy binoculars. What were they seeking so earnestly? Who were they – so composed and steely-eyed? Timidly we stopped a policeman to ask him. 'They are publishers' he said mildly. Publishers! Our hearts stopped beating. 'They are on the look out for new talent.' Great God! It was for *us* they were waiting and watching! Then the kindly policeman lowered his voice confidentially and said in hollow and reverent tones: *'They are waiting for the new Trollope to be born!'* Do you remember, at these words, how heavy our suitcases suddenly felt? How our blood slowed, our footsteps lagged? Brother Ass, we had been bashfully thinking of a kind of illumination such as Rimbaud dreamed of – a nagging poem which was not didactic or expository but which *infected* – was not simply a rationalised intuition, I mean, clothed in isinglass! We had come to the wrong shop, with the wrong change! A chill struck us as we saw the mist falling in

10 on 12pt

Walking along the Mall we wondered who all those men were – tall hawk-featured men perched on balconies and high places, scanning the city with heavy binoculars. What were they seeking so earnestly? Who were they – so composed and steely-eyed? Timidly we stopped a policeman to ask him. 'They are publishers' he said mildly. Publishers! Our hearts stopped beating. 'They are on the look out for new talent.' Great God! It was for *us* they were waiting and watching! Then the kindly policeman lowered his voice confidentially and said in hollow and reverent tones: *'They are waiting for the new Trollope to be born!'* Do you remember, at these words, how heavy our suitcases suddenly felt? How our blood slowed, our footsteps lagged? Brother Ass, we had been bashfully thinking of a kind of illumination such as Rimbaud dreamed of – a nagging poem which was not didactic or expository but which *infected* – was not simply a rationalised intuition, I mean, clothed in isinglass! We had come to the wrong shop,

10 on 13.5pt

Walking along the Mall we wondered who all those men were – tall hawk-featured men perched on balconies and high places, scanning the city with heavy binoculars. What were they seeking so earnestly? Who were they – so composed and steely-eyed? Timidly we stopped a policeman to ask him. 'They are publishers' he said mildly. Publishers! Our hearts stopped beating. 'They are on the look out for new talent.' Great God! It was for *us* they were waiting and watching! Then the kindly policeman lowered his voice confidentially and said in hollow and reverent tones: *'They are waiting for the new Trollope to be born!'* Do you remember, at these words, how heavy our suitcases suddenly felt? How our blood slowed, our footsteps lagged? Brother Ass, we had been bashfully thinking of a kind of illumination such as Rimbaud dreamed of – a nagging poem which was not didactic or expository but which *infected* – was

11 on 13pt

Walking along the Mall we wondered who all those me were – tall hawk-featured men perched on balconies and high places, scanning the city with heavy binoculars. What were they seeking so earnestly? Who were they – so composed and steely-eyed? Timidly we stopped a policeman to ask him. 'They are publishers' he said mildly. Publishers! Our hearts stopped beating. 'They are on the look out for new talent.' Great God! It was for *us* they were waiting and watching! Then the kindly policeman lowered his voice confidentially and said in hollow and reverent tones: *'They are waiting for the new Trollope to be born!'* Do you remember, at these words, how heavy our suitcases suddenly felt? How our blood slowed, our footsteps lagged? Brother Ass, we had been bashfully thinking of a kind of illumination such as Rimbaud dreamed of – a nagging poem

11 on 14.5pt

Linotype SCOTCH 2

roman (05233), **italic** (13233)
Linotype *c.*1910
Copyfitting code 127/117

Derived from types cut by Richard Austin for
William Miller, about 1813

ABCDEFGHIJKLMNOP
QRSTUVWXYZ abcdefg
hijklmnopqrstuvwxyz
1234567890
fifl ()[]&£$.,;:-!?''

ABCDEFGHIJKLMNOP
QRSTUVWXYZ abcdefg
hijklmnopqrstuvwxyz
1234567890
fifl ()[]&£$.,;:-!?''

24 on 27pt

These examples show *normal* letterspacing and the effect of *reduced* letterspacing on roman setting *as well as on words in italic*: they also show the appearance of figures, for example 28 May 1964, within text. These & the ampersand are not included in the setting opposite.
Normal letterspacing

These examples show *normal* letterspacing and the effect of *reduced* letterspacing on roman setting *as well as on words in italic*: they also show the appearance of figures, for example 28 May 1964, within text. These & the ampersand are not included in the setting opposite.
Minus one unit spacing

These examples show *normal* letterspacing and the effect of *reduced* letterspacing on roman setting *as well as on words in italic*: they also show the appearance of figures, for example 28 May 1964, within text. These & the ampersand are not included in the setting opposite.
Minus two units spacing

WALKING ALONG THE MALL WE WONDERED WHO ALL
WALKING ALONG THE MALL WE WONDERED WHO
WALKING ALONG THE MALL WE WONDERED
Capitals: normal letterspacing/plus 4 units/plus 9 units

WALKING ALONG THE MALL WE WONDERED WHO ALL THOSE MEN WERE
WALKING ALONG THE MALL WE WONDERED WHO ALL THOSE MEN
WALKING ALONG THE MALL WE WONDERED WHO ALL THOSE
Small caps: normal letterspacing/plus 3 units/plus 6 units

WALKING ALONG THE MALL WE WONDERED WHO ALL THOSE MEN WERE
WALKING ALONG THE MALL WE WONDERED WHO ALL THOSE MEN WERE
True small caps/reduced capitals

WALKING ALONG THE MALL we wondered who all those men were
WALKING ALONG THE MALL we wondered who all those men
True italic/sloped roman

Walking along the Mall we wondered who all those men were – tall hawk-featured men perched on balconies and high places, scanning the city with heavy binoculars. What were they seeking so earnestly? Who were they – so composed and steely-eyed? Timidly we stopped a policeman to ask him. 'They are publishers' he said mildly. Publishers! Our hearts stopped beating. 'They are on the look out for new talent.' Great God! It was for *us* they were waiting and watching! Then the kindly policeman lowered his voice confidentially and said in hollow and reverent tones: *'They are waiting for the new Trollope to be born!'* Do you remember, at these words, how heavy our suitcases suddenly felt? How our blood slowed, our footsteps lagged? Brother Ass, we had been bashfully thinking of a kind of illumination such as Rimbaud dreamed of – a nagging
8 on 9pt

WALKING ALONG THE MALL WE WONDERED WHO ALL THOSE MEN WERE – TALL HAWK-featured men perched on balconies and high places, scanning the city with heavy binoculars. What were they seeking so earnestly? Who were they – so composed and steely-eyed? Timidly we stopped a policeman to ask him. 'They are publishers' he said mildly. Publishers! Our hearts stopped beating. 'They are on the look out for new talent.' Great God! It was for *us* they were waiting and watching! Then the kindly policeman lowered his voice confidentially and said in hollow and reverent tones: *'They are waiting for the new Trollope to be born!'* Do you remember, at these words, how heavy our suitcases suddenly felt? How our blood slowed, our footsteps lagged? Brother
8 on 10.5pt

Walking along the Mall we wondered who all those men were – tall hawk-featured men perched on balconies and high places, scanning the city with heavy binoculars. What were they seeking so earnestly? Who were they – so composed and steely-eyed? Timidly we stopped a policeman to ask him. 'They are publishers' he said mildly. Publishers! Our hearts stopped beating. 'They are on the look out for new talent.' Great God! It was for *us* they were waiting and watching! Then the kindly policeman lowered his voice confidentially and said in hollow and reverent tones: '*They are waiting for the new Trollope to be born!*' Do you remember, at these words, how heavy our suitcases suddenly felt? How our blood slowed, our footsteps lagged? Brother Ass, we had been bashfully thinking of a kind of illumination such as Rimbaud dreamed of – a nagging poem which was not didactic or expository but which *infected* – was not simply a rationalised intuition, I mean, clothed in isinglass! We had come to the wrong shop, with the wrong change! A chill struck us as we saw the mist falling in Trafalgar Square, coiling round us its tendrils of ectoplasm! A million muffin-eating moralists were waiting, not for us, Brother Ass, but for the plucky and tedious Trollope! (If you are dissatisfied with your form, reach for the *curette*.) Now do you wonder if I laugh
9 on 11pt

Walking along the Mall we wondered who all those men were – tall hawk-featured men perched on balconies and high places, scanning the city with heavy binoculars. What were they seeking so earnestly? Who were they – so composed and steely-eyed? Timidly we stopped a policeman to ask him. 'They are publishers' he said mildly. Publishers! Our hearts stopped beating. 'They are on the look out for new talent.' Great God! It was for *us* they were waiting and watching! Then the kindly policeman lowered his voice confidentially and said in hollow and reverent tones: '*They are waiting for the new Trollope to be born!*' Do you remember, at these words, how heavy our suitcases suddenly felt? How our blood slowed, our footsteps lagged? Brother Ass, we had been bashfully thinking of a kind of illumination such as Rimbaud dreamed of – a nagging poem which was not didactic or expository but which *infected* – was not simply a rationalised intuition, I mean, clothed in isinglass! We had come to the wrong shop, with the wrong change! A chill struck us as we saw the mist falling in Trafalgar
10 on 12pt

Walking along the Mall we wondered who all those men were – tall hawk-featured men perched on balconies and high places, scanning the city with heavy binoculars. What were they seeking so earnestly? Who were they – so composed and steely-eyed? Timidly we stopped a policeman to ask him. 'They are publishers' he said mildly. Publishers! Our hearts stopped beating. 'They are on the look out for new talent.' Great God! It was for *us* they were waiting and watching! Then the kindly policeman lowered his voice confidentially and said in hollow and reverent tones: '*They are waiting for the new Trollope to be born!*' Do you remember, at these words, how heavy our suitcases suddenly felt? How our blood slowed, our footsteps lagged? Brother Ass, we had been bashfully thinking of a kind of illumination such as Rimbaud dreamed of – a nagging poem which was not didactic or expository but which *infected* – was
11 on 13pt

WALKING ALONG THE MALL WE WONDERED WHO ALL THOSE MEN WERE – TALL hawk-featured men perched on balconies and high places, scanning the city with heavy binoculars. What were they seeking so earnestly? Who were they – so composed and steely-eyed? Timidly we stopped a policeman to ask him. 'They are publishers' he said mildly. Publishers! Our hearts stopped beating. 'They are on the look out for new talent.' Great God! It was for *us* they were waiting and watching! Then the kindly policeman lowered his voice confidentially and said in hollow and reverent tones: '*They are waiting for the new Trollope to be born!*' Do you remember, at these words, how heavy our suitcases suddenly felt? How our blood slowed, our footsteps lagged? Brother Ass, we had been bashfully thinking of a kind of illumination such as Rimbaud dreamed of – a nagging poem which was not didactic or expository but which *infected* – was not simply a rationalised intuition, I mean, clothed in isinglass! We had come to the wrong shop, with the wrong change! A chill struck us as we saw the mist falling in Trafalgar Square, coiling round us its tendrils of ectoplasm! A million muffin-eating moralists were waiting, not for us, Brother Ass, but for the plucky and tedious Trollope! (If you are dissatisfied with your
9 on 12pt

WALKING ALONG THE MALL WE WONDERED WHO ALL THOSE MEN WERE – tall hawk-featured men perched on balconies and high places, scanning the city with heavy binoculars. What were they seeking so earnestly? Who were they – so composed and steely-eyed? Timidly we stopped a policeman to ask him. 'They are publishers' he said mildly. Publishers! Our hearts stopped beating. 'They are on the look out for new talent.' Great God! It was for *us* they were waiting and watching! Then the kindly policeman lowered his voice confidentially and said in hollow and reverent tones: '*They are waiting for the new Trollope to be born!*' Do you remember, at these words, how heavy our suitcases suddenly felt? How our blood slowed, our footsteps lagged? Brother Ass, we had been bashfully thinking of a kind of illumination such as Rimbaud dreamed of – a nagging poem which was not didactic or expository but which *infected* – was not simply a rationalised intuition, I mean, clothed in isinglass! We had come to the wrong shop,
10 on 13.5pt

WALKING ALONG THE MALL WE WONDERED WHO ALL THOSE MEN were – tall hawk-featured men perched on balconies and high places, scanning the city with heavy binoculars. What were they seeking so earnestly? Who were they – so composed and steely-eyed? Timidly we stopped a policeman to ask him. 'They are publishers' he said mildly. Publishers! Our hearts stopped beating. 'They are on the look out for new talent.' Great God! It was for *us* they were waiting and watching! Then the kindly policeman lowered his voice confidentially and said in hollow and reverent tones: '*They are waiting for the new Trollope to be born!*' Do you remember, at these words, how heavy our suitcases suddenly felt? How our blood slowed, our footsteps lagged? Brother Ass, we had been bashfully thinking of a kind of illumination such as Rimbaud dreamed of – a
11 on 14.5pt

Linotype **Serifa**

roman 55 (05235), **italic 56** (13235)
bold 65 (07235)
Bauer 1968 (Adrian Frutiger)
Copyfitting code 140/138/146

Range also includes thin, thin italic, light, light italic, black, bold condensed

Monotype's version appears to be slightly bolder (copyfitting factor 49.4/50.0; no italic)

ABCDEFGHIJKLMNOP
QRSTUVWXYZ abcdefg
hijklmnopqrstuvwxyz
1234567890
fifl ()[]&£$.,;:-!?"

ABCDEFGHIJKLMNOP
QRSTUVWXYZ abcdefg
hijklmnopqrstuvwxyz
1234567890
fifl ()[]&£$.,;:-!?"

ABCDEFGHIJKLMNOP
QRSTUVWXYZ abcdefg
hijklmnopqrstuvwxyz
1234567890
fifl ()[]&£$.,;:-!?"

24 on 27pt

These examples show *normal* letterspacing and the effect of *reduced* letterspacing on roman setting *as well as on words in italic*: they also show the appearance of figures, for example 28 May 1964, within text. These & the ampersand are not included in the setting opposite.
Normal letterspacing

These examples show *normal* letterspacing and the effect of *reduced* letterspacing on roman setting *as well as on words in italic*: they also show the appearance of figures, for example 28 May 1964, within text. These & the ampersand are not included in the setting opposite.
Minus one unit spacing

These examples show *normal* letterspacing and the effect of *reduced* letterspacing on roman setting *as well as on words in italic*: they also show the appearance of figures, for example 28 May 1964, within text. These & the ampersand are not included in the setting opposite.
Minus two units spacing

WALKING ALONG THE MALL WE WONDERED WHO ALL THOSE
WALKING ALONG THE MALL WE WONDERED WHO ALL THO
WALKING ALONG THE MALL WE WONDERED WHO
Capitals: normal letterspacing/plus 4 units/plus 9 units

WALKING ALONG THE MALL WE WONDERED WHO ALL THOSE MEN WERE
WALKING ALONG THE MALL WE WONDERED WHO ALL THOSE MEN
WALKING ALONG THE MALL WE WONDERED WHO ALL THOSE
Small caps: normal letterspacing/plus 3 units/plus 6 units

WALKING ALONG THE MALL WE WONDERED WHO ALL THOSE MEN WERE
WALKING ALONG THE MALL WE WONDERED WHO ALL THOSE MEN WERE
True small caps/reduced capitals

WALKING ALONG THE MALL we wondered who all those men
WALKING ALONG THE MALL we wondered who all those men
True italic/sloped roman

Walking along the Mall we wondered who all those men were – tall hawk-featured men perched on balconies and high places, scanning the city with heavy binoculars. What were they seeking so earnestly? Who were they – so composed and steely-eyed? Timidly we stopped a policeman to ask him. 'They are publishers' he said mildly. Publishers! Our hearts stopped beating. 'They are on the look out for new talent.' Great God! It was for *us* they were waiting and watching! Then the kindly policeman lowered his voice confidentially and said in hollow and reverent tones: *'They are waiting for the new Trollope to be born!'* Do you remember, at these words, how heavy our suitcases suddenly felt? How our blood slowed, our footsteps lagged? Brother Ass, we had been bashfully
8 on 9pt

WALKING ALONG THE MALL WE WONDERED WHO ALL THOSE MEN WERE – TALL HAWK-featured men perched on balconies and high places, scanning the city with heavy binoculars. What were they seeking so earnestly? Who were they – so composed and steely-eyed? Timidly we stopped a policeman to ask him. 'They are publishers' he said mildly. Publishers! Our hearts stopped beating. 'They are on the look out for new talent.' Great God! It was for *us* they were waiting and watching! Then the kindly policeman lowered his voice confidentially and said in hollow and reverent tones: *'They are waiting for the new Trollope to be born!'* Do you remember, at these words, how heavy our suitcases suddenly felt? How
8 on 10.5pt

Walking along the Mall we wondered who all those men were – tall hawk-featured men perched on balconies and high places, scanning the city with heavy binoculars. What were they seeking so earnestly? Who were they – so composed and steely-eyed? Timidly we stopped a policeman to ask him. 'They are publishers' he said mildly. Publishers! Our hearts stopped beating. 'They are on the look out for new talent.' Great God! It was for *us* they were waiting and watching! Then the kindly policeman lowered his voice confidentially and said in hollow and reverent tones: *'They are waiting for the new Trollope to be born!'* Do you remember, at these words, how heavy our suitcases suddenly felt? How our blood slowed, our footsteps lagged? Brother Ass, we had been bashfully thinking of a kind of illumination such as Rimbaud dreamed of – a nagging poem which was not didactic or expository but which *infected* – was not simply a rationalised intuition, I mean, clothed in isinglass! We had come to the wrong shop, with the wrong change! A chill struck us as we saw the mist falling in Trafalgar Square, coiling round us its tendrils of ectoplasm! A million muffin-eating moralists were waiting, not for us, Brother Ass, but for the plucky and tedious

9 on 11pt

Walking along the Mall we wondered who all those men were – tall hawk-featured men perched on balconies and high places, scanning the city with heavy binoculars. What were they seeking so earnestly? Who were they – so composed and steely-eyed? Timidly we stopped a policeman to ask him. 'They are publishers' he said mildly. Publishers! Our hearts stopped beating. 'They are on the look out for new talent.' Great God! It was for *us* they were waiting and watching! Then the kindly policeman lowered his voice confidentially and said in hollow and reverent tones: *'They are waiting for the new Trollope to be born!'* Do you remember, at these words, how heavy our suitcases suddenly felt? How our blood slowed, our footsteps lagged? Brother Ass, we had been bashfully thinking of a kind of illumination such as Rimbaud dreamed of – a nagging poem which was not didactic or expository but which *infected* – was not simply a rationalised intuition, I mean, clothed in isinglass!

10 on 12pt

Walking along the Mall we wondered who all those men were – tall hawk-featured men perched on balconies and high places, scanning the city with heavy binoculars. What were they seeking so earnestly? Who were they – so composed and steely-eyed? Timidly we stopped a policeman to ask him. 'They are publishers' he said mildly. Publishers! Our hearts stopped beating. 'They are on the look out for new talent.' Great God! It was for *us* they were waiting and watching! Then the kindly policeman lowered his voice confidentially and said in hollow and reverent tones: *'They are waiting for the new Trollope to be born!'* Do you remember, at these words, how heavy our suitcases suddenly felt? How our blood slowed, our footsteps lagged? Brother Ass, we had been bashfully thinking of a kind of illumination such as Rimbaud dreamed of – a

11 on 13pt

WALKING ALONG THE MALL WE WONDERED WHO ALL THOSE MEN WERE — TALL hawk-featured men perched on balconies and high places, scanning the city with heavy binoculars. What were they seeking so earnestly? Who were they – so composed and steely-eyed? Timidly we stopped a policeman to ask him. 'They are publishers' he said mildly. Publishers! Our hearts stopped beating. 'They are on the look out for new talent.' Great God! It was for *us* they were waiting and watching! Then the kindly policeman lowered his voice confidentially and said in hollow and reverent tones: *'They are waiting for the new Trollope to be born!'* Do you remember, at these words, how heavy our suitcases suddenly felt? How our blood slowed, our footsteps lagged? Brother Ass, we had been bashfully thinking of a kind of illumination such as Rimbaud dreamed of – a nagging poem which was not didactic or expository but which *infected* – was not simply a rationalised intuition, I mean, clothed in isinglass! We had come to the wrong shop, with the wrong change! A chill struck us as we saw the mist falling in Trafalgar Square, coiling round us its tendrils of ectoplasm! A million muffin-eating moralists

9 on 12pt

WALKING ALONG THE MALL WE WONDERED WHO ALL THOSE MEN WERE — tall hawk-featured men perched on balconies and high places, scanning the city with heavy binoculars. What were they seeking so earnestly? Who were they – so composed and steely-eyed? Timidly we stopped a policeman to ask him. 'They are publishers' he said mildly. Publishers! Our hearts stopped beating. 'They are on the look out for new talent.' Great God! It was for *us* they were waiting and watching! Then the kindly policeman lowered his voice confidentially and said in hollow and reverent tones: *'They are waiting for the new Trollope to be born!'* Do you remember, at these words, how heavy our suitcases suddenly felt? How our blood slowed, our footsteps lagged? Brother Ass, we had been bashfully thinking of a kind of illumination such as Rimbaud dreamed of – a nagging poem which was not didactic or expository but which *infected* – was not

10 on 13.5pt

WALKING ALONG THE MALL WE WONDERED WHO ALL THOSE MEN were – tall hawk-featured men perched on balconies and high places, scanning the city with heavy binoculars. What were they seeking so earnestly? Who were they – so composed and steely-eyed? Timidly we stopped a police-man to ask him. 'They are publishers' he said mildly. Pub-lishers! Our hearts stopped beating. 'They are on the look out for new talent.' Great God! It was for *us* they were waiting and watching! Then the kindly policeman lowered his voice confidentially and said in hollow and reverent tones: *'They are waiting for the new Trollope to be born!'* Do you remember, at these words, how heavy our suit-cases suddenly felt? How our blood slowed, our footsteps lagged? Brother Ass, we had been bashfully thinking of a

11 on 14.5pt

LINOTYPE SERIFA

556 roman and italic
756 semi-bold
Designed by Jan van Krimpen 1952 for
Enschedé; brought out by Monotype 1955
Copyfitting factor 38.8/31.1/42.2

Originally designed for a range of bibles
1941-43, but not used. In the Aldine tradition,
with an italic based on the calligraphy of
Arrighi

The disturbingly small figures are part of Van
Krimpen's design. Janson non-lining figures
might provide a useful alternative

ABCDEFGHIJKLMNOP
QRSTUVWXYZ abcdefg
hijklmnopqrstuvwxyz
1234567890
ff fi fl ffi ffl ()[]&£$.,;:-!?''

ABCDEFGHIJKLMNOP
QRSTUVWXYZ abcdefg
hijklmnopqrstuvwxyz
1234567890
ff fi fl ffi ffl ()[]&£$.,;:-!?''

ABCDEFGHIJKLMNOP
QRSTUVWXYZ abcdefg
hijklmnopqrstuvwxyz
1234567890
ff fi fl ffi ffl ()[]&£$.,;:-!?''

24 on 27pt

252

These examples show *normal* letterspacing and the effect of *reduced*
letterspacing on roman setting *as well as on words in italic*: they also
show the appearance of figures, for example 28 May 1964, within text.
These & the ampersand are not included in the setting opposite.
Normal letterspacing

These examples show *normal* letterspacing and the effect of *reduced*
letterspacing on roman setting *as well as on words in italic*: they also
show the appearance of figures, for example 28 May 1964, within text.
These & the ampersand are not included in the setting opposite.
Minus one unit spacing

These examples show *normal* letterspacing and the effect of *reduced*
letterspacing on roman setting *as well as on words in italic*: they also
show the appearance of figures, for example 28 May 1964, within text.
These & the ampersand are not included in the setting opposite.
Minus two units spacing

WALKING ALONG THE MALL WE WONDERED WHO ALL THOSE MEN WERE
WALKING ALONG THE MALL WE WONDERED WHO ALL THOSE
WALKING ALONG THE MALL WE WONDERED WHO ALL
Capitals: normal letterspacing/plus 9 units/plus 18 units

WALKING ALONG THE MALL WE WONDERED WHO ALL THOSE MEN WERE
WALKING ALONG THE MALL WE WONDERED WHO ALL THOSE MEN WERE
WALKING ALONG THE MALL WE WONDERED WHO ALL THOSE MEN
Small caps: normal letterspacing/plus 6 units/plus 12 units

WALKING ALONG THE MALL we wondered who all those men were
WALKING ALONG THE MALL we wondered who all those men were
True italic/sloped roman

WALKING ALONG THE MALL WE WONDERED WHO ALL THOSE MEN WERE
WALKING ALONG THE MALL WE WONDERED WHO ALL THOSE MEN WERE
True small caps/reduced capitals

Walking along the Mall we wondered who all those men were – tall hawk-featured men
perched on balconies and high places, scanning the city with heavy binoculars. What were they
seeking so earnestly? Who were they – so composed and steely-eyed? Timidly we stopped a
policeman to ask him. 'They are publishers' he said mildly. Publishers! Our hearts stopped beating.
'They are on the look out for new talent.' Great God! It was for *us* they were waiting and
watching! Then the kindly policeman lowered his voice confidentially and said in hollow and
reverent tones: *'They are waiting for the new Trollope to be born!'* Do you remember, at these words, how
heavy our suitcases suddenly felt? How our blood slowed, our footsteps lagged? Brother Ass, we
had been bashfully thinking of a kind of illumination such as Rimbaud dreamed of – a nagging
poem which was not didactic or expository but which *infected* – was not simply a rationalised

8 on 9pt

WALKING ALONG THE MALL WE WONDERED WHO ALL THOSE MEN WERE – TALL HAWK-FEATURED
men perched on balconies and high places, scanning the city with heavy binoculars. What were
they seeking so earnestly? Who were they – so composed and steely-eyed? Timidly we stopped a
policeman to ask him. 'They are publishers' he said mildly. Publishers! Our hearts stopped beating.
'They are on the look out for new talent.' Great God! It was for *us* they were waiting and
watching! Then the kindly policeman lowered his voice confidentially and said in hollow and
reverent tones: *'They are waiting for the new Trollope to be born!'* Do you remember, at these words, how
heavy our suitcases suddenly felt? How our blood slowed, our footsteps lagged? Brother Ass, we
had been bashfully thinking of a kind of illumination such as Rimbaud dreamed of – a nagging

8 on 10.5pt

Walking along the Mall we wondered who all those men were — tall hawk-featured men perched on balconies and high places, scanning the city with heavy binoculars. What were they seeking so earnestly? Who were they — so composed and steely-eyed? Timidly we stopped a policeman to ask him. 'They are publishers' he said mildly. Publishers! Our hearts stopped beating. 'They are on the look out for new talent.' Great God! It was for *us* they were waiting and watching! Then the kindly policeman lowered his voice confidentially and said in hollow and reverent tones: *'They are waiting for the new Trollope to be born!'* Do you remember, at these words, how heavy our suitcases suddenly felt? How our blood slowed, our footsteps lagged? Brother Ass, we had been bashfully thinking of a kind of illumination such as Rimbaud dreamed of — a nagging poem which was not didactic or expository but which *infected* — was not simply a rationalised intuition, I mean, clothed in isinglass! We had come to the wrong shop, with the wrong change! A chill struck us as we saw the mist falling in Trafalgar Square, coiling around us its tendrils of ectoplasm! A million muffin-eating moralists were waiting, not for us, Brother Ass, but for the plucky and tedious Trollope! (If you are dissatisfied with your form, reach for the *curette*.) Now do you wonder if I laugh a little off-key? Do you ask yourself what has turned me into nature's bashful little aphorist? We who are, after all, simply poor co-workers in the psyche of our nation, what can we expect but the natural automatic rejection from a

9 on 11pt

Walking along the Mall we wondered who all those men were — tall hawk-featured men perched on balconies and high places, scanning the city with heavy binoculars. What were they seeking so earnestly? Who were they — so composed and steely-eyed? Timidly we stopped a policeman to ask him. 'They are publishers' he said mildly. Publishers! Our hearts stopped beating. 'They are on the look out for new talent.' Great God! It was for *us* they were waiting and watching! Then the kindly policeman lowered his voice confidentially and said in hollow and reverent tones: *'They are waiting for the new Trollope to be born!'* Do you remember, at these words, how heavy our suitcases suddenly felt? How our blood slowed, our footsteps lagged? Brother Ass, we had been bashfully thinking of a kind of illumination such as Rimbaud dreamed of — a nagging poem which was not didactic or expository but which *infected* — was not simply a rationalised intuition, I mean, clothed in isinglass! We had come to the wrong shop, with the wrong change! A chill struck us as we saw the mist falling in Trafalgar Square, coiling around us its tendrils of ectoplasm! A million muffin-eating moralists were waiting, not for us, Brother Ass, but for the plucky and tedious Trollope! (If

10 on 12pt

Walking along the Mall we wondered who all those men were — tall hawk-featured men perched on balconies and high places, scanning the city with heavy binoculars. What were they seeking so earnestly? Who were they — so composed and steely-eyed? Timidly we stopped a policeman to ask him. 'They are publishers' he said mildly. Publishers! Our hearts stopped beating. 'They are on the look out for new talent.' Great God! It was for *us* they were waiting and watching! Then the kindly policeman lowered his voice confidentially and said in hollow and reverent tones: *'They are waiting for the new Trollope to be born!'* Do you remember, at these words, how heavy our suitcases suddenly felt? How our blood slowed, our footsteps lagged? Brother Ass, we had been bashfully thinking of a kind of illumination such as Rimbaud dreamed of — a nagging poem which was not didactic or expository but which *infected* — was not simply a rationalised intuition, I mean, clothed in isinglass! We had come to the wrong shop, with the wrong change! A chill struck us as we saw the mist

11 on 13pt

WALKING ALONG THE MALL WE WONDERED WHO ALL THOSE MEN WERE — TALL HAWK-featured men perched on balconies and high places, scanning the city with heavy binoculars. What were they seeking so earnestly? Who were they — so composed and steely-eyed? Timidly we stopped a policeman to ask him. 'They are publishers' he said mildly. Publishers! Our hearts stopped beating. 'They are on the look out for new talent.' Great God! It was for *us* they were waiting and watching! Then the kindly policeman lowered his voice confidentially and said in hollow and reverent tones: *'They are waiting for the new Trollope to be born!'* Do you remember, at these words, how heavy our suitcases suddenly felt? How our blood slowed, our footsteps lagged? Brother Ass, we had been bashfully thinking of a kind of illumination such as Rimbaud dreamed of — a nagging poem which was not didactic or expository but which *infected* — was not simply a rationalised intuition, I mean, clothed in isinglass! We had come to the wrong shop, with the wrong change! A chill struck us as we saw the mist falling in Trafalgar Square, coiling around us its tendrils of ectoplasm! A million muffin-eating moralists were waiting, not for us, Brother Ass, but for the plucky and tedious Trollope! (If you are dissatisfied with your form, reach for the *curette*.) Now do you wonder if I laugh a little off-key? Do you ask yourself what has turned me into nature's bashful little aphorist? We who are, after all, simply poor co-workers in the

9 on 12pt

WALKING ALONG THE MALL WE WONDERED WHO ALL THOSE MEN WERE — TALL hawk-featured men perched on balconies and high places, scanning the city with heavy binoculars. What were they seeking so earnestly? Who were they — so composed and steely-eyed? Timidly we stopped a policeman to ask him. 'They are publishers' he said mildly. Publishers! Our hearts stopped beating. 'They are on the look out for new talent.' Great God! It was for *us* they were waiting and watching! Then the kindly policeman lowered his voice confidentially and said in hollow and reverent tones: *'They are waiting for the new Trollope to be born!'* Do you remember, at these words, how heavy our suitcases suddenly felt? How our blood slowed, our footsteps lagged? Brother Ass, we had been bashfully thinking of a kind of illumination such as Rimbaud dreamed of — a nagging poem which was not didactic or expository but which *infected* — was not simply a rationalised intuition, I mean, clothed in isinglass! We had come to the wrong shop, with the wrong change! A chill struck us as we saw the mist falling in Trafalgar Square, coiling around us its tendrils of ectoplasm! A million muffin-eating moralists

10 on 13.5pt

WALKING ALONG THE MALL WE WONDERED WHO ALL THOSE MEN WERE — tall hawk-featured men perched on balconies and high places, scanning the city with heavy binoculars. What were they seeking so earnestly? Who were they — so composed and steely-eyed? Timidly we stopped a policeman to ask him. 'They are publishers' he said mildly. Publishers! Our hearts stopped beating. 'They are on the look out for new talent.' Great God! It was for *us* they were waiting and watching! Then the kindly policeman lowered his voice confidentially and said in hollow and reverent tones: *'They are waiting for the new Trollope to be born!'* Do you remember, at these words, how heavy our suitcases suddenly felt? How our blood slowed, our footsteps lagged? Brother Ass, we had been bashfully thinking of a kind of illumination such as Rimbaud dreamed of — a nagging poem which was not didactic or expository but which *infected* — was not simply a rationalised intuition, I mean, clothed in isinglass! We had come to the

11 on 14.5pt

Linotype **Stempel Schadow**

roman (05475), **italic** (13475)
bold (07475)
Weber 1937 (Georg Trump)
Copyfitting code 145/134/154

Range also includes light, light italic, medium,
medium italic, bold italic, black, black italic,
black condensed

Slightly stronger than the original Schadow-
Antiqua Werk, with thin strokes nearer the
weight of the thicks. Other slight changes. The
bolder weights more closely resemble the
original

ABCDEFGHIJKLMNOP
QRSTUVWXYZ abcdefg
hijklmnopqrstuvwxyz
1234567890
fifl ()[]&£$.,;:-!?″

ABCDEFGHIJKLMNOP
QRSTUVWXYZ abcdefg
hijklmnopqrstuvwxyz
1234567890
fifl ()[]&£$.,;:-!?″

ABCDEFGHIJKLMNOP
QRSTUVWXYZ abcdefg
hijklmnopqrstuvwxyz
1234567890
fifl ()[]&£$.,;:-!?″

24 on 27pt

These examples show *normal* letterspacing and the effect of *reduced*
letterspacing on roman setting *as well as on words in italic*: they also
show the appearance of figures, for example 28 May 1964, within text.
These & the ampersand are not included in the setting opposite.
Normal letterspacing

These examples show *normal* letterspacing and the effect of *reduced*
letterspacing on roman setting *as well as on words in italic*: they also
show the appearance of figures, for example 28 May 1964, within text.
These & the ampersand are not included in the setting opposite.
Minus one unit spacing

These examples show *normal* letterspacing and the effect of *reduced*
letterspacing on roman setting *as well as on words in italic*: they also
show the appearance of figures, for example 28 May 1964, within text.
These & the ampersand are not included in the setting opposite.
Minus two units spacing

WALKING ALONG THE MALL WE WONDERED WHO ALL THOSE
WALKING ALONG THE MALL WE WONDERED WHO ALL
WALKING ALONG THE MALL WE WONDERED WHO
Capitals: normal letterspacing/plus 4 units/plus 9 units

Walking along the Mall we wondered who all those men were – tall
hawk-featured men perched on balconies and high places, scanning
the city with heavy binoculars. WHAT WERE THEY SEEKING SO EARNESTLY?
Who were they – so composed and steely-eyed? Timidly we stopped
a policeman to ask him. 'THEY ARE PUBLISHERS' he said mildly.
Publishers! Our hearts stopped beating. 'They are on the look out for
new talent.' Great God! It was for *us* they were waiting and watching!
Text with reduced caps normal letterspacing/plus 3 units

WALKING ALONG THE MALL we wondered who all those men were
WALKING ALONG THE MALL we wondered who all those men were
True italic/sloped roman

Walking along the Mall we wondered who all those men were – tall hawk-
featured men perched on balconies and high places, scanning the city with
heavy binoculars. What were they seeking so earnestly? Who were they –
so composed and steely-eyed? Timidly we stopped a policeman to ask him.
'They are publishers' he said mildly. Publishers! Our hearts stopped beating.
'They are on the look out for new talent.' Great God! It was for *us* they
were waiting and watching! Then the kindly policeman lowered his voice
confidentially and said in hollow and reverent tones: *'They are waiting for the*
new Trollope to be born!' Do you remember, at these words, how heavy our
suitcases suddenly felt? How our blood slowed, our footsteps lagged?

8 on 9pt

Walking along the Mall we wondered who all those men were – tall hawk-
featured men perched on balconies and high places, scanning the city with
heavy binoculars. What were they seeking so earnestly? Who were they – so
composed and steely-eyed? Timidly we stopped a policeman to ask him.
'They are publishers' he said mildly. Publishers! Our hearts stopped beating.
'They are on the look out for new talent.' Great God! It was for *us* they were
waiting and watching! Then the kindly policeman lowered his voice
confidentially and said in hollow and reverent tones: *'They are waiting for the*
new Trollope to be born!' Do you remember, at these words, how heavy our

8 on 10.5pt

Walking along the Mall we wondered who all those men were – tall hawk-featured men perched on balconies and high places, scanning the city with heavy binoculars. What were they seeking so earnestly? Who were they – so composed and steely-eyed? Timidly we stopped a policeman to ask him. 'They are publishers' he said mildly. Publishers! Our hearts stopped beating. 'They are on the look out for new talent.' Great God! It was for *us* they were waiting and watching! Then the kindly policeman lowered his voice confidentially and said in hollow and reverent tones: *'They are waiting for the new Trollope to be born!'* Do you remember, at these words, how heavy our suitcases suddenly felt? How our blood slowed, our footsteps lagged? Brother Ass, we had been bashfully thinking of a kind of illumination such as Rimbaud dreamed of – a nagging poem which was not didactic or expository but which *infected* – was not simply a rationalised intuition, I mean, clothed in isinglass! We had come to the wrong shop, with the wrong change! A chill struck us as we saw the mist falling in Trafalgar Square, coiling round us its tendrils of ectoplasm! A million muffin-eating moralists were waiting, not for us, Brother

9 on 11pt

Walking along the Mall we wondered who all those men were – tall hawk-featured men perched on balconies and high places, scanning the city with heavy binoculars. What were they seeking so earnestly? Who were they – so composed and steely-eyed? Timidly we stopped a policeman to ask him. 'They are publishers' he said mildly. Publishers! Our hearts stopped beating. 'They are on the look out for new talent.' Great God! It was for *us* they were waiting and watching! Then the kindly policeman lowered his voice confidentially and said in hollow and reverent tones: *'They arc waiting for the new Trollope to be born!'* Do you remember, at these words, how heavy our suitcases suddenly felt? How our blood slowed, our footsteps lagged? Brother Ass, we had been bashfully thinking of a kind of illumination such as Rimbaud dreamed of – a nagging poem which was not didactic or expository but which *infected* – was not simply a rationalised intuition, I mean,

10 on 12pt

Walking along the Mall we wondered who all those men were – tall hawk-featured men perched on balconies and high places, scanning the city with heavy binoculars. What were they seeking so earnestly? Who were they – so composed and steely-eyed? Timidly we stopped a policeman to ask him. 'They are publishers' he said mildly. Publishers! Our hearts stopped beating. 'They are on the look out for new talent.' Great God! It was for *us* they were waiting and watching! Then the kindly policeman lowered his voice confidentially and said in hollow and reverent tones: *'They are waiting for the new Trollope to be born!'* Do you remember, at these words, how heavy our suitcases suddenly felt? How our blood slowed, our footsteps lagged? Brother Ass, we had been bashfully thinking of a kind of illumination such as

11 on 13pt

Walking along the Mall we wondered who all those men were – tall hawk-featured men perched on balconies and high places, scanning the city with heavy binoculars. What were they seeking so earnestly? Who were they – so composed and steely-eyed? Timidly we stopped a policeman to ask him. 'They are publishers' he said mildly. Publishers! Our hearts stopped beating. 'They are on the look out for new talent.' Great God! It was for *us* they were waiting and watching! Then the kindly policeman lowered his voice confidentially and said in hollow and reverent tones: *'They are waiting for the new Trollope to be born!'* Do you remember, at these words, how heavy our suitcases suddenly felt? How our blood slowed, our footsteps lagged? Brother Ass, we had been bashfully thinking of a kind of illumination such as Rimbaud dreamed of – a nagging poem which was not didactic or expository but which *infected* – was not simply a rationalised intuition, I mean, clothed in isinglass! We had come to the wrong shop, with the wrong change! A chill struck us as we saw the mist falling in Trafalgar Square, coiling round us its tendrils of ectoplasm! A million

9 on 12pt

Walking along the Mall we wondered who all those men were – tall hawk-featured men perched on balconies and high places, scanning the city with heavy binoculars. What were they seeking so earnestly? Who were they – so composed and steely-eyed? Timidly we stopped a policeman to ask him. 'They are publishers' he said mildly. Publishers! Our hearts stopped beating. 'They are on the look out for new talent.' Great God! It was for *us* they were waiting and watching! Then the kindly policeman lowered his voice confidentially and said in hollow and reverent tones: *'They are waiting for the new Trollope to be born!'* Do you remember, at these words, how heavy our suitcases suddenly felt? How our blood slowed, our footsteps lagged? Brother Ass, we had been bashfully thinking of a kind of illumination such as Rimbaud dreamed of – a nagging poem which was not didactic or expository but which *infected* – was

10 on 13.5pt

Walking along the Mall we wondered who all those men were – tall hawk-featured men perched on balconies and high places, scanning the city with heavy binoculars. What were they seeking so earnestly? Who were they – so composed and steely-eyed? Timidly we stopped a policeman to ask him. 'They are publishers' he said mildly. Publishers! Our hearts stopped beating. 'They are on the look out for new talent.' Great God! It was for *us* they were waiting and watching! Then the kindly policeman lowered his voice confidentially and said in hollow and reverent tones: *'They are waiting for the new Trollope to be born!'* Do you remember, at these words, how heavy our suitcases suddenly felt? How our blood slowed, our footsteps lagged? Brother Ass, we had been

11 on 14.5pt

Monotype **Times**

327 roman and italic
334 bold
Designed by Stanley Morison and Victor
Lardent 1932 for Monotype and *The Times*
Copyfitting factor 42.9/41.5/41.4

Range also includes semi-bold, semi-bold
italic, bold italic, condensed, condensed italic,
bold condensed, extra bold

Plantin was taken as a basis, refined and
sharpened up

Educational characters available

ABCDEFGHIJKLMNOP
QRSTUVWXYZ abcdefg
hijklmnopqrstuvwxyz
1234567890 1234567890
ff fi fl ffi ffl ()[]&£$.,;:-!?"'

ABCDEFGHIJKLMNOP
QRSTUVWXYZ abcdefg
hijklmnopqrstuvwxyz
1234567890 1234567890
ff fi fl ffi ffl ( ) [ ]&£$.,;:-!?"'

ABCDEFGHIJKLMNOP
QRSTUVWXYZ abcdefg
hijklmnopqrstuvwxyz
1234567890 1234567890
ff fi fl ffi ffl ()[]&£$.,;:-!?"'

24 on 27pt

These examples show *normal* letterspacing and the effect of *reduced* letterspacing on roman setting *as well as on words in italic*: they also show the appearance of figures, for example 28 May 1964, within text. These & the ampersand are not included in the setting opposite.

Normal letterspacing

These examples show *normal* letterspacing and the effect of *reduced* letterspacing on roman setting *as well as on words in italic*: they also show the appearance of figures, for example 28 May 1964, within text. These & the ampersand are not included in the setting opposite.

Minus one unit spacing

These examples show *normal* letterspacing and the effect of *reduced* letterspacing on roman setting *as well as on words in italic*: they also show the appearance of figures, for example 28 May 1964, within text. These & the ampersand are not included in the setting opposite.

Minus two units spacing

WALKING ALONG THE MALL WE WONDERED WHO ALL
WALKING ALONG THE MALL WE WONDERED WHO
WALKING ALONG THE MALL WE WONDERED

Capitals: normal letterspacing/plus 9 units/plus 18 units

WALKING ALONG THE MALL WE WONDERED WHO ALL THOSE MEN WERE
WALKING ALONG THE MALL WE WONDERED WHO ALL THOSE MEN
WALKING ALONG THE MALL WE WONDERED WHO ALL THOSE

Small caps: normal letterspacing/plus 6 units/plus 12 units

WALKING ALONG THE MALL we wondered who all those men were
WALKING ALONG THE MALL we wondered who all those men

True italic/sloped roman

WALKING ALONG THE MALL WE WONDERED WHO ALL THOSE MEN WERE
WALKING ALONG THE MALL WE WONDERED WHO ALL THOSE MEN WERE

True small caps/reduced capitals

Walking along the Mall we wondered who all those men were – tall hawk-featured
men perched on balconies and high places, scanning the city with heavy binoculars. What were they seeking so earnestly? Who were they – so composed and steely-eyed? Timidly we stopped a policeman to ask him. 'They are publishers' he said mildly. Publishers! Our hearts stopped beating. 'They are on the look out for new talent.' Great God! It was for *us* they were waiting and watching! Then the kindly policeman lowered his voice confidentially and said in hollow and reverent tones: *'They are waiting for the new Trollope to be born!'* Do you remember, at these words, how heavy our suitcases suddenly felt? How our blood slowed, our footsteps lagged? Brother Ass, we had been bashfully thinking of a kind of illumination such as Rimbaud dreamed of – a nagging

8 on 9pt

WALKING ALONG THE MALL WE WONDERED WHO ALL THOSE MEN WERE – TALL HAWK-featured men perched on balconies and high places, scanning the city with heavy binoculars. What were they seeking so earnestly? Who were they – so composed and steely-eyed? Timidly we stopped a policeman to ask him. 'They are publishers' he said mildly. Publishers! Our hearts stopped beating. 'They are on the look out for new talent.' Great God! It was for *us* they were waiting and watching! Then the kindly policeman lowered his voice confidentially and said in hollow and reverent tones: *'They are waiting for the new Trollope to be born!'* Do you remember, at these words, how heavy our suitcases suddenly felt? How our blood slowed, our footsteps lagged?

8 on 10.5pt

Walking along the Mall we wondered who all those men were – tall hawk-featured men perched on balconies and high places, scanning the city with heavy binoculars. What were they seeking so earnestly? Who were they – so composed and steely-eyed? Timidly we stopped a policeman to ask him. 'They are publishers' he said mildly. Publishers! Our hearts stopped beating. 'They are on the look out for new talent.' Great God! It was for *us* they were waiting and watching! Then the kindly policeman lowered his voice confidentially and said in hollow and reverent tones: *'They are waiting for the new Trollope to be born!'* Do you remember, at these words, how heavy our suitcases suddenly felt? How our blood slowed, our footsteps lagged? Brother Ass, we had been bashfully thinking of a kind of illumination such as Rimbaud dreamed of – a nagging poem which was not didactic or expository but which *infected* – was not simply a rationalised intuition, I mean, clothed in isinglass! We had come to the wrong shop, with the wrong change! A chill struck us as we saw the mist falling in Trafalgar Square, coiling around us its tendrils of ectoplasm! A million muffin-eating moralists were waiting, not for us, Brother Ass, but for the plucky and tedious Trollope! (If you are dissatisfied with your form, reach for the *curette*.) Now do you wonder if I laugh a little off-key? Do you ask yourself what has turned me into

9 on 11pt

Walking along the Mall we wondered who all those men were – tall hawk-featured men perched on balconies and high places, scanning the city with heavy binoculars. What were they seeking so earnestly? Who were they – so composed and steely-eyed? Timidly we stopped a policeman to ask him. 'They are publishers' he said mildly. Publishers! Our hearts stopped beating. 'They are on the look out for new talent.' Great God! It was for *us* they were waiting and watching! Then the kindly policeman lowered his voice confidentially and said in hollow and reverent tones: *'They are waiting for the new Trollope to be born!'* Do you remember, at these words, how heavy our suitcases suddenly felt? How our blood slowed, our footsteps lagged? Brother Ass, we had been bashfully thinking of a kind of illumination such as Rimbaud dreamed of – a nagging poem which was not didactic or expository but which *infected* – was not simply a rationalised intuition, I mean, clothed in isinglass! We had come to the wrong shop, with the wrong change! A chill struck us as we saw the mist falling in Trafalgar Square, coiling around us its tendrils of

10 on 12pt

Walking along the Mall we wondered who all those men were – tall hawk-featured men perched on balconies and high places, scanning the city with heavy binoculars. What were they seeking so earnestly? Who were they – so composed and steely-eyed? Timidly we stopped a policeman to ask him. 'They are publishers' he said mildly. Publishers! Our hearts stopped beating. 'They are on the look out for new talent.' Great God! It was for *us* they were waiting and watching! Then the kindly policeman lowered his voice confidentially and said in hollow and reverent tones: *'They are waiting for the new Trollope to be born!'* Do you remember, at these words, how heavy our suitcases suddenly felt? How our blood slowed, our footsteps lagged? Brother Ass, we had been bashfully thinking of a kind of illumination such as Rimbaud dreamed of – a nagging poem which was not didactic or expository but which *infected* – was not simply a rationalised intuition, I

11 on 13pt

WALKING ALONG THE MALL WE WONDERED WHO ALL THOSE MEN WERE – TALL hawk-featured men perched on balconies and high places, scanning the city with heavy binoculars. What were they seeking so earnestly? Who were they – so composed and steely-eyed? Timidly we stopped a policeman to ask him. 'They are publishers' he said mildly. Publishers! Our hearts stopped beating. 'They are on the look out for new talent.' Great God! It was for *us* they were waiting and watching! Then the kindly policeman lowered his voice confidentially and said in hollow and reverent tones: *'They are waiting for the new Trollope to be born!'* Do you remember, at these words, how heavy our suitcases suddenly felt? How our blood slowed, our footsteps lagged? Brother Ass, we had been bashfully thinking of a kind of illumination such as Rimbaud dreamed of – a nagging poem which was not didactic or expository but which *infected* – was not simply a rationalised intuition, I mean, clothed in isinglass! We had come to the wrong shop, with the wrong change! A chill struck us as we saw the mist falling in Trafalgar Square, coiling around us its tendrils of ectoplasm! A million muffin-eating moralists were waiting, not for us, Brother Ass, but for the plucky and tedious Trollope! (If you are dissatisfied with your form, reach for the

9 on 12pt

WALKING ALONG THE MALL WE WONDERED WHO ALL THOSE MEN WERE – tall hawk-featured men perched on balconies and high places, scanning the city with heavy binoculars. What were they seeking so earnestly? Who were they – so composed and steely-eyed? Timidly we stopped a policeman to ask him. 'They are publishers' he said mildly. Publishers! Our hearts stopped beating. 'They are on the look out for new talent.' Great God! It was for *us* they were waiting and watching! Then the kindly policeman lowered his voice confidentially and said in hollow and reverent tones: *'They are waiting for the new Trollope to be born!'* Do you remember, at these words, how heavy our suitcases suddenly felt? How our blood slowed, our footsteps lagged? Brother Ass, we had been bashfully thinking of a kind of illumination such as Rimbaud dreamed of – a nagging poem which was not didactic or expository but which *infected* – was not simply a rationalised intuition, I mean, clothed in isinglass! We had come to the wrong shop, with the wrong change! A chill struck us as

10 on 13.5pt

WALKING ALONG THE MALL WE WONDERED WHO ALL THOSE men were – tall hawk-featured men perched on balconies and high places, scanning the city with heavy binoculars. What were they seeking so earnestly? Who were they – so composed and steely-eyed? Timidly we stopped a policeman to ask him. 'They are publishers' he said mildly. Publishers! Our hearts stopped beating. 'They are on the look out for new talent.' Great God! It was for *us* they were waiting and watching! Then the kindly policeman lowered his voice confidentially and said in hollow and reverent tones: *'They are waiting for the new Trollope to be born!'* Do you remember, at these words, how heavy our suitcases suddenly felt? How our blood slowed, our footsteps lagged? Brother Ass, we had been bashfully thinking of a kind of illumination such as Rimbaud dreamed of – a nagging poem which was not didactic or

11 on 14.5pt

Linotype **Times**

roman (05249), **italic** (13249)
bold (07249)
Designed by Stanley Morison and Victor
Lardent 1932 for Monotype and *The Times*
Copyfitting code 127/126/127

Range also includes semi-bold, semi-bold
italic, bold italic, extra bold, black, black
outline

Educational characters available

ABCDEFGHIJKLMNOP
QRSTUVWXYZ abcdefg
hijklmnopqrstuvwxyz
1234567890 1234567890
fifl ()[]&£$.,;:-!?''

ABCDEFGHIJKLMNOP
QRSTUVWXYZ abcdefg
hijklmnopqrstuvwxyz
1234567890 1234567890
fifl ()[]&£$.,;:-!?''

ABCDEFGHIJKLMNOP
QRSTUVWXYZ abcdefg
hijklmnopqrstuvwxyz
1234567890
fifl ()[]&£$.,;:-!?''

24 on 27pt

These examples show *normal* letterspacing and the effect of *reduced* letterspacing on roman setting *as well as on words in italic*: they also show the appearance of figures, for example 28 May 1964, within text. These & the ampersand are not included in the setting opposite.
Normal letterspacing

These examples show *normal* letterspacing and the effect of *reduced* letterspacing on roman setting *as well as on words in italic*: they also show the appearance of figures, for example 28 May 1964, within text. These & the ampersand are not included in the setting opposite.
Minus one unit spacing

These examples show *normal* letterspacing and the effect of *reduced* letterspacing on roman setting *as well as on words in italic*: they also show the appearance of figures, for example 28 May 1964, within text. These & the ampersand are not included in the setting opposite.
Minus two units spacing

WALKING ALONG THE MALL WE WONDERED WHO ALL
WALKING ALONG THE MALL WE WONDERED WHO
WALKING ALONG THE MALL WE WONDERED
Capitals: normal letterspacing/plus 4 units/plus 9 units

WALKING ALONG THE MALL WE WONDERED WHO ALL THOSE MEN WERE
WALKING ALONG THE MALL WE WONDERED WHO ALL THOSE MEN
WALKING ALONG THE MALL WE WONDERED WHO ALL THOSE
Small caps: normal letterspacing/plus 3 units/plus 6 units

WALKING ALONG THE MALL WE WONDERED WHO ALL THOSE MEN WERE
WALKING ALONG THE MALL WE WONDERED WHO ALL THOSE MEN WERE
True small caps/reduced capitals

WALKING ALONG THE MALL we wondered who all those men
WALKING ALONG THE MALL we wondered who all those men
True italic/sloped roman

Walking along the Mall we wondered who all those men were – tall hawk-featured men perched on balconies and high places, scanning the city with heavy binoculars. What were they seeking so earnestly? Who were they – so composed and steely-eyed? Timidly we stopped a policeman to ask him. 'They are publishers' he said mildly. Publishers! Our hearts stopped beating. 'They are on the look out for new talent.' Great God! It was for *us* they were waiting and watching! Then the kindly policeman lowered his voice confidentially and said in hollow and reverent tones: *'They are waiting for the new Trollope to be born!'* Do you remember, at these words, how heavy our suitcases suddenly felt? How our blood slowed, our footsteps lagged? Brother Ass, we had been bashfully thinking of a kind of illumination such as Rimbaud dreamed of –
8 on 9pt

WALKING ALONG THE MALL WE WONDERED WHO ALL THOSE MEN WERE – TALL HAWK-featured men perched on balconies and high places, scanning the city with heavy binoculars. What were they seeking so earnestly? Who were they – so composed and steely-eyed? Timidly we stopped a policeman to ask him. 'They are publishers' he said mildly. Publishers! Our hearts stopped beating. 'They are on the look out for new talent.' Great God! It was for *us* they were waiting and watching! Then the kindly policeman lowered his voice confidentially and said in hollow and reverent tones: *'They are waiting for the new Trollope to be born!'* Do you remember, at these words, how heavy our suitcases suddenly felt? How our blood slowed, our footsteps lagged?
8 on 10.5pt

Walking along the Mall we wondered who all those men were – tall hawk-featured men perched on balconies and high places, scanning the city with heavy binoculars. What were they seeking so earnestly? Who were they – so composed and steely-eyed? Timidly we stopped a policeman to ask him. 'They are publishers' he said mildly. Publishers! Our hearts stopped beating. 'They are on the look out for new talent.' Great God! It was for *us* they were waiting and watching! Then the kindly policeman lowered his voice confidentially and said in hollow and reverent tones: *'They are waiting for the new Trollope to be born!'* Do you remember, at these words, how heavy our suitcases suddenly felt? How our blood slowed, our footsteps lagged? Brother Ass, we had been bashfully thinking of a kind of illumination such as Rimbaud dreamed of – a nagging poem which was not didactic or expository but which *infected* – was not simply a rationalised intuition, I mean, clothed in isinglass! We had come to the wrong shop, with the wrong change! A chill struck us as we saw the mist falling in Trafalgar Square, coiling round us its tendrils of ectoplasm! A million muffin-eating moralists were waiting, not for us, Brother Ass, but for the plucky and tedious Trollope! (If you are dissatisfied with your form, reach for the *curette*.) Now do you wonder if I laugh
9 on 11pt

Walking along the Mall we wondered who all those men were – tall hawk-featured men perched on balconies and high places, scanning the city with heavy binoculars. What were they seeking so earnestly? Who were they – so composed and steely-eyed? Timidly we stopped a policeman to ask him. 'They are publishers' he said mildly. Publishers! Our hearts stopped beating. 'They are on the look out for new talent.' Great God! It was for *us* they were waiting and watching! Then the kindly policeman lowered his voice confidentially and said in hollow and reverent tones: *'They are waiting for the new Trollope to be born!'* Do you remember, at these words, how heavy our suitcases suddenly felt? How our blood slowed, our footsteps lagged? Brother Ass, we had been bashfully thinking of a kind of illumination such as Rimbaud dreamed of – a nagging poem which was not didactic or expository but which *infected* – was not simply a rationalised intuition, I mean, clothed in isinglass! We had come to the wrong shop, with the wrong change! A chill struck us as we saw the mist falling in Trafalgar
10 on 12pt

Walking along the Mall we wondered who all those men were – tall hawk-featured men perched on balconies and high places, scanning the city with heavy binoculars. What were they seeking so earnestly? Who were they – so composed and steely-eyed? Timidly we stopped a policeman to ask him. 'They are publishers' he said mildly. Publishers! Our hearts stopped beating. 'They are on the look out for new talent.' Great God! It was for *us* they were waiting and watching! Then the kindly policeman lowered his voice confidentially and said in hollow and reverent tones: *'They are waiting for the new Trollope to be born!'* Do you remember, at these words, how heavy our suitcases suddenly felt? How our blood slowed, our footsteps lagged? Brother Ass, we had been bashfully thinking of a kind of illumination such as Rimbaud dreamed of – a nagging poem which was not didactic or expository but which *infected* – was
11 on 13pt

WALKING ALONG THE MALL WE WONDERED WHO ALL THOSE MEN WERE – TALL hawk-featured men perched on balconies and high places, scanning the city with heavy binoculars. What were they seeking so earnestly? Who were they – so composed and steely-eyed? Timidly we stopped a policeman to ask him. 'They are publishers' he said mildly. Publishers! Our hearts stopped beating. 'They are on the look out for new talent.' Great God! It was for *us* they were waiting and watching! Then the kindly policeman lowered his voice confidentially and said in hollow and reverent tones: *'They are waiting for the new Trollope to be born!'* Do you remember, at these words, how heavy our suitcases suddenly felt? How our blood slowed, our footsteps lagged? Brother Ass, we had been bashfully thinking of a kind of illumination such as Rimbaud dreamed of – a nagging poem which was not didactic or expository but which *infected* – was not simply a rationalised intuition, I mean, clothed in isinglass! We had come to the wrong shop, with the wrong change! A chill struck us as we saw the mist falling in Trafalgar Square, coiling round us its tendrils of ectoplasm! A million muffin-eating moralists were waiting, not for us, Brother Ass, but for the plucky and tedious Trollope! (If you are dissatisfied with
9 on 12pt

WALKING ALONG THE MALL WE WONDERED WHO ALL THOSE MEN WERE – tall hawk-featured men perched on balconies and high places, scanning the city with heavy binoculars. What were they seeking so earnestly? Who were they – so composed and steely-eyed? Timidly we stopped a policeman to ask him. 'They are publishers' he said mildly. Publishers! Our hearts stopped beating. 'They are on the look out for new talent.' Great God! It was for *us* they were waiting and watching! Then the kindly policeman lowered his voice confidentially and said in hollow and reverent tones: *'They are waiting for the new Trollope to be born!'* Do you remember, at these words, how heavy our suitcases suddenly felt? How our blood slowed, our footsteps lagged? Brother Ass, we had been bashfully thinking of a kind of illumination such as Rimbaud dreamed of – a nagging poem which was not didactic or expository but which *infected* – was not simply a rationalised intuition, I mean, clothed in isinglass! We had come to the wrong
10 on 13.5pt

WALKING ALONG THE MALL WE WONDERED WHO ALL THOSE MEN were – tall hawk-featured men perched on balconies and high places, scanning the city with heavy binoculars. What were they seeking so earnestly? Who were they – so composed and steely-eyed? Timidly we stopped a policeman to ask him. 'They are publishers' he said mildly. Publishers! Our hearts stopped beating. 'They are on the look out for new talent.' Great God! It was for *us* they were waiting and watching! Then the kindly policeman lowered his voice confidentially and said in hollow and reverent tones: *'They are waiting for the new Trollope to be born!'* Do you remember, at these words, how heavy our suitcases suddenly felt? How our blood slowed, our footsteps lagged? Brother Ass, we had been bashfully thinking of a kind of illumination such as Rimbaud dreamed of – a nagging poem
11 on 14.5pt

LINOTYPE TIMES

1147 roman and italic
1148 bold
Weber 1956 (Georg Trump)
Copyfitting factor 43.1/43.1/44.0

ABCDEFGHIJKLMNOP
QRSTUVWXYZ abcdefg
hijklmnopqrstuvwxyz
1234567890
ff fi fl ffi ffl (|)[]&£$.,;:-!?''

ABCDEFGHIJKLMNOP
QRSTUVWXYZ abcdefg
hijklmnopqrstuvwxyz
1234567890
ff fi fl ffi ffl (|)[]&£$.,;:-!?''

ABCDEFGHIJKLMNOP
QRSTUVWXYZ abcdefg
hijklmnopqrstuvwxyz
1234567890
ff fi fl ffi ffl (|)[]&£$.,;:-!?''

24 on 27pt

These examples show *normal* letterspacing and the effect of *reduced* letterspacing on roman setting *as well as on words in italic*: they also show the appearance of figures, for example 28 May 1964, within text. These & the ampersand are not included in the setting opposite.

Normal letterspacing

These examples show *normal* letterspacing and the effect of *reduced* letterspacing on roman setting *as well as on words in italic*: they also show the appearance of figures, for example 28 May 1964, within text. These & the ampersand are not included in the setting opposite.

Minus one unit spacing

These examples show *normal* letterspacing and the effect of *reduced* letterspacing on roman setting *as well as on words in italic*: they also show the appearance of figures, for example 28 May 1964, within text. These & the ampersand are not included in the setting opposite.

Minus two units spacing

WALKING ALONG THE MALL WE WONDERED WHO ALL THOSE
WALKING ALONG THE MALL WE WONDERED WHO ALL
WALKING ALONG THE MALL WE WONDERED WHO

Capitals: normal letterspacing/plus 9 units/plus 18 units

WALKING ALONG THE MALL WE WONDERED WHO ALL THOSE MEN WERE
WALKING ALONG THE MALL WE WONDERED WHO ALL THOSE MEN WERE
WALKING ALONG THE MALL WE WONDERED WHO ALL THOSE MEN

Small caps: normal letterspacing/plus 6 units/plus 12 units

WALKING ALONG THE MALL we wondered who all those men were
WALKING ALONG THE MALL we wondered who all those men were

True italic/sloped roman

WALKING ALONG THE MALL WE WONDERED WHO ALL THOSE MEN WERE
WALKING ALONG THE MALL WE WONDERED WHO ALL THOSE MEN WERE

True small caps/reduced capitals

Walking along the Mall we wondered who all those men were – tall hawk-featured men perched on balconies and high places, scanning the city with heavy binoculars. What were they seeking so earnestly? Who were they – so composed and steely-eyed? Timidly we stopped a policeman to ask him. 'They are publishers' he said mildly. Publishers! Our hearts stopped beating. 'They are on the look out for new talent.' Great God! It was for *us* they were waiting and watching! Then the kindly policeman lowered his voice confidentially and said in hollow and reverent tones: *'They are waiting for the new Trollope to be born!'* Do you remember, at these words, how heavy our suitcases suddenly felt? How our blood slowed, our footsteps lagged? Brother Ass, we had been bashfully thinking of a kind of illumination such as Rimbaud dreamed of – a nagging

8 on 9pt

WALKING ALONG THE MALL WE WONDERED WHO ALL THOSE MEN WERE – TALL HAWK- featured men perched on balconies and high places, scanning the city with heavy binoculars. What were they seeking so earnestly? Who were they – so composed and steely-eyed? Timidly we stopped a policeman to ask him. 'They are publishers' he said mildly. Publishers! Our hearts stopped beating. 'They are on the look out for new talent.' Great God! It was for *us* they were waiting and watching! Then the kindly policeman lowered his voice confidentially and said in hollow and reverent tones: *'They are waiting for the new Trollope to be born!'* Do you remember, at these words, how heavy our suitcases suddenly felt? How our blood slowed, our footsteps lagged? Brother

8 on 10.5pt

Walking along the Mall we wondered who all those men were – tall hawk-featured men perched on balconies and high places, scanning the city with heavy binoculars. What were they seeking so earnestly? Who were they – so composed and steely-eyed? Timidly we stopped a policeman to ask him. 'They are publishers' he said mildly. Publishers! Our hearts stopped beating. 'They are on the look out for new talent.' Great God! It was for *us* they were waiting and watching! Then the kindly policeman lowered his voice confidentially and said in hollow and reverent tones: *'They are waiting for the new Trollope to be born!'* Do you remember, at these words, how heavy our suitcases suddenly felt? How our blood slowed, our footsteps lagged? Brother Ass, we had been bashfully thinking of a kind of illumination such as Rimbaud dreamed of – a nagging poem which was not didactic or expository but which *infected* – was not simply a rationalised intuition, I mean, clothed in isinglass! We had come to the wrong shop, with the wrong change! A chill struck us as we saw the mist falling in Trafalgar Square, coiling around us its tendrils of ectoplasm! A million muffin-eating moralists were waiting, not for us, Brother Ass, but for the plucky and tedious Trollope! (If you are dissatisfied with your form, reach for the *curette*.) Now do you wonder if I laugh a little off-key? Do you ask yourself what

9 on 11pt

Walking along the Mall we wondered who all those men were – tall hawk-featured men perched on balconies and high places, scanning the city with heavy binoculars. What were they seeking so earnestly? Who were they – so composed and steely-eyed? Timidly we stopped a police-man to ask him. 'They are publishers' he said mildly. Publishers! Our hearts stopped beating. 'They are on the look out for new talent.' Great God! It was for *us* they were waiting and watching! Then the kindly policeman lowered his voice confidentially and said in hollow and reverent tones: *'They are waiting for the new Trollope to be born!'* Do you remember, at these words, how heavy our suitcases suddenly felt? How our blood slowed, our footsteps lagged? Brother Ass, we had been bash-fully thinking of a kind of illumination such as Rimbaud dreamed of – a nagging poem which was not didactic or expository but which *infected* – was not simply a rationalised intuition, I mean, clothed in isinglass! We had come to the wrong shop, with the wrong change! A chill struck us as we saw the mist falling in Trafalgar Square, coiling around us its tendrils

10 on 12pt

Walking along the Mall we wondered who all those men were – tall hawk-featured men perched on balconies and high places, scanning the city with heavy binoculars. What were they seeking so earnestly? Who were they – so composed and steely-eyed? Timidly we stopped a policeman to ask him. 'They are pub-lishers' he said mildly. Publishers! Our hearts stopped beating. 'They are on the look out for new talent.' Great God! It was for *us* they were waiting and watching! Then the kindly policeman low-ered his voice confidentially and said in hollow and reverent tones: *'They are waiting for the new Trollope to be born!'* Do you remember, at these words, how heavy our suitcases suddenly felt? How our blood slowed, our footsteps lagged? Brother Ass, we had been bashfully thinking of a kind of illumination such as Rim-baud dreamed of – a nagging poem which was not didactic or expository but which *infected* – was not simply a rationalised

11 on 13pt

WALKING ALONG THE MALL WE WONDERED WHO ALL THOSE MEN WERE – TALL hawk-featured men perched on balconies and high places, scanning the city with heavy binoculars. What were they seeking so earnestly? Who were they – so composed and steely-eyed? Timidly we stopped a policeman to ask him. 'They are publishers' he said mildly. Publishers! Our hearts stopped beating. 'They are on the look out for new talent.' Great God! It was for *us* they were waiting and watching! Then the kindly policeman lowered his voice confidentially and said in hollow and reverent tones: *'They are waiting for the new Trollope to be born!'* Do you remember, at these words, how heavy our suitcases suddenly felt? How our blood slowed, our footsteps lagged? Brother Ass, we had been bashfully thinking of a kind of illumination such as Rimbaud dreamed of – a nagging poem which was not didactic or expository but which *infected* – was not simply a rationalised intuition, I mean, clothed in isinglass! We had come to the wrong shop, with the wrong change! A chill struck us as we saw the mist falling in Trafalgar Square, coiling around us its tendrils of ectoplasm! A million muffin-eating moralists were waiting, not for us, Brother Ass, but for the plucky and tedious Trollope! (If you are dissatisfied with your form, reach for the

9 on 12pt

WALKING ALONG THE MALL WE WONDERED WHO ALL THOSE MEN WERE – tall hawk-featured men perched on balconies and high places, scanning the city with heavy binoculars. What were they seeking so earnestly? Who were they – so composed and steely-eyed? Timidly we stopped a policeman to ask him. 'They are publishers' he said mildly. Publishers! Our hearts stopped beating. 'They are on the look out for new talent.' Great God! It was for *us* they were waiting and watching! Then the kindly policeman lowered his voice confidentially and said in hollow and reverent tones: *'They are waiting for the new Trollope to be born!'* Do you remember, at these words, how heavy our suitcases suddenly felt? How our blood slowed, our footsteps lagged? Brother Ass, we had been bashfully thinking of a kind of illumination such as Rimbaud dreamed of – a nagging poem which was not didactic or expository but which *infected* – was not simply a rationalised intuition, I mean, clo-thed in isinglass! We had come to the wrong shop, with the wrong

10 on 13.5pt

WALKING ALONG THE MALL WE WONDERED WHO ALL THOSE MEN were – tall hawk-featured men perched on balconies and high places, scanning the city with heavy binoculars. What were they seeking so earnestly? Who were they – so composed and steely-eyed? Timidly we stopped a policeman to ask him. 'They are publishers' he said mildly. Publishers! Our hearts stopped beat-ing. 'They are on the look out for new talent.' Great God! It was for *us* they were waiting and watching! Then the kindly police-man lowered his voice confidentially and said in hollow and rev-erent tones: *'They are waiting for the new Trollope to be born!'* Do you remember, at these words, how heavy our suitcases sud-denly felt? How our blood slowed, our footsteps lagged? Brother Ass, we had been bashfully thinking of a kind of illumination such as Rimbaud dreamed of – a nagging poem which was not

11 on 14.5pt

MONOTYPE TRUMP MEDIEVAL

Linotype **Trump Medieval**

roman (05257), **italic** (13257)
bold (07257)
Weber 1956 (Georg Trump)
Copyfitting code 136/139/137

Range also includes bold italic, black

ABCDEFGHIJKLMNOP
QRSTUVWXYZ abcdefg
hijklmnopqrstuvwxyz
1234567890 1234567890
fifl (|)[]&£$.,;:-!?"

ABCDEFGHIJKLMNOP
QRSTUVWXYZ abcdefg
hijklmnopqrstuvwxyz
1234567890 1234567890
fifl (|)[]&£$.,;:-!?"

ABCDEFGHIJKLMNOP
QRSTUVWXYZ abcdefg
hijklmnopqrstuvwxyz
1234567890 1234567890
fifl (|)[]&£$.,;:-!?"

24 on 27pt

These examples show *normal* letterspacing and the effect of *reduced* letterspacing on roman setting *as well as on words in italic*: they also show the appearance of figures, for example 28 May 1964, within text. These & the ampersand are not included in the setting opposite.
Normal letterspacing

These examples show *normal* letterspacing and the effect of *reduced* letterspacing on roman setting *as well as on words in italic*: they also show the appearance of figures, for example 28 May 1964, within text. These & the ampersand are not included in the setting opposite.
Minus one unit spacing

These examples show *normal* letterspacing and the effect of *reduced* letterspacing on roman setting *as well as on words in italic*: they also show the appearance of figures, for example 28 May 1964, within text. These & the ampersand are not included in the setting opposite.
Minus two units spacing

WALKING ALONG THE MALL WE WONDERED WHO ALL THOSE
WALKING ALONG THE MALL WE WONDERED WHO ALL
WALKING ALONG THE MALL WE WONDERED WHO
Capitals: normal letterspacing/plus 4 units/plus 9 units

WALKING ALONG THE MALL WE WONDERED WHO ALL THOSE MEN WERE
WALKING ALONG THE MALL WE WONDERED WHO ALL THOSE MEN
WALKING ALONG THE MALL WE WONDERED WHO ALL THOSE
Small caps: normal letterspacing/plus 3 units/plus 6 units

WALKING ALONG THE MALL WE WONDERED WHO ALL THOSE MEN WERE
WALKING ALONG THE MALL WE WONDERED WHO ALL THOSE MEN WERE
True small caps/reduced capitals

WALKING ALONG THE MALL we wondered who all those men were
WALKING ALONG THE MALL we wondered who all those men were
True italic/sloped roman

Walking along the Mall we wondered who all those men were – tall hawk- featured men perched on balconies and high places, scanning the city with heavy binoculars. What were they seeking so earnestly? Who were they – so composed and steely-eyed? Timidly we stopped a policeman to ask him. 'They are publishers' he said mildly. Publishers! Our hearts stopped beating. 'They are on the look out for new talent.' Great God! It was for *us* they were waiting and watching! Then the kindly policeman lowered his voice confidentially and said in hollow and reverent tones: *'They are waiting for the new Trollope to be born!'* Do you remember, at these words, how heavy our suitcases suddenly felt? How our blood slowed, our footsteps lagged? Brother Ass, we had been bashfully thinking of
8 on 9pt

WALKING ALONG THE MALL WE WONDERED WHO ALL THOSE MEN WERE – TALL hawk-featured men perched on balconies and high places, scanning the city with heavy binoculars. What were they seeking so earnestly? Who were they – so composed and steely-eyed? Timidly we stopped a policeman to ask him. 'They are publishers' he said mildly. Publishers! Our hearts stopped beating. 'They are on the look out for new talent.' Great God! It was for *us* they were waiting and watching! Then the kindly policeman lowered his voice confidentially and said in hollow and reverent tones: *'They are waiting for the new Trollope to be born!'* Do you remember, at these words, how heavy our suitcases suddenly felt? How our
8 on 10.5pt

Walking along the Mall we wondered who all those men were – tall hawk-featured men perched on balconies and high places, scanning the city with heavy binoculars. What were they seeking so earnestly? Who were they – so composed and steely-eyed? Timidly we stopped a policeman to ask him. 'They are publishers' he said mildly. Publishers! Our hearts stopped beating. 'They are on the look out for new talent.' Great God! It was for *us* they were waiting and watching! Then the kindly policeman lowered his voice confidentially and said in hollow and reverent tones: *'They are waiting for the new Trollope to be born!'* Do you remember, at these words, how heavy our suitcases suddenly felt? How our blood slowed, our footsteps lagged? Brother Ass, we had been bashfully thinking of a kind of illumination such as Rimbaud dreamed of – a nagging poem which was not didactic or expository but which *infected* – was not simply a rationalised intuition, I mean, clothed in isinglass! We had come to the wrong shop, with the wrong change! A chill struck us as we saw the mist falling in Trafalgar Square, coiling round us its tendrils of ectoplasm! A million muffin-eating moralists were waiting, not for us, Brother Ass, but for the plucky and tedious Trollope! (If you are dis-

9 on 11pt

Walking along the Mall we wondered who all those men were – tall hawk-featured men perched on balconies and high places, scanning the city with heavy binoculars. What were they seeking so earnestly? Who were they – so composed and steely-eyed? Timidly we stopped a policeman to ask him. 'They are publishers' he said mildly. Publishers! Our hearts stopped beating. 'They are on the look out for new talent.' Great God! It was for *us* they were waiting and watching! Then the kindly policeman lowered his voice confidentially and said in hollow and reverent tones: *'They are waiting for the new Trollope to be born!'* Do you remember, at these words, how heavy our suitcases suddenly felt? How our blood slowed, our footsteps lagged? Brother Ass, we had been bashfully thinking of a kind of illumination such as Rimbaud dreamed of – a nagging poem which was not didactic or expository but which *infected* – was not simply a rationalised intuition, I mean, clothed in isinglass! We had come to the wrong shop,

10 on 12pt

Walking along the Mall we wondered who all those men were – tall hawk-featured men perched on balconies and high places, scanning the city with heavy binoculars. What were they seeking so earnestly? Who were they – so composed and steely-eyed? Timidly we stopped a policeman to ask him. 'They are publishers' he said mildly. Publishers! Our hearts stopped beating. 'They are on the look out for new talent.' Great God! It was for *us* they were waiting and watching! Then the kindly policeman lowered his voice confidentially and said in hollow and reverent tones: *'They are waiting for the new Trollope to be born!'* Do you remember, at these words, how heavy our suitcases suddenly felt? How our blood slowed, our footsteps lagged? Brother Ass, we had been bashfully thinking of a kind of illumination such as Rimbaud dreamed of – a nagging poem which

11 on 13pt

WALKING ALONG THE MALL WE WONDERED WHO ALL THOSE MEN WERE – tall hawk-featured men perched on balconies and high places, scanning the city with heavy binoculars. What were they seeking so earnestly? Who were they – so composed and steely-eyed? Timidly we stopped a policeman to ask him. 'They are publishers' he said mildly. Publishers! Our hearts stopped beating. 'They are on the look out for new talent.' Great God! It was for *us* they were waiting and watching! Then the kindly policeman lowered his voice confidentially and said in hollow and reverent tones: *'They are waiting for the new Trollope to be born!'* Do you remember, at these words, how heavy our suitcases suddenly felt? How our blood slowed, our footsteps lagged? Brother Ass, we had been bashfully thinking of a kind of illumination such as Rimbaud dreamed of – a nagging poem which was not didactic or expository but which *infected* – was not simply a rationalised intuition, I mean, clothed in isinglass! We had come to the wrong shop, with the wrong change! A chill struck us as we saw the mist falling in Trafalgar Square, coiling round us its tendrils of ectoplasm! A million muffin-eating moralists were waiting, not for us,

9 on 12pt

WALKING ALONG THE MALL WE WONDERED WHO ALL THOSE MEN were – tall hawk-featured men perched on balconies and high places, scanning the city with heavy binoculars. What were they seeking so earnestly? Who were they – so composed and steely-eyed? Timidly we stopped a policeman to ask him. 'They are publishers' he said mildly. Publishers! Our hearts stopped beating. 'They are on the look out for new talent.' Great God! It was for *us* they were waiting and watching! Then the kindly policeman lowered his voice confidentially and said in hollow and reverent tones: *'They are waiting for the new Trollope to be born!'* Do you remember, at these words, how heavy our suitcases suddenly felt? How our blood slowed, our footsteps lagged? Brother Ass, we had been bashfully thinking of a kind of illumination such as Rimbaud dreamed of – a nagging poem which was not didactic or expository but which *infected* – was not simply a rationalised

10 on 13.5pt

WALKING ALONG THE MALL WE WONDERED WHO ALL THOSE men were – tall hawk-featured men perched on balconies and high places, scanning the city with heavy binoculars. What were they seeking so earnestly? Who were they – so composed and steely-eyed? Timidly we stopped a policeman to ask him. 'They are publishers' he said mildly. Publishers! Our hearts stopped beating. 'They are on the look out for new talent.' Great God! It was for *us* they were waiting and watching! Then the kindly policeman lowered his voice confidentially and said in hollow and reverent tones: *'They are waiting for the new Trollope to be born!'* Do you remember, at these words, how heavy our suitcases suddenly felt? How our blood slowed, our footsteps lagged? Brother Ass, we had been bashfully thinking of a kind of

11 on 14.5pt

LINOTYPE TRUMP MEDIEVAL

Monotype **Univers**

689 medium and italic
696 extra bold
Deberney & Peignot and Monotype 1957
(Adrian Frutiger)
Copyfitting factor 44.7/44.7/51.3

There is an extensive range of weights and
variations

Originally designed to be suitable for
founder's type, hot metal and filmsetting. It is
not entirely monoline, and has a slight vertical
stress – characteristics which help to make it
particularly useful as a text face

Educational characters available

ABCDEFGHIJKLMNOP
QRSTUVWXYZ abcdefg
hijklmnopqrstuvwxyz
1234567890
()[]&£$.,;:-!?''

ABCDEFGHIJKLMNOP
QRSTUVWXYZ abcdefg
hijklmnopqrstuvwxyz
1234567890
()[]&£$.,;:-!?''

ABCDEFGHIJKLMNOP
QRSTUVWXYZ abcdefg
hijklmnopqrstuvwxyz
1234567890
()[]&£$.,;:-!?''

24 on 27pt

These examples show *normal* letterspacing and the effect of *reduced*
letterspacing on roman setting *as well as on words in italic:* they also
show the appearance of figures, for example 28 May 1964, within text.
These & the ampersand are not included in the setting opposite.

Normal letterspacing

These examples show *normal* letterspacing and the effect of *reduced*
letterspacing on roman setting *as well as on words in italic:* they also
show the appearance of figures, for example 28 May 1964, within
text. These & the ampersand are not included in the setting opposite.

Minus one unit spacing

These examples show *normal* letterspacing and the effect of *reduced*
letterspacing on roman setting *as well as on words in italic:* they also
show the appearance of figures, for example 28 May 1964, within
text. These & the ampersand are not included in the setting opposite.

Minus two units spacing

WALKING ALONG THE MALL WE WONDERED WHO ALL THOSE
WALKING ALONG THE MALL WE WONDERED WHO ALL
WALKING ALONG THE MALL WE WONDERED WHO

Capitals: normal letterspacing/plus 9 units/plus 18 units

Walking along the Mall we wondered who all those men were –
tall hawk-featured men perched on balconies and high places,
scanning the city with heavy binoculars. WHAT WERE THEY SEEKING
SO EARNESTLY? Who were they – so composed and steely-eyed?
Timidly we stopped a policeman to ask him. 'They are publishers'
he said mildly. Publishers! OUR HEARTS STOPPED BEATING. 'They
are on the look out for new talent.' Great God! It was for *us* they

Text with reduced capitals normal letterspacing/plus 6 units

WALKING ALONG THE MALL we wondered who all those men were
WALKING ALONG THE MALL we wondered who all those men were

True italic/sloped roman

Walking along the Mall we wondered who all those men were – tall
hawk-featured men perched on balconies and high places, scanning the city with
heavy binoculars. What were they seeking so earnestly? Who were they – so
composed and steely-eyed? Timidly we stopped a policeman to ask him. 'They are
publishers' he said mildly. Publishers! Our hearts stopped beating. 'They are on the
look out for new talent.' Great God! It was for *us* they were waiting and watching!
Then the kindly policeman lowered his voice confidentially and said in hollow
and reverent tones: *'They are waiting for the new Trollope to be born!'* Do you
remember, at these words, how heavy our suitcases suddenly felt? How our blood
slowed, our footsteps lagged? Brother Ass, we had been bashfully thinking of a kind

8 on 9pt

Walking along the Mall we wondered who all those men were – tall hawk-featured
men perched on balconies and high places, scanning the city with heavy binoculars.
What were they seeking so earnestly? Who were they – so composed and steely-
eyed? Timidly we stopped a policeman to ask him. 'They are publishers' he said
mildly. Publishers! Our hearts stopped beating. 'They are on the look out for new
talent.' Great God! It was for *us* they were waiting and watching! Then the kindly
policeman lowered his voice confidentially and said in hollow and reverent tones:
'They are waiting for the new Trollope to be born!' Do you remember, at these
words, how heavy our suitcases suddenly felt? How our blood slowed, our footsteps

8 on 10.5pt

Walking along the Mall we wondered who all those men were – tall hawk-featured men perched on balconies and high places, scanning the city with heavy binoculars. What were they seeking so earnestly? Who were they – so composed and steely-eyed? Timidly we stopped a policeman to ask him. 'They are publishers' he said mildly. Publishers! Our hearts stopped beating. 'They are on the look out for new talent.' Great God! It was for *us* they were waiting and watching! Then the kindly policeman lowered his voice confidentially and said in hollow and reverent tones: *'They are waiting for the new Trollope to be born!'* Do you remember, at these words, how heavy our suitcases suddenly felt? How our blood slowed, our footsteps lagged? Brother Ass, we had been bashfully thinking of a kind of illumination such as Rimbaud dreamed of – a nagging poem which was not didactic or expository but which *infected* – was not simply a rationalised intuition, I mean, clothed in isinglass! We had come to the wrong shop, with the wrong change! A chill struck us as we saw the mist falling in Trafalgar Square, coiling around us its tendrils of ectoplasm! A million muffin-eating moralists were waiting, not for us, Brother Ass, but for the plucky and tedious Trollope! (If you are dissatisfied with your form, reach for the *curette*.) Now do you wonder if I laugh a

9 on 11pt

Walking along the Mall we wondered who all those men were – tall hawk-featured men perched on balconies and high places, scanning the city with heavy binoculars. What were they seeking so earnestly? Who were they – so composed and steely-eyed? Timidly we stopped a policeman to ask him. 'They are publishers' he said mildly. Publishers! Our hearts stopped beating. 'They are on the look out for new talent.' Great God! It was for *us* they were waiting and watching! Then the kindly policeman lowered his voice confidentially and said in hollow and reverent tones: *'They are waiting for the new Trollope to be born!'* Do you remember, at these words, how heavy our suitcases suddenly felt? How our blood slowed, our footsteps lagged? Brother Ass, we had been bashfully thinking of a kind of illumination such as Rimbaud dreamed of – a nagging poem which was not didactic or expository but which *infected* – was not simply a rationalised intuition, I mean, clothed in isinglass! We had come to the wrong shop, with the wrong change! A chill struck us as we saw

10 on 12pt

Walking along the Mall we wondered who all those men were – tall hawk-featured men perched on balconies and high places, scanning the city with heavy binoculars. What were they seeking so earnestly? Who were they – so composed and steely-eyed? Timidly we stopped a policeman to ask him. 'They are publishers' he said mildly. Publishers! Our hearts stopped beating. 'They are on the look out for new talent.' Great God! It was for *us* they were waiting and watching! Then the kindly policeman lowered his voice confidentially and said in hollow and reverent tones: *'They are waiting for the new Trollope to be born!'* Do you remember, at these words, how heavy our suitcases suddenly felt? How our blood slowed, our footsteps lagged? Brother Ass, we had been bashfully thinking of a kind of illumination such as Rimbaud dreamed of – a nagging poem which was not didactic or expository but which

11 on 13pt

Walking along the Mall we wondered who all those men were – tall hawk-featured men perched on balconies and high places, scanning the city with heavy binoculars. What were they seeking so earnestly? Who were they – so composed and steely-eyed? Timidly we stopped a policeman to ask him. 'They are publishers' he said mildly. Publishers! Our hearts stopped beating. 'They are on the look out for new talent.' Great God! It was for *us* they were waiting and watching! Then the kindly policeman lowered his voice confidentially and said in hollow and reverent tones: *'They are waiting for the new Trollope to be born!'* Do you remember, at these words, how heavy our suitcases suddenly felt? How our blood slowed, our footsteps lagged? Brother Ass, we had been bashfully thinking of a kind of illumination such as Rimbaud dreamed of – a nagging poem which was not didactic or expository but which *infected* – was not simply a rationalised intuition, I mean, clothed in isinglass! We had come to the wrong shop, with the wrong change! A chill struck us as we saw the mist falling in Trafalgar Square, coiling around us its tendrils of ectoplasm! A million muffin-eating moralists were waiting, not for us, Brother Ass, but for the plucky and tedious Trollope! (If you are dissa-

9 on 12pt

Walking along the Mall we wondered who all those men were – tall hawk-featured men perched on balconies and high places, scanning the city with heavy binoculars. What were they seeking so earnestly? Who were they – so composed and steely-eyed? Timidly we stopped a policeman to ask him. 'They are publishers' he said mildly. Publishers! Our hearts stopped beating. 'They are on the look out for new talent.' Great God! It was for *us* they were waiting and watching! Then the kindly policeman lowered his voice confidentially and said in hollow and reverent tones: *'They are waiting for the new Trollope to be born!'* Do you remember, at these words, how heavy our suitcases suddenly felt? How our blood slowed, our footsteps lagged? Brother Ass, we had been bashfully thinking of a kind of illumination such as Rimbaud dreamed of – a nagging poem which was not didactic or expository but which *infected* – was not simply a rationalised intuition, I mean, clothed in isinglass! We had come to the wrong

10 on 13.5pt

Walking along the Mall we wondered who all those men were – tall hawk-featured men perched on balconies and high places, scanning the city with heavy binoculars. What were they seeking so earnestly? Who were they – so composed and steely-eyed? Timidly we stopped a policeman to ask him. 'They are publishers' he said mildly. Publishers! Our hearts stopped beating. 'They are on the look out for new talent.' Great God! It was for *us* they were waiting and watching! Then the kindly policeman lowered his voice confidentially and said in hollow and reverent tones: *'They are waiting for the new Trollope to be born!'* Do you remember, at these words, how heavy our suitcases suddenly felt? How our blood slowed, our footsteps lagged? Brother Ass, we had been bashfully thinking of a kind of illumination such as Rimbaud dreamed of – a nagging poem

11 on 14.5pt

Linotype **Univers**

roman 55 (05258), **italic 56** (13258)
black 75 (09258)
Deberney & Peignot and Monotype 1957
(Adrian Frutiger)
Copyfitting code 138/138/157

There is an extensive range of weights and
variations

Educational characters available

See Monotype Univers

ABCDEFGHIJKLMNOP
QRSTUVWXYZ abcdefg
hijklmnopqrstuvwxyz
1234567890
fifl ()[]&£$.,;:-!?"

ABCDEFGHIJKLMNOP
QRSTUVWXYZ abcdefg
hijklmnopqrstuvwxyz
1234567890
fifl ()[]&£$.,;:-!?"

ABCDEFGHIJKLMNOP
QRSTUVWXYZ abcdefg
hijklmnopqrstuvwxyz
1234567890
fifl ()[]&£$.,;:-!?"

24 on 27pt

These examples show *normal* letterspacing and the effect of *reduced*
letterspacing on roman setting *as well as on words in italic*: they also
show the appearance of figures, for example 28 May 1964, within text.
These & the ampersand are not included in the setting opposite.
Normal letterspacing

These examples show *normal* letterspacing and the effect of *reduced*
letterspacing on roman setting *as well as on words in italic*: they also
show the appearance of figures, for example 28 May 1964, within text.
These & the ampersand are not included in the setting opposite.
Minus one unit spacing

These examples show *normal* letterspacing and the effect of *reduced*
letterspacing on roman setting *as well as on words in italic*: they also
show the appearance of figures, for example 28 May 1964, within text.
These & the ampersand are not included in the setting opposite.
Minus two units spacing

WALKING ALONG THE MALL WE WONDERED WHO ALL THOSE MEN
WALKING ALONG THE MALL WE WONDERED WHO ALL
WALKING ALONG THE MALL WE WONDERED WHO ALL
Capitals: normal letterspacing/plus 4 units/plus 9 units

Walking along the Mall we wondered who all those men were – tall
hawk-featured men perched on balconies and high places, scanning
the city with heavy binoculars. WHAT WERE THEY SEEKING SO EARNESTLY?
Who were they – so composed and steely-eyed? Timidly we stopped a
policeman to ask him. 'THEY ARE PUBLISHERS' he said mildly. Publishers!
Our hearts stopped beating. 'They are on the look out for new talent.'
Great God! It was for *us* they were waiting and watching! Then the
Text with reduced caps normal letterspacing/plus 3 units

WALKING ALONG THE MALL we wondered who all those men were
WALKING ALONG THE MALL we wondered who all those men were
True italic/sloped roman

Walking along the Mall we wondered who all those men were – tall
hawk-featured men perched on balconies and high places, scanning the city
with heavy binoculars. What were they seeking so earnestly? Who were they –
so composed and steely-eyed? Timidly we stopped a policeman to ask him.
'They are publishers' he said mildly. Publishers! Our hearts stopped beating.
'They are on the look out for new talent.' Great God! It was for *us* they
were waiting and watching! Then the kindly policeman lowered his voice
confidentially and said in hollow and reverent tones: *'They are waiting for the*
new Trollope to be born!' Do you remember, at these words, how heavy our
suitcases suddenly felt? How our blood slowed, our footsteps lagged? Brother
8 on 9pt

Walking along the Mall we wondered who all those men were – tall hawk-
featured men perched on balconies and high places, scanning the city with
heavy binoculars. What were they seeking so earnestly? Who were they – so
composed and steely-eyed? Timidly we stopped a policeman to ask him. 'They
are publishers' he said mildly. Publishers! Our hearts stopped beating. 'They are
on the look out for new talent.' Great God! It was for *us* they were waiting and
watching! Then the kindly policeman lowered his voice confidentially and said
in hollow and reverent tones: *'They are waiting for the new Trollope to be born!'*
Do you remember, at these words, how heavy our suitcases suddenly felt? How
8 on 10.5pt

Walking along the Mall we wondered who all those men were — tall hawk-featured men perched on balconies and high places, scanning the city with heavy binoculars. What were they seeking so earnestly? Who were they – so composed and steely-eyed? Timidly we stopped a policeman to ask him. 'They are publishers' he said mildly. Publishers! Our hearts stopped beating. 'They are on the look out for new talent.' Great God! It was for *us* they were waiting and watching! Then the kindly policeman lowered his voice confidentially and said in hollow and reverent tones: *'They are waiting for the new Trollope to be born!'* Do you remember, at these words, how heavy our suitcases suddenly felt? How our blood slowed, our footsteps lagged? Brother Ass, we had been bashfully thinking of a kind of illumination such as Rimbaud dreamed of – a nagging poem which was not didactic or expository but which *infected* – was not simply a rationalised intuition, I mean, clothed in isinglass! We had come to the wrong shop, with the wrong change! A chill struck us as we saw the mist falling in Trafalgar Square, coiling round us its tendrils of ectoplasm! A million muffin-eating moralists were waiting, not for us, Brother Ass, but for the plucky and tedious
9 on 11pt

Walking along the Mall we wondered who all those men were – tall hawk-featured men perched on balconies and high places, scanning the city with heavy binoculars. What were they seeking so earnestly? Who were they – so composed and steely-eyed? Timidly we stopped a policeman to ask him. 'They are publishers' he said mildly. Publishers! Our hearts stopped beating. 'They are on the look out for new talent.' Great God! It was for *us* they were waiting and watching! Then the kindly policeman lowered his voice confidentially and said in hollow and reverent tones: *'They are waiting for the new Trollope to be born!'* Do you remember, at these words, how heavy our suitcases suddenly felt? How our blood slowed, our footsteps lagged? Brother Ass, we had been bashfully thinking of a kind of illumination such as Rimbaud dreamed of – a nagging poem which was not didactic or expository but which *infected* – was not simply a rationalised intuition, I mean, clothed in isinglass!
10 on 12pt

Walking along the Mall we wondered who all those men were – tall hawk-featured men perched on balconies and high places, scanning the city with heavy binoculars. What were they seeking so earnestly? Who were they – so composed and steely-eyed? Timidly we stopped a policeman to ask him. 'They are publishers' he said mildly. Publishers! Our hearts stopped beating. 'They are on the look out for new talent.' Great God! It was for *us* they were waiting and watching! Then the kindly policeman lowered his voice confidentially and said in hollow and reverent tones: *'They are waiting for the new Trollope to be born!'* Do you remember, at these words, how heavy our suitcases suddenly felt? How our blood slowed, our footsteps lagged? Brother Ass, we had been bashfully thinking of a kind of illumination such as Rimbaud dreamed of – a
11 on 13pt

Walking along the Mall we wondered who all those men were – tall hawk-featured men perched on balconies and high places, scanning the city with heavy binoculars. What were they seeking so earnestly? Who were they – so composed and steely-eyed? Timidly we stopped a policeman to ask him. 'They are publishers' he said mildly. Publishers! Our hearts stopped beating. 'They are on the look out for new talent.' Great God! It was for *us* they were waiting and watching! Then the kindly policeman lowered his voice confidentially and said in hollow and reverent tones: *'They are waiting for the new Trollope to be born!'* Do you remember, at these words, how heavy our suitcases suddenly felt? How our blood slowed, our footsteps lagged? Brother Ass, we had been bashfully thinking of a kind of illumination such as Rimbaud dreamed of – a nagging poem which was not didactic or expository but which *infected* – was not simply a rationalised intuition, I mean, clothed in isinglass! We had come to the wrong shop, with the wrong change! A chill struck us as we saw the mist falling in Trafalgar Square, coiling round us its tendrils of ectoplasm! A million muffin-eating moralists
9 on 12pt

Walking along the Mall we wondered who all those men were – tall hawk-featured men perched on balconies and high places, scanning the city with heavy binoculars. What were they seeking so earnestly? Who were they – so composed and steely-eyed? Timidly we stopped a policeman to ask him. 'They are publishers' he said mildly. Publishers! Our hearts stopped beating. 'They are on the look out for new talent.' Great God! It was for *us* they were waiting and watching! Then the kindly policeman lowered his voice confidentially and said in hollow and reverent tones: *'They are waiting for the new Trollope to be born!'* Do you remember, at these words, how heavy our suitcases suddenly felt? How our blood slowed, our footsteps lagged? Brother Ass, we had been bashfully thinking of a kind of illumination such as Rimbaud dreamed of – a nagging poem which was not didactic or expository but which *infected* – was not simply a
10 on 13.5pt

Walking along the Mall we wondered who all those men were – tall hawk-featured men perched on balconies and high places, scanning the city with heavy binoculars. What were they seeking so earnestly? Who were they – so composed and steely-eyed? Timidly we stopped a policeman to ask him. 'They are publishers' he said mildly. Publishers! Our hearts stopped beating. 'They are on the look out for new talent.' Great God! It was for *us* they were waiting and watching! Then the kindly policeman lowered his voice confidentially and said in hollow and reverent tones: *'They are waiting for the new Trollope to be born!'* Do you remember, at these words, how heavy our suitcases suddenly felt? How our blood slowed, our footsteps lagged? Brother Ass, we had been bashfully thinking of a kind of
11 on 14.5pt

Monotype VAN DIJCK

203 roman and italic
Monotype 1937 (with the assistance of Jan van Krimpen)
Copyfitting factor 37.5/32.8

Derived from a roman (not definitely by Van Dijck) appearing in an Amsterdam edition of Ovid, printed 1670

Normally supplied with Bembo figures, but here shown with a set designed for Van Dijck by Matthew Carter

ABCDEFGHIJKLMNOP
QRSTUVWXYZ abcdefg
hijklmnopqrstuvwxyz
1234567890
ffffiflffiffl ()[]&£$.,;:-!?''

ABCDEFGHIJKLMNOP
QRSTUVWXYZ abcdefg
hijklmnopqrstuvwxyz
1234567890
ffffiflffiffl ()[]&£$.,;:-!?''

24 on 27pt

268

These examples show *normal* letterspacing and the effect of *reduced* letterspacing on roman setting *as well as on words in italic*: they also show the appearance of figures, for example 28 May 1964, within text. These & the ampersand are not included in the setting opposite.

Normal letterspacing

These examples show *normal* letterspacing and the effect of *reduced* letterspacing on roman setting *as well as on words in italic*: they also show the appearance of figures, for example 28 May 1964, within text. These & the ampersand are not included in the setting opposite.

Minus one unit spacing

These examples show *normal* letterspacing and the effect of *reduced* letterspacing on roman setting *as well as on words in italic*: they also show the appearance of figures, for example 28 May 1964, within text. These & the ampersand are not included in the setting opposite.

Minus two units spacing

WALKING ALONG THE MALL WE WONDERED WHO ALL THOSE MEN
WALKING ALONG THE MALL WE WONDERED WHO ALL
WALKING ALONG THE MALL WE WONDERED WHO ALL

Capitals: normal letterspacing/plus 9 units/plus 18 units

WALKING ALONG THE MALL WE WONDERED WHO ALL THOSE MEN WERE
WALKING ALONG THE MALL WE WONDERED WHO ALL THOSE MEN WERE
WALKING ALONG THE MALL WE WONDERED WHO ALL THOSE MEN

Small caps: normal letterspacing/plus 6 units/plus 12 units

WALKING ALONG THE MALL we wondered who all those men were
WALKING ALONG THE MALL we wondered who all those men were

True italic/sloped roman

WALKING ALONG THE MALL WE WONDERED WHO ALL THOSE MEN WERE
WALKING ALONG THE MALL WE WONDERED WHO ALL THOSE MEN WERE

True small caps/reduced capitals

Walking along the Mall we wondered who all those men were – tall hawk-featured men perched on balconies and high places, scanning the city with heavy binoculars. What were they seeking so earnestly? Who were they – so composed and steely-eyed? Timidly we stopped a policeman to ask him. 'They are publishers' he said mildly. Publishers! Our hearts stopped beating. 'They are on the look out for new talent.' Great God! It was for *us* they were waiting and watching! Then the kindly policeman lowered his voice confidentially and said in hollow and reverent tones: *'They are waiting for the new Trollope to be born!'* Do you remember, at these words, how heavy our suitcases suddenly felt? How our blood slowed, our footsteps lagged? Brother Ass, we had been bashfully thinking of a kind of illumination such as Rimbaud dreamed of – a nagging poem which was not didactic or expository but which *infected* – was not simply a rationalised intuition, I mean, clothed in isinglass! We had come to

8 on 9pt

WALKING ALONG THE MALL WE WONDERED WHO ALL THOSE MEN WERE – TALL hawk-featured men perched on balconies and high places, scanning the city with heavy binoculars. What were they seeking so earnestly? Who were they – so composed and steely-eyed? Timidly we stopped a policeman to ask him. 'They are publishers' he said mildly. Publishers! Our hearts stopped beating. 'They are on the look out for new talent.' Great God! It was for *us* they were waiting and watching! Then the kindly policeman lowered his voice confidentially and said in hollow and reverent tones: *'They are waiting for the new Trollope to be born!'* Do you remember, at these words, how heavy our suitcases suddenly felt? How our blood slowed, our footsteps lagged? Brother Ass, we had been bashfully thinking of a kind of illumination such as Rimbaud dreamed of – a nagging poem which

8 on 10.5pt

Walking along the Mall we wondered who all those men were – tall hawk-featured men perched on balconies and high places, scanning the city with heavy binoculars. What were they seeking so earnestly? Who were they – so composed and steely-eyed? Timidly we stopped a policeman to ask him. 'They are publishers' he said mildly. Publishers! Our hearts stopped beating. 'They are on the look out for new talent.' Great God! It was for *us* they were waiting and watching! Then the kindly policeman lowered his voice confidentially and said in hollow and reverent tones: *'They are waiting for the new Trollope to be born!'* Do you remember, at these words, how heavy our suitcases suddenly felt? How our blood slowed, our footsteps lagged? Brother Ass, we had been bashfully thinking of a kind of illumination such as Rimbaud dreamed of – a nagging poem which was not didactic or expository but which *infected* – was not simply a rationalised intuition, I mean, clothed in isinglass! We had come to the wrong shop, with the wrong change! A chill struck us as we saw the mist falling in Trafalgar Square, coiling around us its tendrils of ectoplasm! A million muffin-eating moralists were waiting, not for us, Brother Ass, but for the plucky and tedious Trollope! (If you are dissatisfied with your form, reach for the *curette*.) Now do you wonder if I laugh a little off-key? Do you ask yourself what has turned me into nature's bashful little aphorist? We who are, after all, simply poor co-workers in the psyche of our nation, what can we expect but the natural automatic rejection from a public which resents interference? And quite right too.

9 on 11pt

Walking along the Mall we wondered who all those men were – tall hawk-featured men perched on balconies and high places, scanning the city with heavy binoculars. What were they seeking so earnestly? Who were they – so composed and steely-eyed? Timidly we stopped a policeman to ask him. 'They are publishers' he said mildly. Publishers! Our hearts stopped beating. 'They are on the look out for new talent.' Great God! It was for *us* they were waiting and watching! Then the kindly policeman lowered his voice confidentially and said in hollow and reverent tones: *'They are waiting for the new Trollope to be born!'* Do you remember, at these words, how heavy our suitcases suddenly felt? How our blood slowed, our footsteps lagged? Brother Ass, we had been bashfully thinking of a kind of illumination such as Rimbaud dreamed of – a nagging poem which was not didactic or expository but which *infected* – was not simply a rationalised intuition, I mean, clothed in isinglass! We had come to the wrong shop, with the wrong change! A chill struck us as we saw the mist falling in Trafalgar Square, coiling around us its tendrils of ectoplasm! A million muffin-eating moralists were waiting, not for us, Brother Ass, but for the plucky and tedious Trollope! (If you are dissatisfied with your form, reach for the *curette*.) Now do you wonder if I laugh a little off-key? Do you ask yourself what has turned me into nature's bashful little aphorist? We who are, after all, simply poor co-workers in the psyche of our nation, what can

9 on 12pt

Walking along the Mall we wondered who all those men were – tall hawk-featured men perched on balconies and high places, scanning the city with heavy binoculars. What were they seeking so earnestly? Who were they – so composed and steely-eyed? Timidly we stopped a policeman to ask him. 'They are publishers' he said mildly. Publishers! Our hearts stopped beating. 'They are on the look out for new talent.' Great God! It was for *us* they were waiting and watching! Then the kindly policeman lowered his voice confidentially and said in hollow and reverent tones: *'They are waiting for the new Trollope to be born!'* Do you remember, at these words, how heavy our suitcases suddenly felt? How our blood slowed, our footsteps lagged? Brother Ass, we had been bashfully thinking of a kind of illumination such as Rimbaud dreamed of – a nagging poem which was not didactic or expository but which *infected* – was not simply a rationalised intuition, I mean, clothed in isinglass! We had come to the wrong shop, with the wrong change! A chill struck us as we saw the mist falling in Trafalgar Square, coiling around us its tendrils of ectoplasm! A million muffin-eating moralists were waiting, not for us, Brother Ass, but for the plucky and tedious Trollope! (If you are dissatisfied with your form, reach for the

10 on 12pt

Walking along the Mall we wondered who all those men were – tall hawk-featured men perched on balconies and high places, scanning the city with heavy binoculars. What were they seeking so earnestly? Who were they – so composed and steely-eyed? Timidly we stopped a policeman to ask him. 'They are publishers' he said mildly. Publishers! Our hearts stopped beating. 'They are on the look out for new talent.' Great God! It was for *us* they were waiting and watching! Then the kindly policeman lowered his voice confidentially and said in hollow and reverent tones: *'They are waiting for the new Trollope to be born!'* Do you remember, at these words, how heavy our suitcases suddenly felt? How our blood slowed, our footsteps lagged? Brother Ass, we had been bashfully thinking of a kind of illumination such as Rimbaud dreamed of – a nagging poem which was not didactic or expository but which *infected* – was not simply a rationalised intuition, I mean, clothed in isinglass! We had come to the wrong shop, with the wrong change! A chill struck us as we saw the mist falling in Trafalgar Square, coiling around us its tendrils of ectoplasm! A million muffin-eating moralists were waiting, not for us, Brother

10 on 13.5pt

Walking along the Mall we wondered who all those men were – tall hawk-featured men perched on balconies and high places, scanning the city with heavy binoculars. What were they seeking so earnestly? Who were they – so composed and steely-eyed? Timidly we stopped a policeman to ask him. 'They are publishers' he said mildly. Publishers! Our hearts stopped beating. 'They are on the look out for new talent.' Great God! It was for *us* they were waiting and watching! Then the kindly policeman lowered his voice confidentially and said in hollow and reverent tones: *'They are waiting for the new Trollope to be born!'* Do you remember, at these words, how heavy our suitcases suddenly felt? How our blood slowed, our footsteps lagged? Brother Ass, we had been bashfully thinking of a kind of illumination such as Rimbaud dreamed of – a nagging poem which was not didactic or expository but which *infected* – was not simply a rationalised intuition, I mean, clothed in isinglass! We had come to the wrong shop, with the wrong change! A chill struck us as we saw the mist falling in Trafalgar Square, coiling around us its

11 on 13pt

Walking along the Mall we wondered who all those men were – tall hawk-featured men perched on balconies and high places, scanning the city with heavy binoculars. What were they seeking so earnestly? Who were they – so composed and steely-eyed? Timidly we stopped a policeman to ask him. 'They are publishers' he said mildly. Publishers! Our hearts stopped beating. 'They are on the look out for new talent.' Great God! It was for *us* they were waiting and watching! Then the kindly policeman lowered his voice confidentially and said in hollow and reverent tones: *'They are waiting for the new Trollope to be born!'* Do you remember, at these words, how heavy our suitcases suddenly felt? How our blood slowed, our footsteps lagged? Brother Ass, we had been bashfully thinking of a kind of illumination such as Rimbaud dreamed of – a nagging poem which was not didactic or expository but which *infected* – was not simply a rationalised intuition, I mean, clothed in isinglass! We had come to the wrong shop, with

11 on 14.5pt

MONOTYPE VAN DIJCK

Linotype **Versailles**

roman 55 (05311), **italic 56** (13311)
black 95 (09311)
Stempel 1984 (Adrian Frutiger)
Copyfitting code 142/139/161

Range also includes light, light italic, bold,
bold italic, black italic

ABCDEFGHIJKLMNOP
QRSTUVWXYZ abcdefg
hijklmnopqrstuvwxyz
1234567890 1234567890
fifl ()[]&£$.,;:-!?"

ABCDEFGHIJKLMNOP
QRSTUVWXYZ abcdefg
hijklmnopqrstuvwxyz
1234567890 1234567890
fifl ()[]&£$.,;:-!?"

ABCDEFGHIJKLMNOP
QRSTUVWXYZ abcdefg
hijklmnopqrstuvwxyz
1234567890 1234567890
fifl ()[]&£$.,;:-!?"

24 on 27pt

270

These examples show *normal* letterspacing and the effect of *reduced*
letterspacing on roman setting *as well as on words in italic*: they also
show the appearance of figures, for example 28 May 1964, within text.
These & the ampersand are not included in the setting opposite.
Normal letterspacing

These examples show *normal* letterspacing and the effect of *reduced*
letterspacing on roman setting *as well as on words in italic*: they also
show the appearance of figures, for example 28 May 1964, within text.
These & the ampersand are not included in the setting opposite.
Minus one unit spacing

These examples show *normal* letterspacing and the effect of *reduced*
letterspacing on roman setting *as well as on words in italic*: they also
show the appearance of figures, for example 28 May 1964, within text.
These & the ampersand are not included in the setting opposite.
Minus two units spacing

WALKING ALONG THE MALL WE WONDERED WHO ALL
WALKING ALONG THE MALL WE WONDERED WHO ALL
WALKING ALONG THE MALL WE WONDERED WHO
Capitals: normal letterspacing/plus 4 units/plus 9 units

WALKING ALONG THE MALL WE WONDERED WHO ALL THOSE MEN WERE
WALKING ALONG THE MALL WE WONDERED WHO ALL THOSE MEN
WALKING ALONG THE MALL WE WONDERED WHO ALL THOSE
Small caps: normal letterspacing/plus 3 units/plus 6 units

WALKING ALONG THE MALL WE WONDERED WHO ALL THOSE MEN WERE
WALKING ALONG THE MALL WE WONDERED WHO ALL THOSE MEN WERE
True small caps/reduced capitals

WALKING ALONG THE MALL we wondered who all those men were
WALKING ALONG THE MALL we wondered who all those men were
True italic/sloped roman

Walking along the Mall we wondered who all those men were – tall hawk-
featured men perched on balconies and high places, scanning the city with
heavy binoculars. What were they seeking so earnestly? Who were they – so
composed and steely-eyed? Timidly we stopped a policeman to ask him. 'They
are publishers' he said mildly. Publishers! Our hearts stopped beating. 'They
are on the look out for new talent.' Great God! It was for *us* they were waiting
and watching! Then the kindly policeman lowered his voice confidentially and
said in hollow and reverent tones: *'They are waiting for the new Trollope to be*
born!' Do you remember, at these words, how heavy our suitcases suddenly
felt? How our blood slowed, our footsteps lagged? Brother Ass, we had been
8 on 9pt

WALKING ALONG THE MALL WE WONDERED WHO ALL THOSE MEN WERE – TALL
hawk-featured men perched on balconies and high places, scanning the city
with heavy binoculars. What were they seeking so earnestly? Who were they –
so composed and steely-eyed? Timidly we stopped a policeman to ask him.
'They are publishers' he said mildly. Publishers! Our hearts stopped beating.
'They are on the look out for new talent.' Great God! It was for *us* they
were waiting and watching! Then the kindly policeman lowered his voice
confidentially and said in hollow and reverent tones: *'They are waiting for the*
new Trollope to be born!' Do you remember, at these words, how heavy our
8 on 10.5pt

Walking along the Mall we wondered who all those men were – tall hawk-featured men perched on balconies and high places, scanning the city with heavy binoculars. What were they seeking so earnestly? Who were they – so composed and steely-eyed? Timidly we stopped a policeman to ask him. 'They are publishers' he said mildly. Publishers! Our hearts stopped beating. 'They are on the look out for new talent.' Great God! It was for *us* they were waiting and watching! Then the kindly policeman lowered his voice confidentially and said in hollow and reverent tones: *'They are waiting for the new Trollope to be born!'* Do you remember, at these words, how heavy our suitcases suddenly felt? How our blood slowed, our footsteps lagged? Brother Ass, we had been bashfully thinking of a kind of illumination such as Rimbaud dreamed of – a nagging poem which was not didactic or expository but which *infected* – was not simply a rationalised intuition, I mean, clothed in isinglass! We had come to the wrong shop, with the wrong change! A chill struck us as we saw the mist falling in Trafalgar Square, coiling round us its tendrils of ectoplasm! A million muffin-eating moralists were waiting, not for us, Brother Ass, but for the

9 on 11pt

Walking along the Mall we wondered who all those men were – tall hawk-featured men perched on balconies and high places, scanning the city with heavy binoculars. What were they seeking so earnestly? Who were they – so composed and steely-eyed? Timidly we stopped a policeman to ask him. 'They are publishers' he said mildly. Publishers! Our hearts stopped beating. 'They are on the look out for new talent.' Great God! It was for *us* they were waiting and watching! Then the kindly policeman lowered his voice confidentially and said in hollow and reverent tones: *'They are waiting for the new Trollope to be born!'* Do you remember, at these words, how heavy our suit-cases suddenly felt? How our blood slowed, our footsteps lagged? Brother Ass, we had been bashfully thinking of a kind of illumination such as Rimbaud dreamed of – a nagging poem which was not didactic or expository but which *infected* – was not simply a rationalised intuition, I mean, clothed in isinglass!

10 on 12pt

Walking along the Mall we wondered who all those men were – tall hawk-featured men perched on balconies and high places, scanning the city with heavy binoculars. What were they seeking so earnestly? Who were they – so composed and steely-eyed? Timidly we stopped a policeman to ask him. 'They are publishers' he said mildly. Publishers! Our hearts stopped beating. 'They are on the look out for new talent.' Great God! It was for *us* they were waiting and watching! Then the kindly policeman lowered his voice confidentially and said in hollow and reverent tones: *'They are waiting for the new Trollope to be born!'* Do you remember, at these words, how heavy our suitcases suddenly felt? How our blood slowed, our footsteps lagged? Brother Ass, we had been bashfully thinking of a kind of illumination such as Rimbaud

11 on 13pt

WALKING ALONG THE MALL WE WONDERED WHO ALL THOSE MEN WERE – tall hawk-featured men perched on balconies and high places, scanning the city with heavy binoculars. What were they seeking so earnestly? Who were they – so composed and steely-eyed? Timidly we stopped a policeman to ask him. 'They are publishers' he said mildly. Publishers! Our hearts stopped beating. 'They are on the look out for new talent.' Great God! It was for *us* they were waiting and watching! Then the kindly policeman lowered his voice confidentially and said in hollow and reverent tones: *'They are waiting for the new Trollope to be born!'* Do you remember, at these words, how heavy our suitcases suddenly felt? How our blood slowed, our footsteps lagged? Brother Ass, we had been bashfully thinking of a kind of illumination such as Rimbaud dreamed of – a nagging poem which was not didactic or expository but which *infected* – was not simply a rationalised intuition, I mean, clothed in isinglass! We had come to the wrong shop, with the wrong change! A chill struck us as we saw the mist falling in Trafalgar Square, coiling round us its tendrils of ectoplasm! A million muffin-

9 on 12pt

WALKING ALONG THE MALL WE WONDERED WHO ALL THOSE MEN were – tall hawk-featured men perched on balconies and high places, scanning the city with heavy binoculars. What were they seeking so earnestly? Who were they – so composed and steely-eyed? Timidly we stopped a policeman to ask him. 'They are publishers' he said mildly. Publishers! Our hearts stopped beating. 'They are on the look out for new talent.' Great God! It was for *us* they were waiting and watching! Then the kindly policeman lowered his voice confidentially and said in hollow and reverent tones: *'They are waiting for the new Trollope to be born!'* Do you remember, at these words, how heavy our suit-cases suddenly felt? How our blood slowed, our footsteps lagged? Brother Ass, we had been bashfully thinking of a kind of illumination such as Rimbaud dreamed of – a nagging poem which was not didactic or expository but which *infected* – was

10 on 13.5pt

WALKING ALONG THE MALL WE WONDERED WHO ALL THOSE men were – tall hawk-featured men perched on balconies and high places, scanning the city with heavy binoculars. What were they seeking so earnestly? Who were they – so composed and steely-eyed? Timidly we stopped a policeman to ask him. 'They are publishers' he said mildly. Publishers! Our hearts stopped beating. 'They are on the look out for new talent.' Great God! It was for *us* they were waiting and watching! Then the kindly policeman lowered his voice confidentially and said in hollow and reverent tones: *'They are waiting for the new Trollope to be born!'* Do you remember, at these words, how heavy our suitcases suddenly felt? How our blood slowed, our footsteps lagged? Brother Ass, we had been bashfully

11 on 14.5pt

Linotype **Video**

medium (06261), **medium oblique** (75261)
black (09261)
Mergenthaler 1974 (Matthew Carter)
Copyfitting code 128/127/160

Range also includes light, light oblique, bold,
bold oblique, black oblique

ABCDEFGHIJKLMNOP
QRSTUVWXYZ abcdefg
hijklmnopqrstuvwxyz
1234567890
fifl ()[]&£$.,;:-!?"

*ABCDEFGHIJKLMNOP
QRSTUVWXYZ abcdefg
hijklmnopqrstuvwxyz
1234567890
fifl ()[]&£$.,;:-!?"*

**ABCDEFGHIJKLMNOP
QRSTUVWXYZ abcdefg
hijklmnopqrstuvwxyz
1234567890
fifl ()[]&£$.,;:-!?"**

24 on 27pt

These examples show *normal* letterspacing and the effect of *reduced* letterspacing on roman setting *as well as on words in italic*: they also show the appearance of figures, for example 28 May 1964, within text. These & the ampersand are not included in the setting opposite.
Normal letterspacing

These examples show *normal* letterspacing and the effect of *reduced* letterspacing on roman setting *as well as on words in italic*: they also show the appearance of figures, for example 28 May 1964, within text. These & the ampersand are not included in the setting opposite.
Minus one unit spacing

These examples show *normal* letterspacing and the effect of *reduced* letterspacing on roman setting *as well as on words in italic*: they also show the appearance of figures, for example 28 May 1964, within text. These & the ampersand are not included in the setting opposite.
Minus two units spacing

WALKING ALONG THE MALL WE WONDERED WHO ALL THOSE
WALKING ALONG THE MALL WE WONDERED WHO ALL
WALKING ALONG THE MALL WE WONDERED WHO
Capitals: normal letterspacing/plus 4 units/plus 9 units

Walking along the Mall we wondered who all those men were – tall hawk-featured men perched on balconies and high places, scanning the city with heavy binoculars. WHAT WERE THEY SEEKING SO EARNESTLY? Who were they – so composed and steely-eyed? Timidly we stopped a policeman to ask him. 'THEY ARE PUBLISHERS' he said mildly. Publishers! Our hearts stopped beating. 'They are on the look out for new talent.' Great God! It was for *us* they were waiting
Text with reduced caps normal letterspacing/plus 3 units

WALKING ALONG THE MALL we wondered who all those men were
WALKING ALONG THE MALL we wondered who all those men were
True italic/sloped roman

Walking along the Mall we wondered who all those men were – tall hawk-featured men perched on balconies and high places, scanning the city with heavy binoculars. What were they seeking so earnestly? Who were they – so composed and steely-eyed? Timidly we stopped a policeman to ask him. 'They are publishers' he said mildly. Publishers! Our hearts stopped beating. 'They are on the look out for new talent.' Great God! It was for *us* they were waiting and watching! Then the kindly policeman lowered his voice confidentially and said in hollow and reverent tones: *'They are waiting for the new Trollope to be born!'* Do you remember, at these words, how heavy our suitcases suddenly felt? How our blood slowed, our footsteps lagged? Brother Ass, we had been bashfully thinking of a kind of
8 on 9pt

Walking along the Mall we wondered who all those men were – tall hawk-featured men perched on balconies and high places, scanning the city with heavy binoculars. What were they seeking so earnestly? Who were they – so composed and steely-eyed? Timidly we stopped a policeman to ask him. 'They are publishers' he said mildly. Publishers! Our hearts stopped beating. 'They are on the look out for new talent.' Great God! It was for *us* they were waiting and watching! Then the kindly policeman lowered his voice confidentially and said in hollow and reverent tones: *'They are waiting for the new Trollope to be born!'* Do you remember, at these words, how heavy our suitcases suddenly felt? How our blood slowed, our footsteps
8 on 10.5pt

Walking along the Mall we wondered who all those men were — tall hawk-featured men perched on balconies and high places, scanning the city with heavy binoculars. What were they seeking so earnestly? Who were they – so composed and steely-eyed? Timidly we stopped a policeman to ask him. 'They are publishers' he said mildly. Publishers! Our hearts stopped beating. 'They are on the look out for new talent.' Great God! It was for *us* they were waiting and watching! Then the kindly policeman lowered his voice confidentially and said in hollow and reverent tones: *'They are waiting for the new Trollope to be born!'* Do you remember, at these words, how heavy our suitcases suddenly felt? How our blood slowed, our footsteps lagged? Brother Ass, we had been bashfully thinking of a kind of illumination such as Rimbaud dreamed of – a nagging poem which was not didactic or expository but which *infected* – was not simply a rationalised intuition, I mean, clothed in isinglass! We had come to the wrong shop, with the wrong change! A chill struck us as we saw the mist falling in Trafalgar Square, coiling round us its tendrils of ectoplasm! A million muffin-eating moralists were waiting, not for us, Brother Ass, but for the plucky and tedious Trollope! (If you are dissatisfied with your form, reach

9 on 11pt

Walking along the Mall we wondered who all those men were – tall hawk-featured men perched on balconies and high places, scanning the city with heavy binoculars. What were they seeking so earnestly? Who were they – so composed and steely-eyed? Timidly we stopped a policeman to ask him. 'They are publishers' he said mildly. Publishers! Our hearts stopped beating. 'They are on the look out for new talent.' Great God! It was for *us* they were waiting and watching! Then the kindly policeman lowered his voice confidentially and said in hollow and reverent tones: *'They are waiting for the new Trollope to be born!'* Do you remember, at these words, how heavy our suitcases suddenly felt? How our blood slowed, our footsteps lagged? Brother Ass, we had been bashfully thinking of a kind of illumination such as Rimbaud dreamed of – a nagging poem which was not didactic or expository but which *infected* – was not simply a rationalised intuition, I mean, clothed in isinglass! We had come to the wrong shop, with the wrong change!

10 on 12pt

Walking along the Mall we wondered who all those men were – tall hawk-featured men perched on balconies and high places, scanning the city with heavy binoculars. What were they seeking so earnestly? Who were they – so composed and steely-eyed? Timidly we stopped a policeman to ask him. 'They are publishers' he said mildly. Publishers! Our hearts stopped beating. 'They are on the look out for new talent.' Great God! It was for *us* they were waiting and watching! Then the kindly policeman lowered his voice confidentially and said in hollow and reverent tones: *'They are waiting for the new Trollope to be born!'* Do you remember, at these words, how heavy our suitcases suddenly felt? How our blood slowed, our footsteps lagged? Brother Ass, we had been bashfully thinking of a kind of illumination such as Rimbaud dreamed of – a nagging poem which was not didactic or

11 on 13pt

Walking along the Mall we wondered who all those men were – tall hawk-featured men perched on balconies and high places, scanning the city with heavy binoculars. What were they seeking so earnestly? Who were they – so composed and steely-eyed? Timidly we stopped a policeman to ask him. 'They are publishers' he said mildly. Publishers! Our hearts stopped beating. 'They are on the look out for new talent.' Great God! It was for *us* they were waiting and watching! Then the kindly policeman lowered his voice confidentially and said in hollow and reverent tones: *'They are waiting for the new Trollope to be born!'* Do you remember, at these words, how heavy our suitcases suddenly felt? How our blood slowed, our footsteps lagged? Brother Ass, we had been bashfully thinking of a kind of illumination such as Rimbaud dreamed of – a nagging poem which was not didactic or expository but which *infected* – was not simply a rationalised intuition, I mean, clothed in isinglass! We had come to the wrong shop, with the wrong change! A chill struck us as we saw the mist falling in Trafalgar Square, coiling round us its tendrils of ectoplasm! A million muffin-eating moralists were waiting, not for us, Brother Ass, but for the plucky and tedious

9 on 12pt

Walking along the Mall we wondered who all those men were – tall hawk-featured men perched on balconies and high places, scanning the city with heavy binoculars. What were they seeking so earnestly? Who were they – so composed and steely-eyed? Timidly we stopped a policeman to ask him. 'They are publishers' he said mildly. Publishers! Our hearts stopped beating. 'They are on the look out for new talent.' Great God! It was for *us* they were waiting and watching! Then the kindly policeman lowered his voice confidentially and said in hollow and reverent tones: *'They are waiting for the new Trollope to be born!'* Do you remember, at these words, how heavy our suitcases suddenly felt? How our blood slowed, our footsteps lagged? Brother Ass, we had been bashfully thinking of a kind of illumination such as Rimbaud dreamed of – a nagging poem which was not didactic or expository but which *infected* – was not simply a rationalised intuition, I mean, clothed in isinglass! We had

10 on 13.5pt

Walking along the Mall we wondered who all those men were – tall hawk-featured men perched on balconies and high places, scanning the city with heavy binoculars. What were they seeking so earnestly? Who were they – so composed and steely-eyed? Timidly we stopped a policeman to ask him. 'They are publishers' he said mildly. Publishers! Our hearts stopped beating. 'They are on the look out for new talent.' Great God! It was for *us* they were waiting and watching! Then the kindly policeman lowered his voice confidentially and said in hollow and reverent tones: *'They are waiting for the new Trollope to be born!'* Do you remember, at these words, how heavy our suitcases suddenly felt? How our blood slowed, our footsteps lagged? Brother Ass, we had been bashfully thinking of a kind of illumination such as Rimbaud

11 on 14.5pt

Monotype **Walbaum**

374 roman and italic
375 medium
Monotype 1934
Copyfitting factor 39.2/37.9/41.2

Range also includes medium italic

The original hot metal design was virtually a facsimile of Justus Erich Walbaum's type of *c*.1800. Although bracketting to the serifs is visible in display sizes, text sizes of the digitised version are still very close to the original, in both roman and italic. It is to be hoped that the alternative non-lining figures provided in the hot metal version will eventually be made available in the digitised designs

ABCDEFGHIJKLMNOP
QRSTUVWXYZ abcdefg
hijklmnopqrstuvwxyz
1234567890
ff fi fl ffi ffl ()[]&£$.,;:-!?""

ABCDEFGHIJKLMNOP
QRSTUVWXYZ abcdefg
hijklmnopqrstuvwxyz
1234567890
ff fi fl ffi ffl ()[]&£$.,;:-!?""

ABCDEFGHIJKLMNOP
QRSTUVWXYZ abcdefg
hijklmnopqrstuvwxyz
1234567890
ff fi fl ffi ffl ()[]&£$.,;:-!?""

24 on 27pt

These examples show *normal* letterspacing and the effect of *reduced* letterspacing on roman setting *as well as on words in italic*: they also show the appearance of figures, for example 28 May 1964, within text. These & the ampersand are not included in the setting opposite.

Normal letterspacing

These examples show *normal* letterspacing and the effect of *reduced* letterspacing on roman setting *as well as on words in italic*: they also show the appearance of figures, for example 28 May 1964, within text. These & the ampersand are not included in the setting opposite.

Minus one unit spacing

These examples show *normal* letterspacing and the effect of *reduced* letterspacing on roman setting *as well as on words in italic*: they also show the appearance of figures, for example 28 May 1964, within text. These & the ampersand are not included in the setting opposite.

Minus two units spacing

WALKING ALONG THE MALL WE WONDERED WHO ALL THOSE MEN
WALKING ALONG THE MALL WE WONDERED WHO ALL
WALKING ALONG THE MALL WE WONDERED WHO

Capitals: normal letterspacing/plus 9 units/plus 18 units

WALKING ALONG THE MALL WE WONDERED WHO ALL THOSE MEN WERE
WALKING ALONG THE MALL WE WONDERED WHO ALL THOSE MEN WERE
WALKING ALONG THE MALL WE WONDERED WHO ALL THOSE MEN

Small caps: normal letterspacing/plus 6 units/plus 12 units

WALKING ALONG THE MALL we wondered who all those men were
WALKING ALONG THE MALL we wondered who all those men were

True italic/sloped roman

WALKING ALONG THE MALL WE WONDERED WHO ALL THOSE MEN WERE
WALKING ALONG THE MALL WE WONDERED WHO ALL THOSE MEN WERE

True small caps/reduced capitals

Walking along the Mall we wondered who all those men were – tall hawk-featured men perched on balconies and high places, scanning the city with heavy binoculars. What were they seeking so earnestly? Who were they – so composed and steely-eyed? Timidly we stopped a policeman to ask him. 'They are publishers' he said mildly. Publishers! Our hearts stopped beating. 'They are on the look out for new talent.' Great God! It was for *us* they were waiting and watching! Then the kindly policeman lowered his voice confidentially and said in hollow and reverent tones: *'They are waiting for the new Trollope to be born!'* Do you remember, at these words, how heavy our suitcases suddenly felt? How our blood slowed, our footsteps lagged? Brother Ass, we had been bashfully thinking of a kind of illumination such as Rimbaud dreamed of – a nagging poem which was not didactic or expository but which *infected* – was not simply a

8 on 9pt

WALKING ALONG THE MALL WE WONDERED WHO ALL THOSE MEN WERE – TALL HAWK-featured men perched on balconies and high places, scanning the city with heavy binoculars. What were they seeking so earnestly? Who were they – so composed and steely-eyed? Timidly we stopped a policeman to ask him. 'They are publishers' he said mildly. Publishers! Our hearts stopped beating. 'They are on the look out for new talent.' Great God! It was for *us* they were waiting and watching! Then the kindly policeman lowered his voice confidentially and said in hollow and reverent tones: *'They are waiting for the new Trollope to be born!'* Do you remember, at these words, how heavy our suitcases suddenly felt? How our blood slowed, our footsteps lagged? Brother Ass, we had been bashfully thinking of a kind of illumination such as Rimbaud

8 on 10.5pt

Walking along the Mall we wondered who all those men were – tall hawk-featured men perched on balconies and high places, scanning the city with heavy binoculars. What were they seeking so earnestly? Who were they – so composed and steely-eyed? Timidly we stopped a policeman to ask him. 'They are publishers' he said mildly. Publishers! Our hearts stopped beating. 'They are on the look out for new talent.' Great God! It was for *us* they were waiting and watching! Then the kindly policeman lowered his voice confidentially and said in hollow and reverent tones: *'They are waiting for the new Trollope to be born!'* Do you remember, at these words, how heavy our suitcases suddenly felt? How our blood slowed, our footsteps lagged? Brother Ass, we had been bashfully thinking of a kind of illumination such as Rimbaud dreamed of – a nagging poem which was not didactic or expository but which *infected* – was not simply a rationalised intuition, I mean, clothed in isinglass! We had come to the wrong shop, with the wrong change! A chill struck us as we saw the mist falling in Trafalgar Square, coiling around us its tendrils of ectoplasm! A million muffin-eating moralists were waiting, not for us, Brother Ass, but for the plucky and tedious Trollope! (If you are dissatisfied with your form, reach for the *curette*.) Now do you wonder if I laugh a little off-key? Do you ask yourself what has turned me into nature's bashful little aphorist? We who are, after all, simply poor co-workers in the psyche of our nation, what can we expect

9 on 11pt .

Walking along the Mall we wondered who all those men were – tall hawk-featured men perched on balconies and high places, scanning the city with heavy binoculars. What were they seeking so earnestly? Who were they – so composed and steely-eyed? Timidly we stopped a policeman to ask him. 'They are publishers' he said mildly. Publishers! Our hearts stopped beating. 'They are on the look out for new talent.' Great God! It was for *us* they were waiting and watching! Then the kindly policeman lowered his voice confidentially and said in hollow and reverent tones: *'They are waiting for the new Trollope to be born!'* Do you remember, at these words, how heavy our suitcases suddenly felt? How our blood slowed, our footsteps lagged? Brother Ass, we had been bashfully thinking of a kind of illumination such as Rimbaud dreamed of – a nagging poem which was not didactic or expository but which *infected* – was not simply a rationalised intuition, I mean, clothed in isinglass! We had come to the wrong shop, with the wrong change! A chill struck us as we saw the mist falling in Trafalgar Square, coiling around us its tendrils of ectoplasm! A million muffin-eating moralists were waiting, not for us, Brother Ass, but for the plucky and tedious Trollope! (If you are dissatisfied with your form, reach for the *curette*.) Now do you wonder if I laugh a little off-key? Do you ask yourself what has turned me into nature's bashful little aphorist? We

9 on 12pt

Walking along the Mall we wondered who all those men were – tall hawk-featured men perched on balconies and high places, scanning the city with heavy binoculars. What were they seeking so earnestly? Who were they – so composed and steely-eyed? Timidly we stopped a policeman to ask him. 'They are publishers' he said mildly. Publishers! Our hearts stopped beating. 'They are on the look out for new talent.' Great God! It was for *us* they were waiting and watching! Then the kindly policeman lowered his voice confidentially and said in hollow and reverent tones: *'They are waiting for the new Trollope to be born!'* Do you remember, at these words, how heavy our suitcases suddenly felt? How our blood slowed, our footsteps lagged? Brother Ass, we had been bashfully thinking of a kind of illumination such as Rimbaud dreamed of – a nagging poem which was not didactic or expository but which *infected* – was not simply a rationalised intuition, I mean, clothed in isinglass! We had come to the wrong shop, with the wrong change! A chill struck us as we saw the mist falling in Trafalgar Square, coiling around us its tendrils of ectoplasm! A million muffin-eating moralists were waiting, not for us, Brother Ass, but for the plucky and

10 on 12pt

Walking along the Mall we wondered who all those men were – tall hawk-featured men perched on balconies and high places, scanning the city with heavy binoculars. What were they seeking so earnestly? Who were they – so composed and steely-eyed? Timidly we stopped a policeman to ask him. 'They are publishers' he said mildly. Publishers! Our hearts stopped beating. 'They are on the look out for new talent.' Great God! It was for *us* they were waiting and watching! Then the kindly policeman lowered his voice confidentially and said in hollow and reverent tones: *'They are waiting for the new Trollope to be born!'* Do you remember, at these words, how heavy our suitcases suddenly felt? How our blood slowed, our footsteps lagged? Brother Ass, we had been bashfully thinking of a kind of illumination such as Rimbaud dreamed of – a nagging poem which was not didactic or expository but which *infected* – was not simply a rationalised intuition, I mean, clothed in isinglass! We had come to the wrong shop, with the wrong change! A chill struck us as we saw the mist falling in Trafalgar Square, coiling around us its tendrils of ectoplasm! A million

10 on 13.5pt

Walking along the Mall we wondered who all those men were – tall hawk-featured men perched on balconies and high places, scanning the city with heavy binoculars. What were they seeking so earnestly? Who were they – so composed and steely-eyed? Timidly we stopped a policeman to ask him. 'They are publishers' he said mildly. Publishers! Our hearts stopped beating. 'They are on the look out for new talent.' Great God! It was for *us* they were waiting and watching! Then the kindly policeman lowered his voice confidentially and said in hollow and reverent tones: *'They are waiting for the new Trollope to be born!'* Do you remember, at these words, how heavy our suitcases suddenly felt? How our blood slowed, our footsteps lagged? Brother Ass, we had been bashfully thinking of a kind of illumination such as Rimbaud dreamed of – a nagging poem which was not didactic or expository but which *infected* – was not simply a rationalised intuition, I mean, clothed in isinglass! We had come to the wrong shop, with the wrong change! A chill struck us as

11 on 13pt

Walking along the Mall we wondered who all those men were – tall hawk-featured men perched on balconies and high places, scanning the city with heavy binoculars. What were they seeking so earnestly? Who were they – so composed and steely-eyed? Timidly we stopped a policeman to ask him. 'They are publishers' he said mildly. Publishers! Our hearts stopped beating. 'They are on the look out for new talent.' Great God! It was for *us* they were waiting and watching! Then the kindly policeman lowered his voice confidentially and said in hollow and reverent tones: *'They are waiting for the new Trollope to be born!'* Do you remember, at these words, how heavy our suitcases suddenly felt? How our blood slowed, our footsteps lagged? Brother Ass, we had been bashfully thinking of a kind of illumination such as Rimbaud dreamed of – a nagging poem which was not didactic or expository but which *infected* – was not simply a rationalised intuition, I mean, clothed in isinglass! We

11 on 14.5pt

Linotype **Walbaum**

roman (05263), **italic** (13263)
bold (07263)
Berthold 1919 (bold: 1933)
Copyfitting code 140/138/149

Range also includes bold italic

The original 1919 fount was cast from
J E Walbaum's matrices of *c*.1800, but the
digitised version is very different, especially in
text sizes. Bolder, more condensed, with a
vertical stress, more mechanical in feeling.
The italic is effectively a new design

ABCDEFGHIJKLMNOP
QRSTUVWXYZ abcdefg
hijklmnopqrstuvwxyz
1234567890 1234567890
fifl ()[]&£$.,;:-!?"

ABCDEFGHIJKLMNOP
QRSTUVWXYZ abcdefg
hijklmnopqrstuvwxyz
1234567890 1234567890
fifl ()[]&£$.,;:-!?"

ABCDEFGHIJKLMNOP
QRSTUVWXYZ abcdefg
hijklmnopqrstuvwxyz
1234567890 1234567890
fifl ()[]&£$.,;:-!?"

24 on 27pt

These examples show *normal* letterspacing and the effect of *reduced* letterspacing on roman setting *as well as on words in italic*: they also show the appearance of figures, for example 28 May 1964, within text. These & the ampersand are not included in the setting opposite.
Normal letterspacing

These examples show *normal* letterspacing and the effect of *reduced* letterspacing on roman setting *as well as on words in italic*: they also show the appearance of figures, for example 28 May 1964, within text. These & the ampersand are not included in the setting opposite.
Minus one unit spacing

These examples show *normal* letterspacing and the effect of *reduced* letterspacing on roman setting *as well as on words in italic*: they also show the appearance of figures, for example 28 May 1964, within text. These & the ampersand are not included in the setting opposite.
Minus two units spacing

WALKING ALONG THE MALL WE WONDERED WHO ALL THOSE
WALKING ALONG THE MALL WE WONDERED WHO ALL
WALKING ALONG THE MALL WE WONDERED WHO
Capitals: normal letterspacing/plus 4 units/plus 9 units

WALKING ALONG THE MALL WE WONDERED WHO ALL THOSE MEN WERE
WALKING ALONG THE MALL WE WONDERED WHO ALL THOSE MEN
WALKING ALONG THE MALL WE WONDERED WHO ALL THOSE
Small caps: normal letterspacing/plus 3 units/plus 6 units

WALKING ALONG THE MALL WE WONDERED WHO ALL THOSE MEN WERE
WALKING ALONG THE MALL WE WONDERED WHO ALL THOSE MEN WERE
True small caps/reduced capitals

WALKING ALONG THE MALL we wondered who all those men were
WALKING ALONG THE MALL we wondered who all those men were
True italic/sloped roman

Walking along the Mall we wondered who all those men were – tall hawk-featured men perched on balconies and high places, scanning the city with heavy binoculars. What were they seeking so earnestly? Who were they – so composed and steely-eyed? Timidly we stopped a policeman to ask him. 'They are publishers' he said mildly. Publishers! Our hearts stopped beating. 'They are on the look out for new talent.' Great God! It was for *us* they were waiting and watching! Then the kindly policeman lowered his voice confidentially and said in hollow and reverent tones: *'They are waiting for the new Trollope to be born!'* Do you remember, at these words, how heavy our suitcases suddenly felt? How our blood slowed, our footsteps lagged? Brother Ass, we had been bashfully
8 on 9pt

WALKING ALONG THE MALL WE WONDERED WHO ALL THOSE MEN WERE – TALL hawk-featured men perched on balconies and high places, scanning the city with heavy binoculars. What were they seeking so earnestly? Who were they – so composed and steely-eyed? Timidly we stopped a policeman to ask him. 'They are publishers' he said mildly. Publishers! Our hearts stopped beating. 'They are on the look out for new talent.' Great God! It was for *us* they were waiting and watching! Then the kindly policeman lowered his voice confidentially and said in hollow and reverent tones: *'They are waiting for the new Trollope to be born!'* Do you remember, at these words, how heavy our
8 on 10.5pt

Walking along the Mall we wondered who all those men were – tall hawk-featured men perched on balconies and high places, scanning the city with heavy binoculars. What were they seeking so earnestly? Who were they – so composed and steely-eyed? Timidly we stopped a policeman to ask him. 'They are publishers' he said mildly. Publishers! Our hearts stopped beating. 'They are on the look out for new talent.' Great God! It was for *us* they were waiting and watching! Then the kindly policeman lowered his voice confidentially and said in hollow and reverent tones: *'They are waiting for the new Trollope to be born!'* Do you remember, at these words, how heavy our suitcases suddenly felt? How our blood slowed, our footsteps lagged? Brother Ass, we had been bashfully thinking of a kind of illumination such as Rimbaud dreamed of – a nagging poem which was not didactic or expository but which *infected* – was not simply a rationalised intuition, I mean, clothed in isinglass! We had come to the wrong shop, with the wrong change! A chill struck us as we saw the mist falling in Trafalgar Square, coiling round us its tendrils of ectoplasm! A million muffin-eating moralists were waiting, not for us, Brother Ass, but for the plucky and tedious

9 on 11pt

Walking along the Mall we wondered who all those men were – tall hawk-featured men perched on balconies and high places, scanning the city with heavy binoculars. What were they seeking so earnestly? Who were they – so composed and steely-eyed? Timidly we stopped a policeman to ask him. 'They are publishers' he said mildly. Publishers! Our hearts stopped beating. 'They are on the look out for new talent.' Great God! It was for *us* they were waiting and watching! Then the kindly policeman lowered his voice confidentially and said in hollow and reverent tones: *'They are waiting for the new Trollope to be born!'* Do you remember, at these words, how heavy our suitcases suddenly felt? How our blood slowed, our footsteps lagged? Brother Ass, we had been bashfully thinking of a kind of illumination such as Rimbaud dreamed of – a nagging poem which was not didactic or expository but which *infected* – was not simply a rationalised intuition, I mean, clothed in isinglass! We

10 on 12pt

Walking along the Mall we wondered who all those men were – tall hawk-featured men perched on balconies and high places, scanning the city with heavy binoculars. What were they seeking so earnestly? Who were they – so composed and steely-eyed? Timidly we stopped a policeman to ask him. 'They are publishers' he said mildly. Publishers! Our hearts stopped beating. 'They are on the look out for new talent.' Great God! It was for *us* they were waiting and watching! Then the kindly policeman lowered his voice confidentially and said in hollow and reverent tones: *'They are waiting for the new Trollope to be born!'* Do you remember, at these words, how heavy our suitcases suddenly felt? How our blood slowed, our footsteps lagged? Brother Ass, we had been bashfully thinking of a kind of illumination such as Rimbaud dreamed of – a

11 on 13pt

WALKING ALONG THE MALL WE WONDERED WHO ALL THOSE MEN WERE – tall hawk-featured men perched on balconies and high places, scanning the city with heavy binoculars. What were they seeking so earnestly? Who were they – so composed and steely-eyed? Timidly we stopped a policeman to ask him. 'They are publishers' he said mildly. Publishers! Our hearts stopped beating. 'They are on the look out for new talent.' Great God! It was for *us* they were waiting and watching! Then the kindly policeman lowered his voice confidentially and said in hollow and reverent tones: *'They are waiting for the new Trollope to be born!'* Do you remember, at these words, how heavy our suitcases suddenly felt? How our blood slowed, our footsteps lagged? Brother Ass, we had been bashfully thinking of a kind of illumination such as Rimbaud dreamed of – a nagging poem which was not didactic or expository but which *infected* – was not simply a rationalised intuition, I mean, clothed in isinglass! We had come to the wrong shop, with the wrong change! A chill struck us as we saw the mist falling in Trafalgar Square, coiling round us its tendrils of ectoplasm! A million muffin-

9 on 12pt

WALKING ALONG THE MALL WE WONDERED WHO ALL THOSE MEN were – tall hawk-featured men perched on balconies and high places, scanning the city with heavy binoculars. What were they seeking so earnestly? Who were they – so composed and steely-eyed? Timidly we stopped a policeman to ask him. 'They are publishers' he said mildly. Publishers! Our hearts stopped beating. 'They are on the look out for new talent.' Great God! It was for *us* they were waiting and watching! Then the kindly policeman lowered his voice confidentially and said in hollow and reverent tones: *'They are waiting for the new Trollope to be born!'* Do you remember, at these words, how heavy our suitcases suddenly felt? How our blood slowed, our footsteps lagged? Brother Ass, we had been bashfully thinking of a kind of illumination such as Rimbaud dreamed of – a nagging poem which was not didactic or expository but which *infected* – was not

10 on 13.5pt

WALKING ALONG THE MALL WE WONDERED WHO ALL THOSE men were – tall hawk-featured men perched on balconies and high places, scanning the city with heavy binoculars. What were they seeking so earnestly? Who were they – so composed and steely-eyed? Timidly we stopped a police-man to ask him. 'They are publishers' he said mildly. Pub-lishers! Our hearts stopped beating. 'They are on the look out for new talent.' Great God! It was for *us* they were waiting and watching! Then the kindly policeman lowered his voice confidentially and said in hollow and reverent tones: *'They are waiting for the new Trollope to be born!'* Do you remember, at these words, how heavy our suit-cases suddenly felt? How our blood slowed, our footsteps lagged? Brother Ass, we had been bashfully thinking of a

11 on 14.5pt

roman (05478), **italic** (13478)
Linotype 1960
Copyfitting code 129/126

ABCDEFGHIJKLMNOP
QRSTUVWXYZ abcdefg
hijklmnopqrstuvwxyz
1234567890 1234567890
fifl ()[]&£$.,;:-!?''

ABCDEFGHIJKLMNOP
QRSTUVWXYZ abcdefg
hijklmnopqrstuvwxyz
1234567890
fifl ()[]&£$.,;:-!?''

24 on 27pt

These examples show *normal* letterspacing and the effect of *reduced* letterspacing on roman setting *as well as on words in italic*: they also show the appearance of figures, for example 28 May 1964, within text. These & the ampersand are not included in the setting opposite.
Normal letterspacing

These examples show *normal* letterspacing and the effect of *reduced* letterspacing on roman setting *as well as on words in italic*: they also show the appearance of figures, for example 28 May 1964, within text. These & the ampersand are not included in the setting opposite.
Minus one unit spacing

These examples show *normal* letterspacing and the effect of *reduced* letterspacing on roman setting *as well as on words in italic*: they also show the appearance of figures, for example 28 May 1964, within text. These & the ampersand are not included in the setting opposite.
Minus two units spacing

WALKING ALONG THE MALL WE WONDERED WHO ALL
WALKING ALONG THE MALL WE WONDERED WHO
WALKING ALONG THE MALL WE WONDERED
Capitals: normal letterspacing/plus 4 units/plus 9 units

WALKING ALONG THE MALL WE WONDERED WHO ALL THOSE MEN WERE
WALKING ALONG THE MALL WE WONDERED WHO ALL THOSE MEN
WALKING ALONG THE MALL WE WONDERED WHO ALL THOSE
Small caps: normal letterspacing/plus 3 units/plus 6 units

WALKING ALONG THE MALL WE WONDERED WHO ALL THOSE MEN WERE
WALKING ALONG THE MALL WE WONDERED WHO ALL THOSE MEN WERE
True small caps/reduced capitals

WALKING ALONG THE MALL we wondered who all those men
WALKING ALONG THE MALL we wondered who all those men
True italic/sloped roman

Walking along the Mall we wondered who all those men were – tall hawk-featured men perched on balconies and high places, scanning the city with heavy binoculars. What were they seeking so earnestly? Who were they – so composed and steely-eyed? Timidly we stopped a policeman to ask him. 'They are publishers' he said mildly. Publishers! Our hearts stopped beating. 'They are on the look out for new talent.' Great God! It was for *us* they were waiting and watching! Then the kindly policeman lowered his voice confidentially and said in hollow and reverent tones: *'They are waiting for the new Trollope to be born!'* Do you remember, at these words, how heavy our suitcases suddenly felt? How our blood slowed, our footsteps lagged? Brother Ass, we had been bashfully thinking of a kind of illumination such as Rimbaud
8 on 9pt

WALKING ALONG THE MALL WE WONDERED WHO ALL THOSE MEN WERE – TALL HAWK-featured men perched on balconies and high places, scanning the city with heavy binoculars. What were they seeking so earnestly? Who were they – so composed and steely-eyed? Timidly we stopped a policeman to ask him. 'They are publishers' he said mildly. Publishers! Our hearts stopped beating. 'They are on the look out for new talent.' Great God! It was for *us* they were waiting and watching! Then the kindly policeman lowered his voice confidentially and said in hollow and reverent tones: *'They are waiting for the new Trollope to be born!'* Do you remember, at these words, how heavy our suitcases suddenly felt? How our blood slowed, our footsteps lagged?
8 on 10.5pt

Walking along the Mall we wondered who all those men were — tall hawk-featured men perched on balconies and high places, scanning the city with heavy binoculars. What were they seeking so earnestly? Who were they — so composed and steely-eyed? Timidly we stopped a policeman to ask him. 'They are publishers' he said mildly. Publishers! Our hearts stopped beating. 'They are on the look out for new talent.' Great God! It was for *us* they were waiting and watching! Then the kindly policeman lowered his voice confidentially and said in hollow and reverent tones: *'They are waiting for the new Trollope to be born!'* Do you remember, at these words, how heavy our suitcases suddenly felt? How our blood slowed, our footsteps lagged? Brother Ass, we had been bashfully thinking of a kind of illumination such as Rimbaud dreamed of — a nagging poem which was not didactic or expository but which *infected* — was not simply a rationalised intuition, I mean, clothed in isinglass! We had come to the wrong shop, with the wrong change! A chill struck us as we saw the mist falling in Trafalgar Square, coiling round us its tendrils of ectoplasm! A million muffin-eating moralists were waiting, not for us, Brother Ass, but for the plucky and tedious Trollope! (If you are dissatisfied with your form, reach for the *curette*.) Now do you wonder if I laugh a

9 on 11pt

Walking along the Mall we wondered who all those men were — tall hawk-featured men perched on balconies and high places, scanning the city with heavy binoculars. What were they seeking so earnestly? Who were they — so composed and steely-eyed? Timidly we stopped a policeman to ask him. 'They are publishers' he said mildly. Publishers! Our hearts stopped beating. 'They are on the look out for new talent.' Great God! It was for *us* they were waiting and watching! Then the kindly policeman lowered his voice confidentially and said in hollow and reverent tones: *'They are waiting for the new Trollope to be born!'* Do you remember, at these words, how heavy our suitcases suddenly felt? How our blood slowed, our footsteps lagged? Brother Ass, we had been bashfully thinking of a kind of illumination such as Rimbaud dreamed of — a nagging poem which was not didactic or expository but which *infected* — was not simply a rationalised intuition, I mean, clothed in isinglass! We had come to the wrong shop, with the wrong change! A chill struck us as we saw

10 on 12pt

Walking along the Mall we wondered who all those men were — tall hawk-featured men perched on balconies and high places, scanning the city with heavy binoculars. What were they seeking so earnestly? Who were they — so composed and steely-eyed? Timidly we stopped a policeman to ask him. 'They are publishers' he said mildly. Publishers! Our hearts stopped beating. 'They are on the look out for new talent.' Great God! It was for *us* they were waiting and watching! Then the kindly policeman lowered his voice confidentially and said in hollow and reverent tones: *'They are waiting for the new Trollope to be born!'* Do you remember, at these words, how heavy our suitcases suddenly felt? How our blood slowed, our footsteps lagged? Brother Ass, we had been bashfully thinking of a kind of illumination such as Rimbaud dreamed of — a nagging poem which was not didactic or

11 on 13pt

WALKING ALONG THE MALL WE WONDERED WHO ALL THOSE MEN WERE — TALL hawk-featured men perched on balconies and high places, scanning the city with heavy binoculars. What were they seeking so earnestly? Who were they — so composed and steely-eyed? Timidly we stopped a policeman to ask him. 'They are publishers' he said mildly. Publishers! Our hearts stopped beating. 'They are on the look out for new talent.' Great God! It was for *us* they were waiting and watching! Then the kindly policeman lowered his voice confidentially and said in hollow and reverent tones: *'They are waiting for the new Trollope to be born!'* Do you remember, at these words, how heavy our suitcases suddenly felt? How our blood slowed, our footsteps lagged? Brother Ass, we had been bashfully thinking of a kind of illumination such as Rimbaud dreamed of — a nagging poem which was not didactic or expository but which *infected* — was not simply a rationalised intuition, I mean, clothed in isinglass! We had come to the wrong shop, with the wrong change! A chill struck us as we saw the mist falling in Trafalgar Square, coiling round us its tendrils of ectoplasm! A million muffin-eating moralists were waiting, not for us, Brother Ass, but for the plucky and

9 on 12pt

WALKING ALONG THE MALL WE WONDERED WHO ALL THOSE MEN WERE — tall hawk-featured men perched on balconies and high places, scanning the city with heavy binoculars. What were they seeking so earnestly? Who were they — so composed and steely-eyed? Timidly we stopped a policeman to ask him. 'They are publishers' he said mildly. Publishers! Our hearts stopped beating. 'They are on the look out for new talent.' Great God! It was for *us* they were waiting and watching! Then the kindly policeman lowered his voice confidentially and said in hollow and reverent tones: *'They are waiting for the new Trollope to be born!'* Do you remember, at these words, how heavy our suitcases suddenly felt? How our blood slowed, our footsteps lagged? Brother Ass, we had been bashfully thinking of a kind of illumination such as Rimbaud dreamed of — a nagging poem which was not didactic or expository but which *infected* — was not simply a rationalised intuition, I mean, clothed in isinglass! We had

10 on 13.5pt

WALKING ALONG THE MALL WE WONDERED WHO ALL THOSE MEN were — tall hawk-featured men perched on balconies and high places, scanning the city with heavy binoculars. What were they seeking so earnestly? Who were they — so composed and steely-eyed? Timidly we stopped a policeman to ask him. 'They are publishers' he said mildly. Publishers! Our hearts stopped beating. 'They are on the look out for new talent.' Great God! It was for *us* they were waiting and watching! Then the kindly policeman lowered his voice confidentially and said in hollow and reverent tones: *'They are waiting for the new Trollope to be born!'* Do you remember, at these words, how heavy our suitcases suddenly felt? How our blood slowed, our footsteps lagged? Brother Ass, we had been bashfully thinking of a kind of illumination such as Rimbaud

11 on 14.5pt

Monotype **Zapf International**

1055 medium and italic
1056 demi
ITC 1977 (Hermann Zapf)
Copyfitting factor 44.0/42.6/47.6

The Linotype version is slightly smaller on the
body (copyfitting code 124/124/137), and the
range also includes light, light italic, demi-
italic, heavy, heavy italic

ABCDEFGHIJKLMNOP
QRSTUVWXYZ abcdefg
hijklmnopqrstuvwxyz
1234567890
fffifl ffiffl () []&£$.,;:-!?''

ABCDEFGHIJKLMNOP
QRSTUVWXYZ abcdefg
hijklmnopqrstuvwxyz
1234567890
fffiflffiffl ()[]&£$.,;:-!?''

ABCDEFGHIJKLMNOP
QRSTUVWXYZ abcdefg
hijklmnopqrstuvwxyz
1234567890
fffi fl ffiffl () []&£$.,;:-!?''

24 on 27pt

These examples show *normal* letterspacing and the effect of *reduced* letterspacing on roman setting *as well as on words in italic*: they also show the appearance of figures, for example 28 May 1964, within text. These & the ampersand are not included in the setting opposite.

Normal letterspacing

These examples show *normal* letterspacing and the effect of *reduced* letterspacing on roman setting *as well as on words in italic*: they also show the appearance of figures, for example 28 May 1964, within text. These & the ampersand are not included in the setting opposite.

Minus one unit spacing

These examples show *normal* letterspacing and the effect of *reduced* letterspacing on roman setting *as well as on words in italic*: they also show the appearance of figures, for example 28 May 1964, within text. These & the ampersand are not included in the setting opposite.

Minus two units spacing

WALKING ALONG THE MALL WE WONDERED WHO ALL THOSE
WALKING ALONG THE MALL WE WONDERED WHO ALL
WALKING ALONG THE MALL WE WONDERED WHO

Capitals: normal letterspacing/plus 9 units/plus 18 units

Walking along the Mall we wondered who all those men were – tall hawk-featured men perched on balconies and high places, scanning the city with heavy binoculars. WHAT WERE THEY SEEKING SO EARNESTLY? Who were they – so composed and steely-eyed? Timidly we stopped a policeman to ask him. 'They are publishers' he said mildly. Publishers! OUR HEARTS STOPPED BEATING. 'They are on the look out for new talent.' Great God! It was for *us* they were waiting

Text with reduced capitals normal letterspacing/plus 6 units

WALKING ALONG THE MALL we wondered who all those men were
WALKING ALONG THE MALL we wondered who all those men were

True italic/sloped roman

Walking along the Mall we wondered who all those men were – tall hawk-featured men perched on balconies and high places, scanning the city with heavy binoculars. What were they seeking so earnestly? Who were they – so composed and steely-eyed? Timidly we stopped a policeman to ask him. 'They are publishers' he said mildly. Publishers! Our hearts stopped beating. 'They are on the look out for new talent.' Great God! It was for *us* they were waiting and watching! Then the kindly policeman lowered his voice confidentially and said in hollow and reverent tones: *'They are waiting for the new Trollope to be born!'* Do you remember, at these words, how heavy our suitcases suddenly felt? How our blood slowed, our footsteps lagged? Brother Ass, we had been bashfully thinking of a kind of illumination such as

8 on 9pt

Walking along the Mall we wondered who all those men were – tall hawk-featured men perched on balconies and high places, scanning the city with heavy binoculars. What were they seeking so earnestly? Who were they – so composed and steely-eyed? Timidly we stopped a policeman to ask him. 'They are publishers' he said mildly. Publishers! Our hearts stopped beating. 'They are on the look out for new talent.' Great God! It was for *us* they were waiting and watching! Then the kindly policeman lowered his voice confidentially and said in hollow and reverent tones: *'They are waiting for the new Trollope to be born!'* Do you remember, at these words, how heavy our suitcases suddenly felt? How our blood slowed, our footsteps lagged? Brother Ass,

8 on 10.5pt

Walking along the Mall we wondered who all those men were – tall hawk-featured men perched on balconies and high places, scanning the city with heavy binoculars. What were they seeking so earnestly? Who were they – so composed and steely-eyed? Timidly we stopped a policeman to ask him. 'They are publishers' he said mildly. Publishers! Our hearts stopped beating. 'They are on the look out for new talent.' Great God! It was for *us* they were waiting and watching! Then the kindly policeman lowered his voice confidentially and said in hollow and reverent tones: *'They are waiting for the new Trollope to be born!'* Do you remember, at these words, how heavy our suitcases suddenly felt? How our blood slowed, our footsteps lagged? Brother Ass, we had been bashfully thinking of a kind of illumination such as Rimbaud dreamed of – a nagging poem which was not didactic or expository but which *infected* – was not simply a rationalised intuition, I mean, clothed in isinglass! We had come to the wrong shop, with the wrong change! A chill struck us as we saw the mist falling in Trafalgar Square, coiling around us its tendrils of ectoplasm! A million muffin-eating moralists were waiting, not for us, Brother Ass, but for the plucky and tedious Trollope! (If you are dissatisfied with your form, reach for the *curette*.) Now do you wonder if I laugh a little off-key? Do

9 on 11pt

Walking along the Mall we wondered who all those men were – tall hawk-featured men perched on balconies and high places, scanning the city with heavy binoculars. What were they seeking so earnestly? Who were they – so composed and steely-eyed? Timidly we stopped a policeman to ask him. 'They are publishers' he said mildly. Publishers! Our hearts stopped beating. 'They are on the look out for new talent.' Great God! It was for *us* they were waiting and watching! Then the kindly policeman lowered his voice confidentially and said in hollow and reverent tones: *'They are waiting for the new Trollope to be born!'* Do you remember, at these words, how heavy our suitcases suddenly felt? How our blood slowed, our footsteps lagged? Brother Ass, we had been bashfully thinking of a kind of illumination such as Rimbaud dreamed of – a nagging poem which was not didactic or expository but which *infected* – was not simply a rationalised intuition, I mean, clothed in isinglass! We had come to the wrong shop, with the wrong change! A chill struck us as we saw the mist falling in Trafalgar Square, coiling around us its tendrils of ectoplasm! A million muffin-eating moralists were waiting, not for us, Brother Ass, but for the plucky and tedious Trollope! (If you are dissatisfied with your form, reach for

9 on 12pt

Walking along the Mall we wondered who all those men were – tall hawk-featured men perched on balconies and high places, scanning the city with heavy binoculars. What were they seeking so earnestly? Who were they – so composed and steely-eyed? Timidly we stopped a policeman to ask him. 'They are publishers' he said mildly. Publishers! Our hearts stopped beating. 'They are on the look out for new talent.' Great God! It was for *us* they were waiting and watching! Then the kindly policeman lowered his voice confidentially and said in hollow and reverent tones: *'They are waiting for the new Trollope to be born!'* Do you remember, at these words, how heavy our suitcases suddenly felt? How our blood slowed, our footsteps lagged? Brother Ass, we had been bashfully thinking of a kind of illumination such as Rimbaud dreamed of – a nagging poem which was not didactic or expository but which *infected* – was not simply a rationalised intuition, I mean, clothed in isinglass! We had come to the wrong shop, with the

10 on 12pt

Walking along the Mall we wondered who all those men were – tall hawk-featured men perched on balconies and high places, scanning the city with heavy binoculars. What were they seeking so earnestly? Who were they – so composed and steely-eyed? Timidly we stopped a policeman to ask him. 'They are publishers' he said mildly. Publishers! Our hearts stopped beating. 'They are on the look out for new talent.' Great God! It was for *us* they were waiting and watching! Then the kindly policeman lowered his voice confidentially and said in hollow and reverent tones: *'They are waiting for the new Trollope to be born!'* Do you remember, at these words, how heavy our suitcases suddenly felt? How our blood slowed, our footsteps lagged? Brother Ass, we had been bashfully thinking of a kind of illumination such as Rimbaud dreamed of – a nagging poem which was not didactic or expository but which *infected* – was not simply a rationalised intuition, I mean, clothed in isinglass! We had come to the wrong shop, with the

10 on 13.5pt

Walking along the Mall we wondered who all those men were – tall hawk-featured men perched on balconies and high places, scanning the city with heavy binoculars. What were they seeking so earnestly? Who were they – so composed and steely-eyed? Timidly we stopped a policeman to ask him. 'They are publishers' he said mildly. Publishers! Our hearts stopped beating. 'They are on the look out for new talent.' Great God! It was for *us* they were waiting and watching! Then the kindly policeman lowered his voice confidentially and said in hollow and reverent tones: *'They are waiting for the new Trollope to be born!'* Do you remember, at these words, how heavy our suitcases suddenly felt? How our blood slowed, our footsteps lagged? Brother Ass, we had been bashfully thinking of a kind of illumination such as Rimbaud dreamed of – a nagging poem which was not didactic or expository but which *infected* – was not simply a

11 on 13pt

Walking along the Mall we wondered who all those men were – tall hawk-featured men perched on balconies and high places, scanning the city with heavy binoculars. What were they seeking so earnestly? Who were they – so composed and steely-eyed? Timidly we stopped a policeman to ask him. 'They are publishers' he said mildly. Publishers! Our hearts stopped beating. 'They are on the look out for new talent.' Great God! It was for *us* they were waiting and watching! Then the kindly policeman lowered his voice confidentially and said in hollow and reverent tones: *'They are waiting for the new Trollope to be born!'* Do you remember, at these words, how heavy our suitcases suddenly felt? How our blood slowed, our footsteps lagged? Brother Ass, we had been bashfully thinking of a kind of illumination such as Rimbaud dreamed of – a nagging poem which was not didactic

11 on 14.5pt

6 | Points of Style

Our suggestions for the detailing of text setting are to be taken as a general guide requiring possible adjustment to particular problems or typefaces. They are based on the criterion of minimum complication and maximum clarity. For example, if an abbreviation is unambiguous without a full point, why use one? Our aims are to achieve a clean, even texture without unnecessary punctuation – Morison's 'maximum repose'.

In text setting of lower case letters, the normal letterspacing as recommended by the manufacturers, and for which the type has been designed, should generally be followed. It should never be increased (with the possible exceptions of Cartier and Galliard, the latter designed during the height of the fashion, in some quarters, for minimum letterspacing). Occasionally, some slight closing-up is possible. Spacing should never be varied from line to line.

In *display* sizes of lower case letters (18 pt and over), some reduction of letterspacing is usually desirable.

For text and display, word spacing should be even and close: the optimum is between 18 and 24 units Mono, 4 units Lino, in justified setting; and a constant 24 (or preferably 21) units Mono, 4 units Lino, in unjustified setting.

In justified setting, and in unjustified setting of continuous text, word breaks at the ends of lines are preferable to erratic setting and ragged lines. Short captions, and certain kinds of setting with many short lines and, maybe, many names (such as catalogue entries) are best set without word breaks, unjustified.

The optimum measure for continuous text in bookwork is one accomodating 60-70 characters per line. Longer lines can be made more acceptable by more generous leading (or line feed), but anything above 90 characters is undesirable. Forty-five characters is about the minimum acceptable, although brief captions might be set with as few as 25.

Short lines ending a paragraph at the top of a page should be avoided, particularly in justified setting. If neither editing nor resetting can solve the problem, it is often better to allow the page (and perhaps its fellow opposite) to carry an extra line.

All setting is made more readable by leading.

Word breaks

The computer commanding the typesetter will have a programme for word breaks, but many awkward or bizarre breaks will need later correction if the keyboard operator has not over-ridden the basic instructions. Some dictionaries, such as *Collins English Dictionary*, show where word breaks may (and must not) occur for every word.

The full point

The full point should be used sparingly. Its chief purpose is to denote the end of a sentence. Unnecessary use is disturbing and confusing. It should be used only if its absence creates ambiguity. Commonly, it is not used after contractions (Mr, Mrs, Dr, St, Ltd, and so on), but *is* used after abbreviations (Esq., Co., Inc.). However, most abbreviations are quite unambiguous without it, and the following rules are suggested.

Omit after all contractions.

Omit after all common abbreviations: Esq, Rev, Co, Inc, etc, mm, cm, km, kg, MS, ibid, per cent; and after *any* abbreviation so long as clarity is maintained.

Omit after ft, yd, yds, cwt, lb, oz.

The word *inch* is best spelt out if it occurs within a sentence. If used repeatedly as in a catalogue (especially if preceded or followed by metric equivalents) it should be abbreviated to 'in' (never 'ins') with no full point.

Omit from mph, kph.

Omit from all groups of initials: BL, BM, BBC, USA, UNESCO.

Omit from awards and honours: MA, PhD, FRIBA, MIEFE, DSO, CH.

Omit from all postal codes.

Omit in BC, AD.

Eg and *ie* should either be set in italic without full points or space or, preferably, translated (for instance, that is).

Use *either:* p 63, pp 80-95, vol 89, fig 204, pl 43, no 6 (no full point but half word space after). *No* without a full point can sometimes be ambiguous.

Or: p.63, pp.80-95, vol.89, fig.204, pl.43, no.6 (with full point but no space after).

Use *either:* c1900, *fl*1800, d1643 (in italic with no full point and no space after).

Or: c.1900, *fl*.1800, d.1643 (in italic with full point and no space after).

Print 6 am, 11.30 pm with half word space after figures, no full points within or following am, pm.

Initials before a name are best without full points, with normal word space: A R Brown, Alfred R Brown. But if full points are used, they should be followed by a half word space: A. R. Brown, Alfred R. Brown. Initials should never be closed up: never A.R.Brown *nor* A.R. Brown.

Spell out Professor (not Prof.).

Lt Col, Maj Gen, Capt: either omit full points or, preferably, spell out.

Rt Hon without full points, MP without full points.

The comma

Omit after street numbers and between name of city/town and postal code.

Omit between a name and the honour/award, and between awards:
A R Brown FSA FRSL FBA.

The dash

Use en dash (not a hyphen) with word space either side.

Marks of omission

Should consist of three full points (never more), half word spaced, preceded and followed by one word space . . . It has become common practice to add a fourth full point if the omission is at the end of a sentence, but it is doubtful if the general reader recognises this refinement, and it is best forgotten.

Quotations

Use single quotes; double quotes for quotations within quotations. Extended quotations should normally be set in a smaller type size, without quote marks, with a half line space above and below, and not indented.

If a smaller type size is undesirable (for instance, there is a large amount of quoted matter throughout the book, or the main text size is already rather small), use the text size, with quote marks, half line space above and below, and not indented. It is sometimes a good idea, if the main text is justified, to unjustify the quotation, ranging left and not indenting.

Capitals, small capitals and non-lining figures

If the typeface is available with non-lining figures, they should always be used in preference to lining figures, except sometimes for tabular matter.

If the typeface includes small capitals, they should be used for groups of initials, postal codes (in combination with non-lining figures), complete words or phrases in capitals within the text, and so on. The practice of using reduced full capitals should be avoided, particularly within continuous text, as they will appear too light in relation to the lower case letters.

Within text, capitals and small caps are usually better *slightly* letterspaced: not more than 12 units Mono, 6 units Lino for capitals; and 6 units Mono, 3 units Lino for small caps. Anything more is likely to weaken the line.

For headings, running heads and display, the letterspacing might be increased up to 18 units Mono, 9 units Lino for capitals; and 12 units Mono, 6 units Lino for small caps.

The Linotron unit spacing is unfortunately confusing, there being 18 units to the em for word spacing and 54 units to the em for letter spacing. In the above paragraphs, the 54 unit system is used. Monotype uses a consistent 96 units to the em.

Groups of initials consisting of more than three letters should be set in small caps if possible (possibly slightly letterspaced), although names of countries should perhaps always be in full capitals: UK, USA, USSR.

If a group of initials is followed by a word commencing with a capital, this group is best in capitals: ICI Chemicals, not ICI Chemicals.

Roman figures can be a problem. Charles I looks diminutive, Henry VIII is rather strong. In this situation it is perhaps best to use full caps throughout; but otherwise, roman numerals are usually best in small caps. A possible compromise is to use caps up to V, small caps thereafter: vol IV, vols XVIII-XXII. Thereby the confusion of vol II (two or eleven?) is avoided – at least if non-lining figures are used elsewhere.

MS, MSS should always be in small caps, if available, with no full points.

BSC, PhD, FIInfSc, FIBiol are problems. Nevertheless, if many names with honours and awards are shown, the lesser evil is probably to use small caps, with lower case where necessary, rather than spattering the page with capitals and overwhelming the name.

Figures and dimensions

Print: from 500 to 600 *or* 500-600, *not* from 500-600. Use a hyphen with a thin space (1 unit) either side.

Dates: 1808-9, 1809-12, 1820-21. Use a hyphen with a thin space (1 unit) either side. Strictly speaking, no extra space is needed before or after a 1. Do not repeat the century: 1780-1820, 1820-30, but not 1820-1830.

Print 18 May 1962, in that order, no commas, no *th*.

Print 500 BC, but AD 500.

Print 18 ft, 21 mm with half word space.

Print 180 × 220 mm, 23 × 16 × 6 in; 'mm' or 'in' to appear only after final dimension, and should be preceded by half word space. The × should be of x-height, align on base line, and have half word spaces either side (not more). Some Monotype multiplication signs have spaces incorporated. If the typesetter does not hold a multiplication sign aligning on the base line, use a lower case x (preferably from a sans serif or grotesque type).

Monotype and Linotype employ different systems of copyfitting. Their factors or codes are shown on our specimen pages in the order in which the types are described. For example, the Linotype codes 125/123/142 refer respectively to the roman, its italic, and the bold.

The **Monotype** system employs the following formula:

For pica measurements

$$\frac{\text{measure (in picas)} \times 1152}{\text{copyfitting factor} \times \text{type size}} = \begin{array}{l}\text{the average number}\\ \text{of characters per line}\end{array}$$

If the point size and measure are both in mm, or both in cicero, the equation remains the same.

If the point size is in pica, measure in mm, multiply the top line by 2.82.
If the point size is in mm, measure in pica, multiply the bottom line by 2.82.

If the point size is in pica, measure in cicero, multiply the top line by 1.07.
If the point size is in cicero, measure in pica, multiply the top line by 1.07.

The **Linotype** system employs the following tables.
1. Note the code given on our specimen pages.
2. Find this code in the first column of Table 1, and move horizontally across until you meet the column with the required type size; note this alphabet length number.
3. Turn to the table for the system of measurement you are using (Table 2 for pica, Table 3 for mm). In the first column find your determined alphabet length number. Move horizontally across until you meet the column for the required line length. The figure found is the average number of characters for that line length.

Linotype Table 1. Alphabet lengths for different sizes

pt	6	7	8	9	10	11	12	14	16	18	20	24	30	36	42	48
mm	2,25	2,63	3,00	3,38	3,75	4,13	4,50	5,25	6,00	6,75	7,50	9,00	11,25	13,50	15,75	18,00
85	51	59	68	76	85	93	102	119	136	153	170	204	255	306	357	408
87	52	60	69	78	87	95	104	121	139	156	174	208	261	313	365	417
88	52	61	70	79	88	96	105	123	140	158	176	211	264	316	369	422
90	54	63	72	81	90	99	108	126	144	162	180	216	270	324	378	432
92	55	64	73	82	92	101	110	128	147	165	184	220	276	331	386	441
93	55	65	74	83	93	102	111	130	148	167	186	223	279	334	390	446
95	57	66	76	85	95	104	114	133	152	171	190	228	285	342	399	456
97	58	67	77	87	97	106	116	135	155	174	194	232	291	349	407	465
98	58	68	78	88	98	107	117	137	156	176	196	235	294	352	411	470
100	60	70	80	90	100	110	120	140	160	180	200	240	300	360	420	480
102	61	71	81	91	102	112	122	142	163	183	204	244	306	367	428	489
103	61	72	82	92	103	113	123	144	164	185	206	247	309	370	432	494
105	63	73	84	94	105	115	126	147	168	189	210	252	315	378	441	504
107	64	74	85	96	107	117	128	149	171	192	214	256	321	385	449	513
108	64	75	86	97	108	118	129	151	172	194	216	259	324	388	453	518
110	66	77	88	99	110	121	132	154	176	198	220	264	330	396	462	528
112	67	78	89	100	112	123	134	156	179	201	224	268	336	403	470	537
113	67	79	90	101	113	124	135	158	180	203	226	271	339	406	474	542
115	69	80	92	103	115	126	138	161	184	207	230	276	345	414	483	552
117	70	81	93	105	117	128	140	163	187	210	234	280	351	421	491	561
118	70	82	94	106	118	129	141	165	188	212	236	283	354	424	495	566
120	72	84	96	108	120	132	144	168	192	216	240	288	360	432	504	576
122	73	85	97	109	122	134	146	170	195	219	244	292	366	439	512	585
123	73	86	98	110	123	135	147	172	196	221	246	295	369	442	516	590
125	75	87	100	112	125	137	150	175	200	225	250	300	375	450	525	600
127	76	88	101	114	127	139	152	177	203	228	254	304	381	457	533	609
128	76	89	102	115	128	140	153	179	204	230	256	307	384	460	537	614
130	78	91	104	117	130	143	156	182	208	234	260	312	390	468	546	624
132	79	92	105	118	132	145	158	184	211	237	264	316	396	475	554	633
133	79	93	106	119	133	146	159	186	212	239	266	319	399	478	558	638
135	81	94	108	121	135	148	162	189	216	243	270	324	405	486	567	648
137	82	95	109	123	137	150	164	191	219	246	274	328	411	493	575	657
138	82	96	110	124	138	151	165	193	220	248	276	331	414	496	579	662
140	84	98	112	126	140	154	168	196	224	252	280	336	420	504	588	672
142	85	99	113	127	142	156	170	198	227	255	284	340	426	511	596	681
143	85	100	114	128	143	157	171	200	228	257	286	343	429	514	600	686
145	87	101	116	130	145	159	174	203	232	261	290	348	435	522	609	696
147	88	102	117	132	147	161	176	205	235	264	294	352	441	529	617	705
148	88	103	118	133	148	162	177	207	236	266	296	355	444	532	621	710
150	90	105	120	135	150	165	180	210	240	270	300	360	450	540	630	720
152	91	106	121	136	152	167	182	212	243	273	304	364	456	547	638	729
153	91	107	122	137	153	168	183	214	244	275	306	367	459	550	642	734
155	93	108	124	139	155	170	186	217	248	279	310	372	465	558	651	744
157	94	109	125	141	157	172	188	219	251	282	314	376	471	565	659	753
158	94	110	126	142	158	173	189	221	252	284	316	379	474	568	663	758
160	96	112	128	144	160	176	192	224	256	288	320	384	480	576	672	768
162	97	113	129	145	162	178	194	226	259	291	324	388	486	583	680	777
163	97	114	130	146	163	179	195	228	260	293	326	391	489	586	684	782
165	99	115	132	148	165	181	198	231	264	297	330	396	495	594	693	792
167	100	116	133	150	167	183	200	233	267	300	334	400	501	601	701	801
168	100	117	134	151	168	184	201	235	268	302	336	403	504	604	705	806
170	102	119	136	153	170	187	204	238	272	306	340	408	510	612	714	816
172	103	120	137	154	172	189	206	240	275	309	344	412	516	619	722	825
173	103	121	138	155	173	190	207	242	276	311	346	415	519	622	726	830
175	105	122	140	157	175	192	210	245	280	315	350	420	525	630	735	840
177	106	123	141	159	177	194	212	247	283	318	354	424	531	637	743	849
178	106	124	142	160	178	195	213	249	284	320	356	427	534	640	747	854
180	108	126	144	162	180	198	216	252	288	324	360	432	540	648	756	864
182	109	127	145	163	182	200	218	254	291	327	364	436	546	655	764	873
183	109	128	146	164	183	201	219	256	292	329	366	439	549	658	768	878

Linotype Table 2. Characters per line (pica)

Pica	1.00	10	12	14	16	18	20	22	24	26	28	30	32	36	40	45
50	6.74	67	81	94	108	121	135	148	162	175	189	202	216	243	270	303
52	6.48	65	78	91	104	117	130	143	156	168	181	194	207	233	259	292
54	6.24	62	75	87	100	112	125	137	150	162	175	187	200	225	250	281
56	6.02	60	72	84	96	108	120	132	144	156	168	181	193	217	241	271
58	5.81	58	70	81	93	105	116	128	139	151	163	174	186	209	232	261
60	5.62	56	67	79	90	101	112	124	135	146	157	168	180	202	225	253
62	5.43	54	65	76	87	98	109	120	130	141	152	163	174	196	217	245
64	5.27	53	63	74	84	95	105	116	126	137	147	158	168	190	211	237
66	5.11	51	61	71	82	92	102	112	123	133	143	153	163	184	204	230
68	4.96	50	59	69	79	89	99	109	119	129	139	149	159	178	198	223
70	4.81	48	58	67	77	87	96	106	116	125	135	144	154	173	193	217
72	4.68	47	56	66	75	84	94	103	112	122	131	140	150	168	187	211
74	4.55	46	55	64	73	82	91	100	109	118	127	137	146	164	182	205
76	4.43	44	53	62	71	80	89	98	106	115	124	133	142	160	177	200
78	4.32	43	52	60	69	78	86	95	104	112	121	130	138	156	173	194
80	4.21	42	51	59	67	76	84	93	101	110	118	126	135	152	168	190
82	4.11	41	49	58	66	74	82	90	99	107	115	123	131	148	164	185
84	4.01	40	48	56	64	72	80	88	96	104	112	120	128	144	160	181
86	3.92	39	47	55	63	71	78	86	94	102	110	118	125	141	157	176
88	3.83	38	46	54	61	69	77	84	92	100	107	115	123	138	153	172
90	3.74	37	45	52	60	67	75	82	90	97	105	112	120	135	150	168
92	3.66	37	44	51	59	66	73	81	88	95	103	110	117	132	147	165
94	3.58	36	43	50	57	65	72	79	86	93	100	108	115	129	143	161
96	3.51	35	42	49	56	63	70	77	84	91	98	105	112	126	140	158
98	3.44	34	41	48	55	62	69	76	83	89	96	103	110	124	138	155
100	3.37	34	40	47	54	61	67	74	81	88	94	101	108	121	135	152
102	3.30	33	40	46	53	59	66	73	79	86	92	99	106	119	132	149
104	3.24	32	39	45	52	58	65	71	78	84	91	97	104	117	130	146
106	3.18	32	38	45	51	57	64	70	76	83	89	95	102	114	127	143
108	3.12	31	37	44	50	56	62	69	75	81	87	94	100	112	125	140
110	3.06	31	37	43	49	55	61	67	74	80	86	92	98	110	123	138
112	3.01	30	36	42	48	54	60	66	72	78	84	90	96	108	120	135
114	2.96	30	35	41	47	53	59	65	71	77	83	89	95	106	118	133
116	2.90	29	35	41	46	52	58	64	70	76	81	87	93	105	116	131
118	2.86	29	34	40	46	51	57	63	69	74	80	86	91	103	114	129
120	2.81	28	34	39	45	51	56	62	67	73	79	84	90	101	112	126
122	2.76	28	33	39	44	50	55	61	66	72	77	83	88	99	110	124
124	2.72	27	33	38	43	49	54	60	65	71	76	82	87	98	109	122
126	2.67	27	32	37	43	48	53	59	64	70	75	80	86	96	107	120
128	2.63	26	32	37	42	47	53	58	63	68	74	79	84	95	105	118
130	2.59	26	31	36	41	47	52	57	62	67	73	78	83	93	104	117
132	2.55	26	31	36	41	46	51	56	61	66	71	77	82	92	102	115
134	2.51	25	30	35	40	45	50	55	60	65	70	75	80	91	101	113
136	2.48	25	30	35	40	45	50	55	59	64	69	74	79	89	99	111
138	2.44	24	29	34	39	44	49	54	59	63	68	73	78	88	98	110
140	2.41	24	29	34	39	43	48	53	58	63	67	72	77	87	96	108
145	2.32	23	28	33	37	42	46	51	56	60	65	70	74	84	93	105
150	2.25	22	27	31	36	40	45	49	54	58	63	67	72	81	90	101
155	2.17	22	26	30	35	39	43	48	52	57	61	65	70	78	87	98
160	2.11	21	25	29	34	38	42	46	51	55	59	63	67	76	84	95
165	2.04	20	25	29	33	37	41	45	49	53	57	61	65	74	82	92
170	1.98	20	24	28	32	36	40	44	48	52	55	59	63	71	79	89
175	1.93	19	23	27	31	35	39	42	46	50	54	58	62	69	77	87
180	1.87	19	22	26	30	34	37	41	45	49	52	56	60	67	75	84
185	1.82	18	22	25	29	33	36	40	44	47	51	55	58	66	73	82
190	1.77	18	21	25	28	32	35	39	43	46	50	53	57	64	71	80
195	1.73	17	21	24	28	31	35	38	41	45	48	52	55	62	69	78
200	1.68	17	20	24	27	30	34	37	40	44	47	51	54	61	67	76
220	1.53	15	18	21	25	28	31	34	37	40	43	46	49	55	61	69
240	1.40	14	17	20	22	25	28	31	34	37	39	42	45	51	56	63

Linotype Table 3. Characters per line (mm)

mm	1.00	40	50	60	70	80	90	100	110	120	130	140	150	160	170	190
50	1.60	64	80	96	112	128	144	160	176	192	208	224	240	256	272	304
52	1.54	62	77	92	108	123	138	154	169	185	200	215	231	246	262	292
54	1.48	59	74	89	104	119	133	148	163	178	193	207	222	237	252	281
56	1.43	57	71	86	100	114	129	143	157	171	186	200	214	229	243	271
58	1.38	55	69	83	97	110	124	138	152	166	179	193	207	221	234	262
60	1.33	53	67	80	93	107	120	133	147	160	173	187	200	213	227	253
62	1.29	52	65	77	90	103	116	129	142	155	168	181	194	206	219	245
64	1.25	50	63	75	88	100	113	125	138	150	163	175	188	200	213	238
66	1.21	48	61	73	85	97	109	121	133	145	158	170	182	194	206	230
68	1.18	47	59	71	82	94	106	118	129	141	153	165	176	188	200	224
70	1.14	46	57	69	80	91	103	114	126	137	149	160	171	183	194	217
72	1.11	44	56	67	78	89	100	111	122	133	144	156	167	178	189	211
74	1.08	43	54	65	76	86	97	108	119	130	141	151	162	173	184	205
76	1.05	42	53	63	74	84	95	105	116	126	137	147	158	168	179	200
78	1.03	41	51	62	72	82	92	103	113	123	133	144	154	164	174	195
80	1.00	40	50	60	70	80	90	100	110	120	130	140	150	160	170	190
82	0.98	39	49	59	68	78	88	98	107	117	127	137	146	156	166	185
84	0.95	38	48	57	67	76	86	95	105	114	124	133	143	152	162	181
86	0.93	37	47	56	65	74	84	93	102	112	121	130	140	149	158	177
88	0.91	36	45	55	64	73	82	91	100	109	118	127	136	145	155	173
90	0.89	36	44	53	62	71	80	89	98	107	116	124	133	142	151	169
92	0.87	35	43	52	61	70	78	87	96	104	113	122	130	139	148	165
94	0.85	34	43	51	60	68	77	85	94	102	111	119	128	136	145	162
96	0.83	33	42	50	58	67	75	83	92	100	108	117	125	133	142	158
98	0.82	33	41	49	57	65	73	82	90	98	106	114	122	131	139	155
100	0.80	32	40	48	56	64	72	80	88	96	104	112	120	128	136	152
102	0.78	31	39	47	55	63	71	78	86	94	102	110	118	125	133	149
104	0.77	31	38	46	54	62	69	77	85	92	100	108	115	123	131	146
106	0.75	30	38	45	53	60	68	75	83	91	98	106	113	121	128	143
108	0.74	30	37	44	52	59	67	74	81	89	96	104	111	119	126	141
110	0.73	29	36	44	51	58	65	73	80	87	95	102	109	116	124	138
112	0.71	29	36	43	50	57	64	71	79	86	93	100	107	114	121	136
114	0.70	28	35	42	49	56	63	70	77	83	89	98	105	112	119	133
116	0.69	28	34	41	48	55	62	69	76	83	90	97	103	110	117	131
118	0.68	27	34	41	47	54	61	68	75	81	88	95	102	108	113	129
120	0.67	27	33	40	47	53	60	67	73	80	87	93	100	107	113	127
122	0.66	26	33	39	46	52	59	66	72	79	85	92	98	105	111	125
124	0.65	26	32	39	45	52	58	65	71	77	84	90	97	103	110	123
126	0.63	25	32	38	44	51	57	63	70	76	83	89	95	102	108	121
128	0.63	25	31	38	44	50	56	63	69	75	81	88	94	100	106	119
130	0.62	25	31	37	43	49	55	62	68	74	80	86	92	98	105	117
132	0.61	24	30	36	42	48	55	61	67	73	79	85	91	97	103	115
134	0.60	24	30	36	42	48	54	60	66	72	78	84	90	96	101	113
136	0.59	24	29	35	41	47	53	59	65	71	76	82	88	94	100	112
138	0.58	23	29	35	41	46	52	58	64	70	75	81	87	93	99	110
140	0.57	23	29	34	40	46	51	57	63	69	74	80	86	91	97	109
145	0.55	22	28	33	39	44	50	55	61	66	72	77	83	88	94	105
150	0.53	21	27	32	37	43	48	53	59	64	69	75	80	85	91	101
155	0.52	21	26	31	36	41	46	52	57	62	67	72	77	83	88	98
160	0.50	20	25	30	35	40	45	50	55	60	65	70	75	80	85	95
165	0.48	19	24	29	34	39	44	48	53	58	63	68	73	78	82	92
170	0.47	19	24	28	33	38	42	47	52	56	61	66	71	75	80	89
175	0.46	18	23	27	32	37	41	46	50	55	59	64	69	73	78	87
180	0.44	18	22	27	31	36	40	44	49	53	58	62	67	71	76	84
185	0.43	17	22	26	30	35	39	43	48	52	56	61	65	69	74	82
190	0.42	17	21	25	29	34	38	42	46	51	55	59	63	67	72	80
195	0.41	16	21	25	29	33	37	41	45	49	53	57	62	66	70	78
200	0.40	16	20	24	28	32	36	40	44	48	52	56	60	64	68	76
220	0.36	15	18	22	25	29	33	36	40	44	47	51	55	58	62	69
240	0.33	13	17	20	23	27	30	33	37	40	43	47	50	53	57	63

Rules

.25 pt	.09 mm	
.5 pt	.18 mm	
.75 pt	.27 mm	
1 pt	.35 mm	
2 pt	.70 mm	
3 pt	1.05 mm	
4 pt	1.41 mm	
5 pt	1.76 mm	
6 pt	2.11 mm	
9 pt	8.16 mm	
12 pt	4.22 mm	

Dotted rules

Filmsetting dotted rules are created from the full point of the type size used

8 pt close spaced
8 pt 3-dot per em of set
8 pt 2-dot per em of set

9 pt close spaced
9 pt 3-dot per em of set
9 pt 2-dot per em of set

10 pt close spaced
10 pt 3-dot per em of set
10 pt 2-dot per em of set

12 pt close spaced
12 pt 3-dot per em of set
12 pt 2-dot per em of set

14 pt close spaced
14 pt 3-dot per em of set
14 pt 2-dot per em of set

18 pt close spaced
18 pt 3-dot per em of set
18 pt 2-dot per em of set

24 pt close spaced
24 pt 3-dot per em of set
24 pt 2-dot per em of set

Typographic signs

The design of these may vary with the typeface.
Stars and asterisks are shown here spaced one em of set.

8 pt	★ ★ ★ ★ ★ ★ ★	· · · · · · ·	‡ † ¶ §
9 pt	★ ★ ★ ★ ★ ★	· · · · · ·	‡ † ¶ §
10 pt	★ ★ ★ ★ ★	· · · · · ·	‡ † ¶ §
12 pt	★ ★ ★ ★ ★	* * * * *	‡ † ¶ §
14 pt	★ ★ ★ ★	* * * *	‡ † ¶ §
18 pt	★ ★ ★	* * *	‡ † ¶ §

Circles, squares and triangles

4 pt	•	◦	▪	◻	▸	▷
6 pt	•	◦	▪	◻	▸	▷
8 pt	•	◦	▪	◻	▸	▷
10 pt	●	○	■	◻	▶	▷
12 pt	●	○	■	▢	▶	▷

Equivalents to pica sizes

The following table gives direct translations of pica point body sizes to mm and didot (cicero) measurements. Specification would normally be made to the nearest 0.25 mm or 0.5 ptD. However, the tendency is for the pica system to be used. If faced with mm specifications, many typesetters will convert them to pica points.

7 pt	2.46 mm	6.54 Didot pts
7.5	2.64	7.01
8	2.82	7.48
8.5	2.99	7.95
9	3.16	8.41
9.5	3.34	8.88
10	3.52	9.35
10.5	3.69	9.82
11	3.87	10.28
11.5	4.05	10.75
12	4.22	11.21
12.5	4.40	11.68
13	4.57	12.15
13.5	4.75	12.62

Bibliography

J Barr	*The Officina Bodoni 1923-1977*, London 1978
W Berry, A Johnson and W Jaspert	*The Encyclopedia of Typefaces*. London 1962, 1970
J Blumenthal	*The Art of the Printed Book 1455-1955*. London 1974
J Blumenthal	*The Printed Book in America*. London & Boston 1978
S Carter	*Twentieth Century Type Designers*. London 1987
C Clair	*A History of European Printing*. London & New York 1976
S Compton	*The World Backwards: Russian Futurist Books 1912-16*. London 1978
J Craig	*Phototypesetting: a design manual*. New York 1970
G Dowding	*An Introduction to the History of Printing Types*. London 1961
A Frutiger	*Type, Sign, Symbol*. Zurich 1980
A E R Gill	*An Essay on Typography*. 1931, reprinted London 1960, 1988
G Glaister	*Glaister's Glossary of the Book*. London 1979
E Gottschall	*Typographic Communication Today*. Cambridge (Mass) & London 1989
A Harbert (ed)	*Hans Schmoller*. Monotype Recorder 6. Salfords 1987
D Hewison	*Introduction to Desktop Publishing*. London 1988
J Hochuli	*Detail in Typography*. Wilmington (Mass) 1987
J Lewis	*The Twentieth Century Book*. London & New York 1967, 1984
R McLean	*Jan Tschichold: Typographer*. London 1975, 1990
R McLean	*Typography*. London 1980
J Miles	*Design for Desktop Publishing*. London 1987
S Morison	*Four Centuries of Fine Printing*. London 1960
S Morison	*A Tally of Types*. Cambridge 1973
C Perfect and G Rookledge	*Rookledge's International Typefinder*. London 1983
A Pryce-Jones	'The Visual Impact of Books'. *Penrose Annual*. London 1952
J Russell Taylor	*The Art Nouveau Book in Britain*. London 1966
H Schmoller	*Two Titans: Mardersteig and Tschichold*. London & New York 1990
H Spencer	*Pioneers of Modern Typography*. London 1968, 1990
H Spencer	*The Liberated Page*. London 1987, 1990
S Steinberg	*Five Hundred Years of Printing*. Harmondsworth 1962
J Sutton and A Bartram	*An Atlas of Typeforms*. London 1968
C Swann	*Techniques of Typography*. London 1969, 1980
J Taylor and S Heale	*Editing for Desktop Publishing*. London 1990
W Tracy	*Letters of Credit*. London 1986
W Tracy	*The Typographic Scene*. London 1988
J Tschichold	*Designing Books*. New York 1951
J Tschichold	*Assymetric Typography*. London & New York 1967
M Twyman	*Printing 1770-1970*. London 1970
D Updike	*Printing Types*. Cambridge (Mass) 1962
L Wallis	*A Concise Chronology of Typesetting Developments 1886-1986*. London 1988
L Wallis	*Modern Encyclopedia of Typefaces 1960-90*. London 1990
H Williamson	*Methods of Book Design*. London 1956, 1966
H Zapf	*Manuale Typographicum*. Frankfurt A-M 1968
	Hart's Rules for Compositors and Readers. Oxford, regularly revised
	A Manual of Style. Chicago, regularly revised

Index

Abbreviation 282
Akzidenz-Grotesk 166
Aldine roman 11, 12, 158, 252
Aldus (*see* Manutius)
Alternative characters 88, 90, 158
Arrighi, Ludovico 11, 12, 236, 252
Austin, Richard 12, 88, 202, 248
Baskerville, John 12, 18, 20, 36, 84, 86
Baskerville type 84
Bauhaus 19, 64, 66
Bell, John 88
Bell type 12
Bembo type 31, 216, 268
Benton, Linn Boyd 116, 118, 120
Benton, Morris Fuller 98, 100, 118, 120, 138
Bewick, Thomas 52
Bilz W 150
Blado, Antonio 236
Bodoni, Giambattista 13, 28, 98
Bodoni type 13, 67
Brand, Chris 76
Bulmer, William 13, 52, 106
Bunyan type 226
Burne-Jones, Edward 15
Californian type 94
Calvert, Margaret 110
Carolingian 9, 10
Carpenter, Ron 108, 122
Carroll, Lewis 28, 29
Carter, Matthew 144, 146, 268, 272
Carter, Will 206
Cartier type 282
Caruso, Victor 138
Caslon foundry 14
Caslon, William 12, 172
Century magazine 118
Century type 67
Chaucer type 15
Ciceros 284
Clarendons 13, 14, 202
Clark, R & R 246
de Colines, Simon 12
Dair, Carl 112
Deutschen Arbeitsfront, Verlag der 64
Desktop publishing 9
Didot, François Ambroise 12
Didot type 13
Digital/CRT/Scan 8
Dimensions 283
Display setting 282
Dooijes, Dick 194
Doves Press 34
Dutch Old Face 11, 16
Dwiggins, William A 106

Educational characters 73, 80, 90, 92, 118, 142, 154, 166, 172, 174, 198, 212, 228, 232, 256, 258, 264, 266
Ehrhardt type 71
Eisen, Charles 55
Egyptians 13, 14, 17, 32
Estienne, Robert 12
Everyman Library 41
Fatfaces 14
Felicity type 20, 222
Figgins, Vincent 13
Figures, non-lining 283
Forsberg, Karl-Erik 96
Fournier, Pierre Simon (le jeune) 134
Freedman, Barnett 60
French Old Face 11, 16
Frutiger, Adrian 80, 104, 156, 178, 200, 250, 264, 266, 270
Fry's Baskerville 12
Futura type 15
Galliard type 282
Garamond, Claude 12, 148, 160
Garamond type 160, 242
Gill, Arthur Eric Rowton 15, 26, 28, 154, 188, 190, 222, 226
Gill Sans type 15
Golden type 15
Goudy, Frederic W 94, 158, 192
Grandjean, Phillipe 12
Granjon, Robert 12, 144, 146, 148, 228
Grids 47, 69, 71
Griffith C H 86, 160, 184
Griffo, Francesco 11, 12
Grotesques 14, 17, 32, 58, 63
Gürtler, André 82, 126
Gutenberg, Johannes 9, 10
Harvey, Michael 132
Haus, Reinhard 164
Headline type 71
Helvetica type 14
Hollis, Richard 32
Humanistic Book Script 10
Imprimerie Royale 13
Imprint magazine 172
Initials 283
Ionic 13
Italian Old Face 11, 16
Italic 11
Jannon, Jean 148
Janson type 252
Jenson, Nicholas 10, 11, 15, 180, 192
Joanna type 26
Johnston, Edward 15, 154, 172
Johnston's Railway Type 15, 154
Jones G W 86, 160
Jost, Heinrich 102

Kelmscott Press 15, 56
Kerver, Jacques 11, 12
Kindersley, David 206
Kirchner, Ludwig 58
Kis, Nicholas 128, 184, 186
Lange, Günter Gehrhard 124
Lardent, Victor 256, 258
Laser/Scan 8
Leading 282
Letterspacing 282
Lewis, John 19
Lhose, Richard P 68
Limited Editions Club, NY 226
Linotron/Linotronic 8
Linotron 202 8, 9, 73
Linotronic 300 8, 9, 73
London Underground 15
Malin, Charles 222
Manutius, Aldus 11, 35, 36, 90, 236
Martin, William 12, 106
Mason J H 172
Measure, text 282
Meidinger, Max 166
Memphis type 67
Mendoza, José 224
Meynell, Gerald 172
Meynell, Francis 20, 22, 40
Minton, John 62
Modern type style 13, 17
Moholy-Nagy, Laszlo 65, 66
Monotype Lasercomp 8, 9, 73
Morison, Stanley 11, 15, 19, 148, 256, 258, 282
Morris, William 15, 28, 56, 57
Muche, Georg 65
Multiplication signs 283
New Caledonia type 106
Neue Helvetica type 166
Nicholas, Robin 122
Nonesuch Press 20, 40
Oxford University Press 24
Palatino type 78
Pannartz (*see* Sweynheym)
Penguin Books 31, 44, 62
Perpetua type 20, 60
Phemister, Alexander 208
Photo/Optic 8
Photo/Scan 8
Pierpont, Frank 228, 232
Plantin, Christopher 22, 24, 54, 228
Plantin type 20, 45, 60, 256
Private presses 15, 34
PostScript 9
Potter, Beatrix 57
Punctuation 282
Quadflieg, Roswitha 58

Renaissance script 10, 36
Renner, Paul 15, 140, 142
Ritzel, Arthur 240
Rockwell type 13
Rules (*see* Typographic rules)
St Augustin Ordinaire type 134
Sans-serifs 14, 15, 17
Schadow-Antiqua Werk type 254
Schmidt, Joost 63
Schmoller, Hans 31, 45, 62
Scotch Roman type 12
Silber, Eucharius 26
Simoncini, Francesco 150
Slab serifs 13, 17
Small caps 283
Stan, Tony 94
Steam press 13
da Spira, Johann 11
Sweynheym and Pannartz 10
Swiss typography 69, 71
Tagliente, Giovantonio 90
Textura 10
Themerson, Stefan 33
Times, The 13, 202, 256, 258
Times Roman type 71
de Tournes, Jean 12
Tory, Geoffrey 12
Transitional type styles 13, 16
Troy type 15
Trump, Georg 254, 260, 262
Tschichold, Jan 39, 242, 244
Twentieth-century romans 127
Tyne and Wear Metro 110
Type families 16
Type sizes 286
Typographica 33
Typographic rules 286
Typographic signs 286
Univers type 42
van Dijck, Christopher 12, 268
Van Dijck type 268
van Krimpen, Jan 252, 268
Vector fonts 8
Venetian type style 11, 16
Visscher, Claes 52
Voskens, Dirk 12
Walbaum, Justus Erich 274, 276
Walbaum type 13, 44
Walpergen, Peter 24
Whistler, James McNeill 29
Wolpe, Berthold 220
Word breaks 282
Zapf, Hermann 7, 78, 196, 198, 212, 214, 216, 218, 280